Pro ASP.NET Core MVC 2

Seventh Edition

Adam Freeman

Apress®

Pro ASP.NET Core MVC 2

Adam Freeman
London, UK

ISBN-13 (pbk): 978-1-4842-3149-4
https://doi.org/10.1007/978-1-4842-3150-0

ISBN-13 (electronic): 978-1-4842-3150-0

Library of Congress Control Number: 2017958033

Cover image by Freepik (`www.freepik.com`)

Managing Director: Welmoed Spahr
Editorial Director: Todd Green
Acquisitions Editor: Gwenan Spearing
Development Editor: Laura Berendson
Technical Reviewer: Fabio Claudio Ferracchiati
Coordinating Editor: Mark Powers
Copy Editor: Kim Wimpsett

Distributed to the book trade worldwide by Springer Science+Business Media New York, 233 Spring Street, 6th Floor, New York, NY 10013. Phone 1-800-SPRINGER, fax (201) 348-4505, e-mail orders-ny@springer-sbm.com, or visit www.springeronline.com. Apress Media, LLC is a California LLC and the sole member (owner) is Springer Science + Business Media Finance Inc (SSBM Finance Inc). SSBM Finance Inc is a **Delaware** corporation.

For information on translations, please e-mail rights@apress.com, or visit www.apress.com/rights-permissions.

Apress titles may be purchased in bulk for academic, corporate, or promotional use. eBook versions and licenses are also available for most titles. For more information, reference our Print and eBook Bulk Sales web page at www.apress.com/bulk-sales.

Any source code or other supplementary material referenced by the author in this book is available to readers on GitHub via the book's product page, located at www.apress.com/9781484231494. For more detailed information, please visit www.apress.com/source-code.

Printed on acid-free paper

Dedicated to my lovely wife, Jacqui Griffyth.
(And also to Peanut.)

Contents at a Glance

Contents

About the Author

Adam Freeman is an experienced IT professional who has held senior positions in a range of companies, most recently serving as chief technology officer and chief operating officer of a global bank. Now retired, he spends his time writing and long-distance running.

About the Technical Reviewer

Fabio Claudio Ferracchiati is a senior consultant and a senior analyst/developer using Microsoft technologies. He works for BluArancio (`www.bluarancio.com`). He is a Microsoft Certified Solution Developer for .NET, a Microsoft Certified Application Developer for .NET, a Microsoft Certified Professional, and a prolific author and technical reviewer. Over the past ten years, he's written articles for Italian and international magazines and coauthored more than ten books on a variety of computer topics.

PART I

Introducing ASP.NET Core MVC 2

ASP.NET Core MVC is a radical shift for web developers using the Microsoft platform. It emphasizes clean architecture, design patterns, and testability, and it doesn't try to conceal how the Web works.

The first part of this book is designed to help you understand broadly the foundational ideas of MVC development, including the new features in ASP.NET Core MVC, and to experience in practice what the framework is like to use.

CHAPTER 1

■ ■ ■

ASP .NET Core MVC in Context

ASP.NET Core MVC is a web application development framework from Microsoft that combines the effectiveness and tidiness of model-view-controller (MVC) architecture, ideas and techniques from agile development, and the best parts of the .NET platform. In this chapter, you'll learn why Microsoft created ASP.NET Core MVC, see how it compares to its predecessors and alternatives, and, finally, get an overview of what's new in ASP.NET Core MVC and what's covered in this book.

Understanding the History of ASP.NET Core MVC

The original ASP.NET was introduced in 2002, at a time when Microsoft was keen to protect a dominant position in traditional desktop application development and saw the Internet as a threat. Figure 1-1 illustrates Microsoft's technology stack as it appeared then.

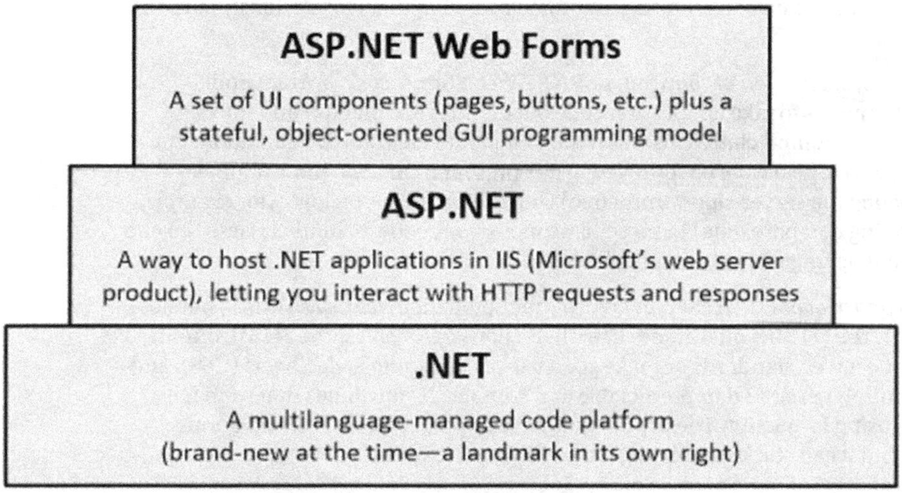

ASP.NET Web Forms
A set of UI components (pages, buttons, etc.) plus a stateful, object-oriented GUI programming model

ASP.NET
A way to host .NET applications in IIS (Microsoft's web server product), letting you interact with HTTP requests and responses

.NET
A multilanguage-managed code platform
(brand-new at the time—a landmark in its own right)

Figure 1-1. *The ASP.NET Web Forms technology stack*

© Adam Freeman 2017
A. Freeman, *Pro ASP.NET Core MVC 2*, https://doi.org/10.1007/978-1-4842-3150-0_1

ASP.NET Web Forms

With Web Forms, Microsoft attempted to hide both Hypertext Transfer Protocol (HTTP), with its intrinsic statelessness, and Hypertext Markup Language (HTML), which at the time was unfamiliar to many developers, by modeling the user interface (UI) as a hierarchy of server-side control objects. Each control kept track of its own state across requests, rendering itself as HTML when needed and automatically connecting client-side events (for example, a button click) with the corresponding server-side event handler code. In effect, Web Forms is a giant abstraction layer designed to deliver a classic event-driven graphical user interface (GUI) over the Web.

The idea was to make web development feel just the same as developing a desktop application. Developers could think in terms of a stateful UI and didn't need to work with a series of independent HTTP requests and responses. Microsoft could seamlessly transition the army of Windows desktop developers into the new world of web applications.

What Was Wrong with ASP.NET Web Forms?

Traditional ASP.NET Web Forms development was good in principle, but reality proved more complicated.

- *View State weight*: The actual mechanism for maintaining state across requests (known as View State) resulted in large blocks of data being transferred between the client and server. This data could reach hundreds of kilobytes in even modest web applications, and it went back and forth with every request, leading to slower response times and increasing the bandwidth demands of the server.

- *Page life cycle*: The mechanism for connecting client-side events with server-side event handler code, part of the page life cycle, could be complicated and delicate. Few developers had success manipulating the control hierarchy at runtime without creating View State errors or finding that some event handlers mysteriously failed to execute.

- *False sense of separation of concerns*: ASP.NET Web Forms' *code-behind* model provided a means to take application code out of its HTML markup and into a separate code-behind class. This was done to separate logic and presentation, but, in reality, developers were encouraged to mix presentation code (for example, manipulating the server-side control tree) with their application logic (for example, manipulating database data) in these same monstrous code-behind classes. The end result could be fragile and unintelligible.

- *Limited control over HTML*: Server controls rendered themselves as HTML, but not necessarily the HTML you wanted. In early versions of ASP.NET, the HTML output failed to meet web standards or make good use of Cascading Style Sheets (CSS), and server controls generated unpredictable and complex ID attributes that were hard to access using JavaScript. These problems have improved in recent Web Forms releases, but it can still be tricky to get the HTML you expect.

- *Leaky abstraction*: Web Forms tried to hide HTML and HTTP wherever possible. As you tried to implement custom behaviors, you frequently fell out of the abstraction, which forced you to reverse-engineer the postback event mechanism or perform obtuse acts to make it generate the desired HTML.

- *Low testability*: The designers of Web Forms could not have anticipated that automated testing would become an essential component of software development. The tightly coupled architecture they designed was unsuitable for unit testing. Integration testing could be a challenge, too.

Web Forms wasn't all bad, and eventually, Microsoft put effort into improving standards compliance and simplifying the development process and even took some features from the original ASP.NET MVC Framework and applied them to Web Forms. Web Forms excelled when you needed quick results, and you could have a reasonably complex web app up and running within a day. But unless you were careful during development, you would find that the application you created was hard to test and hard to maintain.

The Original MVC Framework

In October 2007, Microsoft announced a new development platform, built on the existing ASP.NET platform, that was intended as a direct response to the criticisms of Web Forms and the popularity of competing platforms such as Ruby on Rails. The new platform was called the ASP.NET MVC Framework and reflected the emerging trends in web application development, such as HTML and CSS standardization, RESTful web services, effective unit testing, and the idea that developers should embrace the stateless nature of HTTP.

The concepts that underpin the original MVC Framework seem natural and obvious now, but they were lacking from the world of .NET web development in 2007. The introduction of the ASP.NET MVC Framework brought Microsoft's web development platform back into the modern age.

The MVC Framework also signaled an important change in attitude from Microsoft, which had previously tried to control every component in the web application toolchain. With the MVC Framework, Microsoft built on open source tools such as jQuery, took on design conventions and best practices from competing (and more successful) platforms, and released the source code to the MVC Framework for developers to inspect.

What Was Wrong with the Original MVC Framework?

At the time the MVC Framework was created, it made sense for Microsoft to create it on top of the existing ASP.NET platform, which had a lot of solid low-level functionality that provided a head start in the development process and which was already well-known and understood by ASP.NET developers.

But compromises were required to graft the MVC Framework onto a platform that was originally designed for Web Forms. MVC Framework developers became used to using configuration settings and code tweaks that disabled or reconfigured features that didn't have any bearing on their web application but were required to get everything working.

As the MVC Framework grew in popularity, Microsoft started to take some of the core features and add them to Web Forms. The result was increasingly odd, where features with design quirks required to support the MVC Framework were extended to support Web Forms, with further design quirks to make everything fit together. At the same time, Microsoft started to expand ASP.NET with new frameworks for creating web services (Web API) and real-time communication (SignalR). The new frameworks added their own configuration and development conventions, each of which had its own benefits and oddities, and the overall result was a fragmented mess.

Understanding ASP.NET Core

In 2015, Microsoft announced a new direction for ASP.NET and the MVC Framework, which would eventually produce ASP.NET Core MVC, the topic of this book.

ASP.NET Core is built on .NET Core, which is a cross-platform version of the .NET Framework without the Windows-specific application programming interfaces (APIs). Windows is still a dominant operating system, but web applications are increasingly hosted in small and simple containers in cloud platforms, and by embracing a cross-platform approach, Microsoft has extended the reach of .NET, made it possible to deploy ASP.NET Core applications to a broader set of hosting environments, and, as a bonus, made it possible for developers to create ASP.NET Core web applications on Linux and macOS.

ASP.NET Core is a completely new framework. It is simpler, it is easier to work with, and it is free of the legacy that comes from Web Forms. And, since it is based on .NET Core, it supports the development of web applications on a range of platforms and containers.

ASP.NET Core MVC provides the functionality of the original ASP.NET MVC Framework built on the new ASP.NET Core platform. It integrates the features that were previously provided by Web API, it includes a more natural way of generating complex content, and it makes key development tasks, such as unit testing, simpler and more predictable.

What's New in ASP.NET Core MVC 2

The ASP.NET Core MVC 2 release focuses on consolidation, working through some of the tooling and platform changes that were introduced in earlier versions. ASP.NET Core MVC 2 requires .NET Core 2, which has a much-expanded API surface and is now supported on additional Linux distributions. Useful changes include a new meta-package system, which simplifies the management of NuGet packages, a new configuration system for ASP.NET Core, and support for Entity Framework Core 2. The biggest new feature is Razor Pages, which is an attempt to re-create the development style associated with Web Pages using a more modern platform, but Razor Pages will not be of interest for MVC developers (and I do not describe it in this book).

Key Benefits of ASP.NET Core MVC

The following sections briefly describe how the new MVC platform overcomes the legacy of Web Forms and the original MVC Framework and how it has brought ASP.NET back to the cutting edge.

MVC Architecture

ASP.NET Core MVC follows a pattern called *model-view-controller*, which guides the shape of an ASP.NET web application and the interactions between the components it contains.

It is important to distinguish between the MVC architectural pattern and the ASP.NET Core MVC implementation. The MVC pattern is not new—it dates back to 1978 and the Smalltalk project at Xerox PARC—but it has gained popularity today as a pattern for web applications for the following reasons:

- User interaction with an application that adheres to the MVC pattern follows a natural cycle: the user takes an action, and in response, the application changes its data model and delivers an updated view to the user. Then the cycle repeats. This is a convenient fit for web applications delivered as a series of HTTP requests and responses.

- Web applications necessitate combining several technologies (databases, HTML, and executable code, for example), usually split into a set of tiers or layers. The patterns that arise from these combinations map naturally onto the concepts in the MVC pattern.

ASP.NET Core MVC implements the MVC pattern and, in doing so, provides a greatly improved separation of concerns when compared to Web Forms. In fact, ASP.NET Core MVC implements a variant of the MVC pattern that is especially suitable for web applications. You will learn more about the theory and practice of this architecture in Chapter 3.

Extensibility

ASP.NET Core and ASP.NET Core MVC are built as a series of independent components that have well-defined characteristics, satisfy a .NET interface, or are built on an abstract base class. You can easily replace key components with ones of your own implementation. In general, ASP.NET Core MVC gives you these three options for each component:

- Use the *default* implementation of the component as it stands (which should be enough for most applications).

- Derive a *subclass* of the default implementation to tweak its behavior.

- *Replace* the component entirely with a new implementation of the interface or abstract base class.

You'll learn all about the various components and how and why you might want to tweak or replace each of them, starting in Chapter 14.

Tight Control over HTML and HTTP

ASP.NET Core MVC produces clean, standards-compliant markup. Its built-in tag helpers produce standards-compliant output, but there is a more significant philosophical change compared with Web Forms. Instead of generating out swathes of HTML over which you have little control, ASP.NET Core MVC encourages you to craft simple, elegant markup styled with CSS.

Of course, if you do want to throw in some ready-made widgets for complex UI elements such as date pickers or cascading menus, the "no special requirements" approach taken by ASP.NET Core MVC makes it easy to use best-of-breed client-side libraries such as jQuery, Angular, React, or the Bootstrap CSS library. ASP.NET Core MVC meshes so well with these libraries that Microsoft includes templates that incorporate them to jump-start new development projects.

ASP.NET Core MVC works in tune with HTTP. You have control over the requests passing between the browser and server, so you can fine-tune your user experience as much as you like. Ajax is made easy, and creating web services to receive browser HTTP requests is a simple process, as described in Chapter 20.

Testability

The ASP.NET Core MVC architecture gives you a great start in making your application maintainable and testable because you naturally separate different application concerns into independent pieces. In addition, each piece of the ASP.NET Core platform and the ASP.NET Core MVC framework can be isolated and replaced for unit testing, which can be performed using any popular open source testing framework, such as xUnit, which I introduce in Chapter 7.

In this book, you will see examples of how to write clean, simple unit tests for ASP.NET MVC controllers and actions that supply fake or mock implementations of framework components to simulate any scenario, using a variety of testing and mocking strategies. Even if you have never written a unit test before, you will be off to a great start.

Testability is not only a matter of unit testing. ASP.NET Core MVC applications work well with UI automation testing tools, too. You can write test scripts that simulate user interactions without needing to guess which HTML element structures, CSS classes, or IDs the framework will generate, and you do not have to worry about the structure changing unexpectedly.

Powerful Routing System

The style of uniform resource locators (URLs) has evolved as web application technology has improved. URLs like this one:

```
/App_v2/User/Page.aspx?action=show%20prop&prop_id=82742
```

are increasingly rare, replaced by a simpler, cleaner format like this:

```
/to-rent/chicago/2303-silver-street
```

There are some good reasons for caring about the structure of URLs. First, search engines give weight to keywords found in a URL. A search for "rent in Chicago" is much more likely to turn up the simpler URL. Second, many web users are now savvy enough to understand a URL and appreciate the option of navigating by typing it into their browser's address bar. Third, when someone understands the structure of a URL, they are more likely to link to it, share it with a friend, or even read it aloud over the phone. Fourth, it doesn't expose the technical details, folder, and file name structure of your application to the public Internet, so you are free to change the underlying implementation without breaking all your incoming links.

Clean URLs were hard to implement in earlier frameworks, but ASP.NET Core MVC uses a feature known as *URL routing* to provide clean URLs by default. This gives you control over your URL schema and its relationship to your application, offering you the freedom to create a pattern of URLs that is meaningful and useful to your users, without the need to conform to a predefined pattern. And, of course, this means you can easily define a modern REST-style URL schema if you want. You'll find a thorough description of URL routing in Chapters 15 and 16.

Modern API

Microsoft's .NET platform has evolved with each major release, supporting—and even defining—the state-of-the-art aspects of modern programming. ASP.NET Core MVC is built for .NET Core, so its API can take full advantage of language and runtime innovations familiar to C# programmers, including the await keyword, extension methods, lambda expressions, anonymous and dynamic types, and Language Integrated Query (LINQ).

Many of the ASP.NET Core MVC API methods and coding patterns follow a cleaner, more expressive composition than was possible with earlier platforms. Don't worry if you are not up to speed with the latest C# language features; I provide a summary of the most important C# features for MVC development in Chapter 4.

Cross-Platform

Previous versions of ASP.NET were specific to Windows, requiring a Windows desktop to write web applications and a Windows server to deploy and run them. Microsoft made ASP.NET Core cross-platform, both for development and for deployment. .NET Core is available for different platforms, including macOS and a range of popular Linux distributions. Cross-platform support makes it easier to deploy ASP.NET Core MVC applications, and there is good support for working with application container platforms, such as Docker.

Most ASP.NET Core MVC development is likely to be done using Visual Studio for the immediate future, but Microsoft has also created a cross-platform development tool called Visual Studio Code, which means that ASP.NET Core MVC development is no longer restricted to Windows.

ASP.NET Core MVC Is Open Source

Unlike previous Microsoft web development platforms, you are free to download the source code for ASP. NET Core and ASP.NET Core MVC and even modify and compile your own version of it. This is invaluable when your debugging trail leads into a system component and you want to step into its code (and even read the original programmer's comments). It is also useful if you are building an advanced component and want to see what development possibilities exist or how the built-in components actually work.

You can download the ASP.NET Core and ASP.NET Core MVC source code from `https://github.com/aspnet`.

What Do I Need to Know?

To get the most from this book, you should be familiar with the basics of web development, understand how HTML and CSS work, and have a working knowledge of C#. Don't worry if you are a little hazy on the client-side details, such as JavaScript. My emphasis is on server-side development in this book, and you can pick up what you need through the examples. In Chapter 4, I summarize the most useful C# language features for MVC development, which you'll find useful if you are moving to the latest .NET versions from an earlier release.

What Is the Structure of This Book?

This book is split into two parts, each of which covers a set of related topics.

Part 1: Introducing ASP.NET Core MVC

I start this book by putting ASP.NET Core MVC in context. I explain the benefits and practical impact of the MVC pattern, cover the way in which ASP.NET Core MVC fits into modern web development, and describe the tools and C# language features that every ASP.NET Core MVC programmer needs.

In Chapter 2, you will dive right in by creating a simple web application and will get an idea of what the major components and building blocks are and how they fit together. Most of this part of the book, however, is given over to the development of a project called SportsStore, through which I show you a realistic development process from inception to deployment, touching on the major features of ASP.NET Core MVC.

Part 2: ASP.NET Core MVC in Detail

In Part 2, I explain the inner workings of ASP.NET Core MVC features that I used to build the SportsStore application. I show you how each feature works, explain the role it plays, and show you the configuration and customization options that are available. Having set the broad context in Part 1, I dig right into the details in Part 2.

Where Can You Get the Example Code?

You can download the example projects for all the chapters in this book from `https://github.com/apress/pro-asp.net-core-mvc-2`. The download is available without charge and includes all the supporting resources that are required to re-create the examples without having to type them in. You don't have to download the code, but it is the easiest way of experimenting with the examples and makes it easy to copy and paste code into your own projects.

Where Can You Get Corrections for This Book?

You can find corrections for this book in the Errata file in the GitHub repository for this book
(`https://github.com/apress/pro-asp.net-core-mvc-2`).

Contacting the Author

If you have problems making the examples in this chapter work or if you find a problem in the book, then
you can e-mail me at adam@adam-freeman.com, and I will try my best to help. Please check the errata for
this book at `https://github.com/apress/pro-asp.net-core-mvc-2` to see if it contains a solution to your
problem before contacting me.

Summary

In this chapter, I explained the context in which ASP.NET Core MVC exists and how it has evolved from
Web Forms and the original ASP.NET MVC Framework. I described the benefits of using the ASP.NET Core
MVC and the structure of this book. In the next chapter, you'll see ASP.NET Core MVC in action in a simple
demonstration of the features that deliver these benefits.

CHAPTER 2

■ ■ ■

Your First MVC Application

The best way to appreciate a software development framework is to jump right in and use it. In this chapter, you'll create a simple data-entry application using ASP.NET Core MVC. I take things one step at a time so you can see how an MVC application is constructed. To keep things simple, I skip over some of the technical details for the moment. But don't worry. If you are new to MVC, you will find plenty to keep you interested. Where I use something without explaining it, I provide a reference to the chapter in which you can find all the details.

UPDATES TO THIS BOOK

Microsoft has an active development schedule for .NET Core and ASP.NET Core MVC, which means that there may be new releases available by the time you read this book. It doesn't seem fair to expect readers to buy a new book every few months, especially since most changes are relatively minor. Instead, I will post free updates to the GitHub repository for this book (`https://github.com/apress/pro-asp.net-core-mvc-2`) for breaking changes caused by minor releases.

This kind of update is an experiment for me (and for Apress), and I don't yet know what form those updates may take—not least because I don't know what the future major releases of ASP.NET Core MVC will contain—but the goal is to extend the life of this book by supplementing the examples it contains.

I am not making any promises about what the updates will be like, what form they will take, or how long I will produce them before folding them into a new edition of this book. Please keep an open mind and check the repository for this book when new ASP.NET Core MVC versions are released. If you have ideas about how the updates could be improved, then e-mail me at `adam@adam-freeman.com` and let me know.

Installing Visual Studio

This book relies on Visual Studio 2017, which provides the development environment for ASP.NET Core MVC projects. I use the free *Visual Studio 2017 Community* edition, which can be downloaded from `www.visualstudio.com`. When installing Visual Studio 2017, you must select the .NET Core cross-platform development workload, as shown in Figure 2-1.

■ **Note** Visual Studio 2017 predates the release of ASP.NET Core MVC 2. You must apply the latest updates if you have installed Visual Studio for earlier versions of ASP.NET Core MVC. You can apply updates by running the Visual Studio installer and selecting Update for the Visual Studio edition you are using.

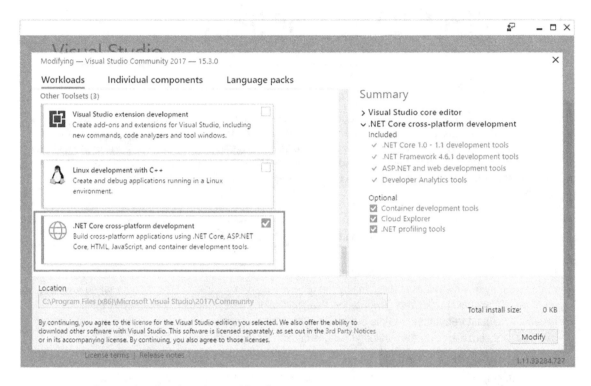

Figure 2-1. *Selecting the Visual Studio workload*

■ **Tip** Visual Studio only supports Windows. You can create ASP.NET Core MVC applications on other platforms using Visual Studio Code. Visual Studio Code doesn't provide all of the features of Visual Studio, but it is an excellent editor and does everything required for MVC application development. See Chapter 13 for details.

Installing the .NET Core 2.0 SDK

The Visual Studio installation includes all of the features required for ASP.NET Core MVC development, but it doesn't include .NET Core 2.0, which must be downloaded and installed separately.

Go to https://www.microsoft.com/net/core and download and run the .NET Core SDK installer for Windows. Once the installer has finished, open a new command prompt or PowerShell window and run the following command to display the version of .NET that has been installed:

```
dotnet --version
```

If the installation has been successful, the result of this command will be 2.0.0.

Creating a New ASP.NET Core MVC Project

I am going to start by creating a new ASP.NET Core MVC project in Visual Studio. Select New ➤ Project from the File menu to open the New Project dialog. If you navigate to the Installed ➤ Visual C# ➤ Web section in the left panel, you will see the ASP.NET Core Web Application (.NET Core) project template. Select this project type, as shown in Figure 2-2.

■ **Tip**　The choice of project template can be confusing because their names are so similar. The ASP.NET Web Application (.NET Framework) template is for creating projects using the legacy versions of ASP.NET and the MVC Framework, which predated ASP.NET Core. The other two templates are for creating ASP.NET Core applications, and they differ in the runtime they use, allowing you to select either the .NET Framework or .NET Core. I explain the difference between them in Chapter 6, but I use the .NET Core option throughout this book, so it is the one you should select to ensure that you get the same results from the example applications.

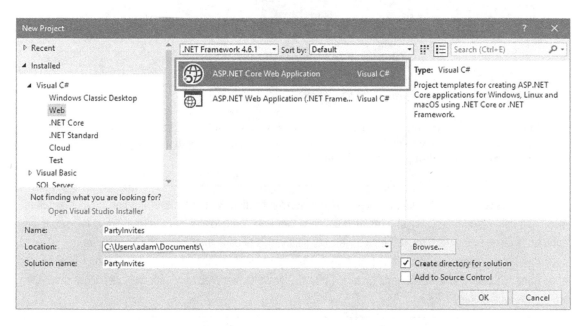

Figure 2-2.　*The ASP.NET Core Web Application project template*

Enter **PartyInvites** in the Name field for the new project. Click the OK button to continue and you will see another dialog box, shown in Figure 2-3, which asks you to set the initial content for the project. Ensure that .NET Core and ASP.NET Core 2.0 are selected from the drop-down menus, as shown in the figure.

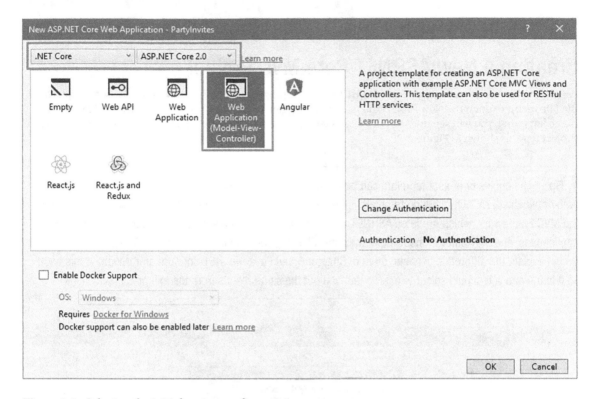

Figure 2-3. *Selecting the initial project configuration*

There are several template options, each of which creates a project with different starting content. For this chapter, select the Web Application (Model-View-Controller) option, which sets up an MVC application with predefined content to jump-start development.

▬ **Note** This is the only chapter in which I use the Web Application (Model-View-Controller) project template. I don't like using predefined project templates because they encourage developers to treat some important features, such as authentication, as black boxes. My goal in this book is to give you the knowledge to understand and manage every aspect of your MVC applications, so I use the Empty template throughout the rest of the book. This chapter is about getting started quickly, for which the Web Application (Model-View-Controller) template is well-suited.

Click the Change Authentication button and ensure that the No Authentication option is selected, as shown in Figure 2-4. This project doesn't require any authentication, but I explain how to secure ASP.NET applications in Chapters 28, 29, and 30.

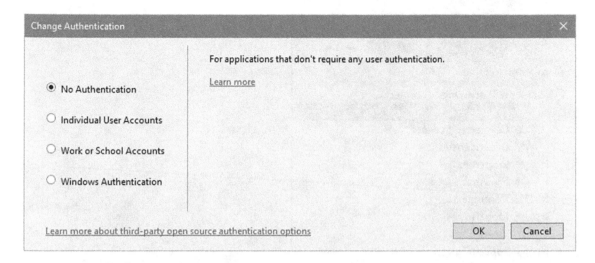

Figure 2-4. Selecting the authentication settings

Click OK to close the Change Authentication dialog. Ensure that the Enable Docker Support option is unchecked and then click OK to create the PartyInvites project.

Once Visual Studio has created the project, you will see a number of files and folders displayed in the Solution Explorer window, as shown in Figure 2-5. This is the default project structure for a new MVC project created using the Web Application (Model-View-Controller) template, and you will soon understand the purpose of each file and folder that Visual Studio creates.

■ **Tip**   If you see a Pages folder, rather than Controllers, Models, and Views folders, then you have selected the Web Application template and not the (confusingly similar) Web Application (Model-View-Controller) template. I have no idea why Microsoft thought that such similar names were a good idea, but you will have to delete the project you created and start over.

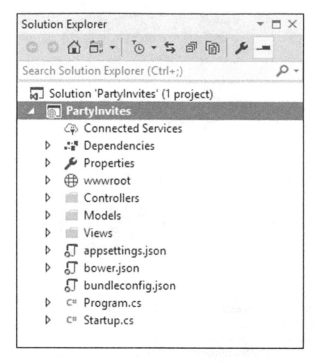

Figure 2-5. *The initial file and folder structure of an ASP.NET Core MVC project*

You can run the application by selecting Start Debugging from the Debug menu (if it prompts you to enable debugging, just click the OK button). When you do this, Visual Studio compiles the application, uses an application server called IIS Express to run it, and opens a web browser to request the application content. It can take Visual Studio some time to run the project for the first time, and when the process is complete, you will see the results shown in Figure 2-6.

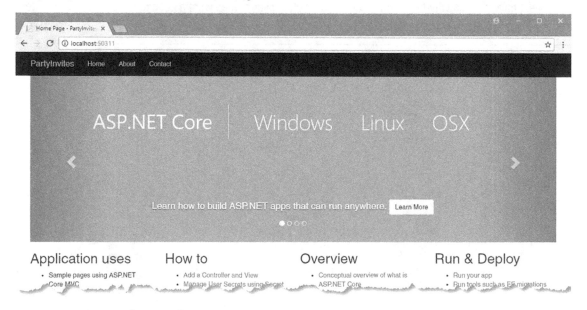

Figure 2-6. *Running the example project*

When Visual Studio creates a project with the Web Application (Model-View-Controller) template, it adds some basic code and content, which is what you see when you run the application. Throughout the rest of the chapter, I will replace this content to create a simple MVC application.

When you are finished, be sure to stop debugging by closing the browser window or by going back to Visual Studio and selecting Stop Debugging from the Debug menu.

As you have just seen, Visual Studio opens the browser to display the project. You can select any browser that you have installed by clicking the arrow to the right of the IIS Express toolbar button and choosing from the list of options in the Web Browser menu, as shown in Figure 2-7.

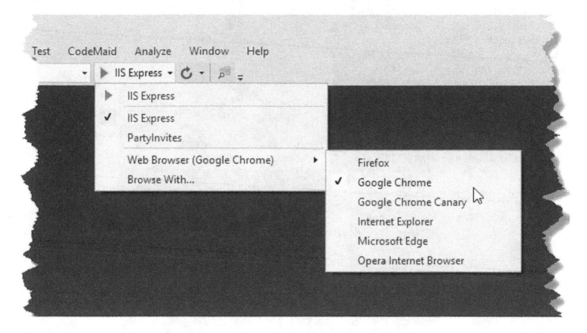

Figure 2-7. *Selecting a browser*

From here on, I will use Google Chrome or Google Chrome Canary for all the screenshots in this book, but you can use any modern browser to display the examples in the books, including Microsoft Edge.

Adding the Controller

In the MVC pattern, incoming requests are handled by *controllers*. In ASP.NET Core MVC, controllers are just C# classes (usually inheriting from the Microsoft.AspNetCore.Mvc.Controller class, which is the built-in MVC controller base class).

Each public method in a controller is known as an *action method*, meaning you can invoke it from the Web via some URL to perform an action. The MVC convention is to put controllers in the Controllers folder, which Visual Studio created when it set up the project.

■ **Tip** You do not need to follow this or most other MVC conventions, but I recommend that you do—not least because it will help you make sense of the examples in this book.

Visual Studio adds a default controller class to the project, which you can see if you expand the Controllers folder in the Solution Explorer. The file is called HomeController.cs. Controller classes contain a name followed by the word Controller, which means that when you see a file called HomeController. cs, you know that it contains a controller called Home, which is the default controller that is used in MVC applications. Click the HomeController.cs file in the Solution Explorer so that Visual Studio opens it for editing. You will see the C# code shown in Listing 2-1.

Listing 2-1. The Initial Contents of the HomeController.cs File in the Controllers Folder

```csharp
using System;
using System.Collections.Generic;
using System.Diagnostics;
using System.Linq;
using System.Threading.Tasks;
using Microsoft.AspNetCore.Mvc;
using PartyInvites.Models;

namespace PartyInvites.Controllers {
    public class HomeController : Controller {
        public IActionResult Index() {
            return View();
        }

        public IActionResult About() {
            ViewData["Message"] = "Your application description page.";

            return View();
        }

        public IActionResult Contact() {
            ViewData["Message"] = "Your contact page.";

            return View();
        }

        public IActionResult Error() {
            return View(new ErrorViewModel { RequestId = Activity.Current?.Id
                ?? HttpContext.TraceIdentifier });
        }
    }
}
```

Replace the code in the HomeController.cs file so that it matches Listing 2-2. I have removed all but one of the methods, changed the result type and its implementation, and removed the using statements for unused namespaces.

Listing 2-2. Changing the HomeController.cs File in the Controllers Folder

```
using Microsoft.AspNetCore.Mvc;

namespace PartyInvites.Controllers {

    public class HomeController : Controller {

        public string Index() {
            return "Hello World";
        }
    }
}
```

These changes don't produce a dramatic effect, but they make for a nice demonstration. I have changed the method called Index so that it returns the string Hello World. Run the project again by selecting Start Debugging from the Visual Studio Debug menu.

■ **Tip**   If you left the application running from the previous section, then select Restart from the Debugging menu or, if you prefer, select Stop Debugging and then Start Debugging.

The browser will make an HTTP request to the server. The default MVC configuration means that the request will be handled using the Index method (known as an *action method* or just an *action*) and the result from the method will be sent back to the browser, as shown in Figure 2-8.

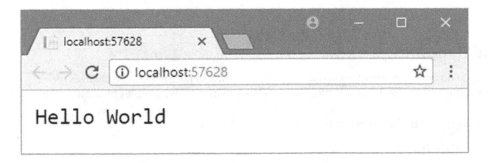

Figure 2-8. The output from the action method

■ **Tip**   Notice that Visual Studio has directed the browser to port 57628. You will almost certainly see a different port number in the URL that your browser requests because Visual Studio allocates a random port when the project is created. If you look in the Windows taskbar notification area, you will find an icon for IIS Express. This is a cut-down version of the full IIS application server that is included with Visual Studio and is used to deliver ASP.NET Core content and services during development. I'll show you how to deploy an MVC project into a production environment in Chapter 12.

Understanding Routes

As well as models, views, and controllers, MVC applications use the ASP.NET *routing system*, which decides how URLs map to controllers and actions. A route is a rule that is used to decide how a request is handled. When Visual Studio creates the MVC project, it adds some default routes to get you started. You can request any of the following URLs, and they will be directed to the Index action on the HomeController:

- /

- /Home

- /Home/Index

So, when a browser requests http://yoursite/ or http://yoursite/Home, it gets back the output from HomeController's Index method. You can try this yourself by changing the URL in the browser. At the moment, it will be http://localhost:57628/, except that the port part may be different. If you append /Home or /Home/Index to the URL, you will see the same Hello World result from the MVC application.

This is a good example of benefiting from following conventions implemented by ASP.NET Core MVC. In this case, the convention is that I will have a controller called HomeController and it will be the starting point for the MVC application. The default configuration that Visual Studio creates for a new project assumes I will follow this convention. Since I *did* follow the convention, I automatically got support for the URLs in the preceding list. If I had *not* followed the convention, I would need to modify the configuration to point to whatever controller I had created instead. For this simple example, the default configuration is all I need.

Rendering Web Pages

The output from the previous example wasn't HTML—it was just the string Hello World. To produce an HTML response to a browser request, I need a *view*, which tells MVC how to generate a response to a request from a browser.

Creating and Rendering a View

The first thing I need to do is modify my Index action method, as shown in Listing 2-3. The changes are shown in bold, which is a convention I follow throughout this book to make the examples easier to follow.

Listing 2-3. Rendering a View in the HomeController.cs File in the Controllers Folder

```
using Microsoft.AspNetCore.Mvc;

namespace PartyInvites.Controllers {

    public class HomeController : Controller {

        public ViewResult Index() {
            return View("MyView");
        }
    }
}
```

When I return a ViewResult object from an action method, I am instructing MVC to *render* a view. I create the ViewResult object by calling the View method, specifying the name of the view that I want to use, which is MyView. If you run the application, you can see MVC trying to find the view, as shown in the error message displayed in Figure 2-9.

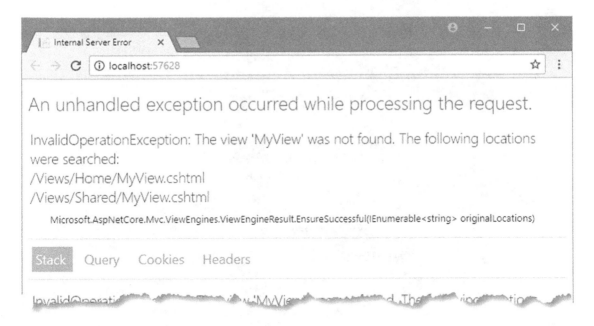

Figure 2-9. *MVC trying to find a view*

This is a helpful error message. It explains that MVC could not find the view I specified for the action method and also shows where it looked. Views are stored in the Views folder, organized into subfolders. Views that are associated with the Home controller, for example, are stored in a folder called Views/Home. Views that are not specific to a single controller are stored in a folder called Views/Shared. Visual Studio creates the Home and Shared folders automatically when the Web Application (Model-View-Controller) template is used and puts in some placeholder views to get the project started.

To create the view needed for this example, expand the Views folder in the Solution Explorer, right-click the Home folder, and select Add ➤ New Item from the pop-up menu. Visual Studio will present you with a list of item templates. Drill down to the ASP.NET Core ➤ Web ➤ ASP.NET category using the left pane and then select the MVC View Page item in the central pane, as shown in Figure 2-10. (Don't use the Razor Page template, which is not related to the MVC Framework.)

▪ **Tip**   You will see some existing files in the Views folder, which were added to the project by Visual Studio to provide some initial content, some of which you saw in Figure 2-6. You can ignore these files.

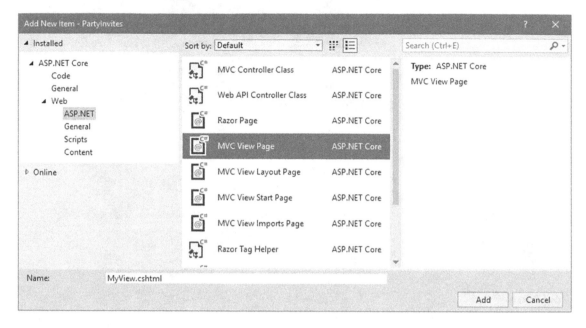

Figure 2-10. *Creating a view*

Set the Name field to MyView.cshtml and click the Add button to create the view. Visual Studio will create the Views/Home/MyView.cshtml file and open it for editing. The initial content of the view file is just some comments and a placeholder. Replace them with the content shown in Listing 2-4.

▓ **Tip**   It is easy to end up creating the view file in the wrong folder. If you didn't end up with a file called MyView.cshtml in the Views/Home folder, then delete the file you did create and try again.

Listing 2-4. Replacing the Content of the MyView.cshtml File in the Views/Home Folder

```
@{
    Layout = null;
}

<!DOCTYPE html>

<html>
<head>
    <meta name="viewport" content="width=device-width" />
    <title>Index</title>
</head>
<body>
    <div>
        Hello World (from the view)
    </div>
</body>
```

```
</html>
```
The new contents of the view file are mostly HTML. The exception is the part that looks like this:
```
...
@{
    Layout = null;
}
...
```

This is an expression that will be interpreted by the Razor view engine, which processes the contents of views and generates HTML that is sent to the browser. This is a simple Razor expression, and it tells Razor that I chose not to use a layout, which is like a template for the HTML that will be sent to the browser (and which I describe in Chapter 5). I am going to ignore Razor for the moment and come back to it later. To see the effect of creating the view, select Start Debugging from the Debug menu to run the application. You should see the result in Figure 2-11.

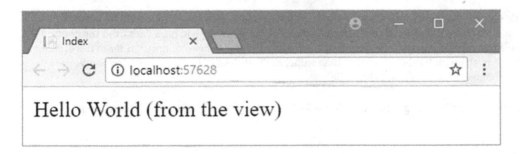

Figure 2-11. *Testing the view*

When I first edited the Index action method, it returned a string value. This meant that MVC did nothing except pass the string value as is to the browser. Now that the Index method returns a ViewResult, MVC renders a view and returns the HTML it produces. I told MVC which view should be used, so it used the naming convention to find it automatically. The convention is that the view has the name of the action method and is contained in a folder named after the controller: /Views/Home/MyView.cshtml.

I can return other results from action methods besides strings and ViewResult objects. For example, if I return a RedirectResult, the browser will be redirected to another URL. If I return an HttpUnauthorizedResult, I can prompt the user to log in. These objects are collectively known as *action results*. The action result system lets you encapsulate and reuse common responses in actions. I'll tell you more about them and explain the different ways they can be used in Chapter 17.

Adding Dynamic Output

The whole point of a web application platform is to construct and display *dynamic* output. In MVC, it is the controller's job to construct some data and pass it to the view, which is responsible for rendering it to HTML.

One way to pass data from the controller to the view is by using the ViewBag object, which is a member of the Controller base class. ViewBag is a dynamic object to which you can assign arbitrary properties, making those values available in whatever view is subsequently rendered. Listing 2-5 demonstrates passing some simple dynamic data in this way in the HomeController.cs file.

Listing 2-5. Setting View Data in the HomeController.cs File in the Controllers Folder

```
using System;
using Microsoft.AspNetCore.Mvc;

namespace PartyInvites.Controllers {

    public class HomeController : Controller {

        public ViewResult Index() {
            int hour = DateTime.Now.Hour;
            ViewBag.Greeting = hour < 12 ? "Good Morning" : "Good Afternoon";
            return View("MyView");
        }
    }
}
```

I provide data for the view when I assign a value to the ViewBag.Greeting property. The Greeting property didn't exist until the moment I assigned the value—this allows me to pass data from the controller to the view in a free and fluid manner, without having to define classes ahead of time. I refer to the ViewBag. Greeting property again in the view to get the data value, as illustrated in Listing 2-6, which shows the corresponding change to the MyView.cshtml file.

Listing 2-6. Retrieving a ViewBag Data Value in the MyView.cshtml File in the Views/Home Folder

```
@{
    Layout = null;
}

<!DOCTYPE html>

<html>
<head>
    <meta name="viewport" content="width=device-width" />
    <title>Index</title>
</head>
<body>
    <div>
        @ViewBag.Greeting World (from the view)
    </div>
</body>
</html>
```

The addition to the listing is a Razor expression that is evaluated when MVC uses the view to generate a response. When I call the View method in the controller's Index method, MVC locates the MyView.cshtml view file and asks the Razor view engine to parse the file's content. Razor looks for expressions like the one I added in the listing and processes them. In this example, processing the expression means inserting the value assigned to the ViewBag.Greeting property in the action method into the view.

There's nothing special about the property name Greeting; you could replace this with any property name and it would work the same, just as long as the name you use in the controller matches the name you use in the view. You can pass multiple data values from your controller to the view by assigning values to more than one property. You can see the effect of these changes by starting the project, as shown in Figure 2-12.

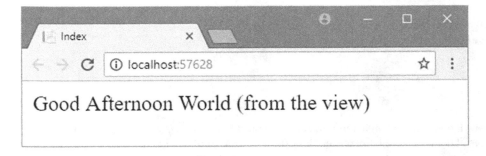

Figure 2-12. *A dynamic response from MVC*

Creating a Simple Data-Entry Application

In the rest of this chapter, I will explore more of the basic MVC features by building a simple data-entry application. I am going to pick up the pace in this section. My goal is to demonstrate MVC in action, so I will skip over some of the explanations as to how things work behind the scenes. But don't worry; I'll revisit these topics in depth in later chapters.

Setting the Scene

Imagine that a friend has decided to host a New Year's Eve party and that she has asked me to create a web app that allows her invitees to electronically RSVP. She has asked for these four key features:

- A home page that shows information about the party
- A form that can be used to RSVP
- Validation for the RSVP form, which will display a thank-you page
- A summary page that shows who is coming to the party

In the following sections, I will build up the MVC project I created at the start of the chapter and add these features. I can check the first item off the list by applying what I covered earlier and add some HTML to my existing view to give details of the party. To get started, Listing 2-7 shows the additions I made to the Views/Home/MyView.cshtml file.

Listing 2-7. Displaying Details of the Party in the MyView.cshtml File in the Views/Home Folder

```
@{
    Layout = null;
}

<!DOCTYPE html>

<html>
<head>
    <meta name="viewport" content="width=device-width" />
    <title>Index</title>
</head>
<body>
    <div>
```

```
        @ViewBag.Greeting World (from the view)
        <p>We're going to have an exciting party.<br />
        (To do: sell it better. Add pictures or something.)
        </p>
    </div>
</body>
</html>
```

I am on my way. If you run the application, by selecting Start Debugging from the Debug menu, you'll see the details of the party (well, the placeholder for the details, but you get the idea), as shown in Figure 2-13.

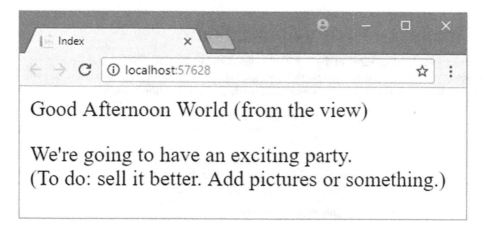

Figure 2-13. *Adding to the view HTML*

Designing a Data Model

In MVC, the *M* stands for *model*, and it is the most important part of the application. The model is the representation of the real-world objects, processes, and rules that define the subject, known as the *domain*, of the application. The model, often referred to as a *domain model*, contains the C# objects (known as *domain objects*) that make up the universe of the application and the methods that manipulate them. The views and controllers expose the domain to the clients in a consistent manner, and a well-designed MVC application starts with a well-designed model, which is then the focal point as controllers and views are added.

I don't need a complex model for the PartyInvites project because it is such a simple application and I need just one domain class that I will call GuestResponse. This object will be responsible for storing, validating, and confirming a RSVP.

The MVC convention is that the classes that make up a model are placed inside a folder called Models, which Visual Studio creates automatically when you use the Web Application (Model-View-Controller) template.

To create the class file, right-click the Models folder in the Solution Explorer and select Add ➤ Class from the pop-up menu. Set the name of the new class to GuestResponse.cs and click the Add button. Edit the contents of the new class file to match Listing 2-8.

Listing 2-8. The Contents of the GuestResponse.cs File in the Models Folder

```
namespace PartyInvites.Models {

    public class GuestResponse {

        public string Name { get; set; }
        public string Email { get; set; }
        public string Phone { get; set; }
        public bool? WillAttend { get; set; }
    }
}
```

■ **Tip** You may have noticed that the `WillAttend` property is a nullable `bool`, which means that it can be `true`, `false`, or `null`. I explain the rationale for this in the "Adding Validation" section later in the chapter.

Creating a Second Action and a Strongly Typed View

One of my application goals is to include an RSVP form, which means I need to define an action method that can receive requests for that form. A single controller class can define multiple action methods, and the convention is to group related actions together in the same controller. Listing 2-9 shows the addition of a new action method to the Home controller.

Listing 2-9. Adding an Action Method in the HomeController.cs File in the Controllers Folder

```
using System;
using Microsoft.AspNetCore.Mvc;

namespace PartyInvites.Controllers {

    public class HomeController : Controller {

        public ViewResult Index() {
            int hour = DateTime.Now.Hour;
            ViewBag.Greeting = hour < 12 ? "Good Morning" : "Good Afternoon";
            return View("MyView");
        }

        public ViewResult RsvpForm() {
            return View();
        }
    }
}
```

The `RsvpForm` action method calls the `View` method without an argument, which tells MVC to render the default view associated with the action method, which is a view with the same name as the action method, in this case, `RsvpForm.cshtml`.

Right-click the Views/Home folder and select Add ➤ New Item from the pop-up menu. Select the MVC View Page template, set the name of the new file to RsvpForm.cshtml, and click the Add button to create the file. Change the content of the file so that it matches Listing 2-10.

Listing 2-10. Setting the Content of the RsvpForm.cshtml File in the Views/Home Folder

```
@model PartyInvites.Models.GuestResponse

@{
    Layout = null;
}

<!DOCTYPE html>

<html>
<head>
    <meta name="viewport" content="width=device-width" />
    <title>RsvpForm</title>
</head>
<body>
    <div>
        This is the RsvpForm.cshtml View
    </div>
</body>
</html>
```

This content is mostly HTML but with the addition of a @model Razor expression, which is used to create a *strongly typed view*. A strongly typed view is intended to render a specific model type, and if I specify the type I want to work with (the GuestResponse class in the PartyInvites.Models namespace in this case), MVC can create some helpful shortcuts to make it easier. I will take advantage of the strongly typed feature shortly.

To test the new action method and its view, start the application by selecting Start Debugging from the Debug menu and use the browser to navigate to the /Home/RsvpForm URL.

MVC will use the naming convention I described earlier to direct the request to the RsvpForm action method defined by the Home controller. This action method tells MVC to render the default view, which, with another application of the naming convention, renders RsvpForm.cshtml from the Views/Home folder. Figure 2-14 shows the result.

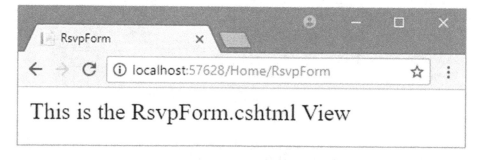

Figure 2-14. *Rendering the second view*

Linking Action Methods

I want to be able to create a link from the MyView view so that guests can see the RsvpForm view without having to know the URL that targets a specific action method, as shown in Listing 2-11.

Listing 2-11. Adding a Link to the RSVP Form in the MyView.cshtml File in the Views/Home Folder

```
@{
    Layout = null;
}

<!DOCTYPE html>

<html>
<head>
    <meta name="viewport" content="width=device-width" />
    <title>Index</title>
</head>
<body>
    <div>
        @ViewBag.Greeting World (from the view)
        <p>We're going to have an exciting party.<br />
        (To do: sell it better. Add pictures or something.)
        </p>
        <a asp-action="RsvpForm">RSVP Now</a>
    </div>
</body>
</html>
```

The addition to the listing is an a element that has an asp-action attribute. The attribute is an example of a *tag helper* attribute, which is an instruction for Razor that will be performed when the view is rendered. The asp-action attribute is an instruction to add an href attribute to the a element that contains a URL for an action method. I explain how tag helpers work in Chapters 24, 25, and 26, but this is the simplest type of tag helper attribute for a elements, and it tells Razor to insert a URL for an action method defined by the same controller for which the current view is being rendered. You can see the link that the helper creates by starting the project, as shown in Figure 2-15.

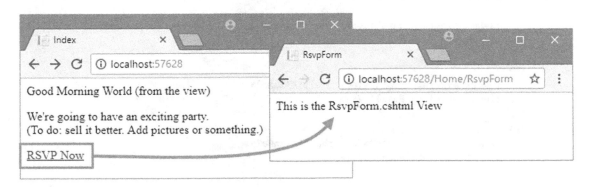

Figure 2-15. *Linking between action methods*

Start the application and roll the mouse over the RSVP Now link the browser. You will see that the link points to the following URL (allowing for the different port number that Visual Studio will have assigned to your project):

```
http://localhost:57628/Home/RsvpForm
```

There is an important principle at work here, which is that you should use the features provided by MVC to generate URLs, rather than hard-code them into your views. When the tag helper created the href attribute for the a element, it inspected the configuration of the application to figure out what the URL should be. This allows the configuration of the application to be changed to support different URL formats without needing to update any views. I explain how this works in Chapter 15.

Building the Form

Now that I have created the strongly typed view and can reach it from the Index view, I am going to build out the contents of the RsvpForm.cshtml file to make it into an HTML form for editing GuestResponse objects, as shown in Listing 2-12.

Listing 2-12. Creating a Form View in the RsvpForm.cshtml File in the Views/Home Folder

```
@model PartyInvites.Models.GuestResponse

@{
    Layout = null;
}

<!DOCTYPE html>

<html>
<head>
    <meta name="viewport" content="width=device-width" />
    <title>RsvpForm</title>
</head>
<body>
    <form asp-action="RsvpForm" method="post">
        <p>
            <label asp-for="Name">Your name:</label>
            <input asp-for="Name" />
        </p>
        <p>
            <label asp-for="Email">Your email:</label>
            <input asp-for="Email" />
        </p>
        <p>
            <label asp-for="Phone">Your phone:</label>
            <input asp-for="Phone" /></p>
```

```
    <p>
        <label>Will you attend?</label>
        <select asp-for="WillAttend">
            <option value="">Choose an option</option>
            <option value="true">Yes, I'll be there</option>
            <option value="false">No, I can't come</option>
        </select>
    </p>
    <button type="submit">Submit RSVP</button>
</form>
</body>
</html>
```

I have defined a label and input element for each property of the GuestResponse model class (or, in the case of the WillAttend property, a select element). Each element is associated with the model property using the asp-for attribute, which is another tag helper attribute. The tag helper attributes configure the elements to tie them to the model object. Here is an example of the HTML that the tag helpers produce and that is sent to the browser:

```
<p>
    <label for="Name">Your name:</label>
    <input type="text" id="Name" name="Name" value="">
</p>
```

The asp-for attribute on the label element sets the value of the for attribute. The asp-for attribute on the input element sets the id and name elements. This doesn't look especially useful at the moment, but you will see that associating elements with a model property offers additional advantages as the application functionality is defined.

Of more immediate use is the asp-action attribute applied to the form element, which uses the application's URL routing configuration to set the action attribute to a URL that will target a specific action method, like this:

```
<form method="post" action="/Home/RsvpForm">
```

As with the helper attribute I applied to the a element, the benefit of this approach is that you can change the system of URLs that the application uses and the content generated by the tag helpers will reflect the changes automatically.

You can see the form by running the application and clicking the RSVP Now link, as shown in Figure 2-16.

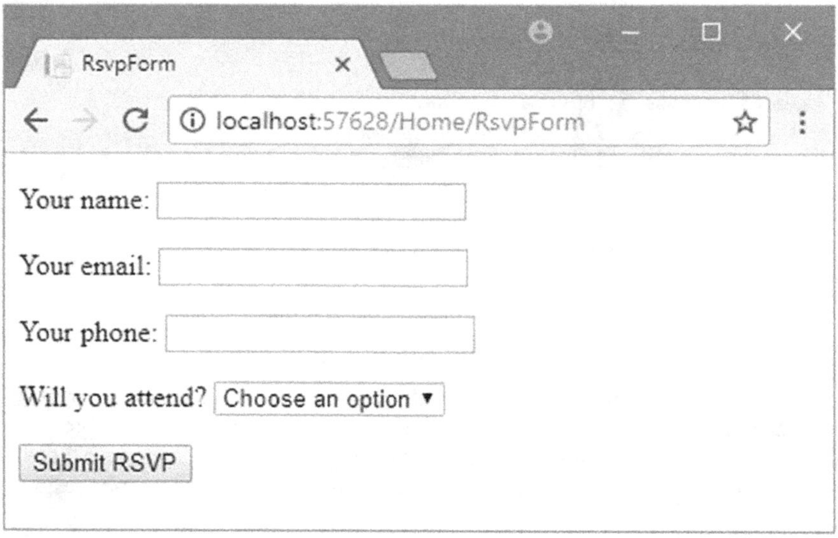

Figure 2-16. *Adding an HTML form to the application*

Receiving Form Data

I have not yet told MVC what I want to do when the form is posted to the server. As things stand, clicking the Submit RSVP button just clears any values you have entered into the form. That is because the form posts back to the RsvpForm action method in the Home controller, which just tells MVC to render the view again. To receive and process submitted form data, I am going to use a core controller feature. I will add a second RsvpForm action method to create the following:

- *A method that responds to HTTP GET requests*: A GET request is what a browser issues normally each time someone clicks a link. This version of the action will be responsible for displaying the initial blank form when someone first visits /Home/ RsvpForm.

- *A method that responds to HTTP POST requests*: By default, forms rendered using Html.BeginForm() are submitted by the browser as a POST request. This version of the action will be responsible for receiving submitted data and deciding what to do with it.

Handing GET and POST requests in separate C# methods helps to keep my controller code tidy since the two methods have different responsibilities. Both action methods are invoked by the same URL, but MVC makes sure that the appropriate method is called, based on whether I am dealing with a GET or POST request. Listing 2-13 shows the changes to the HomeController class.

Listing 2-13. Adding a Method in the HomeController.cs File in the Controllers Folder

```
using System;
using Microsoft.AspNetCore.Mvc;
using PartyInvites.Models;

namespace PartyInvites.Controllers {
```

```
public class HomeController : Controller {

    public ViewResult Index() {
        int hour = DateTime.Now.Hour;
        ViewBag.Greeting = hour < 12 ? "Good Morning" : "Good Afternoon";
        return View("MyView");
    }

    [HttpGet]
    public ViewResult RsvpForm() {
        return View();
    }

    [HttpPost]
    public ViewResult RsvpForm(GuestResponse guestResponse) {
        // TODO: store response from guest
        return View();
    }
}
}
```

I have added the HttpGet attribute to the existing RsvpForm action method. This tells MVC that this method should be used only for GET requests. I then added an overloaded version of the RsvpForm method, which accepts a GuestResponse object. I applied the HttpPost attribute to this method, which tells MVC that the new method will deal with POST requests. I explain how these additions to the listing work in the following sections. I also imported the PartyInvites.Models namespace—this is just so I can refer to the GuestResponse model type without needing to qualify the class name.

Using Model Binding

The first overload of the RsvpForm action method renders the same view as before—the RsvpForm.cshtml file—to generate the form shown in Figure 2-16. The second overload is more interesting because of the parameter, but given that the action method will be invoked in response to an HTTP POST request and that the GuestResponse type is a C# class, how are the two connected?

The answer is *model binding*, a useful MVC feature whereby incoming data is parsed and the key/value pairs in the HTTP request are used to populate properties of domain model types.

Model binding is a powerful and customizable feature that eliminates the grind of dealing with HTTP requests directly and lets you work with C# objects rather than dealing with individual data values sent by the browser. The GuestResponse object that is passed as the parameter to the action method is automatically populated with the data from the form fields. I dive into the detail of model binding, including how it can be customized, in Chapter 26.

One of the application goals is to present a summary page with details of who is attending, which means that I need to keep track of the responses that I receive. I am going to do this by creating an in-memory collection of objects. This isn't useful in a real application because the response data will be lost when the application is stopped or restarted, but this approach will allow me to keep the focus on MVC and create an application that can easily be reset to its initial state.

■ **Tip**   I demonstrate how MVC can be used to store and access data persistently in Chapter 8 as part of a more realistic example application called SportsStore.

I added a file to the project by right-clicking the Models folder and selecting Add ➤ Class from the pop-up menu. I set the name of the file to Repository.cs and used it to define the class shown in Listing 2-14.

Listing 2-14. The Contents of the Repository.cs File in the Models Folder

```
using System.Collections.Generic;

namespace PartyInvites.Models {
    public static class Repository {
        private static List<GuestResponse> responses = new List<GuestResponse>();

        public static IEnumerable<GuestResponse> Responses {
            get {
                return responses;
            }
        }

        public static void AddResponse(GuestResponse response) {
            responses.Add(response);
        }
    }
}
```

The Repository class and its members are set to static, which will make it easy for me to store and retrieve data from different places in the application. MVC provides a more sophisticated approach for defining common functionality, called *dependency injection*, which I describe in Chapter 18, but a static class is a good way to get started for a simple application like this one.

Storing Responses

Now that I have somewhere to store the data, I can update the action method that receives the HTTP POST requests, as shown in Listing 2-15.

Listing 2-15. Updating an Action Method in the HomeController.cs File

```
using System;
using Microsoft.AspNetCore.Mvc;
using PartyInvites.Models;

namespace PartyInvites.Controllers {

    public class HomeController : Controller {

        public ViewResult Index() {
            int hour = DateTime.Now.Hour;
            ViewBag.Greeting = hour < 12 ? "Good Morning" : "Good Afternoon";
            return View("MyView");
        }

        [HttpGet]
        public ViewResult RsvpForm() {
```

```
        return View();
    }

    [HttpPost]
    public ViewResult RsvpForm(GuestResponse guestResponse) {
        Repository.AddResponse(guestResponse);
        return View("Thanks", guestResponse);
    }
  }
}
```

All I have to do to deal with the form data sent in a request is to work with the GuestResponse object that is passed to the action method—in this case, to pass it as an argument to the Repository.AddResponse method so that the response can be stored.

WHY MODEL BINDING IS NOT LIKE WEB FORMS

In Chapter 1, I explained that one of the disadvantages of traditional ASP.NET Web Forms is that it hides the details of HTTP and HTML from the developers. You may be wondering whether the MVC model binding that I used to create a GuestResponse object from an HTTP POST request in Listing 2-15 is doing the same thing.

It isn't. Model binding frees me from the tedious and error-prone task of having to inspect an HTTP request and extract all the data values that I require, but (and this is the important part) if I wanted to process a request manually, I could do so because MVC provides easy access to all of the request data. Nothing is hidden from the developer, but there are a number of useful features that make working with HTTP and HTML simpler and easier; however, using these features is optional.

This may seem like a subtle difference, but as you learn more about MVC, you will see that the development experience is completely different from traditional Web Forms and that you are always aware of how the requests your application receives are handled.

The call to the View method in the RsvpForm action method tells MVC to render a view called Thanks and to pass the GuestResponse object to the view. To create the view, right-click the Views/Home folder in the Solution Explorer and select Add ➤ New Item from the pop-up menu. Select the MVC View Page template in the ASP.NET category, set the name to Thanks.cshtml, and click the Add button. Visual Studio will create the Views/Home/Thanks.cshtml file and open it for editing. Change the contents of the file to match Listing 2-16.

Listing 2-16. The Contents of the Thanks.cshtml File in the Views/Home Folder

```
@model PartyInvites.Models.GuestResponse

@{
    Layout = null;
}

<!DOCTYPE html>

<html>
```

```
<head>
    <meta name="viewport" content="width=device-width" />
    <title>Thanks</title>
</head>
<body>
    <p>
        <h1>Thank you, @Model.Name!</h1>
        @if (Model.WillAttend == true) {
            @:It's great that you're coming. The drinks are already in the fridge!
        } else {
            @:Sorry to hear that you can't make it, but thanks for letting us know.
        }
    </p>
    <p>Click <a asp-action="ListResponses">here</a> to see who is coming.</p>
</body>
</html>
```

The Thanks.cshtml view uses Razor to display content based on the value of the GuestResponse properties that I passed to the View method in the RsvpForm action method. The Razor @model expression specifies the domain model type with which the view is strongly typed.

To access the value of a property in the domain object, I use Model.PropertyName. For example, to get the value of the Name property, I call Model.Name. Don't worry if the Razor syntax doesn't make sense—I explain it in more detail in Chapter 5.

Now that I have created the Thanks view, I have a basic working example of handling a form with MVC. Start the application in Visual Studio by selecting Start Debugging from the Debug menu, click the RSVP Now link, add some data to the form, and click the Submit RSVP button. You will see the result shown in Figure 2-17 (although it will differ if your name is not Joe or you said you could not attend).

Figure 2-17. *The Thanks view*

Displaying the Responses

At the end of the Thanks.cshtml view, I added an a element to create a link to display the list of people who are coming to the party. I used the asp-action tag helper attribute to create a URL that targets an action method called ListResponses, like this:

```
...
<p>Click <a asp-action="ListResponses">here</a> to see who is coming.</p>
...
```

If you hover the mouse over the link that is displayed by the browser, you will see that it targets the / Home/ListResponses URL. This doesn't correspond to any of the action methods in the Home controller, and if you click the link, you will see a 404 Not Found error page

I am going to fix the problem by creating the action method that the URL targets in the Home controller, as shown in Listing 2-17.

Listing 2-17. Adding an Action Method in the HomeController.cs File in the Controllers Folder

```
using System;
using Microsoft.AspNetCore.Mvc;
using PartyInvites.Models;
using System.Linq;

namespace PartyInvites.Controllers {

    public class HomeController : Controller {

        public ViewResult Index() {
            int hour = DateTime.Now.Hour;
            ViewBag.Greeting = hour < 12 ? "Good Morning" : "Good Afternoon";
            return View("MyView");
        }

        [HttpGet]
        public ViewResult RsvpForm() {
            return View();
        }

        [HttpPost]
        public ViewResult RsvpForm(GuestResponse guestResponse) {
            Repository.AddResponse(guestResponse);
            return View("Thanks", guestResponse);
        }

        public ViewResult ListResponses() {
            return View(Repository.Responses.Where(r => r.WillAttend == true));
        }
    }
}
```

The new action method is called `ListResponses`, and it calls the `View` method, using the `Repository.Responses` property as the argument. This is how an action method provides data to a strongly typed view. The collection of `GuestResponse` objects is filtered using LINQ so that only positive responses are used.

The `ListResponses` action method doesn't specify the name of the view that should be used to display the collection of `GuestResponse` objects, which means that the default naming convention will be used and MVC will look for a view called `ListResponses.cshtml` in the Views/Home and Views/Shared folders. To create the view, right-click the Views/Home folder in the Solution Explorer and select Add ➤ New Item from the pop-up menu. Select the MVC View Page template, set the name to `ListResponses.cshtml`, and click the Add button. Edit the contents of the new view to match Listing 2-18.

Listing 2-18. Displaying the Acceptances in the ListResponses.cshtml File in the Views/Home Folder

```
@model IEnumerable<PartyInvites.Models.GuestResponse>

@{
    Layout = null;
}

<!DOCTYPE html>

<html>
<head>
    <meta name="viewport" content="width=device-width" />
    <title>Responses</title>
</head>
<body>
    <h2>Here is the list of people attending the party</h2>
    <table>
        <thead>
            <tr>
                <th>Name</th>
                <th>Email</th>
                <th>Phone</th>
            </tr>
        </thead>
        <tbody>
            @foreach (PartyInvites.Models.GuestResponse r in Model) {
                <tr>
                    <td>@r.Name</td>
                    <td>@r.Email</td>
                    <td>@r.Phone</td>
                </tr>
            }
        </tbody>
    </table>
</body>
</html>
```

Razor view files have the cshtml file extension because they are a mix of C# code and HTML elements. You can see this in Listing 2-18 where I have used a foreach loop to process each of the GuestResponse objects that the action method passes to the view using the View method. Unlike a normal C# foreach loop, the body of a Razor foreach loop contains HTML elements that are added to the response that will be sent back to the browser. In this view, each GuestResponse object generates a tr element that contains td elements populated with the value of an object property.

To see the list at work, run the application by selecting Start Debugging from the Start menu, submit some form data, and then click the link to see the list of responses. You will see a summary of the data you have entered since the application was started, as shown in Figure 2-18. The view does not present the data in an appealing way, but it is enough for the moment, and I will address the styling of the application later in this chapter.

Figure 2-18. *Showing a list of party attendees*

Adding Validation

I am now in a position to add data validation to my application. Without validation, users could enter nonsense data or even submit an empty form. In an MVC application, you typically apply validation to the domain model rather than in the user interface. This means that you define validation in one place, but it takes effect anywhere in the application that the model class is used. MVC supports *declarative validation rules* defined with attributes from the System.ComponentModel.DataAnnotations namespace, meaning that validation constraints are expressed using the standard C# attribute features. Listing 2-19 shows how I applied these attributes to the GuestResponse model class.

Listing 2-19. Applying Validation in the GuestResponse.cs File in the Models Folder

```
using System.ComponentModel.DataAnnotations;

namespace PartyInvites.Models {

    public class GuestResponse {

        [Required(ErrorMessage = "Please enter your name")]
        public string Name { get; set; }
```

```
    [Required(ErrorMessage = "Please enter your email address")]
    [RegularExpression(".+\\@.+\\..+",
        ErrorMessage = "Please enter a valid email address")]
    public string Email { get; set; }

    [Required(ErrorMessage = "Please enter your phone number")]
    public string Phone { get; set; }

    [Required(ErrorMessage = "Please specify whether you'll attend")]
    public bool? WillAttend { get; set; }
    }
}
```

MVC automatically detects the attributes and uses them to validate data during the model-binding process. I imported the namespace that contains the validation attributes, so I can refer to them without needing to qualify their names.

■ **Tip** As noted earlier, I used a nullable bool for the WillAttend property. I did this so that I could apply the Required validation attribute. If I had used a regular bool, the value I received through model binding could be only true or false, and I would not be able to tell whether the user had selected a value. A nullable bool has three possible values: true, false, and null. The browser sends a null value if the user has not selected a value, and this causes the Required attribute to report a validation error. This is a nice example of how MVC elegantly blends C# features with HTML and HTTP.

I check to see whether there has been a validation problem using the ModelState.IsValid property in the controller class. Listing 2-20 shows how I have done this in the POST-enabled RsvpForm action method in the Home controller class.

Listing 2-20. Checking for Validation Errors in the HomeController.cs File in the Controllers Folder

```
using System;
using Microsoft.AspNetCore.Mvc;
using PartyInvites.Models;
using System.Linq;

namespace PartyInvites.Controllers {

    public class HomeController : Controller {

        public ViewResult Index() {
            int hour = DateTime.Now.Hour;
            ViewBag.Greeting = hour < 12 ? "Good Morning" : "Good Afternoon";
            return View("MyView");
        }

        [HttpGet]
        public ViewResult RsvpForm() {
            return View();
        }
```

```
        [HttpPost]
        public ViewResult RsvpForm(GuestResponse guestResponse) {
            if (ModelState.IsValid) {
                Repository.AddResponse(guestResponse);
                return View("Thanks", guestResponse);
            } else {
                // there is a validation error
                return View();
            }
        }

        public ViewResult ListResponses() {
            return View(Repository.Responses.Where(r => r.WillAttend == true));
        }
    }
}
```

The Controller base class provides a property called ModelState that provides information about the conversion of HTTP request data into C# objects. If the ModelState.IsValid property returns true, then I know that MVC has been able to satisfy the validation constraints I specified through the attributes on the GuestResponse class. When this happens, I render the Thanks view, just as I did previously.

If the ModelState.IsValid property returns false, then I know that there are validation errors. The object returned by the ModelState property provides details of each problem that has been encountered, but I don't need to get into that level of detail because I can rely on a useful feature that automates the process of asking the user to address any problems by calling the View method without any parameters.

When MVC renders a view, Razor has access to the details of any validation errors associated with the request, and tag helpers can access the details to display validation errors to the user. Listing 2-21 shows the addition of validation tag helper attributes to the RsvpForm view.

Listing 2-21. Adding a Validation Summary to the RsvpForm.cshtml File in the Views/Home Folder

```
@model PartyInvites.Models.GuestResponse

@{
    Layout = null;
}

<!DOCTYPE html>

<html>
<head>
    <meta name="viewport" content="width=device-width" />
    <title>RsvpForm</title>
</head>
<body>
    <form asp-action="RsvpForm" method="post">
        <div asp-validation-summary="All"></div>
        <p>
            <label asp-for="Name">Your name:</label>
            <input asp-for="Name" />
        </p>
        <p>
```

```
                <label asp-for="Email">Your email:</label>
                <input asp-for="Email" />
        </p>
        <p>
                <label asp-for="Phone">Your phone:</label>
                <input asp-for="Phone" /></p>
        <p>
                <label>Will you attend?</label>
                <select asp-for="WillAttend">
                    <option value="">Choose an option</option>
                    <option value="true">Yes, I'll be there</option>
                    <option value="false">No, I can't come</option>
                </select>
        </p>
        <button type="submit">Submit RSVP</button>
    </form>
</body>
</html>
```

The asp-validation-summary attribute is applied to a div element, and it displays a list of validation errors when the view is rendered. The value for the asp-validation-summary attribute is a value from an enumeration called ValidationSummary, which specifies what types of validation errors the summary will contain. I specified All, which is a good starting point for most applications, and I describe the other values and explain how they work in Chapter 27.

To see how the validation summary works, run the application, fill out the Name field, and submit the form without entering any other data. You will see a summary of validation errors, as shown in Figure 2-19.

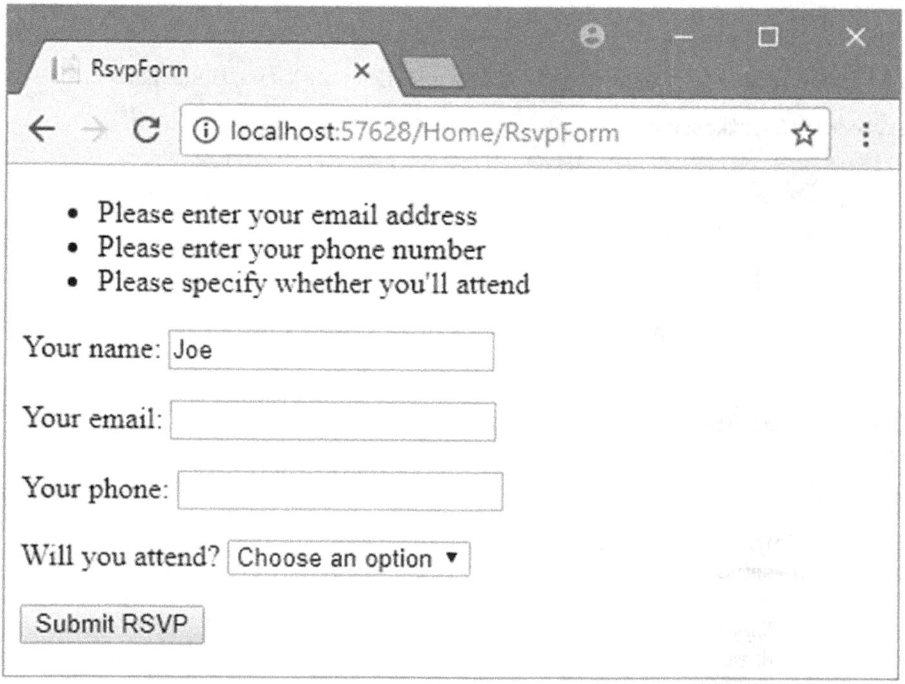

Figure 2-19. *Displaying validation errors*

The RsvpForm action method will not render the Thanks view until all of the validation constraints applied to the GuestResponse class have been satisfied. Notice that the data entered into the Name field was preserved and displayed again when Razor rendered the view with the validation summary. This is another benefit of model binding, and it simplifies working with form data.

▪ **Note**   If you have worked with ASP.NET Web Forms, you will know that Web Forms has a concept of *server controls* that retain state by serializing values into a hidden form field called __VIEWSTATE. MVC model binding is not related to the Web Forms concepts of server controls, postbacks, or View State. MVC does not inject a hidden __VIEWSTATE field into your rendered HTML pages. Instead, it includes the data by setting the value attributes of the input element.

Highlighting Invalid Fields

The tag helper attributes that associate model properties with elements have a handy feature that can be used in conjunction with model binding. When a model class property has failed validation, the helper attributes will generate slightly different HTML. Here is the input element that is generated for the Phone field when there is no validation error:

```
<input type="text" data-val="true" data-val-required="Please enter your phone number"
id="Phone" name="Phone" value="">
```

For comparison, here is the same HTML element after the user has submitted the form without entering any data into the text field (which is a validation error because I applied the Required validation attribute to the Phone property of the GuestResponse class):

```
<input type="text" class="input-validation-error" data-val="true"
    data-val-required="Please enter your phone number" id="Phone"
    name="Phone" value="">
```

I have highlighted the difference: the asp-for tag helper attribute added the input element to a class called input-validation-error. I can take advantage of this feature by creating a stylesheet that contains CSS styles for this class and the others that different HTML helper attributes use.

The convention in MVC projects is that static content delivered to clients is placed into the wwwroot folder, organized by content type, so that CSS stylesheets go into the wwwroot/css folder, JavaScript files go into the wwwroot/js folder, and so on.

To create the stylesheet, right-click the wwwroot/css folder in the Visual Studio Solution Explorer, select Add ➤ New Item, navigate to the ASP.NET Core ➤ Web ➤ Content section, and select Style Sheet from the list of templates, as shown in Figure 2-20.

▪ **Tip**   Visual Studio creates a site.css file in the wwwroot/css folder when a project is created using the Web Application template. You can ignore this file, which I don't use in this chapter.

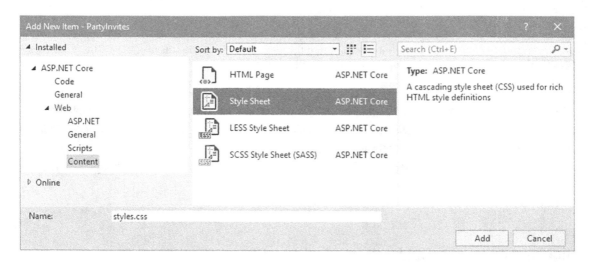

Figure 2-20. *Creating a CSS stylesheet*

Set the name of the file to `styles.css`, click the Add button to create the stylesheet, and edit the new file so that it contains the styles shown in Listing 2-22.

Listing 2-22. The Contents of the styles.css File in the wwwroot/css Folder

```
.field-validation-error    {color: #f00;}
.field-validation-valid    { display: none;}
.input-validation-error    { border: 1px solid #f00; background-color: #fee; }
.validation-summary-errors { font-weight: bold; color: #f00;}
.validation-summary-valid  { display: none;}
To apply this stylesheet, I have added a link element to the head section of the RsvpForm
view, as shown in Listing 2-23.
```

Listing 2-23. Applying a Stylesheet in the RsvpForm.cshtml File in the Views/Home Folder

```
...
<head>
    <meta name="viewport" content="width=device-width" />
    <title>RsvpForm</title>
    <link rel="stylesheet" href="/css/styles.css" />
</head>
...
```

The link element uses the href attribute to specify the location of the stylesheet. Notice that the wwwroot folder is omitted from the URL. The default configuration for ASP.NET includes support for serving static content, such as images, CSS stylesheets, and JavaScript files, and it maps requests to the wwwroot folder automatically. I describe the ASP.NET and MVC configuration process in Chapter 14.

■ **Tip**   There is a special tag helper for dealing with stylesheets that can be useful if you have a lot of files to manage. See Chapter 25 for details.

With the application of the stylesheet, a more visually obvious validation error will be displayed when data is submitted that causes a validation error, as shown in Figure 2-21.

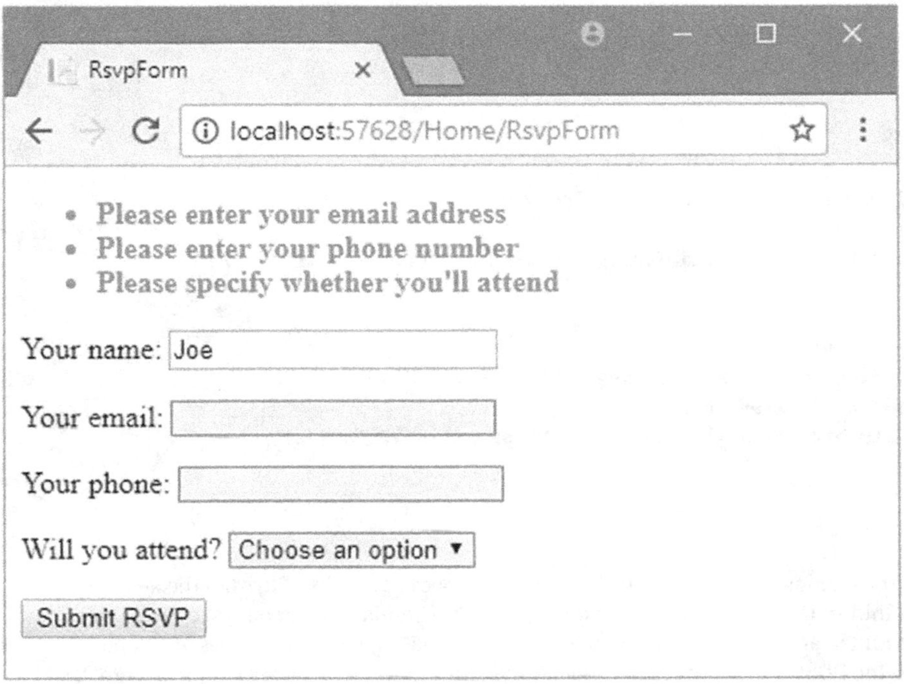

Figure 2-21. *Automatically highlighted validation errors*

Styling the Content

All of the functional goals for the application are complete, but the overall appearance of the application is poor. When you create a project using the Web Application template, as I did for the example in this chapter, Visual Studio installs some common client-side development packages. While I am not a fan of using template projects, I do like the client-side libraries that Microsoft has chosen. One of them is called Bootstrap, which is a nice CSS framework originally developed by Twitter that has become a major open source project in its own right and which has become a mainstay of web application development.

___

■ **Note** Bootstrap 3 is the current version as I write this, but version 4 is under development. Microsoft may choose to update the version of Bootstrap used by the Web Application template in later releases of Visual Studio, which may cause the content to display differently. This won't be a problem for the other chapters in the book because I show you how to explicitly specify a package version so that you get the expected results.

___

Styling the Welcome View

The basic Bootstrap features work by applying classes to elements that correspond to CSS selectors defined in the files added to the wwwroot/lib/bootstrap folder. You can get full details of the classes that Bootstrap defines from http://getbootstrap.com, but you can see how I have applied some basic styling to the MyView.cshtml view file in Listing 2-24.

45

Listing 2-24. Adding Bootstrap to the MyView.cshtml File in the Views/Home Folder

```
@{
    Layout = null;
}

<!DOCTYPE html>

<html>
<head>
    <meta name="viewport" content="width=device-width" />
    <title>Index</title>
    <link rel="stylesheet" href="/lib/bootstrap/dist/css/bootstrap.css" />
</head>
<body>
    <div class="text-center">
        <h3>We're going to have an exciting party!</h3>
        <h4>And you are invited</h4>
        <a class="btn btn-primary" asp-action="RsvpForm">RSVP Now</a>
    </div>
</body>
</html>
```

I have added a link element whose href attribute loads the bootstrap.css file from the wwwroot/lib/ bootstrap/dist/css folder. The convention is that third-party CSS and JavaScript packages are installed into the wwwroot/lib folder, and I describe the tool that is used to manage these packages in Chapter 6.

Having imported the Bootstrap stylesheets, I need to style my elements. This is a simple example, so I only need to use a small number of Bootstrap CSS classes: text-center, btn, and btn-primary.

The text-center class centers the content of an element and its children. The btn class styles a button, input, or a element as a pretty button, and the btn-primary class specifies which of a range of colors I want the button to be. You can see the effect by running the application, as shown in Figure 2-22.

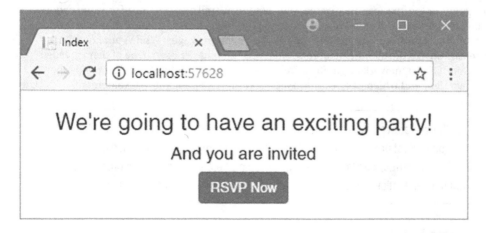

Figure 2-22. *Styling a view*

It will be obvious to you that I am not a web designer. In fact, as a child, I was excused from art lessons on the basis that I had absolutely no talent whatsoever. This had the happy result of making more time for math lessons but meant that my artistic skills have not developed beyond those of the average 10-year-old child. For a real project, I would seek a professional to help design and style the content, but for this example, I am going it alone, and that means applying Bootstrap with as much restraint and consistency as I can muster.

Styling the RsvpForm View

Bootstrap defines classes that can be used to style forms. I am not going to go into detail, but you can see how I have applied these classes in Listing 2-25.

Listing 2-25. Adding Bootstrap to the RsvpForm.cshtml File in the Views/Home Folder

```
@model PartyInvites.Models.GuestResponse

@{
    Layout = null;
}

<!DOCTYPE html>

<html>
<head>
    <meta name="viewport" content="width=device-width" />
    <title>RsvpForm</title>
    <link rel="stylesheet" href="/css/styles.css" />
    <link rel="stylesheet" href="/lib/bootstrap/dist/css/bootstrap.css" />
</head>
<body>
    <div class="panel panel-success">
        <div class="panel-heading text-center"><h4>RSVP</h4></div>
        <div class="panel-body">
            <form class="p-a-1" asp-action="RsvpForm" method="post">
                <div asp-validation-summary="All"></div>
                <div class="form-group">
                    <label asp-for="Name">Your name:</label>
                    <input class="form-control" asp-for="Name" />
                </div>
                <div class="form-group">
                    <label asp-for="Email">Your email:</label>
                    <input class="form-control" asp-for="Email" />
                </div>
                <div class="form-group">
                    <label asp-for="Phone">Your phone:</label>
                    <input class="form-control" asp-for="Phone" />
                </div>
                <div class="form-group">
                    <label>Will you attend?</label>
                    <select class="form-control" asp-for="WillAttend">
                        <option value="">Choose an option</option>
                        <option value="true">Yes, I'll be there</option>
                        <option value="false">No, I can't come</option>
                    </select>
```

47

```
                </div>
                <div class="text-center">
                    <button class="btn btn-primary" type="submit">
                        Submit RSVP
                    </button>
                </div>
            </form>
        </div>
    </div>
</body>
</html>
```

The Bootstrap classes in this example create a header, just to give structure to the layout. To style the form, I have used the form-group class, which is used to style the element that contains the label and the associated input or select element. You can see the effect of the styles in Figure 2-23.

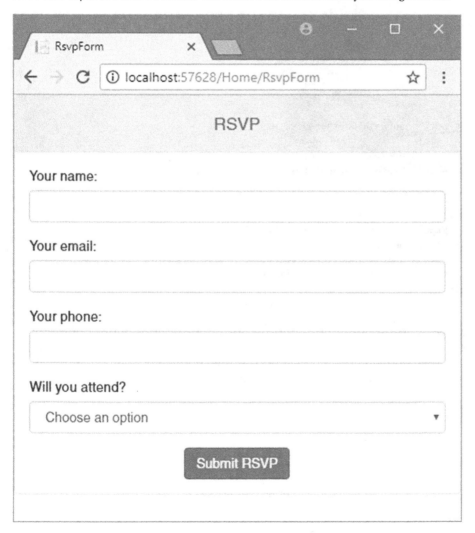

Figure 2-23. *Styling the RsvpForm view*

Styling the Thanks View

The next view file to style is Thanks.cshtml, and you can see how I have done this in Listing 2-26, using CSS classes that are similar to the ones I used for the other views. To make an application easier to manage, it is a good principle to avoid duplicating code and markup wherever possible. MVC provides several features to help reduce duplication, which I describe in later chapters. These features include Razor layouts (Chapter 5), partial views (Chapter 21), and view components (Chapter 22).

Listing 2-26. Applying Bootstrap to the Thanks.cshtml File in the Views/Home Folder

```
@model PartyInvites.Models.GuestResponse

@{
    Layout = null;
}

<!DOCTYPE html>

<html>
<head>
    <meta name="viewport" content="width=device-width" />
    <title>Thanks</title>
    <link rel="stylesheet" href="/lib/bootstrap/dist/css/bootstrap.css" />
</head>
<body class="text-center">
    <p>
        <h1>Thank you, @Model.Name!</h1>
        @if (Model.WillAttend == true) {
            @:It's great that you're coming. The drinks are already in the fridge!
        } else {
            @:Sorry to hear that you can't make it, but thanks for letting us know.
        }
    </p>
    Click <a class="nav-link" asp-action="ListResponses">here</a>
    to see who is coming.
</body>
</html>
```

Figure 2-24 shows the effect of the styles.

Figure 2-24. *Styling the Thanks view*

Styling the List View

The final view to style is ListResponses, which presents the list of attendees. Styling the content follows the same basic approach as used for all Bootstrap styles, as shown in Listing 2-27.

Listing 2-27. Adding Bootstrap to the ListResponses.cshtml File in the Views/Home Folder

```
@model IEnumerable<PartyInvites.Models.GuestResponse>

@{
    Layout = null;
}

<!DOCTYPE html>

<html>
<head>
    <meta name="viewport" content="width=device-width" />
    <link rel="stylesheet" href="/lib/bootstrap/dist/css/bootstrap.css" />
    <title>Responses</title>
</head>
<body>
    <div class="panel-body">
        <h2>Here is the list of people attending the party</h2>
        <table class="table table-sm table-striped table-bordered">
            <thead>
                <tr>
                    <th>Name</th>
                    <th>Email</th>
                    <th>Phone</th>
                </tr>
            </thead>
            <tbody>
```

```
@foreach (PartyInvites.Models.GuestResponse r in Model) {
    <tr>
        <td>@r.Name</td>
        <td>@r.Email</td>
        <td>@r.Phone</td>
    </tr>
}
        </tbody>
    </table>
</div>
</body>
</html>
```

Figure 2-25 shows the way that the table of attendees is presented. Adding these styles to the view completes the example application, which now meets all of the development goals and has an improved appearance.

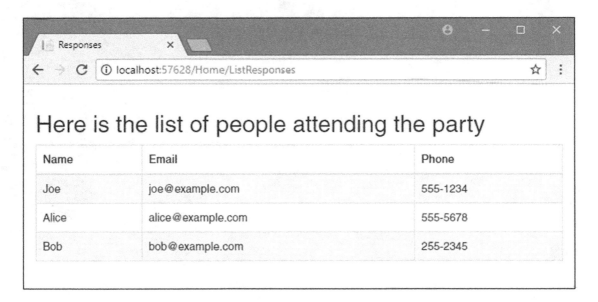

Figure 2-25. Styling the ListResponses view

Summary

In this chapter, I created a new MVC project and used it to construct a simple data-entry application, giving you a first glimpse of the ASP.NET Core MVC architecture and approach. I skipped some key features (including Razor syntax, routing, and testing), but I return to these topics in depth in later chapters. In the next chapter, I describe the MVC design patterns, which form the foundation for effective development with ASP.NET Core MVC.

■ ■ ■

CHAPTER 3

The MVC Pattern, Projects, and Conventions

Before digging into the details of ASP.NET Core MVC, I want to make sure you are familiar with the MVC design pattern, the thinking behind it, and the way it is translated into ASP.NET Core MVC projects. You might already know about some of the ideas and conventions I discuss in this chapter, especially if you have done advanced ASP.NET or C# development. If not, I encourage you to read carefully—a good understanding of what lies behind MVC can help put the features of the framework into context as you continue through the book.

The History of MVC

The term *model-view-controller* has been in use since the late 1970s and arose from the Smalltalk project at Xerox PARC, where it was conceived as a way to organize some early GUI applications. Some of the fine detail of the original MVC pattern was tied to Smalltalk-specific concepts, such as *screens* and *tools*, but the broader concepts are still applicable to applications, and they are especially well-suited to web applications.

Understanding the MVC Pattern

In high-level terms, the MVC pattern means that an MVC application will be split into at least three pieces.

- *Models*, which contain or represent the data that users work with

- *Views*, which are used to render some part of the model as a user interface

- *Controllers*, which process incoming requests, perform operations on the model, and select views to render to the user

Each piece of the MVC architecture is well-defined and self-contained, which is referred to as the *separation of concerns*. The logic that manipulates the data in the model is contained *only* in the model, the logic that displays data is *only* in the view, and the code that handles user requests and input is contained *only* in the controller. With a clear division between each of the pieces, your application will be easier to maintain and extend over its lifetime, no matter how large it becomes.

Understanding Models

Models—the *M* in *MVC*—contain the data that users work with. There are two broad types of model: *view models*, which represent just data passed from the controller to the view, and *domain models*, which contain the data in a business domain, along with the operations, transformations, and rules for creating, storing, and manipulating that data, collectively referred to as the *model logic*.

© Adam Freeman 2017
A. Freeman, *Pro ASP.NET Core MVC 2*, https://doi.org/10.1007/978-1-4842-3150-0_3

Models are the definition of the universe your application works in. In a banking application, for example, the model represents everything in the bank that the application supports, such as accounts, the general ledger, and credit limits for customers, as well as the operations that can be used to manipulate the data in the model, such as depositing funds and making withdrawals from the accounts. The model is also responsible for preserving the overall state and consistency of the data—for example, making sure that all transactions are added to the ledger and that a client doesn't withdraw more money than he is entitled to or more money than the bank has.

For each of the components in the MVC pattern, I'll describe what should and should not be included. The model in an application built using the MVC pattern *should*

- Contain the domain data

- Contain the logic for creating, managing, and modifying the domain data

- Provide a clean API that exposes the model data and operations on it

The model *should not*

- Expose details of how the model data is obtained or managed (in other words, details of the data storage mechanism should not be exposed to controllers and views)

- Contain logic that transforms the model based on user interaction (because that is the controller's job)

- Contain logic for displaying data to the user (that is the view's job)

The benefits of ensuring that the model is isolated from the controller and views are that you can test your logic more easily (I describe unit testing in Chapter 7) and that enhancing and maintaining the overall application is simpler and easier.

■ **Tip**   Many developers new to the MVC pattern get confused with the idea of including logic in the data model, believing that the goal of the MVC pattern is to separate data from logic. This is a misapprehension: the goal of the MVC pattern is to divide an application into three functional areas, each of which may contain both logic *and* data. The goal isn't to eliminate logic from the model. Rather, it is to ensure that the model only contains logic for creating and managing the model data.

Understanding Controllers

Controllers are the connective tissue in the MVC pattern, acting as conduits between the data model and views. Controllers define actions that provide the business logic that operates on the data model and that provide the data that views display to the user.

A controller built using the MVC pattern *should*

- Contain the actions required to update the model based on user interaction

The controller *should not*

- Contain logic that manages the appearance of data (that is the job of the view)

- Contain logic that manages the persistence of data (that is the job of the model)

Understanding Views

Views contain the logic required to display data to the user or to capture data from the user so that it can be processed by a controller action. Views *should*

- Contain the logic and markup required to present data to the user

Views *should not*

- Contain complex logic (this is better placed in a controller)
- Contain logic that creates, stores, or manipulates the domain model

Views *can* contain logic, but it should be simple and used sparingly. Putting anything but the simplest method calls or expressions in a view makes the overall application harder to test and maintain.

The ASP.NET Implementation of MVC

As its name suggests, the ASP.NET Core MVC adapts the abstract MVC pattern to the world of ASP.NET and C# development. In ASP.NET Core MVC, controllers are C# classes, usually derived from the `Microsoft.AspNetCore.Mvc.Controller` class. Each `public` method in a class derived from `Controller` is an *action method*, which is associated with a URL. When a request is sent to the URL associated with an action method, the statements in that action method are executed in order to perform some operation on the domain model and then to select a view to display to the client. Figure 3-1 shows the interactions between the controller, model, and view.

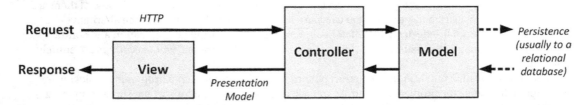

Figure 3-1. *The interactions in an MVC application*

ASP.NET Core MVC uses a *view engine*, known as Razor, which is the component responsible for processing a view in order to generate a response for the browser. Razor views are HTML templates that contain C# logic that is used to process model data to generate dynamic content that responds to changes in the model. I explain how Razor works in Chapter 5.

ASP.NET Core MVC doesn't apply any constraints on the implementation of your domain model. You can create a model using regular C# objects and implement persistence using any of the databases, object-relational mapping frameworks, or other data tools supported by .NET.

UNDERSTANDING SINGLE-PAGE APPLICATIONS

The history of web application development has tended to treat browsers as a simple display device for rendering HTML and responding to mouse clicks. This is known as the *round-trip* style of web application. Each time the user clicks a link, an HTTP request is sent to the ASP.NET Core MVC application, where a controller selects a view that is rendered by Razor and sent back to the browser so that a new HTML page can be displayed to the user. All the logic, data, and state resides in the ASP.NET

Core MVC server, which simplifies development and means you don't have to pay much attention to the browser, other than ensuring that it can handle the HTML features you include in your Razor views.

By contrast, *single-page applications* incorporate the browser into the application platform. The server is responsible for managing the application's data, while JavaScript code running the browser requests that data, displays it to the user, and responds to user interaction. In a single-page application, the responsibilities for the model, view, and controller are shared between the browser and the server. Rather than send complete HTML pages to the browser, the ASP.NET Core MVC part of the application provides access to the application's data, which is queried and displayed by a JavaScript framework such as Angular or React.

Single-page applications can be more responsive than round-trip applications, but they are more complex to create and require both C# and JavaScript skills for effective development, the difficulty of which should not be underestimated. In Chapter 20, I demonstrate how ASP.NET Core MVC can be used to provide data in this kind of application, but I don't demonstrate single-page application development, which is a topic in its own right. My preferred JavaScript framework is Angular, which I have written about in *Pro Angular*. If you want to use Angular with ASP.NET Core MVC, then see my book *Essential Angular for ASP.NET Core MVC*.

Comparing MVC to Other Patterns

MVC is not the only software architecture pattern, of course. There are many others, and some of them are, or at least have been, extremely popular. You can learn a lot about MVC by looking at the alternatives. In the following sections, I briefly describe different approaches to structuring an application and contrast them with MVC. Some of the patterns are close variations on the MVC theme, whereas others are entirely different.

I am not suggesting that MVC is the perfect pattern for all situations. I am a proponent of picking the best approach to solve the problem at hand. As you will see, there are situations where some competing patterns are as useful as or better than MVC. I encourage you to make an *informed* and *deliberate* choice when selecting a pattern. The fact that you are reading this book suggests that you already have a certain commitment to the MVC pattern, but it is always helpful to maintain the widest possible perspective.

Understanding the Smart UI Pattern

One of the most common design patterns is known as the *smart user interface* (smart UI). Most programmers have created a smart UI application at some point in their careers—I certainly have. If you have used Windows Forms or ASP.NET Web Forms, you have too.

To build a smart UI application, developers construct a user interface, often by dragging a set of *components* or *controls* onto a design surface or canvas. The controls report interactions with the user by emitting events for button presses, keystrokes, mouse movements, and so on. The developer adds code to respond to these events in a series of *event handlers*; these are small blocks of code that are called when a specific event on a specific component is emitted. This creates a monolithic application, as shown in Figure 3-2. The code that handles the user interface and the business is all mixed together with no separation of concerns at all. The code that defines the acceptable values for data input and that queries for data or modifies a user account ends up in little pieces, coupled together by the order in which events are expected.

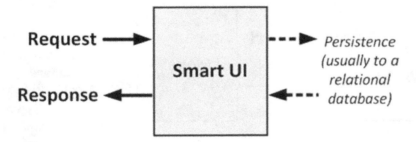

Figure 3-2. *The smart UI pattern*

Smart UIs are ideal for simple projects because you can get some good results quickly (by comparison to MVC development, which, as you'll see in Chapter 8, requires an initial investment of time before delivering results). Smart UIs are also suited to user interface prototyping. These design surface tools can be *really* good, and if you are sitting with a customer and want to capture the requirements for the look and flow of the interface, a smart UI tool can be a quick and responsive way to generate and test different ideas.

The biggest drawback is that smart UIs are difficult to maintain and extend. Mixing the domain model and business logic code in with the user interface code leads to duplication, where the same fragment of business logic is copied and pasted to support a newly added component. Finding all the duplicate parts and applying a fix can be difficult. It can be almost impossible to add a new feature without breaking an existing one. Testing a smart UI application can also be difficult. The only way is to simulate user interactions, which is far from ideal and a difficult basis from which to provide full test coverage.

In the world of MVC, the smart UI is often referred to as an *anti-pattern*: something that should be avoided at all costs. This antipathy arises, at least in part, because people come to MVC looking for an alternative after spending part of their careers trying to develop and maintain smart UI applications that grew out of control.

That said, it is a mistake to reject the smart UI pattern out of hand. Not everything is rotten in the smart UI pattern, and there are positive aspects to this approach. Smart UI applications are quick and easy to develop. The component and design tool producers have put a lot of effort into making the development experience a pleasant one, and even the most inexperienced programmer can produce something professional-looking and reasonably functional in just a few hours.

The biggest weakness of smart UI applications—maintainability—doesn't arise in small development efforts. If you are producing a simple tool for a small audience, a smart UI application can be a good solution. The additional complexity of an MVC application simply isn't warranted.

Understanding the Model-View Architecture

The area in which maintenance problems tend to arise in a smart UI application is in the business logic, which ends up so diffused across the application that making changes or adding features becomes a fraught process. An improvement in this area is offered by the *model-view* architecture, which pulls out the business logic into a separate domain model. In doing this, the data, processes, and rules are all concentrated in one part of the application, as shown in Figure 3-3.

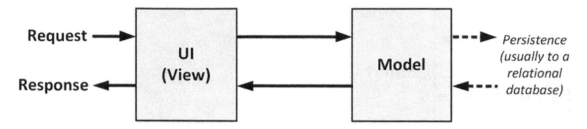

Figure 3-3. *The model-view pattern*

The model-view architecture can be an improvement over the monolithic smart UI pattern—it is much easier to maintain, for example—but two problems arise. The first is that since the UI and the domain model are closely integrated, it can be difficult to perform unit testing on either. The second problem arises from practice, rather than the definition of the pattern. The model typically contains a mass of data access code— this need not be the case, but it usually is—and this means that the data model does not contain just the business data, operations, and rules.

Understanding Classic Three-Tier Architecture

To address the problems of the model-view architecture, the *three-tier* or *three-layer* pattern separates the persistence code from the domain model and places it in a new component called the *data access layer* (DAL). This is shown in Figure 3-4.

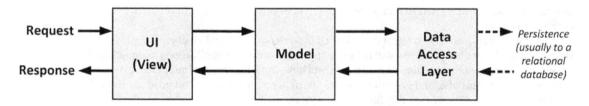

Figure 3-4. *The three-tier pattern*

The three-tier architecture is the most widely used pattern for business applications. It has no constraints on how the UI is implemented and provides good separation of concerns without being too complicated. And, with some care, the DAL can be created so that unit testing is relatively easy. You can see the obvious similarities between a classic three-tier application and the MVC pattern. The difference is that when the UI layer is directly coupled to a click-and-event GUI framework (such as Windows Forms or ASP.NET Web Forms), it becomes almost impossible to perform automated unit tests. And because the UI part of a three-tier application can be complex, there's a lot of code that can't be rigorously tested.

In the worst scenario, the three-tier pattern's lack of enforced discipline in the UI tier means that many such applications end up as thinly disguised smart UI applications, with no real separation of concerns. This gives the worst possible outcome: an untestable, unmaintainable application that is excessively complex.

Understanding Variations on MVC

I have already described the core design principles of MVC applications, especially as they apply to the ASP. NET Core MVC. Others interpret aspects of the pattern differently and have added to, adjusted, or otherwise adapted MVC to suit the scope and subject of their projects. In the following sections, I provide a brief overview of the two most prevalent variations on the MVC theme. Understanding these variations is not essential to working with ASP.NET Core MVC, and I have included this information just for completeness because you will hear the terms used in most discussions of software patterns.

Understanding the Model-View-Presenter Pattern

Model-view-presenter (MVP) is a variation on MVC that is designed to fit more easily with stateful GUI platforms such as Windows Forms or ASP.NET Web Forms. This is a worthwhile attempt to get the best aspects of the smart UI pattern without the problems it usually brings.

In this pattern, the presenter has the same responsibilities as an MVC controller, but it also takes a more direct relationship to a stateful view, directly managing the values displayed in the UI components according to the user's inputs and actions. There are two implementations of this pattern.

- The *passive view* implementation, in which the view contains no logic. The view is a container for UI controls that are directly manipulated by the presenter.

- The *supervising controller* implementation, in which the view may be responsible for some elements of presentation logic, such as data binding, and has been given a reference to a data source from the domain models.

The difference between these two approaches relates to how intelligent the view is. Either way, the presenter is decoupled from the GUI framework, which makes the presenter logic simpler and suitable for unit testing.

Understanding the Model-View-View Model Pattern

The *model-view-view model* (MVVM) pattern is a recent variation on MVC. It originated from Microsoft and is used in the Windows Presentation Foundation (WPF). In the MVVM pattern, models and views have the same roles as they do in MVC. The difference is the MVVM concept of a *view model*, which is an abstract representation of a user interface. Typically the view model is a C# class that exposes both properties for the data to be displayed in the UI and operations on the data that can be invoked from the UI. Unlike an MVC controller, an MVVM view model has no notion that a view (or any specific UI technology) exists. An MVVM view uses the WPF *binding* feature to bidirectionally associate properties exposed by controls in the view (items in a drop-down menu or the effect of pressing a button) with the properties exposed by the view model.

■ **Tip**   The MVC pattern also uses the term *view model* but refers to a simple model class that is used only to pass data from a controller to a view, as opposed to *domain models*, which are sophisticated representations of data, operations, and rules.

Understanding ASP.NET Core MVC Projects

When you create a new ASP.NET Core MVC project, Visual Studio gives you some choices about the initial content that you want in the project. The idea is to ease the learning process for new developers and apply some time-saving best practices for common features and tasks. I am not a fan of this kind of approach to cookie-cutter projects or code. The intent is good, but the execution is underwhelming. One of the characteristics I like most about ASP.NET Core and MVC is just how much flexibility I have in tailoring the platform to suit my development style. The projects, classes, and views that Visual Studio creates and populates make me feel constrained to work in someone else's style. I also find the content and configuration too generic and too bland to be useful. Microsoft can't possibly know what kind of application is needed and so it covers all the bases, but in such a generalized way that I end up just ripping out the default content anyway.

My advice (given to anyone who makes the mistake of asking) is to start with an empty project and add the folders, files, and packages that you need. Not only will you learn more about the way that MVC works, but you will have complete control over what your application contains.

But my preferences should not color your development experience. You may find the templates more useful than I do, especially if you are new to ASP.NET development and you have not yet developed a development style that suits you. You may also find the project templates a useful resource and a source of ideas, although you should be cautious about adding any functionality to an application before you completely understand how it works.

Creating the Project

When you first create a new ASP.NET Core project, you will be presented with a range of starting points, as shown in Figure 3-5.

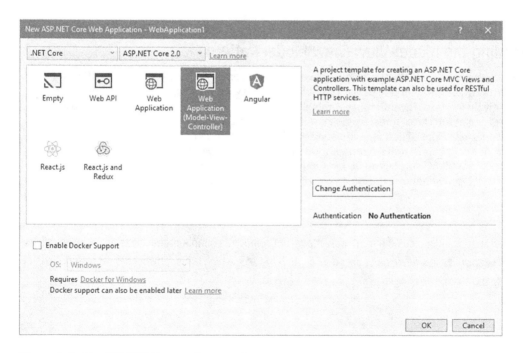

Figure 3-5. *The ASP.NET Core project templates*

The Empty project template contains the plumbing for ASP.NET Core but doesn't include the libraries or configuration required for an MVC application. The Web API project template includes ASP.NET Core and MVC, with a sample application that demonstrates how to receive and process data requests from clients, using an API controller, which I describe in Chapter 20.

The Web Application (Model-View-Controller) project template includes ASP.NET Core and MVC, with a sample application that demonstrates how to generate HTML content. The Web API and Web Application (Model-View-Controller) templates can be configured with different schemes for authenticating users and authorizing their access to the application.

The other templates provide initial content suitable for working with single-page application frameworks (Angular and React) and with Razor Pages (which allows code and markup to be mixed in a file, merging the roles of controllers and views, and which trades off some of the benefits of the MVC model for simplicity).

The project templates can give the impression that you need to follow a specific path to create a certain kind of ASP.NET Core application, but that's not the case. The templates are just different starting points into the same functionality, and you can add whatever functionality you need to projects created with any of the templates. For example, I explain how to deal with HTTP data requests in Chapter 20 and authentication and authorization in Chapters 28, 29, and 30, all of which I do by starting with the Empty project template.

The real difference between the project templates is the initial set of libraries, configuration files, code, and content that Visual Studio adds when it creates the project. There are a lot of differences between the simplest template (Empty) and the most complex (Web Application (Model-View-Controller)), as you can see in Figure 3-6, which shows the Solution Explorer after a project has been created with each one. For the Web Application (Model-View-Controller) template, I had to focus the Solution Explorer on different folders because a single listing was too long for the printed page.

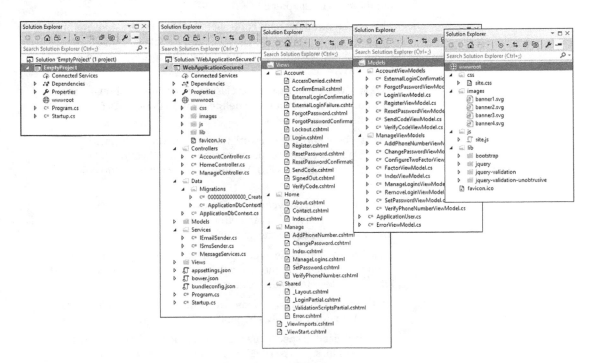

Figure 3-6. *The default content added to a project by the Empty and Web Application (MVC) templates*

The extra files that the Web Application (Model-View-Controller) template adds to the project look daunting, but many of them are just placeholders or example implementations of common features. Some of the other files set up MVC or configure ASP.NET Core. Others are client-side libraries, which you will incorporate into the HTML generated by an application. The list of files may seem overwhelming now, but you'll understand what everything does by the time you finish this book.

Regardless of the template you use to create a project, some common folders and files will appear. Some of the items in a project have special roles that are hard-coded into ASP.NET Core or MVC or one of the tools that Visual Studio provides support for. Others are subject to naming conventions that are used in most ASP.NET Core or MVC projects. In Table 3-1, I have described the important files and folders that you will encounter in an ASP.NET Core MVC project, some of which are not present in the project by default but which I introduce in later chapters.

Table 3-1. *Summary of MVC Project Items*

Folder or File	Description
/Areas	Areas are a way of partitioning a large application into smaller pieces. I describe areas in Chapter 16.
/Dependencies	The Dependencies item provides details of all the packages a project relies on. I describe the package managers that Visual Studio uses in Chapter 6.
/Components	This is where view component classes, which are used to display self-contained features such as shopping carts, are defined. I describe view components in Chapter 22.
/Controllers	This is where you put your controller classes. This is a convention. You can put your controller classes anywhere you like because they are all compiled into the same assembly. I describe controllers in detail in Chapter 17.
/Data	This is where database context classes are defined, although I prefer to ignore this convention and define them in the Models folder, as demonstrated in Chapter 8.
/Data/Migrations	This is where Entity Framework Core migrations are stored so that databases can be prepared to store the application data. I use migrations in Chapters 8, 9, 10, and 11 as part of the SportsStore project.
/Models	This is where you put your view model and domain model classes. This is a convention. You can define your model classes anywhere in the project or in a separate project.
/Views	This directory holds views and partial views, usually grouped together in folders named after the controller with which they are associated. I describe views in detail in Chapter 21.
/Views/Shared	This directory holds layouts and views that are not specific to a single controller. I describe views in detail in Chapter 21.
/Views/_ViewImports.cshtml	This file is used to specify the namespaces that will be included in Razor view files, as described in Chapter 5. It is also used to set up tag helpers, as described in Chapter 23.

(*continued*)

Table 3-1. (*continued*)

Folder or File	Description
/Views/_ViewStart.cshtml	This file is used to specify a default layout for the Razor view engine, as described in Chapter 5.
/appsettings.json	This file contains configuration settings that can be tailored for different environments, such as development, testing, and production. The most common uses for this file are to define database server connection strings and logging/debug settings, which I describe in Chapter 14.
/bower.json	This file contains the list of packages managed by the Bower package manager, as described in Chapter 6.
/<project>.csproj	This file contains the configuration for the project, including the NuGet packages that the application requires, as described in Chapters 6 and 14. This file is hidden and can be edited only by right-clicking the project item in the Solution Explorer window and selecting the Edit <project>.csproj menu item.
/Program.cs	This class configures the hosting platform for the application, as described in Chapter 14.
/Startup.cs	This class configures the application, as described in Chapter 14.
/wwwroot	This is where you put static content such as CSS files and images. It is also where the Bower package manager installs JavaScript and CSS packages, as described in Chapter 6.

Understanding MVC Conventions

There are two kinds of conventions in an MVC project. The first kind is just suggestions as to how you might like to structure your project. For example, it is conventional to put the third-party JavaScript and CSS packages you rely on in the wwwroot/lib folder. This is where other MVC developers would expect to find them and where the package manager will install them. But you are free to rename the lib folder or remove it entirely and put your packages somewhere else. That would not prevent MVC from running your application as long as the script and link elements in your views refer to the location you settle on.

,The other kind of convention arises from the principle of *convention over configuration*, which was one of the main selling points that made Ruby on Rails so popular. Convention over configuration means that you don't need to explicitly configure associations between controllers and their views, for example. You just follow a certain naming convention for your files, and everything just works. There is less flexibility in changing your project structure when dealing with this kind of convention. The following sections explain the conventions that are used in place of configuration.

■ **Tip** All of the conventions can be changed by replacing the standard MVC components with your own implementations. I describe different ways of doing this throughout the book to help explain how MVC applications work, but these are the conventions you will be dealing with in most projects.

Following Conventions for Controller Classes

Controller classes have names that end with `Controller`, such as `ProductController`, `AdminController`, and `HomeController`. When referencing a controller from elsewhere in the project, such as when using an HTML helper method, you specify the first part of the name (such as `Product`), and MVC automatically appends `Controller` to the name and starts looking for the controller class.

■ **Tip**   You can change this by creating a model convention, which I describe in Chapter 31.

Following Conventions for Views

Views go into the folder named `/Views/Controllername`. For example, a view associated with the `ProductController` class would go in the `/Views/Product` folder.

■ **Tip**   Notice that I omit the `Controller` part of the class from the `Views` folder: `/Views/Product`, *not* `/Views/ProductController`. This may seem counterintuitive at first, but it quickly becomes second nature.

MVC expects that the default view for an action method should be named after that method. For example, the default view associated with an action method called `List` should be called `List.cshtml`. Thus, for the `List` action method in the `ProductController` class, the default view is expected to be `/Views/Product/List.cshtml`. The default view is used when you return the result of calling the `View` method in an action method, like this:

```
...
return View();
...
```

You can specify a different view by name, like this:

```
...
return View("MyOtherView");
...
```

Notice that I do not include the file name extension or the path to the view. When looking for a view, MVC looks in the folder named after the controller and then in the `/Views/Shared` folder. This means that I can put views that will be used by more than one controller in the `/Views/Shared` folder and MVC will find them.

Following Conventions for Layouts

The naming convention for layouts is to prefix the file with an underscore (_) character, and layout files are placed in the /Views/Shared folder. This layout is applied to all views by default through the /Views/_ ViewStart.cshtml file. If you do not want the default layout applied to views, you can change the settings in _ViewStart.cshtml (or delete the file entirely) to specify another layout in the view, like this:

```
@{
    Layout = "~/_MyLayout.cshtml";
}
```

Or you can disable any layout for a given view, like this:

```
@{
    Layout = null;
}
```

Summary

In this chapter, I introduced you to the MVC architectural pattern and compared it to some other patterns you may have seen or heard of before. I discussed the significance of the domain model and introduced dependency injection, which allows you to decouple components to enforce a strict separation between the parts of an application. In the next chapter, I describe the essential C# language features that are used in MVC web application development.

CHAPTER 4

■ ■ ■

Essential C# Features

In this chapter, I describe C# features used in web application development that are not widely understood or that often cause confusion. This is not a book about C#, however, and so I provide only a brief example for each feature so that you can follow the examples in the rest of the book and take advantage of these features in your own projects. Table 4-1 summarizes this chapter.

Table 4-1. *Chapter Summary*

Problem	Solution	Listing
Avoid accessing properties on null references	Use the null conditional operator	5–8
Simplify C# properties	Use automatically implemented properties	9–11
Simplify string composition	Use string interpolation	12
Create an object and set its properties in a single step	Use an object or collection initializer	13–16
Test an object's type or characteristics	Use pattern matching	17–18
Add functionality to a class that cannot be modified	Use an extension method	19–26
Simplify the use of delegates and single-statement methods	Use a lambda expression	27–34
Use implicit typing	Use the var keyword	35
Create objects without defining a type	Use an anonymous type	36–37
Simplify the use of asynchronous methods	Use the async and await keywords	38–41
Get the name of a class method or property without defining a static string	Use a nameof expression	42–43

© Adam Freeman 2017
A. Freeman, *Pro ASP.NET Core MVC 2*, https://doi.org/10.1007/978-1-4842-3150-0_4

Preparing the Example Project

For this chapter, I created a new Visual Studio project called LanguageFeatures using the ASP.NET Core Web Application (.NET Core) template, as shown in Figure 4-1.

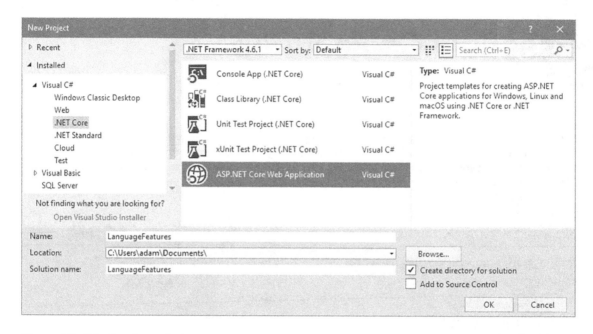

Figure 4-1. *Selecting the project type*

When presented with the different project configurations, I selected the Empty template, as shown in Figure 4-2. I selected .NET Core and ASP.NET Core 2.0 from the lists at the top of the dialog window, ensured that Authentication option was set to No Authentication and that the Enable Docker Support option was unchecked before clicking the OK button to create the project.

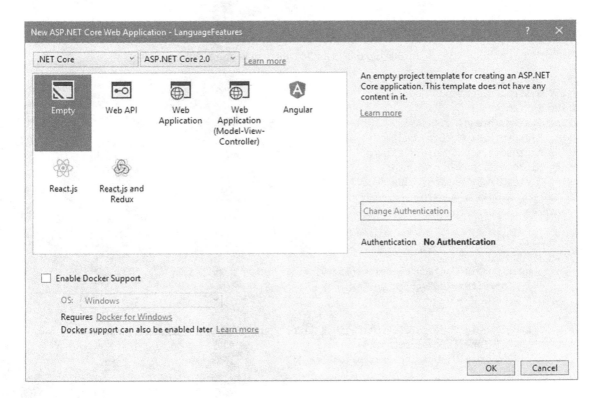

Figure 4-2. Selecting the project template

Enabling ASP.NET Core MVC

The Empty project template creates a project that contains a minimal ASP.NET Core configuration without any MVC support. This means that the placeholder content that is added by the Web Application (Model-View-Controller) template isn't present, but it also means that some extra steps are required to enable MVC so that features such as controllers and views work. In this section, I make the changes required to add enable an MVC setup in the project, but I won't get into the details of what each step does for the moment.

To enable the MVC framework, make the changes shown in Listing 4-1 to the Startup class.

Listing 4-1. Enabling MVC in the Startup.cs File in the LanguageFeatures Folder

```
using System;
using System.Collections.Generic;
using System.Linq;
using System.Threading.Tasks;
using Microsoft.AspNetCore.Builder;
using Microsoft.AspNetCore.Hosting;
using Microsoft.AspNetCore.Http;
using Microsoft.Extensions.DependencyInjection;

namespace LanguageFeatures {

    public class Startup {

        public void ConfigureServices(IServiceCollection services) {
            services.AddMvc();
        }

        public void Configure(IApplicationBuilder app, IHostingEnvironment env) {
            if (env.IsDevelopment()) {
                app.UseDeveloperExceptionPage();
            }

            //app.Run(async (context) => {
            //    await context.Response.WriteAsync("Hello World!");
            //});

            app.UseMvcWithDefaultRoute();
        }
    }
}
```

I explain how to configure ASP.NET Core MVC applications in Chapter 14, but the two statements added in Listing 4-1 provide a basic MVC setup using the default configuration and conventions.

Creating the MVC Application Components

Now that MVC is set up, I can add the MVC application components that I will use to demonstrate important C# language features.

Creating the Model

I started by creating a simple model class so that I can have some data to work with. I added a folder called Models and created a class file called Product.cs within it, which I used to define the class shown in Listing 4-2.

Listing 4-2. The Contents of the Product.cs File in the Models Folder

```
namespace LanguageFeatures.Models {
    public class Product {

        public string Name { get; set; }
        public decimal? Price { get; set; }

        public static Product[] GetProducts() {

            Product kayak = new Product {
                Name = "Kayak", Price = 275M
            };

            Product lifejacket = new Product {
                Name = "Lifejacket", Price = 48.95M
            };

            return new Product[] { kayak, lifejacket, null };
        }
    }
}
```

The Products class defines Name and Price properties, and there is a static method called GetProducts that returns a Products array. One of the elements contained in the array returned by the GetProducts method is set to null, which I will use to demonstrate some useful language features later in the chapter.

Creating the Controller and View

For the examples in this chapter, I use a simple controller to demonstrate different language features. I created a Controllers folder and added to it a class file called HomeController.cs, the contents of which are shown in Listing 4-3. When using the default MVC configuration, the Home controller is where MVC will send HTTP requests by default.

Listing 4-3. The Contents of the HomeController.cs File in the Controllers Folder

```
using Microsoft.AspNetCore.Mvc;

namespace LanguageFeatures.Controllers {
    public class HomeController : Controller {

        public ViewResult Index() {
            return View(new string[] { "C#", "Language", "Features" });
        }
    }
}
```

The Index action method tells MVC to render the default view and passes it an array of strings to be included in the HTML sent to the client. To create the corresponding view, I added a Views/Home folder (by creating a Views folder and then adding a Home folder within it) and added a view file called Index.cshtml, the contents of which are shown in Listing 4-4.

Listing 4-4. The Contents of the Index.cshtml File in the Views/Home Folder

```
@model IEnumerable<string>
@{ Layout = null; }

<!DOCTYPE html>
<html>
<head>
    <meta name="viewport" content="width=device-width" />
    <title>Language Features</title>
</head>
<body>
    <ul>
        @foreach (string s in Model) {
            <li>@s</li>
        }
    </ul>
</body>
</html>
```

If you run the example application by selecting Start Debugging from the Debug menu, you will see the output shown in Figure 4-3.

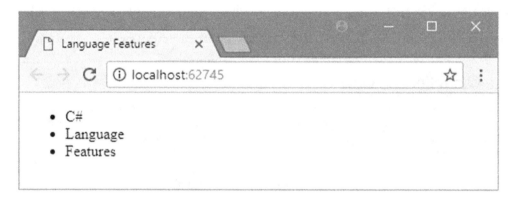

Figure 4-3. Running the example application

Since the output from all the examples in this chapter is text, I will show the messages displayed by the browser like this:

```
C#
Language
Features
```

Using the Null Conditional Operator

The null conditional operator allows for null values to be detected more elegantly. There can be a lot of checking for nulls in MVC development as you work out whether a request contains a specific header or value or whether the model contains a particular data item. Traditionally, dealing with nulls requires making an explicit check, and this can become tedious and error-prone when both an object and its properties have to be inspected. The null conditional operator makes this process simpler and more concise, as shown in Listing 4-5.

Listing 4-5. Detecting null Values in the HomeController.cs File in the Controllers Folder

```
using Microsoft.AspNetCore.Mvc;
using System.Collections.Generic;
using LanguageFeatures.Models;

namespace LanguageFeatures.Controllers {
    public class HomeController : Controller {

        public ViewResult Index() {

            List<string> results = new List<string>();

            foreach (Product p in Product.GetProducts()) {
                string name = p?.Name;
                decimal? price = p?.Price;
                results.Add(string.Format("Name: {0}, Price: {1}", name, price));
            }

            return View(results);
        }
    }
}
```

The static GetProducts method defined by the Product class returns an array of objects that I inspect in the controller's Index action method in order to get a list of the Name and Price values. The problem is that both the object in the array and the value of the properties could be null, which means I can't just refer to p.Name or p.Price within the foreach loop without causing a NullReferenceException. To avoid this, I used the null conditional operator, like this:

```
...
string name = p?.Name;
decimal? price = p?.Price;
...
```

The null conditional operator is a single question mark (the ? character). If p is null, then name will be set to null as well. If p is not null, then name will be set to the value of the Person.Name property. The Price property is subject to the same test. Notice that the variable you assign to when using the null conditional operator must be able to be assigned null, which is why the price variable is declared as a nullable decimal (decimal?).

Chaining the Null Conditional Operator

The null conditional operator can be chained to navigate through a hierarchy of objects, which is where it really becomes an effective tool for simplifying code and allowing safe navigation. In Listing 4-6, I have added a property to the Product class that nests references, creating a more complex object hierarchy.

Listing 4-6. Adding a Property in the Product.cs File in the Models Folder

```
namespace LanguageFeatures.Models {
    public class Product {

        public string Name { get; set; }
        public decimal? Price { get; set; }
        public Product Related { get; set; }

        public static Product[] GetProducts() {

            Product kayak = new Product {
                Name = "Kayak", Price = 275M
            };
            Product lifejacket = new Product {
                Name = "Lifejacket", Price = 48.95M
            };

            kayak.Related = lifejacket;

            return new Product[] { kayak, lifejacket, null };
        }
    }
}
```

Each Product object has a Related property that can refer to another Product object. In the GetProducts method, I set the Related property for the Product object that represents a kayak. Listing 4-7 shows how I can chain the null conditional operator to navigate through the object properties without causing an exception.

Listing 4-7. Detecting Nested null Values in the HomeController.cs File in the Controllers Folder

```
using Microsoft.AspNetCore.Mvc;
using System.Collections.Generic;
using LanguageFeatures.Models;

namespace LanguageFeatures.Controllers {
    public class HomeController : Controller {

        public ViewResult Index() {

            List<string> results = new List<string>();

            foreach (Product p in Product.GetProducts()) {
                string name = p?.Name;
                decimal? price = p?.Price;
                string relatedName = p?.Related?.Name;
```

```
        results.Add(string.Format("Name: {0}, Price: {1}, Related: {2}",
            name, price, relatedName));
    }

    return View(results);
  }
 }
}
```

The null conditional operator can be applied to each part of a chain of properties, like this:

```
...
string relatedName = p?.Related?.Name;
...
```

The result is that the relatedName variable will be null when p is null or when p.Related is null. Otherwise, the variable will be assigned the value of the p.Related.Name property. If you run the example, you will see the following output in the browser window:

```
Name: Kayak, Price: 275, Related: Lifejacket
Name: Lifejacket, Price: 48.95, Related:
Name: , Price: , Related:
```

Combining the Conditional and Coalescing Operators

It can be useful to combine the null conditional operator (a single question mark) with the null coalescing operator (two question marks) to set a fallback value to present null values being used in the application, as shown in Listing 4-8.

Listing 4-8. Combining Null Operators in the HomeController.cs File in the Controllers Folder

```
using Microsoft.AspNetCore.Mvc;
using System.Collections.Generic;
using LanguageFeatures.Models;

namespace LanguageFeatures.Controllers {
    public class HomeController : Controller {

        public ViewResult Index() {

            List<string> results = new List<string>();

            foreach (Product p in Product.GetProducts()) {
                string name = p?.Name ?? "<No Name>";
                decimal? price = p?.Price ?? 0;
                string relatedName = p?.Related?.Name ?? "<None>";
                results.Add(string.Format("Name: {0}, Price: {1}, Related: {2}",
                    name, price, relatedName));
            }
```

```
                return View(results);
        }
    }
}
```

The null conditional operator ensures that I don't get a NullReferenceException when navigating through the object properties, and the null coalescing operator ensures that I don't include null values in the results displayed in the browser. If you run the example, you will see the following results displayed in the browser window:

```
Name: Kayak, Price: 275, Related: Lifejacket
Name: Lifejacket, Price: 48.95, Related: <None>
Name: <No Name>, Price: 0, Related: <None>
```

Using Automatically Implemented Properties

C# supports automatically implemented properties, and I used them when defining properties for the Person class in the previous section, like this:

```
namespace LanguageFeatures.Models {
    public class Product {

        public string Name { get; set; }
        public decimal? Price { get; set; }
        public Product Related { get; set; }

        public static Product[] GetProducts() {

            Product kayak = new Product {
                Name = "Kayak", Price = 275M
            };
            Product lifejacket = new Product {
                Name = "Lifejacket", Price = 48.95M
            };

            kayak.Related = lifejacket;

            return new Product[] { kayak, lifejacket, null };
        }
    }
}
```

This feature allows me to define properties without having to implement the get and set bodies. Using the auto-implemented property feature means that defining a property like this:

```
...
public string Name { get; set; }
...
```

is equivalent to the following code:

```
...
public string Name {
    get { return name; }
    set { name = value; }
}
...
```

This type of feature is known as *syntactic sugar*, which means that it makes C# more pleasant to work with—in this case by eliminating redundant code that ends up being duplicated for every property—without substantially altering the way the language behaves. The term *sugar* may seem pejorative, but any enhancements that make code easier to write and maintain can be beneficial, especially in large and complex projects.

Using Auto-Implemented Property Initializers

Automatically implemented properties have been supported since C# 3.0. The latest version of C# supports initializers for automatically implemented properties, which allows an initial value to be set without having to use the constructor, as shown in Listing 4-9.

Listing 4-9. Using an Auto-Implemented Property Initializer in the Product.cs File in the Models Folder

```
namespace LanguageFeatures.Models {
    public class Product {

        public string Name { get; set; }
        public string Category { get; set; } = "Watersports";
        public decimal? Price { get; set; }
        public Product Related { get; set; }

        public static Product[] GetProducts() {
            Product kayak = new Product {
                Name = "Kayak",
                Category = "Water Craft",
                Price = 275M
            };
            Product lifejacket = new Product {
                Name = "Lifejacket", Price = 48.95M
            };

            kayak.Related = lifejacket;

            return new Product[] { kayak, lifejacket, null };
        }
    }
}
```

Assigning a value to an auto-implemented property doesn't prevent the setter from being used to change the property later and just tidies up the code for simple types that ended up with a constructor that contained a list of property assignments to provide default values. In the example, the initializer assigns a value of Watersports to the Category property. The initial value can be changed, which I do when I create the kayak object and specify a value of Water Craft instead.

Creating Read-Only Automatically Implemented Properties

You can create a read-only property by using an initializer and omitting the set keyword from an auto-implemented property that has an initializer, as shown in Listing 4-10.

Listing 4-10. Creating a Read-Only Property in the Product.cs File in the Models Folder

```
namespace LanguageFeatures.Models {
    public class Product {

        public string Name { get; set; }
        public string Category { get; set; } = "Watersports";
        public decimal? Price { get; set; }
        public Product Related { get; set; }
        public bool InStock { get; } = true;

        public static Product[] GetProducts() {

            Product kayak = new Product {
                Name = "Kayak",
                Category = "Water Craft",
                Price = 275M
            };
            Product lifejacket = new Product {
                Name = "Lifejacket", Price = 48.95M
            };

            kayak.Related = lifejacket;

            return new Product[] { kayak, lifejacket, null };
        }
    }
}
```

The InStock property is initialized to true and cannot be changed; however, the value can be assigned to in the type's constructor, as shown in Listing 4-11.

Listing 4-11. Assigning a Value to a Read-Only Property in the Product.cs File in the Models Folder

```
namespace LanguageFeatures.Models {
    public class Product {

        public Product(bool stock = true) {
            InStock = stock;
        }

        public string Name { get; set; }
        public string Category { get; set; } = "Watersports";
        public decimal? Price { get; set; }
        public Product Related { get; set; }
        public bool InStock { get; }
```

```
        public static Product[] GetProducts() {
            Product kayak = new Product {
                Name = "Kayak",
                Category = "Water Craft",
                Price = 275M
            };

            Product lifejacket = new Product(false) {
                Name = "Lifejacket",
                Price = 48.95M
            };

            kayak.Related = lifejacket;

            return new Product[] { kayak, lifejacket, null };
        }
    }
}
```

The constructor allows the value for the read-only property to be specified as an argument and defaults to true if no value is provided. The property value cannot be changed once set by the constructor.

Using String Interpolation

The string.Format method is the traditional C# tool for composing strings that contain data values. Here is an example of this technique from the Home controller:

```
...
results.Add(string.Format("Name: {0}, Price: {1}, Related: {2}",
                    name, price, relatedName));
...
```

C# also supports a different approach, known as *string interpolation*, that avoids the need to ensure that the {0} references in the string template match up with the variables specified as arguments. Instead, string interpolation uses the variable names directly, as shown in Listing 4-12.

Listing 4-12. Using String Interpolation in the HomeController.cs File in the Controllers Folder

```
using Microsoft.AspNetCore.Mvc;
using System.Collections.Generic;
using LanguageFeatures.Models;

namespace LanguageFeatures.Controllers {
    public class HomeController : Controller {

        public ViewResult Index() {

            List<string> results = new List<string>();

            foreach (Product p in Product.GetProducts()) {
                string name = p?.Name ?? "<No Name>";
```

```
            decimal? price = p?.Price ?? 0;
            string relatedName = p?.Related?.Name ?? "<None>";
            results.Add($"Name: {name}, Price: {price}, Related: {relatedName}");
        }

        return View(results);
    }
  }
}
```

Interpolated strings are prefixed with the $ character and contain *holes*, which are references to values contained within the { and } characters. When the string is evaluated, the holes are filled in with the current values of the variables or constants that are specified.

Visual Studio provides IntelliSense support for creating interpolated strings and offers a list of the available members when the { character is typed; this helps to minimize typos, and the result is a string format that is easier to understand.

■ **Tip**   String interpolation supports all the format specifiers that are available with the string.Format method. The format specifiers are included as part of the hole, so $"Price: {price:C2}" would format the price value as a currency value with two decimal digits.

Using Object and Collection Initializers

When I create an object in the static GetProducts method of the Product class, I use an *object initializer*, which allows me to create an object and specify its property values in a single step, like this:

```
...
Product kayak = new Product {
    Name = "Kayak",
    Category = "Water Craft",
    Price = 275M
};
...
```

This is another syntactic sugar feature that makes C# easier to use. Without this feature, I would have to call the Product constructor and then use the newly created object to set each of the properties, like this:

```
...
Product kayak = new Product();
kayak.Name = "Kayak";
kayak.Category = "Water Craft";
kayak.Price = 275M;
...
```

A related feature is the *collection initializer*, which allows the creation of a collection and its contents to be specified in a single step. Without an initializer, creating a string array, for example, requires the size of the array and the array elements to be specified separately, as shown in Listing 4-13.

Listing 4-13. Initializing an Object in the HomeController.cs File in the Controllers Folder

```
using Microsoft.AspNetCore.Mvc;
using System.Collections.Generic;
using LanguageFeatures.Models;

namespace LanguageFeatures.Controllers {
    public class HomeController : Controller {

        public ViewResult Index() {
            string[] names = new string[3];
            names[0] = "Bob";
            names[1] = "Joe";
            names[2] = "Alice";
            return View("Index", names);
        }
    }
}
```

Using a collection initializer allows the contents of the array to be specified as part of the construction, which implicitly provides the compiler with the size of the array, as shown in Listing 4-14.

Listing 4-14. Using a Collection Initializer in the HomeController.cs File in the Controllers Folder

```
using Microsoft.AspNetCore.Mvc;
using System.Collections.Generic;
using LanguageFeatures.Models;

namespace LanguageFeatures.Controllers {
    public class HomeController : Controller {

        public ViewResult Index() {
            return View("Index", new string[] { "Bob", "Joe", "Alice" });
        }
    }
}
```

The array elements are specified between the { and } characters, which allows for a more concise definition of the collection and makes it possible to define a collection inline within a method call. The code in Listing 4-14 has the same effect as the code in Listing 4-13, and if you run the example application, you will see the following output in the browser window:

```
Bob
Joe
Alice
```

Using an Index Initializer

Recent versions of C# tidy up the way collections that use indexes, such as dictionaries, are initialized. Listing 4-15 shows the Index action rewritten to define a collection using the traditional C# approach to initializing a dictionary.

Listing 4-15. Initializing a Dictionary in the HomeController.cs File in the Controllers Folder

```
using Microsoft.AspNetCore.Mvc;
using System.Collections.Generic;
using LanguageFeatures.Models;

namespace LanguageFeatures.Controllers {
    public class HomeController : Controller {

        public ViewResult Index() {
            Dictionary<string, Product> products = new Dictionary<string, Product> {
                { "Kayak", new Product { Name = "Kayak", Price = 275M } },
                { "Lifejacket",  new Product{ Name = "Lifejacket", Price = 48.95M } }
            };
            return View("Index", products.Keys);
        }
    }
}
```

The syntax for initializing this type of collection relies too much on the { and } characters, especially when the collection values are created using object initializers. The latest versions of C# support a more natural approach to initializing indexed collections that is consistent with the way that values are retrieved or modified once the collection has been initialized, as shown in Listing 4-16.

Listing 4-16. Using Collection Initializer Syntax in the HomeController.cs File in the Controllers Folder

```
using Microsoft.AspNetCore.Mvc;
using System.Collections.Generic;
using LanguageFeatures.Models;

namespace LanguageFeatures.Controllers {
    public class HomeController : Controller {

        public ViewResult Index() {
            Dictionary<string, Product> products = new Dictionary<string, Product> {
                ["Kayak"] = new Product { Name = "Kayak", Price = 275M },
                ["Lifejacket"] = new Product { Name = "Lifejacket", Price = 48.95M }
            };

            return View("Index", products.Keys);
        }
    }
}
```

The effect is the same—to create a dictionary whose keys are Kayak and Lifejacket and whose values are Product objects—but the elements are created using the index notation that is used for other collection operations. If you run the application, you will see the following results in the browser:

```
Kayak
Lifejacket
```

Pattern Matching

One of the most useful recent additions to C# is support for pattern matching, which can be used to test that an object is of a specific type or has specific characteristics. This is another form is syntactic sugar, and it can dramatically simplify complex blocks of conditional statements. The is keyword is used to perform a type test, as demonstrated in Listing 4-17.

Listing 4-17. Performing a Type Test in the HomeController.cs File in the Controllers Folder

```csharp
using Microsoft.AspNetCore.Mvc;
using System.Collections.Generic;
using LanguageFeatures.Models;

namespace LanguageFeatures.Controllers {
    public class HomeController : Controller {

        public ViewResult Index() {

            object[] data = new object[] { 275M, 29.95M,
            "apple", "orange", 100, 10 };
            decimal total = 0;
            for (int i = 0; i < data.Length; i++) {
                if (data[i] is decimal d) {
                    total += d;
                }
            }

            return View("Index", new string[] { $"Total: {total:C2}" });
        }
    }
}
```

The is keyword performs a type check, and if a value is of the specified type, it will assign the value to a new variable, like this:

```csharp
...
if (data[i] is decimal d) {
...
```

This expression will evaluate as true if the value stored in data[i] is a decimal. The value of data[i] will be assigned to the variable d, which allows it to be used in subsequent statements without needing to perform any type conversions. The is keyword will only match the specified type, which means that only two of the values in the data array will be processed (the other items in the array are string and int values). If you run the application, you will see the following output in the browser window:

```
Total: $304.95
```

Pattern Matching in Switch Statements

Pattern matching can also be used in switch statements, which support the when keyword for restricting when a value is matched by a case statement, as shown in Listing 4-18.

Listing 4-18. Pattern Matching in the HomeController.cs File in the Controllers Folder

```
using Microsoft.AspNetCore.Mvc;
using System.Collections.Generic;
using LanguageFeatures.Models;

namespace LanguageFeatures.Controllers {
    public class HomeController : Controller {

        public ViewResult Index() {

            object[] data = new object[] { 275M, 29.95M,
                "apple", "orange", 100, 10 };
            decimal total = 0;
            for (int i = 0; i < data.Length; i++) {
                switch (data[i]) {
                    case decimal decimalValue:
                        total += decimalValue;
                        break;
                    case int intValue when intValue > 50:
                        total += intValue;
                        break;
                }
            }

            return View("Index", new string[] { $"Total: {total:C2}" });
        }
    }
}
```

To match any value of a specific type, use the type and variable name in the case statement, like this:

```
...
case decimal decimalValue:
...
```

This case statement matches any decimal value and assigns it to a new variable called decimalValue. To be more selective, the when keyword can be included, like this:

```
...
case int intValue when intValue > 50:
...
```

This case statement matches int values and assigns them to a variable called intValue, but only when the value is greater than 50. If you run the application, you will see the following output in the browser window:

```
Total: $404.95
```

Using Extension Methods

Extension methods are a convenient way of adding methods to classes that you do not own and cannot modify directly. Listing 4-19 shows the definition of the ShoppingCart class, which I added to the Models folder in a file called ShoppingCart.cs and which represents a collection of Product objects.

Listing 4-19. The Contents of the ShoppingCart.cs File in the Models Folder

```
using System.Collections.Generic;

namespace LanguageFeatures.Models {

    public class ShoppingCart {
        public IEnumerable<Product> Products { get; set; }
    }
}
```

This is a simple class that acts as a wrapper around a sequence of Product objects (I only need a basic class for this example). Suppose I need to be able to determine the total value of the Product objects in the ShoppingCart class but I cannot modify the class itself, perhaps because it comes from a third party and I do not have the source code. I can use an extension method to add the functionality I need. Listing 4-20 shows the MyExtensionMethods class that I added to the Models folder in the MyExtensionMethods.cs file.

Listing 4-20. The Contents of the MyExtensionMethods.cs File in the Models Folder

```
namespace LanguageFeatures.Models {

    public static class MyExtensionMethods {

        public static decimal TotalPrices(this ShoppingCart cartParam) {
            decimal total = 0;
            foreach (Product prod in cartParam.Products) {
                total += prod?.Price ?? 0;
            }
            return total;
        }
    }
}
```

The this keyword in front of the first parameter marks TotalPrices as an extension method. The first parameter tells .NET which class the extension method can be applied to—ShoppingCart in this case. I can refer to the instance of the ShoppingCart class that the extension method has been applied to by using the cartParam parameter. My method enumerates the Product objects in ShoppingCart and returns the sum of the Product.Price property values. Listing 4-21 shows how I apply the extension method in the Home controller's action method.

■ **Note** Extension methods do not let you break through the access rules that classes define for methods, fields, and properties. You can extend the functionality of a class by using an extension method but only using the class members that you had access to anyway.

Listing 4-21. Applying an Extension Method in the HomeController.cs File in the Controllers Folder

```
using Microsoft.AspNetCore.Mvc;
using System.Collections.Generic;
using LanguageFeatures.Models;

namespace LanguageFeatures.Controllers {
    public class HomeController : Controller {

        public ViewResult Index() {
            ShoppingCart cart
            = new ShoppingCart { Products = Product.GetProducts() };
            decimal cartTotal = cart.TotalPrices();
            return View("Index", new string[] { $"Total: {cartTotal:C2}" });
        }
    }
}
```

The key statement is this one:

```
...
decimal cartTotal = cart.TotalPrices();
...
```

I call the TotalPrices method on a ShoppingCart object as though it were part of the ShoppingCart class, even though it is an extension method defined by a different class altogether. .NET will find extension classes if they are in the scope of the current class, meaning that they are part of the same namespace or in a namespace that is the subject of a using statement. If you run the application, you will see the following output in the browser window:

```
Total: $323.95
```

Applying Extension Methods to an Interface

I can also create extension methods that apply to an interface, which allows me to call the extension method on all the classes that implement the interface. Listing 4-22 shows the ShoppingCart class updated to implement the IEnumerable<Product> interface.

Listing 4-22. Implementing an Interface in the ShoppingCart.cs File in the Models Folder

```
using System.Collections;
using System.Collections.Generic;

namespace LanguageFeatures.Models {

    public class ShoppingCart : IEnumerable<Product> {
        public IEnumerable<Product> Products { get; set; }

        public IEnumerator<Product> GetEnumerator() {
            return Products.GetEnumerator();
        }

        IEnumerator IEnumerable.GetEnumerator() {
            return GetEnumerator();
        }
    }
}
```

I can now update the extension method so that it deals with IEnumerable<Product>, as shown in Listing 4-23.

Listing 4-23. Updating an Extension Method in the MyExtensionMethods.cs File in the Models Folder

```
using System.Collections.Generic;

namespace LanguageFeatures.Models {

    public static class MyExtensionMethods {

        public static decimal TotalPrices(this IEnumerable<Product> products) {
            decimal total = 0;
            foreach (Product prod in products) {
                total += prod?.Price ?? 0;
            }
            return total;
        }
    }
}
```

The first parameter type has changed to IEnumerable<Product>, which means that the foreach loop in the method body works directly on Product objects. The change to using the interface means that I can calculate the total value of the Product objects enumerated by any IEnumerable<Product>, which includes instances of ShoppingCart but also arrays of Product objects, as shown in Listing 4-24.

Listing 4-24. Applying an Extension Method in the HomeController.cs File in the Controllers Folder

```
using Microsoft.AspNetCore.Mvc;
using System.Collections.Generic;
using LanguageFeatures.Models;

namespace LanguageFeatures.Controllers {
    public class HomeController : Controller {
```

```
    public ViewResult Index() {

        ShoppingCart cart
            = new ShoppingCart { Products = Product.GetProducts() };

        Product[] productArray = {
            new Product {Name = "Kayak", Price = 275M},
            new Product {Name = "Lifejacket", Price = 48.95M}
        };

        decimal cartTotal = cart.TotalPrices();
        decimal arrayTotal = productArray.TotalPrices();

        return View("Index", new string[] {
            $"Cart Total: {cartTotal:C2}",
            $"Array Total: {arrayTotal:C2}" });
        }
    }
}
```

If you start the project, you will see the following results, which demonstrate that I get the same result from the extension method, irrespective of how the Product objects are collected:

```
Cart Total: $323.95
Array Total: $323.95
```

Creating Filtering Extension Methods

The last thing I want to show you about extension methods is that they can be used to filter collections of objects. An extension method that operates on an IEnumerable<T> and that also returns an IEnumerable<T> can use the yield keyword to apply selection criteria to items in the source data to produce a reduced set of results. Listing 4-25 demonstrates such a method, which I have added to the MyExtensionMethods class.

Listing 4-25. A Filtering Extension Method in the MyExtensionMethods.cs File in the Controllers Folder

```
using System.Collections.Generic;

namespace LanguageFeatures.Models {

    public static class MyExtensionMethods {

        public static decimal TotalPrices(this IEnumerable<Product> products) {
            decimal total = 0;
            foreach (Product prod in products) {
                total += prod?.Price ?? 0;
            }
            return total;
        }
```

```
    public static IEnumerable<Product> FilterByPrice(
            this IEnumerable<Product> productEnum, decimal minimumPrice) {

        foreach (Product prod in productEnum) {
            if ((prod?.Price ?? 0) >= minimumPrice) {
                yield return prod;
            }
        }
    }
}
```

This extension method, called FilterByPrice, takes an additional parameter that allows me to filter products so that Product objects whose Price property matches or exceeds the parameter are returned in the result. Listing 4-26 shows this method being used.

Listing 4-26. Using the Filtering Extension Method in the HomeController.cs File in the Controllers Folder

```
using Microsoft.AspNetCore.Mvc;
using System.Collections.Generic;
using LanguageFeatures.Models;

namespace LanguageFeatures.Controllers {
    public class HomeController : Controller {

        public ViewResult Index() {

            Product[] productArray = {
                new Product {Name = "Kayak", Price = 275M},
                new Product {Name = "Lifejacket", Price = 48.95M},
                new Product {Name = "Soccer ball", Price = 19.50M},
                new Product {Name = "Corner flag", Price = 34.95M}
            };

            decimal arrayTotal = productArray.FilterByPrice(20).TotalPrices();

            return View("Index", new string[] { $"Array Total: {arrayTotal:C2}" });
        }
    }
}
```

When I call the FilterByPrice method on the array of Product objects, only those that cost more than $20 are received by the TotalPrices method and used to calculate the total. If you run the application, you will see the following output in the browser window:

```
Total: $358.90
```

Using Lambda Expressions

Lambda expressions are a feature that causes a lot of confusion, not least because the feature they simplify is also confusing. To understand the problem that is being solved, consider the FilterByPrice extension method that I defined in the previous section. This method is written so that it can filter Product objects by price, which means that if I want to filter by name, I have to create a second method, like the one shown in Listing 4-27.

Listing 4-27. Adding a Filter Method in the MyExtensionMethods.cs File in the Models Folder

```
using System.Collections.Generic;

namespace LanguageFeatures.Models {

    public static class MyExtensionMethods {

        public static decimal TotalPrices(this IEnumerable<Product> products) {
            decimal total = 0;
            foreach (Product prod in products) {
                total += prod?.Price ?? 0;
            }
            return total;
        }

        public static IEnumerable<Product> FilterByPrice(
                this IEnumerable<Product> productEnum, decimal minimumPrice) {

            foreach (Product prod in productEnum) {
                if ((prod?.Price ?? 0) >= minimumPrice) {
                    yield return prod;
                }
            }
        }

        public static IEnumerable<Product> FilterByName(
                this IEnumerable<Product> productEnum, char firstLetter) {

            foreach (Product prod in productEnum) {
                if (prod?.Name?[0] == firstLetter) {
                    yield return prod;
                }
            }
        }
    }
}
```

Listing 4-28 shows the use of both filter methods applied in the controller to create two different totals.

Listing 4-28. Using Two Filter Methods in the HomeController.cs File in the Controllers Folder

```
using Microsoft.AspNetCore.Mvc;
using System.Collections.Generic;
using LanguageFeatures.Models;

namespace LanguageFeatures.Controllers {
    public class HomeController : Controller {

        public ViewResult Index() {

            Product[] productArray = {
                new Product {Name = "Kayak", Price = 275M},
                new Product {Name = "Lifejacket", Price = 48.95M},
                new Product {Name = "Soccer ball", Price = 19.50M},
                new Product {Name = "Corner flag", Price = 34.95M}
            };

            decimal priceFilterTotal = productArray.FilterByPrice(20).TotalPrices();
            decimal nameFilterTotal = productArray.FilterByName('S').TotalPrices();

            return View("Index", new string[] {
                $"Price Total: {priceFilterTotal:C2}",
                $"Name Total: {nameFilterTotal:C2}" });
        }
    }
}
```

The first filter selects all of the products with a price of $20 or more, and the second filter selects products whose name starts with the letter *S*. You will see the following output in the browser window if you run the example application:

```
Price Total: $358.90
Name Total: $19.50
```

Defining Functions

I can repeat this process indefinitely to create filter methods for every property and every combination of properties that I am interested in. A more elegant approach is to separate out the code that processes the enumeration from the selection criteria. C# makes this easy by allowing functions to be passed around as objects. Listing 4-29 shows a single extension method that filters an enumeration of Product objects but that delegates the decision about which ones are included in the results to a separate function.

Listing 4-29. Creating a General Filter Method in the MyExtensionMethods.cs File in the Models Folder

```
using System.Collections.Generic;
using System;

namespace LanguageFeatures.Models {

    public static class MyExtensionMethods {

        public static decimal TotalPrices(this IEnumerable<Product> products) {
            decimal total = 0;
            foreach (Product prod in products) {
                total += prod?.Price ?? 0;
            }
            return total;
        }

        public static IEnumerable<Product> Filter(
                this IEnumerable<Product> productEnum,
                Func<Product, bool> selector) {

            foreach (Product prod in productEnum) {
                if (selector(prod)) {
                    yield return prod;
                }
            }
        }
    }
}
```

The second argument to the Filter method is a function that accepts a Product object and that returns a bool value. The Filter method calls the function for each Product object and includes it in the result if the function returns true. To use the Filter method, I can specify a method or create a stand-alone function, as shown in Listing 4-30.

Listing 4-30. Using a Function to Filter Objects in the HomeController.cs File in the Controllers Folder

```
using Microsoft.AspNetCore.Mvc;
using System.Collections.Generic;
using LanguageFeatures.Models;
using System;

namespace LanguageFeatures.Controllers {
    public class HomeController : Controller {

        bool FilterByPrice(Product p) {
            return (p?.Price ?? 0) >= 20;
        }

        public ViewResult Index() {

            Product[] productArray = {
```

```
            new Product {Name = "Kayak", Price = 275M},
            new Product {Name = "Lifejacket", Price = 48.95M},
            new Product {Name = "Soccer ball", Price = 19.50M},
            new Product {Name = "Corner flag", Price = 34.95M}
        };

        Func<Product, bool> nameFilter = delegate (Product prod) {
            return prod?.Name?[0] == 'S';
        };

        decimal priceFilterTotal = productArray
            .Filter(FilterByPrice)
            .TotalPrices();
        decimal nameFilterTotal = productArray
            .Filter(nameFilter)
            .TotalPrices();

        return View("Index", new string[] {
            $"Price Total: {priceFilterTotal:C2}",
            $"Name Total: {nameFilterTotal:C2}" });
    }
  }
}
```

Neither approach is ideal. Defining methods like FilterByPrice clutters up a class definition. Creating a Func<Product, bool> object avoids this problem but uses an awkward syntax that is hard to read and hard to maintain. It is this issue that lambda expressions address by allowing functions to be defined in a more elegant and expressive way, as shown in Listing 4-31.

Listing 4-31. Using Lambda Expression in the HomeController.cs File in the Controllers Folder

```
using Microsoft.AspNetCore.Mvc;
using System.Collections.Generic;
using LanguageFeatures.Models;
using System;

namespace LanguageFeatures.Controllers {
    public class HomeController : Controller {

        public ViewResult Index() {

            Product[] productArray = {
                new Product {Name = "Kayak", Price = 275M},
                new Product {Name = "Lifejacket", Price = 48.95M},
                new Product {Name = "Soccer ball", Price = 19.50M},
                new Product {Name = "Corner flag", Price = 34.95M}
            };

            decimal priceFilterTotal = productArray
                .Filter(p => (p?.Price ?? 0) >= 20)
                .TotalPrices();
            decimal nameFilterTotal = productArray
```

```
        .Filter(p => p?.Name?[0] == 'S')
        .TotalPrices();

    return View("Index", new string[] {
        $"Price Total: {priceFilterTotal:C2}",
        $"Name Total: {nameFilterTotal:C2}" });
    }
  }
}
```

The lambda expressions are shown in bold. The parameters are expressed without specifying a type, which will be inferred automatically. The => characters are read aloud as "goes to" and link the parameter to the result of the lambda expression. In my examples, a Product parameter called p goes to a bool result, which will be true if the Price property is equal or greater than 20 in the first expression or if the Name property starts with S in the second expression. This code works in the same way as the separate method and the function delegate but is more concise and is—for most people—easier to read.

OTHER FORMS FOR LAMBDA EXPRESSIONS

I don't need to express the logic of my delegate in the lambda expression. I can as easily call a method, like this:

```
prod => EvaluateProduct(prod)
```

If I need a lambda expression for a delegate that has multiple parameters, I must wrap the parameters in parentheses, like this:

```
(prod, count) => prod.Price > 20 && count > 0
```

Finally, if I need logic in the lambda expression that requires more than one statement, I can do so by using braces ({}) and finishing with a return statement, like this:

```
(prod, count) => {
    // ...multiple code statements...
    return result;
}
```

You do not need to use lambda expressions in your code, but they are a neat way of expressing complex functions simply and in a manner that is readable and clear. I like them a lot, and you will see them used liberally throughout this book.

Using Lambda Expression Methods and Properties

Lambda expressions can be used to implement constructors, methods, and properties. In MVC development, especially when writing controllers, you will often end up with methods that contain a single statement that selects the data to display and the view to render. In Listing 4-32, I have rewritten the Index action method so that it follows this common pattern.

Listing 4-32. Creating a Common Action Pattern in the HomeController.cs File in the Controllers Folder

```
using Microsoft.AspNetCore.Mvc;
using System.Collections.Generic;
using LanguageFeatures.Models;
using System;
using System.Linq;

namespace LanguageFeatures.Controllers {
    public class HomeController : Controller {

        public ViewResult Index() {
            return View(Product.GetProducts().Select(p => p?.Name));
        }
    }
}
```

The action method gets a collection of Product objects from the static Product.GetProducts method and uses LINQ to project the values of the Name properties, which are then used as the view model for the default view. If you run the application, you will see the following output displayed in the browser window:

```
Kayak
Lifejacket
```

There will be an empty list item in the browser window as well because the GetProducts method includes a null reference in its results, but that doesn't matter for this section of the chapter.

When a constructor or method body consists of a single statement, it can be rewritten as a lambda expression, as shown in Listing 4-33.

Listing 4-33. An Action Method Expressed as a Lambda Expression in the HomeController.cs File

```
using Microsoft.AspNetCore.Mvc;
using System.Collections.Generic;
using LanguageFeatures.Models;
using System;
using System.Linq;

namespace LanguageFeatures.Controllers {
    public class HomeController : Controller {

        public ViewResult Index() =>
            View(Product.GetProducts().Select(p => p?.Name));
    }
}
```

Lambda expressions for methods omit the return keyword and use => (goes to) to associate the method signature (including its arguments) with its implementation. The Index method shown in Listing 4-33 works in the same way as the one shown in Listing 4-32 but is expressed more concisely. The same basic approach can also be used to define properties. Listing 4-34 shows the addition of a property that uses a lambda express to the Product class.

Listing 4-34. Expressing a Property as a Lambda Expression in the Product.cs File in the Models Folder

```
namespace LanguageFeatures.Models {
    public class Product {

        public Product(bool stock = true) {
            InStock = stock;
        }

        public string Name { get; set; }
        public string Category { get; set; } = "Watersports";
        public decimal? Price { get; set; }
        public Product Related { get; set; }
        public bool InStock { get; }
        public bool NameBeginsWithS => Name?[0] == 'S';

        public static Product[] GetProducts() {

            Product kayak = new Product {
                Name = "Kayak",
                Category = "Water Craft",
                Price = 275M
            };

            Product lifejacket = new Product(false) {
                Name = "Lifejacket",
                Price = 48.95M
            };

            kayak.Related = lifejacket;

            return new Product[] { kayak, lifejacket, null };
        }
    }
}
```

Using Type Inference and Anonymous Types

The var keyword allows you to define a local variable without explicitly specifying the variable type, as demonstrated by Listing 4-35. This is called *type inference* or *implicit typing*.

Listing 4-35. Using Type Inference in the HomeController.cs File in the Controllers Folder

```
using Microsoft.AspNetCore.Mvc;
using System.Collections.Generic;
using LanguageFeatures.Models;
using System;
using System.Linq;

namespace LanguageFeatures.Controllers {
    public class HomeController : Controller {
```

```
    public ViewResult Index() {
        var names = new [] { "Kayak", "Lifejacket", "Soccer ball" };
        return View(names);
    }
  }
}
```

It is not that the names variable does not have a type; instead, I am asking the compiler to infer the type from the code. The compiler examines the array declaration and works out that it is a string array. Running the example produces the following output:

```
Kayak
Lifejacket
Soccer ball
```

Using Anonymous Types

By combining object initializers and type inference, I can create simple view model objects that are useful for transferring data between a controller and a view without having to define a class or struct, as shown in Listing 4-36.

Listing 4-36. Creating an Anonymous Type in the HomeController.cs File in the Controllers Folder

```
using Microsoft.AspNetCore.Mvc;
using System.Collections.Generic;
using LanguageFeatures.Models;
using System;
using System.Linq;

namespace LanguageFeatures.Controllers {
    public class HomeController : Controller {

        public ViewResult Index() {
            var products = new [] {
                new { Name = "Kayak", Price = 275M },
                new { Name = "Lifejacket", Price = 48.95M },
                new { Name = "Soccer ball", Price = 19.50M },
                new { Name = "Corner flag", Price = 34.95M }
            };

            return View(products.Select(p => p.Name));
        }
    }
}
```

Each of the objects in the products array is an anonymously typed object. This does not mean that it is dynamic in the sense that JavaScript variables are dynamic. It just means that the type definition will be created automatically by the compiler. Strong typing is still enforced. You can get and set only the properties that have been defined in the initializer, for example. If you run the example, you will see the following output in the browser window:

```
Kayak
Lifejacket
Soccer ball
Corner flag
```

The C# compiler generates the class based on the name and type of the parameters in the initializer. Two anonymously typed objects that have the same property names and types will be assigned to the same automatically generated class. This means that all the objects in the products array will have the same type because they define the same properties.

Tip I have to use the var keyword to define the array of anonymously typed objects because the type isn't created until the code is compiled and so I don't know the name of the type to use. The elements in an array of anonymously typed objects must all define the same properties; otherwise, the compiler can't work out what the array type should be.

To demonstrate this, I have changed the output from the example in Listing 4-37 so that it shows the type name rather than the value of the Name property.

Listing 4-37. Displaying the Type Name in the HomeController.cs File in the Controllers Folder

```
using Microsoft.AspNetCore.Mvc;
using System.Collections.Generic;
using LanguageFeatures.Models;
using System;
using System.Linq;

namespace LanguageFeatures.Controllers {
    public class HomeController : Controller {

        public ViewResult Index() {
            var products = new [] {
                new { Name = "Kayak", Price = 275M },
                new { Name = "Lifejacket", Price = 48.95M },
                new { Name = "Soccer ball", Price = 19.50M },
                new { Name = "Corner flag", Price = 34.95M }
            };

            return View(products.Select(p => p.GetType().Name));
        }
    }
}
```

All the objects in the array have been assigned the same type, which you can see if you run the example. The type name isn't user-friendly but isn't intended to be used directly, and you may see a different name than the one shown in the following output:

```
<>f__AnonymousType0`2
<>f__AnonymousType0`2
<>f__AnonymousType0`2
<>f__AnonymousType0`2
```

Using Asynchronous Methods

Asynchronous methods go off and do work in the background and notify you when they are complete, allowing your code to take care of other business while the background work is performed. Asynchronous methods are an important tool in removing bottlenecks from code and allow applications to take advantage of multiple processors and processor cores to perform work in parallel.

In MVC, asynchronous methods can be used to improve the overall performance of an application by allowing the server more flexibility in the way that requests are scheduled and executed. Two C# keywords—async and await—are used to perform work asynchronously.

To prepare for this section, I need to add a new .NET assembly to the example project so that I can make asynchronous HTTP requests. Right-click the LanguageFeatures project item in the Solution Explorer, select Edit LanguageFeatures.csproj from the pop-up menu, and add the element shown in Listing 4-38.

Listing 4-38. Adding a Package in the LanguageFeatures.csproj File in the LanguageFeatures Folder

```
<Project Sdk="Microsoft.NET.Sdk.Web">

  <PropertyGroup>
    <TargetFramework>netcoreapp2.0</TargetFramework>
  </PropertyGroup>

  <ItemGroup>
    <Folder Include="wwwroot\" />
  </ItemGroup>

  <ItemGroup>
    <PackageReference Include="Microsoft.AspNetCore.All" Version="2.0.0" />
    <PackageReference Include="System.Net.Http" Version="4.3.2" />
  </ItemGroup>

</Project>
```

When you save the file, Visual Studio will download the System.Net.Http assembly and add it to the project. I describe this process in more detail in Chapter 6.

Working with Tasks Directly

C# and .NET have excellent support for asynchronous methods, but the code has tended to be verbose, and developers who are not used to parallel programming often get bogged down by the unusual syntax. As an example, Listing 4-39 shows an asynchronous method called GetPageLength, which I defined in a class called MyAsyncMethods and added to the Models folder in a class file called MyAsyncMethods.cs.

Listing 4-39. The Contents of the MyAsyncMethods.cs File in the Models Folder

```
using System.Net.Http;
using System.Threading.Tasks;

namespace LanguageFeatures.Models {

    public class MyAsyncMethods {

        public static Task<long?> GetPageLength() {

            HttpClient client = new HttpClient();

            var httpTask = client.GetAsync("http://apress.com");

            return httpTask.ContinueWith((Task<HttpResponseMessage> antecedent) => {
                return antecedent.Result.Content.Headers.ContentLength;
            });
        }
    }
}
```

This method uses a System.Net.Http.HttpClient object to request the contents of the Apress home page and returns its length. .NET represents work that will be done asynchronously as a Task. Task objects are strongly typed based on the result that the background work produces. So, when I call the HttpClient. GetAsync method, what I get back is a Task<HttpResponseMessage>. This tells me that the request will be performed in the background and that the result of the request will be an HttpResponseMessage object.

■ **Tip**   When I use words like *background*, I am skipping over a lot of detail to make just the key points that are important to the world of MVC. The .NET support for asynchronous methods and parallel programming is excellent, and I encourage you to learn more about it if you want to create truly high-performing applications that can take advantage of multicore and multiprocessor hardware. You will see how MVC makes it easy to create asynchronous web applications throughout this book as I introduce different features.

The part that most programmers get bogged down with is the *continuation*, which is the mechanism by which you specify what you want to happen when the background task is complete. In the example, I have used the ContinueWith method to process the HttpResponseMessage object I get from the HttpClient. GetAsync method, which I do using a lambda expression that returns the value of a property that contains the length of the content I get from the Apress web server. Here is the continuation code:

```
...
return httpTask.ContinueWith((Task<HttpResponseMessage> antecedent) => {
    return antecedent.Result.Content.Headers.ContentLength;
});
...
```

Notice that I use the return keyword twice. This is the part that causes confusion. The first use of the return keyword specifies that I am returning a Task<HttpResponseMessage> object, which, when the task is complete, will return the length of the ContentLength header. The ContentLength header returns a long? result (a nullable long value), and this means that the result of my GetPageLength method is Task<long?>, like this:

```
...
public static Task<long?> GetPageLength() {
...
```

Do not worry if this does not make sense—you are not alone in your confusion. It is for this reason that Microsoft added keywords to C# to simplify asynchronous methods.

Applying the async and await Keywords

Microsoft introduced two keywords to C# that are specifically intended to simplify using asynchronous methods like HttpClient.GetAsync. The keywords are async and await, and you can see how I have used them to simplify my example method in Listing 4-40.

Listing 4-40. Using the async and await Keywords in the MyAsyncMethods.cs File in the Models Folder

```
using System.Net.Http;
using System.Threading.Tasks;

namespace LanguageFeatures.Models {

    public class MyAsyncMethods {

        public async static Task<long?> GetPageLength() {

            HttpClient client = new HttpClient();

            var httpMessage = await client.GetAsync("http://apress.com");

            return httpMessage.Content.Headers.ContentLength;
        }
    }
}
```

I used the await keyword when calling the asynchronous method. This tells the C# compiler that I want to wait for the result of the Task that the GetAsync method returns and then carry on executing other statements in the same method.

Applying the await keyword means I can treat the result from the GetAsync method as though it were a regular method and just assign the HttpResponseMessage object that it returns to a variable. Even better, I can then use the return keyword in the normal way to produce a result from another method—in this case, the value of the ContentLength property. This is a much more natural technique, and it means I do not have to worry about the ContinueWith method and multiple uses of the return keyword.

When you use the await keyword, you must also add the async keyword to the method signature, as I have done in the example. The method result type does not change—my example GetPageLength method still returns a Task<long?>. This is because await and async are implemented using some clever compiler tricks, meaning that they allow a more natural syntax, but they do not change what is happening in the methods to which they are applied. Someone who is calling my GetPageLength method still has to deal with a Task<long?> result because there is still a background operation that produces a nullable long— although, of course, that programmer can also choose to use the await and async keywords as well.

This pattern follows through into the MVC controller, which makes it easy to write asynchronous action methods, as shown in Listing 4-41.

Listing 4-41. An Asynchronous Action Methods in the HomeController.cs File in the Controllers Folder

```
using Microsoft.AspNetCore.Mvc;
using System.Collections.Generic;
using LanguageFeatures.Models;
using System;
using System.Linq;
using System.Threading.Tasks;

namespace LanguageFeatures.Controllers {
    public class HomeController : Controller {

        public async Task<ViewResult> Index() {
            long? length = await MyAsyncMethods.GetPageLength();
            return View(new string[] { $"Length: {length}" });
        }
    }
}
```

I have changed the result of the Index action method to Task<ViewResult>, which tells MVC that the action method will return a Task that will produce a ViewResult object when it completes, which will provide details of the view that should be rendered and the data that it requires. I have added the async keyword to the method's definition, which allows me to use the await keyword when calling the MyAsyncMethods.GetPathLength method. MVC and .NET take care of dealing with the continuations, and the result is asynchronous code that is easy to write, easy to read, and easy to maintain. If you run the application, you will see output similar to the following (although with a different length since the content of the Apress web site changes often):

```
Length: 54576
```

Getting Names

There are many tasks in web application development in which you need to refer to the name of an argument, variable, method, or class. Common examples include when you throw an exception or create a validation error when processing input from the user. The traditional approach has been to use a string value hard-coded with the name, as shown in Listing 4-42.

Listing 4-42. Hard-Coding a Name in the HomeController.cs File in the Controllers Folder

```
using Microsoft.AspNetCore.Mvc;
using System.Collections.Generic;
using LanguageFeatures.Models;
using System;
using System.Linq;

namespace LanguageFeatures.Controllers {
    public class HomeController : Controller {

        public ViewResult Index() {

            var products = new [] {
                new { Name = "Kayak", Price = 275M },
                new { Name = "Lifejacket", Price = 48.95M },
                new { Name = "Soccer ball", Price = 19.50M },
                new { Name = "Corner flag", Price = 34.95M }
            };

            return View(products.Select(p => $"Name: {p.Name}, Price: {p.Price}"));
        }
    }
}
```

The call to the LINQ Select method generates a sequence of strings, each of which contains a hard-coded reference to the Name and Price properties. Running the application produces the following output in the browser window:

```
Name: Kayak, Price: 275
Name: Lifejacket, Price: 48.95
Name: Soccer ball, Price: 19.50
Name: Corner flag, Price: 34.95
```

The problem with this approach is that it is prone to errors, either because the name was mistyped or the code was refactored and the name in the string isn't correctly updated. The result can be misleading, which can be especially problematic for messages that are displayed to the user. C# supports the nameof expression, in which the compiler takes responsibility for producing a name string, as shown in Listing 4-43.

Listing 4-43. Using nameof Expressions in the HomeController.cs File in the Controllers Folder

```
using Microsoft.AspNetCore.Mvc;
using System.Collections.Generic;
using LanguageFeatures.Models;
using System;
using System.Linq;

namespace LanguageFeatures.Controllers {
    public class HomeController : Controller {
```

```
    public ViewResult Index() {

        var products = new [] {
            new { Name = "Kayak", Price = 275M },
            new { Name = "Lifejacket", Price = 48.95M },
            new { Name = "Soccer ball", Price = 19.50M },
            new { Name = "Corner flag", Price = 34.95M }
        };

        return View(products.Select(p =>
            $"{nameof(p.Name)}: {p.Name}, {nameof(p.Price)}: {p.Price}"));
    }
  }
}
```

The compiler processes a reference such as p.Name so that only the last part is included in the string, producing the same output as in previous examples. Visual Studio includes IntelliSense support for nameof expressions, so you will be prompted to select references, and expressions will be correctly updated when you refactor code. Since the compiler is responsible for dealing with nameof, using an invalid reference causes a compiler error, which prevents incorrect or outdated references from escaping notice.

Summary

In this chapter, I gave you an overview of the key C# language features that an effective MVC programmer needs to know. C# is a sufficiently flexible language that there are usually different ways to approach any problem, but these are the features that you will encounter most often during web application development and see throughout the examples in this book. In the next chapter, I introduce the Razor view engine and explain how it is used to generate dynamic content in MVC web applications.

CHAPTER 5

■ ■ ■

Working with Razor

In an ASP.NET Core MVC application, a component called the *view engine* is used to produce the content sent to clients. The default view engine is called Razor, and it processes annotated HTML files for instructions that insert dynamic content into the output sent to the browser.

In this chapter, I give you a quick tour of the Razor syntax so you can recognize Razor expressions when you see them. I am not going to supply an exhaustive Razor reference in this chapter; think of this more as a crash course in the syntax. I explore Razor in depth as I continue through the book, within the context of other MVC features. Table 5-1 puts Razor in context.

Table 5-1. *Putting Razor in Context*

Question	Answer
What is it?	Razor is the view engine responsible for incorporating data into HTML documents.
Why is it useful?	The ability to dynamically generate content is essential to being able to write a web application. Razor provides features that make it easy to work with the rest of the ASP.NET Core MVC using C# statements.
How is it used?	Razor expressions are added to static HTML in view files. The expressions are evaluated to generate responses to client requests.
Are there any pitfalls or limitations?	Razor expressions can contain almost any C# statement, and it can be hard to decide whether logic should belong in the view or in the controller, which can erode the separation of concerns that is central to the MVC pattern.
Are there any alternatives?	You can write your own view engine, as I explain in Chapter 21. There are some third-party view engines available, but they tend to be useful for niche situations and don't attract long-term support.

© Adam Freeman 2017
A. Freeman, *Pro ASP.NET Core MVC 2*, https://doi.org/10.1007/978-1-4842-3150-0_5

Table 5-2 summarizes the chapter.

Table 5-2. *Chapter Summary*

Problem	Solution	Listing
Access the view model	Use an @model expression to define the model type and @Model expressions to access the model object	5, 14, 17
Use type names without qualifying them with namespaces	Create a view imports file	6, 7
Define content that will be used by multiple views	Use a layout	8–10
Specify a default layout	Use a view start file	11–13
Pass data from the controller to the view outside of the view model	Use the view bag	15–16
Generate content selectively	Use Razor conditional expressions	18, 19
Generate content for each item in an array or collection	Use a Razor foreach expression	20–21

Preparing the Example Project

To demonstrate how Razor works, I created an ASP.NET Core Web Application (.NET Core) project called Razor using the Empty template, just as in the previous chapter. I enabled the MVC framework by make the changes shown in Listing 5-1 to the Startup class.

Listing 5-1. Enabling MVC in the Startup.cs File in the Razor Folder

```
using System;
using System.Collections.Generic;
using System.Linq;
using System.Threading.Tasks;
using Microsoft.AspNetCore.Builder;
using Microsoft.AspNetCore.Hosting;
using Microsoft.AspNetCore.Http;
using Microsoft.Extensions.DependencyInjection;

namespace Razor {
    public class Startup {

        public void ConfigureServices(IServiceCollection services) {
            services.AddMvc();
        }

        public void Configure(IApplicationBuilder app, IHostingEnvironment env) {
            if (env.IsDevelopment()) {
                app.UseDeveloperExceptionPage();
            }
```

```
    //app.Run(async (context) => {
    //    await context.Response.WriteAsync("Hello World!");
    //});
    app.UseMvcWithDefaultRoute();
        }
    }
}
```

Defining the Model

Next, I created a Models folder and added to it a class file called Product.cs, which I used to define the simple model class shown in Listing 5-2.

Listing 5-2. The Contents of the Product.cs File in the Models Folder

```
namespace Razor.Models {

    public class Product {

        public int ProductID { get; set; }
        public string Name { get; set; }
        public string Description { get; set; }
        public decimal Price { get; set; }
        public string Category { set; get; }
    }
}
```

Creating the Controller

The default configuration that I set up in the Startup.cs file follows the MVC convention of sending requests to a controller called Home by default. I created a Controllers folder and added to it a class file called HomeController.cs, which I used to define the simple controller shown in Listing 5-3.

Listing 5-3. The Contents of the HomeController.cs File in the Controllers Folder

```
using Microsoft.AspNetCore.Mvc;
using Razor.Models;

namespace Razor.Controllers {
    public class HomeController : Controller {

        public ViewResult Index() {
            Product myProduct = new Product {
                ProductID = 1,
                Name = "Kayak",
                Description = "A boat for one person",
                Category = "Watersports",
                Price = 275M
            };

            return View(myProduct);
        }
    }
}
```

The controller defines an action method called Index, in which I create and populate the properties of a Product object. I pass the Product to the View method so that it is used as the model when the view is rendered. I do not specify the name of a view file when I call the View method, so the default view for the action method will be used.

Creating the View

To create the default view for the Index action method, I created a Views/Home folder and added to it an MVC View Page file called Index.cshtml, to which I added the content shown in Listing 5-4.

Listing 5-4. The Contents of the Index.cshtml File in the Views/Home Folder

```
@model Razor.Models.Product

@{
    Layout = null;
}

<!DOCTYPE html>
<html>
<head>
    <meta name="viewport" content="width=device-width" />
    <title>Index</title>
</head>
<body>
    Content will go here
</body>
</html>
```

In the sections that follow, I go through the different parts of a Razor view and demonstrate some of the different things you can do with one. When learning about Razor, it is helpful to bear in mind that views exist to express one or more parts of the model to the user—and that means generating HTML that displays data that is retrieved from one or more objects. If you remember that I am always trying to build an HTML page that can be sent to the client, then everything that Razor does begins to make sense. If you run the application, you will see the simple output shown in Figure 5-1.

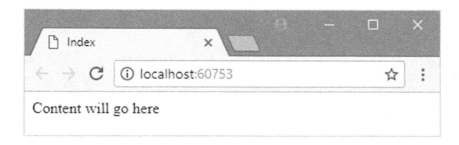

Figure 5-1. *Running the example application*

Working with the Model Object

Let's start with the first line in the Index.cshtml view file:

```
...
@model Razor.Models.Product
...
```

Razor expressions start with the @ character. In this case, the @model expression declares the type of the model object that I will pass to the view from the action method. This allows me to refer to the methods, fields, and properties of the view model object through @Model, as shown in Listing 5-5, which displays a simple addition to the Index view.

Listing 5-5. Referring to a View Model Object Property in the Index.cshtml File in the Views/Home Folder

```
@model Razor.Models.Product

@{
    Layout = null;
}

<!DOCTYPE html>
<html>
<head>
    <meta name="viewport" content="width=device-width" />
    <title>Index</title>
</head>
<body>
    @Model.Name
</body>
</html>
```

■ **Note**   Notice that I declare the view model object type using @model (a lowercase m) and access the Name property using @Model (an uppercase M). This is slightly confusing when you start working with Razor, but it quickly becomes second nature.

If you run the application, you will see the output shown in Figure 5-2.

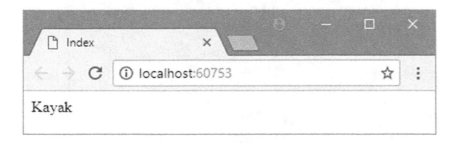

Figure 5-2. *The effect of reading a property value in the view*

A view that uses the @model expression to specify a type is known as a *strongly typed view*. Visual Studio is able to use the @model expression to pop up suggestions of member names when you type @Model followed by a period, as shown in Figure 5-3.

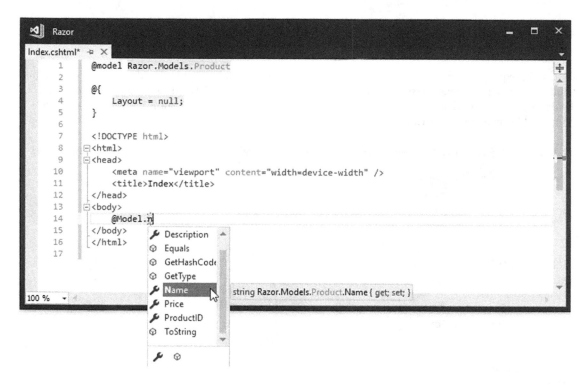

Figure 5-3. *Visual Studio offering suggestions for member names based on the @Model expression*

The Visual Studio suggestions for member names help avoid errors in Razor views. You can ignore the suggestions if you prefer, and Visual Studio will highlight problems with member names so that you make corrections, just as it does with regular C# class files. You can see an example of problem highlighting in Figure 5-4, where I have tried to reference @Model.NotARealProperty. Visual Studio has realized that the Product class I specified at the model type does not have such a property and has highlighted an error in the editor.

```
   ∟  .r.
⊟<head>
      <meta name="viewport" content="width=device-width" />
      <title>Index</title>
   </head>
⊟<body>
      @Model.NotARealProperty
   </body>
   </html>
```

Figure 5-4. *Visual Studio reporting a problem with an @Model expression*

Using View Imports

When I defined the model object at the start of the Index.cshtml file, I had to include the namespace that contains the model class, like this:

```
...
@model Razor.Models.Product
...
```

By default, all types that are referenced in a strongly typed Razor view must be qualified with a namespace. This isn't a big deal when the only type reference is for the model object, but it can make a view more difficult to read when writing more complex Razor expressions such as the ones I describe later in this chapter.

You can specify a set of namespaces that should be searched for types by adding a *view imports* file to the project. The view imports file is placed in the Views folder and is named _ViewImports.cshtml.

■ **Note**   Files in the Views folder whose names begin with an underscore (the _ character) are not returned to the user, which allows the file name to differentiate between views that you want to render and the files that support them. View imports files and layouts (which I describe shortly) are prefixed with an underscore.

To create the view imports file, right-click the Views folder in the Solution Explorer, select Add ➤ New Item from the pop-up menu, and select the MVC View Imports Page template from the ASP.NET Core ➤ Web category, as shown in Figure 5-5.

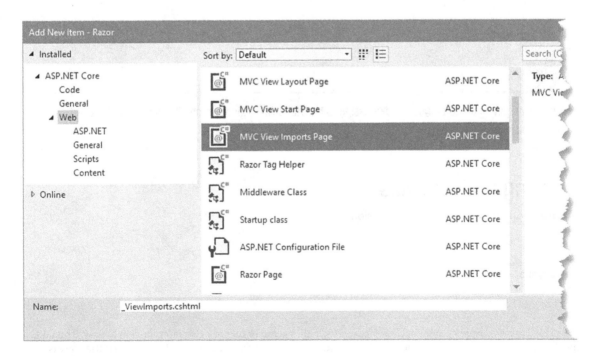

Figure 5-5. *Creating a view imports file*

Visual Studio will automatically set the name of the file to _ViewImports.cshtml, and clicking the Add button will create the file, which will be empty. Add the expression shown in Listing 5-6.

Listing 5-6. The Content of the _ViewImports.cshtml File in the Views Folder

```
@using Razor.Models
```

The namespaces that should be searched for classes used in Razor views are specified using the @ using expression, followed by the namespace. In Listing 5-6, I have added an entry for the Razor.Models namespace that contains the model class in the example application.

Now that the Razor.Models namespace is included in the view imports file, I can remove the namespace from the Index.cshtml file, as shown in Listing 5-7.

Listing 5-7. Omitting the Model Namespace in the Index.cshtml File in the Views/Home Folder

```
@model Product

@{
    Layout = null;
}

<!DOCTYPE html>
<html>
<head>
    <meta name="viewport" content="width=device-width" />
    <title>Index</title>
</head>
<body>
    @Model.Name
</body>
</html>
```

■ **Tip**   You can also add an @using expression to individual view files, which allows types to be used without namespaces in a single view.

Working with Layouts

There is another important Razor expression in the Index.cshtml view file:

```
...
@{
    Layout = null;
}
...
```

This is an example of a Razor *code block*, which allows me to include C# statements in a view. The code block is opened with @{ and closed with }, and the statements it contains are evaluated when the view is rendered.

This code block sets the value of the Layout property to null. Razor views are compiled into C# classes in an MVC application, and the base class that is used defines the Layout property. I'll show you how this all works in Chapter 21, but the effect of setting the Layout property to null is to tell MVC that the view is self-contained and will render all of the content required for the client.

Self-contained views are fine for simple example apps, but a real project can have dozens of views, and some views will have shared content. Duplicating shared content in views becomes hard to manage, especially when you need to make a change and have to track down all of the views that need to be altered.

A better approach is to use a Razor layout, which is a template that contains common content and that can be applied to one or more views. When you make a change to a layout, the change will automatically affect all the views that use it.

Creating the Layout

Layouts are typically shared by views used by multiple controllers and are stored in a folder called Views/Shared, which is one of the locations that Razor looks in when it tries to find a file. To create a layout, create the Views/Shared folder, right-click it, and select Add ➤ New Item from the pop-up menu. Select the MVC View Layout Page template from the ASP.NET category and set the file name to _BasicLayout.cshtml, as shown in Figure 5-6. Click the Add button to create the file. (Like view import files, the names of layout files begin with an underscore.)

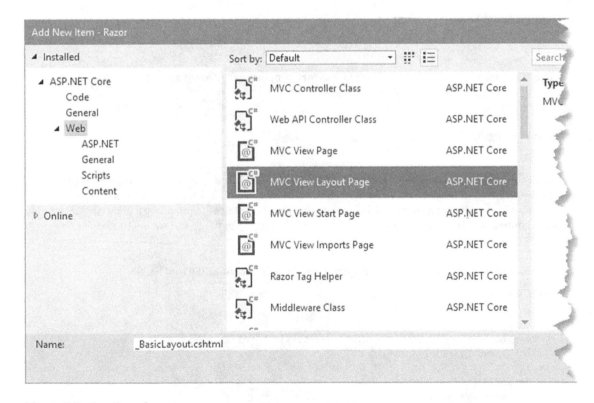

Figure 5-6. *Creating a layout*

Listing 5-8 shows the initial contents of the _BasicLayout.cshtml file, added by Visual Studio when it creates the file.

113

Listing 5-8. The Initial Contents of the _BasicLayout.cshtml File in the Views/Shared Folder

```
<!DOCTYPE html>
<html>
<head>
    <meta name="viewport" content="width=device-width" />
    <title>@ViewBag.Title</title>
</head>
<body>
    <div>
        @RenderBody()
    </div>
</body>
</html>
```

Layouts are a specialized form of view, and there are two @ expressions in the listing. The call to the @ RenderBody method inserts the contents of the view specified by the action method into the layout markup, like this:

```
...
<div>
    @RenderBody()
</div>
...
```

The other Razor expression in the layout looks for a property called ViewBag.Title in order to set the contents of the title element, like this:

```
...
<title>@ViewBag.Title</title>
...
```

The ViewBag is a handy feature that allows data values to be passed around an application and, in this case, between a view and its layout. You will see how this works when I apply the layout to a view.

The HTML elements in a layout will be applied to any view that uses it, providing a template for defining common content. In Listing 5-9, I have added some simple markup to the layout so that its template effect will be obvious.

Listing 5-9. Adding Content to the _BasicLayout.cshtml File in the Views/Shared Folder

```
<!DOCTYPE html>
<html>
<head>
    <meta name="viewport" content="width=device-width" />
    <title>@ViewBag.Title</title>
    <style>
        #mainDiv {
            padding: 20px;
            border: solid medium black;
            font-size: 20pt
        }
    </style>
```

```
</head>
<body>
    <h1>Product Information</h1>
    <div id="mainDiv">
        @RenderBody()
    </div>
</body>
</html>
```

I have added a header element as well as some CSS to style the contents of the div element that contains the @RenderBody expression, just to make it clear what content comes from the layout and what comes from the view.

Applying a Layout

To apply the layout to the view, I need to set the value of the Layout property and remove the HTML that will now be provided by the layout, such as the html, head, and body elements, as shown in Listing 5-10.

Listing 5-10. Applying a Layout in the Index.cshtml File in the Views/Home Folder

```
@model Product

@{
    Layout = "_BasicLayout";
    ViewBag.Title = "Product Name";
}

Product Name: @Model.Name
```

The Layout property specifies the name of the layout file that will be used for the view, without the cshtml file extension. Razor will look for the specified layout file in the /Views/Home and Views/Shared folders.

I also set the ViewBag.Title property in the listing. This will be used by the layout to set the contents of the title element when the view is rendered.

The transformation of the view is dramatic, even for such a simple application. The layout contains all the structure required for any HTML response, which leaves the view to focus on just the dynamic content that presents the data to the user. When MVC processes the Index.cshtml file, it applies the layout to create a unified HTML response, as shown in Figure 5-7.

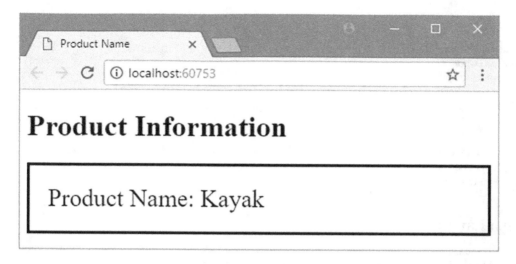

Figure 5-7. *The effect of applying a layout to a view*

Using a View Start File

I still have a tiny wrinkle to sort out, which is that I have to specify the layout file I want in every view. If I need to rename the layout file, I am going to have to find every view that refers to it and make a change, which will be an error-prone process and counter to the general theme of easy maintenance that runs through MVC development.

I can resolve this by using a *view start file*. When it renders a view, MVC will look for a file called _ViewStart.cshtml. The contents of this file will be treated as though they were contained in the view file itself, and I can use this feature to automatically set a value for the Layout property.

To create a view start file, right-click the Views folder, select Add ➤ New Item from the pop-up menu, and choose the MVC View Start Page template from the ASP.NET category, as shown in Figure 5-8.

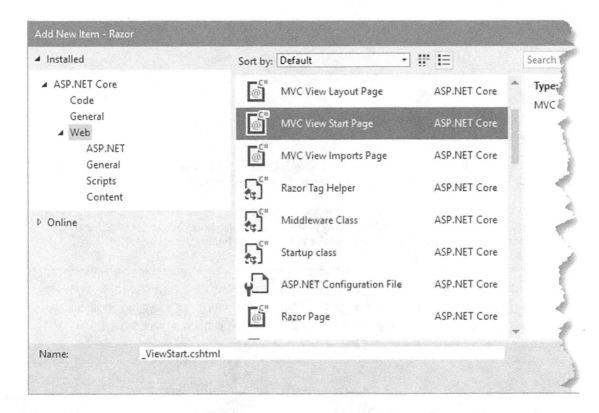

Figure 5-8. *Creating a view start file*

Visual Studio will set the name of the file to _ViewStart.cshtml, and clicking the Add button will create the file with the initial content shown in Listing 5-11.

Listing 5-11. The Initial Contents of the _ViewStart.cshtml File in the Views Folder

```
@{
    Layout = "_Layout";
}
```

To apply my layout to all the views in the application, I changed the value assigned to the Layout property, as shown in Listing 5-12.

Listing 5-12. Applying a Default View in the _ViewStart.cshtml File in the Views Folder

```
@{
    Layout = "_BasicLayout";
}
```

Since the view start file contains a value for the Layout property, I can remove the corresponding expression from the Index.cshtml file, as shown in Listing 5-13.

Listing 5-13. Applying a View Start File in the Index.cshtml File in the Views/Home Folder

```
@model Product

@{
    ViewBag.Title = "Product Name";
}

Product Name: @Model.Name
```

I do not have to specify that I want to use the view start file. MVC will locate the file and use its contents automatically. The values defined in the view file take precedence, which makes it easy to override the view start file.

You can also use multiple view start files to set defaults for different parts of the application. Razor looks for the closest view start file to the view that it being processed, which means you can override the default setting by adding a view start file to the Views/Home or Views/Shared folders, for example.

■ **Caution**   It is important to understand the difference between omitting the Layout property from the view file and setting it to null. If your view is self-contained and you do not want to use a layout, then set the Layout property to null. If you omit the Layout property, then MVC will assume that you *do* want a layout and that it should use the value it finds in the view start file.

Using Razor Expressions

Now that I have shown you the basics of views and layouts, I am going to turn to the different kinds of expressions that Razor supports and how you can use them to create view content. In a good MVC application, there is a clear separation between the roles that the action method and view perform. The rules are simple; I have summarized them in Table 5-3.

Table 5-3. The Roles Played by the Action Method and the View

Component	Does Do	Doesn't Do
Action method	Passes a view model object to the view	Passes formatted data to the view
View	Uses the view model object to present content to the user	Changes any aspect of the view model object

I come back to this theme throughout this book. To get the best from MVC, you need to respect and enforce the separation between the different parts of the app. As you will see, you can do quite a lot with Razor, including using C# statements—but you should not use Razor to perform business logic or manipulate your domain model objects in any way. Listing 5-14 shows the addition of a new expression to the Index view.

Listing 5-14. Adding an Expression to the Index.cshtml File in the Views/Home Folder

```
@model Product

@{
    ViewBag.Title = "Product Name";
}
```

```
<p>Product Name: @Model.Name</p>
<p>Product Price: @($"{Model.Price:C2}")</p>
```

I could have formatted the value of the Price property in the action method and passed it to the view. It would have worked, but taking this approach undermines the benefit of the MVC pattern and reduces my ability to respond to changes in the future. As I said, I will return to this theme again, but you should remember that ASP.NET Core MVC does not enforce proper use of the MVC pattern and that you must remain aware of the effect of the design and coding decisions you make.

PROCESSING VERSUS FORMATTING DATA

It is important to differentiate between *processing* data and *formatting* it. Views *format* data, which is why I passed the Product object in the previous section to the view, rather than formatting the object's properties into a display string. Processing data—including selecting the data objects to display—is the responsibility of the controller, which will call on the model to get and modify the data it requires. It can sometimes be hard to figure out where the line between processing and formatting is, but as a rule of thumb, I recommend erring on the side of caution and pushing anything but the simplest of expressions out of the view and into the controller.

Inserting Data Values

The simplest thing you can do with a Razor expression is to insert a data value into the markup. The most common way to do this is with the @Model expression. The Index view already includes examples of this approach, like this:

```
...
<p>Product Name: @Model.Name</p>
...
```

You can also insert values using the ViewBag feature, which is the feature I used in the layout to set the content of the title element. The ViewBag can be used to pass data from the controller to the view, supplementing the model, as shown in Listing 5-15.

Listing 5-15. Using the View Bag in the HomeController.cs File in the Controllers Folder

```
using Microsoft.AspNetCore.Mvc;
using Razor.Models;

namespace Razor.Controllers {
    public class HomeController : Controller {
```

```
    public ViewResult Index() {
        Product myProduct = new Product {
            ProductID = 1,
            Name = "Kayak",
            Description = "A boat for one person",
            Category = "Watersports",
            Price = 275M
        };

        ViewBag.StockLevel = 2;

        return View(myProduct);
    }
  }
}
```

The ViewBag property returns a dynamic object that can be used to define arbitrary properties. In the listing, I have defined a property called StockLevel and assigned a value of 2 to it. Since the ViewBag property is dynamic, I don't have to declare the property names in advance, but it does mean that Visual Studio is unable to provide autocomplete suggestions for view bag properties.

Knowing when to use the view bag and when the model should be extended is a matter of experience and personal preference. My personal style is to use the view bag only to give a view hints about how to render data and not to use it for data values that are displayed to the user. But that's just what works for me. If you do use the view bag for data you want to display to the user, then you access values using the @ViewBag expression, as shown in Listing 5-16.

Listing 5-16. Displaying a View Bag Value in the Index.cshtml File in the Views/Home Folder

```
@model Product

@{
    ViewBag.Title = "Product Name";
}

<p>Product Name: @Model.Name</p>
<p>Product Price: @($"{Model.Price:C2}")</p>
<p>Stock Level: @ViewBag.StockLevel</p>
```

Figure 5-9 shows the result of the new data value.

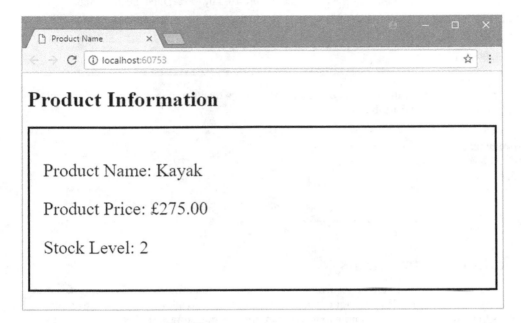

Figure 5-9. *Using Razor expressions to insert data values*

Setting Attribute Values

All the examples so far have set the content of elements, but you can also use Razor expressions to set the value of element *attributes*. Listing 5-17 shows the user of the @Model and @ViewBag expressions to set the contents of attributes on elements in the Index view.

Listing 5-17. Set Attribute Values in the Index.cshtml File in the Views/Home Folder

```
@model Product

@{
    ViewBag.Title = "Product Name";
}

<div data-productid="@Model.ProductID" data-stocklevel="@ViewBag.StockLevel">
    <p>Product Name: @Model.Name</p>
    <p>Product Price: @($"{Model.Price:C2}")</p>
    <p>Stock Level: @ViewBag.StockLevel</p>
</div>
```

I used the Razor expressions to set the value for some data attributes on a div element.

■ **Tip**   Data attributes, which are attributes whose names are prefixed by `data-`, have been an informal way of creating custom attributes for many years and have been made part of the formal standard as part of HTML5. They are most often applied so that JavaScript code can locate specific elements or so that CSS styles can be more narrowly applied.

If you run the example application and look at the HTML source that is sent to the browser, you will see that Razor has set the values of the attributes, like this:

```html
<div data-productid="1" data-stocklevel="2">
    <p>Product Name: Kayak</p>
    <p>Product Price: £275.00</p>
    <p>Stock Level: 2</p>
</div>
```

Using Conditional Statements

Razor is able to process conditional statements, which means that I can tailor the output from a view based on values in the view data. This kind of technique is at the heart of Razor and allows you to create complex and fluid layouts that are still reasonably simple to read and maintain. In Listing 5-18, I have updated the Index view so that it includes a conditional statement.

Listing 5-18. Using a Conditional Razor Statement in the Index.cshtml File in the Views/Home Folder

```
@model Product

@{
    ViewBag.Title = "Product Name";
}

<div data-productid="@Model.ProductID" data-stocklevel="@ViewBag.StockLevel">
    <p>Product Name: @Model.Name</p>
    <p>Product Price: @($"{Model.Price:C2}")</p>
    <p>Stock Level:
        @switch (ViewBag.StockLevel) {
            case 0:
                @:Out of Stock
                break;
            case 1:
            case 2:
            case 3:
                <b>Low Stock (@ViewBag.StockLevel)</b>
                break;
            default:
                @: @ViewBag.StockLevel in Stock
                break;
        }
    </p>
</div>
```

To start a conditional statement, you place an @ character in front of the C# conditional keyword, which is switch in this example. You terminate the code block with a close brace character (}) just as you would with a regular C# code block.

Inside the Razor code block, you can include HTML elements and data values into the view output just by defining the HTML and Razor expressions, like this:

```
...
<b>Low Stock (@ViewBag.StockLevel)</b>
...
```

I do not have to put the elements or expressions in quotes or denote them in any special way—the Razor engine will interpret these as output to be processed. However, if you want to insert literal text into the view when it is not contained in an HTML element, then you need to give Razor a helping hand and prefix the line like this:

```
...
@: Out of Stock
...
```

The @: characters prevent Razor from interpreting this as a C# statement, which is the default behavior when it encounters text. You can see the result of the conditional statement in Figure 5-10.

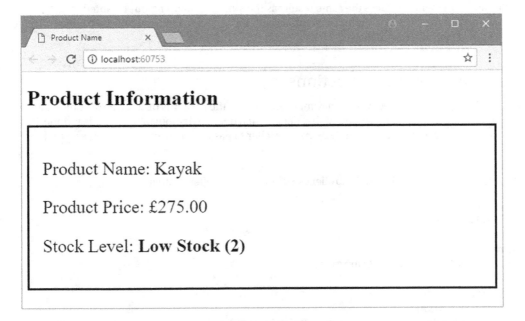

Figure 5-10. *Using a switch statement in a Razor view*

Conditional statements are important in Razor views because they allow content to be varied based on the data values that the view receives from the action method. As an additional demonstration, Listing 5-19 shows the addition of an if statement to the Index.cshtml view. As you might imagine, this is a commonly used conditional statement.

Listing 5-19. Using an if Statement in a Razor View in the Index.cshtml File in Views/Home Folder

```
@model Product

@{
    ViewBag.Title = "Product Name";
}

<div data-productid="@Model.ProductID" data-stocklevel="@ViewBag.StockLevel">
    <p>Product Name: @Model.Name</p>
    <p>Product Price: @($"{Model.Price:C2}")</p>
    <p>Stock Level:
        @if (ViewBag.StockLevel == 0) {
            @:Out of Stock
        } else if (ViewBag.StockLevel > 0 && ViewBag.StockLevel <= 3) {
            <b>Low Stock (@ViewBag.StockLevel)</b>
        } else {
            @: @ViewBag.StockLevel in Stock
        }
    </p>
</div>
```

This conditional statement produces the same results as the switch statement, but I wanted to demonstrate how you can mesh C# conditional statements with Razor views. I explain how this works in Chapter 21, when I describe views in depth.

Enumerating Arrays and Collections

When writing an MVC application, you will often want to enumerate the contents of an array or some other kind of collection of objects and generate content that details each one. To demonstrate how this is done, in Listing 5-20 I have revised the Index action in the Home controller to pass an array of Product objects to the view.

Listing 5-20. Using an Array in the HomeController.cs File in the Controllers Folder

```
using Microsoft.AspNetCore.Mvc;
using Razor.Models;

namespace Razor.Controllers {
    public class HomeController : Controller {

        public IActionResult Index() {
            Product[] array = {
                new Product {Name = "Kayak", Price = 275M},
                new Product {Name = "Lifejacket", Price = 48.95M},
                new Product {Name = "Soccer ball", Price = 19.50M},
                new Product {Name = "Corner flag", Price = 34.95M}
            };
            return View(array);
        }
    }
}
```

This action method creates a Product[] object that contains simple data values and passes them to the View method so that the data is rendered using the default view. In Listing 5-21, I have changed the model type for the Index view and used a foreach loop to enumerate the objects in the array.

■ **Tip**   The Model term in Listing 5-21 doesn't need to be prefixed with an @ character because it is part of a larger C# expression. It can be difficult to figure out when an @ character is required and when it is not, but the Visual Studio IntelliSense for Razor files will tell you when you get it wrong by underlining errors.

Listing 5-21. Enumerating an Array in the Index.cshtml File in the Views/Home Folder

```
@model Product[]

@{
    ViewBag.Title = "Product Name";
}

<table>
    <thead>
        <tr><th>Name</th><th>Price</th></tr>
    </thead>
    <tbody>
        @foreach (Product p in Model) {
            <tr>
                <td>@p.Name</td>
                <td>@($"{p.Price:C2}")</td>
            </tr>
        }
    </tbody>
</table>
```

The @foreach statement enumerates the contents of the model array and generates a row in a table for each of them. You can see how I created a local variable called p in the foreach loop and then referred to its properties using the Razor expressions @p.Name and @p.Price. You can see the result in Figure 5-11.

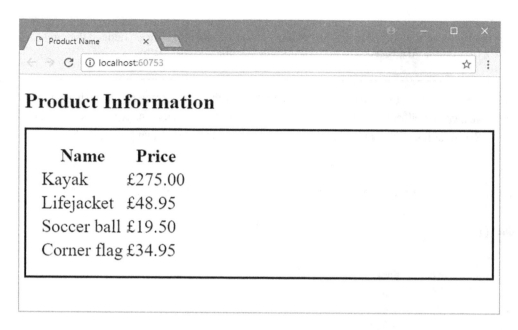

Figure 5-11. *Using Razor to enumerate an array*

Summary

In this chapter, I gave you an overview of the Razor view engine and how it can be used to generate HTML. I showed you how to refer to data passed from the controller via the view model object and the view bag and how Razor expressions can be used to tailor responses to the user based on data values. You will see many different examples of how Razor can be used in the rest of the book, and I describe how the MVC view mechanism works in detail in Chapter 21. In the next chapter, I introduce some of the features provided by Visual Studio for working with ASP.NET Core MVC projects.

CHAPTER 6

■ ■ ■

Working with Visual Studio

In this chapter, I describe the key features that Visual Studio provides for developing ASP.NET Core MVC projects. Table 6-1 summarizes the chapter.

Table 6-1. *Chapter Summary*

Problem	Solution	Listing
Add packages to a project	Use the NuGet tool for .NET packages and Bower for client-side packages	6-8
See the effect of view or class changes	Use the iterative development model	9–11
Display detailed messages in the browser	Use developer exception pages	12
Get detailed information and control about application execution	Use the debugger	13
Reload one or more browsers using Visual Studio	Use Browser Link	14–15
Reduce the number of HTTP requests and the amount of bandwidth required for JavaScript and CSS files	Use the Bundler & Minifier extension	16–23

Preparing the Example Project

For this chapter, I created a new ASP.NET Core Web Application (.NET Core) project called Working WithVisualStudio using the Empty template. I enabled MVC with its default configuration in the Startup.cs file, as shown in Listing 6-1.

Listing 6-1. Enabling MVC in the Startup.cs File in the WorkingWithVisualStudio Folder

```
using System;
using System.Collections.Generic;
using System.Linq;
using System.Threading.Tasks;
using Microsoft.AspNetCore.Builder;
using Microsoft.AspNetCore.Hosting;
using Microsoft.AspNetCore.Http;
using Microsoft.Extensions.DependencyInjection;
```

© Adam Freeman 2017
A. Freeman, *Pro ASP.NET Core MVC 2*, https://doi.org/10.1007/978-1-4842-3150-0_6

```
namespace WorkingWithVisualStudio {
    public class Startup {

        public void ConfigureServices(IServiceCollection services) {
            services.AddMvc();
        }

        public void Configure(IApplicationBuilder app, IHostingEnvironment env) {
            app.UseMvcWithDefaultRoute();
        }
    }
}
```

Creating the Model

I created a Models folder and added to it a class file called Product.cs, which I used to define the class shown in Listing 6-2.

Listing 6-2. The Contents of the Product.cs File in the Models Folder

```
namespace WorkingWithVisualStudio.Models {

    public class Product {
        public string Name { get; set; }
        public decimal Price { get; set; }
    }
}
```

To create a simple store of Product objects, I added a class file called SimpleRepository.cs to the Models folder and used it to define the class shown in Listing 6-3.

Listing 6-3. The Contents of the SimpleRepository.cs File in the Models Folder

```
using System.Collections.Generic;

namespace WorkingWithVisualStudio.Models {
    public class SimpleRepository {
        private static SimpleRepository sharedRepository = new SimpleRepository();
        private Dictionary<string, Product> products
            = new Dictionary<string, Product>();

        public static SimpleRepository SharedRepository => sharedRepository;

        public SimpleRepository() {
            var initialItems = new[] {
                new Product { Name = "Kayak", Price = 275M },
                new Product { Name = "Lifejacket", Price = 48.95M },
                new Product { Name = "Soccer ball", Price = 19.50M },
                new Product { Name = "Corner flag", Price = 34.95M }
            };
```

```
        foreach (var p in initialItems) {
            AddProduct(p);
        }
    }

    public IEnumerable<Product> Products => products.Values;

    public void AddProduct(Product p) => products.Add(p.Name, p);
    }
}
```

This class stores model objects in memory, which means that any changes to the model are lost when the application is stopped or restarted. A nonpersistent store is sufficient for the examples in this chapter, but it isn't an approach that can be used in many real projects; see Chapter 8 for an example of creating a repository that stores model objects persistently using a relational database.

■ **Note**   In Listing 6-3, I defined a static property called `SharedRepository` that provides access to a single `SimpleRepository` object that can be used throughout the application. This isn't best practice, but I want to demonstrate a common problem that you will encounter in MVC development; I describe a better way to work with shared components in Chapter 18.

Creating the Controller and View

I added a `Controllers` folder to the project and added to it a class file called `HomeController.cs`, which I used to define the controller shown in Listing 6-4.

Listing 6-4. The Contents of the HomeController.cs File in the Controllers Folder

```
using Microsoft.AspNetCore.Mvc;
using WorkingWithVisualStudio.Models;

namespace WorkingWithVisualStudio.Controllers {
    public class HomeController : Controller {

        public IActionResult Index()
            => View(SimpleRepository.SharedRepository.Products);
    }
}
```

There is a single action—called `Index`—that gets all of the model objects and passes them to the `View` method to render the default view. To add that view, I created the `Views/Home` folder and added a view file called `Index.cshtml`, the contents of which are shown in Listing 6-5.

Listing 6-5. The Contents of the Index.cshtml File in the Views/Home Folder

```
@model IEnumerable<WorkingWithVisualStudio.Models.Product>
@{ Layout = null; }

<!DOCTYPE html>
<html>
<head>
    <meta name="viewport" content="width=device-width" />
    <title>Working with Visual Studio</title>
</head>
<body>
    <table>
        <thead>
            <tr><td>Name</td><td>Price</td></tr>
        </thead>
        <tbody>
            @foreach (var p in Model) {
                <tr>
                    <td>@p.Name</td>
                    <td>@p.Price</td>
                </tr>
            }
        </tbody>
    </table>
</body>
</html>
```

The view contains a table that uses a Razor foreach loop to create rows for each model object, where each row contains cells for the Name and Price properties. If you run the example application, you will see the results shown in Figure 6-1.

Figure 6-1. *Running the example application*

Managing Software Packages

There are two different types of software package required for ASP.NET Core MVC projects. In the sections that follow, I describe each type of package and the tools that are provided by Visual Studio for managing them.

Understanding NuGet

Visual Studio provides a graphical tool for managing the .NET packages that are included in a project. To open the tool, select Manage NuGet Packages for Solution from the Tools ➤ NuGet Package Manager menu. The NuGet tool opens and displays a list of the packages that are already installed, as shown in Figure 6-2.

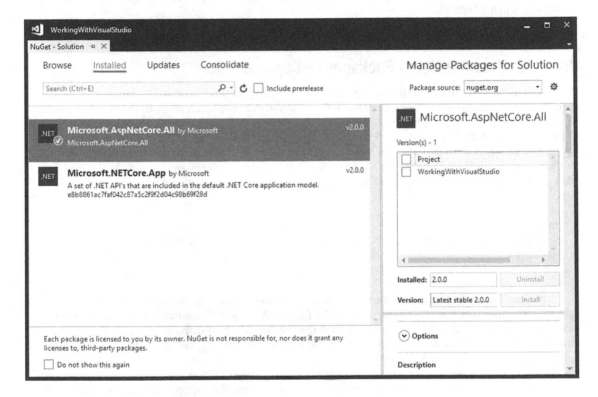

Figure 6-2. Using the NuGet package manager

The Installed tab provides a summary of the packages that are already installed in the project. The Browse tab can be used to locate and install new packages, and the Updates tab can be used to list packages for which more recent versions have been released.

UNDERSTANDING THE MICROSOFT.ASPNETCORE.ALL PACKAGE

If you have used earlier versions of ASP.NET Core, you will have become familiar with the need to add a long list of NuGet packages to a new project. ASP.NET Core 2 takes a different approach and relies on a single package called `Microsoft.AspNetCore.All`.

The `Microsoft.AspNetCore.All` package is a meta-package, which contains all the individual NuGet packages required by ASP.NET Core and the MVC framework, which means you don't need to add packages one by one. When you publish your application, any individual packages that are part of the meta-package but not used by the application will be removed, ensuring that you don't deploy more packages that you need.

Understanding the NuGet Packages List and Location

The NuGet tool keeps track of the project's packages in the `<projectname>.csproj` file, where `<projectname>` is replaced by the name of the project. For the example application, this means that details of the NuGet packages are stored in a file called `WorkingWithVisualStudio.csproj`. Visual Studio doesn't display the `.csproj` file in the Solution Explorer window. To edit the file, right-click the project item in the Solution Explorer window and select Edit WorkingWithVisualStudio.csproj from the pop-up menu. Visual Studio will open the file for editing. The `.csproj` file is XML, and you will see an element like this one that adds the ASP.NET Core meta-package to the project, like this:

```
...
<ItemGroup>
  <PackageReference Include="Microsoft.AspNetCore.All" Version="2.0.0" />
</ItemGroup>
...
```

A package is specified with its name and the version number that is required. Although the meta-package includes all the features required for ASP.NET Core MVC, you will still have to add packages to the project so that additional features can be used. Packages can be added using the interface shown in Figure 6-2 or using command-line tools. You can also edit the `.csproj` file directly and Visual Studio will detect changes and download and install the packages add.

When you use NuGet to add a package to a project, it is automatically installed along with any packages it depends on. You can explore the NuGet packages and their dependencies by opening the Dependencies ➤ NuGet item in the Solution Explorer, which shows each of the packages in the `.csproj` file and its dependencies. The ASP.NET Core meta-package has a large number of dependencies, some of which can be seen in Figure 6-3.

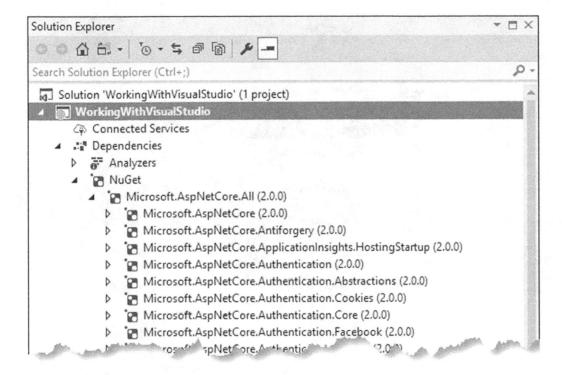

Figure 6-3. The References section of the Solution Explorer

Understanding Bower

A client-side package is one that contains content that is sent to the client, such as JavaScript files, CSS stylesheets, or images. NuGet used to manage these projects as well, but ASP.NET Core MVC now relies on a tool called Bower. Bower is an open source tool that has been developed outside of Microsoft and the .NET world and is widely used in non-ASP.NET Core web application development.

■ **Note**   Bower has recently been deprecated. You may see warnings that recommend alternative tools; however, Bower is still being actively maintained, and support for Bower is integrated into Visual Studio. At some point, you can expect Microsoft to support a different tool for managing client-side packages, but you should continue to use Bower until that happens.

Understanding the Bower Packages List

Bower packages are specified through the bower.json file. To create this file, right-click the WorkingWithVisualStudio project item in the Solution Explorer, select Add ➤ New Item from the pop-up menu, and choose the Bower Configuration File item template from the ASP.NET Core ➤ Web ➤ General category, as shown in Figure 6-4.

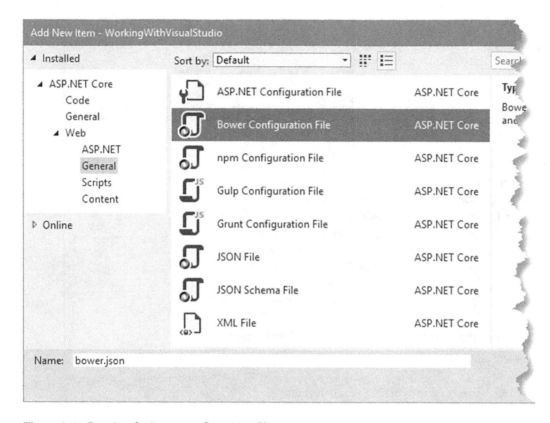

Figure 6-4. Creating the Bower configuration file

Visual Studio sets the name to bower.json, and clicking the Add button adds the file to the project with the default content shown in Listing 6-6.

Listing 6-6. The Default Contents of the bower.json File

```
{
  "name": "asp.net",
  "private": true,
  "dependencies": {
  }
}
```

Listing 6-7 shows the addition of a client-side package to the bower.json file, which is done by adding an entry to the dependencies section.

■ **Tip**   The repository for Bower packages is http://bower.io/search, where you can search for packages to add to your project.

Listing 6-7. Adding Packages to the bower.json File

```json
{
  "name": "asp.net",
  "private": true,
  "dependencies": {
    "bootstrap": "3.3.7"
  }
}
```

The addition in the listing adds the Bootstrap CSS package to the example project. When you edit the bower.json file, Visual Studio will offer you a list of package names and list the versions of the packages that are available, as shown in Figure 6-5.

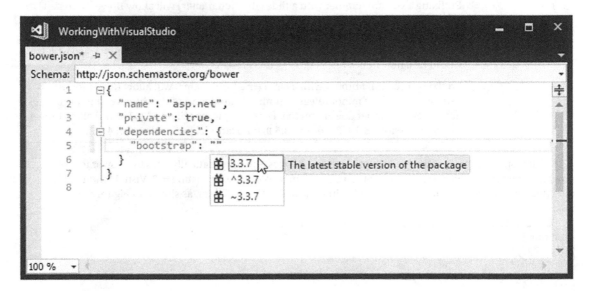

Figure 6-5. *Listing the available versions of the client-side package*

At the time of writing, the latest version of the bootstrap package is 3.3.7. Notice, however, that there are three options offered by Visual Studio: 3.3.7, ^3.3.7, and ~3.3.7. Version numbers can be specified in a range of different ways in the bower.json file, the most useful of which are described in Table 6-2. The safest way to specify a package is to use an explicit version number. This ensures you will always be working with the same version unless you deliberately update the bower.json file to request a different one.

■ **Tip** For the examples in this book, I create and edit the bower.json file directly. The file is simple to edit, and it helps ensure that you get the expected results if you are following along. Visual Studio also provides a graphical tool for managing Bower packages, which can be opened by right-clicking the bower.json file and selecting Manage Bower Packages from the pop-up menu.

Table 6-2. Common Formats for Version Numbers in the bower.json File

Format	Description
3.3.7	Expressing a version number directly will install the package with the exact matching version number, e.g., 3.3.7.
*	Using an asterisk will allow Bower to download and install any version of the package.
>3.3.7 >=3.3.7	Prefixing a version number with > or >= will allow Bower to install any version of the package that is greater than or greater than or equal to a given version.
<3.3.7 <=3.3.7	Prefixing a version number with < or <= will allow Bower to install any version of the package that is less than or less than or equal to a given version.
~3.3.7	Prefixing a version number with a tilde (the ~ character) will allow Bower to install versions even if the patch level number (the last of the three version numbers) doesn't match. For example, specifying ~3.3.7 will allow Bower to install version 3.3.8 or 3.3.9 (which would be patches to version 3.3.7) but not version 3.4.0 (which would be a new minor release).
^3.3.7	Prefixing a version number with a caret (the ^ character) will allow Bower to install versions even if the minor release number (the second of the three version numbers) or the patch number doesn't match. For example, specifying ^3.3.0 will allow Bower to install versions 3.3.1, 3.4.0, and 3.5.0, for example, but not version 4.0.0.

Visual Studio monitors the bower.json files for changes and automatically uses the Bower tool to download and install packages. When you save the change to the file for Listing 6-7, Visual Studio will download the Bootstrap package and install it into the wwwroot/lib folder, as shown in Figure 6-6.

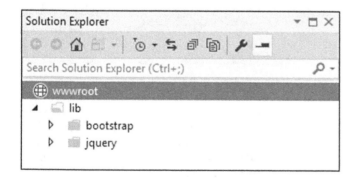

Figure 6-6. Adding client-side packages to the project

Like NuGet, Bower manages the dependencies of the packages you add to a project. Bootstrap relies on the jQuery JavaScript library for some of its advanced features, which is why there are two packages shown in the figure. You can see the list of packages and their dependencies by expanding the Dependencies item in the Solution Explorer, as shown in Figure 6-7.

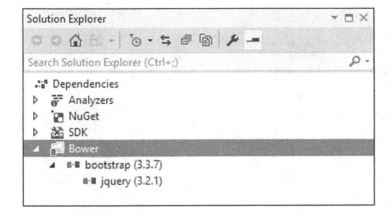

Figure 6-7. *Examining the client-side packages and their dependencies*

Updating the Bootstrap Package

Throughout the rest of this book, I use a prerelease version of the Bootstrap CSS framework. As I write this, the Bootstrap team is in the process of developing Bootstrap version 4 and has made several early releases. These releases have been labeled as "alpha," but the quality is high, and they are stable enough for use in the examples in this book. Given the choice of writing this book using the soon-to-be-obsolete Bootstrap 3 and a prerelease version of Bootstrap 4, I decided to use the new version even though some of the class names that are used to style HTML elements are likely to change before the final release. This means you must use the same version of Bootstrap to get the expected results from the examples.

To update the Bootstrap package, change the version number in the bower.json file, as shown in Listing 6-8.

Listing 6-8. Changing a Package Version in the bower.json File in the WorkingWithVisualStudio Folder

```
{
  "name": "asp.net",
  "private": true,
  "dependencies": {
    "bootstrap": "4.0.0-alpha.6"
  }
}
```

Visual Studio will download the new version of the Bootstrap package when you save the change to the bower.json file.

Understanding Iterative Development

Web application development can often be an iterative process, where you make small changes to views or classes and run the application to test their effect. MVC and Visual Studio work together to support this iterative approach to make seeing the impact of changes quick and easy.

Making Changes to Razor Views

During development, changes to Razor views take effect as soon as an HTTP request is received from the browser. To demonstrate how this works, start the application by selecting Start Debugging from the Debug menu and, once a browser tab has been opened and the data displayed, make the changes shown in Listing 6-9 to the Index.cshtml file.

Listing 6-9. Making Changes to the Index.cshtml File

```
@model IEnumerable<WorkingWithVisualStudio.Models.Product>
@{ Layout = null; }

<!DOCTYPE html>
<html>
<head>
    <meta name="viewport" content="width=device-width" />
    <title>Working with Visual Studio</title>
</head>
<body>
    <h3>Products</h3>
    <table>
        <thead>
            <tr><td>Name</td><td>Price</td></tr>
        </thead>
        <tbody>
            @foreach (var p in Model) {
                <tr>
                    <td>@p.Name</td>
                    <td>@($"{p.Price:C2}")</td>
                </tr>
            }
        </tbody>
    </table>
</body>
</html>
```

Save the changes to the Index view and reload the web page using the browser reload button. The changes to the view (the addition of a header element and formatting the Price model property as a currency) take effect and are shown in the browser, as illustrated in Figure 6-8.

■ **Tip**   I explain the process by which Razor views are prepared for use in Chapter 21.

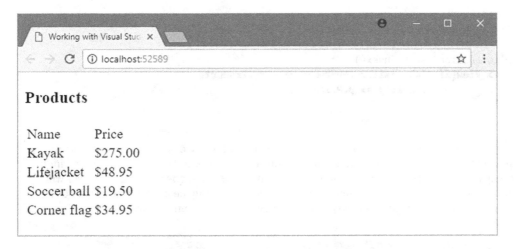

Figure 6-8. *Making a change to a view*

Making Changes to C# Classes

For C# classes, including controllers and models, the way that changes are handled depend on how you start the application. In the sections that follow, I describe the two approaches available, which are selected through different items in the Debug menu, as described in Table 6-3 for quick reference.

Table 6-3. *The Debug Menu Items*

Menu Item	Description
Start Without Debugging	The classes in the project are compiled automatically when an HTTP request is received, allowing for a more dynamic development experience. The application is run without the debugger, which cannot be used to take control of code execution.
Start Debugging	You must explicitly compile your project and restart the application for changes to take effect. The debugger is attached to the application when it runs, allowing inspection of its state and analysis of any problems.

Compiling Classes Automatically

During normal development, a fast iterative cycle lets you see the effect of your changes immediately, whether it is the effect of adding a new action or changing the way that view model data is selected. For this kind of development, Visual Studio supports detecting changes as soon as an HTTP request is received from the browser and recompiling classes automatically. To see how this works, select Start Without Debugging from the Visual Studio Debug menu. Once the browser displays the application data, make the changes shown in Listing 6-10 to the Home controller.

Listing 6-10. Filtering Model Data in the HomeController.cs File

```
using Microsoft.AspNetCore.Mvc;
using WorkingWithVisualStudio.Models;
using System.Linq;
```

```
namespace WorkingWithVisualStudio.Controllers {
    public class HomeController : Controller {

        public IActionResult Index()
            => View(SimpleRepository.SharedRepository.Products
                         .Where(p => p.Price < 50));
    }
}
```

The changes use LINQ to filter the Product objects so that only those whose Price property is less than 50 are passed to the view. Save the changes to the controller class file and reload the browser window without stopping or restarting the application in Visual Studio. The HTTP request from the browser will trigger the compilation process, and the application will be restarted using the modified controller class, producing the results shown in Figure 6-9, which omit the Kayak product from the table.

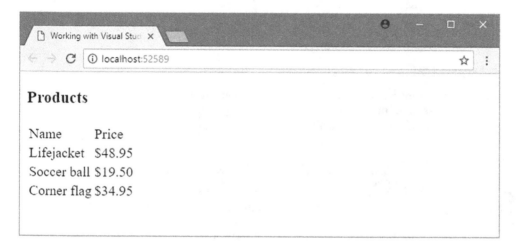

Figure 6-9. *Automatically compiling classes*

The automated compilation feature is useful when everything is going to plan. The drawback is that compiler and runtime errors are displayed in the browser rather than Visual Studio, which can make it hard to figure out what is happening when there is a problem. As an example, Listing 6-11 shows the addition of a null reference to the collection of model objects in the repository.

Listing 6-11. Adding a null Reference in the SimpleRepository.cs File

```
using System.Collections.Generic;

namespace WorkingWithVisualStudio.Models {
    public class SimpleRepository {
        private static SimpleRepository sharedRepository = new SimpleRepository();
        private Dictionary<string, Product> products
            = new Dictionary<string, Product>();

        public static SimpleRepository SharedRepository => sharedRepository;
```

```
    public SimpleRepository() {
        var initialItems = new[] {
            new Product { Name = "Kayak", Price = 275M },
            new Product { Name = "Lifejacket", Price = 48.95M },
            new Product { Name = "Soccer ball", Price = 19.50M },
            new Product { Name = "Corner flag", Price = 34.95M }
        };
        foreach (var p in initialItems) {
            AddProduct(p);
        }
        products.Add("Error", null);
    }

    public IEnumerable<Product> Products => products.Values;

    public void AddProduct(Product p) => products.Add(p.Name, p);
    }
}
```

A problem like a null reference won't show up until the application is running. Reloading the browser page will cause the SimpleRepository class to be compiled, and the application will be restarted. When MVC creates an instance of the controller class to process the HTTP request from the browser, the HomeController constructor will instantiate the SimpleRepository class, which will, in turn, try to process the null reference added in the listing. The null value causes a problem, but it isn't obvious what the problem is because the browser doesn't display a helpful message.

Enabling Developer Exception Pages

During the development process, it can be helpful to display more useful information in the browser window when there is a problem. This can be done by enabling developer exception pages, which requires a configuration change in the Startup class, as shown in Listing 6-12.

I explain the role of the Startup class in detail in Chapter 14, but for now, it is enough to know that calling the UseDeveloperExceptionPage extension method sets up the descriptive error pages.

Listing 6-12. Enabling Developer Exception Pages in the Startup.cs File

```
using System;
using System.Collections.Generic;
using System.Linq;
using System.Threading.Tasks;
using Microsoft.AspNetCore.Builder;
using Microsoft.AspNetCore.Hosting;
using Microsoft.AspNetCore.Http;
using Microsoft.Extensions.DependencyInjection;

namespace WorkingWithVisualStudio {
    public class Startup {

        public void ConfigureServices(IServiceCollection services) {
            services.AddMvc();
        }
```

```
    public void Configure(IApplicationBuilder app, IHostingEnvironment env) {
        app.UseDeveloperExceptionPage();
        app.UseMvcWithDefaultRoute();
    }
  }
}
```

If you reload the browser window, the automatically compilation process will rebuild the application and produce a more useful error message in the browser, as shown in Figure 6-10.

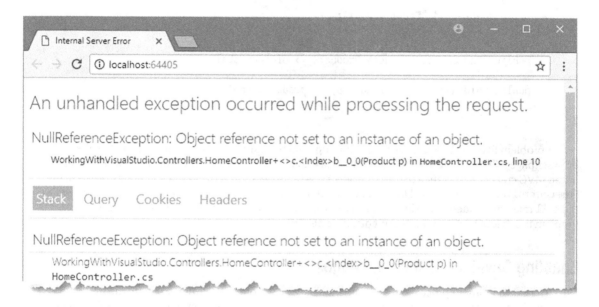

Figure 6-10. *A developer exception page*

The error message shown by the browser can be sufficient to figure out simple problems, especially since the iterative style of development means that the most recent changes made are likely to be the cause. But for more complex problems—and for problems that don't become immediately apparent—the Visual Studio debugger is required.

Using the Debugger

Visual Studio also supports running an MVC application using a debugger, which allows execution to be halted to inspect the application's state and the path that a request follows through the code. This requires a different style of development because modifications to C# classes are not applied until the application is restarted (although changes to Razor views still take effect automatically).

This style of development isn't as dynamic as using the automatic compilation feature, but the Visual Studio debugger is excellent and can provide deeper insights into the way an application works.

To run an application using the debugger, select Start Debugging from the Visual Studio Debug menu. Visual Studio will compile the C# classes in the project before launching the application, but you can also manually compile your code by using the items in the Build menu.

The example application still contains the null reference, which means that the unhandled NullReferenceException that is thrown by the SimpleRepository class will interrupt the application and pass execution control to the developer, as shown in Figure 6-11.

■ **Tip** If the debugger doesn't intercept the exception, then select Windows ➤ Exception Settings from the Visual Studio Debug menu and make sure that all the exception types in the Common Language Runtime Exceptions list are checked.

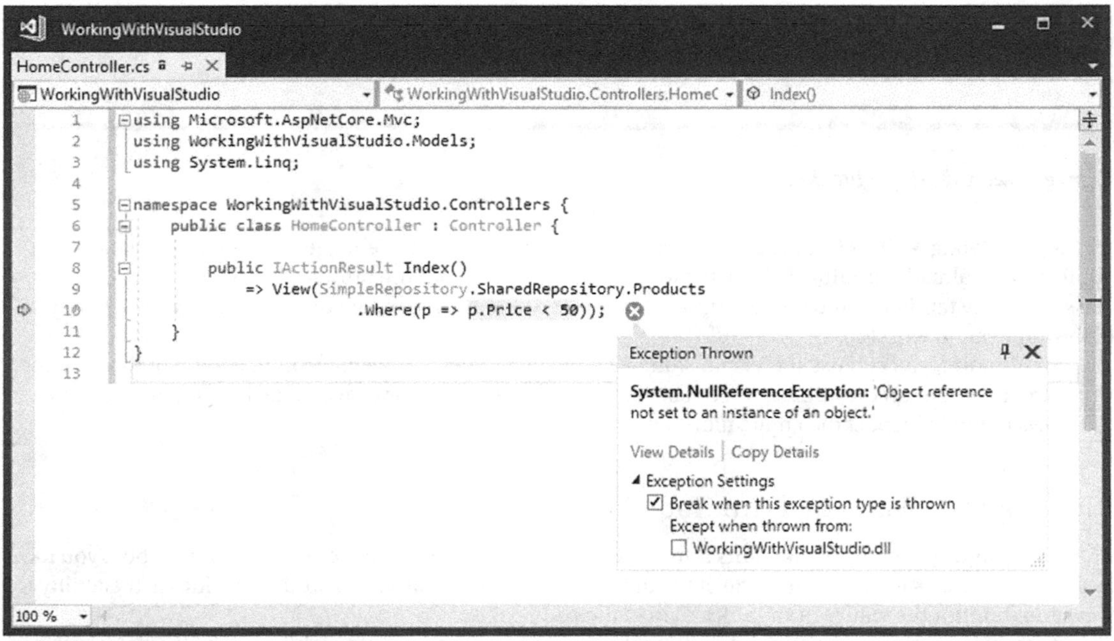

Figure 6-11. Dealing with an unhandled exception

Setting a Breakpoint

The debugger doesn't indicate the root cause of the problem, only where it manifested itself. The statement that Visual Studio highlights indicates that the problem occurs when filtering the objects using LINQ, but a little work is required to dig into the detail and get to the underlying cause.

A *breakpoint* is an instruction that tells the debugger to halt execution of the application and hand control to the programmer. You can inspect the state of the application and see what is happening and, optionally, resume execution again.

To create a breakpoint, right-click a code statement and select Breakpoint ➤ Insert Breakpoint from the pop-up menu. As a demonstration, apply a breakpoint to the AddProduct method in the SimpleRepository class, as shown in Figure 6-12.

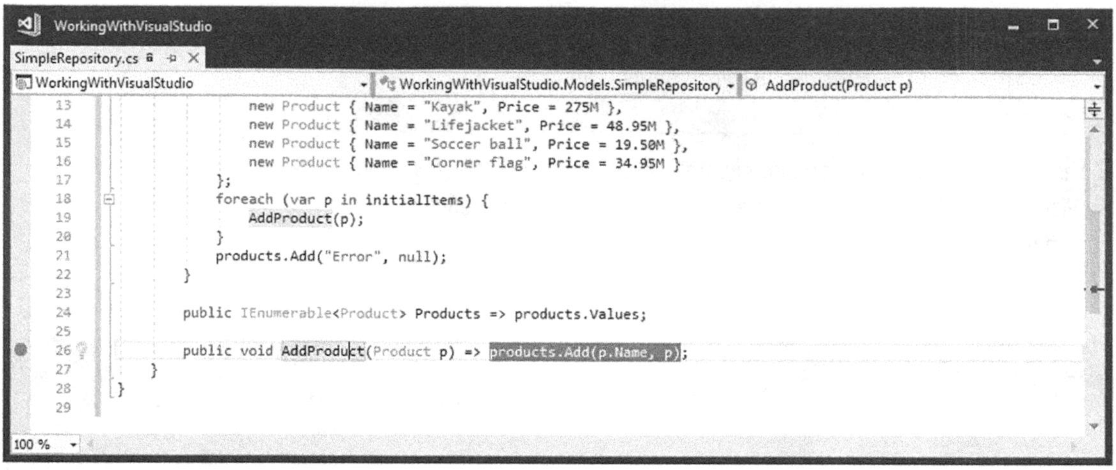

```
 WorkingWithVisualStudio                                                                    —  □  ×

SimpleRepository.cs  🔒  ⊣   ×

 WorkingWithVisualStudio              ▼  🔧 WorkingWithVisualStudio.Models.SimpleRepositor ▼  ⊕ AddProduct(Product p)                    ▼

     13                    new Product { Name = "Kayak", Price = 275M },                                              ╬
     14                    new Product { Name = "Lifejacket", Price = 48.95M },
     15                    new Product { Name = "Soccer ball", Price = 19.50M },
     16                    new Product { Name = "Corner flag", Price = 34.95M }
     17                };
     18    ⊟          foreach (var p in initialItems) {
     19                    AddProduct(p);
     20                }
     21                products.Add("Error", null);
     22            }
     23
     24            public IEnumerable<Product> Products => products.Values;
     25
●    26 ⚲          public void AddProduct(Product p) => products.Add(p.Name, p);
     27        }
     28    └ }
     29

100 %    ▼
```

Figure 6-12. *Creating a breakpoint*

Select Debug ➤ Start Debugging to start the application using the debugger or Debug ➤ Restart if the application is already running. During the initial HTTP request from the browser, the SimpleRepository class will be instantiated, and the execution of the code will reach the breakpoint, at which point execution of the application will stop.

At this point, you can use the Visual Studio Debug menu items or the controls at the top of the window to control execution of the application or use the different debugger views available through the Debug ➤ Windows menu to inspect the application state.

Viewing Data Values in the Code Editor

The most common use for breakpoints is to track down bugs in your code. Before you can fix a bug, you have to figure out what is going on, and one of the most useful features that Visual Studio provides is the ability to view and monitor the values of variables right in the code editor.

If you move the mouse over the p argument to the AddProduct method highlighted by the debugger, a pop-up will appear that shows you the current value of p, as shown in Figure 6-13. It can be hard to make out the pop-up, so I have shown a magnified version in the figure.

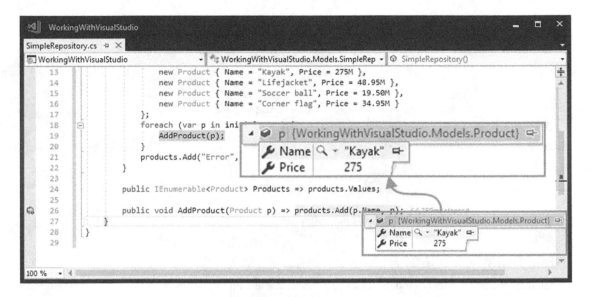

Figure 6-13. *Inspecting a data value*

This may not seem impressive since the data object is defined in the same constructor as the breakpoint, but this feature works for any variable. You can explore values to see their property and field values. Each value has a small pin button to its right that you can use to monitor a value when code execution continues.

Hover the mouse over the p variable and pin the Product reference. Expand the pinned reference so that you can also pin the Name and Price properties, creating the effect shown in Figure 6-14.

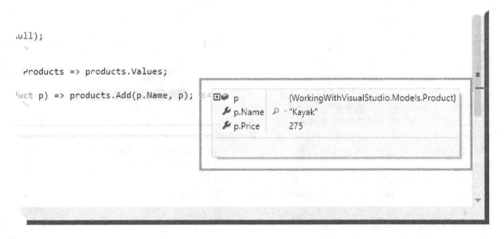

Figure 6-14. *Pinning values in the code editor*

Select Continue from the Visual Studio Debug menu to continue execution of the application. Since the application is executing a foreach loop, execution will be halted again when the breakpoint is encountered again. The pinned values show how the object assigned to the p variable and its properties change, as illustrated by Figure 6-15.

Figure 6-15. *Monitoring state change using pinned values*

Using the Locals Window

A related feature is the Locals window, which is opened by selecting the Debug ➤ Windows ➤ Locals menu item. The Locals window displays data values in a similar way to pinning, but it displays all of the local objects relative to the breakpoint, as shown in Figure 6-16.

Locals			▾ □ ✕
Name	Value	Type	
⏴ ◉ this	{WorkingWithVisualStudio.Models.SimpleRepository}	WorkingWithVisualStudio.Models.SimpleReposit	
▸ ⚲ Products	Count = 2	System.Collections.Generic.IEnumerable<Workir	
▸ ⚙ products	Count = 2	System.Collections.Generic.Dictionary<string, W	
▸ ⚙ Static members			
⏴ ◉ p	{WorkingWithVisualStudio.Models.Product}	WorkingWithVisualStudio.Models.Product	
⚲ Name	"Soccer ball"	⌕ ▾ string	
⚲ Price	19.50	decimal	

Figure 6-16. *The Locals window*

Each time you select Continue, execution of the application will resume, and another object will be processed by the foreach loop. If you keep going, you will see the null reference appear, both in the Locals window and in the pinned values displayed in the code editor. By using the debugger to control the execution of the application, you can follow the flow through your code and get a sense of what is going on.

I could fix the null reference problem by cleaning up the collection of Product objects, but an alternative approach is to make the controller more robust, as shown in Listing 6-13, where I have applied the null conditional operator to check for null values (as described in Chapter 4).

Listing 6-13. Fixing the null Reference Problem in the HomeController.cs File

```
using Microsoft.AspNetCore.Mvc;
using WorkingWithVisualStudio.Models;
using System.Linq;

namespace WorkingWithVisualStudio.Controllers {
    public class HomeController : Controller {
```

```
    public IActionResult Index()
        => View(SimpleRepository.SharedRepository.Products
            .Where(p => p?.Price < 50));
    }
}
```

Disable the breakpoint by right-clicking the code statement to which it has been applied and selecting Delete Breakpoint from the pop-up menu. Restart the application and you will see the simple data table shown in Figure 6-17.

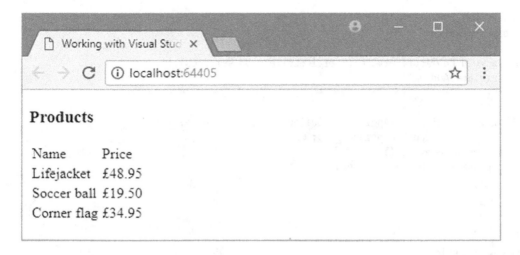

Figure 6-17. *Fixing the bug*

This is a simple problem to solve compared to the problems that require real bug hunting, but the Visual Studio debugger is excellent, and by using the many different views of the application that are available and controlling execution, you can really dig into the detail to figure out what is going wrong.

Using Browser Link

The Browser Link feature can simplify the development process by putting one or more browsers under the control of Visual Studio. This feature is especially useful if you need to see the effect of changes on a range of browsers. The Browser Link feature works with or without the debugger, but I find it most useful when using the automatic class compilation feature because it means I can modify any file in the project and see the effect of the change without having to switch to the browser and manually reload the page.

Setting Up Browser Link

Enabling Browser Link requires a configuration change to the Startup class, as shown in Listing 6-14.

Listing 6-14. Enabling Browser Link in the Startup.cs File in the WorkingWithVisualStudio Folder

```
using System;
using System.Collections.Generic;
using System.Linq;
using System.Threading.Tasks;
using Microsoft.AspNetCore.Builder;
using Microsoft.AspNetCore.Hosting;
using Microsoft.AspNetCore.Http;
using Microsoft.Extensions.DependencyInjection;

namespace WorkingWithVisualStudio {
    public class Startup {

        public void ConfigureServices(IServiceCollection services) {
            services.AddMvc();
        }

        public void Configure(IApplicationBuilder app, IHostingEnvironment env) {
            app.UseDeveloperExceptionPage();
            app.UseBrowserLink();
            app.UseMvcWithDefaultRoute();
        }
    }
}
```

Using Browser Link

To understand how Browser Link works, select Start Without Debugging from the Visual Studio Debug menu. Visual Studio will start the application and open a new browser tab to display the results. Inspect the HTML sent to the browser and you will see that it contains an additional section like this:

```
<!DOCTYPE html>
<html>
<head>
    <meta name="viewport" content="width=device-width" />
    <title>Working with Visual Studio</title>
</head>
<body>
    <h3>Products</h3>
    <table>
        <thead>
            <tr><td>Name</td><td>Price</td></tr>
        </thead>
        <tbody>
                <tr><td>Lifejacket</td><td>&#xA3;48.95</td></tr>
                <tr><td>Soccer ball</td><td>&#xA3;19.50</td></tr>
                <tr><td>Corner flag</td><td>&#xA3;34.95</td></tr>
        </tbody>
    </table>
```

```
<!-- Visual Studio Browser Link -->
<script type="application/json" id="__browserLink_initializationData">
    {"requestId":"968949d8affc47c4a9c6326de21dfa03","requestMappingFromServer":false}
</script>
<script type="text/javascript"
    src="http://localhost:55356/d1a038413c804e178ef009a3be07b262/browserLink"
    async="async">
</script>
<!-- End Browser Link -->
</body>
</html>
```

■ **Tip**   If you don't see the additional section, select Enable Browser Link from the menu shown in Figure 6-18 and reload the browser.

Visual Studio adds a pair of script elements to the HTML sent to the browser, which are used to open a long-lived HTTP connection back to the application server so that Visual Studio can force the browser to reload the page. (If you don't see the script elements, then make sure that Enable Browser Link is selected in the menu shown in Figure 6-18.) Listing 6-15 shows a change to the Index view that will illustrate the effect of using Browser Link.

Listing 6-15. Adding a Timestamp in the Index.cshtml File

```
@model IEnumerable<WorkingWithVisualStudio.Models.Product>
@{ Layout = null; }

<!DOCTYPE html>
<html>
<head>
    <meta name="viewport" content="width=device-width" />
    <title>Working with Visual Studio</title>
</head>
<body>
    <h3>Products</h3>
    <p>Request Time: @DateTime.Now.ToString("HH:mm:ss")</p>
    <table>
        <thead>
            <tr><td>Name</td><td>Price</td></tr>
        </thead>
        <tbody>
            @foreach (var p in Model) {
                <tr>
                    <td>@p.Name</td>
                    <td>@($"{p.Price:C2}")</td>
                </tr>
            }
        </tbody>
    </table>
</body>
</html>
```

Save the change to the view file and select Refresh Linked Browsers from the Browser Link menu on the Visual Studio toolbar, as shown in Figure 6-18. (If Browser Link doesn't work, try reloading the browser or restarting Visual Studio and trying again.)

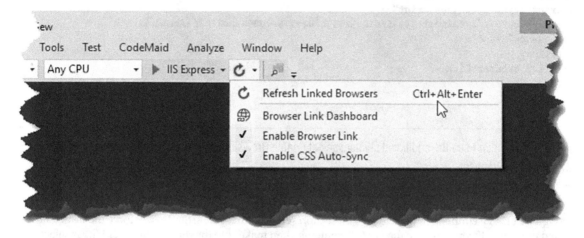

Figure 6-18. *Using Browser Link to reload a browser*

The JavaScript code embedded in the HTML sent to the browser will reload the page, showing the effect of the addition, which is to add a simple timestamp. Each time you select the Visual Studio menu item, the browser will make a new request to the server. The request will result in the Index view being rendered to generate a new HTML page with an updated timestamp.

■ **Note** Browser Link's `script` elements are embedded only in successful responses, meaning that if an exception is thrown when compiling a class, rendering a Razor view, or handling a request, then the connection between the browser and Visual Studio is lost and you will have to reload the page using the browser once you have resolved the problem.

Using Multiple Browsers

Browser Link can be used to display an application in multiple browsers simultaneously, which can be useful when you want to iron out implementation differences between browsers or see how an application is rendered on a mix of desktop and mobile browsers.

To pick the browsers that will be used, select Browse With from the IIS Express button on the Visual Studio toolbar, as shown in Figure 6-19.

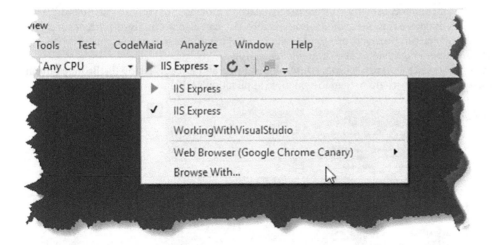

Figure 6-19. *Selecting multiple browsers*

Visual Studio displays a list of the browsers that it knows about. Figure 6-20 shows the browsers I have installed on my system, some of which are installed with Windows (Internet Explorer and Edge) and others that I install because they are in widespread use.

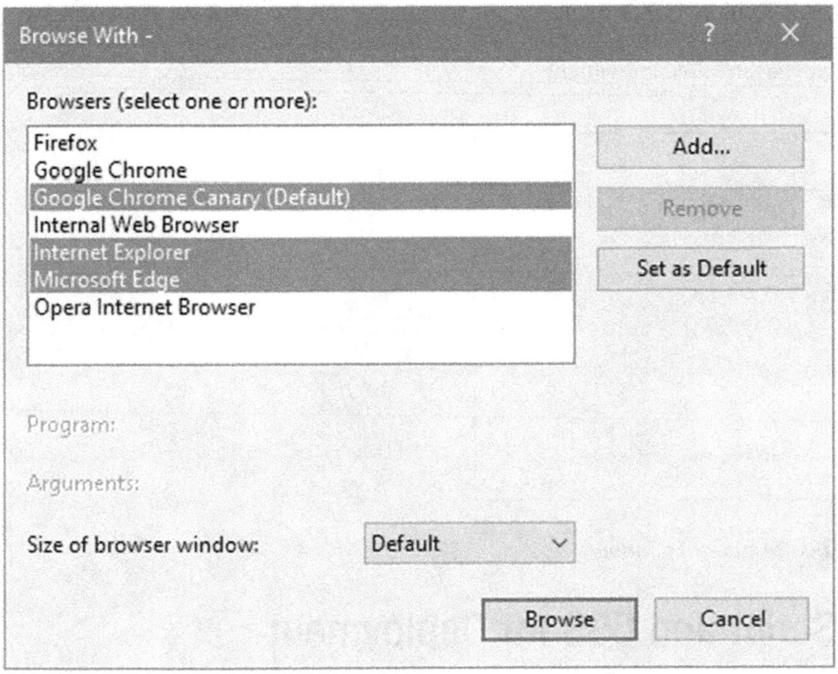

Figure 6-20. *Picking browsers from the list*

Visual Studio looks for common browsers during the installation process, but you can use the Add button to set up browsers that were not discovered automatically. You can also set up third-party testing tools like Browser Stack, which run browsers on cloud-hosted virtual machines so that you don't have to manage a large matrix of operating systems and browsers for testing.

I selected three browsers in the figure: Chrome, Internet Explorer, and Edge. Clicking the Browse button starts all three browsers and causes them to load the example application's URL, as shown in Figure 6-21.

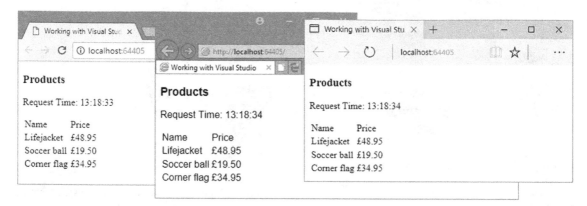

Figure 6-21. *Working with multiple browsers*

You can see which browsers Browser Link is managing by selecting the Browser Link Dashboard menu item, which opens the window shown in Figure 6-22. The dashboard shows the URL displayed by each browser, and each browser can be refreshed individually.

Figure 6-22. *The Browser Link Dashboard window*

Preparing JavaScript and CSS for Deployment

When you create the client-side part of a web application, you will usually create a number of custom JavaScript and CSS files, which are used to supplement those in the packages installed by Bower. These files require processing to optimize them for delivery in a production environment in order to minimize the number of HTTP requests and the amount of network bandwidth required to deliver them to the client. This process is known as *bundling* and *minification*. In this section, I explain how to enable delivery of static content and how that content can be prepared for deployment.

Enabling Static Content Delivery

ASP.NET Core includes support for delivering static files from the wwwroot folder to clients, but it isn't enabled by default when the Empty template is used to create the project. Enable support for static content by adding the statement shown in Listing 6-16 to the Startup class.

Listing 6-16. Enabling Static Content in the Startup.cs File in the Working WithVisualStudio Folder

```
using System;
using System.Collections.Generic;
using System.Linq;
using System.Threading.Tasks;
using Microsoft.AspNetCore.Builder;
using Microsoft.AspNetCore.Hosting;
using Microsoft.AspNetCore.Http;
using Microsoft.Extensions.DependencyInjection;

namespace WorkingWithVisualStudio {
    public class Startup {

        public void ConfigureServices(IServiceCollection services) {
            services.AddMvc();
        }

        public void Configure(IApplicationBuilder app, IHostingEnvironment env) {
            app.UseDeveloperExceptionPage();
            app.UseBrowserLink();
            app.UseStaticFiles();
            app.UseMvcWithDefaultRoute();
        }
    }
}
```

Adding Static Content to the Project

To demonstrate the bundling and minification process, I need to add some static content to the project and incorporate it into the example application. First, I created the wwwroot/css folder, which is the conventional location for custom CSS files. I then added a file called first.css using the Style Sheet item template, as shown in Figure 6-23. The Style Sheet template is found in the ASP.NET Core ➤ Web ➤ Content section.

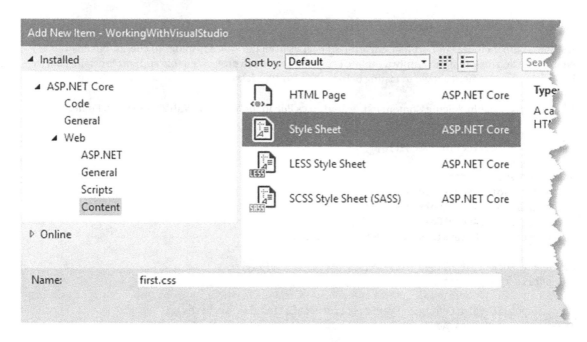

Figure 6-23. *Creating a CSS stylesheet*

I edited the first.css file to add the CSS styles shown in Listing 6-17.

Listing 6-17. The Contents of the first.css File in the wwwroot/css Folder

```
h3 {
    font-size: 18pt;
    font-family: sans-serif;
}
table, td {
    border: 2px solid black;
    border-collapse:collapse;
    padding: 5px;
    font-family: sans-serif;
}
```

I repeated the process to create another style sheet called second.css in the wwwroot/css folder, with the content shown in Listing 6-18.

Listing 6-18. The Contents of the second.css File in the wwwroot/css Folder

```
p {
    font-family: sans-serif;
    font-size: 10pt;
    color: darkgreen;
    background-color:antiquewhite;
    border: 1px solid black;
    padding: 2px;
}
```

Custom JavaScript files are conventionally stored in the wwwroot/js folder. I created this folder and used the JavaScript File item template to create a file called third.js, as shown in Figure 6-24. The JavaScript File template is in the ASP.NET Core ➤ Web ➤ Scripts section.

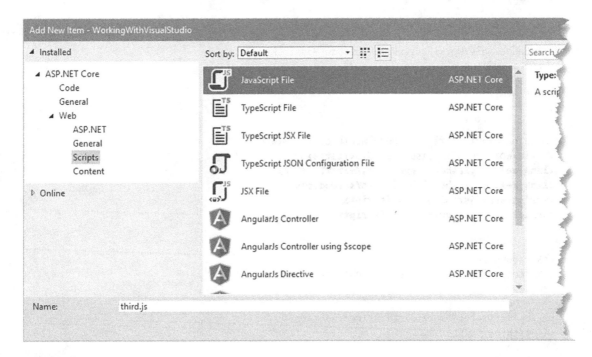

Figure 6-24. *Creating a JavaScript File*

I added some simple JavaScript code to the new file, as shown in Listing 6-19.

Listing 6-19. The Contents of the third.js File in the wwwroot/js Folder

```
document.addEventListener("DOMContentLoaded", function () {
    var element = document.createElement("p");
    element.textContent = "This is the element from the third.js file";
    document.querySelector("body").appendChild(element);
});
```

I need one more JavaScript file. I created a file called fourth.js in the wwwroot/js folder and added the code shown in Listing 6-20.

Listing 6-20. The Contents of the fourth.js File in the wwwroot/js Folder

```
document.addEventListener("DOMContentLoaded", function () {
    var element = document.createElement("p");
    element.textContent = "This is the element from the fourth.js file";
    document.querySelector("body").appendChild(element);
});
```

Updating the View

The final preparatory step is to update the Index.cshtml view to use the new CSS stylesheets and JavaScript files, as shown in Listing 6-21.

Listing 6-21. Adding script and link Elements to the Index.cshtml File in the Views/Home Folder

```
@model IEnumerable<WorkingWithVisualStudio.Models.Product>
@{ Layout = null; }

<!DOCTYPE html>
<html>
<head>
    <meta name="viewport" content="width=device-width" />
    <title>Working with Visual Studio</title>
    <link rel="stylesheet" href="css/first.css" />
    <link rel="stylesheet" href="css/second.css" />
    <script src="js/third.js"></script>
    <script src="js/fourth.js"></script>
</head>
<body>
    <h3>Products</h3>
    <p>Request Time: @DateTime.Now.ToString("HH:mm:ss")</p>
    <table>
        <thead>
            <tr><td>Name</td><td>Price</td></tr>
        </thead>
        <tbody>
            @foreach (var p in Model) {
                <tr>
                    <td>@p.Name</td>
                    <td>@($"{p.Price:C2}")</td>
                </tr>
            }
        </tbody>
    </table>
</body>
</html>
```

If you run the example application, you will see the content shown in Figure 6-25. The existing content has been styled by the CSS stylesheets, and the JavaScript code has added new content.

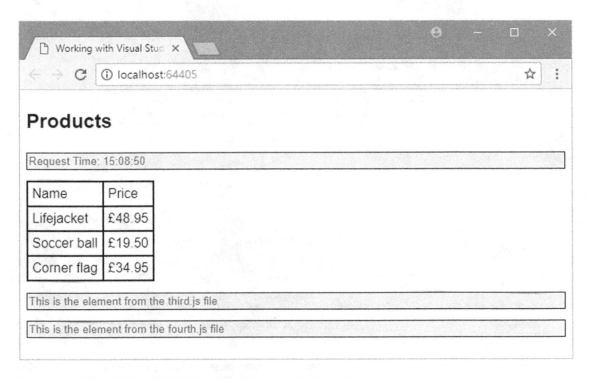

Figure 6-25. *Running the example application*

Bundling and Minifying in MVC Applications

At the moment, there are four static files, and the browser has to make four requests in order to get the static files. And each of those files requires more bandwidth than it should to be delivered to the client because they contain whitespace and variable names that are meaningful to the developer but have no significance to the browser.

Combining files of the same type is called *bundling*. Making files smaller is called *minification*. Both of these tasks are performed in ASP.NET Core MVC applications by the Bundler & Minifier extension for Visual Studio.

Installing the Visual Studio Extension

The first step is to install an extension. Select the Tools ➤ Extensions and Updates menu and click the Online category to display the gallery of available Visual Studio extensions. Enter Bundler into the search box in the top-right corner of the window, as shown in Figure 6-26. Locate the Bundler & Minifier extension and click the Download button to add it to Visual Studio. Restart Visual Studio to complete the installation process.

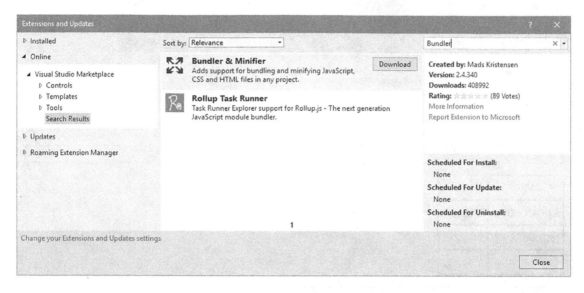

Figure 6-26. *Finding the Visual Studio extension*

Bundling and Minifying Files

Once the extension has been installed, restart Visual Studio and open the example project. With the addition of the extension, you can select multiple files of the same type in the Solution Explorer, bundle them together, and minify their contents. As an example, select the first.css and second.css files in the Solution Explorer, right-click, and then select Bundler & Minifier ➤ Bundle and Minify Files from the pop-up menu, as shown in Figure 6-27.

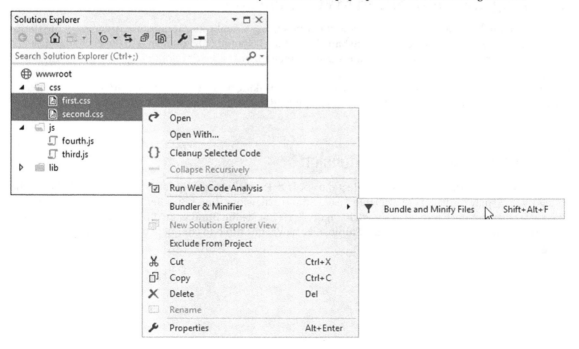

Figure 6-27. *Bundling and minifying CSS files*

Save the output file as bundle.css, and the extension will process the CSS files. The Solution Explorer will show a new bundle.css item, which you can expand to reveal the minified file, called bundle.min.css. If you open the minified file, you will see that the contents of both separate CSS files have been combined and all of the whitespace has been removed. You won't want to work directly with this file, but it is smaller and requires only a single HTTP connection to deliver the CSS styles to the client.

Repeat the process with the third.js and fourth.js files in order to create new files called bundle.js and bundle.min.js in the wwwroot/js folder.

■ **Caution**   Make sure you select the files in the order in which they are loaded by the browser in order to preserve the order of the styles or code statements in the output files. So, for example, ensure that you select the third.js file before selecting the fourth.js file to ensure that the code is executed in the right order.

In Listing 6-22, I have replaced the link elements for the separate files with one that requests the bundled and minified files in the Index.cshtml view.

Listing 6-22. Using the Bundled and Minified Files in the Index.cshtml File

```
@model IEnumerable<WorkingWithVisualStudio.Models.Product>
@{ Layout = null; }

<!DOCTYPE html>
<html>
<head>
    <meta name="viewport" content="width=device-width" />
    <title>Working with Visual Studio</title>
    <link rel="stylesheet" href="css/bundle.min.css" />
    <script src="js/bundle.min.js"></script>
</head>
<body>
    <h3>Products</h3>
    <p>Request Time: @DateTime.Now.ToString("HH:mm:ss")</p>
    <table>
        <thead>
            <tr><td>Name</td><td>Price</td></tr>
        </thead>
        <tbody>
            @foreach (var p in Model) {
                <tr>
                    <td>@p.Name</td>
                    <td>@($"{p.Price:C2}")</td>
                </tr>
            }
        </tbody>
    </table>
</body>
</html>
```

There isn't any visual change if you run the application, but the bundled and minified files are used to provide the browser with all the styles and code that were defined in the separate files.

As you perform bundling and minification operations, the extension keeps a record of the files that have been processed in a file called bundleconfig.json in the root folder of the project. Here is the configuration that was produced for the files in the example application:

```
[
  {
    "outputFileName": "wwwroot/css/bundle.css",
    "inputFiles": [
      "wwwroot/css/first.css",
      "wwwroot/css/second.css"
    ]
  },
  {
    "outputFileName": "wwwroot/js/bundle.js",
    "inputFiles": [
      "wwwroot/js/third.js",
      "wwwroot/js/fourth.js"
    ]
  }
]
```

The extension automatically monitors the input files for changes and regenerates the output files when there are changes, ensuring that any edits you make are reflected in the bundled and minified files. To demonstrate, Listing 6-23 shows a change to the third.js file.

Listing 6-23. Making a Change in the third.js File

```
document.addEventListener("DOMContentLoaded", function () {
    var element = document.createElement("p");
    element.textContent = "This is the element from the (modified) third.js file";
    document.querySelector("body").appendChild(element);
});
```

As soon as the file is saved, the extension regenerates the bundle.min.js file. If you reload the browser, you will see the change shown in Figure 6-28.

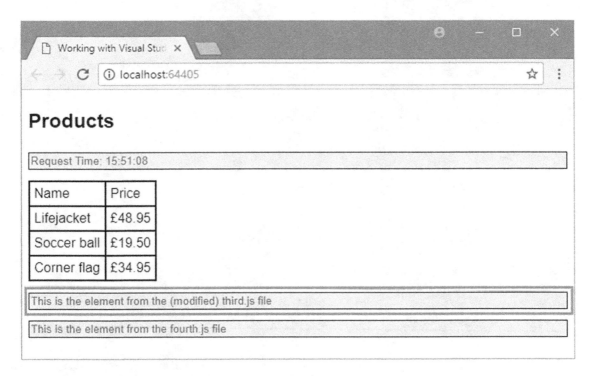

Figure 6-28. *Change detection in bundled and minified files*

Summary

In this chapter, I described the features that Visual Studio provides for web application development, including automatic class compilation, Browser Link, and bundling and minification. In the next chapter, I explain how ASP.NET Core MVC projects lend themselves to unit testing.

CHAPTER 7

■ ■ ■

Unit Testing MVC Applications

In this chapter, I demonstrate how to unit test MVC applications. Unit testing is a form of testing in which individual components are isolated from the rest of the application so their behavior can be thoroughly validated. ASP.NET Core MVC has been designed to make it easy to create unit tests, and Visual Studio provides support for a wide range of unit testing frameworks. I show you how to set up a unit test project, explain how to install one of the most popular testing frameworks, and describe the process for writing and running tests. Table 7-1 summarizes the chapter.

DECIDING WHETHER TO UNIT TEST

Being able to easily perform unit testing is one of the benefits of using ASP.NET Core MVC, but it isn't for everyone, and I have no intention of pretending otherwise.

I like unit testing and I use it in my own projects, but not in all of them and not as consistently as you might expect. I tend to focus on writing unit tests for features and functions that I know will be hard to write and that are likely to be the source of bugs in deployment. In these situations, unit testing helps structure my thoughts about how to best implement what I need. I find that just thinking about what I need to test helps produce ideas about potential problems, and that's before I start dealing with actual bugs and defects.

That said, unit testing is a tool and not a religion, and only you know how much testing you require. If you don't find unit testing useful or if you have a different methodology that suits you better, then don't feel you need to unit test just because it is fashionable. (However, if you *don't* have a better methodology and you are not testing at all, then you are probably letting users find your bugs, which is rarely ideal. You don't *have* to unit test, but you really should consider doing *some* testing of *some* kind.)

If you have not encountered unit testing before, then I encourage you to give it a try and see how it works. If you are not a fan unit testing, then you can skip this chapter and move on to Chapter 8, where I start to build a more realistic MVC application.

© Adam Freeman 2017
A. Freeman, *Pro ASP.NET Core MVC 2*, https://doi.org/10.1007/978-1-4842-3150-0_7

Table 7-1. *Chapter Summary*

Problem	Solution	Listing
Create a unit test	Create a unit test project, install a test package, and add classes that contain tests	5, 6
Isolate components for unit testing	Use interfaces to separate application components and use fake implementations with restricted test data in the unit tests	7–14
Run the same xUnit tests with different data values	Use a parameterized unit test or get the test data from a method or property	15–17
Simplify the process of creating fake test objects	Use a mocking framework	18–19

Preparing the Example Project

In this chapter, I continue to use the WorkingWithVisualStudio project that I created in Chapter 6. For this chapter, I will add support for creating new Product objects in the repository.

Enabling the Built-in Tag Helpers

I use one of the built-in tag helpers in this chapter to set the href attribute of an anchor element. I explain how tag helpers work in detail in Chapters 23, 24, and 25, but to simply enable them, I created a view imports file by right-clicking the Views folder, selecting Add ➤ New Item from the pop-up menu, and choosing the MVC View Imports Page item template from the ASP.NET category. Visual Studio automatically sets the name of the file to _ViewImports.cshtml, and clicking the Add button created the file, which allowed me to add the statements shown in Listing 7-1.

Listing 7-1. The Contents of the _ViewImports.cshtml File in the Views Folder

```
@addTagHelper *, Microsoft.AspNetCore.Mvc.TagHelpers
```

This statement enables the built-in tag helpers, including the one that I use in the Index view shortly. I could add using statements to import namespaces from the projects, but the views are not important parts of the example application in this chapter, and referring to model types with their namespaces isn't a problem.

Adding Actions to the Controller

The first step is to add actions to the Home controller that will render a view for entering data and for receiving that data from the browser, as shown in Listing 7-2. These actions follow the same pattern that I used in Chapter 2 and that I explain in detail in Chapter 17.

Listing 7-2. Adding Action Methods in the HomeController.cs File in the Controllers Folder

```
using Microsoft.AspNetCore.Mvc;
using WorkingWithVisualStudio.Models;
using System.Linq;
```

```
namespace WorkingWithVisualStudio.Controllers {
    public class HomeController : Controller {

        SimpleRepository Repository = SimpleRepository.SharedRepository;

        public IActionResult Index() => View(Repository.Products
                    .Where(p => p?.Price < 50));

        [HttpGet]
        public IActionResult AddProduct() => View(new Product());

        [HttpPost]
        public IActionResult AddProduct(Product p) {
            Repository.AddProduct(p);
            return RedirectToAction("Index");
        }
    }
}
```

Creating the Data Entry Form

To allow the user to create a new product, I created a Razor view called AddProduct.cshtml in the Views/
Home folder. This is the file name and location conventions that correspond to the default view rendered by
the AddProduct method in the Home controller. Listing 7-3 shows the contents of the new view, which relies
on the Bootstrap package that I added to the project using Bower in Chapter 6.

Listing 7-3. The Contents of the AddProduct.cshtml File in the Views/Home Folder

```
@model WorkingWithVisualStudio.Models.Product
@{ Layout = null; }

<!DOCTYPE html>
<html>
<head>
    <meta name="viewport" content="width=device-width" />
    <title>Working with Visual Studio</title>
    <link rel="stylesheet" href="/lib/bootstrap/dist/css/bootstrap.min.css" />
</head>
<body class="p-2">
    <h3 class="text-center">Create Product</h3>
    <form asp-action="AddProduct" method="post">
        <div class="form-group">
            <label asp-for="Name">Name:</label>
            <input asp-for="Name" class="form-control" />
        </div>
        <div class="form-group">
            <label asp-for="Price">Price:</label>
            <input asp-for="Price" class="form-control" />
        </div>
        <div class="text-center">
            <button type="submit" class="btn btn-primary">Add</button>
```

```
            <a asp-action="Index" class="btn btn-secondary">Cancel</a>
        </div>
    </form>
</body>
</html>
```

This view contains an HTML form that uses an HTTP POST request to send Name and Price values to the AddProduct action on the Home controller. The content is styled using the Bootstrap CSS package.

Updating the Index View

The final preparatory step is to update the Index view so that it contains a link to the new form, as shown in Listing 7-4. I have also taken the opportunity to remove the JavaScript files I used in the previous chapter and to replace the custom CSS stylesheets with Bootstrap, which I have applied to the HTML elements in the view.

Listing 7-4. Updating the Content in the Index.cshtml File in the Views/Home Folder

```
@model IEnumerable<WorkingWithVisualStudio.Models.Product>
@{ Layout = null; }

<!DOCTYPE html>
<html>
<head>
    <meta name="viewport" content="width=device-width" />
    <title>Working with Visual Studio</title>
    <link rel="stylesheet" href="/lib/bootstrap/dist/css/bootstrap.min.css" />
</head>
<body class="p-1">
    <h3 class="text-center">Products</h3>
    <table class="table table-bordered table-striped">
        <thead>
            <tr><td>Name</td><td>Price</td></tr>
        </thead>
        <tbody>
            @foreach (var p in Model) {
                <tr>
                    <td>@p.Name</td>
                    <td>@($"{p.Price:C2}")</td>
                </tr>
            }
        </tbody>
    </table>
    <div class="text-center">
        <a class="btn btn-primary" asp-action="AddProduct">
            Add New Product
        </a>
    </div>
</body>
</html>
```

If you run the example, you will see the newly styled content and the Add New Product button, which leads to the data entry form. Submitting the form will add a new Product object to the repository and redirect the browser so that the initial application view is displayed, as shown in Figure 7-1.

■ **Tip**   Remember that the repository in this example stores its objects only in memory, which means that any new products you create will be lost when the application is restarted.

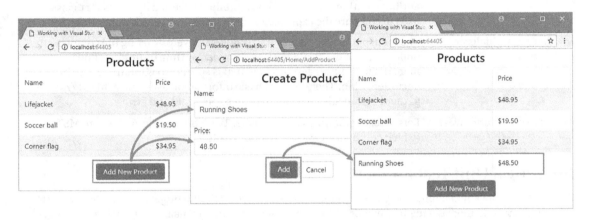

Figure 7-1. *Running the example application*

Unit Testing MVC Applications

Unit tests are used to validate the behavior of individual components and features in an application, and ASP.NET Core and the MVC framework have been designed to make it as easy as possible to set up and run unit tests for web applications. In the sections that follow, I explain how to set up unit testing in Visual Studio and demonstrate how to write unit tests for MVC applications. I also introduce some useful tools that make unit testing simpler and more reliable.

There is a range of different unit test packages available. The one I use in this book is called xUnit.net; I selected it because it integrates well with Visual Studio and because it is used by the Microsoft team to write its unit tests for ASP.NET Core. Table 7-2 puts xUnit.net in context.

■ **Note**   Just about everything in unit testing is a matter of personal preference and a subject of vociferous disagreement. Some developers don't like separating their unit tests from their application code and prefer to define tests in the same project or even in the same class file. The approach I describe here is commonly used and is the approach that I follow, but if it doesn't feel right, you should experiment with different styles of testing until you find something you like.

Table 7-2. *Putting xUnit.net in Context*

Question	Answer
What is it?	xUnit.net is a unit test framework that can be used to test ASP.NET Core MVC applications.
Why is it useful?	xUnit is a well-written test framework that integrates easily into Visual Studio.
How is it used?	Tests are defined as methods that are annotated with the Fact or Theory attribute. Within the method body, methods defined by the Assert class are used to compare the expected result of a test with what actually happened.
Are there any pitfalls or limitations?	The main pitfall with unit testing is not effectively isolating the component under test. See the "Isolating Components for Unit Testing" section for more details. The biggest problem that is specific to xUnit.net is a lack of documentation. There is some basic information available at http://xunit.github.io, but advanced use requires some trial and error.
Are there any alternatives?	Lots of test frameworks are available. Two popular alternatives are MSTest (which comes from Microsoft) and NUnit.

Creating a Unit Test Project

For ASP.NET Core applications, you generally create a separate Visual Studio project to hold the unit tests, each of which is defined as a method in a C# class. Using a separate project means you can deploy your application without also deploying the tests.

To create the test project, right-click the WorkingWithVisualStudio solution item in the Solution Explorer and select Add ➤ New Project from the pop-up menu. Select the xUnit Test Project (.NET Core) template from the Visual C# ➤ .NET Core category, as shown in Figure 7-2.

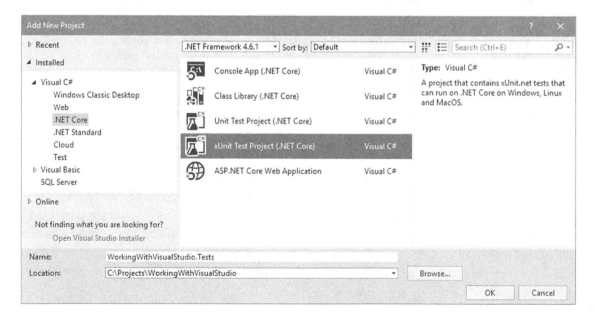

Figure 7-2. *Selecting the unit test project template*

■ **Caution**   Make sure you select the right project template. Visual Studio provides a number of templates for unit test projects and they have similar names.

The convention is to name the unit test project <ApplicationName>.Tests. Set the name of the new project to WorkingWithVisualStudio.Tests and click the OK button to create the new project. Visual Studio will create the project and install the NuGet packages for xUnit and its dependencies.

Removing the Default Test Class

Visual Studio adds a C# class file to the test project, which will confuse the results of later examples. Right-click the UnitTest1.cs file in the WorkingWithVisualStudio.Tests project and select Delete from the pop-up menu. Click OK when prompted and Visual Studio will delete the class file.

Creating the Project Reference

To make the classes in the main project available for testing, right-click the WorkingWithVisualStudio.Tests item in the Solution Explorer and select Add ➤ Reference from the pop-up menu.

Check the option for the WorkingWithVisualStudio item in the Solution section, as shown in Figure 7-3.

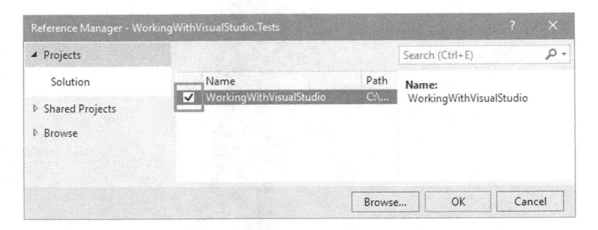

Figure 7-3. *Creating a reference to the application project*

Click the OK button to create the reference to the application project. You may see a working icon displayed on the Dependencies item for the test project in the Solution Explorer, but this will disappear once you have built the projects.

Writing and Running Unit Tests

Now that all the preparation is complete, I can write some tests. To get started, I added a class file called ProductTests.cs to the WorkingWithVisualStudio.Tests project and defined the class shown in Listing 7-5. This is a simple class, but it contains everything required to get started with unit testing.

■ **Note**   The CanChangeProductPrice method contains a deliberate error that I resolve later in this section.

Listing 7-5. The Contents of the ProductTests.cs File in the WorkingWithVisualStudio.Tests Folder

```
using WorkingWithVisualStudio.Models;
using Xunit;

namespace WorkingWithVisualStudio.Tests {

    public class ProductTests {

        [Fact]
        public void CanChangeProductName() {

            // Arrange
            var p = new Product { Name = "Test", Price = 100M };

            // Act
            p.Name = "New Name";

            //Assert
            Assert.Equal("New Name", p.Name);
        }

        [Fact]
        public void CanChangeProductPrice() {

            // Arrange
            var p = new Product { Name = "Test", Price = 100M };

            // Act
            p.Price = 200M;

            //Assert
            Assert.Equal(100M, p.Price);
        }
    }
}
```

There are two unit tests in the ProductTests class, each of which tests a different behavior of the Product model class from the WorkingWithVisualStudio project. A test project can contain many classes, each of which can contain many unit tests.

Conventionally, the name of the test methods describes what the test does, and the name of the class describes what is being tested. This makes it easier to structure the tests in a project and to understand what the results of all the tests are when they are run by Visual Studio. The name ProductTests indicates that the class contains tests for the Product class, and the method names indicate that they test the ability to change the name and price of a Product object.

The Fact attribute is applied to each method to indicate that it is a test. Within the method body, a unit test follows a pattern called *arrange, act, assert* (A/A/A). *Arrange* refers to setting up the conditions for the test, *act* refers to performing the test, and *assert* refers to verifying that the result was the one that was expected.

The arrange and act sections of these tests are regular C# code, but the assert section is handled by xUnit.net, which provides a class called Assert, whose methods are used to check that the outcome of an action is the one that is expected.

■ **Tip**　The Fact attribute and the Asset class are defined in the Xunit namespace, for which there must be a using statement in every test class.

The methods of the Assert class are static and are used to perform different kinds of comparison between the expected and actual results. Table 7-3 shows the most commonly used Assert methods.

Table 7-3. *Commonly Used xUnit.net Assert Methods*

Name	Description
Equal(expected, result)	This method asserts that the result is equal to the expected outcome. There are overloaded versions of this method for comparing different types and for comparing collections. There is also a version of this method that accepts an additional argument of an object that implements the IEqualityComparer<T> interface for comparing objects.
NotEqual(expected, result)	This method asserts that the result is not equal to the expected outcome.
True(result)	This method asserts that the result is true.
False(result)	This method asserts that the result is false.
IsType(expected, result)	This method asserts that the result is of a specific type.
IsNotType(expected, result)	This method asserts that the result is not a specific type.
IsNull(result)	This method asserts that the result is null.
IsNotNull(result)	This method asserts that the result is not null.
InRange(result, low, high)	This method asserts that the result falls between low and high.
NotInRange(result, low, high)	This method asserts that the result falls outside low and high.
Throws(exception, expression)	This method asserts that the specified expression throws a specific exception type.

Each Assert method allows different types of comparison to be made and throws an exception if the result is not what was expected. The exception is used to indicate that a test has failed. In the tests in Listing 7-5, I used the Equal method to determine whether the value of a property has been changed correctly.

```
...
Assert.Equal("New Name", p.Name);
...
```

Running Tests with the Test Explorer

Visual Studio includes support for finding and running unit tests through the Test Explorer window, which is available through the Test ➤ Windows ➤ Test Explorer menu and which is shown in Figure 7-4.

■ **Tip**   Build the solution if you don't see the unit tests in the Test Explorer window. Compilation triggers the process by which unit tests are discovered.

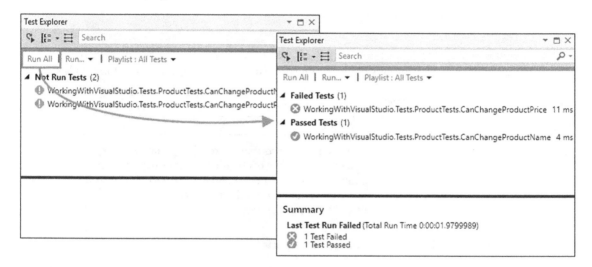

Figure 7-4. *The Visual Studio Test Explorer*

Run the tests by clicking Run All in the Test Explorer window. Visual Studio will use xUnit.net to run the tests in the project and display the results. As noted, the CanChangeProductPrice test contains an error that causes the test to fail. The problem is with the arguments to the Assert.Equal method, which compares the test result to the original Price property value rather than the value it has been changed to. Listing 7-6 corrects the problem.

■ **Tip**   When a test fails, it is always a good idea to check the accuracy of the test before looking at the component it targets, especially if the test is new or has been recently modified.

Listing 7-6. Correcting a Test in the ProductTests.cs File

```
using WorkingWithVisualStudio.Models;
using Xunit;

namespace WorkingWithVisualStudio.Tests {

    public class ProductTests {

        [Fact]
        public void CanChangeProductName() {
```

```
        // Arrange
        var p = new Product { Name = "Test", Price = 100M };

        // Act
        p.Name = "New Name";

        //Assert
        Assert.Equal("New Name", p.Name);
    }

    [Fact]
    public void CanChangeProductPrice() {

        // Arrange
        var p = new Product { Name = "Test", Price = 100M };

        // Act
        p.Price = 200M;

        //Assert
        Assert.Equal(200M, p.Price);
    }
  }
}
```

If you have a lot of tests, it can take a while for them all to be performed. So that you can work rapidly and iteratively, the Test Explorer window offers different options for selecting subsets of tests to perform. The most useful subset is the set of tests that have failed, as shown in Figure 7-5. Run the corrected test again and the Test Explorer will show that no tests have failed.

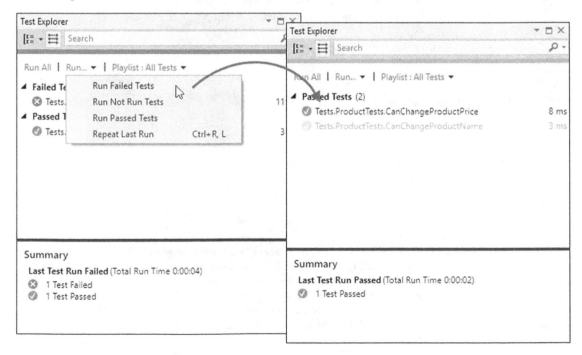

Figure 7-5. *Selectively running tests*

Isolating Components for Unit Testing

Writing unit tests for model classes like Product is easy. Not only is the Product class simple, but it is self-contained, which means that when I perform an action on a Product object, I can be confident that I am testing the functionality provided by the Product class.

The situation is more complicated with other components in an MVC application because there are dependencies between them. The next set of tests that I define will operate on the controller, examining the sequence of Product objects that are passed between the controller and the view.

When comparing objects instantiated from custom classes, you will need to use the xUnit.net Assert. Equal method that accepts an argument that implements the IEqualityComparer<T> interface so that the objects can be compared. My first step is to add a class file called Comparer.cs to the unit test project and use it to define the helper classes shown in Listing 7-7.

Listing 7-7. The Contents of the Comparer.cs File in the WorkingWithVisualStudio.Tests Folder

```
using System;
using System.Collections.Generic;

namespace WorkingWithVisualStudio.Tests {

    public class Comparer {

        public static Comparer<U> Get<U>(Func<U, U, bool> func) {
            return new Comparer<U>(func);
        }
    }

    public class Comparer<T> : Comparer, IEqualityComparer<T> {
        private Func<T, T, bool> comparisonFunction;

        public Comparer(Func<T, T, bool> func) {
            comparisonFunction = func;
        }

        public bool Equals(T x, T y) {
            return comparisonFunction(x, y);
        }

        public int GetHashCode(T obj) {
            return obj.GetHashCode();
        }
    }
}
```

These classes will allow me to create IEqualityComparer<T> objects using lambda expressions rather than having to define a new class for each type of comparison that I want to make. This isn't essential, but it will simplify the code in my unit test classes and make them easier to read and maintain.

Now that I can easily make comparisons, I can illustrate the problem of dependencies between components in the application. I added a new class called HomeControllerTests.cs to the WorkingWith VisualStudio.Tests project and used it to define the unit test shown in Listing 7-8.

Listing 7-8. The HomeControllerTests.cs File in the WorkingWithVisualStudio.Tests Folder

```
using Microsoft.AspNetCore.Mvc;
using System.Collections.Generic;
using WorkingWithVisualStudio.Controllers;
using WorkingWithVisualStudio.Models;
using Xunit;

namespace WorkingWithVisualStudio.Tests {
    public class HomeControllerTests {

        [Fact]
        public void IndexActionModelIsComplete() {
            // Arrange
            var controller = new HomeController();

            // Act
            var model = (controller.Index() as ViewResult)?.ViewData.Model
                as IEnumerable<Product>;

            // Assert
            Assert.Equal(SimpleRepository.SharedRepository.Products, model,
                Comparer.Get<Product>((p1, p2) => p1.Name == p2.Name
                    && p1.Price == p2.Price));
        }
    }
}
```

The unit test in the listing checks that the Index action method passes all the objects in the repository to the view. (Ignore the act section of the test for the moment; I explain the ViewResult class and the role it plays in MVC applications in Chapter 17. For the moment, it is enough to know that I am getting the model data returned by the Index action method.)

If you run the test, you will see that it fails, indicating that the set of objects in the repository differs from the set of objects returned by the Index method. But when it comes to figuring out why the test fails, there is a problem: the test is supposed to act on the Home controller, but the controller class depends on the SimpleRepository class, which makes it difficult to figure out whether the test is revealing a problem with the class it is intended to target or a problem with another part of the application.

The example application is simple enough that you could easily figure out the problem just by looking at the code for the HomeController and SimpleRepository classes. Visual inspection isn't as easy in a real application, where the chain of dependencies can make it difficult to understand what causes a test to fail. Typically, the repository would rely on some kind of persistent storage system, such as a database, and a library that provides access to it, and a unit test can act on a whole chain of complex components, any of which could be causing the problem.

Unit tests are effective when they target small parts of an application, such as an individual method or class. What I need is the ability to isolate the Home controller from the rest of the application so that I can limit the scope of the test and rule out any impact caused by the repository.

Isolating a Component

The key to isolating components is to use C# interfaces. To separate the controller from the repository, I added a new class file called IRepository.cs to the Models folder and used it to define the interface shown in Listing 7-9.

Listing 7-9. The Contents of the IRepository.cs File in the Models Folder

```
using System.Collections.Generic;

namespace WorkingWithVisualStudio.Models {

    public interface IRepository {

        IEnumerable<Product> Products { get; }
        void AddProduct(Product p);
    }
}
```

There is nothing special about this interface (except that it doesn't define the full set of operations that would usually be needed in a web application; see Chapter 8 for a more realistic and complete example). However, adding an interface like this allows me to easily isolate a component for testing. The first step is to update the SimpleRepository class so that it implements the new interface, as shown in Listing 7-10.

Listing 7-10. Implementing an Interface in the SimpleRepository.cs File in the Models Folder

```
using System.Collections.Generic;

namespace WorkingWithVisualStudio.Models {
    public class SimpleRepository : IRepository {
        private static SimpleRepository sharedRepository = new SimpleRepository();
        private Dictionary<string, Product> products
            = new Dictionary<string, Product>();

        public static SimpleRepository SharedRepository => sharedRepository;

        public SimpleRepository() {
            var initialItems = new[] {
                new Product { Name = "Kayak", Price = 275M },
                new Product { Name = "Lifejacket", Price = 48.95M },
                new Product { Name = "Soccer ball", Price = 19.50M },
                new Product { Name = "Corner flag", Price = 34.95M }
            };
            foreach (var p in initialItems) {
                AddProduct(p);
            }
            products.Add("Error", null);
        }

        public IEnumerable<Product> Products => products.Values;

        public void AddProduct(Product p) => products.Add(p.Name, p);
    }
}
```

The next step is to modify the controller so that the property used to refer to the repository uses the interface and not the class type, as shown in Listing 7-11.

■ **Tip**   ASP.NET Core MVC supports a more elegant approach for solving this problem, known as *dependency injection*, which I describe in Chapter 18. Dependency injection often causes confusion, so I isolate components in a simpler and more manual way in this chapter.

Listing 7-11. Adding a Repository Property in the HomeController.cs File in the Controllers Folder

```
using Microsoft.AspNetCore.Mvc;
using WorkingWithVisualStudio.Models;
using System.Linq;

namespace WorkingWithVisualStudio.Controllers {
    public class HomeController : Controller {
        public IRepository Repository = SimpleRepository.SharedRepository;

        public IActionResult Index() => View(Repository.Products
                    .Where(p => p?.Price < 50));

        [HttpGet]
        public IActionResult AddProduct() => View();

        [HttpPost]
        public IActionResult AddProduct(Product p) {
            Repository.AddProduct(p);
            return RedirectToAction("Index");
        }
    }
}
```

This may not seem like a significant change, but it allows me to change the repository that the controller uses during testing, which is how I can isolate the controller. In Listing 7-12, I have updated the controller unit tests so they use a special version of the repository.

Listing 7-12. Isolating the Controller in the Unit Test in the HomeControllerTests.cs File

```
using Microsoft.AspNetCore.Mvc;
using System.Collections.Generic;
using WorkingWithVisualStudio.Controllers;
using WorkingWithVisualStudio.Models;
using Xunit;

namespace WorkingWithVisualStudio.Tests {
    public class HomeControllerTests {

        class ModelCompleteFakeRepository : IRepository {

            public IEnumerable<Product> Products { get; } = new Product[] {
                new Product { Name = "P1", Price = 275M },
                new Product { Name = "P2", Price = 48.95M },
                new Product { Name = "P3", Price = 19.50M },
                new Product { Name = "P3", Price = 34.95M }};
```

```
        public void AddProduct(Product p) {
            // do nothing - not required for test
        }
    }

    [Fact]
    public void IndexActionModelIsComplete() {
        // Arrange
        var controller = new HomeController();
        controller.Repository = new ModelCompleteFakeRepository();

        // Act
        var model = (controller.Index() as ViewResult)?.ViewData.Model
            as IEnumerable<Product>;

        // Assert
        Assert.Equal(controller.Repository.Products, model,
            Comparer.Get<Product>((p1, p2) => p1.Name == p2.Name
                && p1.Price == p2.Price));
    }
  }
}
```

I have defined a fake implementation of the IRepository interface that implements only the property I need for the test and uses test data that will always be consIstent (something that may not be the case when working with a real database, especially if you are sharing it with other developers who will be making their own changes).

The revised unit test still fails, which indicates that the problem is caused by the Index action method in the HomeController class and not the components it depends on. The action method that is being acted on by the unit test is sufficiently simple that the problem is obvious from inspecting it.

```
...
public IActionResult Index() => View(Repository.Products.Where(p => p.Price < 50));
...
```

The problem is caused by the use of the LINQ Where method, which is being used to filter out any Product objects whose Price property has a value of 50 or more. At this point, I have a solid lead as to the cause of the problem, but it is good practice to create a test that confirms the problem before making a corrective change, as shown in Listing 7-13.

■ **Tip**   There is a lot of duplication in these tests. I describe how to simplify tests in the next section.

Listing 7-13. Adding a Test to HomeControllerTests.cs in the WorkingWithVisualStudio.Tests Folder

```
using Microsoft.AspNetCore.Mvc;
using System.Collections.Generic;
using WorkingWithVisualStudio.Controllers;
using WorkingWithVisualStudio.Models;
using Xunit;
```

```
namespace WorkingWithVisualStudio.Tests {
    public class HomeControllerTests {

        class ModelCompleteFakeRepository : IRepository {

            public IEnumerable<Product> Products { get; } = new Product[] {
                new Product { Name = "P1", Price = 275M },
                new Product { Name = "P2", Price = 48.95M },
                new Product { Name = "P3", Price = 19.50M },
                new Product { Name = "P3", Price = 34.95M }};

            public void AddProduct(Product p) {
                // do nothing - not required for test
            }
        }

        [Fact]
        public void IndexActionModelIsComplete() {
            // Arrange
            var controller = new HomeController();
            controller.Repository = new ModelCompleteFakeRepository();

            // Act
            var model = (controller.Index() as ViewResult)?.ViewData.Model
                as IEnumerable<Product>;

            // Assert
            Assert.Equal(controller.Repository.Products, model,
                Comparer.Get<Product>((p1, p2) => p1.Name == p2.Name
                    && p1.Price == p2.Price));
        }

        class ModelCompleteFakeRepositoryPricesUnder50 : IRepository {

            public IEnumerable<Product> Products { get; } = new Product[] {
                new Product { Name = "P1", Price = 5M },
                new Product { Name = "P2", Price = 48.95M },
                new Product { Name = "P3", Price = 19.50M },
                new Product { Name = "P3", Price = 34.95M }};

            public void AddProduct(Product p) {
                // do nothing - not required for test
            }
        }

        [Fact]
        public void IndexActionModelIsCompletePricesUnder50() {
            // Arrange
            var controller = new HomeController();
            controller.Repository = new ModelCompleteFakeRepositoryPricesUnder50();
```

```
    // Act
    var model = (controller.Index() as ViewResult)?.ViewData.Model
        as IEnumerable<Product>;

    // Assert
    Assert.Equal(controller.Repository.Products, model,
        Comparer.Get<Product>((p1, p2) => p1.Name == p2.Name
            && p1.Price == p2.Price));
        }
    }
}
```

I have defined a new fake repository that only contains Product objects with Price values that are less than 50 and used it in a new test. If you run this test, you will see that it succeeds, which adds weight to the idea that the problem is caused by the use of the Where method in the Index action method.

In a real project, understanding why a test fails is the point at which you need to reconcile the purpose of the test with the specification for the application. It may well be the case that the Index method is supposed to filter Product objects by Price, in which case the test will need to be revised. This is a common outcome, and a failed test doesn't always indicate a real problem in the application. On the other hand, if the Index action method shouldn't be filtering the model objects, then a corrective change is required, as shown in Listing 7-14.

UNDERSTANDING TEST-DRIVEN DEVELOPMENT

I have followed the most commonly used unit testing style in this chapter, in which an application feature is written and then tested to make sure it works as required. This is popular because most developers think about application code first and testing comes second (this is certainly the category that I fall into).

The problem with this approach is that it tends to produce unit tests that focus only on the parts of the application code that were difficult to write or that needed some serious debugging, leaving some aspects of a feature only partially tested or untested altogether.

An alternative approach is Test-Driven Development (TDD). There are lots of variations on TDD, but the core idea is that you write the tests for a feature before implementing the feature itself. Writing the tests first makes you think more carefully about the specification you are implementing and how you will know that a feature has been implemented correctly. Rather than diving into the implementation detail, TDD makes you consider what the measures of success or failure will be in advance.

The tests that you write will all fail initially because your new feature will not be implemented. But as you add code to the application, your tests will gradually move from red to green and all of your tests will pass by the time that the feature is complete. TDD requires discipline, but it does produce a more comprehensive set of tests and can lead to more robust and reliable code.

Listing 7-14. Removing the LINQ Filter in the HomeController.cs File in the Controllers Folder

```
using Microsoft.AspNetCore.Mvc;
using WorkingWithVisualStudio.Models;
using System.Linq;

namespace WorkingWithVisualStudio.Controllers {
    public class HomeController : Controller {
        public IRepository Repository = SimpleRepository.SharedRepository;

        public IActionResult Index() => View(Repository.Products);

        [HttpGet]
        public IActionResult AddProduct() => View(new Product());

        [HttpPost]
        public IActionResult AddProduct(Product p) {
            Repository.AddProduct(p);
            return RedirectToAction("Index");
        }
    }
}
```

If you run the tests again, you will see that they all pass, as shown in Figure 7-6.

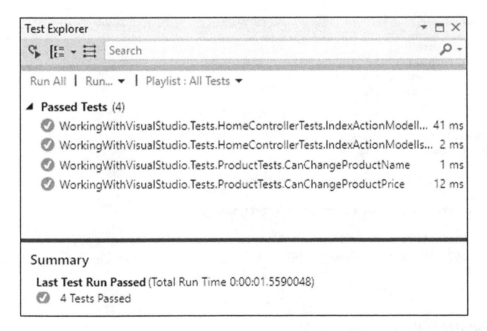

Figure 7-6. *Passing all tests*

This may seem like a lot of work to go to for such a simple problem, but the ability to test a specific component is essential in a real application. Reaching the point where you have identified the problem and have written tests to validate the fix is possible only when you can effectively isolate components.

Improving Unit Tests

The previous section introduced the basic approach to writing unit tests and running tests in Visual Studio and emphasized the importance of isolating the component that is being tested. In this section, I will introduce some more advanced tools and features that you can use to write tests more concisely and expressively. If you get immersed in the culture of unit testing, then you can end up with a lot of test code and the clarity of that code becomes important, especially as you will need to revise tests to reflect changes in the application they apply to during development and into maintenance.

Parameterizing a Unit Test

The tests I wrote for the HomeController class revealed a problem that was present only for some data values. To test for this condition, I ended up creating two similar tests, each of which had its own fake repository. This is a duplicative approach, especially since the only difference between these tests is the set of decimal values used for the Price properties of the Product objects in the fake repositories.

xUnit.net provides supports for *parameterized tests*, where the data used in a test is removed from the test so that a single method can be used for multiple tests. In Listing 7-15, I have used the parameterized test feature to remove duplication in tests for the HomeController class.

Listing 7-15. Parameterizing a Unit Test in the HomeControllerTests.cs File in the Tests Project

```
using Microsoft.AspNetCore.Mvc;
using System.Collections.Generic;
using WorkingWithVisualStudio.Controllers;
using WorkingWithVisualStudio.Models;
using Xunit;

namespace WorkingWithVisualStudio.Tests {
    public class HomeControllerTests {

        class ModelCompleteFakeRepository : IRepository {

            public IEnumerable<Product> Products { get; set; }

            public void AddProduct(Product p) {
                // do nothing - not required for test
            }
        }

        [Theory]
        [InlineData(275, 48.95, 19.50, 24.95)]
        [InlineData(5, 48.95, 19.50, 24.95)]
        public void IndexActionModelIsComplete(decimal price1, decimal price2,
                decimal price3, decimal price4) {
```

```
        // Arrange
        var controller = new HomeController();
        controller.Repository = new ModelCompleteFakeRepository {
            Products = new Product[] {
                new Product {Name = "P1", Price = price1 },
                new Product {Name = "P2", Price = price2 },
                new Product {Name = "P3", Price = price3 },
                new Product {Name = "P4", Price = price4 },
            }
        };

        // Act
        var model = (controller.Index() as ViewResult)?.ViewData.Model
            as IEnumerable<Product>;

        // Assert
        Assert.Equal(controller.Repository.Products, model,
            Comparer.Get<Product>((p1, p2) => p1.Name == p2.Name
                && p1.Price == p2.Price));
    }
}
}
```

Parameterized unit tests are denoted with the Theory attribute rather than the Fact attribute that is used for standard tests. I have also used the InlineData attribute, which allows me to specify values for arguments defined by the unit test method. C# restricts the way that data values are expressed in attributes, so I have defined four decimal arguments on the test method and used the InlineData attribute to provide values for them. I use the decimal values within the test method to generate an array of Product objects, which I use to set the Products property of the fake repository object.

Each Inline attribute defines a separate unit test that is shown as a distinct item in the Visual Studio Test Explorer, as Figure 7-7 illustrates. The Test Explorer entry reveals the values that will be used for the unit test method arguments.

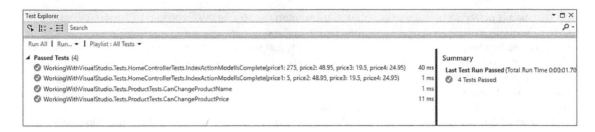

Figure 7-7. Parameterized tests in the Visual Studio Test Explorer

Getting Test Data from a Method or Property

The limitations imposed on expressing data in attributes restrict the usefulness of the InlineData attribute, but an alternative approach is to create a static method or property that returns the object required for testing. In this situation, there are no restrictions on the way that data is defined, and you can create a wider range of test values. To demonstrate how this works, I added a class file called ProductTestData.cs to the unit test project and used it to define the class shown in Listing 7-16.

Listing 7-16. The Contents of the ProductTestData.cs File in the WorkingWithVisualStudio.Tests Folder

```
using System.Collections;
using System.Collections.Generic;
using WorkingWithVisualStudio.Models;

namespace WorkingWithVisualStudio.Tests {

    public class ProductTestData : IEnumerable<object[]> {

        public IEnumerator<object[]> GetEnumerator() {
            yield return new object[] { GetPricesUnder50() };
            yield return new object[] { GetPricesOver50 };
        }

        IEnumerator IEnumerable.GetEnumerator() {
            return this.GetEnumerator();
        }

        private IEnumerable<Product> GetPricesUnder50() {
            decimal[] prices = new decimal[] { 275, 49.95M, 19.50M, 24.95M };
            for (int i = 0; i < prices.Length; i++) {
                yield return new Product { Name = $"P{i + 1}", Price = prices[i] };
            }
        }

        private Product[] GetPricesOver50 => new Product[] {
            new Product { Name = "P1", Price = 5 },
            new Product { Name = "P2", Price = 48.95M },
            new Product { Name = "P3", Price = 19.50M },
            new Product { Name = "P4", Price = 24.95M }};
    }
}
```

Test data is provided through a class that implemented the IEnumerable<object[]> interface, which returns a sequence of object arrays. Each object array in the sequence contains one set of arguments that will be passed to a test method. I am going to redefine my test method so that it accepts an array of Product objects, which adds another layer to the test data. The layer is an enumeration of object arrays, each of which contains a single array of Product objects. This depth of structure in the test data can be confusing, but it is important to get right because your tests won't work if the number of arguments that Xunit.net tries to pass to the test method doesn't match the method signature.

I like to structure my test data classes so that private methods or properties define individual sets of test data, which is then combined into sequences of object arrays by the GetEnumerator method. To demonstrate different techniques, I have created arrays of Product objects using both a method and a property, but I tend to use one approach in my own projects (the choice of which is driven by the kind of data that I am testing with). Listing 7-17 shows how I can use the test data class with the Theory attribute to set up my tests.

■ **Tip**   If you want to include the test data in the same class as the unit tests, then you can use the
`MemberData` attribute instead of `ClassData`. The `MemberData` attribute is configured using a string that specifies
the name of a static method that will provide an `IEnumerable<object[]>`, where each object array in the
sequence is a set of arguments for the test method.

Listing 7-17. Using a Test Data Class in the HomeControllerTests.cs File in the Tests Project

```
using Microsoft.AspNetCore.Mvc;
using System.Collections.Generic;
using WorkingWithVisualStudio.Controllers;
using WorkingWithVisualStudio.Models;
using Xunit;

namespace WorkingWithVisualStudio.Tests {
    public class HomeControllerTests {

        class ModelCompleteFakeRepository : IRepository {

            public IEnumerable<Product> Products { get; set; }

            public void AddProduct(Product p) {
                // do nothing - not required for test
            }
        }

        [Theory]
        [ClassData(typeof(ProductTestData))]
        public void IndexActionModelIsComplete(Product[] products ) {
            // Arrange
            var controller = new HomeController();
            controller.Repository = new ModelCompleteFakeRepository {
                Products = products
            };

            // Act
            var model = (controller.Index() as ViewResult)?.ViewData.Model
                as IEnumerable<Product>;

            // Assert
            Assert.Equal(controller.Repository.Products, model,
                Comparer.Get<Product>((p1, p2) => p1.Name == p2.Name
                    && p1.Price == p2.Price));
        }
    }
}
```

The `ClassData` attribute is configured with the type of the test data class, which is `ProductTestData` in this case. When the tests are run, Xunit.net will create a new instance of the `ProductTestData` class and use it to get the sequence of test data for the test.

■ **Note**   If you look at the list of tests in the Test Explorer, you will see that there is a single entry for the `IndexActionModelIsComplete` tests, even though the `ProductTestData` class provides two sets of test data. This happens when the test data objects cannot be serialized and can be resolved by applying the `Serializable` attribute to the test objects.

Improving Fake Implementations

Isolating components effectively requires fake implementations of classes to provide test data or to check that a component behaves the way it should. In previous examples, I created a class that implemented the `IRepository` interface. This can be an effective approach, but it does lead to creating implementation classes for every kind of test you want to run. As an example, Listing 7-18 shows the addition of a test that checks that the `Index` action method calls the `Products` method in the repository only once. (This kind of test is common when there is concern that a component is making duplicate queries to the repository, leading to multiple database queries.)

Listing 7-18. Adding a Unit Test to the HomeControllerTests.cs File in the Tests Folder

```
using Microsoft.AspNetCore.Mvc;
using System.Collections.Generic;
using WorkingWithVisualStudio.Controllers;
using WorkingWithVisualStudio.Models;
using Xunit;
using System;

namespace WorkingWithVisualStudio.Tests {
    public class HomeControllerTests {

        class ModelCompleteFakeRepository : IRepository {

            public IEnumerable<Product> Products { get; set; }

            public void AddProduct(Product p) {
                // do nothing - not required for test
            }
        }

        [Theory]
        [ClassData(typeof(ProductTestData))]
        public void IndexActionModelIsComplete(Product[] products ) {
            // Arrange
            var controller = new HomeController();
            controller.Repository = new ModelCompleteFakeRepository {
                Products = products
            };
```

```
            // Act
            var model = (controller.Index() as ViewResult)?.ViewData.Model
                as IEnumerable<Product>;

            // Assert
            Assert.Equal(controller.Repository.Products, model,
                Comparer.Get<Product>((p1, p2) => p1.Name == p2.Name
                    && p1.Price == p2.Price));
        }

        class PropertyOnceFakeRepository : IRepository {
            public int PropertyCounter { get; set; } = 0;

            public IEnumerable<Product> Products {
                get {
                    PropertyCounter++;
                    return new[] { new Product { Name = "P1", Price = 100 } };
                }
            }

            public void AddProduct(Product p) {
                // do nothing - not required for test
            }
        }

        [Fact]
        public void RepositoryPropertyCalledOnce() {
            // Arrange
            var repo = new PropertyOnceFakeRepository();
            var controller = new HomeController { Repository = repo };

            // Act
            var result = controller.Index();

            // Assert
            Assert.Equal(1, repo.PropertyCounter);
        }
    }
}
```

Fake implementations are not always simple sources of data; they can also be used to assess the way that components perform their work. In this case, I added a simple counter property that is incremented each time that the Products property of the fake repository is read, and I used the Assert.Equal method to make sure that the property is called only once.

Adding a Mocking Framework

Creating fake objects like this gets out of hand, and the best way to get things back under control is to use a *fakes framework*, also known as a *mocking framework*. (There is a technical difference between fake and mock objects, but modern test tools blur them together for ease of use, so I will use these terms interchangeably.) The framework I use in this chapter is called Moq and is described in Table 7-4.

Table 7-4. *Putting Moq in Context*

Question	Answer
What is it?	Moq is a software package for creating fake implementations of components in an application.
Why is it useful?	A mocking framework makes it easier to create fake components to isolate parts of the application for unit testing.
How is it used?	Moq uses lambda expressions to define functionality for the fake component and only requires the features that are used for testing to be defined.
Are there any pitfalls or limitations?	Getting used to the syntax can take some effort. See `https://github.com/Moq/moq4` for documentation and examples.
Are there any alternatives?	There are several alternatives frameworks available including NSubstitute (`http://nsubstitute.github.io`) and FakeItEasy (`http://fakeiteasy.github.io`). All of these frameworks offer similar features, and choosing between them is a matter of selecting the syntax that you prefer.

To install Moq, right-click the WorkingWithVisualStudio.Tests project in the Solution Explorer and select Manage NuGet Packages from the pop-up menu. Click on Browse and enter Moq into the search box. Select Moq from the list of packages, as shown in Figure 7-8, and click Install to add the package to the project.

■ **Note**   The Moq package is added to the unit test project and not the application project.

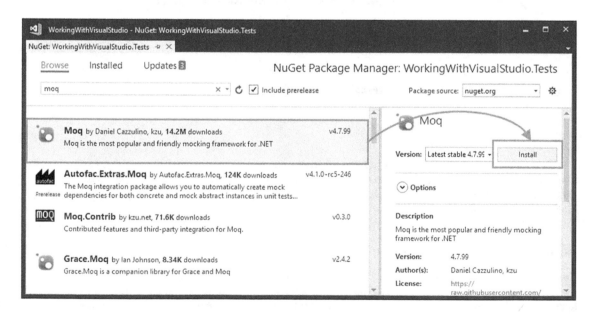

Figure 7-8. *Adding a package to the unit test project*

Close the NuGet package management window once Visual Studio has installed the Moq package.

Creating a Mock Object

Creating a mock object means telling Moq what kind of object you want, configuring its behavior, and applying the object to the subject of the test. In Listing 7-19, I have used Moq to replace the two fake repositories in the tests for the HomeController.

Listing 7-19. Using Mock Objects in the HomeControllerTests.cs File

```
using Microsoft.AspNetCore.Mvc;
using System.Collections.Generic;
using WorkingWithVisualStudio.Controllers;
using WorkingWithVisualStudio.Models;
using Xunit;
using System;
using Moq;

namespace WorkingWithVisualStudio.Tests {
    public class HomeControllerTests {

        [Theory]
        [ClassData(typeof(ProductTestData))]
        public void IndexActionModelIsComplete(Product[] products ) {

            // Arrange
            var mock = new Mock<IRepository>();
            mock.SetupGet(m => m.Products).Returns(products);
            var controller = new HomeController { Repository = mock.Object };

            // Act
            var model = (controller.Index() as ViewResult)?.ViewData.Model
                as IEnumerable<Product>;

            // Assert
            Assert.Equal(controller.Repository.Products, model,
                Comparer.Get<Product>((p1, p2) => p1.Name == p2.Name
                    && p1.Price == p2.Price));
        }

        [Fact]
        public void RepositoryPropertyCalledOnce() {

            // Arrange
            var mock = new Mock<IRepository>();
            mock.SetupGet(m => m.Products)
                .Returns(new[] { new Product { Name = "P1", Price = 100 } });
            var controller = new HomeController { Repository = mock.Object };
```

```
            // Act
            var result = controller.Index();

            // Assert
            mock.VerifyGet(m => m.Products, Times.Once);
        }
    }
}
```

The use of Moq has allowed me to remove the fake implementations of the IRepository interface and replace them with just a few lines of code. I am not going to go into detail about the different features that Moq supports, but I will explain the way that I used Moq in the examples. (See https://github.com/Moq/moq4 for examples and documentation for Moq. There are also examples in later chapters as I explain how to unit test different types of MVC component.)

The first step is to create a new instance of the Mock object, specifying the interface that should be implemented, like this:

```
...
var mock = new Mock<IRepository>();
...
```

The Mock object I created will fake the IRepository interface. The next step is to define the functionality that is required for the test. Unlike a regular class implementation of an interface, a mock object is only configured with the behavior required for the test. For the first mock repository, I need to implement the Product property so that it returns the set of Product objects that are passed to the test method through the ClassData attribute, as follows:

```
...
mock.SetupGet(m => m.Products).Returns(products);
...
```

The SetupGet method is used to implement the getter for a property. The argument to this method is a lambda expression that specifies the property to be implemented, which is Products in this example. The Returns method is called on the result of the SetupGet method to specify the result that will be returned when the property value is read. I used the same approach for the second mock repository but specified a fixed value, like this:

```
...
mock.SetupGet(m => m.Products)
            .Returns(new[] { new Product { Name = "P1", Price = 100 } });
...
```

The Mock class defines an Object property, which returns the object that implements the specified interface and with the behaviors that have been defined. In both unit tests, I use the Object property to get the repository to configure the controller, like this:

```
...
var controller = new HomeController { Repository = mock.Object };
...
```

The final Moq feature I used was to check that the `Products` property was called once, like this:

```
...
mock.VerifyGet(m => m.Products, Times.Once);
...
```

The `VerifyGet` method is one of the methods defined by the `Mock` class to inspect the state of the mock object when the test has completed. In this case, the `VerifyGet` method allows me to check the number of times that the `Products` property method has been read. The `Times.Once` value specifies that the `VerifyGet` method should throw an exception if the property has not been read exactly once, which will cause the test to fail. (The `Assert` methods usually used in tests work by throwing an exception when a test fails, which is why the `VerifyGet` method can be used to replace an `Assert` method when working with mock objects.)

Summary

This chapter focused on unit testing, which can be a powerful tool for improving the quality of code. Unit testing doesn't suit every developer, but it is worth experimenting with and can be useful even if used only for complex features or problem diagnosis. I described the use of the xUnit.net test framework, explained the importance of isolating components for testing, and demonstrated some tools and techniques for simplifying unit test code. In the next chapter, I start the process of creating a more realistic MVC application called SportsStore.

CHAPTER 8

■ ■ ■

SportsStore: A Real Application

In the previous chapters, I built quick and simple MVC applications. I described the MVC pattern, the essential C# features, and the kinds of tools that good MVC developers require. Now it is time to put everything together and build a simple but realistic e-commerce application.

My application, called *SportsStore*, will follow the classic approach taken by online stores everywhere. I will create an online product catalog that customers can browse by category and page, a shopping cart where users can add and remove products, and a checkout where customers can enter their shipping details. I will also create an administration area that includes create, read, update, and delete (CRUD) facilities for managing the catalog, and I will protect it so that only logged-in administrators can make changes.

My goal in this chapter and those that follow is to give you a sense of what real MVC development is like by creating as realistic an example as possible. I want to focus on ASP.NET Core MVC, of course, so I have simplified the integration with external systems, such as the database, and omitted others entirely, such as payment processing.

You might find the going a little slow as I build up the levels of infrastructure I need, but the initial investment in an MVC application pays dividends, resulting in maintainable, extensible, well-structured code with excellent support for unit testing.

UNIT TESTING

I have made quite a big deal about the ease of unit testing in MVC and about how unit testing can be an important and useful part of the development process. You will see this demonstrated throughout this part of the book because I have included details of unit tests and techniques as they relate to key MVC features.

I know this is not a universal opinion. If you do not want to unit test, that is fine with me. To that end, when I have something to say that is purely about testing, I put it in a sidebar like this one. If you are not interested in unit testing, you can skip right over these sections, and the SportsStore application will work just fine. You do not need to do any kind of unit testing to get the technology benefits of ASP.NET Core MVC, although, of course, support for testing is a key reason for adopting ASP.NET Core MVC.

Most of the MVC features I use for the SportsStore application have their own chapters later in the book. Rather than duplicate everything here, I tell you just enough to make sense for the example application and point you to the other chapter for in-depth information.

I will call out each step needed to build the application so that you can see how the MVC features fit together. You should pay particular attention when I create views. You will get some odd results if you do not follow the examples closely.

© Adam Freeman 2017
A. Freeman, *Pro ASP.NET Core MVC 2*, https://doi.org/10.1007/978-1-4842-3150-0_8

Getting Started

You will need to install Visual Studio if you are planning to code the SportsStore application on your own computer as you read through this part of the book and make sure that you install the LocalDB option, which is required to store data persistently. LocalDB will be installed automatically if you follow the instructions in Chapter 2.

■ **Note**   If you just want to follow the project without having to re-create it, then you can download the SportsStore project from the GitHub repository for this book, `https://github.com/apress/pro-asp.net-core-mvc-2`. You do not need to follow along, of course. I have tried to make the screenshots and code listings as easy to follow as possible, just in case you are reading this book on a train, in a coffee shop, or the like.

Creating the MVC Project

I am going to follow the same basic approach that I used in earlier chapters, which is to start with an empty project and add all of the configuration files and components that I require. I started by selecting New ➤ Project from the Visual Studio File menu and selecting the ASP.NET Core Web Application project template, as shown in Figure 8-1. I set the name of the project to be **SportsStore** and clicked the OK button.

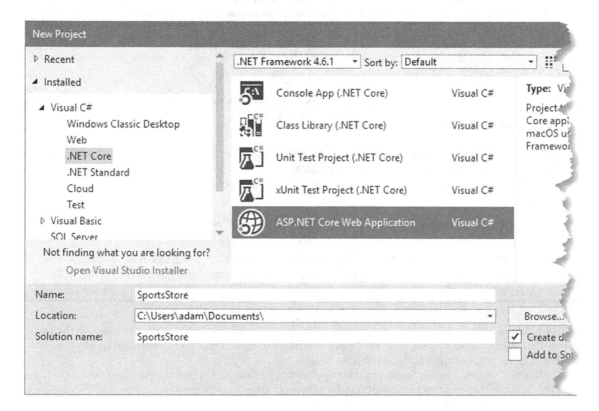

Figure 8-1. *Selecting the project type*

I selected the Empty template, as shown in Figure 8-2. I ensured that .NET Core and ASP.NET Core 2.0 were selected in the menus at the top of the dialog window and that the Enable Docker Support option was unchecked before clicking the OK button to create the SportsStore project.

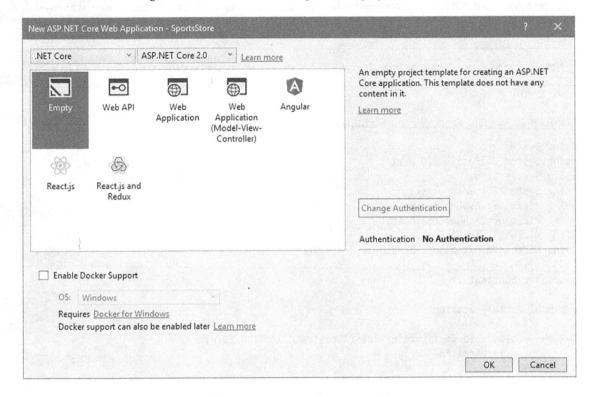

Figure 8-2. *Selecting the project template*

Creating the Folder Structure

The next step is to add the folders that will contain the application components required for an MVC application: models, controllers, and views. For each of the folders described in Table 8-1, right-click the SportsStore project item in the Solution Explorer, select Add ➤ New Folder from the pop-up menu, and set the folder name. Additional folders will be required later, but these reflect the main parts of the MVC application and are enough to get started with.

Table 8-1. *The Folders Required for the SportsStore Project*

Name	Description
Models	This folder will contain the model classes.
Controllers	This folder will contain the controller classes.
Views	This folder holds everything related to views, including individual Razor files, the view start file, and the view imports file.

Configuring the Application

The Startup class is responsible for configuring the ASP.NET Core application. Listing 8-1 shows the changes I made to the Startup class to enable the MVC framework and some related features that are useful for development.

■ **Note**   The Startup class is an important ASP.NET Core feature. I describe it in detail in Chapter 14.

Listing 8-1. Enabling Features in the Startup.cs File in the SportsStore Folder

```
using System;
using System.Collections.Generic;
using System.Linq;
using System.Threading.Tasks;
using Microsoft.AspNetCore.Builder;
using Microsoft.AspNetCore.Hosting;
using Microsoft.AspNetCore.Http;
using Microsoft.Extensions.DependencyInjection;

namespace SportsStore {

    public class Startup {

        public void ConfigureServices(IServiceCollection services) {
            services.AddMvc();
        }

        public void Configure(IApplicationBuilder app, IHostingEnvironment env) {
            app.UseDeveloperExceptionPage();
            app.UseStatusCodePages();
            app.UseStaticFiles();
            app.UseMvc(routes => {

            });
        }
    }
}
```

The ConfigureServices method is used to set up shared objects that can be used throughout the application through the dependency injection feature, which I describe in Chapter 18. The AddMvc method that I call in the ConfigureServices method is an extension method that sets up the shared objects used in MVC applications.

The Configure method is used to set up the features that receive and process HTTP requests. Each method that I call in the Configure method is an extension method that sets up an HTTP request processor, as described in Table 8-2.

Table 8-2. *The Initial Feature Methods Called in the Start Class*

Method	Description
UseDeveloperExceptionPage()	This extension method displays details of exceptions that occur in the application, which is useful during the development process. It should not be enabled in deployed applications, and I disable this feature when I deploy the application in Chapter 12.
UseStatusCodePages()	This extension method adds a simple message to HTTP responses that would not otherwise have a body, such as 404 - Not Found responses.
UseStaticFiles()	This extension method enables support for serving static content from the wwwroot folder.
UseMvc()	This extension method enables ASP.NET Core MVC.

Next, I need to prepare the application for Razor views. Right-click the Views folder, select Add ➤ New Item from the pop-up menu, and select the MVC View Imports Page item from the ASP.NET category, as shown in Figure 8-3.

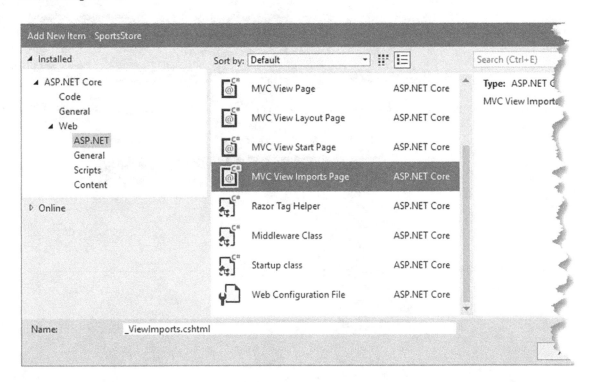

Figure 8-3. *Creating the view imports file*

Click the Add button to create the _ViewImports.cshtml file and set the contents of the new file to match Listing 8-2.

Listing 8-2. The Contents of the _ViewImports.cshtml File in the Views Folder

```
@using SportsStore.Models
@addTagHelper *, Microsoft.AspNetCore.Mvc.TagHelpers
```

The @using statement will allow me to use the types in the SportsStore.Models namespace in views without needing to refer to the namespace. The @addTagHelper statement enables the built-in tag helpers, which I use later to create HTML elements that reflect the configuration of the SportsStore application.

Creating the Unit Test Project

Creating the unit test project requires the same process as described Chapter 7. Right-click the SportsStore solution item in the Solution Explorer and select Add ➤ New Project from the pop-up menu. Select the xUnit Test Project (.NET Core) project template, as shown in Figure 8-4, and set the name of the project to SportsStore.Tests. Click OK to create the unit test project.

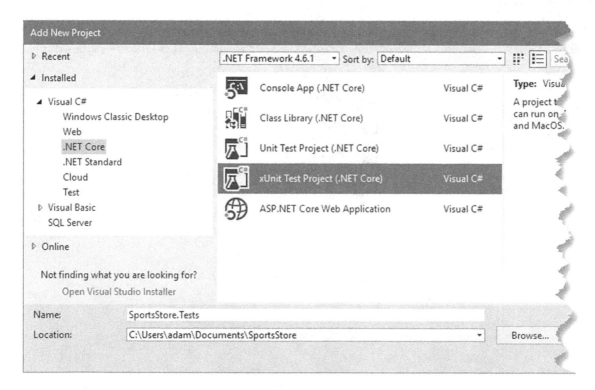

Figure 8-4. Creating the unit test project

Once the unit test project has been created, right-click the SportsStore.Tests project in the Solution Explorer and select Edit SportsStore.Tests.csproj from the pop-up menu. Add the new elements shown in Listing 8-3 to add the Moq package to the tests project and to create a reference to the main SportsStore project. Ensure that you specify the version shown in the listing for the Moq package.

Listing 8-3. Adding a Package in the SportsStore.Tests.csproj File in the SportsStore.Tests Folder

```
<Project Sdk="Microsoft.NET.Sdk">

  <PropertyGroup>
    <TargetFramework>netcoreapp2.0</TargetFramework>

    <IsPackable>false</IsPackable>
  </PropertyGroup>

  <ItemGroup>
    <ProjectReference Include="..\SportsStore\SportsStore.csproj" />
  </ItemGroup>

  <ItemGroup>
    <PackageReference Include="Microsoft.NET.Test.Sdk"
        Version="15.3.0-preview-20170628-02" />
    <PackageReference Include="xunit" Version="2.2.0" />
    <PackageReference Include="xunit.runner.visualstudio" Version="2.2.0" />
    <PackageReference Include="Moq" Version="4.7.99" />
  </ItemGroup>

</Project>
```

When you save the changes to the csproj file, Visual Studio will download and install the Moq package into the unit test project and create a reference to the main SportsStore project so that the classes it contains can be used in tests.

Checking and Running the Application

The application and unit test projects are created and configured and ready for development. The Solution Explorer should contain the items shown in Figure 8-5. You will have problems if you see different items or items are not in the same locations, so take a moment to check that everything is present and in the right place.

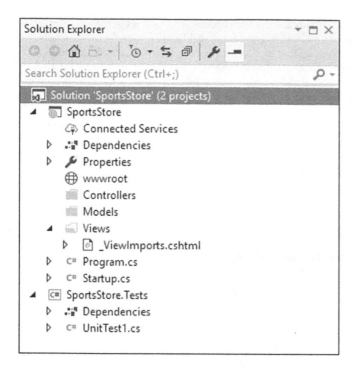

Figure 8-5. *The Solution Explorer for the SportsStore application and unit test projects*

If you select Start Debugging from the Debug menu (or Start Without Debugging if you prefer the iterative development style I described in Chapter 6), you will see an error page, as shown in Figure 8-6. The error message is shown because there are no controllers in the application to handle requests at the moment, which is something that I will address shortly.

Figure 8-6. *Running the SportsStore application*

Starting the Domain Model

All projects start with the domain model, which is the heart of an MVC application. Since this is an e-commerce application, the most obvious model I need is for a product. I added a class file called `Product.cs` to the `Models` folder and used it to define the class shown in Listing 8-4.

Listing 8-4. The Contents of the Product.cs File in the Models Folder

```
namespace SportsStore.Models {

    public class Product {
        public int ProductID { get; set; }
        public string Name { get; set; }
        public string Description { get; set; }
        public decimal Price { get; set; }
        public string Category { get; set; }
    }
}
```

Creating a Repository

I need some way of getting Product objects from a database. As I explained in Chapter 3, the model includes the logic for storing and retrieving the data from the persistent data store. I won't worry about how I am going to implement data persistence for the moment, but I will start the process of defining an interface for it. I added a new C# interface file called IProductRepository.cs to the Models folder and used it to define the interface shown in Listing 8-5.

Listing 8-5. The Contents of the IProductRepository.cs File in the Models Folder

```
using System.Linq;

namespace SportsStore.Models {

    public interface IProductRepository {

        IQueryable<Product> Products { get; }
    }
}
```

This interface uses IQueryable<T> to allow a caller to obtain a sequence of Product objects. The IQueryable<T> interface is derived from the more familiar IEnumerable<T> interface and represents a collection of objects that can be queried, such as those managed by a database.

A class that depends on the IProductRepository interface can obtain Product objects without needing to know the details of how they are stored or how the implementation class will deliver them.

UNDERSTANDING IENUMERABLE<T> AND IQUERYABLE<T> INTERFACES

The IQueryable<T> interface is useful because it allows a collection of objects to be queried efficiently. Later in this chapter, I add support for retrieving a subset of Product objects from a database, and using the IQueryable<T> interface allows me to ask the database for just the objects that I require using standard LINQ statements and without needing to know what database server stores the data or how it processes the query. Without the IQueryable<T> interface, I would have to retrieve all of the Product objects from the database and then discard the ones I don't want, which becomes an expensive operation as the amount of data used by an application increases. It is for this reason that the IQueryable<T> interface is typically used instead of IEnumerable<T> in database repository interfaces and classes.

However, care must be taken with the IQueryable<T> interface because each time the collection of objects is enumerated, the query will be evaluated again, which means that a new query will be sent to the database. This can undermine the efficiency gains of using IQueryable<T>. In such situations, you can convert IQueryable<T> to a more predictable form using the ToList or ToArray extension method.

Creating a Fake Repository

Now that I have defined an interface, I could implement the persistence mechanism and hook it up to a database, but I want to add some of the other parts of the application first. To do this, I am going to create a fake implementation of the IProductRepository interface that will stand in until I return to the topic of data storage. To create the fake repository, I added a class file called FakeProductRepository.cs to the Models folder and used it to define the class shown in Listing 8-6.

Listing 8-6. The Contents of FakeProductRepository.cs File in the Models Folder

```
using System.Collections.Generic;
using System.Linq;

namespace SportsStore.Models {

    public class FakeProductRepository : IProductRepository {

        public IQueryable<Product> Products => new List<Product> {
            new Product { Name = "Football", Price = 25 },
            new Product { Name = "Surf board", Price = 179 },
            new Product { Name = "Running shoes", Price = 95 }
        }.AsQueryable<Product>();
    }
}
```

The FakeProductRepository class implements the IProductRepository interface by returning a fixed collection of Product objects as the value of the Products property. The AsQueryable method is used to convert the fixed collection of objects to an IQueryable<Product>, which is required to implement the IProductRepository interface and allows me to create a compatible fake repository without having to deal with real queries.

Registering the Repository Service

MVC emphasizes the use of *loosely coupled components*, which means you can make a change in one part of the application without having to make corresponding changes elsewhere. This approach categorizes parts of the application as *services*, which provide features that other parts of the application use. The class that provides a service can then be altered or replaced without requiring changes in the classes that use it. I explain this in depth in Chapter 18, but for the SportsStore application, I want to create a repository service, which allows controllers to get objects that implement the IProductRepository interface without knowing which class is being used. This will allow me to start developing the application using the simple FakeProductRepository class I created in the previous section and then replace it with a real repository later without having to make changes in all of the classes that need access to the repository. Services are registered in the ConfigureServices method of the Startup class, and in Listing 8-7, I have defined a new service for the repository.

Listing 8-7. Creating the Repository Service in the Startup.cs File in the SportsStore Folder

```
using System;
using System.Collections.Generic;
using System.Linq;
using System.Threading.Tasks;
using Microsoft.AspNetCore.Builder;
using Microsoft.AspNetCore.Hosting;
using Microsoft.AspNetCore.Http;
using Microsoft.Extensions.DependencyInjection;
using SportsStore.Models;

namespace SportsStore {

    public class Startup {

        public void ConfigureServices(IServiceCollection services) {
            services.AddTransient<IProductRepository, FakeProductRepository>();
            services.AddMvc();
        }

        public void Configure(IApplicationBuilder app, IHostingEnvironment env) {
            app.UseDeveloperExceptionPage();
            app.UseStatusCodePages();
            app.UseStaticFiles();
            app.UseMvc(routes => {

            });
        }
    }
}
```

The statement I added to the ConfigureServices method tells ASP.NET Core that when a component, such as a controller, needs an implementation of the IProductRepository interface, it should receive an instance of the FakeProductRepository class. The AddTransient method specifies that a new FakeProductRepository object should be created each time the IProductRepository interface is needed. Don't worry if this doesn't make sense at the moment; you will see how it fits into the application shortly, and I explain what is happening in detail in Chapter 18.

Displaying a List of Products

I could spend the rest of this chapter building out the domain model and the repository and not touch the rest of the application at all. I think you would find that boring, though, so I am going to switch tracks and start using MVC in earnest and come back to add model and repository features as I need them.

In this section, I am going to create a controller and an action method that can display details of the products in the repository. For the moment, this will be for only the data in the fake repository, but I will sort that out later. I will also set up an initial *routing configuration* so that MVC knows how to map requests for the application to the controller I create.

```
┌─────────────────────────────────────────────────────────────────────┐
│            USING THE VISUAL STUDIO MVC SCAFFOLDING                     │
└─────────────────────────────────────────────────────────────────────┘
```

Throughout this book, I create MVC controllers and views by right-clicking a folder in the Solution Explorer, selecting Add ➤ New Item from the pop-up menu, and then choosing an item template from the Add New Item window. There is an alternative, known as scaffolding, in which Visual Studio provides items in the Add menu specifically for creating controllers and views. When you select these menu items, you are prompted to choose a scenario for the component that you want to create, such as a controller with read/write actions or a view that contains a form that will be used to create a specific model object.

I don't use the scaffolding in this book. The code and markup that the scaffolding generates are so generic as to be all but useless, while the set of scenarios that are supported are narrow and don't address common development problems. My goal in this book is not only to make sure you know how to create MVC applications but also to explain how everything works behind the scenes, and that is harder to do when responsibility for creating components is handed to the scaffolding.

That said, this is another situation where your development style may be different from mine, and you may find that you prefer working with the scaffolding in your own projects. That's perfectly reasonable, although I recommend you take the time to understand what the scaffolding does so you know where to look if you don't get the results you expect.

Adding a Controller

To create the first controller in the application, I added a class file called ProductController.cs to the Controllers folder and defined the class shown in Listing 8-8.

Listing 8-8. The Contents of the ProductController.cs File in the Controllers Folder

```
using Microsoft.AspNetCore.Mvc;
using SportsStore.Models;

namespace SportsStore.Controllers {

    public class ProductController : Controller {
        private IProductRepository repository;

        public ProductController(IProductRepository repo) {
            repository = repo;
        }
    }
}
```

When MVC needs to create a new instance of the ProductController class to handle an HTTP request, it will inspect the constructor and see that it requires an object that implements the IProductRepository interface. To determine what implementation class should be used, MVC consults the configuration in the Startup class, which tells it that FakeRepository should be used and that a new instance should be created every time. MVC creates a new FakeRepository object and uses it to invoke the ProductController constructor in order to create the controller object that will process the HTTP request.

This is known as *dependency injection,* and its approach allows the ProductController constructor to access the application's repository through the IProductRepository interface without having any need to know which implementation class has been configured. Later, I'll replace the fake repository with the real one, and dependency injection means that the controller will continue to work without changes.

■ **Note**   Some developers don't like dependency injection and believe it makes applications more complicated. That's not my view, but if you are new to dependency injection, then I recommend you wait until you have read Chapter 18 before you make up your mind.

Next, I have added an action method, called List, which will render a view showing the complete list of the products in the repository, as shown in Listing 8-9.

Listing 8-9. Adding an Action Method in the ProductController.cs File in the Controllers Folder

```
using Microsoft.AspNetCore.Mvc;
using SportsStore.Models;

namespace SportsStore.Controllers {

    public class ProductController : Controller {
        private IProductRepository repository;

        public ProductController(IProductRepository repo) {
            repository = repo;
        }

        public ViewResult List() => View(repository.Products);
    }
}
```

Calling the View method like this (without specifying a view name) tells MVC to render the default view for the action method. Passing the collection of Product objects from the repository to the View method provides the framework with the data with which to populate the Model object in a strongly typed view.

Adding and Configuring the View

I need to create a view to present the content to the user, but there are some preparatory steps required that will make writing the view simpler. The first is to create a shared layout that will define common content that will be included in all HTML responses sent to clients. Shared layouts are a useful way of ensuring that views are consistent and contain important JavaScript files and CSS stylesheets, and I explained how they worked in Chapter 5.

I created the Views/Shared folder and added to it a new MVC View Layout Page called _Layout.cshtml, which is the default name that Visual Studio assigns to this item type. Listing 8-10 shows the _Layout. cshtml file. I made one change to the default content, which is to set the contents of the title element to SportsStore.

Listing 8-10. The Contents of the _Layout.cshtml File in the Views/Shared Folder

```
<!DOCTYPE html>

<html>
<head>
    <meta name="viewport" content="width=device-width" />
    <title>SportsStore</title>
```

```
</head>
<body>
    <div>
        @RenderBody()
    </div>
</body>
</html>
```

Next, I need to configure the application so that the _Layout.cshtml file is applied by default. This is done by adding an MVC View Start Page file called _ViewStart.cshtml to the Views folder. The default content added by Visual Studio, shown in Listing 8-11, selects a layout called _Layout.cshtml, which corresponds to the file shown in Listing 8-10.

Listing 8-11. The Contents of the _ViewStart.cshtml File in the Views Folder

```
@{
    Layout = "_Layout";
}
```

Now I need to add the view that will be displayed when the List action method is used to handle a request. I created the Views/Product folder and added to it a Razor view file called List.cshtml. I then added the markup shown in Listing 8-12.

Listing 8-12. The Contents of the List.cshtml File in the Views/Product Folder

```
@model IEnumerable<Product>

@foreach (var p in Model) {
    <div>
        <h3>@p.Name</h3>
        @p.Description
        <h4>@p.Price.ToString("c")</h4>
    </div>
}
```

The @model expression at the top of the file specifies that the view will receive a sequence of Product objects from the action method as its model data. I use a @foreach expression to work through the sequence and generate a simple set of HTML elements for each Product object that is received.

The view doesn't know where the Product objects came from, how they were obtained, or whether they represent all of the products known to the application. Instead, the view deals only with how details of each Product is displayed using HTML elements, which is consistent with the separation of concerns that I described in Chapter 3.

■ **Tip**   I converted the Price property to a string using the ToString("c") method, which renders numerical values as currency according to the culture settings that are in effect on your server. For example, if the server is set up as en-US, then (1002.3).ToString("c") will return $1,002.30, but if the server is set to en-GB, then the same method will return £1,002.30.

Setting the Default Route

I need to tell MVC that it should send requests that arrive for the root URL of my application (http://mysite/) to the List action method in the ProductController class. I do this by editing the statement in the Startup class that sets up the MVC classes that handle HTTP requests, as shown in Listing 8-13.

Listing 8-13. Changing the Default Route in the Startup.cs File in the SportsStore Folder

```
using System;
using System.Collections.Generic;
using System.Linq;
using System.Threading.Tasks;
using Microsoft.AspNetCore.Builder;
using Microsoft.AspNetCore.Hosting;
using Microsoft.AspNetCore.Http;
using Microsoft.Extensions.DependencyInjection;
using SportsStore.Models;

namespace SportsStore {

    public class Startup {

        public void ConfigureServices(IServiceCollection services) {
            services.AddTransient<IProductRepository, FakeProductRepository>();
            services.AddMvc();
        }

        public void Configure(IApplicationBuilder app, IHostingEnvironment env) {
            app.UseDeveloperExceptionPage();
            app.UseStatusCodePages();
            app.UseStaticFiles();
            app.UseMvc(routes => {
                routes.MapRoute(
                    name: "default",
                    template: "{controller=Product}/{action=List}/{id?}");
            });
        }
    }
}
```

The Configure method of the Startup class is used to set up the request pipeline, which consists of classes (known as *middleware*) that will inspect HTTP requests and generate responses. The UseMvc method sets up the MVC middleware, and one of the configuration options is the scheme that will be used to map URLs to controllers and action methods. I describe the routing system in detail in Chapters 15 and 16, but the change in Listing 8-13 tells MVC to send requests to the List action method of the Product controller unless the request URL specifies otherwise.

■ **Tip** Notice that I have set the name of the controller in Listing 8-13 to be Product and not ProductController, which is the name of the class. This is part of the MVC naming convention, in which controller class names generally end in Controller, but you omit this part of the name when referring to the class. I explain the naming convention and its effect in Chapter 31.

Running the Application

All the basics are in place. I have a controller with an action method that MVC will use when the default URL for the application is requested. MVC will create an instance of the FakeRepository class and use it to create a new controller object to handle the request. The fake repository will provide the controller with some simple test data, which its action method passes to the Razor view so that the HTML response to the browser will include details for each Product object. When generating the HTML response, MVC will combine the data from the view selected by the action method with the content from the shared layout, producing a complete HTML document that the browser can parse and display. You can see the result by starting the application, as shown in Figure 8-7.

This is the typical pattern of development for ASP.NET Core MVC. An initial investment of time setting everything up is necessary, and then the basic features of the application snap together quickly.

Figure 8-7. *Viewing the basic application functionality*

Preparing a Database

I can display a simple view that contains details of the products, but it uses the test data that the fake repository contains. Before I can implement a real repository with real data, I need to set up a database and populate it with some data.

I am going to use SQL Server as the database, and I will access the database using the Entity Framework Core (EF Core), which is the Microsoft .NET object-relational mapping (ORM) framework. An ORM framework presents the tables, columns, and rows of a relational database through regular C# objects.

■ **Note** This is an area where you can choose from a wide range of tools and technologies. Not only are there different relational databases available, but you can also work with object repositories, document stores, and some esoteric alternatives. There are other .NET ORM frameworks as well, each of which takes a slightly different approach; these variations may give you a better fit for your projects.

I am using Entity Framework Core for several reasons: it is simple to get working, the integration with LINQ is first-rate (and I like using LINQ), and it works nicely with ASP.NET Core MVC. The earlier releases were a bit hit-and-miss, but the current versions are elegant and feature-rich.

A nice feature of SQL Server is *LocalDB*, which is an administration-free implementation of the basic SQL Server features specifically designed for developers. Using this feature, I can skip the process of setting up a database while I build my project and then deploy to a full SQL Server instance later. Most MVC applications are deployed to hosted environments that are run by professional administrators, so the LocalDB feature means that database configuration can be left in the hands of DBAs, and developers can get on with coding.

■ **Tip** If you didn't select the LocalDB when you installed Visual Studio, then you need to do so now. It can be selected through the Individual Components section of the Visual Studio installer. If you followed the instructions in Chapter 2, then the LocalDB feature should be installed and ready to use.

Installing the Entity Framework Core Tools Package

The main Entity Framework Core functionality is added to the project by default when Visual Studio creates the project. One additional NuGet package is required to provide the command-line tools that are used to create the classes that prepare the database to store the application data, known as *migrations*.

To add the package to the project, right-click the SportsStore project item in the Solution Explorer, select Edit SportsStore.csproj from the pop-up window, and make the change to the file shown in Listing 8-14. Take care to use the version specified in the listing, and note that the package is added using the DotNetCliToolReference element and not the PackageReference element that is used for the existing package.

■ **Note** You must install this package by editing the file. This type of package cannot be added using the NuGet Package Manager or the dotnet command-line tools.

Listing 8-14. Adding a Package in the SportsStore.csproj File in the SportsStore Folder

```
<Project Sdk="Microsoft.NET.Sdk.Web">

  <PropertyGroup>
    <TargetFramework>netcoreapp2.0</TargetFramework>
  </PropertyGroup>

  <ItemGroup>
    <Folder Include="wwwroot\" />
  </ItemGroup>

  <ItemGroup>
    <PackageReference Include="Microsoft.AspNetCore.All" Version="2.0.0" />
    <DotNetCliToolReference Include="Microsoft.EntityFrameworkCore.Tools.DotNet"
        Version="2.0.0" />
  </ItemGroup>

</Project>
```

When you save the file, Visual Studio will download and install the Entity Framework Core command-line tools and add them to the project.

Creating the Database Classes

The *database context class* is the bridge between the application and Entity Framework Core and provides access to the application's data using model objects. To create the database context class for the SportsStore application, I added a class file called ApplicationDbContext.cs to the Models folder and defined the class shown in Listing 8-15.

Listing 8-15. The Contents of the ApplicationDbContext.cs File in the Models Folder

```
using Microsoft.EntityFrameworkCore;
using Microsoft.EntityFrameworkCore.Design;
using Microsoft.Extensions.DependencyInjection;

namespace SportsStore.Models {

    public class ApplicationDbContext : DbContext {

        public ApplicationDbContext(DbContextOptions<ApplicationDbContext> options)
            : base(options) { }

        public DbSet<Product> Products { get; set; }
    }
}
```

The DbContext base class provides access to the Entity Framework Core's underlying functionality, and the Products property will provide access to the Product objects in the database. The ApplicationDbContext class is derived from DbContext and adds the properties that will be used to read and write the application's data. There is only one property at the moment, which will provide access to Product objects.

Creating the Repository Class

It may not seem like it at the moment, but most of the work required to set up the database is complete. The next step is to create a class that implements the IProductRepository interface and gets its data using Entity Framework Core. I added a class file called EFProductRepository.cs to the Models folder and used it to define the repository class shown in Listing 8-16.

Listing 8-16. The Contents of the EFProductRepository.cs File in the Models Folder

```
using System.Collections.Generic;
using System.Linq;

namespace SportsStore.Models {

    public class EFProductRepository : IProductRepository {
        private ApplicationDbContext context;
```

```
        public EFProductRepository(ApplicationDbContext ctx) {
            context = ctx;
        }

        public IQueryable<Product> Products => context.Products;
    }
}
```

I'll add functionality as I add features to the application, but for the moment, the repository implementation just maps the Products property defined by the IProductRepository interface onto the Products property defined by the ApplicationDbContext class. The Products property in the context class returns a DbSet<Product> object, which implements the IQueryable<T> interface and makes it easy to implement the IProductRepository interface when using Entity Framework Core. This ensures that queries to the database will retrieve only the objects that are required, as explained earlier in this chapter.

Defining the Connection String

A *connection string* specifies the location and name of the database and provides configuration settings for how the application should connect to the database server. Connection strings are stored in a JSON file called appsettings.json, which I created in the SportsStore project using the ASP.NET Configuration File item template in the General section of the Add New Item window.

Visual Studio adds a placeholder connection string to the appsettings.json file when it creates the file, which I have replaced in Listing 8-17.

■ **Tip** Connection strings must be expressed as a single unbroken line, which is fine in the Visual Studio editor but doesn't fit on the printed page and explains the awkward formatting in Listing 8-17. When you define the connection string in your own project, make sure that the value of the ConnectionString item is on a single line.

Listing 8-17. Editing the Connection String in the appsettings.json File in the SportsStore Folder

```
{
  "Data": {
    "SportStoreProducts": {
      "ConnectionString": "Server=(localdb)\\MSSQLLocalDB;Database=SportsStore;Trusted_Conne
      ction=True;MultipleActiveResultSets=true"
    }
  }
}
```

Within the Data section of the configuration file, I have set the name of the connection string to SportsStoreProducts. The value of the ConnectionString item specifies that the LocalDB feature should be used for a database called SportsStore.

Configuring the Application

The next steps are to read the connection string and to configure the application to use it to connect to the database. Listing 8-18 shows the changes required to the Startup class required to receive details of the configuration data contained in the appsettings.json file and use it to configure Entity Framework Core. (The job of reading the JSON file is handled by the Program class, which I describe in Chapter 14).

Listing 8-18. Configuring the Application in the Startup.cs File in the SportsStore Folder

```
using System;
using System.Collections.Generic;
using System.Linq;
using System.Threading.Tasks;
using Microsoft.AspNetCore.Builder;
using Microsoft.AspNetCore.Hosting;
using Microsoft.AspNetCore.Http;
using Microsoft.Extensions.DependencyInjection;
using SportsStore.Models;
using Microsoft.Extensions.Configuration;
using Microsoft.EntityFrameworkCore;

namespace SportsStore {

    public class Startup {

        public Startup(IConfiguration configuration) =>
            Configuration = configuration;

        public IConfiguration Configuration { get; }

        public void ConfigureServices(IServiceCollection services) {
            services.AddDbContext<ApplicationDbContext>(options =>
                options.UseSqlServer(
                    Configuration["Data:SportStoreProducts:ConnectionString"]));
            services.AddTransient<IProductRepository, EFProductRepository>();
            services.AddMvc();
        }

        public void Configure(IApplicationBuilder app, IHostingEnvironment env) {
            app.UseDeveloperExceptionPage();
            app.UseStatusCodePages();
            app.UseStaticFiles();
            app.UseMvc(routes => {
                routes.MapRoute(
                    name: "default",
                    template: "{controller=Product}/{action=List}/{id?}");
            });
        }
    }
}
```

The constructor I added to the Startup class receives the configuration data loaded from the appsettings.json file, which is presented through an object that implements the IConfiguration interface. The constructor assigns the IConfiguration object to a property called Configuration so that it can be used by the rest of the Startup class.

I explain how to read and access configuration data in Chapter 14. For the SportsStore application, I have added a sequence of method calls that set up Entity Framework Core within the ConfigureServices method.

```
...
services.AddDbContext<ApplicationDbContext>(options =>
    options.UseSqlServer(Configuration["Data:SportStoreProducts:ConnectionString"]));
...
```

The AddDbContext extension method sets up the services provided by Entity Framework Core for the database context class I created in Listing 8-15. As I explain in Chapter 14, many of the methods that are used in the Startup class allow services and middleware features to be configured using options arguments. The argument to the AddDbContext method is a lambda expression that receives an options object that configures the database for the context class. In this case, I configured the database with the UseSqlServer method and specified the connection string, which is obtained from the Configuration property.

The next change I made in the Startup class was to replace the fake repository with the real one, like this:

```
...
services.AddTransient<IProductRepository, EFProductRepository>();
...
```

The components in the application that use the IProductRepository interface, which is just the Product controller at the moment, will receive an EFProductRepository object when they are created, which will provide them with access to the data in the database. I explain how this works in detail in Chapter 18, but the effect is that the fake data will be seamlessly replaced by the real data in the database without having to change the ProductController class.

Disabling Scope Verification

Using Entity Framework Core requires a configuration change to the dependency injection feature, which I describe in Chapter 18. The Program class is responsible for starting and configuring ASP.NET Core before handing control to the Startup class, and Listing 8-19 shows the change required. Without this change, an exception will be thrown when you try to create the database schema in the next section.

Listing 8-19. Preparing for Entity Framework Core in the Program.cs File in the SportsStore Folder

```
using System;
using System.Collections.Generic;
using System.IO;
using System.Linq;
using System.Threading.Tasks;
using Microsoft.AspNetCore;
using Microsoft.AspNetCore.Hosting;
using Microsoft.Extensions.Configuration;
using Microsoft.Extensions.Logging;
```

```
namespace SportsStore {
    public class Program {
        public static void Main(string[] args) {
            BuildWebHost(args).Run();
        }

        public static IWebHost BuildWebHost(string[] args) =>
            WebHost.CreateDefaultBuilder(args)
                .UseStartup<Startup>()
                .UseDefaultServiceProvider(options =>
                    options.ValidateScopes = false)
                .Build();
    }
}
```

I explain how ASP.NET Core is configured in detail in Chapter 14, but this is the only change to the Program class required by the SportsStore application.

Creating the Database Migration

Entity Framework Core is able to generate the schema for the database using the model classes through a feature called *migrations*. When you prepare a migration, EF Core creates a C# class that contains the SQL commands required to prepare the database. If you need to modify your model classes, then you can create a new migration that contains the SQL commands required to reflect the changes. In this way, you don't have to worry about manually writing and testing SQL commands and can just focus on the C# model classes in the application.

Entity Framework Core commands are performed from the command line. Open a new command prompt or PowerShell window, navigate to the SportsStore project folder (the one that contains the Startup.cs and appsettings.json files), and run the following command to create the migration class that will prepare the database for its first use:

```
dotnet ef migrations add Initial
```

When this command has finished, you will see a Migrations folder in the Visual Studio Solution Explorer window. This is where Entity Framework Core stores its migration classes. One of the file names will be a timestamp followed by _Initial.cs, and this is the class that will be used to create the initial schema for the database. If you examine the contents of this file, you can see how the Product model class has been used to create the schema.

WHAT ABOUT THE ADD-MIGRATION AND UPDATE-DATABASE COMMANDS?

If you are an experienced Entity Framework developer, you may be used to using the Add-Migration command to create a database migration and the Update-Database command to apply it to a database.

With the introduction of .NET Core, Entity Framework Core has added commands that are integrated into the dotnet command-line tool, using the Microsoft.EntityFrameworkCore.Tools.DotNet package added to the project in Listing 8-14. These are the commands that I have used in this chapter because they are consistent with other .NET commands and they can be used in any command prompt or PowerShell window, unlike the Add-Migration and Update-Database commands, which work only in a specific Visual Studio window.

Creating the Seed Data

To populate the database and provide some sample data, I added a class file called SeedData.cs to the Models folder and defined the class shown in Listing 8-20.

Listing 8-20. The Contents of the SeedData.cs File in the Models Folder

```
using System.Linq;
using Microsoft.AspNetCore.Builder;
using Microsoft.Extensions.DependencyInjection;
using Microsoft.EntityFrameworkCore;

namespace SportsStore.Models {

    public static class SeedData {

        public static void EnsurePopulated(IApplicationBuilder app) {
            ApplicationDbContext context = app.ApplicationServices
                .GetRequiredService<ApplicationDbContext>();
            context.Database.Migrate();
            if (!context.Products.Any()) {
                context.Products.AddRange(
                    new Product {
                        Name = "Kayak", Description = "A boat for one person",
                        Category = "Watersports", Price = 275 },
                    new Product {
                        Name = "Lifejacket",
                        Description = "Protective and fashionable",
                        Category = "Watersports", Price = 48.95m },
                    new Product {
                        Name = "Soccer Ball",
                        Description = "FIFA-approved size and weight",
                        Category = "Soccer", Price = 19.50m },
                    new Product {
                        Name = "Corner Flags",
                        Description = "Give your playing field a professional touch",
                        Category = "Soccer", Price = 34.95m },
                    new Product {
                        Name = "Stadium",
                        Description = "Flat-packed 35,000-seat stadium",
                        Category = "Soccer", Price = 79500 },
                    new Product {
                        Name = "Thinking Cap",
                        Description = "Improve brain efficiency by 75%",
                        Category = "Chess", Price = 16 },
                    new Product {
                        Name = "Unsteady Chair",
                        Description = "Secretly give your opponent a disadvantage",
                        Category = "Chess", Price = 29.95m },
                    new Product {
                        Name = "Human Chess Board",
                        Description = "A fun game for the family",
```

```
                        Category = "Chess", Price = 75 },
                new Product {
                    Name = "Bling-Bling King",
                    Description = "Gold-plated, diamond-studded King",
                    Category = "Chess", Price = 1200
                }
            );
            context.SaveChanges();
        }
    }
    }
}
```

The static EnsurePopulated method receives an IApplicationBuilder argument, which is the interface used in the Configure method of the Startup class to register middleware components to handle HTTP requests, and this is where I will ensure that the database has content.

The EnsurePopulated method obtains an ApplicationDbContext object through the IApplicationBuilder interface and calls the Database.Migrate method to ensure that the migration has been applied, which means that the database will be created and prepared so that it can store Product objects. Next, the number of Product objects in the database is checked. If there are no objects in the database, then the database is populated using a collection of Product objects using the AddRange method and then written to the database using the SaveChanges method.

The final change is to seed the database when the application starts, which I have done by adding a call to the EnsurePopulated method from the Startup class, as shown in Listing 8-21.

Listing 8-21. Seeding the Database in the Startup.cs File in the SportsStore Folder

```
using System;
using System.Collections.Generic;
using System.Linq;
using System.Threading.Tasks;
using Microsoft.AspNetCore.Builder;
using Microsoft.AspNetCore.Hosting;
using Microsoft.AspNetCore.Http;
using Microsoft.Extensions.DependencyInjection;
using SportsStore.Models;
using Microsoft.Extensions.Configuration;
using Microsoft.EntityFrameworkCore;

namespace SportsStore {

    public class Startup {

        public Startup(IConfiguration configuration) =>
            Configuration = configuration;

        public IConfiguration Configuration { get; }
```

```
public void ConfigureServices(IServiceCollection services) {
    services.AddDbContext<ApplicationDbContext>(options =>
        options.UseSqlServer(
            Configuration["Data:SportStoreProducts:ConnectionString"]));
    services.AddTransient<IProductRepository, EFProductRepository>();
    services.AddMvc();
}

public void Configure(IApplicationBuilder app, IHostingEnvironment env) {
    app.UseDeveloperExceptionPage();
    app.UseStatusCodePages();
    app.UseStaticFiles();
    app.UseMvc(routes => {
        routes.MapRoute(
            name: "default",
            template: "{controller=Product}/{action=List}/{id?}");
    });
    SeedData.EnsurePopulated(app);
}
}
}
```

Start the application, and the database will be created and seeded and used to provide the application with its data. (Be patient; it can take a moment for the database to be created).

When the browser requests the default URL for the application, the application configuration tells MVC that it needs to create a Product controller to handle the request. Creating a new Product controller means invoking the ProductController constructor, which requires an object that implements the IProductRepository interface, and the new configuration tells MVC that an EFProductRepository object should be created and used for this. The EFProductRepository object taps into the Entity Framework Core functionality that loads data from SQL Server and converts it into Product objects. All of this is hidden from the ProductController class, which just receives an object that implements the IProductRepository interface and works with the data it provides. The result is that the browser window shows the sample data in the database, as illustrated in Figure 8-8.

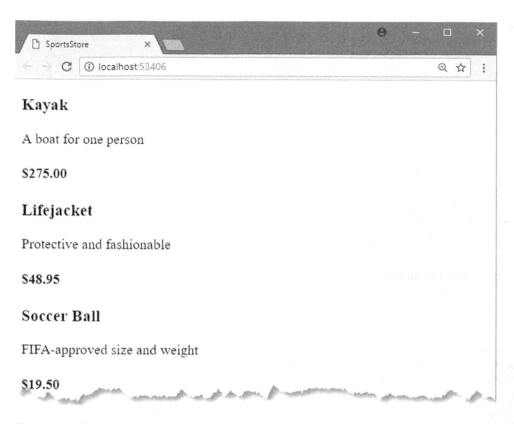

Figure 8-8. *Using the database repository*

This approach to getting Entity Framework Core to present a SQL Server database as a series of model objects is simple and easy to work with, and it allows me to keep my focus on ASP.NET Core MVC. I am skipping over a lot of the detail in how EF Core operates and the huge number of configuration options that are available. I like Entity Framework Core a lot, and I recommend that you spend some time getting to know it in detail. A good place to start is the Microsoft site for Entity Framework Core (http://ef.readthedocs.io) or my forthcoming book on Entity Framework Core, which will be published by Apress.

Adding Pagination

You can see from Figure 8-8 that the List.cshtml view displays the products in the database on a single page. In this section, I will add support for pagination so that the view displays a smaller number of products on a page and the user can move from page to page to view the overall catalog. To do this, I am going to add a parameter to the List method in the Product controller, as shown in Listing 8-22.

Listing 8-22. Adding Pagination in the ProductController.cs File in the Controllers Folder

```
using Microsoft.AspNetCore.Mvc;
using SportsStore.Models;
using System.Linq;
```

```
namespace SportsStore.Controllers {

    public class ProductController : Controller {
        private IProductRepository repository;
        public int PageSize = 4;

        public ProductController(IProductRepository repo) {
            repository = repo;
        }

        public ViewResult List(int productPage = 1)
            => View(repository.Products
                .OrderBy(p => p.ProductID)
                .Skip((productPage - 1) * PageSize)
                .Take(PageSize));
    }
}
```

The PageSize field specifies that I want four products per page. I have added an optional parameter to the List method, which means that if I call the method without a parameter (List()), my call is treated as though I had supplied the value specified in the parameter definition (List(1)). The effect is that the action method displays the first page of products when MVC invokes it without an argument. Within the body of the action method, I get the Product objects, order them by the primary key, skip over the products that occur before the start of the current page, and take the number of products specified by the PageSize field.

UNIT TEST: PAGINATION

I can unit test the pagination feature by creating a mock repository, injecting it into the constructor of the ProductController class, and then calling the List method to request a specific page. I can then compare the Product objects I get with what I would expect from the test data in the mock implementation. See Chapter 7 for details of how to set up unit tests. Here is the unit test I created for this purpose, in a class file called ProductControllerTests.cs that I added to the SportsStore. Tests project:

```
using System.Collections.Generic;
using System.Linq;
using Moq;
using SportsStore.Controllers;
using SportsStore.Models;
using Xunit;

namespace SportsStore.Tests {

    public class ProductControllerTests {

        [Fact]
        public void Can_Paginate() {
            // Arrange
            Mock<IProductRepository> mock = new Mock<IProductRepository>();
```

```
        mock.Setup(m => m.Products).Returns((new Product[] {
            new Product {ProductID = 1, Name = "P1"},
            new Product {ProductID = 2, Name = "P2"},
            new Product {ProductID = 3, Name = "P3"},
            new Product {ProductID = 4, Name = "P4"},
            new Product {ProductID = 5, Name = "P5"}
        }).AsQueryable<Product>());

        ProductController controller = new ProductController(mock.Object);
        controller.PageSize = 3;

        // Act
        IEnumerable<Product> result =
            controller.List(2).ViewData.Model as IEnumerable<Product>;

        // Assert
        Product[] prodArray = result.ToArray();
        Assert.True(prodArray.Length == 2);
        Assert.Equal("P4", prodArray[0].Name);
        Assert.Equal("P5", prodArray[1].Name);
    }
  }
}
```

It is a little awkward to get the data returned from the action method. The result is a `ViewResult` object, and I have to cast the value of its `ViewData.Model` property to the expected data type. I explain the different result types that can be returned by action methods and how to work with them in Chapter 17.

Displaying Page Links

If you run the application, you will see that there are now four items shown on the page. If you want to view another page, you can append query string parameters to the end of the URL, like this:

```
http://localhost:5000/?productPage=2
```

You will need to change the port part of the URL to match whatever port has been assigned to your project. Using these query strings, you can navigate through the catalog of products.

There is no way for customers to figure out that these query string parameters exist, and even if there were, they are not going to want to navigate this way. Instead, I need to render some page links at the bottom of each list of products so that customers can navigate between pages. To do this, I am going to create a *tag helper*, which generates the HTML markup for the links I require.

Adding the View Model

To support the tag helper, I am going to pass information to the view about the number of pages available, the current page, and the total number of products in the repository. The easiest way to do this is to create a view model class, which is used specifically to pass data between a controller and a view. I created a `Models/ViewModels` folder in the `SportsStore` project and added to it a class file called `PagingInfo.cs` defined in Listing 8-23.

Listing 8-23. The Contents of the PagingInfo.cs File in the Models/ViewModels Folder

```
using System;

namespace SportsStore.Models.ViewModels {

    public class PagingInfo {
        public int TotalItems { get; set; }
        public int ItemsPerPage { get; set; }
        public int CurrentPage { get; set; }

        public int TotalPages =>
            (int)Math.Ceiling((decimal)TotalItems / ItemsPerPage);
    }
}
```

Adding the Tag Helper Class

Now that I have a view model, I can create a tag helper class. I created the Infrastructure folder in the SportsStore project and added to it a class file called PageLinkTagHelper.cs, which I used to define the class shown in Listing 8-24. Tag helpers are a big part of ASP.NET Core MVC, and I explain how they work and how to create them in Chapters 23, 24, and 25.

■ **Tip** The Infrastructure folder is where I put classes that deliver the plumbing for an application but that are not related to the application's domain.

Listing 8-24. The Contents of the PageLinkTagHelper.cs File in the Infrastructure Folder

```
using Microsoft.AspNetCore.Mvc;
using Microsoft.AspNetCore.Mvc.Rendering;
using Microsoft.AspNetCore.Mvc.Routing;
using Microsoft.AspNetCore.Mvc.ViewFeatures;
using Microsoft.AspNetCore.Razor.TagHelpers;
using SportsStore.Models.ViewModels;

namespace SportsStore.Infrastructure {

    [HtmlTargetElement("div", Attributes = "page-model")]
    public class PageLinkTagHelper : TagHelper {
        private IUrlHelperFactory urlHelperFactory;

        public PageLinkTagHelper(IUrlHelperFactory helperFactory) {
            urlHelperFactory = helperFactory;
        }

        [ViewContext]
        [HtmlAttributeNotBound]
```

```
    public ViewContext ViewContext { get; set; }

    public PagingInfo PageModel { get; set; }

    public string PageAction { get; set; }

    public override void Process(TagHelperContext context,
            TagHelperOutput output) {
        IUrlHelper urlHelper = urlHelperFactory.GetUrlHelper(ViewContext);
        TagBuilder result = new TagBuilder("div");
        for (int i = 1; i <= PageModel.TotalPages; i++) {
            TagBuilder tag = new TagBuilder("a");
            tag.Attributes["href"] = urlHelper.Action(PageAction,
                new { productPage = i });
            tag.InnerHtml.Append(i.ToString());
            result.InnerHtml.AppendHtml(tag);
        }
        output.Content.AppendHtml(result.InnerHtml);
    }
}
}
```

This tag helper populates a div element with a elements that correspond to pages of products. I am not going to go into detail about tag helpers now; it is enough to know that they are one of the most useful ways that you can introduce C# logic into your views. The code for a tag helper can look tortured because C# and HTML don't mix easily. But using tag helpers is preferable to including blocks of C# code in a view because a tag helper can be easily unit tested.

Most MVC components, such as controllers and views, are discovered automatically, but tag helpers have to be registered. In Listing 8-25, I have added a statement to the _ViewImports.cshtml file in the Views folder that tells MVC to look for tag helper classes in the SportsStore.Infrastructure namespace. I also added a @using expression so that I can refer to the view model classes in views without having to qualify their names with the namespace.

Listing 8-25. Registering a Tag Helper in the _ViewImports.cshtml File in the Views/Shared Folder

```
@using SportsStore.Models
@using SportsStore.Models.ViewModels
@addTagHelper *, Microsoft.AspNetCore.Mvc.TagHelpers
@addTagHelper SportsStore.Infrastructure.*, SportsStore
```

UNIT TEST: CREATING PAGE LINKS

To test the PageLinkTagHelper tag helper class, I call the Process method with test data and provide a TagHelperOutput object that I inspect to see the HTML that is generated, as follows, which I defined in a new PageLinkTagHelperTests.cs file in the SportsStore.Tests project:

```
using System.Collections.Generic;
using System.Threading.Tasks;
using Microsoft.AspNetCore.Mvc;
using Microsoft.AspNetCore.Mvc.Routing;
using Microsoft.AspNetCore.Razor.TagHelpers;
```

```csharp
using Moq;
using SportsStore.Infrastructure;
using SportsStore.Models.ViewModels;
using Xunit;

namespace SportsStore.Tests {

    public class PageLinkTagHelperTests {

        [Fact]
        public void Can_Generate_Page_Links() {
            // Arrange
            var urlHelper = new Mock<IUrlHelper>();
            urlHelper.SetupSequence(x => x.Action(It.IsAny<UrlActionContext>()))
                .Returns("Test/Page1")
                .Returns("Test/Page2")
                .Returns("Test/Page3");

            var urlHelperFactory = new Mock<IUrlHelperFactory>();
            urlHelperFactory.Setup(f =>
                    f.GetUrlHelper(It.IsAny<ActionContext>()))
                        .Returns(urlHelper.Object);

            PageLinkTagHelper helper =
                    new PageLinkTagHelper(urlHelperFactory.Object) {
                PageModel = new PagingInfo {
                    CurrentPage = 2,
                    TotalItems = 28,
                    ItemsPerPage = 10
                },
                PageAction = "Test"
            };

            TagHelperContext ctx = new TagHelperContext(
                new TagHelperAttributeList(),
                new Dictionary<object, object>(), "");

            var content = new Mock<TagHelperContent>();
            TagHelperOutput output = new TagHelperOutput("div",
                new TagHelperAttributeList(),
                (cache, encoder) => Task.FromResult(content.Object));

            // Act
            helper.Process(ctx, output);

            // Assert
            Assert.Equal(@"<a href=""Test/Page1"">1</a>"
                + @"<a href=""Test/Page2"">2</a>"
                + @"<a href=""Test/Page3"">3</a>",
                 output.Content.GetContent());
        }
    }
}
```

The complexity in this test is in creating the objects that are required to create and use a tag helper. Tag helpers use IUrlHelperFactory objects to generate URLs that target different parts of the application, and I have used Moq to create an implementation of this interface and the related IUrlHelper interface that provides test data.

The core part of the test verifies the tag helper output by using a literal string value that contains double quotes. C# is perfectly capable of working with such strings, as long as the string is prefixed with @ and uses two sets of double quotes ("") in place of one set of double quotes. You must remember not to break the literal string into separate lines unless the string you are comparing to is similarly broken. For example, the literal I use in the test method has wrapped onto several lines because the width of a printed page is narrow. I have not added a newline character; if I did, the test would fail.

Adding the View Model Data

I am not quite ready to use the tag helper because I have yet to provide an instance of the PagingInfo view model class to the view. I could do this using the view bag feature, but I would rather wrap all of the data I am going to send from the controller to the view in a single view model class. To do this, I added a class file called ProductsListViewModel.cs to the Models/ViewModels folder of the SportsStore project. Listing 8-26 shows the contents of the new file.

Listing 8-26. The Contents of the ProductsListViewModel.cs File in the Models/ViewModels Folder

```
using System.Collections.Generic;
using SportsStore.Models;

namespace SportsStore.Models.ViewModels {

    public class ProductsListViewModel {
        public IEnumerable<Product> Products { get; set; }
        public PagingInfo PagingInfo { get; set; }
    }
}
```

I can update the List action method in the ProductController class to use the ProductsListViewModel class to provide the view with details of the products to display on the page and details of the pagination, as shown in Listing 8-27.

Listing 8-27. Updating the List Method in the ProductController.cs File in the Controllers Folder

```
using Microsoft.AspNetCore.Mvc;
using SportsStore.Models;
using System.Linq;
using SportsStore.Models.ViewModels;

namespace SportsStore.Controllers {

    public class ProductController : Controller {
        private IProductRepository repository;
        public int PageSize = 4;
```

```
    public ProductController(IProductRepository repo) {
        repository = repo;
    }

    public ViewResult List(int productPage = 1)
        => View(new ProductsListViewModel {
            Products = repository.Products
                .OrderBy(p => p.ProductID)
                .Skip((productPage - 1) * PageSize)
                .Take(PageSize),
            PagingInfo = new PagingInfo {
                CurrentPage = productPage,
                ItemsPerPage = PageSize,
                TotalItems = repository.Products.Count()
            }
        });
    }
}
```

These changes pass a ProductsListViewModel object as the model data to the view.

UNIT TEST: PAGE MODEL VIEW DATA

I need to ensure that the controller sends the correct pagination data to the view. Here is the unit test I added to the ProductControllerTests class in the test project to make sure:

```
...
[Fact]
public void Can_Send_Pagination_View_Model() {

    // Arrange
    Mock<IProductRepository> mock = new Mock<IProductRepository>();
    mock.Setup(m => m.Products).Returns((new Product[] {
        new Product {ProductID = 1, Name = "P1"},
        new Product {ProductID = 2, Name = "P2"},
        new Product {ProductID = 3, Name = "P3"},
        new Product {ProductID = 4, Name = "P4"},
        new Product {ProductID = 5, Name = "P5"}
    }).AsQueryable<Product>());

    // Arrange
    ProductController controller =
        new ProductController(mock.Object) { PageSize = 3 };

    // Act
    ProductsListViewModel result =
        controller.List(2).ViewData.Model as ProductsListViewModel;

    // Assert
    PagingInfo pageInfo = result.PagingInfo;
```

```
        Assert.Equal(2, pageInfo.CurrentPage);
        Assert.Equal(3, pageInfo.ItemsPerPage);
        Assert.Equal(5, pageInfo.TotalItems);
        Assert.Equal(2, pageInfo.TotalPages);
}
...
```

I also need to modify the earlier pagination unit test, contained in the Can_Paginate method. It relies on the List action method returning a ViewResult whose Model property is a sequence of Product objects, but I have wrapped that data inside another view model type. Here is the revised test:

```
...
[Fact]
public void Can_Paginate() {
    // Arrange
    Mock<IProductRepository> mock = new Mock<IProductRepository>();
    mock.Setup(m => m.Products).Returns((new Product[] {
        new Product {ProductID = 1, Name = "P1"},
        new Product {ProductID = 2, Name = "P2"},
        new Product {ProductID = 3, Name = "P3"},
        new Product {ProductID = 4, Name = "P4"},
        new Product {ProductID = 5, Name = "P5"}
    }).AsQueryable<Product>());

    ProductController controller = new ProductController(mock.Object);
    controller.PageSize = 3;

    // Act
    ProductsListViewModel result =
        controller.List(2).ViewData.Model as ProductsListViewModel;

    // Assert
    Product[] prodArray = result.Products.ToArray();
    Assert.True(prodArray.Length == 2);
    Assert.Equal("P4", prodArray[0].Name);
    Assert.Equal("P5", prodArray[1].Name);
}
...
```

I would usually create a common setup method, given the degree of duplication between these two test methods. However, since I am delivering the unit tests in individual sidebars like this one, I am going to keep everything separate so you can see each test on its own.

The view is currently expecting a sequence of Product objects, so I need to update the List.cshtml file, as shown in Listing 8-28, to deal with the new view model type.

Listing 8-28. Updating the List.cshtml File in the Views/Product Folder

@model ProductsListViewModel

@foreach (var p in Model.Products) {
        <div>
            <h3>@p.Name</h3>
            @p.Description
            <h4>@p.Price.ToString("c")</h4>
        </div>
}

I have changed the @model directive to tell Razor that I am now working with a different data type. I updated the foreach loop so that the data source is the Products property of the model data.

Displaying the Page Links

I have everything in place to add the page links to the List view. I created the view model that contains the paging information, updated the controller so that it passes this information to the view, and changed the @model directive to match the new model view type. All that remains is to add an HTML element that the tag help will process to create the page links, as shown in Listing 8-29.

Listing 8-29. Adding the Pagination Links in the List.cshtml File in the Views/Product Folder

```
@model ProductsListViewModel

@foreach (var p in Model.Products) {
    <div>
        <h3>@p.Name</h3>
        @p.Description
        <h4>@p.Price.ToString("c")</h4>
    </div>
}
```

<div page-model="@Model.PagingInfo" page-action="List"></div>

If you run the application, you will see the new page links, as illustrated in Figure 8-9. The style is still basic, which I will fix later in the chapter. What is important for the moment is that the links take the user from page to page in the catalog and allow for exploration of the products for sale. When Razor finds the page-model attribute on the div element, it asks the PageLinkTagHelper class to transform the element, which produces the set of links shown in the figure.

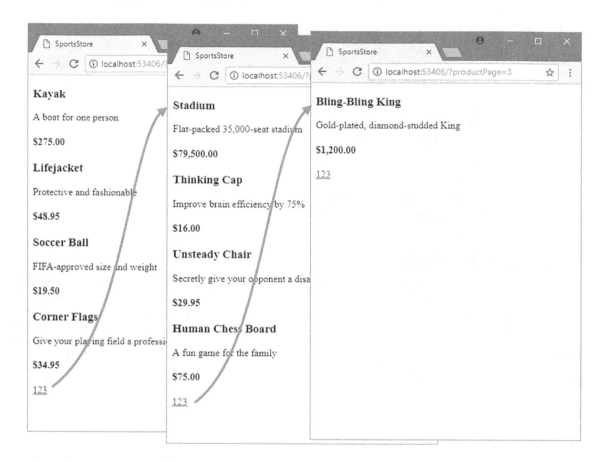

Figure 8-9. *Displaying page navigation links*

WHY NOT JUST USE A GRIDVIEW?

If you have worked with ASP.NET before, you might think that was a lot of work for an unimpressive result. It has taken me pages and pages just to get a simple paginated product list. If I were using Web Forms, I could have done the same thing using the ASP.NET Web Forms GridView or ListView control, right out of the box, by hooking them up directly to the Products database table.

What I have accomplished in this chapter may not look like much, but it is profoundly different from dragging a control onto a design surface. First, I am building an application with a sound and maintainable architecture that involves proper separation of concerns. Unlike the simplest use of the ListView control, I have not directly coupled the UI and the database, which is an approach that gives quick results but that causes pain and misery over time. Second, I have been creating unit tests as I go, and these allow me to validate the behavior of the application in a natural way that is nearly impossible with a complex Web Forms control. Finally, bear in mind that I have given over a lot of this chapter to the process of creating the underlying infrastructure on which I am building the application. I need to define and implement the repository only once, for example, and now that I have, I will be able to build and test new features quickly and easily, as the following chapters will demonstrate.

None of this detracts from the immediate results that Web Forms can deliver, of course, but as I explained in Chapter 3, that immediacy comes with a cost that can be expensive and painful in large and complex projects.

Improving the URLs

I have the page links working, but they still use the query string to pass page information to the server, like this:

```
http://localhost/?productPage=2
```

I can create URLs that are more appealing by creating a scheme that follows the pattern of *composable URLs*. A composable URL is one that makes sense to the user, like this one:

```
http://localhost/Page2
```

MVC makes it easy to change the URL scheme in an application because it uses the ASP.NET Core *routing* feature, which is responsible for processing URLs to figure out what part of the application they target. All I need to do is add a new route when registering the MVC middleware in the Configure method of the Startup class, as shown in Listing 8-30.

Listing 8-30. Adding a New Route in the Startup.cs File in the SportsStore Folder

```csharp
using System;
using System.Collections.Generic;
using System.Linq;
using System.Threading.Tasks;
using Microsoft.AspNetCore.Builder;
using Microsoft.AspNetCore.Hosting;
using Microsoft.AspNetCore.Http;
using Microsoft.Extensions.DependencyInjection;
using SportsStore.Models;
using Microsoft.Extensions.Configuration;
using Microsoft.EntityFrameworkCore;

namespace SportsStore {

    public class Startup {

        public Startup(IConfiguration configuration) =>
            Configuration = configuration;

        public IConfiguration Configuration { get; }

        public void ConfigureServices(IServiceCollection services) {
            services.AddDbContext<ApplicationDbContext>(options =>
                options.UseSqlServer(
                    Configuration["Data:SportStoreProducts:ConnectionString"]));
```

```
        services.AddTransient<IProductRepository, EFProductRepository>();
        services.AddMvc();
    }

    public void Configure(IApplicationBuilder app, IHostingEnvironment env) {
        app.UseDeveloperExceptionPage();
        app.UseStatusCodePages();
        app.UseStaticFiles();
        app.UseMvc(routes => {
            routes.MapRoute(
                name: "pagination",
                template: "Products/Page{productPage}",
                defaults: new { Controller = "Product", action = "List" });

            routes.MapRoute(
                name: "default",
                template: "{controller=Product}/{action=List}/{id?}");
        });
        SeedData.EnsurePopulated(app);
    }
  }
}
```

It is important that you add the new route before the Default one that is already in the method. As you will learn in Chapter 15, the routing system processes routes in the order they are listed, and I need the new route to take precedence over the existing one.

This is the only alteration required to change the URL scheme for product pagination. MVC and the routing function are tightly integrated, so the application automatically reflects a change like this in the URLs used by the application, including those generated by tag helpers like the one I use to generate the page navigation links. Do not worry if routing does not make sense to you now. I explain it in detail in Chapters 15 and 16.

If you run the application and click a pagination link, you will see the new URL scheme in action, as illustrated in Figure 8-10.

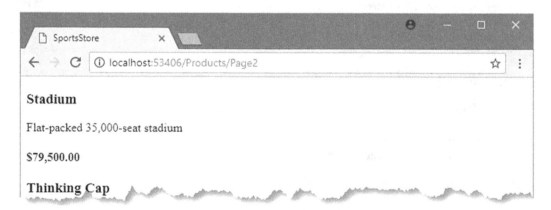

Figure 8-10. *The new URL scheme displayed in the browser*

Styling the Content

I have built a great deal of infrastructure and the basic features of the application are starting to come together, but I have not paid any attention to appearance. Even though this book is not about design or CSS, the SportsStore application design is so miserably plain that it undermines its technical strengths. In this section, I will put some of that right. I am going to implement a classic two-column layout with a header, as shown in Figure 8-11.

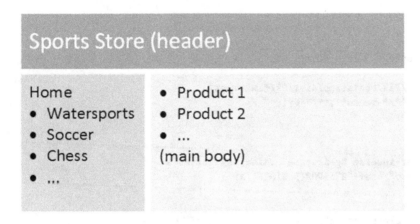

Figure 8-11. *The design goal for the SportsStore application*

Installing the Bootstrap Package

I am going to use the Bootstrap package to provide the CSS styles I will apply to the application. I will rely on the Visual Studio support for Bower to install the Bootstrap package for me, so I selected the Bower Configuration File item template from the General category of the Add New Item dialog to create a file called bower.json in the SportsStore project, as demonstrated in Chapter 6. I then added the Bootstrap package to the dependencies section of the file that was created, as shown in Listing 8-31. As explained previously, I am using a prerelease version of Bootstrap for the examples in this book.

Listing 8-31. Adding Bootstrap to the bower.json File in the SportsStore Project

```
{
  "name": "asp.net",
  "private": true,
  "dependencies": {
    "bootstrap": "4.0.0-alpha.6"
  }
}
```

When the changes to the bower.json file are saved, Visual Studio uses Bower to download the Bootstrap package into the wwwroot/lib/bootstrap folder. Bootstrap depends on the jQuery package, and this will be automatically added to the project as well.

Applying Bootstrap Styles to the Layout

In Chapter 5, I explained how Razor layouts work, how they are used, and how they incorporate layouts. The view start file that I added at the start of the chapter specified that a file called _Layout.cshtml should be used as the default layout, and that is where the initial Bootstrap styling will be applied, as shown in Listing 8-32.

Listing 8-32. Applying Bootstrap CSS to the _Layout.cshtml File in the Views/Shared Folder

```
<!DOCTYPE html>

<html>
<head>
    <meta name="viewport" content="width=device-width" />
    <link rel="stylesheet"
        asp-href-include="/lib/bootstrap/dist/**/*.min.css"
        asp-href-exclude="**/*-reboot*,**/*-grid*" />
    <title>SportsStore</title>
</head>
<body>
    <div class="navbar navbar-inverse bg-inverse" role="navigation">
        <a class="navbar-brand" href="#">SPORTS STORE</a>
    </div>
    <div class="row m-1 p-1">
        <div id="categories" class="col-3">
            Put something useful here later
        </div>
        <div class="col-9">
            @RenderBody()
        </div>
    </div>
</body>
</html>
```

The link element in this listing has asp-href-include and asp-href-exclude attributes, which represents an example of a built-in tag helper class. In this case, the tag helper looks at the value of the attributes and generates link elements for all the files that match the path specified by the include attribute and by the paths specified by the exclude attributes. The paths used by the attributes can contain wildcards, which makes this a useful feature to ensure that you can add and remove files from the wwwroot folder structure without breaking the application. But, as I explain in Chapter 25, caution is required to make sure that the paths you specify select only the files you expect.

Adding the Bootstrap CSS stylesheet to the layout means that I can use the styles it defines in any of the views that rely on the layout. In Listing 8-33, you can see the styling I applied to the List.cshtml file.

Listing 8-33. Styling Content in the List.cshtml File in the Views/Product Folder

```
@model ProductsListViewModel

@foreach (var p in Model.Products) {
    <div class="card card-outline-primary m-1 p-1">
        <div class="bg-faded p-1">
            <h4>
                @p.Name
```

```html
        <span class="badge badge-pill badge-primary" style="float:right">
            <small>@p.Price.ToString("c")</small>
        </span>
    </h4>
    </div>
    <div class="card-text p-1">@p.Description</div>
</div>
}

<div page-model="@Model.PagingInfo" page-action="List" page-classes-enabled="true"
    page-class="btn" page-class-normal="btn-secondary"
    page-class-selected="btn-primary" class="btn-group pull-right m-1">
</div>
```

I need to style the buttons that are generated by the PageLinkTagHelper class, but I don't want to hardwire the Bootstrap classes into the C# code because it makes it harder to reuse the tag helper elsewhere in the application or change the appearance of the buttons. Instead, I have defined custom attributes on the div element that specify the classes that I require, and these correspond to properties I added to the tag helper class, which are then used to style the a elements that are produced, as shown in Listing 8-34.

Listing 8-34. Adding Classes to Generated Elements in the PageLinkTagHelper.cs File

```csharp
using Microsoft.AspNetCore.Mvc;
using Microsoft.AspNetCore.Mvc.Rendering;
using Microsoft.AspNetCore.Mvc.Routing;
using Microsoft.AspNetCore.Mvc.ViewFeatures;
using Microsoft.AspNetCore.Razor.TagHelpers;
using SportsStore.Models.ViewModels;

namespace SportsStore.Infrastructure {

    [HtmlTargetElement("div", Attributes = "page-model")]
    public class PageLinkTagHelper : TagHelper {
        private IUrlHelperFactory urlHelperFactory;

        public PageLinkTagHelper(IUrlHelperFactory helperFactory) {
            urlHelperFactory = helperFactory;
        }

        [ViewContext]
        [HtmlAttributeNotBound]
        public ViewContext ViewContext { get; set; }

        public PagingInfo PageModel { get; set; }

        public string PageAction { get; set; }

        public bool PageClassesEnabled { get; set; } = false;
        public string PageClass { get; set; }
        public string PageClassNormal { get; set; }
        public string PageClassSelected { get; set; }
```

```
    public override void Process(TagHelperContext context,
            TagHelperOutput output) {
        IUrlHelper urlHelper = urlHelperFactory.GetUrlHelper(ViewContext);
        TagBuilder result = new TagBuilder("div");
        for (int i = 1; i <= PageModel.TotalPages; i++) {
            TagBuilder tag = new TagBuilder("a");
            tag.Attributes["href"] = urlHelper.Action(PageAction,
                new { productPage = i });
            if (PageClassesEnabled) {
                tag.AddCssClass(PageClass);
                tag.AddCssClass(i == PageModel.CurrentPage
                    ? PageClassSelected : PageClassNormal);
            }
            tag.InnerHtml.Append(i.ToString());
            result.InnerHtml.AppendHtml(tag);
        }
        output.Content.AppendHtml(result.InnerHtml);
    }
  }
}
```

The values of the attributes are automatically used to set the tag helper property values, with the mapping between the HTML attribute name format (page-class-normal) and the C# property name format (PageClassNormal) taken into account. This allows tag helpers to respond differently based on the attributes of an HTML element, creating a more flexible way to generate content in an MVC application.

If you run the application, you will see that the appearance of the application has been improved—at least a little, anyway—as illustrated by Figure 8-12.

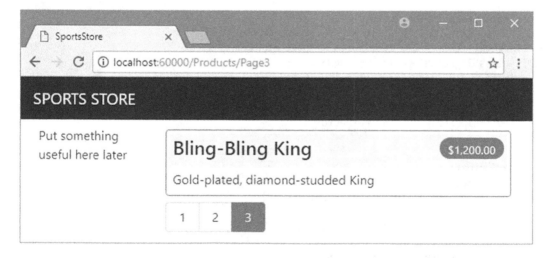

Figure 8-12. *The design-enhanced SportsStore application*

Creating a Partial View

As a finishing flourish for this chapter, I am going to refactor the application to simplify the List.cshtml view. I am going to create a *partial view*, which is a fragment of content that you can embed into another view, rather like a template. I describe partial views in detail in Chapter 21, and they help reduce duplication when you need the same content to appear in different places in an application. Rather than copy and paste the same Razor markup into multiple views, you can define it once in a partial view. To create the partial view, I added a Razor view file called ProductSummary.cshtml to the Views/Shared folder and added the markup shown in Listing 8-35.

Listing 8-35. The Contents of the ProductSummary.cshtml File in the Views/Shared Folder

```
@model Product

<div class="card card-outline-primary m-1 p-1">
    <div class="bg-faded p-1">
        <h4>
            @Model.Name
            <span class="badge badge-pill badge-primary" style="float:right">
                <small>@Model.Price.ToString("c")</small>
            </span>
        </h4>
    </div>
    <div class="card-text p-1">@Model.Description</div>
</div>
```

Now I need to update the List.cshtml file in the Views/Products folder so that it uses the partial view, as shown in Listing 8-36.

Listing 8-36. Using a Partial View in the List.cshtml File

```
@model ProductsListViewModel

@foreach (var p in Model.Products) {
    @Html.Partial("ProductSummary", p)
}

<div page-model="@Model.PagingInfo" page-action="List" page-classes-enabled="true"
    page-class="btn" page-class-normal="btn-secondary"
    page-class-selected="btn-primary" class="btn-group pull-right m-1">
</div>
```

I have taken the markup that was previously in the foreach loop in the List.cshtml view and moved it to the new partial view. I call the partial view using the Html.Partial helper method, with arguments for the name of the view and the view model object. Switching to a partial view like this is good practice because it allows the same markup to be inserted into any view that needs to display a summary of a product. As Figure 8-13 shows, adding the partial view doesn't change the appearance of the application; it just changes where Razor finds the content that is used to generate the response sent to the browser.

Figure 8-13. *Applying a partial view*

Summary

In this chapter, I built the core infrastructure for the SportsStore application. It does not have many features that you could demonstrate to a client at this point, but behind the scenes, there are the beginnings of a domain model with a product repository backed by SQL Server and Entity Framework Core. There is a single controller, ProductController, that can produce paginated lists of products, and I have set up a clean and friendly URL scheme.

If this chapter felt like a lot of setup for little benefit, then the next chapter will balance the equation. Now that the fundamental structure is in place, we can forge ahead and add all the customer-facing features: navigation by category, a shopping cart, and the start of a checkout process.

CHAPTER 9

■ ■ ■

SportsStore: Navigation

In this chapter, I continue to build out the SportsStore example app. In this chapter, I add support for navigating around the application and start building a shopping cart.

Adding Navigation Controls

The SportsStore application will be more useful if customers can navigate products by category. I will do this in three phases.

- Enhance the List action model in the ProductController class so that it is able to filter the Product objects in the repository

- Revisit and enhance the URL scheme

- Create a category list that will go into the sidebar of the site, highlighting the current category and linking to others

Filtering the Product List

I am going to start by enhancing the view model class, ProductsListViewModel, which I added to the SportsStore project in the previous chapter. I need to communicate the current category to the view in order to render the sidebar, and this is as good a place to start as any. Listing 9-1 shows the changes I made to the ProductsListViewModel.cs file in the Models/ViewModels folder.

Listing 9-1. Adding a Property in the ProductsListViewModel .cs File in the Models/ViewModels Folder

```
using System.Collections.Generic;
using SportsStore.Models;

namespace SportsStore.Models.ViewModels {

    public class ProductsListViewModel {
        public IEnumerable<Product> Products { get; set; }
        public PagingInfo PagingInfo { get; set; }
        public string CurrentCategory { get; set; }
    }
}
```

© Adam Freeman 2017

A. Freeman, *Pro ASP.NET Core MVC 2*, https://doi.org/10.1007/978-1-4842-3150-0_9

I added a property called CurrentCategory. The next step is to update the Product controller so that the List action method will filter Product objects by category and use the new property I added to the view model to indicate which category has been selected. Listing 9-2 shows the changes.

Listing 9-2. Adding Category Support to the List Action in the ProductController.cs File in the Controllers

```
using Microsoft.AspNetCore.Mvc;
using SportsStore.Models;
using System.Linq;
using SportsStore.Models.ViewModels;

namespace SportsStore.Controllers {

    public class ProductController : Controller {
        private IProductRepository repository;
        public int PageSize = 4;

        public ProductController(IProductRepository repo) {
            repository = repo;
        }

        public ViewResult List(string category, int productPage = 1)
            => View(new ProductsListViewModel {
                Products = repository.Products
                    .Where(p => category == null || p.Category == category)
                    .OrderBy(p => p.ProductID)
                    .Skip((productPage - 1) * PageSize)
                    .Take(PageSize),
                PagingInfo = new PagingInfo {
                    CurrentPage = productPage,
                    ItemsPerPage = PageSize,
                    TotalItems = repository.Products.Count()
                },
                CurrentCategory = category
            });
    }
}
```

I made three changes to the action method. First, I added a parameter called category. This category parameter is used by the second change in the listing, which is an enhancement to the LINQ query: if category is not null, only those Product objects with a matching Category property are selected. The last change is to set the value of the CurrentCategory property I added to the ProductsListViewModel class. However, these changes mean that the value of PagingInfo.TotalItems is incorrectly calculated because it doesn't take the category filter into account. I will fix this in a while.

UNIT TEST: UPDATING EXISTING UNIT TESTS

I changed the signature of the List action method, which will prevent some of the existing unit test methods from compiling. To address this, I need to pass null as the first parameter to the List method in those unit tests that work with the controller. For example, in the Can_Paginate test in the ProductControllerTests.cs file, the action section of the unit test becomes as follows:

```
...
[Fact]
public void Can_Paginate() {
    // Arrange
    Mock<IProductRepository> mock = new Mock<IProductRepository>();
    mock.Setup(m => m.Products).Returns((new Product[] {
        new Product {ProductID = 1, Name = "P1"},
        new Product {ProductID = 2, Name = "P2"},
        new Product {ProductID = 3, Name = "P3"},
        new Product {ProductID = 4, Name = "P4"},
        new Product {ProductID = 5, Name = "P5"}
    }).AsQueryable<Product>());

    ProductController controller = new ProductController(mock.Object);
    controller.PageSize = 3;

    // Act
    ProductsListViewModel result =
        controller.List(null, 2).ViewData.Model as ProductsListViewModel;

    // Assert
    Product[] prodArray = result.Products.ToArray();
    Assert.True(prodArray.Length == 2);
    Assert.Equal("P4", prodArray[0].Name);
    Assert.Equal("P5", prodArray[1].Name);
}
...
```

By using null for the category argument, I receive all the Product objects that the controller gets from the repository, which is the same situation I had before adding the new parameter. I need to make the same change to the Can_Send_Pagination_View_Model test.

```
...
[Fact]
public void Can_Send_Pagination_View_Model() {
```

```
    // Arrange
    Mock<IProductRepository> mock = new Mock<IProductRepository>();
    mock.Setup(m => m.Products).Returns((new Product[] {
        new Product {ProductID = 1, Name = "P1"},
        new Product {ProductID = 2, Name = "P2"},
        new Product {ProductID = 3, Name = "P3"},
        new Product {ProductID = 4, Name = "P4"},
        new Product {ProductID = 5, Name = "P5"}
    }).AsQueryable<Product>());

    // Arrange
    ProductController controller =
        new ProductController(mock.Object) { PageSize = 3 };

    // Act
    ProductsListViewModel result =
        controller.List(null, 2).ViewData.Model as ProductsListViewModel;

    // Assert
    PagingInfo pageInfo = result.PagingInfo;
    Assert.Equal(2, pageInfo.CurrentPage);
    Assert.Equal(3, pageInfo.ItemsPerPage);
    Assert.Equal(5, pageInfo.TotalItems);
    Assert.Equal(2, pageInfo.TotalPages);
}
...
```

Keeping your unit tests synchronized with your code changes quickly becomes second nature when you get into the testing mind-set.

To see the effect of the category filtering, start the application and select a category using the following query string, changing the port to match the one that Visual Studio assigned for your project (and taking care to use an uppercase S for Soccer):

```
http://localhost:60000/?category=Soccer
```

You will see only the products in the Soccer category, as shown in Figure 9-1.

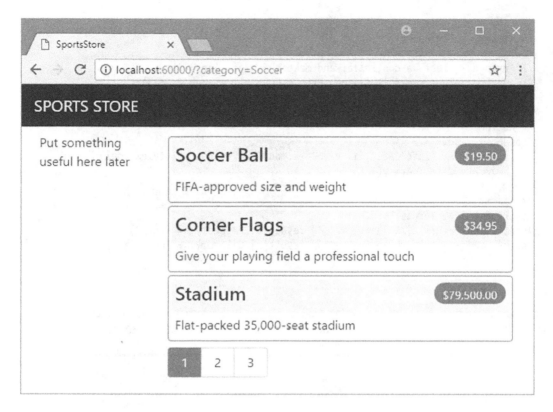

Figure 9-1. *Using the query string to filter by category*

Obviously, users won't want to navigate to categories using URLs, but you can see how small changes can have a big impact in an MVC application once the basic structure is in place.

UNIT TEST: CATEGORY FILTERING

I need a unit test to properly test the category filtering function to ensure that the filter can correctly generate products in a specified category. Here is the test method I added to the ProductControllerTests class:

```
...
[Fact]
public void Can_Filter_Products() {

    // Arrange
    // - create the mock repository
    Mock<IProductRepository> mock = new Mock<IProductRepository>();
    mock.Setup(m => m.Products).Returns((new Product[] {
        new Product {ProductID = 1, Name = "P1", Category = "Cat1"},
        new Product {ProductID = 2, Name = "P2", Category = "Cat2"},
        new Product {ProductID = 3, Name = "P3", Category = "Cat1"},
        new Product {ProductID = 4, Name = "P4", Category = "Cat2"},
```

```
        new Product {ProductID = 5, Name = "P5", Category = "Cat3"}
    }).AsQueryable<Product>());

    // Arrange - create a controller and make the page size 3 items
    ProductController controller = new ProductController(mock.Object);
    controller.PageSize = 3;

    // Action
    Product[] result =
        (controller.List("Cat2", 1).ViewData.Model as ProductsListViewModel)
            .Products.ToArray();

    // Assert
    Assert.Equal(2, result.Length);
    Assert.True(result[0].Name == "P2" && result[0].Category == "Cat2");
    Assert.True(result[1].Name == "P4" && result[1].Category == "Cat2");
}
...
```

This test creates a mock repository containing `Product` objects that belong to a range of categories. One specific category is requested using the action method, and the results are checked to ensure that the results are the right objects in the right order.

Refining the URL Scheme

No one wants to see or use ugly URLs such as /?category=Soccer. To address this, I am going to change the routing configuration in the `Configure` method of the `Startup` class to create a more useful set of URLs, as shown in Listing 9-3.

■ **Caution**   It is important to add the new routes in Listing 9-3 in the order they are shown. Routes are applied in the order in which they are defined, and you will get some odd effects if you change the order.

Listing 9-3. Changing the Routing Schema in the Startup.cs File in the SportsStore Folder

```
...
public void Configure(IApplicationBuilder app, IHostingEnvironment env) {
    app.UseDeveloperExceptionPage();
    app.UseStatusCodePages();
    app.UseStaticFiles();
    app.UseMvc(routes => {

        routes.MapRoute(
            name: null,
            template: "{category}/Page{productPage:int}",
            defaults: new { controller = "Product", action = "List" }
        );
```

```
    routes.MapRoute(
        name: null,
        template: "Page{productPage:int}",
        defaults: new { controller = "Product",
            action = "List", productPage = 1 }
    );

    routes.MapRoute(
        name: null,
        template: "{category}",
        defaults: new { controller = "Product",
            action = "List", productPage = 1 }
    );

    routes.MapRoute(
        name: null,
        template: "",
        defaults: new { controller = "Product", action = "List",
            productPage = 1 });

    routes.MapRoute(name: null, template: "{controller}/{action}/{id?}");
});
    SeedData.EnsurePopulated(app);
}
...
```

Table 9-1 describes the URL scheme that these routes represent. I explain the routing system in detail in Chapters 15 and 16.

Table 9-1. *Route Summary*

URL	Leads To
/	Lists the first page of products from all categories
/Page2	Lists the specified page (in this case, page 2), showing items from all categories
/Soccer	Shows the first page of items from a specific category (in this case, the Soccer category)
/Soccer/Page2	Shows the specified page (in this case, page 2) of items from the specified category (in this case, Soccer)

The ASP.NET Core routing system is used by MVC to handle *incoming* requests from clients, but it also generates *outgoing* URLs that conform to the URL scheme and that can be embedded in web pages. By using the routing system both to handle incoming requests and to generate outgoing URLs, I can ensure that all the URLs in the application are consistent.

The IUrlHelper interface provides access to the URL-generating functionality. I used this interface and the Action method it defines in the tag helper I created in the previous chapter. Now that I want to start generating more complex URLs, I need a way to receive additional information from the view without having to add extra properties to the tag helper class. Fortunately, tag helpers have a nice feature that allows properties with a common prefix to be received all together in a single collection, as shown in Listing 9-4.

Listing 9-4. Receiving Prefixed Values in the PageLinkTagHelper.cs File in the Infrastructure Folder

```
using Microsoft.AspNetCore.Mvc;
using Microsoft.AspNetCore.Mvc.Rendering;
using Microsoft.AspNetCore.Mvc.Routing;
using Microsoft.AspNetCore.Mvc.ViewFeatures;
using Microsoft.AspNetCore.Razor.TagHelpers;
using SportsStore.Models.ViewModels;
using System.Collections.Generic;

namespace SportsStore.Infrastructure {

    [HtmlTargetElement("div", Attributes = "page-model")]
    public class PageLinkTagHelper : TagHelper {
        private IUrlHelperFactory urlHelperFactory;

        public PageLinkTagHelper(IUrlHelperFactory helperFactory) {
            urlHelperFactory = helperFactory;
        }

        [ViewContext]
        [HtmlAttributeNotBound]
        public ViewContext ViewContext { get; set; }

        public PagingInfo PageModel { get; set; }

        public string PageAction { get; set; }

        [HtmlAttributeName(DictionaryAttributePrefix = "page-url-")]
        public Dictionary<string, object> PageUrlValues { get; set; }
            = new Dictionary<string, object>();

        public bool PageClassesEnabled { get; set; } = false;
        public string PageClass { get; set; }
        public string PageClassNormal { get; set; }
        public string PageClassSelected { get; set; }

        public override void Process(TagHelperContext context,
                TagHelperOutput output) {
            IUrlHelper urlHelper = urlHelperFactory.GetUrlHelper(ViewContext);
            TagBuilder result = new TagBuilder("div");
            for (int i = 1; i <= PageModel.TotalPages; i++) {
                TagBuilder tag = new TagBuilder("a");
                PageUrlValues["productPage"] = i;
                tag.Attributes["href"] = urlHelper.Action(PageAction, PageUrlValues);
                if (PageClassesEnabled) {
                    tag.AddCssClass(PageClass);
                    tag.AddCssClass(i == PageModel.CurrentPage
                        ? PageClassSelected : PageClassNormal);
                }
```

```
            tag.InnerHtml.Append(i.ToString());
            result.InnerHtml.AppendHtml(tag);
        }
        output.Content.AppendHtml(result.InnerHtml);
      }
   }
}
```

Decorating a tag helper property with the `HtmlAttributeName` attribute allows me to specify a prefix for attribute names on the element, which in this case will be `page-url-`. The value of any attribute whose name begins with this prefix will be added to the dictionary that is assigned to the `PageUrlValues` property, which is then passed to the `IUrlHelper.Action` method to generate the URL for the `href` attribute of the a elements that the tag helper produces.

In Listing 9-5, I have added a new attribute to the `div` element that is processed by the tag helper, specifying the category that will be used to generate the URL. I have added only one new attribute to the view, but any attribute with the same prefix would be added to the dictionary.

Listing 9-5. Adding a New Attribute in the List.cshtml File in the Views/Home Folder

```
@model ProductsListViewModel

@foreach (var p in Model.Products) {
    @Html.Partial("ProductSummary", p)
}

<div page-model="@Model.PagingInfo" page-action="List" page-classes-enabled="true"
     page-class="btn" page-class-normal="btn-secondary"
     page-class-selected="btn-primary" page-url-category="@Model.CurrentCategory"
     class="btn-group pull-right m-1">
</div>
```

Prior to this change, the links generated for the pagination links were like this:

```
http://<myserver>:<port>/Page1
```

If the user clicked a page link like this, the category filter would be lost, and the application would present a page containing products from all categories. By adding the current category, taken from the view model, I generate URLs like this instead:

```
http://<myserver>:<port>/Chess/Page1
```

When the user clicks this kind of link, the current category will be passed to the `List` action method, and the filtering will be preserved. After you have made this change, you can visit a URL such as `/Chess` or `/Soccer`, and you will see that the page links at the bottom of the page correctly includes the category.

Building a Category Navigation Menu

I need to provide customers with a way to select a category that does not involve typing in URLs. This means presenting them with a list of the categories available and indicating which, if any, is currently selected. As I build out the application, I will use this list of categories in more than one controller, so I need something that is self-contained and reusable.

ASP.NET Core MVC has the concept of *view components*, which are perfect for creating items such as a reusable navigation control. A view component is a C# class that provides a small amount of reusable application logic with the ability to select and display Razor partial views. I describe view components in detail in Chapter 22.

In this case, I will create a view component that renders the navigation menu and integrates it into the application by invoking the component from the shared layout. This approach gives me a regular C# class that can contain whatever application logic I need and that can be unit tested like any other class. It is a nice way of creating smaller segments of an application while preserving the overall MVC approach.

Creating the Navigation View Component

I created a folder called Components, which is the conventional home of view components, and added to it a class called NavigationMenuViewComponent.cs, which I used to define the class shown in Listing 9-6.

Listing 9-6. The Contents of the NavigationMenuViewComponent.cs File in the Components Folder

```
using Microsoft.AspNetCore.Mvc;

namespace SportsStore.Components {

    public class NavigationMenuViewComponent : ViewComponent {

        public string Invoke() {
            return "Hello from the Nav View Component";
        }
    }
}
```

The view component's Invoke method is called when the component is used in a Razor view, and the result of the Invoke method is inserted into the HTML sent to the browser. I have started with a simple view component that returns a string, but I'll replace this with dynamic HTML content shortly.

I want the category list to appear on all pages, so I am going to use the view component in the shared layout, rather than in a specific view. Within a view, view components are used through the @await Component.InvokeAsync expression, as shown in Listing 9-7.

Listing 9-7. Using View Component in the _Layout.cshtml File in the Views/Shared Folder

```
<!DOCTYPE html>

<html>
<head>
    <meta name="viewport" content="width=device-width" />
    <link rel="stylesheet"
        asp-href-include="/lib/bootstrap/dist/**/*.min.css"
```

```
                asp-href-exclude="**/*-reboot*,**/*-grid*" />
    <title>SportsStore</title>
</head>
<body>
    <div class="navbar navbar-inverse bg-inverse" role="navigation">
        <a class="navbar-brand" href="#">SPORTS STORE</a>
    </div>
    <div class="row m-1 p-1">
        <div id="categories" class="col-3">
            @await Component.InvokeAsync("NavigationMenu")
        </div>
        <div class="col-9">
            @RenderBody()
        </div>
    </div>
</body>
</html>
```

I removed the placeholder text and replaced it with a call to the Component.InvokeAsync method. The argument to this method is the name of the component class, omitting the ViewComponent part of the class name, such that NavigationMenu specifies the NavigationMenuViewComponent class. If you run the application, you will see that the output from the Invoke method is included in the HTML sent to the browser, as shown in Figure 9-2.

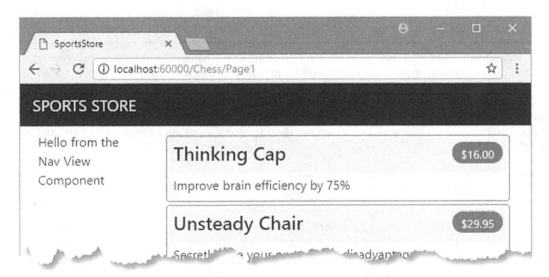

Figure 9-2. *Using a view component*

Generating Category Lists

I can now return to the navigation view controller and generate a real set of categories. I could build the HTML for the categories programmatically, as I did for the page tag helper, but one of the benefits of working with view components is they can render Razor partial views. That means I can use the view component to generate the list of components and then use the more expressive Razor syntax to render the HTML that will display them. The first step is to update the view component, as shown in Listing 9-8.

Listing 9-8. Adding Categories in the NavigationMenuViewComponent.cs File in the Components Folder

```
using Microsoft.AspNetCore.Mvc;
using System.Linq;
using SportsStore.Models;

namespace SportsStore.Components {

    public class NavigationMenuViewComponent : ViewComponent {
        private IProductRepository repository;

        public NavigationMenuViewComponent(IProductRepository repo) {
            repository = repo;
        }

        public IViewComponentResult Invoke() {
            return View(repository.Products
                .Select(x => x.Category)
                .Distinct()
                .OrderBy(x => x));
        }
    }
}
```

The constructor defined in Listing 9-8 defines an IProductRepository argument. When MVC needs to create an instance of the view component class, it will note the need to provide this argument and inspect the configuration in the Startup class to determine which implementation object should be used. This is the same dependency injection feature that I used in the controller in Chapter 8, and it has the same effect, which is to allow the view component to access data without knowing which repository implementation will be used, as described in Chapter 18.

In the Invoke method, I use LINQ to select and order the set of categories in the repository and pass them as the argument to the View method, which renders the default Razor partial view, details of which are returned from the method using an IViewComponentResult object, a process I describe in more detail in Chapter 22.

UNIT TEST: GENERATING THE CATEGORY LIST

The unit test for my ability to produce a category list is relatively simple. The goal is to create a list that is sorted in alphabetical order and contains no duplicates, and the simplest way to do this is to supply some test data that *does* have duplicate categories and that is *not* in order, pass this to the tag helper class, and assert that the data has been properly cleaned up. Here is the unit test, which I defined in a new class file called NavigationMenuViewComponentTests.cs in the SportsStore.Tests project:

```
using System.Collections.Generic;
using System.Linq;
using Microsoft.AspNetCore.Mvc.ViewComponents;
using Moq;
using SportsStore.Components;
using SportsStore.Models;
using Xunit;
```

```
namespace SportsStore.Tests {

    public class NavigationMenuViewComponentTests {

        [Fact]
        public void Can_Select_Categories() {
            // Arrange
            Mock<IProductRepository> mock = new Mock<IProductRepository>();
            mock.Setup(m => m.Products).Returns((new Product[] {
                new Product {ProductID = 1, Name = "P1", Category = "Apples"},
                new Product {ProductID = 2, Name = "P2", Category = "Apples"},
                new Product {ProductID = 3, Name = "P3", Category = "Plums"},
                new Product {ProductID = 4, Name = "P4", Category = "Oranges"},
            }).AsQueryable<Product>());

            NavigationMenuViewComponent target =
                new NavigationMenuViewComponent(mock.Object);

            // Act = get the set of categories
            string[] results = ((IEnumerable<string>)(target.Invoke()
                as ViewViewComponentResult).ViewData.Model).ToArray();

            // Assert
            Assert.True(Enumerable.SequenceEqual(new string[] { "Apples",
                "Oranges", "Plums" }, results));
        }
    }
}
```

I created a mock repository implementation that contains repeating categories and categories that are not in order. I assert that the duplicates are removed and that alphabetical ordering is imposed.

Creating the View

Razor uses different conventions for dealing with views that are selected by view components. Both the default name of the view and the locations that are searched for the view are different from those used for controllers. To that end, I created the Views/Shared/Components/NavigationMenu folder and added to it a view file called Default.cshtml, to which I added the content shown in Listing 9-9.

Listing 9-9. Contents of the Default.cshtml File in the Views/Shared/Components/NavigationMenu Folder

```
@model IEnumerable<string>

<a class="btn btn-block btn-secondary"
   asp-action="List"
   asp-controller="Product"
   asp-route-category="">
     Home
</a>
```

```
@foreach (string category in Model) {
    <a class="btn btn-block btn-secondary"
        asp-action="List"
        asp-controller="Product"
        asp-route-category="@category"
        asp-route-productPage="1">
        @category
    </a>
}
```

This view uses one of the built-in tag helpers, which I describe in Chapters 24 and 25, to create a elements whose href attribute contains a URL that selects a different product category.

You can see the category links if you run the application, as shown in Figure 9-3. If you click a category, the list of items is updated to show only items from the selected category.

Figure 9-3. *Generating category links with a view component*

Highlighting the Current Category

There is no feedback to the user to indicate which category has been selected. It might be possible to infer the category from the items in the list, but some clear visual feedback seems like a good idea. ASP.NET Core MVC components such as controllers and view components can receive information about the current request by asking for a context object. Most of the time, you can rely on the base classes that you use to create components to take care of getting the context object for you, such as when you use the Controller base class to create controllers.

The ViewComponent base class is no exception and provides access to context objects through a set of properties. One of the properties is called RouteData, which provides information about how the request URL was handled by the routing system.

In Listing 9-10, I use the RouteData property to access the request data in order to get the value for the currently selected category. I could pass the category to the view by creating another view model class (and that's what I would do in a real project), but for variety, I am going to use the view bag feature I introduced in Chapter 2.

Listing 9-10. Passing the Selected Category in the NavigationMenuViewComponent.cs File

```
using Microsoft.AspNetCore.Mvc;
using System.Linq;
using SportsStore.Models;

namespace SportsStore.Components {

    public class NavigationMenuViewComponent : ViewComponent {
        private IProductRepository repository;

        public NavigationMenuViewComponent(IProductRepository repo) {
            repository = repo;
        }

        public IViewComponentResult Invoke() {
            ViewBag.SelectedCategory = RouteData?.Values["category"];
            return View(repository.Products
                .Select(x => x.Category)
                .Distinct()
                .OrderBy(x => x));
        }
    }
}
```

Inside the Invoke method, I have dynamically assigned a SelectedCategory property to the ViewBag object and set its value to be the current category, which is obtained through the context object returned by the RouteData property. As I explained in Chapter 2, the ViewBag is a dynamic object that allows me to define new properties simply by assigning values to them.

UNIT TEST: REPORTING THE SELECTED CATEGORY

I can test that the view component correctly adds details of the selected category by reading the value of the ViewBag property in a unit test, which is available through the ViewViewComponentResult class, described in Chapter 22. Here is the test, which I added to the NavigatioMenuViewComponentTests class:

```
...
[Fact]
public void Indicates_Selected_Category() {

    // Arrange
    string categoryToSelect = "Apples";
    Mock<IProductRepository> mock = new Mock<IProductRepository>();
    mock.Setup(m => m.Products).Returns((new Product[] {
        new Product {ProductID = 1, Name = "P1", Category = "Apples"},
        new Product {ProductID = 4, Name = "P2", Category = "Oranges"},
    }).AsQueryable<Product>());
    NavigationMenuViewComponent target =
        new NavigationMenuViewComponent(mock.Object);
```

```
        target.ViewComponentContext = new ViewComponentContext {
            ViewContext = new ViewContext {
                RouteData = new RouteData()
            }
        };
        target.RouteData.Values["category"] = categoryToSelect;

        // Action
        string result = (string)(target.Invoke() as
            ViewViewComponentResult).ViewData["SelectedCategory"];

        // Assert
        Assert.Equal(categoryToSelect, result);
    }
...
```

This unit test provides the view component with routing data through the ViewComponentContext property, which is how view components receive all of their context data. The ViewComponentContext property provides access to view-specific context data through its ViewContext property, which in turns provides access to the routing information through its RouteData property. Most of the code in the unit test goes into creating the context objects that will provide the selected category in the same way that it would be presented when the application is running and the context data is provided by ASP.NET Core MVC.

Now that I am providing information about which category is selected, I can update the view selected by the view component to take advantage of this and vary the CSS classes used to style the links to make the one representing the current category distinct from the others. Listing 9-11 shows the change I made to the Default.cshtml file.

Listing 9-11. Highlighting in the Default.cshtml File in the Views/Shared/Components/NavigationMenu Folder

```
@model IEnumerable<string>

<a class="btn btn-block btn-secondary"
    asp-action="List"
    asp-controller="Product"
    asp-route-category="">
    Home
</a>

@foreach (string category in Model) {
    <a class="btn btn-block
        @(category == ViewBag.SelectedCategory ? "btn-primary": "btn-secondary")"
        asp-action="List"
        asp-controller="Product"
        asp-route-category="@category"
        asp-route-productPage="1">
        @category
    </a>
}
```

I have used a Razor expression within the class attribute to apply the btn-primary class to the element that represents the selected category and the btn-secondary class otherwise. These classes apply different Bootstrap styles and make the active button obvious, as shown in Figure 9-4.

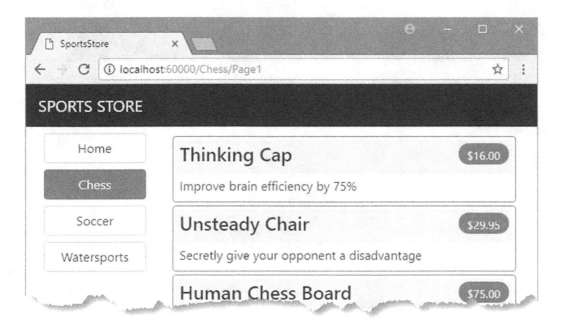

Figure 9-4. *Highlighting the selected category*

Correcting the Page Count

I need to correct the page links so that they work correctly when a category is selected. Currently, the number of page links is determined by the total number of products in the repository and not the number of products in the selected category. This means that the customer can click the link for page 2 of the Chess category and end up with an empty page because there are not enough chess products to fill two pages. You can see the problem in Figure 9-5.

Figure 9-5. *Displaying the wrong page links when a category is selected*

I can fix this by updating the List action method in the Product controller so that the pagination information takes the categories into account, as shown in Listing 9-12.

Listing 9-12. Creating Category Pagination Data in the ProductController.cs File in the Controllers Folder

```
using Microsoft.AspNetCore.Mvc;
using SportsStore.Models;
using System.Linq;
using SportsStore.Models.ViewModels;

namespace SportsStore.Controllers {

    public class ProductController : Controller {
        private IProductRepository repository;
        public int PageSize = 4;

        public ProductController(IProductRepository repo) {
            repository = repo;
        }

        public ViewResult List(string category, int productPage = 1)
            => View(new ProductsListViewModel {
                Products = repository.Products
                    .Where(p => category == null || p.Category == category)
                    .OrderBy(p => p.ProductID)
                    .Skip((productPage - 1) * PageSize)
                    .Take(PageSize),
```

```
        PagingInfo = new PagingInfo {
            CurrentPage = productPage,
            ItemsPerPage = PageSize,
            TotalItems = category == null ?
                repository.Products.Count() :
                repository.Products.Where(e =>
                    e.Category == category).Count()
        },
        CurrentCategory = category
    });
    }
}
```

If a category has been selected, I return the number of items in that category; if not, I return the total number of products. Now when I view a category, the links at the bottom of the page correctly reflect the number of products in the category, as shown in Figure 9-6.

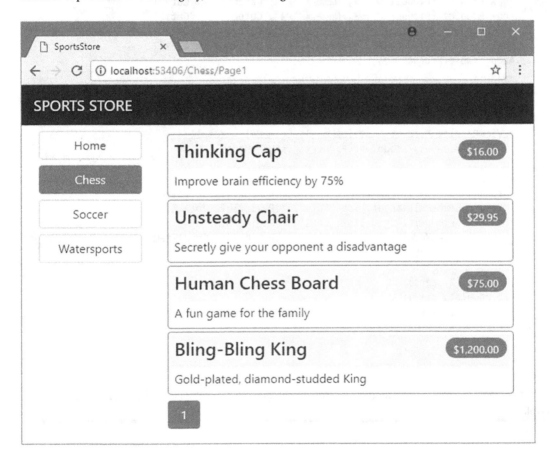

Figure 9-6. *Displaying category-specific page counts*

UNIT TEST: CATEGORY-SPECIFIC PRODUCT COUNTS

Testing that I am able to generate the current product count for different categories is simple. I create a mock repository that contains known data in a range of categories and then call the `List` action method requesting each category in turn. Here is the unit test method that I added to the `ProductControllerTests` class:

```
...
[Fact]
public void Generate_Category_Specific_Product_Count() {
    // Arrange
    Mock<IProductRepository> mock = new Mock<IProductRepository>();
    mock.Setup(m => m.Products).Returns((new Product[] {
        new Product {ProductID = 1, Name = "P1", Category = "Cat1"},
        new Product {ProductID = 2, Name = "P2", Category = "Cat2"},
        new Product {ProductID = 3, Name = "P3", Category = "Cat1"},
        new Product {ProductID = 4, Name = "P4", Category = "Cat2"},
        new Product {ProductID = 5, Name = "P5", Category = "Cat3"}
    }).AsQueryable<Product>());

    ProductController target = new ProductController(mock.Object);
    target.PageSize = 3;

    Func<ViewResult, ProductsListViewModel> GetModel = result =>
        result?.ViewData?.Model as ProductsListViewModel;

    // Action
    int? res1 = GetModel(target.List("Cat1"))?.PagingInfo.TotalItems;
    int? res2 = GetModel(target.List("Cat2"))?.PagingInfo.TotalItems;
    int? res3 = GetModel(target.List("Cat3"))?.PagingInfo.TotalItems;
    int? resAll = GetModel(target.List(null))?.PagingInfo.TotalItems;

    // Assert
    Assert.Equal(2, res1);
    Assert.Equal(2, res2);
    Assert.Equal(1, res3);
    Assert.Equal(5, resAll);
}
...
```

Notice that I also call the `List` method, specifying no category, to make sure I get the correct total count as well.

Building the Shopping Cart

The application is progressing nicely, but I cannot sell any products until I implement a shopping cart. In this section, I will create the shopping cart experience shown in Figure 9-7. This will be familiar to anyone who has ever made a purchase online.

Figure 9-7. *The basic shopping cart flow*

An Add to Cart button will be displayed alongside each of the products in the catalog. Clicking this button will show a summary of the products the customer has selected so far, including the total cost. At this point, the user can click the Continue Shopping button to return to the product catalog or click the Checkout Now button to complete the order and finish the shopping session.

Defining the Cart Model

I started by adding a class file called Cart.cs to the Models folder in and used it to define the classes shown in Listing 9-13.

Listing 9-13. The Contents of the Cart.cs File in the Models Folder

```
using System.Collections.Generic;
using System.Linq;

namespace SportsStore.Models {

    public class Cart {
        private List<CartLine> lineCollection = new List<CartLine>();

        public virtual void AddItem(Product product, int quantity) {
            CartLine line = lineCollection
                .Where(p => p.Product.ProductID == product.ProductID)
                .FirstOrDefault();

            if (line == null) {
                lineCollection.Add(new CartLine {
                    Product = product,
                    Quantity = quantity
                });
```

```
            } else {
                line.Quantity += quantity;
            }
        }

        public virtual void RemoveLine(Product product) =>
            lineCollection.RemoveAll(l => l.Product.ProductID == product.ProductID);

        public virtual decimal ComputeTotalValue() =>
            lineCollection.Sum(e => e.Product.Price * e.Quantity);

        public virtual void Clear() => lineCollection.Clear();

        public virtual IEnumerable<CartLine> Lines => lineCollection;
    }

    public class CartLine {
        public int CartLineID { get; set; }
        public Product Product { get; set; }
        public int Quantity { get; set; }
    }
}
```

The Cart class uses the CartLine class, defined in the same file, to represent a product selected by the customer and the quantity the user wants to buy. I defined methods to add an item to the cart, remove a previously added item from the cart, calculate the total cost of the items in the cart, and reset the cart by removing all the items. I also provided a property that gives access to the contents of the cart using an IEnumerable<CartLine>. This is all straightforward stuff, easily implemented in C# with the help of a little LINQ.

UNIT TEST: TESTING THE CART

The Cart class is relatively simple, but it has a range of important behaviors that must work properly. A poorly functioning cart would undermine the entire SportsStore application. I have broken down the features and tested them individually. I created a new unit test file called CartTests.cs in the SportsStore.Tests project called to contain these tests.

The first behavior relates to when I add an item to the cart. If this is the first time that a given Product has been added to the cart, I want a new CartLine to be added. Here is the test, including the unit test class definition:

```
using System.Linq;
using SportsStore.Models;
using Xunit;

namespace SportsStore.Tests {

    public class CartTests {
```

```
    [Fact]
    public void Can_Add_New_Lines() {

        // Arrange - create some test products
        Product p1 = new Product { ProductID = 1, Name = "P1" };
        Product p2 = new Product { ProductID = 2, Name = "P2" };

        // Arrange - create a new cart
        Cart target = new Cart();

        // Act
        target.AddItem(p1, 1);
        target.AddItem(p2, 1);
        CartLine[] results = target.Lines.ToArray();

        // Assert
        Assert.Equal(2, results.Length);
        Assert.Equal(p1, results[0].Product);
        Assert.Equal(p2, results[1].Product);
    }
}
}
```

However, if the customer has already added a `Product` to the cart, I want to increment the quantity of the corresponding `CartLine` and not create a new one. Here is the test:

```
...
[Fact]
public void Can_Add_Quantity_For_Existing_Lines() {
    // Arrange - create some test products
    Product p1 = new Product { ProductID = 1, Name = "P1" };
    Product p2 = new Product { ProductID = 2, Name = "P2" };

    // Arrange - create a new cart
    Cart target = new Cart();

    // Act
    target.AddItem(p1, 1);
    target.AddItem(p2, 1);
    target.AddItem(p1, 10);
    CartLine[] results = target.Lines
        .OrderBy(c => c.Product.ProductID).ToArray();

    // Assert
    Assert.Equal(2, results.Length);
    Assert.Equal(11, results[0].Quantity);
    Assert.Equal(1, results[1].Quantity);
}
...
```

I also need to check that users can change their mind and remove products from the cart. This feature is implemented by the RemoveLine method. Here is the test:

```
...
[Fact]
public void Can_Remove_Line() {
    // Arrange - create some test products
    Product p1 = new Product { ProductID = 1, Name = "P1" };
    Product p2 = new Product { ProductID = 2, Name = "P2" };
    Product p3 = new Product { ProductID = 3, Name = "P3" };

    // Arrange - create a new cart
    Cart target = new Cart();
    // Arrange - add some products to the cart
    target.AddItem(p1, 1);
    target.AddItem(p2, 3);
    target.AddItem(p3, 5);
    target.AddItem(p2, 1);

    // Act
    target.RemoveLine(p2);

    // Assert
    Assert.Equal(0, target.Lines.Where(c => c.Product == p2).Count());
    Assert.Equal(2, target.Lines.Count());
}
...
```

The next behavior I want to test is the ability to calculate the total cost of the items in the cart. Here's the test for this behavior:

```
...
[Fact]
public void Calculate_Cart_Total() {
    // Arrange - create some test products
    Product p1 = new Product { ProductID = 1, Name = "P1", Price = 100M };
    Product p2 = new Product { ProductID = 2, Name = "P2", Price = 50M };

    // Arrange - create a new cart
    Cart target = new Cart();

    // Act
    target.AddItem(p1, 1);
    target.AddItem(p2, 1);
    target.AddItem(p1, 3);
    decimal result = target.ComputeTotalValue();

    // Assert
    Assert.Equal(450M, result);
}
...
```

The final test is simple. I want to ensure that the contents of the cart are properly removed when reset. Here is the test:

```
...
[Fact]
public void Can_Clear_Contents() {
    // Arrange - create some test products
    Product p1 = new Product { ProductID = 1, Name = "P1", Price = 100M };
    Product p2 = new Product { ProductID = 2, Name = "P2", Price = 50M };

    // Arrange - create a new cart
    Cart target = new Cart();

    // Arrange - add some items
    target.AddItem(p1, 1);
    target.AddItem(p2, 1);

    // Act - reset the cart
    target.Clear();

    // Assert
    Assert.Equal(0, target.Lines.Count());
}
...
```

Sometimes, as in this case, the code required to test the functionality of a class is longer and more complex than the class itself. Do not let that put you off writing the unit tests. Defects in simple classes can have huge impacts, especially ones that play such an important role as Cart does in the example application.

Adding the Add to Cart Buttons

I need to edit the Views/Shared/ProductSummary.cshtml partial view to add the buttons to the product listings. To prepare for this, I added a class file called UrlExtensions.cs to the Infrastructure folder and defined the extension method shown in Listing 9-14.

Listing 9-14. The Contents of the UrlExtensions.cs File in the Infrastructure Folder

```
using Microsoft.AspNetCore.Http;

namespace SportsStore.Infrastructure {

    public static class UrlExtensions {

        public static string PathAndQuery(this HttpRequest request) =>
            request.QueryString.HasValue
                ? $"{request.Path}{request.QueryString}"
                : request.Path.ToString();
    }
}
```

The PathAndQuery extension method operates on the HttpRequest class, which ASP.NET uses to describe an HTTP request. The extension method generates a URL that the browser will be returned to after the cart has been updated, taking into account the query string if there is one. In Listing 9-15, I have added the namespace that contains the extension method to the view imports file so that I can use it in the partial view.

Listing 9-15. Adding a Namespace in the _ViewImports.cshtml File in the Views Folder

```
@using SportsStore.Models
@using SportsStore.Models.ViewModels
@using SportsStore.Infrastructure
@addTagHelper *, Microsoft.AspNetCore.Mvc.TagHelpers
@addTagHelper SportsStore.Infrastructure.*, SportsStore
```

In Listing 9-16, I have updated the partial view that describes each product to contain an Add To Cart button.

Listing 9-16. Adding the Buttons to the ProductSummary.cshtml File View in the Views/Shared Folder

```
@model Product

<div class="card card-outline-primary m-1 p-1">
    <div class="bg-faded p-1">
        <h4>
            @Model.Name
            <span class="badge badge-pill badge-primary" style="float:right">
                <small>@Model.Price.ToString("c")</small>
            </span>
        </h4>
    </div>
    <form id="@Model.ProductID" asp-action="AddToCart"
            asp-controller="Cart" method="post">
        <input type="hidden" asp-for="ProductID" />
        <input type="hidden" name="returnUrl"
                value="@ViewContext.HttpContext.Request.PathAndQuery()" />
        <span class="card-text p-1">
            @Model.Description
            <button type="submit"
                class="btn btn-success btn-sm pull-right" style="float:right">
                Add To Cart
            </button>
        </span>
    </form>
</div>
```

I have added a form element that contains hidden input elements specifying the ProductID value from the view model and the URL that the browser should be returned to after the cart has been updated. The form element and one of the input elements are configured using built-in tag helpers, which are a useful way of generating forms that contain model values and that target controllers and actions in the application, as described in Chapter 24. The other input element uses the extension method I created to set the return URL. I also added a button element that will submit the form to the application.

> ■ **Note**   Notice that I have set the `method` attribute on the form element to `post`, which instructs the browser to submit the form data using an HTTP POST request. You can change this so that forms use the GET method, but you should think carefully about doing so. The HTTP specification requires that GET requests must be *idempotent*, meaning that they must not cause changes, and adding a product to a cart is definitely a change. I have more to say on this topic in Chapter 16, including an explanation of what can happen if you ignore the need for idempotent GET requests.

Enabling Sessions

I am going to store details of a user's cart using session state, which is data that is stored at the server and associated with a series of requests made by a user. ASP.NET provides a range of different ways to store session state, including storing it in memory, which is the approach that I am going to use. This has the advantage of simplicity, but it means that the session data is lost when the application is stopped or restarted. Enabling sessions requires adding services and middleware in the Startup class, as shown in Listing 9-17.

Listing 9-17. Enabling Sessions in the Startup.cs File in the SportsStore Folder

```
using System;
using System.Collections.Generic;
using System.Linq;
using System.Threading.Tasks;
using Microsoft.AspNetCore.Builder;
using Microsoft.AspNetCore.Hosting;
using Microsoft.AspNetCore.Http;
using Microsoft.Extensions.DependencyInjection;
using SportsStore.Models;
using Microsoft.Extensions.Configuration;
using Microsoft.EntityFrameworkCore;

namespace SportsStore {

    public class Startup {

        public Startup(IConfiguration configuration) =>
            Configuration = configuration;

        public IConfiguration Configuration { get; }

        public void ConfigureServices(IServiceCollection services) {
            services.AddDbContext<ApplicationDbContext>(options =>
                options.UseSqlServer(
                    Configuration["Data:SportStoreProducts:ConnectionString"]));
            services.AddTransient<IProductRepository, EFProductRepository>();
            services.AddMvc();
            services.AddMemoryCache();
            services.AddSession();
        }
```

```
    public void Configure(IApplicationBuilder app, IHostingEnvironment env) {
        app.UseDeveloperExceptionPage();
        app.UseStatusCodePages();
        app.UseStaticFiles();
        app.UseSession();
        app.UseMvc(routes => {

            // ...routing configuration omitted for brevity...

        });
        SeedData.EnsurePopulated(app);
    }
  }
}
```

The AddMemoryCache method call sets up the in-memory data store. The AddSession method registers the services used to access session data, and the UseSession method allows the session system to automatically associate requests with sessions when they arrive from the client.

Implementing the Cart Controller

I need a controller to handle the Add to Cart button presses. I added a new class file called CartController.cs to the Controllers folder and used it to define the class shown in Listing 9-18.

Listing 9-18. The Contents of the CartController.cs File in the Controllers Folder

```
using System.Linq;
using Microsoft.AspNetCore.Http;
using Microsoft.AspNetCore.Mvc;
using SportsStore.Infrastructure;
using SportsStore.Models;

namespace SportsStore.Controllers {

    public class CartController : Controller {
        private IProductRepository repository;

        public CartController(IProductRepository repo) {
            repository = repo;
        }

        public RedirectToActionResult AddToCart(int productId, string returnUrl) {
            Product product = repository.Products
                .FirstOrDefault(p => p.ProductID == productId);

            if (product != null) {
                Cart cart = GetCart();
                cart.AddItem(product, 1);
                SaveCart(cart);
            }
```

```
            return RedirectToAction("Index", new { returnUrl });
        }

        public RedirectToActionResult RemoveFromCart(int productId,
        string returnUrl) {
            Product product = repository.Products
                .FirstOrDefault(p => p.ProductID == productId);

            if (product != null) {
                Cart cart = GetCart();
                cart.RemoveLine(product);
                SaveCart(cart);
            }
            return RedirectToAction("Index", new { returnUrl });
        }

        private Cart GetCart() {
            Cart cart = HttpContext.Session.GetJson<Cart>("Cart") ?? new Cart();
            return cart;
        }

        private void SaveCart(Cart cart) {
            HttpContext.Session.SetJson("Cart", cart);
        }
    }
}
```

There are a few points to note about this controller. The first is that I use the ASP.NET session state feature to store and retrieve Cart objects, which is the purpose of the GetCart method. The middleware that I registered in the previous section uses cookies or URL rewriting to associate multiple requests from a user together to form a single browsing session. A related feature is session state, which associates data with a session. This is an ideal fit for the Cart class: I want each user to have their own cart, and I want the cart to be persistent between requests. Data associated with a session is deleted when a session expires (typically because a user has not made a request for a while), which means that I do not need to manage the storage or life cycle of the Cart objects.

For the AddToCart and RemoveFromCart action methods, I have used parameter names that match the input elements in the HTML forms created in the ProductSummary.cshtml view. This allows MVC to associate incoming form POST variables with those parameters, meaning I do not need to process the form myself. This is known as *model binding* and is a powerful tool for simplifying controller classes, as I explain in Chapter 26.

Defining Session State Extension Methods

The session state feature in ASP.NET Core stores only int, string, and byte[] values. Since I want to store a Cart object, I need to define extension methods to the ISession interface, which provides access to the session state data to serialize Cart objects into JSON and convert them back. I added a class file called SessionExtensions.cs to the Infrastructure folder and defined the extension methods shown in Listing 9-19.

Listing 9-19. The Contents of the SessionExtensions.cs File in the Infrastructure Folder

```
using Microsoft.AspNetCore.Http;
using Newtonsoft.Json;

namespace SportsStore.Infrastructure {

    public static class SessionExtensions {

        public static void SetJson(this ISession session, string key, object value) {
            session.SetString(key, JsonConvert.SerializeObject(value));
        }

        public static T GetJson<T>(this ISession session, string key) {
            var sessionData = session.GetString(key);
            return sessionData == null
                ? default(T) : JsonConvert.DeserializeObject<T>(sessionData);
        }
    }
}
```

These methods rely on the Json.Net package to serialize objects into the JavaScript Object Notation format, which you will encounter again in Chapter 20. The Json.Net package doesn't have to be added to the project because it is already used behind the scenes by MVC to provide the JSON helper feature, as described in Chapter 21. (See www.newtonsoft.com/json for information on working directly with Json.Net.)

The extension methods make it easy to store and retrieve Cart objects. To add a Cart to the session state in the controller, I make an assignment like this:

```
...
HttpContext.Session.SetJson("Cart", cart);
...
```

The HttpContext property is provided the Controller base class from which controllers are usually derived and returns an HttpContext object that provides context data about the request that has been received and the response that is being prepared. The HttpContext.Session property returns an object that implements the ISession interface, which is the type on which I defined the SetJson method, which accepts arguments that specify a key and an object that will be added to the session state. The extension method serializes the object and adds it to the session state using the underlying functionality provided by the ISession interface.

To retrieve the Cart again, I use the other extension method, specifying the same key, like this:

```
...
Cart cart = HttpContext.Session.GetJson<Cart>("Cart");
...
```

The type parameter lets me specify the type that I expecting to be retrieved, which is used in the deserialization process.

Displaying the Contents of the Cart

The final point to note about the Cart controller is that both the AddToCart and RemoveFromCart methods call the RedirectToAction method. This has the effect of sending an HTTP redirect instruction to the client browser, asking the browser to request a new URL. In this case, I have asked the browser to request a URL that will call the Index action method of the Cart controller.

I am going to implement the Index method and use it to display the contents of the Cart. If you refer back to Figure 9-7, you will see that this is the workflow when the user clicks the Add to Cart button.

I need to pass two pieces of information to the view that will display the contents of the cart: the Cart object and the URL to display if the user clicks the Continue Shopping button. I created a new class file called CartIndexViewModel.cs in the Models/ViewModels folder of the SportsStore project and used it to define the class shown in Listing 9-20.

Listing 9-20. The Contents of the CartIndexViewModel.cs File in the Models/ViewModels Folder

```
using SportsStore.Models;

namespace SportsStore.Models.ViewModels {

    public class CartIndexViewModel {
        public Cart Cart { get; set; }
        public string ReturnUrl { get; set; }
    }
}
```

Now that I have the view model, I can implement the Index action method in the Cart controller class, as shown in Listing 9-21.

Listing 9-21. Implementing the Index Action Method in the CartController.cs File in the Controllers Folder

```
using System.Linq;
using Microsoft.AspNetCore.Http;
using Microsoft.AspNetCore.Mvc;
using SportsStore.Infrastructure;
using SportsStore.Models;
using SportsStore.Models.ViewModels;

namespace SportsStore.Controllers {

    public class CartController : Controller {
        private IProductRepository repository;

        public CartController(IProductRepository repo) {
            repository = repo;
        }

        public ViewResult Index(string returnUrl) {
            return View(new CartIndexViewModel {
                Cart = GetCart(),
                ReturnUrl = returnUrl
            });
        }

        // ...other methods omitted for brevity...
    }
}
```

The Index action retrieves the Cart object from the session state and uses it to create a CartIndexView Model object, which is then passed to the View method to be used as the view model.

The last step to display the contents of the cart is to create the view that the Index action will render. I created the Views/Cart folder and added to it a Razor view file called Index.cshtml with the markup shown in Listing 9-22.

Listing 9-22. The Contents of the Index.cshtml File in the Views/Cart Folder

```
@model CartIndexViewModel

<h2>Your cart</h2>
<table class="table table-bordered table-striped">
    <thead>
        <tr>
            <th>Quantity</th>
            <th>Item</th>
            <th class="text-right">Price</th>
            <th class="text-right">Subtotal</th>
        </tr>
    </thead>
    <tbody>
        @foreach (var line in Model.Cart.Lines) {
            <tr>
                <td class="text-center">@line.Quantity</td>
                <td class="text-left">@line.Product.Name</td>
                <td class="text-right">@line.Product.Price.ToString("c")</td>
                <td class="text-right">
                    @((line.Quantity * line.Product.Price).ToString("c"))
                </td>
            </tr>
        }
    </tbody>
    <tfoot>
        <tr>
            <td colspan="3" class="text-right">Total:</td>
            <td class="text-right">
                @Model.Cart.ComputeTotalValue().ToString("c")
            </td>
        </tr>
    </tfoot>
</table>

<div class="text-center">
    <a class="btn btn-primary" href="@Model.ReturnUrl">Continue shopping</a>
</div>
```

The view enumerates the lines in the cart and adds rows for each of them to an HTML table, along with the total cost per line and the total cost for the cart. The classes to which I assigned the elements correspond to Bootstrap styles for tables and text alignment.

The result is that the basic functions of the shopping cart are in place. First, products are listed along with a button to add them to the cart, as shown in Figure 9-8.

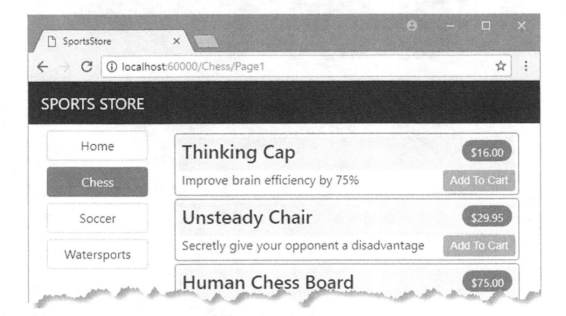

Figure 9-8. *The Add to Cart button*

Second, when the user clicks the Add to Cart button, the appropriate product is added to their cart, and a summary of the cart is displayed, as shown in Figure 9-9. Clicking the Continue Shopping button returns the user to the product page they came from.

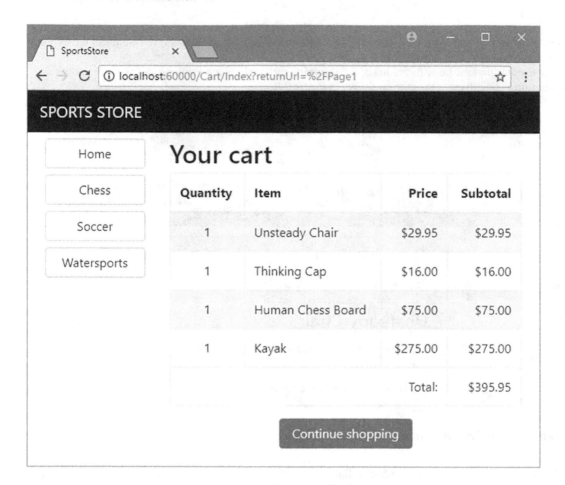

Figure 9-9. *Displaying the contents of the shopping cart*

Summary

In this chapter, I started to flesh out the customer-facing parts of the SportsStore app. I provided the means by which the user can navigate by category and put the basic building blocks in place for adding items to a shopping cart. I have more work to do, and I continue the development of the application in the next chapter.

CHAPTER 10

■ ■ ■

SportsStore: Completing the Cart

In this chapter, I continue to build the SportsStore example app. In the previous chapter, I added the basic support for a shopping cart, and now I am going to improve on and complete that functionality.

Refining the Cart Model with a Service

I defined a Cart model class in the previous chapter and demonstrated how it can be stored using the session feature, allowing the user to build up a set of products for purchase. The responsibility for managing the persistence of the Cart class fell to the Cart controller, which explicitly defines methods for getting and storing Cart objects.

The problem with this approach is that I will have to duplicate the code that obtains and stores Cart objects in any component that uses them. In this section, I am going to use the services feature that sits at the heart of ASP.NET Core to simplify the way that Cart objects are managed, freeing individual components such as the Cart controller from needing to deal with the details directly.

Services are most commonly used to hide details of how interfaces are implemented from the components that depend on them. You saw an example of this when I created a service for the IProductRepository interface, which allowed me to seamlessly replace the fake repository class with the Entity Framework Core repository. But services can be used to solve lots of other problems as well and can be used to shape and reshape an application, even when you are working with concrete classes such as Cart.

Creating a Storage-Aware Cart Class

The first step in tidying up the way that the Cart class is used will be to create a subclass that is aware of how to store itself using session state. I added a class file called SessionCart.cs to the Models folder and used it to define the class shown in Listing 10-1.

Listing 10-1. The Contents of the SessionCart.cs File in the Models Folder

```
using System;
using Microsoft.AspNetCore.Http;
using Microsoft.Extensions.DependencyInjection;
using Newtonsoft.Json;
using SportsStore.Infrastructure;

namespace SportsStore.Models {

    public class SessionCart: Cart {
```

```
    public static Cart GetCart(IServiceProvider services) {
        ISession session = services.GetRequiredService<IHttpContextAccessor>()?
            .HttpContext.Session;
        SessionCart cart = session?.GetJson<SessionCart>("Cart")
            ?? new SessionCart();
        cart.Session = session;
        return cart;
    }

    [JsonIgnore]
    public ISession Session { get; set; }

    public override void AddItem(Product product, int quantity) {
        base.AddItem(product, quantity);
        Session.SetJson("Cart", this);
    }

    public override void RemoveLine(Product product) {
        base.RemoveLine(product);
        Session.SetJson("Cart", this);
    }

    public override void Clear() {
        base.Clear();
        Session.Remove("Cart");
    }
}
}
```

The SessionCart class subclasses the Cart class and overrides the AddItem, RemoveLine, and Clear methods so they call the base implementations and then store the updated state in the session using the extension methods on the ISession interface I defined in Chapter 9. The static GetCart method is a factory for creating SessionCart objects and providing them with an ISession object so they can store themselves.

Getting hold of the ISession object is a little complicated. I have to obtain an instance of the IHttpContextAccessor service, which provides me with access to an HttpContext object that, in turn, provides me with the ISession. This indirect approach is required because the session isn't provided as a regular service.

Registering the Service

The next step is to create a service for the Cart class. My goal is to satisfy requests for Cart objects with SessionCart objects that will seamlessly store themselves. You can see how I created the service in Listing 10-2.

Listing 10-2. Creating the Cart Service in the Startup.cs File in the SportsStore Folder

```
...
public void ConfigureServices(IServiceCollection services) {
    services.AddDbContext<ApplicationDbContext>(options =>
        options.UseSqlServer(
            Configuration["Data:SportStoreProducts:ConnectionString"]));
    services.AddTransient<IProductRepository, EFProductRepository>();
```

```
services.AddScoped<Cart>(sp => SessionCart.GetCart(sp));
services.AddSingleton<IHttpContextAccessor, HttpContextAccessor>();
services.AddMvc();
services.AddMemoryCache();
services.AddSession();
}
...
```

The AddScoped method specifies that the same object should be used to satisfy related requests for Cart instances. How requests are related can be configured, but by default, it means that any Cart required by components handling the same HTTP request will receive the same object.

Rather than provide the AddScoped method with a type mapping, as I did for the repository, I have specified a lambda expression that will be invoked to satisfy Cart requests. The expression receives the collection of services that have been registered and passes the collection to the GetCart method of the SessionCart class. The result is that requests for the Cart service will be handled by creating SessionCart objects, which will serialize themselves as session data when they are modified.

I also added a service using the AddSingleton method, which specifies that the same object should always be used. The service I created tells MVC to use the HttpContextAccessor class when implementations of the IHttpContextAccessor interface are required. This service is required so I can access the current session in the SessionCart class in Listing 10-1.

Simplifying the Cart Controller

The benefit of creating this kind of service is that it allows me to simplify the controllers where Cart objects are used. In Listing 10-3, I have reworked the CartController class to take advantage of the new service.

Listing 10-3. Using the Cart Service in the CartController.cs File in the Controllers Folder

```
using System.Linq;
using Microsoft.AspNetCore.Mvc;
using SportsStore.Models;
using SportsStore.Models.ViewModels;

namespace SportsStore.Controllers {

    public class CartController : Controller {
        private IProductRepository repository;
        private Cart cart;

        public CartController(IProductRepository repo, Cart cartService) {
            repository = repo;
            cart = cartService;
        }

        public ViewResult Index(string returnUrl) {
            return View(new CartIndexViewModel {
                Cart = cart,
                ReturnUrl = returnUrl
            });
        }
```

```
public RedirectToActionResult AddToCart(int productId, string returnUrl) {
    Product product = repository.Products
        .FirstOrDefault(p => p.ProductID == productId);
    if (product != null) {
        cart.AddItem(product, 1);
    }
    return RedirectToAction("Index", new { returnUrl });
}

public RedirectToActionResult RemoveFromCart(int productId,
        string returnUrl) {
    Product product = repository.Products
        .FirstOrDefault(p => p.ProductID == productId);

    if (product != null) {
        cart.RemoveLine(product);
    }
    return RedirectToAction("Index", new { returnUrl });
}
}
}
```

The CartController class indicates that it needs a Cart object by declaring a constructor argument, which has allowed me to remove the methods that read and write data from the session and the steps required to write updates. The result is a controller that is simpler and remains focused on its role in the application without having to worry about how Cart objects are created or persisted. And, since services are available throughout the application, any component can get hold of the user's cart using the same technique.

Completing the Cart Functionality

Now that I have introduced the Cart service, it is time to complete the cart functionality by adding two new features. The first will allow the customer to remove an item from the cart. The second feature will display a summary of the cart at the top of the page.

Removing Items from the Cart

I already defined and tested the RemoveFromCart action method in the controller, so letting the customer remove items is just a matter of exposing this method in a view, which I am going to do by adding a Remove button in each row of the cart summary. Listing 10-4 shows the changes to the Views/Cart/Index.cshtml file.

Listing 10-4. Introducing a Remove Button to the Index.cshtml File in the Views/Cart Folder

```
@model CartIndexViewModel

<h2>Your cart</h2>
<table class="table table-bordered table-striped">
    <thead>
        <tr>
            <th>Quantity</th>
            <th>Item</th>
```

```html
                <th class="text-right">Price</th>
                <th class="text-right">Subtotal</th>
            </tr>
        </thead>
        <tbody>
            @foreach (var line in Model.Cart.Lines) {
                <tr>
                    <td class="text-center">@line.Quantity</td>
                    <td class="text-left">@line.Product.Name</td>
                    <td class="text-right">@line.Product.Price.ToString("c")</td>
                    <td class="text-right">
                        @((line.Quantity * line.Product.Price).ToString("c"))
                    </td>
                    <td>
                        <form asp-action="RemoveFromCart" method="post">
                            <input type="hidden" name="ProductID"
                                    value="@line.Product.ProductID" />
                            <input type="hidden" name="returnUrl"
                                    value="@Model.ReturnUrl" />
                            <button type="submit" class="btn btn-sm btn-danger">
                                Remove
                            </button>
                        </form>
                    </td>
                </tr>
            }
        </tbody>
        <tfoot>
            <tr>
                <td colspan="3" class="text-right">Total:</td>
                <td class="text-right">
                    @Model.Cart.ComputeTotalValue().ToString("c")
                </td>
            </tr>
        </tfoot>
    </table>

    <div class="text-center">
        <a class="btn btn-primary" href="@Model.ReturnUrl">Continue shopping</a>
    </div>
```

I added a new column to each row of the table that contains a form with hidden input elements that specify the product to be removed and the return URL, along with a button that submits the form.

You can see the Remove buttons at work by running the application and adding items to the shopping cart. Remember that the cart already contains the functionality to remove it, which you can test by clicking one of the new buttons, as shown in Figure 10-1.

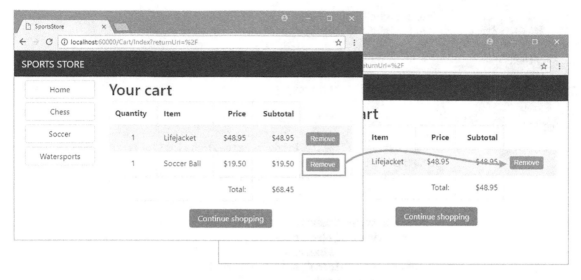

Figure 10-1. *Removing an item from the shopping cart*

Adding the Cart Summary Widget

I may have a functioning cart, but there is an issue with the way it is integrated into the interface. Customers can tell what is in their cart only by viewing the cart summary screen. And they can view the cart summary screen only by adding a new a new item to the cart.

To solve this problem, I am going to add a widget that summarizes the contents of the cart and that can be clicked to display the cart contents throughout the application. I will do this in much the same way that I added the navigation widget—as a view component whose output I can include in the Razor shared layout.

Adding the Font Awesome Package

As part of the cart summary, I am going to display a button that allows the user to check out. Rather than display the word *checkout* in the button, I want to use a cart symbol. Since I have no artistic skills, I am going to use the Font Awesome package, which is an excellent set of open source icons that are integrated into applications as fonts, where each character in the font is a different image. You can learn more about Font Awesome, including inspecting the icons it contains, at http://fortawesome.github.io/Font-Awesome.

I selected the SportsStore project and clicked the Show All Items button at the top of the Solution Explorer to reveal the bower.json file. I then added the Font Awesome package to the dependencies section, as shown in Listing 10-5.

Listing 10-5. Adding the Font Awesome Package in the bower.json File in the SportsStore Folder

```
{
  "name": "asp.net",
  "private": true,
  "dependencies": {
    "bootstrap": "4.0.0-alpha.6",
    "fontawesome": "4.7.0"
  }
}
```

When the bower.json file is saved, Visual Studio uses Bower to download and install the Font Awesome package in the www/lib/fontawesome folder.

Creating the View Component Class and View

I added a class file called CartSummaryViewComponent.cs in the Components folder and used it to define the view component shown in Listing 10-6.

Listing 10-6. The Contents of the CartSummaryViewComponent.cs File in the Components Folder

```
using Microsoft.AspNetCore.Mvc;
using SportsStore.Models;

namespace SportsStore.Components {

    public class CartSummaryViewComponent : ViewComponent {
        private Cart cart;

        public CartSummaryViewComponent(Cart cartService) {
            cart = cartService;
        }

        public IViewComponentResult Invoke() {
            return View(cart);
        }
    }
}
```

This view component is able to take advantage of the service that I created earlier in the chapter in order to receive a Cart object as a constructor argument. The result is a simple view component class that passes on the Cart object to the View method in order to generate the fragment of HTML that will be included in the layout. To create the layout, I created the Views/Shared/Components/CartSummary folder, added to it a Razor view file called Default.cshtml, and added the markup shown in Listing 10-7.

Listing 10-7. The Default.cshtml File in the Views/Shared/Components/CartSummary Folder

```
@model Cart

<div class="">
    @if (Model.Lines.Count() > 0) {
        <small class="navbar-text">
            <b>Your cart:</b>
            @Model.Lines.Sum(x => x.Quantity) item(s)
            @Model.ComputeTotalValue().ToString("c")
        </small>
    }
    <a class="btn btn-sm btn-secondary navbar-btn"
       asp-controller="Cart" asp-action="Index"
       asp-route-returnurl="@ViewContext.HttpContext.Request.PathAndQuery()">
        <i class="fa fa-shopping-cart"></i>
    </a>
</div>
```

The view displays a button with the Font Awesome cart icon and, if there are items in the cart, provides a snapshot that details the number of items and their total value. Now that I have a view component and a view, I can modify the shared layout so that the cart summary is included in the responses generated by the application's controllers, as shown in Listing 10-8.

Listing 10-8. Adding the Cart Summary in the _Layout.cshtml File in the Views/Shared Folder

```
<!DOCTYPE html>

<html>
<head>
    <meta name="viewport" content="width=device-width" />
    <link rel="stylesheet"
        asp-href-include="/lib/bootstrap/dist/**/*.min.css"
        asp-href-exclude="**/*-reboot*,**/*-grid*" />
    <link rel="stylesheet" asp-href-include="/lib/fontawesome/css/*.css" />
    <title>SportsStore</title>
</head>
<body>
    <div class="navbar navbar-inverse bg-inverse" role="navigation">
        <div class="row">
            <a class="col navbar-brand" href="#">SPORTS STORE</a>
            <div class="col-4 text-right">
                @await Component.InvokeAsync("CartSummary")
            </div>
        </div>
    </div>
    <div class="row m-1 p-1">
        <div id="categories" class="col-3">
            @await Component.InvokeAsync("NavigationMenu")
        </div>
        <div class="col-9">
            @RenderBody()
        </div>
    </div>
</body>
</html>
```

You can see the cart summary by starting the application. When the cart is empty, only the checkout button is shown. If you add items to the cart, then the number of items and their combined cost are shown, as illustrated in Figure 10-2. With this addition, customers know what is in their cart and have an obvious way to check out from the store.

Figure 10-2. *Displaying a summary of the cart*

Submitting Orders

I have now reached the final customer feature in SportsStore: the ability to check out and complete an order. In the following sections, I will extend the domain model to provide support for capturing the shipping details from a user and add the application support to process those details.

Creating the Model Class

I added a class file called Order.cs to the Models folder and edited it to match the contents shown in Listing 10-9. This is the class I will use to represent the shipping details for a customer.

Listing 10-9. The Contents of the Order.cs File in the Models Folder

```
using System.Collections.Generic;
using System.ComponentModel.DataAnnotations;
using Microsoft.AspNetCore.Mvc.ModelBinding;

namespace SportsStore.Models {

    public class Order {

        [BindNever]
        public int OrderID { get; set; }
        [BindNever]
        public ICollection<CartLine> Lines { get; set; }

        [Required(ErrorMessage = "Please enter a name")]
        public string Name { get; set; }

        [Required(ErrorMessage = "Please enter the first address line")]
        public string Line1 { get; set; }
        public string Line2 { get; set; }
        public string Line3 { get; set; }
```

```
    [Required(ErrorMessage = "Please enter a city name")]
    public string City { get; set; }

    [Required(ErrorMessage = "Please enter a state name")]
    public string State { get; set; }

    public string Zip { get; set; }

    [Required(ErrorMessage = "Please enter a country name")]
    public string Country { get; set; }

    public bool GiftWrap { get; set; }
    }
}
```

I am using the validation attributes from the System.ComponentModel.DataAnnotations namespace, just as I did in Chapter 2. I describe validation further in Chapter 27.

I also use the BindNever attribute, which prevents the user from supplying values for these properties in an HTTP request. This is a feature of the model binding system, which I describe in Chapter 26; it stops MVC using values from the HTTP request to populate sensitive or important model properties.

Adding the Checkout Process

The goal is to reach the point where users are able to enter their shipping details and submit their order. To start, I need to add a Checkout button to the cart summary view. Listing 10-10 shows the change I applied to the Views/Cart/Index.cshtml file.

Listing 10-10. Adding the Checkout Now Button to the Index.cshtml File in the Views/Cart Folder

```
...
<div class="text-center">
    <a class="btn btn-primary" href="@Model.ReturnUrl">Continue shopping</a>
    <a class="btn btn-primary" asp-action="Checkout" asp-controller="Order">
        Checkout
    </a>
</div>
...
```

This change generates a link that I have styled as a button and that, when clicked, calls the Checkout action method of the Order controller, which I create in the following section. You can see how this button appears in Figure 10-3.

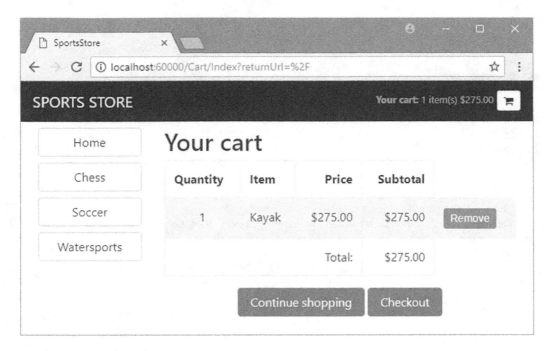

Figure 10-3. *The Checkout button*

I now need to define the Order controller. I added a class file called OrderController.cs to the Controllers folder and used it to define the class shown in Listing 10-11.

Listing 10-11. The Contents of the OrderController.cs File in the Controllers Folder

```
using Microsoft.AspNetCore.Mvc;
using SportsStore.Models;

namespace SportsStore.Controllers {

    public class OrderController : Controller {

        public ViewResult Checkout() => View(new Order());
    }
}
```

The Checkout method returns the default view and passes a new ShippingDetails object as the view model. To create the view, I created the Views/Order folder and added a Razor view file called Checkout.cs html with the markup shown in Listing 10-12.

Listing 10-12. The Contents of the Checkout.cshtml File in the Views/Order Folder

```
@model Order

<h2>Check out now</h2>
<p>Please enter your details, and we'll ship your goods right away!</p>

<form asp-action="Checkout" method="post">
    <h3>Ship to</h3>
    <div class="form-group">
        <label>Name:</label><input asp-for="Name" class="form-control" />
    </div>
    <h3>Address</h3>
    <div class="form-group">
        <label>Line 1:</label><input asp-for="Line1" class="form-control" />
    </div>
    <div class="form-group">
        <label>Line 2:</label><input asp-for="Line2" class="form-control" />
    </div>
    <div class="form-group">
        <label>Line 3:</label><input asp-for="Line3" class="form-control" />
    </div>
    <div class="form-group">
        <label>City:</label><input asp-for="City" class="form-control" />
    </div>
    <div class="form-group">
        <label>State:</label><input asp-for="State" class="form-control" />
    </div>
    <div class="form-group">
        <label>Zip:</label><input asp-for="Zip" class="form-control" />
    </div>
    <div class="form-group">
        <label>Country:</label><input asp-for="Country" class="form-control" />
    </div>
    <h3>Options</h3>
    <div class="checkbox">
        <label>
            <input asp-for="GiftWrap" /> Gift wrap these items
        </label>
    </div>
    <div class="text-center">
        <input class="btn btn-primary" type="submit" value="Complete Order" />
    </div>
</form>
```

For each of the properties in the model, I have created a label element and an input element to capture the user input, formatted with Bootstrap. The asp-for attribute on the input elements is handled by a built-in tag helper that generates the type, id, name, and value attributes based on the specified model property, as described in Chapter 24.

You can see the effect of the new action method and view by starting the application, clicking the cart button at the top of the page, and then clicking the Checkout button, as shown in Figure 10-4. You can also reach this point by requesting the /Cart/Checkout URL.

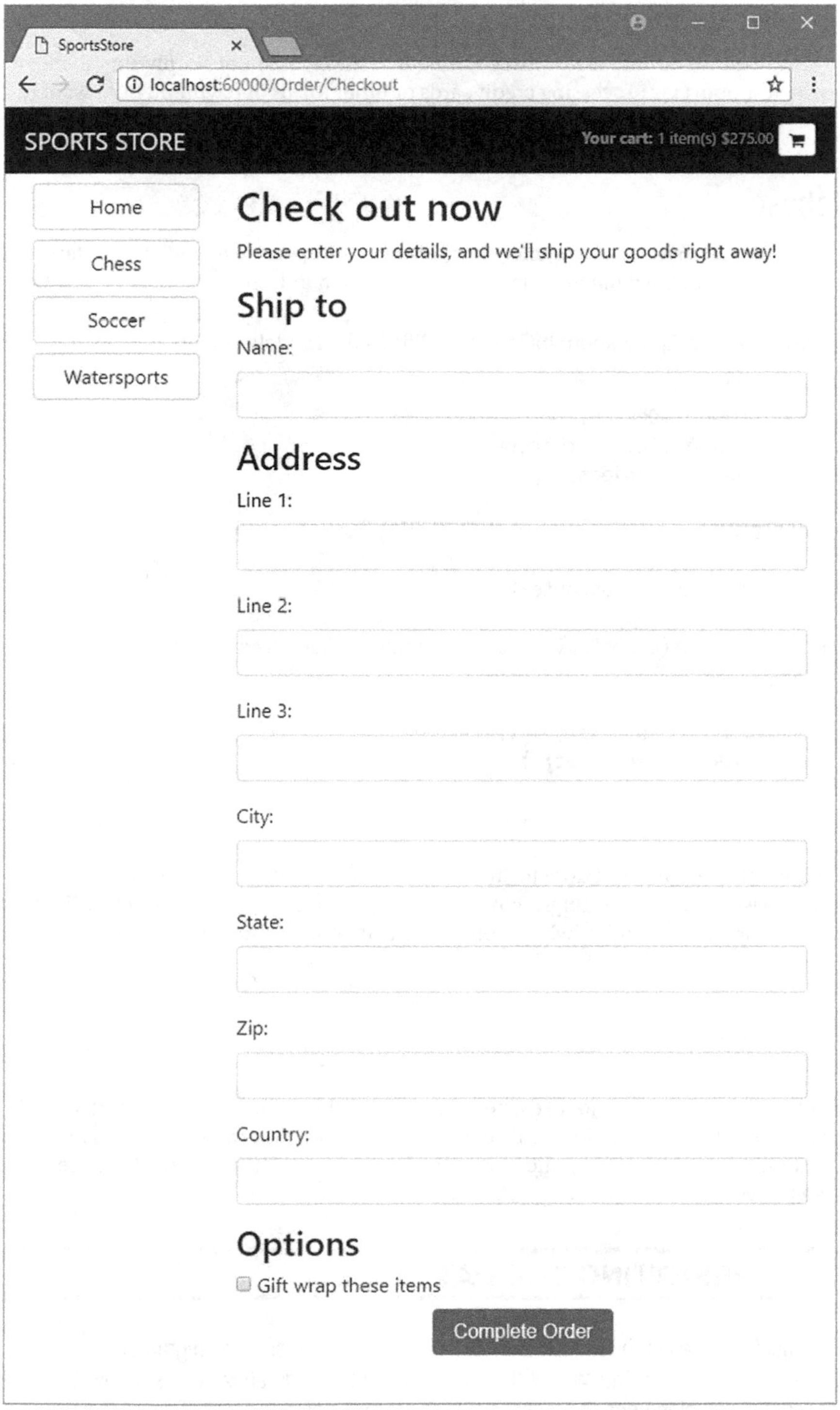

Figure 10-4. *The shipping details form*

Implementing Order Processing

I will process orders by writing them to the database. Most e-commerce sites would not simply stop there, of course, and I have not provided support for processing credit cards or other forms of payment. But I want to keep things focused on MVC, so a simple database entry will do.

Extending the Database

Adding a new kind of model to the database is simple once the basic plumbing that I created in Chapter 8 is in place. First, I added a new property to the database context class, as shown in Listing 10-13.

Listing 10-13. Adding a Property in the ApplicationDbContext.cs File in the Models Folder

```
using Microsoft.EntityFrameworkCore;
using Microsoft.EntityFrameworkCore.Design;
using Microsoft.EntityFrameworkCore.Infrastructure;
using Microsoft.Extensions.DependencyInjection;

namespace SportsStore.Models {

    public class ApplicationDbContext : DbContext {

        public ApplicationDbContext(DbContextOptions<ApplicationDbContext> options)
            : base(options) { }

        public DbSet<Product> Products { get; set; }
        public DbSet<Order> Orders { get; set; }
    }
}
```

This change is enough for Entity Framework Core to create a database migration that will allow Order objects to be stored in the database. To create the migration, open a new command prompt or PowerShell window, navigate to the SportsStore project folder (which contains the Startup.cs file), and run the following command:

```
dotnet ef migrations add Orders
```

This command tells Entity Framework Core to take a new snapshot of the application data model, work out how it differs from the previous database version, and generate a new migration called Orders. The new migration will be applied automatically when the application starts because SeedData calls the Migrate method provided by Entity Framework Core.

RESETTING THE DATABASE

When you are making frequent changes to the model, there will come a point when your migrations and your database schema get out of sync. The easiest thing to do is delete the database and start over. However, this applies only during development, of course, because you will lose any data you have stored.

To delete the database, run the following command in the SportsStore project folder:

```
dotnet ef database drop --force
```

Once the database has been removed, run the following command from the SportsStore folder to re-create the database and apply the migrations you have created by running the following command:

```
dotnet ef database update
```

This will reset the database so that it accurately reflects your model and allow you to return to developing your application.

Creating the Order Repository

I am going to follow the same pattern I used for the product repository to provide access to the Order objects. I added a class file called IOrderRepository.cs to the Models folder and used it to define the interface shown in Listing 10-14.

Listing 10-14. The Contents of the IOrderRepository.cs File in the Models Folder

```
using System.Linq;

namespace SportsStore.Models {

    public interface IOrderRepository {

        IQueryable<Order> Orders { get; }
        void SaveOrder(Order order);
    }
}
```

To implement the order repository interface, I added a class file called EFOrderRepository.cs to the Models folder and defined the class shown in Listing 10-15.

Listing 10-15. The Contents of the EFOrderRepository.cs File in the Models Folder

```
using Microsoft.EntityFrameworkCore;
using System.Linq;

namespace SportsStore.Models {

    public class EFOrderRepository : IOrderRepository {
        private ApplicationDbContext context;

        public EFOrderRepository(ApplicationDbContext ctx) {
            context = ctx;
        }
```

```
        public IQueryable<Order> Orders => context.Orders
                            .Include(o => o.Lines)
                            .ThenInclude(l => l.Product);

        public void SaveOrder(Order order) {
            context.AttachRange(order.Lines.Select(l => l.Product));
            if (order.OrderID == 0) {
                context.Orders.Add(order);
            }
            context.SaveChanges();
        }
    }
}
```

This class implements IOrderRepository using Entity Framework Core, allowing the set of Order objects that have been stored to be retrieved and allowing orders to be created or changed.

UNDERSTANDING THE ORDER REPOSITORY

There is a little extra work required to implement the repository for the orders in Listing 10-15. Entity Framework Core requires instruction to load related data if it spans multiple tables. In the listing, I used the Include and ThenInclude methods to specify that when an Order object is read from the database, the collection associated with the Lines property should also be loaded along with each Product object associated with each collection object.

```
...
public IQueryable<Order> Orders => context.Orders
    .Include(o => o.Lines)
    .ThenInclude(l => l.Product);
...
```

This ensures that I receive all the data objects that I need without having to perform the queries and assemble the data directly.

An additional step is required when I store an Order object in the database. When the user's cart data is deserialized from the session store, the JSON package creates new objects that are not known to Entity Framework Core, which then tries to write all the objects into the database. For the Product objects, this means that Entity Framework Core tries to write objects that have already been stored, which causes an error. To avoid this problem, I notify Entity Framework Core that the objects exist and shouldn't be stored in the database unless they are modified, as follows:

```
...
context.AttachRange(order.Lines.Select(l => l.Product));
...
```

This ensures that Entity Framework Core won't try to write the deserialized Product objects that are associated with the Order object.

In Listing 10-16, I have registered the order repository as a service in the ConfigureServices method of the Startup class.

Listing 10-16. Registering the Order Repository Service in the Startup.cs File in the SportsStore Folder

```
...
public void ConfigureServices(IServiceCollection services) {
    services.AddDbContext<ApplicationDbContext>(options =>
        options.UseSqlServer(
            Configuration["Data:SportStoreProducts:ConnectionString"]));
    services.AddTransient<IProductRepository, EFProductRepository>();
    services.AddScoped<Cart>(sp => SessionCart.GetCart(sp));
    services.AddSingleton<IHttpContextAccessor, HttpContextAccessor>();
    services.AddTransient<IOrderRepository, EFOrderRepository>();
    services.AddMvc();
    services.AddMemoryCache();
    services.AddSession();
}
...
```

Completing the Order Controller

To complete the OrderController class, I need to modify the constructor so that it receives the services it requires to process an order, and I need to add a new action method that will handle the HTTP form POST request when the user clicks the Complete Order button. Listing 10-17 shows both changes.

Listing 10-17. Completing the Controller in the OrderController.cs File in the Controllers Folder

```
using Microsoft.AspNetCore.Mvc;
using SportsStore.Models;
using System.Linq;

namespace SportsStore.Controllers {

    public class OrderController : Controller {
        private IOrderRepository repository;
        private Cart cart;

        public OrderController(IOrderRepository repoService, Cart cartService) {
            repository = repoService;
            cart = cartService;
        }

        public ViewResult Checkout() => View(new Order());

        [HttpPost]
        public IActionResult Checkout(Order order) {
            if (cart.Lines.Count() == 0) {
                ModelState.AddModelError("", "Sorry, your cart is empty!");
            }
```

```
        if (ModelState.IsValid) {
            order.Lines = cart.Lines.ToArray();
            repository.SaveOrder(order);
            return RedirectToAction(nameof(Completed));
        } else {
            return View(order);
        }
    }

    public ViewResult Completed() {
        cart.Clear();
        return View();
    }
    }
}
```

The Checkout action method is decorated with the HttpPost attribute, which means that it will be invoked for a POST request—in this case, when the user submits the form. Once again, I am relying on the model binding system so that I can receive the Order object, which I then complete using data from the Cart and store in the repository.

MVC checks the validation constraints that I applied to the Order class using the data annotation attributes, and any validation problems are passed to the action method through the ModelState property. I can see whether there are any problems by checking the ModelState.IsValid property. I call the ModelState.AddModelError method to register an error message if there are no items in the cart. I will explain how to display such errors shortly, and I have much more to say about model binding and validation in Chapters 27 and 28.

UNIT TEST: ORDER PROCESSING

To perform unit testing for the OrderController class, I need to test the behavior of the POST version of the Checkout method. Although the method looks short and simple, the use of MVC model binding means that there is a lot going on behind the scenes that needs to be tested.

I want to process an order only if there are items in the cart *and* the customer has provided valid shipping details. Under all other circumstances, the customer should be shown an error. Here is the first test method, which I defined in a class file called OrderControllerTests.cs in the SportsStore.Tests project:

```
using Microsoft.AspNetCore.Mvc;
using Moq;
using SportsStore.Controllers;
using SportsStore.Models;
using Xunit;

namespace SportsStore.Tests {

    public class OrderControllerTests {

        [Fact]
        public void Cannot_Checkout_Empty_Cart() {
```

```
        // Arrange - create a mock repository
        Mock<IOrderRepository> mock = new Mock<IOrderRepository>();
        // Arrange - create an empty cart
        Cart cart = new Cart();
        // Arrange - create the order
        Order order = new Order();
        // Arrange - create an instance of the controller
        OrderController target = new OrderController(mock.Object, cart);

        // Act
        ViewResult result = target.Checkout(order) as ViewResult;

        // Assert - check that the order hasn't been stored
        mock.Verify(m => m.SaveOrder(It.IsAny<Order>()), Times.Never);
        // Assert - check that the method is returning the default view
        Assert.True(string.IsNullOrEmpty(result.ViewName));
        // Assert - check that I am passing an invalid model to the view
        Assert.False(result.ViewData.ModelState.IsValid);
    }
  }
}
```

This test ensures that I cannot check out with an empty cart. I check this by ensuring that SaveOrder of the mock IOrderRepository implementation is never called, that the view the method returns is the default view (which will redisplay the data entered by customers and give them a chance to correct it), and that the model state being passed to the view has been marked as invalid. This may seem like a belt-and-braces set of assertions, but I need all three to be sure that I have the right behavior. The next test method works in much the same way but injects an error into the view model to simulate a problem reported by the model binder (which would happen in production when the customer enters invalid shipping data):

```
...
[Fact]
public void Cannot_Checkout_Invalid_ShippingDetails() {

    // Arrange - create a mock order repository
    Mock<IOrderRepository> mock = new Mock<IOrderRepository>();
    // Arrange - create a cart with one item
    Cart cart = new Cart();
    cart.AddItem(new Product(), 1);
    // Arrange - create an instance of the controller
    OrderController target = new OrderController(mock.Object, cart);
    // Arrange - add an error to the model
    target.ModelState.AddModelError("error", "error");

    // Act - try to checkout
    ViewResult result = target.Checkout(new Order()) as ViewResult;

    // Assert - check that the order hasn't been passed stored
    mock.Verify(m => m.SaveOrder(It.IsAny<Order>()), Times.Never);
    // Assert - check that the method is returning the default view
    Assert.True(string.IsNullOrEmpty(result.ViewName));
```

```
        // Assert - check that I am passing an invalid model to the view
        Assert.False(result.ViewData.ModelState.IsValid);
}
...
```

Having established that an empty cart or invalid details will prevent an order from being processed, I need to ensure that I process orders when appropriate. Here is the test:

```
...
[Fact]
public void Can_Checkout_And_Submit_Order() {
    // Arrange - create a mock order repository
    Mock<IOrderRepository> mock = new Mock<IOrderRepository>();
    // Arrange - create a cart with one item
    Cart cart = new Cart();
    cart.AddItem(new Product(), 1);
    // Arrange - create an instance of the controller
    OrderController target = new OrderController(mock.Object, cart);

    // Act - try to checkout
    RedirectToActionResult result =
        target.Checkout(new Order()) as RedirectToActionResult;

    // Assert - check that the order has been stored
    mock.Verify(m => m.SaveOrder(It.IsAny<Order>()), Times.Once);
    // Assert - check that the method is redirecting to the Completed action
    Assert.Equal("Completed", result.ActionName);
}
...
```

I did not need to test that I can identify valid shipping details. This is handled for me automatically by the model binder using the attributes applied to the properties of the Order class.

Displaying Validation Errors

MVC will use the validation attributes applied to the Order class to validate user data. However, I need to make a simple change to display any problems. This relies on another built-in tag helper that inspects the validation state of the data provided by the user and adds warning messages for each problem that has been discovered. Listing 10-18 shows the addition of an HTML element that will be processed by the tag helper to the Checkout.cshtml file.

Listing 10-18. Adding a Validation Summary to the Checkout.cshtml File in the Views/Order Folder

```
@model Order

<h2>Check out now</h2>
<p>Please enter your details, and we'll ship your goods right away!</p>

<div asp-validation-summary="All" class="text-danger"></div>

<form asp-action="Checkout" method="post">
    <h3>Ship to</h3>
...
```

With this simple change, validation errors are reported to the user. To see the effect, go to the /Order/ Checkout URL and try to check out without selecting any products or filling in any shipping details, as shown in Figure 10-5. The tag helper that generates these messages is part of the model validation system, which I describe in detail in Chapter 27.

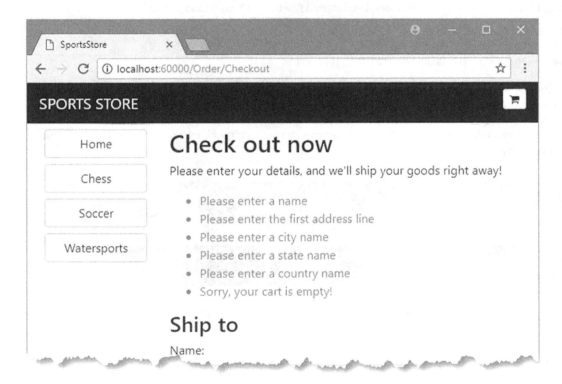

Figure 10-5. *Displaying validation messages*

■ **Tip**   The data submitted by the user is sent to the server before it is validated, which is known as *server-side validation* and for which MVC has excellent support. The problem with server-side validation is that the user isn't told about errors until after the data has been sent to the server and processed and the result page has been generated—something that can take a few seconds on a busy server. For this reason, server-side validation is usually complemented by client-side validation, where JavaScript is used to check the values that the user has entered before the form data is sent to the server. I describe client-side validation in Chapter 27.

Displaying a Summary Page

To complete the checkout process, I need to create the view that will be shown when the browser is redirected to the Completed action on the Order controller. I added a Razor view file called Completed. cshtml to the Views/Order folder and added the markup shown in Listing 10-19.

Listing 10-19.   The Contents of the Completed.cshtml File in the Views/Order Folder

```
<h2>Thanks!</h2>
<p>Thanks for placing your order.</p>
<p>We'll ship your goods as soon as possible.</p>
```

I don't need to make any code changes to integrate this view into the application because I already added the required statements when I defined the Completed action method. Now customers can go through the entire process, from selecting products to checking out. If they provide valid shipping details (and have items in their cart), they will see the summary page when they click the Complete Order button, as shown in Figure 10-6.

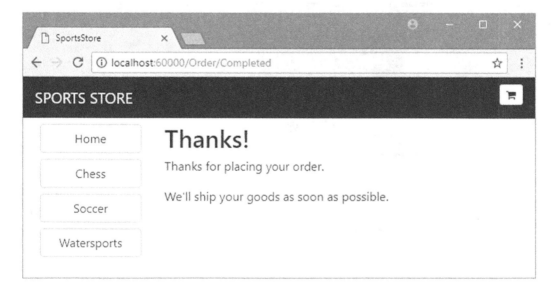

Figure 10-6.   *The completed order summary view*

Summary

I have completed all the major parts of the customer-facing portion of SportsStore. It might not be enough to worry Amazon, but I have a product catalog that can be browsed by category and page, a neat shopping cart, and a simple checkout process.

The well-separated architecture means I can easily change the behavior of any piece of the application without causing problems or inconsistencies elsewhere. For example, I could change the way that orders are stored and it would not have any impact on the shopping cart, the product catalog, or any other area of the application. In the next chapter, I add the features required to administer the SportsStore application.

■ ■ ■

CHAPTER 11

SportsStore: Administration

In this chapter, I continue to build the SportsStore application to give the site administrator a way of managing orders and products.

Managing Orders

In the previous chapter, I added support for receiving orders from customers and storing them in a database. In this chapter, I am going to create a simple administration tool that will let me view the orders that have been received and mark them as shipped.

Enhancing the Model

The first change I need to make is to enhance the model so that I can record which orders have been shipped. Listing 11-1 shows the addition of a new property to the Order class, which is defined in the Order.cs file in the Models folder.

Listing 11-1. Adding a Property in the Order.cs File in the Models Folder

```
using System.Collections.Generic;
using System.ComponentModel.DataAnnotations;
using Microsoft.AspNetCore.Mvc.ModelBinding;

namespace SportsStore.Models {

    public class Order {

        [BindNever]
        public int OrderID { get; set; }
        [BindNever]
        public ICollection<CartLine> Lines { get; set; }

        [BindNever]
        public bool Shipped { get; set; }

        [Required(ErrorMessage = "Please enter a name")]
        public string Name { get; set; }

        [Required(ErrorMessage = "Please enter the first address line")]
        public string Line1 { get; set; }
```

© Adam Freeman 2017
A. Freeman, *Pro ASP.NET Core MVC 2*, https://doi.org/10.1007/978-1-4842-3150-0_11

```
        public string Line2 { get; set; }
        public string Line3 { get; set; }

        [Required(ErrorMessage = "Please enter a city name")]
        public string City { get; set; }

        [Required(ErrorMessage = "Please enter a state name")]
        public string State { get; set; }

        public string Zip { get; set; }

        [Required(ErrorMessage = "Please enter a country name")]
        public string Country { get; set; }

        public bool GiftWrap { get; set; }
    }
}
```

This iterative approach of extending and adapting the model to support different features is typical of MVC development. In an ideal world, you would be able to completely define the model classes at the start of the project and just build the application around them, but that happens only for the simplest of projects, and, in practice, iterative development is to be expected as the understanding of what is required develops and evolves.

Entity Framework Core migrations make this process easier because you don't have to manually keep the database schema synchronized to the model class by writing your own SQL commands. To update the database to reflect the addition of the Shipped property to the Order class, open a new command prompt or PowerShell window, navigate to the SportsStore project folder (which is the one that contains the Startup.cs file) and run the following command:

```
dotnet ef migrations add ShippedOrders
```

The migration will be applied automatically when the application is started and the SeedData class calls the Migrate method provided by Entity Framework Core.

Adding the Actions and View

The functionality required to display and update the set of orders in the database is relatively simple because it builds on the features and infrastructure that I created in previous chapters. In Listing 11-2, I have added two new action methods to the Order controller.

Listing 11-2. Adding Action Methods in the OrderController.cs File in the Controllers Folder

```
using Microsoft.AspNetCore.Mvc;
using SportsStore.Models;
using System.Linq;

namespace SportsStore.Controllers {

    public class OrderController : Controller {
        private IOrderRepository repository;
        private Cart cart;
```

```
public OrderController(IOrderRepository repoService, Cart cartService) {
    repository = repoService;
    cart = cartService;
}

public ViewResult List() =>
    View(repository.Orders.Where(o => !o.Shipped));

[HttpPost]
public IActionResult MarkShipped(int orderID) {
    Order order = repository.Orders
        .FirstOrDefault(o => o.OrderID == orderID);
    if (order != null) {
        order.Shipped = true;
        repository.SaveOrder(order);
    }
    return RedirectToAction(nameof(List));
}

public ViewResult Checkout() => View(new Order());

[HttpPost]
public IActionResult Checkout(Order order) {
    if (cart.Lines.Count() == 0) {
        ModelState.AddModelError("", "Sorry, your cart is empty!");
    }
    if (ModelState.IsValid) {
        order.Lines = cart.Lines.ToArray();
        repository.SaveOrder(order);
        return RedirectToAction(nameof(Completed));
    } else {
        return View(order);
    }
}

public ViewResult Completed() {
    cart.Clear();
    return View();
}
}
}
```

The List method selects all the Order objects in the repository that have a Shipped value of false and passes them to the default view. This is the action method that I will use to display a list of the unshipped orders to the administrator.

The MarkShipped method will receive a POST request that specifies the ID of an order, which is used to locate the corresponding Order object from the repository so that the Shipped property can be set to true and saved.

To display the list of unshipped orders, I added a Razor view file called List.cshtml to the Views/Order folder and added the markup shown in Listing 11-3. A table element is used to display some of the details from each other, including details of which products have been purchased.

Listing 11-3. The Contents of the List.cshtml File in the Views/Order Folder

```
@model IEnumerable<Order>

@{
    ViewBag.Title = "Orders";
    Layout = "_AdminLayout";
}

@if (Model.Count() > 0) {

    <table class="table table-bordered table-striped">
        <tr><th>Name</th><th>Zip</th><th colspan="2">Details</th><th></th></tr>
        @foreach (Order o in Model) {
            <tr>
                <td>@o.Name</td><td>@o.Zip</td><th>Product</th><th>Quantity</th>
                <td>
                    <form asp-action="MarkShipped" method="post">
                        <input type="hidden" name="orderId" value="@o.OrderID" />
                        <button type="submit" class="btn btn-sm btn-danger">
                            Ship
                        </button>
                    </form>
                </td>
            </tr>
            @foreach (CartLine line in o.Lines) {
                <tr>
                    <td colspan="2"></td>
                    <td>@line.Product.Name</td><td>@line.Quantity</td>
                    <td></td>
                </tr>

            }
        }
    </table>
} else {
    <div class="text-center">No Unshipped Orders</div>
}
```

Each order is displayed with a Ship button that submits a form to the MarkShipped action method. I specified a different layout for the List view using the Layout property, which overrides the layout specified in the _ViewStart.cshtml file.

To add the layout, I used the MVC View Layout Page item template to create a file called _AdminLayout. cshtml in the Views/Shared folder, and I added the markup shown in Listing 11-4.

Listing 11-4. The Contents of the _AdminLayout.cshtml File in the Views/Shared Folder

```
<!DOCTYPE html>
<html>
<head>
    <meta name="viewport" content="width=device-width" />
    <link rel="stylesheet" asp-href-include="lib/bootstrap/dist/css/*.min.css" />
    <title>@ViewBag.Title</title>
```

```
</head>
<body class="m-1 p-1">
    <div class="bg-info p-2"><h4>@ViewBag.Title</h4></div>
    @RenderBody()
</body>
</html>
```

To see and manage the orders in the application, start the application, select some products, and then check out. Then navigate to the /Order/List URL and you will see a summary of the order you created, as shown in Figure 11-1. Click the Ship button; the database will be updated, and the list of pending orders will be empty.

■ **Note**   At the moment, there is nothing to stop customers from requesting the /Order/List URL and administering their own orders. I explain how to restrict access to action methods in Chapter 12.

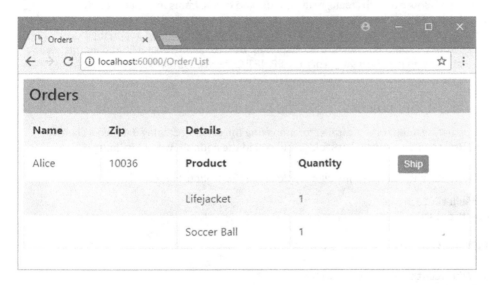

Figure 11-1. *Managing orders*

Adding Catalog Management

The convention for managing more complex collections of items is to present the user with two types of pages: a *list* page and an *edit* page, as shown in Figure 11-2.

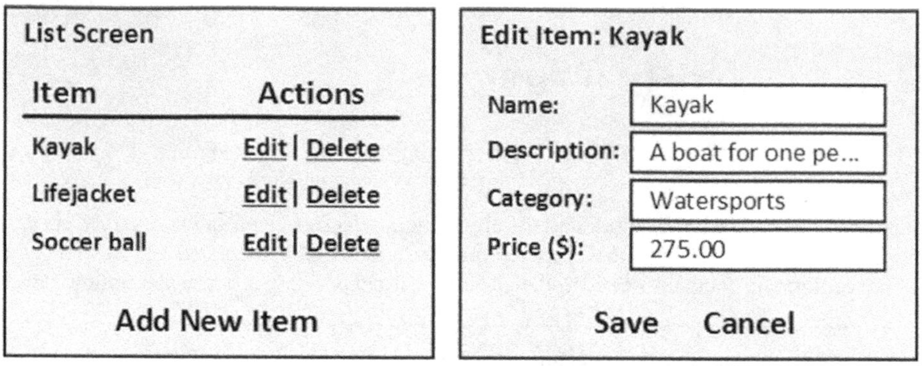

Figure 11-2. *Sketch of a CRUD UI for the product catalog*

Together, these pages allow a user to create, read, update, and delete items in the collection. Collectively, these actions are known as *CRUD*. Developers need to implement CRUD so often that Visual Studio scaffolding includes scenarios for creating CRUD controllers with predefined action methods (I explained how to enable the scaffolding feature in Chapter 8). But like all the Visual Studio templates, I think it is better to learn how to use the features of the ASP.NET Core MVC directly.

Creating a CRUD Controller

I am going to start by creating a separate controller for managing the product catalog. I added a class file called AdminController.cs to the Controllers folder and added the code shown in Listing 11-5.

Listing 11-5. The Contents of the AdminController.cs File in the Controllers Folder

```
using Microsoft.AspNetCore.Mvc;
using SportsStore.Models;

namespace SportsStore.Controllers {

    public class AdminController : Controller {
        private IProductRepository repository;

        public AdminController(IProductRepository repo) {
            repository = repo;
        }

        public ViewResult Index() => View(repository.Products);
    }
}
```

The controller constructor declares a dependency on the IProductRepository interface, which will be resolved when instances are created. The controller defines a single action method, Index, that calls the View method to select the default view for the action, passing the set of products in the database as the view model.

UNIT TEST: THE INDEX ACTION

The behavior that I care about for the Index method of the Admin controller is that it correctly returns the Product objects that are in the repository. I can test this by creating a mock repository implementation and comparing the test data with the data returned by the action method. Here is the unit test, which I placed into a new unit test file called AdminControllerTests.cs in the SportsStore.UnitTests project:

```
using System.Collections.Generic;
using System.Linq;
using Microsoft.AspNetCore.Mvc;
using Moq;
using SportsStore.Controllers;
using SportsStore.Models;
using Xunit;

namespace SportsStore.Tests {

    public class AdminControllerTests {

        [Fact]
        public void Index_Contains_All_Products() {
            // Arrange - create the mock repository
            Mock<IProductRepository> mock = new Mock<IProductRepository>();
            mock.Setup(m => m.Products).Returns(new Product[] {
                new Product {ProductID = 1, Name = "P1"},
                new Product {ProductID = 2, Name = "P2"},
                new Product {ProductID = 3, Name = "P3"},
            }.AsQueryable<Product>());

            // Arrange - create a controller
            AdminController target = new AdminController(mock.Object);

            // Action
            Product[] result
                = GetViewModel<IEnumerable<Product>>(target.Index())?.ToArray();

            // Assert
            Assert.Equal(3, result.Length);
            Assert.Equal("P1", result[0].Name);
            Assert.Equal("P2", result[1].Name);
            Assert.Equal("P3", result[2].Name);
        }

        private T GetViewModel<T>(IActionResult result) where T : class {
            return (result as ViewResult)?.ViewData.Model as T;
        }
    }
}
```

I added a GetViewModel method to the test to unpack the result from the action method and get the view model data. I'll be adding more tests that use this method later in the chapter.

Implementing the List View

The next step is to add a view for the Index action method of the Admin controller. I created the Views/Admin folder and added a Razor file called Index.cshtml, the contents of which are shown in Listing 11-6.

Listing 11-6. The Contents of the Index.cshtml File in the Views/Admin Folder

```
@model IEnumerable<Product>

@{
    ViewBag.Title = "All Products";
    Layout = "_AdminLayout";
}

<table class="table table-striped table-bordered table-sm">
    <tr>
        <th class="text-right">ID</th>
        <th>Name</th>
        <th class="text-right">Price</th>
        <th class="text-center">Actions</th>
    </tr>
    @foreach (var item in Model) {
        <tr>
            <td class="text-right">@item.ProductID</td>
            <td>@item.Name</td>
            <td class="text-right">@item.Price.ToString("c")</td>
            <td class="text-center">
                <form asp-action="Delete" method="post">
                    <a asp-action="Edit" class="btn btn-sm btn-warning"
                       asp-route-productId="@item.ProductID">
                        Edit
                    </a>
                    <input type="hidden" name="ProductID" value="@item.ProductID" />
                    <button type="submit" class="btn btn-danger btn-sm">
                        Delete
                    </button>
                </form>
            </td>
        </tr>
    }
</table>
<div class="text-center">
    <a asp-action="Create" class="btn btn-primary">Add Product</a>
</div>
```

This view contains a table that has a row for each product with cells that contain the name of the product, the price, and buttons that will allow the product to be edited or deleted by sending requests to Edit and Delete actions. In addition to the table, there is an Add Product button that targets the Create action. I'll add the Edit, Delete, and Create actions in the sections that follow, but you can see how the products are displayed by starting the application and requesting the /Admin/Index URL, as shown in Figure 11-3.

■ **Tip**   The Edit button is inside the form element in Listing 11-6 so that the two buttons sit next to each other, working around the spacing that Bootstrap applies. The Edit button will send an HTTP GET request to the server to get the current details of a product; this doesn't require a form element. However, since the Delete button will make a change to the application state, I need to use an HTTP POST request—and that does require the form element.

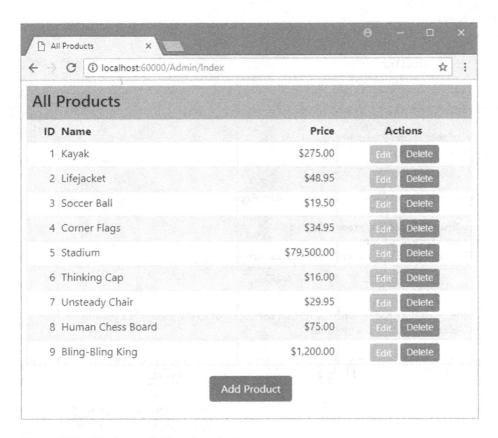

Figure 11-3. *Displaying the list of products*

Editing Products

To provide create and update features, I will add a product-editing page like the one shown in Figure 11-2. These are the two parts of this job:

- Display a page that will allow the administrator to change values for the properties of a product

- Add an action method that can process those changes when they are submitted

Creating the Edit Action Method

Listing 11-7 shows the Edit action method I added to the Admin controller, which will receive the HTTP request sent by the browser when the user clicks an Edit button.

Listing 11-7. Adding an Edit Action Method in the AdminController.cs File in the Controllers Folder

```
using Microsoft.AspNetCore.Mvc;
using SportsStore.Models;
using System.Linq;

namespace SportsStore.Controllers {

    public class AdminController : Controller {
        private IProductRepository repository;

        public AdminController(IProductRepository repo) {
            repository = repo;
        }

        public ViewResult Index() => View(repository.Products);

        public ViewResult Edit(int productId) =>
            View(repository.Products
                .FirstOrDefault(p => p.ProductID == productId));
    }
}
```

This simple method finds the product with the ID that corresponds to the productId parameter and passes it as a view model object to the View method.

UNIT TEST: THE EDIT ACTION METHOD

I want to test for two behaviors in the Edit action method. The first is that I get the product I ask for when I provide a valid ID value to make sure that I am editing the product I expected. The second behavior to test is that I do not get any product at all when I request an ID value that is not in the repository. Here are the test methods I added to the AdminControllerTests.cs class file:

```
...
[Fact]
public void Can_Edit_Product() {
    // Arrange - create the mock repository
    Mock<IProductRepository> mock = new Mock<IProductRepository>();
    mock.Setup(m => m.Products).Returns(new Product[] {
        new Product {ProductID = 1, Name = "P1"},
        new Product {ProductID = 2, Name = "P2"},
        new Product {ProductID = 3, Name = "P3"},
    }.AsQueryable<Product>());
```

```
    // Arrange - create the controller
    AdminController target = new AdminController(mock.Object);

    // Act
    Product p1 = GetViewModel<Product>(target.Edit(1));
    Product p2 = GetViewModel<Product>(target.Edit(2));
    Product p3 = GetViewModel<Product>(target.Edit(3));

    // Assert
    Assert.Equal(1, p1.ProductID);
    Assert.Equal(2, p2.ProductID);
    Assert.Equal(3, p3.ProductID);
}

[Fact]
public void Cannot_Edit_Nonexistent_Product() {
    // Arrange - create the mock repository
    Mock<IProductRepository> mock = new Mock<IProductRepository>();
    mock.Setup(m => m.Products).Returns(new Product[] {
        new Product {ProductID = 1, Name = "P1"},
        new Product {ProductID = 2, Name = "P2"},
        new Product {ProductID = 3, Name = "P3"},
    }.AsQueryable<Product>());

    // Arrange - create the controller
    AdminController target = new AdminController(mock.Object);

    // Act
    Product result = GetViewModel<Product>(target.Edit(4));

    // Assert
    Assert.Null(result);
}
...
```

Creating the Edit View

Now that I have an action method, I can create a view for it to display. I added a Razor view file called Edit.cshtml to the Views/Admin folder and added the markup shown in Listing 11-8.

Listing 11-8. The Contents of the Edit.cshtml File in the Views/Admin Folder

```
@model Product
@{
    ViewBag.Title = "Edit Product";
    Layout = "_AdminLayout";
}

<form asp-action="Edit" method="post">
    <input type="hidden" asp-for="ProductID" />
```

```
<div class="form-group">
    <label asp-for="Name"></label>
    <input asp-for="Name" class="form-control" />
</div>
<div class="form-group">
    <label asp-for="Description"></label>
    <textarea asp-for="Description" class="form-control"></textarea>
</div>
<div class="form-group">
    <label asp-for="Category"></label>
    <input asp-for="Category" class="form-control" />
</div>
<div class="form-group">
    <label asp-for="Price"></label>
    <input asp-for="Price" class="form-control" />
</div>
<div class="text-center">
    <button class="btn btn-primary" type="submit">Save</button>
    <a asp-action="Index" class="btn btn-secondary">Cancel</a>
</div>
</form>
```

The view contains an HTML form that uses tag helpers to generate much of the content, including setting the target for the form and a elements, setting the content of the label elements, and producing the name, 1d, and value attributes for the input and textarea elements.

You can see the HTML produced by the view by starting the application, navigating to the /Admin/Index URL, and clicking the Edit button for one of the products, as shown in Figure 11-4.

■ **Tip**   I have used a hidden input element for the ProductID property for simplicity. The value of the ProductID is generated by the database as a primary key when a new object is stored by Entity Framework Core, and safely changing it can be a complex process. For most applications, the simplest approach is to prevent the user from changing the value.

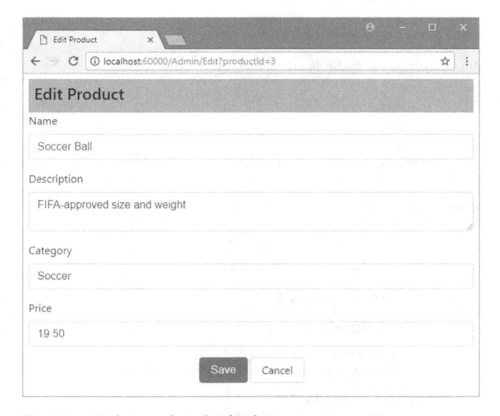

Figure 11-4. *Displaying product values for editing*

Updating the Product Repository

Before I can process edits, I need to enhance the product repository so that it is able to save changes. First, I added a new method to the IProductRepository interface, as shown in Listing 11-9.

Listing 11-9. Adding a Method to the IProductRespository.cs File in the Models Folder

```
using System.Linq;

namespace SportsStore.Models {

    public interface IProductRepository {

        IQueryable<Product> Products { get; }

        void SaveProduct(Product product);
    }
}
```

I can then add the new method to the Entity Framework Core implementation of the repository, which is defined in the EFProductRepository.cs file, as shown in Listing 11-10.

Listing 11-10. Implementing the New Method in the EFProductRepository.cs File in the Models Folder

```
using System.Collections.Generic;
using System.Linq;

namespace SportsStore.Models {

    public class EFProductRepository : IProductRepository {
        private ApplicationDbContext context;

        public EFProductRepository(ApplicationDbContext ctx) {
            context = ctx;
        }

        public IQueryable<Product> Products => context.Products;

        public void SaveProduct(Product product) {
            if (product.ProductID == 0) {
                context.Products.Add(product);
            } else {
                Product dbEntry = context.Products
                    .FirstOrDefault(p => p.ProductID == product.ProductID);
                if (dbEntry != null) {
                    dbEntry.Name = product.Name;
                    dbEntry.Description = product.Description;
                    dbEntry.Price = product.Price;
                    dbEntry.Category = product.Category;
                }
            }
            context.SaveChanges();
        }
    }
}
```

The implementation of the SaveChanges method adds a product to the repository if the ProductID is 0; otherwise, it applies any changes to the existing entry in the database.

I do not want to go into details of Entity Framework Core because, as I explained earlier, it is a topic in itself and not part of ASP.NET Core MVC. But there is something in the SaveProduct method that has a bearing on the design of the MVC application.

I know I need to perform an update when I receive a Product parameter that has a ProductID that is not zero. I do this by getting a Product object from the repository with the same ProductID and updating each of the properties so they match the parameter object.

I can do this because Entity Framework Core keeps track of the objects that it creates from the database. The object passed to the SaveChanges method is created by the MVC model binding feature, which means that Entity Framework Core does not know anything about the new Product object and will not apply an update to the database when it is modified. There are lots of ways of resolving this issue, and I have taken the simplest one, which is to locate the corresponding object that Entity Framework Core *does* know about and update it explicitly.

The addition of a new method in the IProductRepository interface has broken the fake repository class—FakeProductRepository—that I created in Chapter 8. I used the fake repository to kick-start the development process and demonstrate how services can be used to seamlessly replace interface implementations without needing to modify the components that rely on them. I don't need the fake repository any further, and in Listing 11-11, you can see that I have removed the interface from the class declaration so that I don't have to keep modifying the class as I add repository features.

Listing 11-11. Removing the Interface in the FakeProductRepository.cs File in the Models Folder

```
using System.Collections.Generic;
using System.Linq;

namespace SportsStore.Models {

    public class FakeProductRepository /* : IProductRepository */ {

        public IQueryable<Product> Products => new List<Product> {
            new Product { Name = "Football", Price = 25 },
            new Product { Name = "Surf board", Price = 179 },
            new Product { Name = "Running shoes", Price = 95 }
        }.AsQueryable<Product>();
    }
}
```

Handling Edit POST Requests

I am ready to implement an overload of the Edit action method in the Admin controller that will handle POST requests when the administrator clicks the Save button. Listing 11-12 shows the new action method.

Listing 11-12. Defining an Action Method in the AdminController.cs File in the Controllers Folder

```
using Microsoft.AspNetCore.Mvc;
using SportsStore.Models;
using System.Linq;

namespace SportsStore.Controllers {

    public class AdminController : Controller {
        private IProductRepository repository;

        public AdminController(IProductRepository repo) {
            repository = repo;
        }

        public ViewResult Index() => View(repository.Products);

        public ViewResult Edit(int productId) =>
            View(repository.Products
                .FirstOrDefault(p => p.ProductID == productId));

        [HttpPost]
        public IActionResult Edit(Product product) {
```

```
        if (ModelState.IsValid) {
            repository.SaveProduct(product);
            TempData["message"] = $"{product.Name} has been saved";
            return RedirectToAction("Index");
        } else {
            // there is something wrong with the data values
            return View(product);
        }
    }
}
```

I check that the model binding process has been able to validate the data submitted by the user by reading the value of the ModelState.IsValid property. If everything is OK, I save the changes to the repository and redirect the user to the Index action so they see the modified list of products. If there is a problem with the data, I render the default view again so that the user can make corrections.

After I have saved the changes in the repository, I store a message using the *temp data* feature, which is part of the ASP.NET Core session state feature. This is a key/value dictionary similar to the session data and view bag features I used previously. The key difference from session data is that temp data persists until it is read.

I cannot use ViewBag in this situation because ViewBag passes data between the controller and view and it cannot hold data for longer than the current HTTP request. When an edit succeeds, the browser is redirected to a new URL, so the ViewBag data is lost. I could use the session data feature, but then the message would be persistent until I explicitly removed it, which I would rather not have to do.

So, the temp data feature is the perfect fit. The data is restricted to a single user's session (so that users do not see each other's TempData) and will persist long enough for me to read it. I will read the data in the view rendered by the action method to which I have redirected the user, which I define in the next section.

UNIT TEST: EDIT SUBMISSIONS

For the POST-processing Edit action method, I need to make sure that valid updates to the Product object, which is received as the method argument, are passed to the product repository to be saved. I also want to check that invalid updates (where a model validation error exists) are not passed to the repository. Here are the test methods, which I added to the AdminControllerTests.cs file:

```
...
[Fact]
public void Can_Save_Valid_Changes() {
    // Arrange - create mock repository
    Mock<IProductRepository> mock = new Mock<IProductRepository>();
    // Arrange - create mock temp data
    Mock<ITempDataDictionary> tempData = new Mock<ITempDataDictionary>();
    // Arrange - create the controller
    AdminController target = new AdminController(mock.Object) {
        TempData = tempData.Object
    };
    // Arrange - create a product
    Product product = new Product { Name = "Test" };

    // Act - try to save the product
    IActionResult result = target.Edit(product);
```

```
        // Assert - check that the repository was called
        mock.Verify(m => m.SaveProduct(product));
        // Assert - check the result type is a redirection
        Assert.IsType<RedirectToActionResult>(result);
        Assert.Equal("Index", (result as RedirectToActionResult).ActionName);
    }

    [Fact]
    public void Cannot_Save_Invalid_Changes() {
        // Arrange - create mock repository
        Mock<IProductRepository> mock = new Mock<IProductRepository>();
        // Arrange - create the controller
        AdminController target = new AdminController(mock.Object);
        // Arrange - create a product
        Product product = new Product { Name = "Test" };
        // Arrange - add an error to the model state
        target.ModelState.AddModelError("error", "error");

        // Act - try to save the product
        IActionResult result = target.Edit(product);

        // Assert - check that the repository was not called
        mock.Verify(m => m.SaveProduct(It.IsAny<Product>()), Times.Never());
        // Assert - check the method result type
        Assert.IsType<ViewResult>(result);
    }
    ...
```

Displaying a Confirmation Message

I am going to deal with the message I stored using TempData in the _AdminLayout.cshtml layout file, as shown in Listing 11-13. By handling the message in the template, I can create messages in any view that uses the template without needing to create additional Razor expressions.

Listing 11-13. Handling the ViewBag Message in the _AdminLayout.cshtml File

```
<!DOCTYPE html>
<html>
<head>
    <meta name="viewport" content="width=device-width" />
    <link rel="stylesheet" asp-href-include="lib/bootstrap/dist/css/*.min.css" />
    <title>@ViewBag.Title</title>
</head>
<body class="m-1 p-1">
    <div class="bg-info p-2"><h4>@ViewBag.Title</h4></div>
    @if (TempData["message"] != null) {
        <div class="alert alert-success">@TempData["message"]</div>
    }
    @RenderBody()
</body>
</html>
```

311

■ **Tip**   The benefit of dealing with the message in the template like this is that users will see it displayed on whatever page is rendered after they have saved a change. At the moment, I return them to the list of products, but I could change the workflow to render some other view, and the users will still see the message (as long as the next view also uses the same layout).

I now have all the pieces in place to edit products. To see how it all works, start the application, navigate to the /Admin/Index URL, click the Edit button, and make a change. Click the Save button. You will be redirected to the /Admin/Index URL, and the TempData message will be displayed, as shown in Figure 11-5. The message will disappear if you reload the product list screen because TempData is deleted when it is read. That is convenient since I do not want old messages hanging around.

Figure 11-5. *Editing a product and seeing the TempData message*

Adding Model Validation

I have reached the point where I need to add validation rules to the model classes. At the moment, the administrator could enter negative prices or blank descriptions, and SportsStore would happily store that data in the database. Whether or not the bad data would be successfully persisted would depend on whether it conformed to the constraints in the SQL tables created by Entity Framework Core, and that is not enough protection for most applications. To guard against bad data values, I decorated the properties of the Product class with attributes, as shown in Listing 11-14, just as I did for the Order class in Chapter 10.

Listing 11-14. Applying Validation Attributes in the Product.cs File in the Models Folder

```
using System.ComponentModel.DataAnnotations;
using Microsoft.AspNetCore.Mvc.ModelBinding;

namespace SportsStore.Models {

    public class Product {
        public int ProductID { get; set; }

        [Required(ErrorMessage = "Please enter a product name")]
        public string Name { get; set; }

        [Required(ErrorMessage = "Please enter a description")]
        public string Description { get; set; }

        [Required]
        [Range(0.01, double.MaxValue,
            ErrorMessage = "Please enter a positive price")]
        public decimal Price { get; set; }

        [Required(ErrorMessage = "Please specify a category")]
        public string Category { get; set; }
    }
}
```

In Chapter 10, I used a tag helper to display a summary of validation errors at the top of the form. For this example, I am going to use a similar approach, but I am going to display error messages next to individual form elements in the Edit view, as shown in Listing 11-15.

Listing 11-15. Adding Validation Error Elements in the Edit.cshtml File in the Views/Admin Folder

```
@model Product
@{
    ViewBag.Title = "Edit Product";
    Layout = "_AdminLayout";
}

<form asp-action="Edit" method="post">
    <input type="hidden" asp-for="ProductID" />
    <div class="form-group">
        <label asp-for="Name"></label>
        <div><span asp-validation-for="Name" class="text-danger"></span></div>
        <input asp-for="Name" class="form-control" />
    </div>
    <div class="form-group">
        <label asp-for="Description"></label>
        <div><span asp-validation-for="Description" class="text-danger"></span></div>
        <textarea asp-for="Description" class="form-control"></textarea>
    </div>
    <div class="form-group">
        <label asp-for="Category"></label>
```

```
    <div><span asp-validation-for="Category" class="text-danger"></span></div>
    <input asp-for="Category" class="form-control" />
</div>
<div class="form-group">
    <label asp-for="Price"></label>
    <div><span asp-validation-for="Price" class="text-danger"></span></div>
    <input asp-for="Price" class="form-control" />
</div>
<div class="text-center">
    <button class="btn btn-primary" type="submit">Save</button>
    <a asp-action="Index" class="btn btn-secondary">Cancel</a>
</div>
</form>
```

When applied to a span element, the asp-validation-for attribute applies a tag helper that will add a validation error message for the specified property if there are any validation problems.

The tag helpers will insert an error message into the span element and add the element to the input-validation-error class, which makes it easy to apply CSS styles to error message elements, as shown in Listing 11-16.

Listing 11-16. Adding CSS to the _AdminLayout.cshtml File in the Views/Shared Folder

```
<!DOCTYPE html>
<html>
<head>
    <meta name="viewport" content="width=device-width" />
    <link rel="stylesheet" asp-href-include="lib/bootstrap/dist/css/*.min.css" />
    <title>@ViewBag.Title</title>
    <style>
        .input-validation-error { border-color: red; background-color: #fee ; }
    </style>
</head>
<body class="m-1 p-1">
    <div class="bg-info p-2"><h4>@ViewBag.Title</h4></div>
    @if (TempData["message"] != null) {
        <div class="alert alert-success mt-1">@TempData["message"]</div>
    }
    @RenderBody()
</body>
</html>
```

The CSS style I defined selects elements that are members of the input-validation-error class and applies a red border and background color.

■ **Tip**   Explicitly setting styles when using a CSS library like Bootstrap can cause inconsistencies when content themes are applied. In Chapter 27, I show an alternative approach that uses JavaScript code to apply Bootstrap classes to elements with validation errors, which keeps everything consistent but is also more complex.

You can apply the validation message tag helpers anywhere in the view, but it is conventional (and sensible) to put it somewhere near the problem element to give the user some context. Figure 11-6 shows the validation messages and cues that are displayed, which you can see by running the application, editing a product, and submitting invalid data.

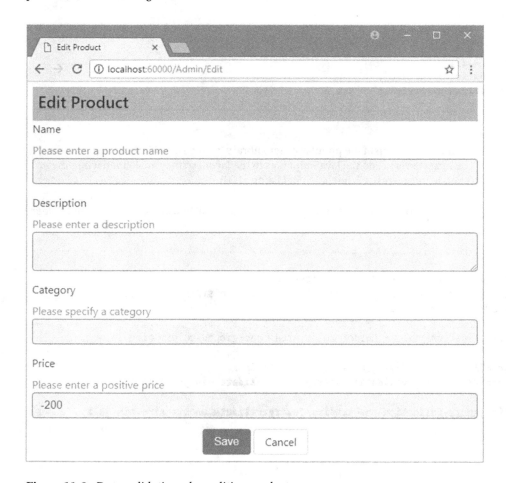

Figure 11-6. *Data validation when editing products*

Enabling Client-Side Validation

Currently, data validation is applied only when the administration user submits edits to the server, but most users expect immediate feedback if there are problems with the data they have entered. This is why developers often want to perform *client-side validation*, where the data is checked in the browser using JavaScript. MVC applications can perform client-side validation based on the data annotations I applied to the domain model class.

The first step is to add the JavaScript libraries that provide the client-side feature to the application, which is done in the bower.json file, as shown in Listing 11-17.

Listing 11-17. Adding JavaScript Packages in the bower.json File

```
{
  "name": "asp.net",
  "private": true,
  "dependencies": {
    "bootstrap": "4.0.0-alpha.6",
    "fontawesome": "4.7.0",
    "jquery": "3.2.1",
    "jquery-validation": "1.17.0",
    "jquery-validation-unobtrusive": "3.2.6"
  }
}
```

Client-side validation is built on top of the popular jQuery library, which simplifies working with the browser's DOM API. The next step is to add the JavaScript files to the layout so they are loaded when the SportsStore administration features are used, as shown in Listing 11-18.

Listing 11-18. Adding the Validation Libraries to the _AdminLayout.cshtml File in the Views/Shared Folder

```
<!DOCTYPE html>
<html>
<head>
    <meta name="viewport" content="width=device-width" />
    <link rel="stylesheet" asp-href-include="lib/bootstrap/dist/css/*.min.css" />
    <title>@ViewBag.Title</title>
    <style>
        .input-validation-error { border-color: red; background-color: #fee ; }
    </style>
    <script src="/lib/jquery/dist/jquery.min.js"></script>
    <script src="/lib/jquery-validation/dist/jquery.validate.min.js"></script>
    <script
      src="/lib/jquery-validation-unobtrusive/jquery.validate.unobtrusive.min.js">
    </script>
</head>
<body class="m-1 p-1">
    <div class="bg-info p-2"><h4>@ViewBag.Title</h4></div>
    @if (TempData["message"] != null) {
        <div class="alert alert-success mt-1">@TempData["message"]</div>
    }
    @RenderBody()
</body>
</html>
```

Enabling client-side validation doesn't cause any visual change, but the constraints specified by the attributes applied to the C# model class are enforced at the browser, preventing the user from submitting the form with bad data and providing immediate feedback when there is a problem. See Chapter 27 for more details.

Creating New Products

Next, I will implement the Create action method, which is the one specified by the Add Product link in the main product list page. This will allow the administrator to add new items to the product catalog. Adding the ability to create new products will require one small addition to the application. This is a great example of the power and flexibility of a well-structured MVC application. First, add the Create method, shown in Listing 11-19, to the Admin controller.

Listing 11-19. Adding the Create Action to the AdminController.cs File in the Controllers Folder

```
using Microsoft.AspNetCore.Mvc;
using SportsStore.Models;
using System.Linq;

namespace SportsStore.Controllers {

    public class AdminController : Controller {
        private IProductRepository repository;

        public AdminController(IProductRepository repo) {
            repository = repo;
        }

        public ViewResult Index() => View(repository.Products);

        public ViewResult Edit(int productId) =>
            View(repository.Products
                .FirstOrDefault(p => p.ProductID == productId));

        [HttpPost]
        public IActionResult Edit(Product product) {
            if (ModelState.IsValid) {
                repository.SaveProduct(product);
                TempData["message"] = $"{product.Name} has been saved";
                return RedirectToAction("Index");
            } else {
                // there is something wrong with the data values
                return View(product);
            }
        }

        public ViewResult Create() => View("Edit", new Product());
    }
}
```

The Create method does not render its default view. Instead, it specifies that the Edit view should be used. It is perfectly acceptable for one action method to use a view that is usually associated with another view. In this case, I provide a new Product object as the view model so that the Edit view is populated with empty fields.

■ **Note**   I have not added a unit test for this action method. Doing so would only be testing the ASP.NET Core MVC ability to process the result from the action method result, which is something you can take for granted. (Tests are not usually written for framework features unless you suspect there is a defect.)

That is the only change that is required because the Edit action method is already set up to receive Product objects from the model binding system and store them in the database. You can test this functionality by starting the application, navigating to /Admin/Index, clicking the Add Product button, and populating and submitting the form. The details you specify in the form will be used to create a new product in the database, which will then appear in the list, as shown in Figure 11-7.

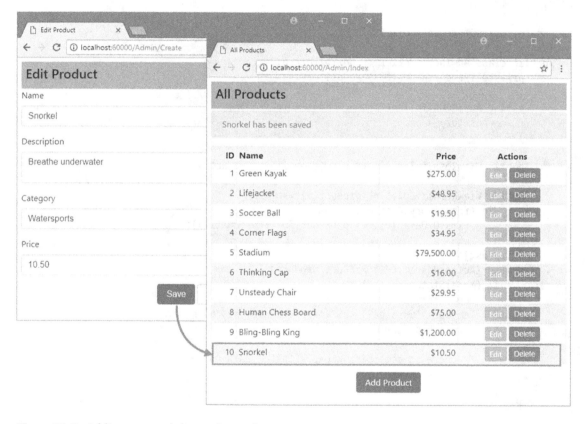

Figure 11-7. *Adding a new product to the catalog*

Deleting Products

Adding support for deleting items is also simple. The first step is to add a new method to the IProductRepository interface, as shown in Listing 11-20.

Listing 11-20. Adding a Method to Delete Products to the IProductRepository.cs File in the Models Folder

```
using System.Linq;

namespace SportsStore.Models {

    public interface IProductRepository {

        IQueryable<Product> Products { get; }

        void SaveProduct(Product product);

        Product DeleteProduct(int productID);
    }
}
```

Next, I implement this method in the Entity Framework Core repository class, EFProductRepository, as shown in Listing 11-21.

Listing 11-21. Implementing Deletion Support in the EFProductRepository.cs File in the Models Folder

```
using System.Collections.Generic;
using System.Linq;

namespace SportsStore.Models {

    public class EFProductRepository : IProductRepository {
        private ApplicationDbContext context;

        public EFProductRepository(ApplicationDbContext ctx) {
            context = ctx;
        }

        public IQueryable<Product> Products => context.Products;

        public void SaveProduct(Product product) {
            if (product.ProductID == 0) {
                context.Products.Add(product);
            } else {
                Product dbEntry = context.Products
                    .FirstOrDefault(p => p.ProductID == product.ProductID);
                if (dbEntry != null) {
                    dbEntry.Name = product.Name;
                    dbEntry.Description = product.Description;
                    dbEntry.Price = product.Price;
                    dbEntry.Category = product.Category;
                }
            }
            context.SaveChanges();
        }
```

```
    public Product DeleteProduct(int productID) {
        Product dbEntry = context.Products
            .FirstOrDefault(p => p.ProductID == productID);
        if (dbEntry != null) {
            context.Products.Remove(dbEntry);
            context.SaveChanges();
        }
        return dbEntry;
    }
  }
}
```

The final step is to implement a Delete action method in the Admin controller. This action method should support only POST requests because deleting objects is not an idempotent operation. As I explain in Chapter 16, browsers and caches are free to make GET requests without the user's explicit consent, so I must be careful to avoid making changes as a consequence of GET requests. Listing 11-22 shows the new action method.

Listing 11-22. Adding the Delete Action Method in the AdminController.cs File in the Controllers Folder

```
using Microsoft.AspNetCore.Mvc;
using SportsStore.Models;
using System.Linq;

namespace SportsStore.Controllers {

    public class AdminController : Controller {
        private IProductRepository repository;

        public AdminController(IProductRepository repo) {
            repository = repo;
        }

        public ViewResult Index() => View(repository.Products);

        public ViewResult Edit(int productId) =>
            View(repository.Products
                .FirstOrDefault(p => p.ProductID == productId));

        [HttpPost]
        public IActionResult Edit(Product product) {
            if (ModelState.IsValid) {
                repository.SaveProduct(product);
                TempData["message"] = $"{product.Name} has been saved";
                return RedirectToAction("Index");
            } else {
                // there is something wrong with the data values
                return View(product);
            }
        }
    }
```

```
    public IActionResult Create() => View("Edit", new Product());

    [HttpPost]
    public IActionResult Delete(int productId) {
        Product deletedProduct = repository.DeleteProduct(productId);
        if (deletedProduct != null) {
            TempData["message"] = $"{deletedProduct.Name} was deleted";
        }
        return RedirectToAction("Index");
    }
}
}
```

UNIT TEST: DELETING PRODUCTS

I want to test the basic behavior of the Delete action method, which is that when a valid ProductID is passed as a parameter, the action method calls the DeleteProduct method of the repository and passes the correct ProductID value to be deleted. Here is the test that I added to the AdminControllerTests.cs file:

```
...
[Fact]
public void Can_Delete_Valid_Products() {
    // Arrange - create a Product
    Product prod = new Product { ProductID = 2, Name = "Test" };

    // Arrange - create the mock repository
    Mock<IProductRepository> mock = new Mock<IProductRepository>();
    mock.Setup(m => m.Products).Returns(new Product[] {
        new Product {ProductID = 1, Name = "P1"},
        prod,
        new Product {ProductID = 3, Name = "P3"},
    }.AsQueryable<Product>());

    // Arrange - create the controller
    AdminController target = new AdminController(mock.Object);

    // Act - delete the product
    target.Delete(prod.ProductID);

    // Assert - ensure that the repository delete method was
    // called with the correct Product
    mock.Verify(m => m.DeleteProduct(prod.ProductID));
}
...
```

You can see the delete feature by starting the application, navigating to /Admin/Index, and clicking one of the Delete buttons in the product list page, as shown in Figure 11-8. As shown in the figure, I have taken advantage of the TempData variable to display a message when a product is deleted from the catalog.

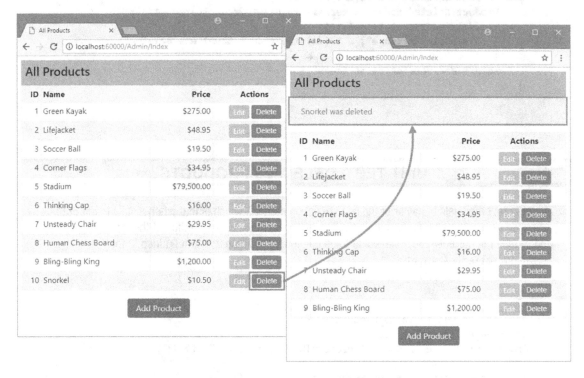

Figure 11-8. *Deleting a product from the catalog*

■ **Note**　You will find that you get an error if you delete a product for which you have previously created an order. When an Order object is stored in the database, it is transformed into an entry in a database table that contains a reference to the Product object with which it is associated, known as a *foreign key relationship*. The means that, by default, the database won't allow a Product object to be deleted if an Order has been created for that Product because doing so would create an inconsistency in the database. There are a number of ways to approach this issue, including automatically deleting Order objects when the Product they relate to is deleted or changing the relationship between Product and Order objects. See the Entity Framework Core documentation for details.

Summary

In this chapter, I introduced the administration capability and showed you how to implement CRUD operations that allow the administrator to create, read, update, and delete products from the repository and mark orders as shipped. In the next chapter, I show you how to secure the administration functions so that they are not available to all users, and I deploy the SportsStore application into production.

CHAPTER 12

SportsStore: Security and Deployment

In the previous chapter, I added support for administering the SportsStore application, and it probably did not escape your attention that anyone could modify the product catalog if I deploy the application as it is. All they would need to know is that the administration features are available using the /Admin/Index and /Order/List URLs. In this chapter, I am going to show you how to prevent random people from using the administration functions by password-protecting them. Once I have the security in place, I will show you how to prepare and deploy the SportsStore application into production.

Securing the Administration Features

Authentication and authorization are provided by the ASP.NET Core Identity system, which integrates neatly into both the ASP.NET Core platform and MVC applications. In the sections that follow, I will create a basic security setup that allows one user, called Admin, to authenticate and access the administration features in the application. ASP.NET Core Identity provides many more features for authenticating users and authorizing access to application features and data, and you can find more detailed information in Chapters 28, 29, and 30, where I show you how to create and manage user accounts, how to use roles and policies, and how to support authentication from third parties such as Microsoft, Google, Facebook, and Twitter. In this chapter, however, my goal is just to get enough functionality in place to prevent customers from being able to access the sensitive parts of the SportsStore application and, in doing so, give you a flavor of how authentication and authorization fit into an MVC application.

Creating the Identity Database

The ASP.NET Identity system is endlessly configurable and extensible and supports lots of options for how its user data is stored. I am going to use the most common, which is to store the data using Microsoft SQL Server accessed using Entity Framework Core.

Creating the Context Class

I need to create a database context file that will act as the bridge between the database and the Identity model objects it provides access to. I added a class file called AppIdentityDbContext.cs to the Models folder and used it to define the class shown in Listing 12-1.

© Adam Freeman 2017
A. Freeman, *Pro ASP.NET Core MVC 2*, https://doi.org/10.1007/978-1-4842-3150-0_12

■ **Note**   You might be used to adding packages to the project to get additional features like security working. But, with the release of ASP.NET Core 2, the NuGet packages required for Identity are already included in the project through the meta-package that was added to the `SportsStore.csproj` file as part of the project template.

Listing 12-1. The Contents of the AppIdentityDbContext.cs File in the Models Folder

```
using Microsoft.AspNetCore.Identity;
using Microsoft.AspNetCore.Identity.EntityFrameworkCore;
using Microsoft.EntityFrameworkCore;

namespace SportsStore.Models {

    public class AppIdentityDbContext : IdentityDbContext<IdentityUser> {

        public AppIdentityDbContext(DbContextOptions<AppIdentityDbContext> options)
            : base(options) { }
    }
}
```

The `AppIdentityDbContext` class is derived from `IdentityDbContext`, which provides Identity-specific features for Entity Framework Core. For the type parameter, I used the `IdentityUser` class, which is the built-in class used to represent users. In Chapter 28, I demonstrate how to use a custom class that you can extend to add extra information about the users of your application.

Defining the Connection String

The next step is to define the connection string that will be for the database. In Listing 12-2, you can see the additions I made to the `appsettings.json` file of the SportsStore project, which follows the same format as the connection string that I defined for the product database in Chapter 8.

Listing 12-2. Defining a Connection String in the appsettings.json File

```
{
  "Data": {
    "SportStoreProducts": {
      "ConnectionString": "Server=(localdb)\\MSSQLLocalDB;Database=SportsStore;Trusted_
                          Connection=True;MultipleActiveResultSets=true"
    },
    "SportStoreIdentity": {
      "ConnectionString": "Server=(localdb)\\MSSQLLocalDB;Database=Identity;Trusted_
                          Connection=True;MultipleActiveResultSets=true"
    }
  }
}
```

Remember that the connection string has to be defined in a single unbroken line in the `appsettings.json` file and is shown across multiple lines in the listing only because of the fixed width of a book page. The addition in the listing defines a connection string called `SportsStoreIdentity` that specifies a LocalDB database called `Identity`.

Configuring the Application

Like other ASP.NET Core features, Identity is configured in the Start class. Listing 12-3 shows the additions I made to set up Identity in the SportsStore project, using the context class and connection string defined previously.

Listing 12-3. Configuring Identity in the Startup.cs File

```
using System;
using System.Collections.Generic;
using System.Linq;
using System.Threading.Tasks;
using Microsoft.AspNetCore.Builder;
using Microsoft.AspNetCore.Hosting;
using Microsoft.AspNetCore.Http;
using Microsoft.Extensions.DependencyInjection;
using SportsStore.Models;
using Microsoft.Extensions.Configuration;
using Microsoft.EntityFrameworkCore;
using Microsoft.AspNetCore.Identity;

namespace SportsStore {

    public class Startup {

        public Startup(IConfiguration configuration) =>
            Configuration = configuration;

        public IConfiguration Configuration { get; }

        public void ConfigureServices(IServiceCollection services) {

            services.AddDbContext<ApplicationDbContext>(options =>
                options.UseSqlServer(
                    Configuration["Data:SportStoreProducts:ConnectionString"]));

            services.AddDbContext<AppIdentityDbContext>(options =>
                options.UseSqlServer(
                    Configuration["Data:SportStoreIdentity:ConnectionString"]));

            services.AddIdentity<IdentityUser, IdentityRole>()
                .AddEntityFrameworkStores<AppIdentityDbContext>()
                .AddDefaultTokenProviders();

            services.AddTransient<IProductRepository, EFProductRepository>();
            services.AddScoped<Cart>(sp => SessionCart.GetCart(sp));
            services.AddSingleton<IHttpContextAccessor, HttpContextAccessor>();
            services.AddTransient<IOrderRepository, EFOrderRepository>();
            services.AddMvc();
            services.AddMemoryCache();
            services.AddSession();
        }
```

```
    public void Configure(IApplicationBuilder app, IHostingEnvironment env) {
        app.UseDeveloperExceptionPage();
        app.UseStatusCodePages();
        app.UseStaticFiles();
        app.UseSession();
        app.UseAuthentication();
        app.UseMvc(routes => {

            // ...routes omitted for brevity...

        });
        SeedData.EnsurePopulated(app);
    }
  }
}
```

In the `ConfigureServices` method, I extended the Entity Framework Core configuration to register the context class and used the `AddIdentity` method to set up the Identity services using the built-in classes to represent users and roles. In the `Configure` method, I called the `UseAuthentication` method to set up the components that will intercept requests and responses to implement the security policy.

Creating and Applying the Database Migration

The basic configuration is in place, and it is time to use the Entity Framework Core migrations feature to define the schema and apply it to the database. Open a new command prompt or PowerShell window and run the following command in the SportsStore project folder to create a new migration for the Identity database:

```
dotnet ef migrations add Initial --context AppIdentityDbContext
```

The important difference from previous database commands is that I have used the `-context` argument to specify the name of the context class associated with the database that I want to work with, which is `AppIdentityDbContext`. When you have multiple databases in the application, it is important to ensure that you are working with the right context class.

Once Entity Framework Core has generated the initial migration, run the following command to create the database and run the migration commands:

```
dotnet ef database update --context AppIdentityDbContext
```

The result is a new LocalDB database called `Identity` that you can inspect using the Visual Studio SQL Server Object Explorer.

Defining the Seed Data

I am going to explicitly create the `Admin` user by seeding the database when the application starts. I added a class file called `IdentitySeedData.cs` to the `Models` folder and defined the static class shown in Listing 12-4.

Listing 12-4. The Contents of the IdentitySeedData.cs File in the Models Folder

```
using Microsoft.AspNetCore.Builder;
using Microsoft.AspNetCore.Identity;
using Microsoft.Extensions.DependencyInjection;

namespace SportsStore.Models {

    public static class IdentitySeedData {
        private const string adminUser = "Admin";
        private const string adminPassword = "Secret123$";

        public static async void EnsurePopulated(IApplicationBuilder app) {

            UserManager<IdentityUser> userManager = app.ApplicationServices
                .GetRequiredService<UserManager<IdentityUser>>();

            IdentityUser user = await userManager.FindByIdAsync(adminUser);
            if (user == null) {
                user = new IdentityUser("Admin");
                await userManager.CreateAsync(user, adminPassword);
            }
        }
    }
}
```

This code uses the UserManager<T> class, which is provided as a service by ASP.NET Core Identity for managing users, as described in Chapter 28. The database is searched for the Admin user account, which is created—with a password of Secret123$—if it is not present. Do not change the hard-coded password in this example because Identity has a validation policy that requires passwords to contain a number and range of characters. See Chapter 28 for details of how to change the validation settings.

■ **Caution**   Hard-coding the details of an administrator account is often required so that you can log into an application once it has been deployed and start administering it. When you do this, you must remember to change the password for the account you have created. See Chapter 28 for details of how to change passwords using Identity.

To ensure that the Identity database is seeded when the application starts, I added the statement shown in Listing 12-5 to the Configure method of the Startup class.

Listing 12-5. Seeding the Identity Database in the Startup.cs File in the SportsStore Folder

```
...
public void Configure(IApplicationBuilder app, IHostingEnvironment env) {
    app.UseDeveloperExceptionPage();
    app.UseStatusCodePages();
    app.UseStaticFiles();
    app.UseSession();
    app.UseAuthentication();
    app.UseMvc(routes => {
```

```
        // ...routes omitted for brevity...

    });
    SeedData.EnsurePopulated(app);
    IdentitySeedData.EnsurePopulated(app);
}
...
```

Applying a Basic Authorization Policy

Now that I have configured ASP.NET Core Identity, I can apply an authorization policy to the parts of the application that I want to protect. I am going to use the most basic authorization policy possible, which is to allow access to any authenticated user. Although this can be a useful policy in real applications as well, there are also options for creating finer-grained authorization controls (as described in Chapters 28,29, and 30), but since the SportsStore application has only one user, distinguishing between anonymous and authenticated requests is sufficient.

The Authorize attribute is used to restrict access to action methods, and in Listing 12-6, you can see that I have used the attribute to protect access to the administrative actions in the Order controller.

Listing 12-6. Restricting Access in the OrderController.cs File

```
using Microsoft.AspNetCore.Mvc;
using SportsStore.Models;
using System.Linq;
using Microsoft.AspNetCore.Authorization;

namespace SportsStore.Controllers {

    public class OrderController : Controller {
        private IOrderRepository repository;
        private Cart cart;

        public OrderController(IOrderRepository repoService, Cart cartService) {
            repository = repoService;
            cart = cartService;
        }

        [Authorize]
        public ViewResult List() =>
            View(repository.Orders.Where(o => !o.Shipped));

        [HttpPost]
        [Authorize]
        public IActionResult MarkShipped(int orderID) {
            Order order = repository.Orders
                .FirstOrDefault(o => o.OrderID == orderID);
            if (order != null) {
                order.Shipped = true;
                repository.SaveOrder(order);
            }
            return RedirectToAction(nameof(List));
        }
```

```
    public ViewResult Checkout() => View(new Order());

    [HttpPost]
    public IActionResult Checkout(Order order) {
        if (cart.Lines.Count() == 0) {
            ModelState.AddModelError("", "Sorry, your cart is empty!");
        }
        if (ModelState.IsValid) {
            order.Lines = cart.Lines.ToArray();
            repository.SaveOrder(order);
            return RedirectToAction(nameof(Completed));
        } else {
            return View(order);
        }
    }

    public ViewResult Completed() {
        cart.Clear();
        return View();
    }
    }
}
```

I don't want to stop unauthenticated users from accessing the other action methods in the Order controller, so I have applied the Authorize attribute only to the List and MarkShipped methods. I want to protect all of the action methods defined by the Admin controller, and I can do this by applying the Authorize attribute to the controller class, which then applies the authorization policy to all the action methods it contains, as shown in Listing 12-7.

Listing 12-7. Restricting Access in the AdminController.cs File

```
using Microsoft.AspNetCore.Mvc;
using SportsStore.Models;
using System.Linq;
using Microsoft.AspNetCore.Authorization;

namespace SportsStore.Controllers {

    [Authorize]
    public class AdminController : Controller {
        private IProductRepository repository;

        public AdminController(IProductRepository repo) {
            repository = repo;
        }

        public ViewResult Index() => View(repository.Products);

        public ViewResult Edit(int productId) =>
            View(repository.Products
                .FirstOrDefault(p => p.ProductID == productId));
```

```
[HttpPost]
public IActionResult Edit(Product product) {
    if (ModelState.IsValid) {
        repository.SaveProduct(product);
        TempData["message"] = $"{product.Name} has been saved";
        return RedirectToAction("Index");
    } else {
        // there is something wrong with the data values
        return View(product);
    }
}

public ViewResult Create() => View("Edit", new Product());

[HttpPost]
public IActionResult Delete(int productId) {
    Product deletedProduct = repository.DeleteProduct(productId);
    if (deletedProduct != null) {
        TempData["message"] = $"{deletedProduct.Name} was deleted";
    }
    return RedirectToAction("Index");
}
    }
}
```

Creating the Account Controller and Views

When an unauthenticated user sends a request that requires authorization, they are redirected to the /Account/Login URL, which the application can use to prompt the user for their credentials. In preparation, I added a view model to represent the user's credentials by adding a class file called LoginModel.cs to the Models/ViewModels folder and using it to define the class shown in Listing 12-8.

Listing 12-8. The Contents of the LoginModel.cs File in the Models/ViewModels Folder

```
using System.ComponentModel.DataAnnotations;

namespace SportsStore.Models.ViewModels {

    public class LoginModel {

        [Required]
        public string Name { get; set; }

        [Required]
        [UIHint("password")]
        public string Password { get; set; }

        public string ReturnUrl { get; set; } = "/";
    }
}
```

The Name and Password properties have been decorated with the Required attribute, which uses model validation to ensure that values have been provided. The Password property has been decorated with the UIHint attribute so that when I use the asp-for attribute on the input element in the login Razor view, the tag helper will set the type attribute to password; that way, the text entered by the user isn't visible on-screen. I describe the use of the UIHint attribute in Chapter 24.

Next, I added a class file called AccountController.cs to the Controllers folder and used it to define the controller shown in Listing 12-9. This is the controller that will respond to requests to the /Account/ Login URL.

Listing 12-9. The Contents of the AccountController.cs File in the Controllers Folder

```
using System.Threading.Tasks;
using Microsoft.AspNetCore.Authorization;
using Microsoft.AspNetCore.Identity;
using Microsoft.AspNetCore.Mvc;
using SportsStore.Models.ViewModels;

namespace SportsStore.Controllers {

    [Authorize]
    public class AccountController : Controller {
        private UserManager<IdentityUser> userManager;
        private SignInManager<IdentityUser> signInManager;

        public AccountController(UserManager<IdentityUser> userMgr,
                SignInManager<IdentityUser> signInMgr) {
            userManager = userMgr;
            signInManager = signInMgr;
        }

        [AllowAnonymous]
        public ViewResult Login(string returnUrl) {
            return View(new LoginModel {
                ReturnUrl = returnUrl
            });
        }

        [HttpPost]
        [AllowAnonymous]
        [ValidateAntiForgeryToken]
        public async Task<IActionResult> Login(LoginModel loginModel) {
            if (ModelState.IsValid) {
                IdentityUser user =
                    await userManager.FindByNameAsync(loginModel.Name);
                if (user != null) {
                    await signInManager.SignOutAsync();
                    if ((await signInManager.PasswordSignInAsync(user,
                            loginModel.Password, false, false)).Succeeded) {
                        return Redirect(loginModel?.ReturnUrl ?? "/Admin/Index");
                    }
                }
            }
```

```
            ModelState.AddModelError("", "Invalid name or password");
            return View(loginModel);
        }

        public async Task<RedirectResult> Logout(string returnUrl = "/") {
            await signInManager.SignOutAsync();
            return Redirect(returnUrl);
        }
    }
}
```

When the user is redirected to the /Account/Login URL, the GET version of the Login action method renders the default view for the page, providing a view model object that includes the URL that the browser should be redirected to if the authentication request is successful.

Authentication credentials are submitted to the POST version of the Login method, which uses the UserManager<IdentityUser> and SignInManager<IdentityUser> services that have been received through the controller's constructor to authenticate the user and log them into the system. I explain how these classes work in Chapters 28, 29, and 30, but for now it is enough to know that if there is an authentication failure, then I create a model validation error and render the default view; however, if authentication is successful, then I redirect the user to the URL that they want to access before they are prompted for their credentials.

■ **Caution**   In general, using client-side data validation is a good idea. It offloads some of the work from your server and gives users immediate feedback about the data they are providing. However, you should not be tempted to perform authentication at the client, as this would typically involve sending valid credentials to the client so they can be used to check the username and password that the user has entered, or at least trusting the client's report of whether they have successfully authenticated. Authentication should always be done at the server.

To provide the Login method with a view to render, I created the Views/Account folder and added a Razor view file called Login.cshtml with the contents shown in Listing 12-10.

Listing 12-10. The Contents of the Login.cshtml File in the Views/Account Folder

```
@model LoginModel
@{
    ViewBag.Title = "Log In";
    Layout = "_AdminLayout";
}

<div class="text-danger" asp-validation-summary="All"></div>

<form asp-action="Login" asp-controller="Account" method="post">
    <input type="hidden" asp-for="ReturnUrl" />
    <div class="form-group">
        <label asp-for="Name"></label>
        <div><span asp-validation-for="Name" class="text-danger"></span></div>
        <input asp-for="Name" class="form-control" />
    </div>
    <div class="form-group">
        <label asp-for="Password"></label>
```

```
            <div><span asp-validation-for="Password" class="text-danger"></span></div>
            <input asp-for="Password" class="form-control" />
        </div>
        <button class="btn btn-primary" type="submit">Log In</button>
</form>
```

The final step is a change to the shared administration layout to add a button that will log the current user out by sending a request to the Logout action, as shown in Listing 12-11. This is a useful feature that makes it easier to test the application, without which you would need to clear the browser's cookies in order to return to the unauthenticated state.

Listing 12-11. Adding a Logout Button in the _AdminLayout.cshtml File

```
<!DOCTYPE html>
<html>
<head>
    <meta name="viewport" content="width=device-width" />
    <link rel="stylesheet" asp-href-include="lib/bootstrap/dist/css/*.min.css" />
    <title>@ViewBag.Title</title>
    <style>
        .input-validation-error {
            border-color: red;
            background-color: #fee;
        }
    </style>
    <script src="/lib/jquery/dist/jquery.min.js"></script>
    <script src="/lib/jquery-validation/dist/jquery.validate.min.js"></script>
    <script
      src="/lib/jquery-validation-unobtrusive/jquery.validate.unobtrusive.min.js">
    </script>
</head>
<body class="m-1 p-1">
    <div class="bg-info p-2 row">
        <div class="col">
            <h4>@ViewBag.Title</h4>
        </div>
        <div class="col-2">
            <a class="btn btn-sm btn-primary"
                asp-action="Logout" asp-controller="Account">Log Out</a>
        </div>
    </div>
    @if (TempData["message"] != null) {
        <div class="alert alert-success mt-1">@TempData["message"]</div>
    }
    @RenderBody()
</body>
</html>
```

Testing the Security Policy

Everything is in place, and you can test the security policy by starting the application and requesting the /Admin/Index URL. Since you are presently unauthenticated and you are trying to target an action that requires authorization, your browser will be redirected to the /Account/Login URL. Enter **Admin** and **Secret123$** as the name and password and submit the form. The Account controller will check the credentials you provided with the seed data added to the Identity database and—assuming you entered the right details—authenticate you and redirect you back to the /Account/Login URL, to which you now have access. Figure 12-1 illustrates the process.

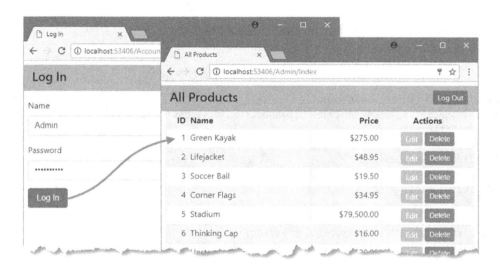

Figure 12-1. *The administration authentication/authorization process*

Deploying the Application

All the features and functionality for the SportsStore application are in place, so it is time to prepare the application and deploy it into production. Lots of hosting options are available for ASP.NET Core MVC applications, and the one that I use in this chapter is the Microsoft Azure platform, which I have chosen because it comes from Microsoft and because it offers free accounts, which means you can follow the SportsStore example all the way through, even if you don't want to use Azure for your own projects.

■ **Note**   You will need an Azure account for this section. If you don't have one, you can create a free account at http://azure.microsoft.com.

Creating the Databases

The starting point is to create the databases that the SportsStore application will use in production. This is something that you can do as part of the Visual Studio deployment process, but it is a chicken-and-egg situation because you need to know the connection strings for the databases before you deploy, which is the process that creates the databases.

■ **Caution**   The Azure portal changes often as Microsoft adds new features and revises existing ones. The instructions in this section were accurate when I wrote them, but the required steps may have changed slightly by the time you read this. The basic approach should still be the same, but the names of data fields and the exact order of steps may require some experimentation to get the right results.

The simplest approach is to log in to http://portal.azure.com using your Azure account and create the databases manually. Once you are logged in, select the SQL Databases resource category and click the Add button to create a new database.

For the first database enter the name **products**. Click the Configure Required Settings link and then the Create a New Server link. Enter a new server name—which must be unique across Azure—and select a database administrator username and password. I entered the server name **sportsstorecore2db**, with the administrator name of **sportsstoreadmin** and a password of **Secret123$**. You will have to use a different server name, and I suggest that you use a more robust password. Select a location for your database; click the Select button to close the options and then the Create button to create the database itself. Azure will take a few minutes to perform the creation process, after which it will appear in the SQL Databases resource category.

Create another SQL server, this time entering the name **identity**. You can use the database server that you created a moment ago, rather than creating a new one. The result is two SQL Server databases hosted by Azure with the details shown in Table 12-1. You will have a different database server name and—ideally—better passwords.

Table 12-1. *The Azure Databases for the SportsStore Application*

Database Name	Server Name	Administrator	Password
products	sportsstorecore2db	sportsstoreadmin	Secret123$
identity	sportsstorecore2db	sportsstoreadmin	Secret123$

Opening Firewall Access for Configuration

I need to populate the databases with their schemas, and the simplest way to do that is by opening Azure firewall access so that I can run the Entity Framework Core commands from my development machine.

Select either of the databases in the SQL Databases resource category, click the Tools button, and then click the Open in Visual Studio link. Now click the Configure Your Firewall link, click the Add Client IP button, and then click Save. This allows your current IP address to reach the database server and perform configuration commands. (You can inspect the database schema by clicking the Open In Visual Studio button, which will open Visual Studio and use the SQL Server Object Explorer to examine the database.)

Getting the Connection Strings

I will need the connection strings for the new database shortly. Azure provides this information when you click a database in the SQL Databases resource category through a Show Database Connection Strings link. Connection strings are provided for different development platforms, and it is the ADO.NET strings that are required for .NET applications. Here is the connection string that the Azure portal provides for the products database:

```
Server=tcp:sportsstorecore2db.database.windows.net,1433;Initial Catalog=products;Persist
Security Info=False;User ID={your_username};Password={your_password};MultipleActiveResultS
ets=True;Encrypt=True;TrustServerCertificate=False;Connection Timeout=30;
```

You will see different configuration options depending on how Azure provisioned your database. Notice that there are placeholders for the username and password, which I have marked in bold, that must be changed when you use the connection string to configure the application.

Preparing the Application

I have some basic preparation to do before I can deploy the application, to make it ready for the production environment. In the sections that follow, I change the way that errors are displayed and set up the production connection strings for the databases.

Creating the Error Controller and View

At the moment, the application is configured to use the developer-friendly error pages, which provide helpful information when a problem occurs. This is not information that end users should see, so I added a class file called ErrorController.cs to the Controllers folder and used it to define the simple controller shown in Listing 12-12.

Listing 12-12. The Contents of the ErrorController.cs File in the Controllers Folder

```
using Microsoft.AspNetCore.Mvc;

namespace SportsStore.Controllers {

    public class ErrorController : Controller {

        public ViewResult Error() => View();
    }
}
```

The controller defines an Error action that renders the default view. To provide the controller with the view, I created the Views/Error folder, added a Razor view file called Error.cshtml, and applied the markup shown in Listing 12-13.

Listing 12-13. The Contents of the Error.cshtml File in the Views/Error Folder

```
@{
    Layout = null;
}
<!DOCTYPE html>
<html>
<head>
    <meta name="viewport" content="width=device-width" />
    <link rel="stylesheet" href="~/lib/bootstrap/dist/css/bootstrap.min.css" />
    <title>Error</title>
</head>
<body>
    <h2 class="text-danger">Error.</h2>
    <h3 class="text-danger">An error occurred while processing your request.</h3>
</body>
</html>
```

This kind of error page is the last resort, and it is best to keep it as simple as possible and not to rely on shared views, view components, or other rich features. In this case, I have disabled shared layouts and defined a simple HTML document that explains that there has been an error, without providing any information about what has happened.

Defining the Production Database Settings

The next step is to create a file that will provide the application with its database connection strings in production. I added a new ASP.NET Configuration File called appsettings.production.json to the SportsStore project and added the content shown in Listing 12-14.

■ **Tip** The Solution Explorer nests this file inside appsettings.json in the file listing, which you will have to expand if you want to edit the file again later.

Listing 12-14. The Contents of the appsettings.production.json File

```
{
  "Data": {
    "SportStoreProducts": {
      "ConnectionString": "Server=tcp:sportsstorecore2db.database.windows.net,1433;Initial
      Catalog=products;Persist Security Info=False;User ID={your_username};Password={your_
      password};MultipleActiveResultSets=True;Encrypt=True;TrustServerCertificate=False;
      Connection Timeout=30;"

    },
    "SportStoreIdentity": {
      "ConnectionString": "Server=tcp:sportsstorecore2db.database.windows.net,1433;Initial
      Catalog=identity;Persist Security Info=False;User ID={your_username};Password={your_
      password};MultipleActiveResultSets=True;Encrypt=True;TrustServerCertificate=False;
      Connection Timeout=30;"
    }
  }
}
```

This file is hard to read because connection strings cannot be split across multiple lines. The contents of this file duplicate the connection strings section of the appsettings.json file but use the Azure connection strings. (Remember to replace the username and password placeholders.) I have also set the MultipleActiveResultSets to True, which allows multiple concurrent queries and avoids a common error condition that arises when performing complex LINQ queries of application data.

■ **Note** Remove the brace characters when you insert your username and password into the connection strings so that you end up with Password=MyPassword and not Password={MyPassword}.

Configuring the Application

Now I can change the Startup class so that the application behaves differently when in production. Listing 12-15 shows the changes I made.

Listing 12-15. Configuring the Application in the Startup.cs File

```
using System;
using System.Collections.Generic;
using System.Linq;
using System.Threading.Tasks;
using Microsoft.AspNetCore.Builder;
using Microsoft.AspNetCore.Hosting;
using Microsoft.AspNetCore.Http;
using Microsoft.Extensions.DependencyInjection;
using SportsStore.Models;
using Microsoft.Extensions.Configuration;
using Microsoft.EntityFrameworkCore;
using Microsoft.AspNetCore.Identity;

namespace SportsStore {

    public class Startup {

        public Startup(IConfiguration configuration) =>
            Configuration = configuration;

        public IConfiguration Configuration { get; }

        public void ConfigureServices(IServiceCollection services) {
            services.AddDbContext<ApplicationDbContext>(options =>
                options.UseSqlServer(
                    Configuration["Data:SportStoreProducts:ConnectionString"]));

            services.AddDbContext<AppIdentityDbContext>(options =>
                options.UseSqlServer(
                    Configuration["Data:SportStoreIdentity:ConnectionString"]));

            services.AddIdentity<IdentityUser, IdentityRole>()
                .AddEntityFrameworkStores<AppIdentityDbContext>()
                .AddDefaultTokenProviders();

            services.AddTransient<IProductRepository, EFProductRepository>();
            services.AddScoped<Cart>(sp => SessionCart.GetCart(sp));
            services.AddSingleton<IHttpContextAccessor, HttpContextAccessor>();
            services.AddTransient<IOrderRepository, EFOrderRepository>();
            services.AddMvc();
            services.AddMemoryCache();
            services.AddSession();
        }
```

```
public void Configure(IApplicationBuilder app, IHostingEnvironment env) {

    if (env.IsDevelopment()) {
        app.UseDeveloperExceptionPage();
        app.UseStatusCodePages();
    } else {
        app.UseExceptionHandler("/Error");
    }

    app.UseStaticFiles();
    app.UseSession();
    app.UseAuthentication();
    app.UseMvc(routes => {
        routes.MapRoute(name: "Error", template: "Error",
            defaults: new { controller = "Error", action = "Error" });
        routes.MapRoute(name: null,
            template: "{category}/Page{productPage:int}",
            defaults: new { controller = "Product", action = "List" }
        );
        routes.MapRoute(name: null,template: "Page{productPage:int}",
            defaults: new { controller = "Product",
            action = "List", productPage = 1 }
        );
        routes.MapRoute(name: null, template: "{category}",
            defaults: new { controller = "Product",
                action = "List", productPage = 1 }
        );
        routes.MapRoute(name: null,template: "",
            defaults: new { controller = "Product",
                action = "List", productPage = 1 });
        routes.MapRoute(name: null, template: "{controller}/{action}/{id?}");
    });
    //SeedData.EnsurePopulated(app);
    //IdentitySeedData.EnsurePopulated(app);
    }
  }
}
```

The IHostingEnvironment interface is used to provide information about the environment in which the application is running, such as development or production. When the hosting environment is set to Production, then ASP.NET Core will load the appsettings.production.json file and its contents to override the settings in the appsettings.json file, which means that the Entity Framework Core will connect to the Azure databases instead of LocalDB. There are a lot of options available for tailoring the configuration of an application in different environments, which I explain in Chapter 14.

I have also commented out the statements that seed the databases, which I explain in the "Managing Database Seeding" section.

Applying the Database Migrations

To set up the databases with the schemas required for the application, open a new command prompt or PowerShell window and navigate to the SportsStore project directory. Setting the environment so that the dotnet command-line tool will use the connection strings for Azure requires setting an environment variable. If you are using PowerShell, use this command to set the environment variable:

```
$env:ASPNETCORE_ENVIRONMENT="Production"
```

If you are using a command prompt, then use this command to set the environment variable instead:

```
set ASPNETCORE_ENVIRONMENT=Production
```

Run the following commands in the SportsStore project folder to apply the migrations in the project to the Azure databases:

```
dotnet ef database update --context ApplicationDbContext
dotnet ef database update --context AppIdentityDbContext
```

The environment variable specifies the hosting environment that is used to obtain the connection strings to reach the databases. If these commands do not work, ensure that you have configured the Azure firewall to allow access to your development machine, as described earlier in this chapter, and that you have correctly copied and modified the connection strings.

Managing Database Seeding

In Listing 12-15, I commented out the statements in the Startup class that seeded the databases. I did this because the Entity Framework Core commands used in the previous section to apply the migrations to the database rely on the services set up by the Startup class, which means that, with those statements enabled, the code to seed the databases would have been called before the migrations were applied, which would have resulted in an error and prevented the migrations from working. This didn't cause a problem when the databases were set up. For the products database, this was because the SeedData.EnsurePopulated method applies the migrations before seeding the data and because I didn't add the Identity seed data to the application until after I had applied the migration to the database.

For the production environment, I want to take a different approach to seed data. For the user accounts, I am going to populate the database with the administrator account when there is a login attempt. I am going to add a feature to the administration tool for seeding the product database so that the production system can be populated with data for testing data or left empty for real data as required.

■ **Note** Seeding authentication data in a production system should be done with care, and your application should use the features described in Chapters 28, 29, and 30 to change the password as soon as the application is deployed.

Seeding Identity Data

The first step in changing the way that user data is seeded is to simplify the code in the `IdentitySeedData` class, as shown in Listing 12-16.

Listing 12-16. Simplifying Code in the IdentitySeedData.cs File in the Models Folder

```
using Microsoft.AspNetCore.Builder;
using Microsoft.AspNetCore.Identity;
using Microsoft.Extensions.DependencyInjection;
using System.Threading.Tasks;

namespace SportsStore.Models {

    public static class IdentitySeedData {
        private const string adminUser = "Admin";
        private const string adminPassword = "Secret123$";

        public static async Task EnsurePopulated(UserManager<IdentityUser>
                userManager) {

            IdentityUser user = await userManager.FindByIdAsync(adminUser);
            if (user == null) {
                user = new IdentityUser("Admin");
                await userManager.CreateAsync(user, adminPassword);
            }
        }
    }
}
```

Rather than obtaining the `UserManager<IdentityUser>` service itself, the `EnsurePopulated` method receives the object as an argument. This allows me to integrate the database seeding in the AccountController class, as shown in Listing 12-17.

Listing 12-17. Seeding Data in the AccountController.cs File in the Controllers Folder

```
using System.Threading.Tasks;
using Microsoft.AspNetCore.Authorization;
using Microsoft.AspNetCore.Identity;
using Microsoft.AspNetCore.Mvc;
using SportsStore.Models.ViewModels;
using SportsStore.Models;

namespace SportsStore.Controllers {

    [Authorize]
    public class AccountController : Controller {
        private UserManager<IdentityUser> userManager;
        private SignInManager<IdentityUser> signInManager;

        public AccountController(UserManager<IdentityUser> userMgr,
                SignInManager<IdentityUser> signInMgr) {
            userManager = userMgr;
            signInManager = signInMgr;
```

341

```
            IdentitySeedData.EnsurePopulated(userMgr).Wait();
        }

        // ...other methods omitted for brevity...
    }
}
```

These changes will ensure that the Identity database is seeded every time that an `AccountController` object is created to handle an HTTP request. This is not ideal, of course, but there is no good way to seed a database, and this approach will ensure that the application can be administered both in production and development, albeit at the cost of some additional database queries.

Seeding the Product Data

For the product data, I am going to present the administrator with a button that will seed the database when it is empty. The first step is to change the seeding code so that it uses an interface that will allow it to access services provided through a controller, rather than through the `Startup` class, as shown in Listing 12-18. I have also commented out the statement that automatically applies any pending migrations, which can cause data loss and should be used only with the greatest care in production systems.

Listing 12-18. Preparing for Manual Seeding in the SeedData.cs File in the Models Folder

```
using System.Linq;
using Microsoft.AspNetCore.Builder;
using Microsoft.Extensions.DependencyInjection;
using Microsoft.EntityFrameworkCore;
using System;

namespace SportsStore.Models {

    public static class SeedData {

        public static void EnsurePopulated(IServiceProvider services) {
            ApplicationDbContext context =
                services.GetRequiredService<ApplicationDbContext>();
            //context.Database.Migrate();
            if (!context.Products.Any()) {
                context.Products.AddRange(

                    // ...statements omiited for brevity...

                );
                context.SaveChanges();
            }
        }
    }
}
```

The next step is to update the `Admin` controller to add an action method that will trigger the seeding operation, as shown in Listing 12-19.

Listing 12-19. Seeding the Database in the AdminController.cs File in the Controllers Folder

```csharp
using Microsoft.AspNetCore.Mvc;
using SportsStore.Models;
using System.Linq;
using Microsoft.AspNetCore.Authorization;

namespace SportsStore.Controllers {

    [Authorize]
    public class AdminController : Controller {
        private IProductRepository repository;

        public AdminController(IProductRepository repo) {
            repository = repo;
        }

        public ViewResult Index() => View(repository.Products);

        // ...other methods omitted for brevity...

        [HttpPost]
        public IActionResult SeedDatabase() {
            SeedData.EnsurePopulated(HttpContext.RequestServices);
            return RedirectToAction(nameof(Index));
        }
    }
}
```

The new action is decorated with the HttpPost attribute so that it can be targeted with POST requests, and it will redirect the browser to the Index action method once the database has been seeded. All that remains is to create a button to seed the database that will be displayed when it is empty, as shown in Listing 12-20.

Listing 12-20. Adding a Button in the Index.cshtml File in the Views/Admin Folder

```html
@model IEnumerable<Product>

@{
    ViewBag.Title = "All Products";
    Layout = "_AdminLayout";
}

@if (Model.Count() == 0) {
    <div class="text-center m-2">
        <form asp-action="SeedDatabase" method="post">
            <button type="submit" class="btn btn-danger">Seed Database</button>
        </form>
    </div>
} else {
    <table class="table table-striped table-bordered table-sm">
        <tr>
            <th class="text-right">ID</th>
```

```
            <th>Name</th>
            <th class="text-right">Price</th>
            <th class="text-center">Actions</th>
        </tr>
        @foreach (var item in Model) {
            <tr>
                <td class="text-right">@item.ProductID</td>
                <td>@item.Name</td>
                <td class="text-right">@item.Price.ToString("c")</td>
                <td class="text-center">
                    <form asp-action="Delete" method="post">
                        <a asp-action="Edit" class="btn btn-sm btn-warning"
                            asp-route-productId="@item.ProductID">
                            Edit
                        </a>
                        <input type="hidden" name="ProductID"
                            value="@item.ProductID" />
                        <button type="submit" class="btn btn-danger btn-sm">
                            Delete
                        </button>
                    </form>
                </td>
            </tr>
        }
    </table>
}
<div class="text-center">
    <a asp-action="Create" class="btn btn-primary">Add Product</a>
</div>
```

Deploying the Application

To deploy the application, right-click the SportsStore project in the Solution Explorer (the project, not the solution) and select Publish from the pop-up menu. Visual Studio will present you with a choice of publishing methods, as shown in Figure 12-2.

WHERE TO START IF DEPLOYMENT FAILS

The single biggest cause of failed deployments is connection strings, either because they were not copied correctly from Azure or because they were edited incorrectly to insert the username and password. If your deployment fails, then the connection strings are the place to start. If you don't get the expected results from the `dotnet ef database update` commands in the "Applying the Database Migrations" sections, then your deployment will fail. If the commands do work but deployment fails, then make sure you have set the environment variable because it is possible that you are preparing the local database and not the one in the cloud.

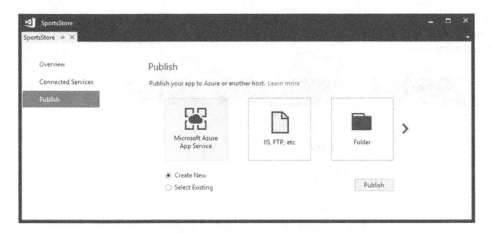

Figure 12-2. *Selecting a publishing method*

Select the Microsoft Azure App Service option and make sure that Create New is selected (the Select Existing option is used to update an existing deployed application). You will be prompted to provide details for the deployment. Start by clicking Add an Account and enter your Azure credentials.

Once you have entered your credentials, you can select a name for the deployed application and enter the details for the service, which will depend on the type of Azure account you have, the region you want to deploy to, and the deployment service you require, as shown in Figure 12-3.

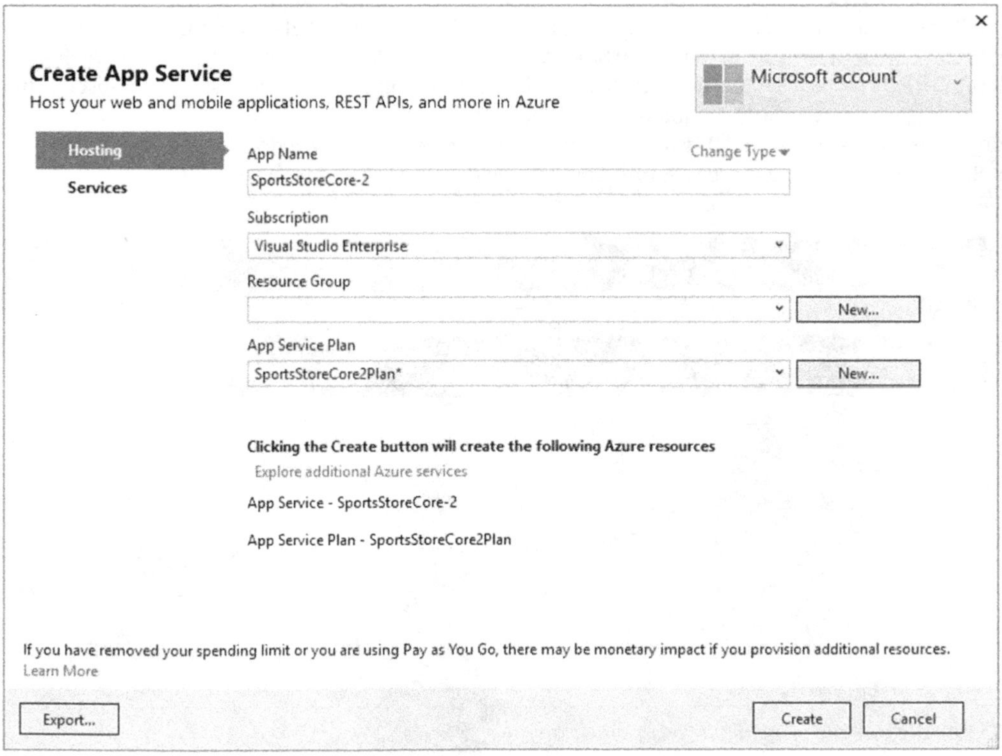

Figure 12-3. *Creating a new Azure app service*

Once you have configured the service, click the Create button. Once the service has been set up, you will be prompted with a summary of the publishing operation, which will send the application to the hosted service, as shown in Figure 12-4.

Figure 12-4. *The service publishing summary*

Click the Publish button to begin the deployment process. You can see details of the publishing progress by selecting Web Publish Activity from the Visual Studio View ➤ Other Windows menu. Be patient during this process because it can take a while to send all of the files in the project to the Azure service. Subsequent updates will be quicker because only modified files will be transferred.

Once deployment has completed, Visual Studio will open a new browser window for the deployed application. Since the product database is empty, you will see the layout shown in Figure 12-5.

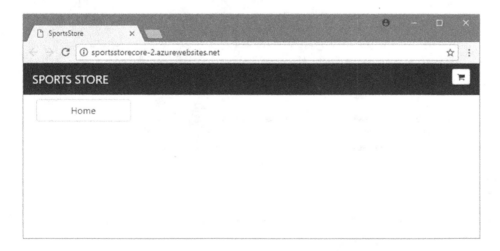

Figure 12-5. *The initial state of the deployed application*

Navigate to the /Admin/Index URL and authenticate with the username **Admin** and the password **Secret123$**. The Identity database will be seeded on-demand, allowing you to log into the administration part of the application, as shown in Figure 12-6.

Figure 12-6. *The administration screen*

Click the Seed Database button to populate the product database, which will produce the result shown in Figure 12-7. You can then navigate back to the root URL for the application and use it as normal.

ID	Name	Price	Actions	
1	Kayak	$275.00	Edit	Delete
2	Lifejacket	$48.95	Edit	Delete
3	Soccer Ball	$19.50	Edit	Delete
4	Corner Flags	$34.95	Edit	Delete
5	Stadium	$79,500.00	Edit	Delete
6	Thinking Cap	$16.00	Edit	Delete
7	Unsteady Chair	$29.95	Edit	Delete
8	Human Chess Board	$75.00	Edit	Delete
9	Bling-Bling King	$1,200.00	Edit	Delete

Figure 12-7. *The populated database*

Summary

In this and previous chapters, I demonstrated how ASP.NET Core MVC can be used to create a realistic e-commerce application. This extended example introduced many key MVC features: controllers, action methods, routing, views, metadata, validation, layouts, authentication, and more. You also saw how some of the key technologies related to MVC can be used. These included Entity Framework Core, dependency injection, and unit testing. The result is an application that has a clean, component-oriented architecture that separates the various concerns and a code base that will be easy to extend and maintain. That's the end of the SportsStore application. In the next chapter, I show you how to use Visual Studio Code to create ASP.NET Core MVC applications.

CHAPTER 13

Working with Visual Studio Code

In this chapter, I show you how to create an ASP.NET Core MVC application using Visual Studio Code, which is an open source, cross-platform editor produced by Microsoft. Despite the name, Visual Studio Code is unrelated to Visual Studio and is based on the Electron framework, which is used by the Atom editor popular with developers of other web application frameworks such as Angular.

Visual Studio Code supports Windows, macOS, and the most popular Linux distributions. Visual Studio Code has matured into a useful and fully featured development environment, even if it lacks all of the bells and whistles provided by Visual Studio. I find myself using Visual Studio Code more and more because it is simple to work with, is fast, and has good support for other languages, such as JavaScript and TypeScript.

Setting Up the Development Environment

The process for setting up Visual Studio Code requires a little work because some of the functionality that is included in Visual Studio is handled by external tools. Some of these tools are the same ones that Visual Studio uses behind the scenes, but others are new to the world of .NET development and may be unfamiliar. The good news is that these tools are widely used by developers of other web application frameworks, and the quality and features are good. In the sections that follow, I walk you through the process of installing Visual Studio Code and the essential tools and add-ons that are required for MVC development.

Installing Node.js

In the world of client-side development, Node.js (also known as Node) has emerged as the runtime on which many popular development tools rely. Node was created in 2009 as a simple and efficient runtime for server-side applications written in JavaScript. It is based on the JavaScript engine used in the Chrome browser and provides an API for executing JavaScript code outside of the browser environment.

Node.js has enjoyed some success as an application server, but for this chapter, it is interesting because it has provided the foundation for a new generation of cross-platform build tools and package managers. Some smart design decisions by the Node team and the cross-platform support provided by the Chrome JavaScript runtime have created an opportunity that has been seized upon by enthusiastic tool writers, especially those who want to support web application development.

Note Two versions of Node.js are available. The Long Term Support (LTS) version provides a stable foundation for deployment into production environments where changes are to be minimized. LTS updates are released every 6 months and maintained for 18 months. The Current version is a more rapidly changing release that favors new features over stability. For this chapter, I have used the Current release.

© Adam Freeman 2017

A. Freeman, *Pro ASP.NET Core MVC 2*, https://doi.org/10.1007/978-1-4842-3150-0_13

Installing Node.js on Windows

Download and run the Node.js installer for Windows from http://nodejs.org. When you install Node.js, ensure that it is added to the path. Figure 13-1 shows the Windows installer, which offers to modify the PATH environment variable as an installation option.

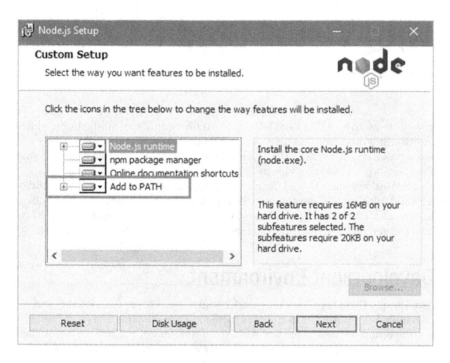

Figure 13-1. *Adding Node to the path*

Installing Node.js on macOS

You can download an installer for macOS from http://nodejs.org. Run the installer and accept the defaults. When the installation has completed, ensure that /usr/local/bin is in your $PATH.

Installing Node.js on Linux

The easiest way to install Node.js on Linux is to use a package manager; the Node team has provided instructions for the main distributions at http://nodejs.org/en/download/package-manager. For Ubuntu, I used the commands in Listing 13-1 to download and install Node.js.

Listing 13-1. Installing Node.js

```
sudo curl -sL https://deb.nodesource.com/setup_6.x | sudo -E bash -
sudo apt-get install -y nodejs
```

Checking the Node Installation

Once you have completed the installation, open a new command prompt and run the command shown in Listing 13-2 to check that Node is working and to display the version that has been installed.

Listing 13-2. Checking the Node Installation

```
node -v
```

You will see the version number if the installation has been successful and Node has been added to the path. At the time of writing, the current version of Node is 6.11.2. If you get unexpected results while following the examples in this chapter, try using this specific version.

Installing Git

Visual Studio Code includes integrated Git support, but a separate installation is required to support the Bower tool, which is used to manage client-side packages.

Installing Git on Windows or macOS

Download and run the installer from `https://git-scm.com/downloads`.

Installing Git on Linux

Git is already installed on most Linux distributions. If you want to install it anyway, then consult the installation instructions for your distribution at `https://git-scm.com/download/linux`. For Ubuntu, I used the command shown in Listing 13-3.

Listing 13-3. Installing Git on Ubuntu

```
sudo apt-get install git
```

Checking the Git Installation

Once you have completed the installation, run the command shown in Listing 13-4 in a new command prompt/Terminal to check that Git is installed and available.

Listing 13-4. Checking the Git Installation

```
git --version
```

This command prints out the version of the Git package that has been installed. At the time of writing, the latest version of Git for Windows and macOS is 2.14.1, and the latest version of Git for Linux is 2.7.4.

Installing Bower

Node.js comes with the Node Package Manager (NPM), which is used to download and install development packages that are written in JavaScript. The only package required for this chapter is Bower, which is used to manage client-side packages and which I described in Chapter 6. Run the command shown in Listing 13-5 to download and install Bower on Windows.

Listing 13-5. Installing the Bower Package on Windows

```
npm install -g bower@1.8.0
```

For Linux and macOS, the same command is used but requires sudo, as shown in Listing 13-6.

Listing 13-6. Installing the Bower Package on Linux or macOS

```
sudo npm install -g bower@1.8.0
```

Installing .NET Core

The .NET Core runtime is required for ASP.NET Core MVC development. Each supported platform has its own installation process, which is described at www.microsoft.com/net/core. Microsoft provides installers for Windows and macOS and provides instructions for Linux using tar archives.

Installing .NET Core on Windows and macOS

To install .NET Core on Windows or macOS, simply download and run the .NET Core SDK installer.

Installing .NET Core on Linux

Microsoft provides instructions for installing .NET Core on the most popular Linux distributions at www.microsoft.com/net/core. I have used Ubuntu for this chapter, and the process requires first setting up a new feed for apt-get using the commands shown in Listing 13-7.

Listing 13-7. Preparing to Install .NET Core on Ubuntu Linux

```
sudo sh -c 'echo "deb [arch=amd64] https://apt-mo.trafficmanager.net/repos/dotnet-release/
xenial main" > /etc/apt/sources.list.d/dotnetdev.list'
sudo apt-key adv --keyserver hkp://keyserver.ubuntu.com:80 --recv-keys 417A0893
sudo apt-get update
```

The next step is to install .NET Core, as shown in Listing 13-8.

Listing 13-8. Installing .NET Core on Ubuntu Linux

```
sudo apt-get install dotnet-sdk-2.0.0
```

Checking the .NET Core Installation

Regardless of the platform you are using, you can check that .NET Core has been installed and is ready for use. Open a new command prompt or Terminal and run the command in Listing 13-9.

Listing 13-9. Checking the .NET Core Version

```
dotnet --version
```

The dotnet command starts the .NET runtime, and the version number for the .NET package you installed will be displayed. At the time of writing, the current release is 2.0.0, but this is likely to have been superseded by the time you read this book.

Installing Visual Studio Code

The most important step is to download and install Visual Studio Code, which is available from http:// code.visualstudio.com. Installation packages are available for WIndows, macOS, and popular Linux distributions. Download and install the package for your chosen platform.

■ **Note** Microsoft makes a new release of Visual Studio Code every month, which means the version you install will be different from the version that is current as I write this. This means some experimentation may be required to complete some of the examples in this chapter, although the fundamentals should remain the same.

Installing Visual Studio Code on Windows

To install Visual Studio Code for Windows, simply run the installer. When the process is complete, Visual Studio Code will start, and you will see the editor window, as shown in Figure 13-2.

Installing Visual Studio Code on macOS

Visual Studio Code is provided as a zip archive for the Mac, which can be downloaded from https:// go.microsoft.com/fwlink/?LinkID=620882. Expand the archive and double-click the Visual Studio Code.app file that it contains to start Visual Studio Code, producing the editor window shown in Figure 13-2.

Installing Visual Studio Code on Linux

Microsoft provides a .deb file for Debian and Ubuntu and an .rpm file for Red Hat, Fedora, and CentOS. Download and install the file for your preferred Linux. Since I am using Ubuntu for this chapter, I downloaded the .deb file and installed it using the Ubuntu Software tool.

When the installation is complete, run the command in Listing 13-10 to start Visual Studio Code, which will produce the editor window shown in Figure 13-2.

Listing 13-10. Starting Visual Studio Code on Linux

```
/usr/share/code/code
```

Checking the Visual Studio Code Installation

The test of a successful installation of Visual Studio Code is simply being able to start the application and see the editor, as shown in Figure 13-2. (I have changed the color scheme because the dark default colors are not well-suited to creating screenshots for a book.)

Figure 13-2. *Running Visual Studio Code on Windows, macOS, and Ubuntu Linux*

Installing the Visual Studio Code C# Extension

Visual Studio Code supports language-specific functionality through extensions, although these are not the same extensions that are supported by Visual Studio 2015. The most important extension for ASP.NET Core MVC development adds support for C#, which may seem like an odd omission from the basic install but reflects the fact that Microsoft has positioned Visual Studio Code as a general-purpose cross-platform editor that supports the widest possible range of languages and frameworks.

To install the C# extension, click the Extensions icon on the left side of the Visual Studio Code window. Enter csharp into the search box and locate the C# for Visual Studio Code extension in the list, as shown in Figure 13-3.

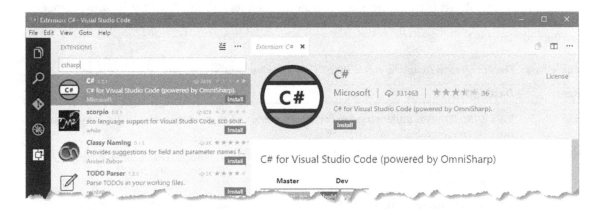

Figure 13-3. *Locating the C# extension*

Click the Install button and Visual Studio Code will download and install the extension. Click the Reload button to restart Visual Studio Code and activate the extension, as shown in Figure 13-4.

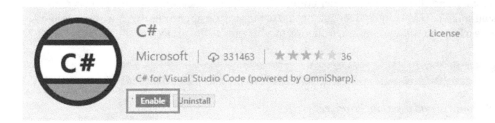

Figure 13-4. *Enabling the C# extension*

Creating an ASP.NET Core Project

Visual Studio Code doesn't have integrated support for creating ASP.NET Core projects, but you can create new projects using the dotnet command line.

It is important to create the right folder structure to get the project set up correctly, especially when it comes to working with unit tests. Create a project called InvitesProjects in a convenient location. This will be the folder that will contain both the ASP.NET Core MVC and unit test projects.

Next, create a folder called PartyInvites inside the InvitesProjects folder and use a command prompt to navigate to that folder and run the command shown in Listing 13-11.

Listing 13-11. Creating a New Project in the PartyInvites Folder

```
dotnet new web --language C# --framework netcoreapp2.0
```

The dotnet new command provides command-line access to project templates, and the web template specified in Listing 13-11 corresponds to the Visual Studio Empty template that I used in earlier chapters. Table 13-1 describes the set of project templates that are available for ASP.NET Core development. (Other templates are available, but they are not used for ASP.NET Core. Run the dotnet new --help command to see the complete list.)

Table 13-1. The dotnet new Templates for ASP.NET Core Development

Name	Description
web	This is the Empty template used in earlier chapters, which creates an ASP.NET Core project but does not enable the MVC framework.
mvc	This is the Web Application (Model-View-Controller) template used in Chapter 2, which creates an ASP.NET Core project that includes the MVC framework and placeholder controllers and views.
xunit	This is the xUnit Test Project (.NET Core) template that sets up unit testing with the xUnit package, as described in Chapter 7.

Preparing the Project with Visual Studio Code

To open the project in Visual Studio Code, select Open Folder from the File menu, navigate to the InvitesProjects folder, and click the Select Folder button. Visual Studio Code will open the project and automatically install some package required for editing and debugging C# applications. A few seconds after you first start editing a file, you will see a message offering to add items to the project, as shown in Figure 13-5.

Figure 13-5. The prompt to add assets to the project

Click the Yes button. VIsual Studio Code will create a .vscode folder and add some files that configure the build process. Visual Studio Code uses a three-section layout by default. The sidebar, which is highlighted in Figure 13-6, provides access to the main areas of functionality.

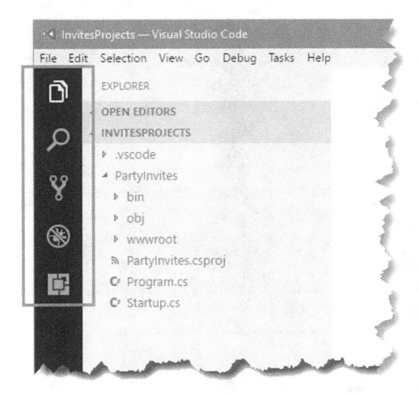

Figure 13-6. *The Visual Studio Code sidebar*

The topmost button opens the explorer pane, which shows the contents of the folder that has been opened. The other buttons provide access to the search feature, the integrated source code management, the debugger, and the set of installed extensions.

Click a file in the explorer pane to open it for editing. Multiple files can be edited simultaneously, and you can create new editor panes by clicking the Split Editor button in the top right of the window. The Visual Studio Code editor is pretty good, with decent IntelliSense support and assistance in completing NuGet and Bower package names and versions.

In addition to the contents of the project folder, the explorer pane shows which files are currently being edited, which makes it easy to remain focused on the subset of files that you are working with, which is a helpful addition when working on a subset of related files in a large project.

Managing Client-Side Packages

Bower is used to manage client-side packages in Visual Studio Code projects, just as it is in Visual Studio, although some additional work is required.

The first step is to add a file called .bowerrc, which is used to tell Bower where to install its packages. Right-click the PartyInvites folder and select New File from the pop-up menu, as shown in Figure 13-7.

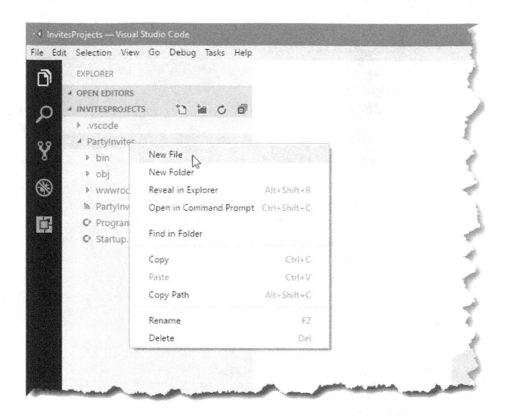

Figure 13-7. *Creating a new file*

Set the name of the file to .bowerrc (note that there are two r's in the file name) and add the content shown in Listing 13-12.

Listing 13-12. The Contents of the .bowerrc File

```
{
  "directory": "wwwroot/lib"
}
```

Next, create a file called bower.json and add the content shown in Listing 13-13.

Listing 13-13. The Contents of the bower.json File

```
{
  "name": "PartyInvites",
  "private": true,
  "dependencies": {
    "bootstrap": "4.0.0-alpha.6"
  }
}
```

Using the command prompt/Terminal to run the command shown in Listing 13-14 in the PartyInvites folder. This command uses the Bower tool to download and install the client-side packages specified in the bower.json file.

Listing 13-14. Installing the Client-Side Packages

```
bower install
```

Configuring the Application

The project initialization process has created an empty project without support for MVC. Listing 13-15 shows the changes to the Startup.cs file to set up MVC using the most basic configuration, the statements for which are described Chapter 14.

Listing 13-15. Adding Support for MVC in the Startup.cs File

```csharp
using System;
using System.Collections.Generic;
using System.Linq;
using System.Threading.Tasks;
using Microsoft.AspNetCore.Builder;
using Microsoft.AspNetCore.Hosting;
using Microsoft.AspNetCore.Http;
using Microsoft.Extensions.DependencyInjection;

namespace PartyInvites {
    public class Startup {

        public void ConfigureServices(IServiceCollection services) {
            services.AddMvc();
        }

        public void Configure(IApplicationBuilder app, IHostingEnvironment env) {
            app.UseDeveloperExceptionPage();
            app.UseStatusCodePages();
            app.UseStaticFiles();
            app.UseMvcWithDefaultRoute();
        }
    }
}
```

Building and Running the Project

To build and run the project, run the command shown in Listing 13-16 in the PartyInvites directory.

Listing 13-16. Running the Application

```
dotnet run
```

Visual Studio Code will compile the code in the project and use the Kestrel application server, described in Chapter 14, to run the application, waiting for HTTP requests on port 5000.

Visual Studio Code doesn't provide support for detecting changes to C# class files, which means that you must stop the application and start it again when you make changes.

To test the application, use a browser to navigate to `http://localhost:5000`. You will see the response shown in Figure 13-8. The 404 error is shown because there are no controllers in the project to handle requests at the moment.

Figure 13-8. *Testing the example application*

Re-creating the PartyInvites Application

All of the preparation is complete, which means that I can switch my focus to creating an MVC application. I am going to re-create the simple `PartyInvites` application from Chapter 2 but with some changes and additions to highlight working with Visual Studio Code.

Creating the Model and Repository

To get started, right-click the `PartyInvites` folder and select New Folder from the pop-up menu, as shown in Figure 13-9. Set the name of the folder to `Models`.

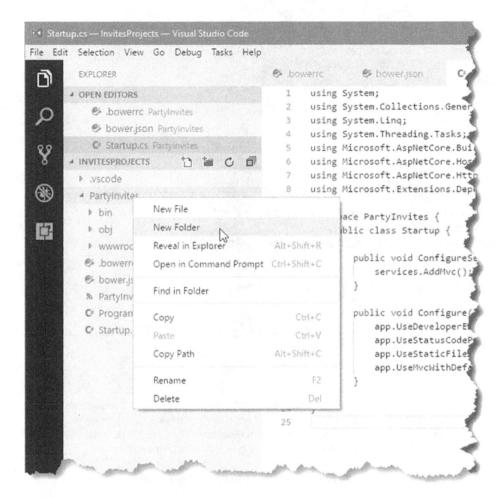

Figure 13-9. *Creating a new folder*

Right-click the Models folder in the explorer pane, select New File from the pop-up menu, set the name of the file to GuestResponse.cs, and add the C# code shown in Listing 13-17.

WORKING WITH THE VISUAL STUDIO CODE EDITOR

Visual Studio Code (and the C# extension installed earlier in the chapter) provides a full editing experience for C# files, as well as for common web formats such as JavaScript, CSS, and plain HTML files. In many ways, writing an MVC application in Visual Studio Code has a lot in common with the Visual Studio editor: there is IntelliSense support, color coding, and highlighting for errors (with suggestions to fix them).

The main deficit in Visual Studio Code is a lack of customization, especially when it comes to formatting code. As I write this, there are configuration options available for other languages, but the C# extension doesn't allow customization, which can make it a little difficult to work with if your preferred coding style isn't the one it supports by default. But overall, the editor is responsive and easy to work with, and writing MVC applications on macOS or Linux doesn't feel like a second-class experience.

Listing 13-17. The Contents of the GuestResponse.cs File in the PartyInvites/Models Folder

```
using System.ComponentModel.DataAnnotations;

namespace PartyInvites.Models {

    public class GuestResponse {

        public int id {get; set; }

        [Required(ErrorMessage = "Please enter your name")]
        public string Name { get; set; }

        [Required(ErrorMessage = "Please enter your email address")]
        [RegularExpression(".+\\@.+\\..+",
            ErrorMessage = "Please enter a valid email address")]
        public string Email { get; set; }

        [Required(ErrorMessage = "Please enter your phone number")]
        public string Phone { get; set; }

        [Required(ErrorMessage = "Please specify whether you'll attend")]
        public bool? WillAttend { get; set; }
    }
}
```

Next, add a file called IRepository.cs to the Models folder and use it to define the interface shown in Listing 13-18. The most important difference between the application in this chapter and the one in Chapter 2 is that I am going to store the model data in a persistent database. The IRepository interface describes how the application will access the model data without specifying its implementation.

Listing 13-18. The Contents of the IRepository.cs File in the PartyInvites/Models Folder

```
using System.Collections.Generic;

namespace PartyInvites.Models {

    public interface IRepository {
        IEnumerable<GuestResponse> Responses {get; }

        void AddResponse(GuestResponse response);
    }
}
```

Add a file called ApplicationDbContext.cs to the Models folder and use it to define the database context class shown in Listing 13-19.

Listing 13-19. The Contents of the ApplicationDbContext.cs File in the PartyInvites/Models Folder

```
using Microsoft.EntityFrameworkCore;

namespace PartyInvites.Models {
    public class ApplicationDbContext : DbContext {
```

```
    public ApplicationDbContext() {}

    protected override void OnConfiguring(DbContextOptionsBuilder builder) {
        builder.UseSqlite("Filename=./PartyInvites.db");
    }

    public DbSet<GuestResponse> Invites {get; set;}
    }
}
```

SQLite stores its data in a file, which is specified by the context class. For the example application, the data will be stored in a file called PartyInvites.db, which is defined in the OnConfiguring method.

To complete the set of classes required to store and access the model data, an implementation of the IRepository interface is required that uses the database context class. Add a new file called EFRepository.cs to the Models folder and add the code shown in Listing 13-20.

Listing 13-20. The Contents of the EFRepository.cs File in the PartyInvites/Models Folder

```
using System.Collections.Generic;

namespace PartyInvites.Models {
    public class EFRepository : IRepository {
        private ApplicationDbContext context = new ApplicationDbContext();

        public IEnumerable<GuestResponse> Responses => context.Invites;

        public void AddResponse(GuestResponse response) {
            context.Invites.Add(response);
            context.SaveChanges();
        }
    }
}
```

The EFRepository class follows a similar pattern to the one I used in Chapter 8 to set up the SportsStore database. In Listing 13-21, I have added a configuration statement to the ConfigureServices method of the Startup class that tells ASP.NET to create the EFRepository class when implementations of the IRepository interface are demanded by the dependency injection feature (which is described in Chapter 18).

Listing 13-21. Configuring the Repository in the Startup.cs File in the PartyInvites Folder

```
using System;
using System.Collections.Generic;
using System.Linq;
using System.Threading.Tasks;
using Microsoft.AspNetCore.Builder;
using Microsoft.AspNetCore.Hosting;
using Microsoft.AspNetCore.Http;
using Microsoft.Extensions.DependencyInjection;
using PartyInvites.Models;

namespace PartyInvites {
    public class Startup {
```

```
    public void ConfigureServices(IServiceCollection services) {
        services.AddTransient<IRepository, EFRepository>();
        services.AddMvc();
    }

    public void Configure(IApplicationBuilder app, IHostingEnvironment env) {
        app.UseDeveloperExceptionPage();
        app.UseStatusCodePages();
        app.UseStaticFiles();
        app.UseMvcWithDefaultRoute();
    }
    }
}
```

Creating the Database

In the rest of the book, whenever I need to demonstrate a feature that requires data persistence, I use the LocalDB feature, which is a simplified version of Microsoft SQL Server. But the LocalDB feature is available only on Windows, which means that an alternative is required when creating ASP.NET Core MVC applications on other platforms. The best alternative to LocalDB is SQLite, which is a cross-platform zero-configuration database that can be embedded in applications and for which Microsoft has included support in Entity Framework Core, which is the data access layer typically used with ASP.NET Core MVC applications. In the sections that follow, I walk through the process of adding SQLite to the project and using it as the data store for party responses.

USING SQLITE FOR DEVELOPMENT

One of the reasons that LocalDB is such a useful tool is because it allows development using the SQL Server database engine, which makes the transition to a production SQL Server environment simple and largely risk-free. SQLite is an excellent database, but it isn't well-suited to large-scale web applications, and that means a transition to another database is required when an MVC application is deployed. The configuration changes can be simplified using the project configuration features that I describe in Chapter 14, but you need to test the application thoroughly in a staging environment to surface any differences introduced by the production database.

See https://www.sqlite.org/whentouse.html if you are unsure whether to use SQLite in production. This page provides a good summary of where SQLite excels and where it doesn't.

One issue to be aware of is that SQLite doesn't support the full set of schema changes that Entity Framework Core can generate for other databases. This isn't generally a problem when using SQLite in development because you can delete the database file and generate a new one with a clean schema. It does complicate matters if you are considering deploying an application using SQLite, however.

If you want to use the same database in development and production, then consult the list of supported Entity Framework Core databases at http://ef.readthedocs.io/en/latest/providers/index.html. The list is short as I write this, but Microsoft has announced support for databases that are more suited to deployment than SQLite and that can also run on non-Windows platforms.

Adding the Database Package

The NuGet package that contains the command-line tools used to create and apply database migrations must be added to the project manually. Open the PartyInvites.csproj file and add the element shown in Listing 13-22.

Listing 13-22. Adding NuGet Package to the PartyInvites.csproj File in the PartyInvites Folder

```
<Project Sdk="Microsoft.NET.Sdk.Web">

  <PropertyGroup>
    <TargetFramework>netcoreapp2.0</TargetFramework>
  </PropertyGroup>

  <ItemGroup>
    <Folder Include="wwwroot\" />
  </ItemGroup>

  <ItemGroup>
    <PackageReference Include="Microsoft.AspNetCore.All" Version="2.0.0" />
    <DotNetCliToolReference Include="Microsoft.EntityFrameworkCore.Tools.DotNet"
        Version="2.0.0" />
  </ItemGroup>

</Project>
```

Save the change and run the command shown in Listing 13-23 in the PartyInvites folder to ensure that the new packages are downloaded and installed.

Listing 13-23. Installing the NuGet Packages

```
dotnet restore
```

Creating and Applying the Database Migration

Creating the database follows the same process as used by Visual Studio. To create an initial database migration, run the command in Listing 13-24 in the PartyInvites folder.

Listing 13-24. Creating a Database Migration

```
dotnet ef migrations add Initial
```

Entity Framework Core will create a folder called Migrations that contains the C# classes that will be used to set up the database schema. To apply the database migration, run the command shown in Listing 13-25 in the PartyInvites folder, which will create the database in the PartyInvites folder.

Listing 13-25. Applying the Database Migration

```
dotnet ef database update
```

Visual Studio Code doesn't include support for inspecting SQLite databases, but you can find an excellent open source tool for Windows, macOS, and Linux at http://sqlitebrowser.org.

Creating the Controllers and Views

In this section, I add the controller and views to the application. I started by creating a PartyInvites/Controllers folder and adding a file called HomeController.cs to it, which I used to create the controller shown in Listing 13-26.

Listing 13-26. The Contents of the HomeController.cs File in the PartyInvites/Controllers Folder

```csharp
using System;
using Microsoft.AspNetCore.Mvc;
using PartyInvites.Models;
using System.Linq;

namespace PartyInvites.Controllers {

    public class HomeController : Controller {
        private IRepository repository;

        public HomeController(IRepository repo) =>
            this.repository = repo;

        public ViewResult Index() {
            int hour = DateTime.Now.Hour;
            ViewBag.Greeting = hour < 12 ? "Good Morning" : "Good Afternoon";
            return View("MyView");
        }

        [HttpGet]
        public ViewResult RsvpForm() => View();

        [HttpPost]
        public ViewResult RsvpForm(GuestResponse guestResponse) {
            if (ModelState.IsValid) {
                repository.AddResponse(guestResponse);
                return View("Thanks", guestResponse);
            } else {
                // there is a validation error
                return View();
            }
        }
    }
```

```
public ViewResult ListResponses() =>
    View(repository.Responses.Where(r => r.WillAttend == true));
}
}
```

To set up the built-in tag helpers, I created a PartyInvites/Views folder and added a file called
_ViewImports.cshtml containing the expression shown in Listing 13-27.

Listing 13-27. The Contents of the _ViewImports.cshtml File in the PartyInvites/Views Folder

```
@addTagHelper *, Microsoft.AspNetCore.Mvc.TagHelpers
```

Next, I created a Views/Home folder and added a file called MyView.cshtml, which is the view selected by
the Index action method in Listing 13-26. I added the markup shown in Listing 13-28

Listing 13-28. The Contents of the MyView.cshtml File in the PartyInvites/Views/Home Folder

```
@{
    Layout = null;
}

<!DOCTYPE html>

<html>
<head>
    <meta name="viewport" content="width=device-width" />
    <title>Index</title>
    <link rel="stylesheet" href="/lib/bootstrap/dist/css/bootstrap.css" />
</head>
<body class="p-2">
    <div class="text-center">
        <h3>We're going to have an exciting party!</h3>
        <h4>And you are invited</h4>
        <a class="btn btn-primary" asp-action="RsvpForm">RSVP Now</a>
    </div>
</body>
</html>
```

I added a file called RsvpForm.cshtml to the Views/Home folder and added the content shown in
Listing 13-29. This view provides the HTML form that invitees will fill in to accept or decline their invitation
to the party.

Listing 13-29. The Contents of the RsvpForm.cshtml File in the PartyInvites/Views/Home Folder

```
@model PartyInvites.Models.GuestResponse

@{
    Layout = null;
}

<!DOCTYPE html>
```

```
<html>
<head>
    <meta name="viewport" content="width=device-width" />
    <title>RsvpForm</title>
    <link rel="stylesheet" href="/lib/bootstrap/dist/css/bootstrap.css" />
</head>
<body>
    <div class="m-2">
        <div class="text-center"><h4>RSVP</h4></div>
        <form class="p-1" asp-action="RsvpForm" method="post">
            <div asp-validation-summary="All"></div>
            <div class="form-group">
                <label asp-for="Name">Your name:</label>
                <input class="form-control" asp-for="Name" />
            </div>
            <div class="form-group">
                <label asp-for="Email">Your email:</label>
                <input class="form-control" asp-for="Email" />
            </div>
            <div class="form-group">
                <label asp-for="Phone">Your phone:</label>
                <input class="form-control" asp-for="Phone" />
            </div>
            <div class="form-group">
                <label>Will you attend?</label>
                <select class="form-control" asp-for="WillAttend">
                    <option value="">Choose an option</option>
                    <option value="true">Yes, I'll be there</option>
                    <option value="false">No, I can't come</option>
                </select>
            </div>
            <div class="text-center">
                <button class="btn btn-primary" type="submit">
                    Submit RSVP
                </button>
            </div>
        </form>
    </div>
</body>
</html>
```

The next view file is called Thanks.cshtml and is also created in the Views/Home folder, with the content shown in Listing 13-30 that is displayed when the guest has submitted their response.

Listing 13-30. The Contents of the Thanks.cshtml File in the PartyInvites/Views/Home Folder

```
@model PartyInvites.Models.GuestResponse

@{
    Layout = null;
}
```

```
<!DOCTYPE html>

<html>
<head>
    <meta name="viewport" content="width=device-width" />
    <title>Thanks</title>
    <link rel="stylesheet" href="/lib/bootstrap/dist/css/bootstrap.css" />
</head>
<body class="text-center">
    <p>
        <h1>Thank you, @Model.Name!</h1>
        @if (Model.WillAttend == true) {
            @:It's great that you're coming. The drinks are already in the fridge!
        } else {
            @:Sorry to hear that you can't make it, but thanks for letting us know.
        }
    </p>
    Click <a asp-action="ListResponses">here</a>
    to see who is coming.
</body>
</html>
```

The final view is called ListResponses.cshtml and, like the other views in this example, is added to the Views/Home folder. This view displays the list of guest responses using the markup shown in Listing 13-31.

Listing 13-31. The Contents of the ListResponses.cshtml File in the PartyInvites/Views/Home Folder

```
@model IEnumerable<PartyInvites.Models.GuestResponse>

@{
    Layout = null;
}

<!DOCTYPE html>
<html>
<head>
    <meta name="viewport" content="width=device-width" />
    <link rel="stylesheet" href="/lib/bootstrap/dist/css/bootstrap.css" />
    <title>Responses</title>
</head>
<body>
    <div class="m-1 p-1">
        <h2>Here is the list of people attending the party</h2>
        <table class="table table-sm table-striped table-bordered">
            <thead>
                <tr><th>Name</th><th>Email</th><th>Phone</th></tr>
            </thead>
            <tbody>
                @foreach (PartyInvites.Models.GuestResponse r in Model) {
                    <tr><td>@r.Name</td><td>@r.Email</td><td>@r.Phone</td></tr>
                }
            </tbody>
```

```
        </table>
    </div>
</body>
</html>
```

Run the dotnet run command in the PartyInvites project to compile the project and start the ASP. NET Core runtime. Once the application has started, you can see the completed application by navigating to http://localhost:5000, as shown in Figure 13-10.

Figure 13-10. *Running the completed application*

Unit Testing in Visual Studio Code

The process for unit testing with Visual Studio Code is similar to Visual Studio. The first step is to create a separate project for unit testing. Create a folder called Tests in the InvitesProject folder and run the command shown in Listing 13-32 in the new folder to create the unit test project.

Listing 13-32. Creating the Unit Test Project

```
dotnet new xunit --language C# --framework netcoreapp2.0
```

Run the command shown in Listing 13-33 in the Tests folder to add a reference to the application project so that the classes it contains are available for testing.

Listing 13-33. Adding a Reference to the Application Project

```
dotnet add reference ../PartyInvites/PartyInvites.csproj
```

Creating a Unit Test

Unit tests are created as described in Chapter 7. I added a new class file called HomeControllerTests.cs to the Tests folder, with the content shown in Listing 13-34.

Listing 13-34. The Contents of the HomeControllerTests.cs File in the Tests Folder

```
using System;
using System.Collections.Generic;
using PartyInvites.Controllers;
using PartyInvites.Models;
using Xunit;
using Microsoft.AspNetCore.Mvc;
using System.Linq;

namespace Tests {
    public class HomeControllerTests {

        [Fact]
        public void ListActionFiltersNonAttendees() {
            //Arrange
            HomeController controller = new HomeController(new FakeRepository());
            // Act
            ViewResult result = controller.ListResponses();
            // Assert
            Assert.Equal(2, (result.Model as IEnumerable<GuestResponse>).Count());
        }
    }

    class FakeRepository : IRepository {
        public IEnumerable<GuestResponse> Responses =>
            new List<GuestResponse> {
                new GuestResponse { Name = "Bob", WillAttend = true },
                new GuestResponse { Name = "Alice", WillAttend = true },
                new GuestResponse { Name = "Joe", WillAttend = false }
            };

        public void AddResponse(GuestResponse response) {
            throw new NotImplementedException();
        }
    }
}
```

This is a standard xUnit test that checks the ListResponses action in the Home controller and correctly filters out GuestResponse objects in the repository for which the WillAttend property is false.

Running Tests

To execute the unit tests in the project, run the command shown in Listing 13-35 in the Tests folder.

Listing 13-35. Running Unit Tests

```
dotnet test
```

All the tests in the project will be run and the results shown, producing output like this:

```
Starting test execution, please wait...
[xUnit.net 00:00:00.6731479]   Discovering: Tests
[xUnit.net 00:00:00.7900132]   Discovered:  Tests
[xUnit.net 00:00:00.8432715]   Starting:    Tests
[xUnit.net 00:00:00.9967614]   Finished:    Tests

Total tests: 2. Passed: 2. Failed: 0. Skipped: 0.
Test Run Successful.
Test execution time: 1.6974 Seconds
```

Two tests are shown in the results because the project template includes a file called UnitTest1.cs that contains an empty unit test. You can delete this file, as demonstrated in Chapter 7.

Summary

In this chapter, I provided a brief overview of working with Visual Studio Code, which is a light-weight development tool that supports ASP.NET Core MVC development on Windows, macOS, and Linux. Visual Studio Code isn't a full replacement for the complete Visual Studio product yet, but it provides the core features required to create MVC applications and is being enhanced by Microsoft with monthly releases.

That's the end of this part of the book. In Part 2, I begin the process of digging into the details and showing you how the features I used to create the application work in depth.

PART II

ASP.NET Core MVC 2 in Detail

So far, you've learned about why ASP.NET Core MVC exists and have gained an understanding of its architecture and underlying design goals. You've taken it for a good, long test-drive by building a realistic e-commerce application. Now it's time to open the hood and expose the full details of the framework's machinery.

In Part 2 of this book, I dig into the details. I start with an exploration of the structure of an ASP.NET Core MVC application and the way that requests are processed. I then focus on individual features, such as routing, controllers and actions, the MVC view and tag helper system, and the way that MVC works with domain models.

CHAPTER 14

■ ■ ■

Configuring Applications

The topic of configuration may not seem interesting, but it reveals a lot about how MVC applications work and how HTTP requests are handled. Resist the temptation to skip this chapter, and take the time to understand the way that the configuration system shapes MVC web applications. It will give you a solid foundation for understanding the chapters that follow.

In this chapter, I explain how these are used to configure MVC applications and show how MVC builds on features provided by the ASP.NET Core platform. Table 14-1 puts configuring applications in context.

Table 14-1. *Putting Configuration in Context*

Question	Answer
What is it?	The `Program` and `Startup` classes and the JSON files are used to configure how an application works and what packages it depends on.
Why is it useful?	The configuration system allows applications to be tailored to their environments and to manage their package dependencies.
How is it used?	The most important component is the `Startup` class, which is used to create services (which are objects that provide common functionality throughout an application) and middleware components (which are used to handle HTTP requests).
Are there any pitfalls or limitations?	In complex applications, the configuration can become difficult to manage. See the "Dealing with Complex Configurations" section for ASP.NET features intended to manage this problem.
Are there any alternatives?	No. The configuration system is an integral part of ASP.NET and the means by which MVC applications are set up.

Table 14-2 summarizes the chapter.

Table 14-2. *Chapter Summary*

Problem	Solution	Listing
Add functionality to the application	Add NuGet packages to the `csproj` file	5–8
Manage the initialization of the ASP.NET application	Use the `Program` class	9–11
Configure the application	Use the `ConfigureServices` and `Configure` methods of the `Startup` class	12–13
Create common functionality	Use the `ConfigureServices` method to create services	14–16
Generate content responses	Create content-generating middleware	17–19
Prevent requests from traversing the request pipeline	Create short-circuiting middleware	20–21
Edit a request before it is processed by other middleware components	Create request-editing middleware	22–24
Edit a response that has been processed by other middleware components	Create response-editing middleware	25–26
Set up MVC functionality	Use the `UseMvc` or `UseMvcWithDefaultRoute` method	27
Change the application configuration for different environments	Use the hosting environment service	28
Handle application errors	Use the developer or production error-handling middleware	29–30
Manage multiple browsers during development	Use Browser Link	31
Enable images, JavaScript files, and CSS files	Enable the static content middleware	32
Separate configuration data from C# code	Create external configuration sources, such as JSON files	33–35
Log application data	Use the logging middleware	36–38
Prepare dependency injection for use with Entity Framework Core	Disable scope validation	39
Configure MVC services	Use the options features	40
Configure complex applications	Use multiple external files or classes	41–45

Preparing the Example Project

For this chapter, I created a new project called ConfiguringApps using the Empty template. I am going to configure the application later in the chapter, but there are some basics that I need to put in place in preparation for the changes I make.

I am going to use Bootstrap to style the HTML content in this chapter, so I created the bower.json file using the Bower Configuration File item template and added the package shown in Listing 14-1.

Listing 14-1. Adding Bootstrap in the bower.json File in the ConfiguringApps Folder

```
{
  "name": "asp.net",
  "private": true,
  "dependencies": {
    "bootstrap": "4.0.0-alpha.6"
  }
}
```

Next, I created the `Controllers` folder and added a class file called `HomeController.cs`, which I used to define the controller shown in Listing 14-2.

Listing 14-2. The Contents of the HomeController.cs File in the Controllers Folder

```
using System.Collections.Generic;
using Microsoft.AspNetCore.Mvc;

namespace ConfiguringApps.Controllers {

    public class HomeController : Controller {

        public ViewResult Index() => View(new Dictionary<string, string> {
                ["Message"] = "This is the Index action"
            });
    }
}
```

I created the Views/Home folder and added a view file called `Index.cshtml` with the content shown in Listing 14-3.

Listing 14-3. The Contents of the Index.cshtml File in the Views/Home Folder

```
@model Dictionary<string, string>
@{ Layout = null; }

<!DOCTYPE html>
<html>
<head>
    <meta name="viewport" content="width=device-width" />
    <link asp-href-include="lib/bootstrap/dist/css/*.min.css" rel="stylesheet" />
    <title>Result</title>
</head>
<body class="p-1">
    <table class="table table-condensed table-bordered table-striped">
        @foreach (var kvp in Model) {
            <tr><th>@kvp.Key</th><td>@kvp.Value</td></tr>
        }
    </table>
</body>
</html>
```

The link element in the view relies on a built-in tag helper to select the Bootstrap CSS files. To enable the built-in tag helpers, I used the MVC View Imports Page item template to create the _ViewImports. cshtml file in the Views folder and added the expression shown in Listing 14-4.

Listing 14-4. The Contents of the _ViewImports.cshtml File in the Views Folder

```
@addTagHelper *, Microsoft.AspNetCore.Mvc.TagHelpers
```

Start the application and you will see the message shown in Figure 14-1.

Figure 14-1. *Running the example application*

Configuring the Project

The most important configuration file is <projectname>.csproj, which replaces the project.json file used in earlier versions of ASP.NET Core. This file, which is called ConfiguringApps.csproj in the example project, is hidden by Visual Studio and must be accessed by right-clicking the project item in the Solution Explorer window and selecting Edit ConfiguringApps.csproj from the pop-up menu. Listing 14-5 shows the initial content of the ConfiguringApps.csproj file, which was created by Visual Studio as part of the Empty project template.

Listing 14-5. The Contents of the ConfiguringApps.csproj File in the ConfiguringApps Folder

```xml
<Project Sdk="Microsoft.NET.Sdk.Web">

  <PropertyGroup>
    <TargetFramework>netcoreapp2.0</TargetFramework>
  </PropertyGroup>

  <ItemGroup>
    <Folder Include="wwwroot\" />
  </ItemGroup>

  <ItemGroup>
    <PackageReference Include="Microsoft.AspNetCore.All" Version="2.0.0" />
  </ItemGroup>

</Project>
```

The `csproj` file is used to configure the MSBuild tool, which is used to build .NET projects. Configuration is performed using XML elements, and Table 14-3 describes the elements that are in the default configuration file. I use other configuration elements in later examples, but the elements in the table are enough to start development on an ASP.NET Core MVC project.

Table 14-3. *The XML Configuration Elements in the Default csproj File*

Element	Description
Project	This is the root element, which denotes that this is an MSBuild configuration file. The Sdk attribute is set to `Microsoft.NET.Sdk.Web` to provide the set of implicit package imports that are required to build the project.
PropertyGroup	This element groups related configuration properties to add structure to the file.
TargetFramework	This element specifies the .NET Framework that is targeted by the build process and must be defined within a PropertyGroup element. The default value is `netcoreapp2.0`, which targets .NET Core 2.0.
ItemGroup	This element groups related configuration items to add structure to the file.
Folder	This element tells MSBuild how to deal with a folder in the project. The element in the listing tells MSBuild to include the wwwroot folder when the application is published.
PackageReference	This element is used to specify a dependency on the NuGet package, which is identified through the Include and Version attributes. The `Microsoft.AspNetCore.All` package is used to provide access to all of the individual packages that provide ASP.NET Core and MVC Framework functionality.

Adding Packages to the Project

The most important role for the `csproj` file is to list the packages that the project depends on. When Visual Studio detects a change to the `csproj` file, it inspects the list of packages, downloads any new additions, and removes any packages that are no longer required.

With the release of ASP.NET Core 2, all of the basic functionality required for ASP.NET Core MVC, the MVC Framework, and Entity Framework Core is included in the `Microsoft.AspNetCore.All` meta-package, which is a convenience feature that avoids the need to start a new development effort by adding a long list of NuGet packages to the project.

Even so, you will still need to add NuGet packages for third-party or advanced features. There are three ways to add packages to a project. The first is to select Tools ➤ NuGet Package Manager ➤ Manage NuGet Packages for Solution, which allows the management of NuGet packages through an easy-to-use interface. If you are new to .NET development, then this is the best approach because it reduces the chance of making a mistake when selecting a package.

To add the `System.Net.Http` package, for example, which provides support for making (rather than receiving) HTTP requests, you can go to the Browse section of the package manager, search by name, and see a complete list of the versions available, including any prerelease versions, as shown in Figure 14-2.

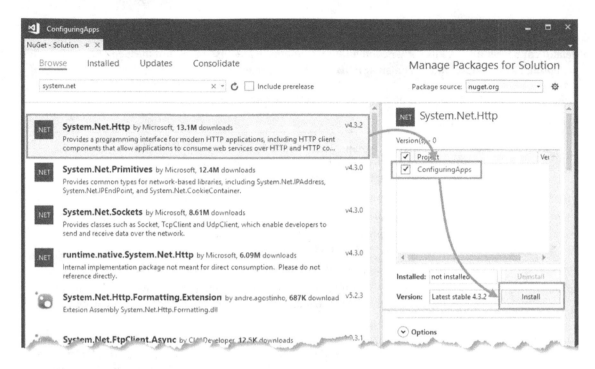

Figure 14-2. *Adding a package using the NuGet package manager*

Select the package and version you need, select the projects that the package is required for, and click the Install button. Visual Studio will download the package and update the csproj file.

You can also add packages using the command line, although this requires you to know the name of the package you require (and, ideally, the version). Listing 14-6 shows the command you would run in the ConfiguringApps folder to add the System.Net.Http package to the project.

Listing 14-6. Adding a Package to the Project

```
dotnet add package System.Net.Http --version 4.3.2
```

The NuGet package manager and the dotnet add package command both add PackageReference elements to the csproj file. If you prefer, you can add packages by editing the configuration file to add the PackageReference element manually. This is the most direct approach but requires care to avoid mistyping the name of the package or specifying a version number that doesn't exist. In Listing 14-7, you can see the addition to the csproj file for the System.Net.Http package.

Listing 14-7. Adding a Package in the ConfiguringApps.csproj File in the ConfiguringApps Folder

```
<Project Sdk="Microsoft.NET.Sdk.Web">

  <PropertyGroup>
    <TargetFramework>netcoreapp2.0</TargetFramework>
  </PropertyGroup>
```

```
<ItemGroup>
  <Folder Include="wwwroot\" />
</ItemGroup>

<ItemGroup>
  <PackageReference Include="Microsoft.AspNetCore.All" Version="2.0.0" />
  <PackageReference Include="System.Net.Http" Version="4.3.2" />
</ItemGroup>
```

The PackageReference element has an Include attribute that specifies the package name and a Version attribute that specifies the version number.

Adding Tools Packages to the Project

Although you can add regular packages in different ways, some packages extend the range of tasks that can be performed with the dotnet command-line tool, and these packages require a different kind of element in the csproj file, which is a DotNetCliToolReference element instead of the PackageReference element used by packages that contain features used directly by the application. These packages can be added to projects only by editing the csproj file directly.

Listing 14-8 shows the addition of the package that allows database migrations to be created and applied using the dotnet ef commands used in Part 1 of this book.

Listing 14-8. Adding Tools Packages to the ConfiguringApps.csprog File in the ConfiguringApps Folder

```
<Project Sdk="Microsoft.NET.Sdk.Web">

  <PropertyGroup>
    <TargetFramework>netcoreapp2.0</TargetFramework>
  </PropertyGroup>

  <ItemGroup>
    <Folder Include="wwwroot\" />
  </ItemGroup>

  <ItemGroup>
    <PackageReference Include="Microsoft.AspNetCore.All" Version="2.0.0" />
    <PackageReference Include="System.Net.Http" Version="4.3.2" />
    <DotNetCliToolReference Include="Microsoft.EntityFrameworkCore.Tools.DotNet"
        Version="2.0.0 " />
  </ItemGroup>

</Project>
```

When you add tools packages to a project, you can either include the DotNetCliToolReference elements in the same ItemGroup as the regular PackageReference elements, as I have done in Listing 14-8, or create a separate ItemGroup element. When you save the changes to the csproj file, Visual Studio will download and install the packages and use them to configure the dotnet command-line tool.

Understanding the Program Class

The Program class is defined in a file called Program.cs and provides the entry point for running the application, providing .NET with a main method that can be executed to configure the hosting environment and select the class that completes the configuration for the ASP.NET Core application. The default contents of the Program class are enough to get most projects up and running, and Listing 14-9 shows the default code added to projects by Visual Studio.

Listing 14-9. The Default Contents of the Program.cs File in the ConfiguringApps Folder

```
using System;
using System.Collections.Generic;
using System.IO;
using System.Linq;
using System.Threading.Tasks;
using Microsoft.AspNetCore;
using Microsoft.AspNetCore.Hosting;
using Microsoft.Extensions.Configuration;
using Microsoft.Extensions.Logging;

namespace ConfiguringApps {
    public class Program {

        public static void Main(string[] args) {
            BuildWebHost(args).Run();
        }

        public static IWebHost BuildWebHost(string[] args) =>
            WebHost.CreateDefaultBuilder(args)
                .UseStartup<Startup>()
                .Build();
    }
}
```

The Main method provides the entry point that all .NET applications must provide so they can be executed by the runtime. The Main method in the Program class calls the BuildWebHost method, which is responsible for configuring ASP.NET Core.

The BuildWebHost method uses static methods defined by the WebHost class to configure ASP.NET Core. With the release of ASP.NET Core 2, the configuration is simplified by the use of the CreateDefaultBuilder method, which configures ASP.NET Core using settings that are likely to suit most projects. The UseStartup method is called to identify the class that will provide application-specific configuration; the convention is to use a class called Startup, which I describe later in this chapter. The Build method processes all the configuration settings and creates an object that implements the IWebHost interface, which is returned to the Main method, which calls Run to start handling HTTP requests.

Digging into the Configuration Detail

The CreateDefaultBuilder method is a convenient way to jump-start the configuration of ASP.NET Core, but it does hide a lot of important detail, which can be a problem if you need to change the way that your application is configured. Listing 14-10 replaces the CreateDefaultBuilder method with individual statements that are called to create the default configuration.

Listing 14-10. Detailed Configuration Statements in the Program.cs File in the ConfiguringApps Folder

```
using System;
using System.Collections.Generic;
using System.IO;
using System.Linq;
using System.Threading.Tasks;
using Microsoft.AspNetCore;
using Microsoft.AspNetCore.Hosting;
using Microsoft.Extensions.Configuration;
using Microsoft.Extensions.Logging;
using System.Reflection;

namespace ConfiguringApps {
    public class Program {

        public static void Main(string[] args) {
            BuildWebHost(args).Run();
        }

        public static IWebHost BuildWebHost(string[] args) {
            return new WebHostBuilder()
                .UseKestrel()
                .UseContentRoot(Directory.GetCurrentDirectory())
                .ConfigureAppConfiguration((hostingContext, config) => {
                    var env = hostingContext.HostingEnvironment;
                    config.AddJsonFile("appsettings.json", optional: true,
                            reloadOnChange: true)
                        .AddJsonFile($"appsettings.{env.EnvironmentName}.json",
                            optional: true, reloadOnChange: true);

                    if (env.IsDevelopment()) {
                        var appAssembly =
                            Assembly.Load(new AssemblyName(env.ApplicationName));
                        if (appAssembly != null) {
                            config.AddUserSecrets(appAssembly, optional: true);
                        }
                    }

                    config.AddEnvironmentVariables();

                    if (args != null) {
                        config.AddCommandLine(args);
                    }
                })
                .ConfigureLogging((hostingContext, logging) => {
                    logging.AddConfiguration(
                        hostingContext.Configuration.GetSection("Logging"));
                    logging.AddConsole();
                    logging.AddDebug();
                })
```

```
            .UseIISIntegration()
            .UseDefaultServiceProvider((context, options) => {
                options.ValidateScopes =
                    context.HostingEnvironment.IsDevelopment();
            })
            .UseStartup<Startup>()
            .Build();
        }
    }
}
```

Table 14-4 lists each of the configuration methods added to the BuildWebHost method and provides a brief description of what they do.

Table 14-4. *The Default ASP.NET Core Configuration Methods*

Name	Description
UseKestrel	This method configures the Kestrel web server, as described in the "Using Kestrel Directly" sidebar.
UseContentRoot	This method configures the root directory for the application, which is used for loading configuration files and delivering static content such as images, JavaScript, and CSS.
ConfigureAppConfiguration	This method is used to prepare the configuration data for the application, as described in the "Configuring the Application" section later in this chapter.
AddUserSecrets	This method is used to store sensitive data outside of code files, as described at https://docs.microsoft.com/en-us/aspnet/core/security/app-secrets. This is a somewhat awkward feature, which I do not use in this book.
ConfigureLogging	This method is used to configure logging for the application, as described in the "Configuring Logging" section later in this chapter.
UseIISIntegration	This method enables integration with IIS and IIS Express.
UseDefaultServiceProvider	This method is used to configure dependency injection, as described in the "Configuring Dependency Injection" section.
UseStartup	This method specifies the class that will be used to configure ASP.NET, as described in the "Understanding the Startup Class" section.

I explain some of the more complex statements shown in Listing 14-10 later in the chapter. For now, I am going to remove some of the configuration statements so that only the basic configuration remains, as shown in Listing 14-11.

Listing 14-11. Simplifying the Configuration in the Program.cs File in the ConfiguringApps Folder

```
using System;
using System.Collections.Generic;
using System.IO;
using System.Linq;
using System.Threading.Tasks;
```

```
using Microsoft.AspNetCore;
using Microsoft.AspNetCore.Hosting;
using Microsoft.Extensions.Configuration;
using Microsoft.Extensions.Logging;
using System.Reflection;

namespace ConfiguringApps {
    public class Program {

        public static void Main(string[] args) {
            BuildWebHost(args).Run();
        }

        public static IWebHost BuildWebHost(string[] args) {

            return new WebHostBuilder()
                .UseKestrel()
                .UseContentRoot(Directory.GetCurrentDirectory())
                .UseIISIntegration()
                .UseStartup<Startup>()
                .Build();
        }
    }
}
```

These are the statements that provide a basic configuration that will work for most ASP.NET Core MVC applications. I'll add back in the other statements as I explain the features they relate to.

USING KESTREL DIRECTLY

Kestrel is a cross-platform web server designed to run ASP.NET Core applications. It is used automatically when you run an ASP.NET Core application using IIS Express (which is the server provided by Visual Studio for use during development) or the full version of IIS, which has been the traditional web platform for .NET applications.

You can also run Kestrel directly if you want, which means you can run your ASP.NET Core MVC applications on any of the supported platforms, bypassing the Windows-only restriction of IIS. There are two ways to run an application using Kestrel. The first is to click the arrow at the right edge of the IIS Express button on the Visual Studio toolbar and select the entry that matches the name of the project. This will open a new command prompt and run the application using Kestrel.

You can achieve the same effect by opening your own command prompt, navigating to the folder that contains the application's configuration files (the one that contains the csproj file), and running the following command:

```
dotnet run
```

By default, the Kestrel server starts listening for HTTP requests on port 5000. If there is a Properties/launchSettings.json file in the project, the HTTP port and environment for the application will be read from this file.

Understanding the Startup Class

The Program class is responsible for jump-starting the application, but the most important configuration work is delegated through the UseStartup method, like this:

```
...
.UseStartup<Startup>()
...
```

The UseStartup method relies on a type parameter to identify the class that will configure ASP.NET Core. The conventional name for this class is Startup, which is the name used by the ASP.NET Core MVC project templates, including the Empty template used to create the example project for this chapter.

Examining how the Startup class works provides insights into the way that HTTP requests are processed and how MVC integrates into the rest of the ASP.NET Core platform.

In this section, I start with the simplest possible Startup class and add features to demonstrate the effect of different configuration options, ending up with a configuration that is suitable for most MVC projects. As the starting point, Listing 14-12 shows the Startup class that Visual Studio adds to Empty projects, which sets up just enough functionality to get ASP.NET Core to handle HTTP requests.

Listing 14-12. The Initial Contents of the Startup.cs File

```
using System;
using System.Collections.Generic;
using System.Linq;
using System.Threading.Tasks;
using Microsoft.AspNetCore.Builder;
using Microsoft.AspNetCore.Hosting;
using Microsoft.AspNetCore.Http;
using Microsoft.Extensions.DependencyInjection;

namespace ConfiguringApps {
    public class Startup {

        public void ConfigureServices(IServiceCollection services) {
        }

        public void Configure(IApplicationBuilder app, IHostingEnvironment env) {

            if (env.IsDevelopment()) {
                app.UseDeveloperExceptionPage();
            }

            app.Run(async (context) => {
                await context.Response.WriteAsync("Hello World!");
            });
        }
    }
}
```

The Startup class defines two methods, ConfigureServices and Configure, that set up the shared features required by an application and tell ASP.NET Core how they should be used.

When the application starts, ASP.NET Core creates a new instance of the Startup class and calls its ConfigureServices method so that the application can create its *services*. As I explain in the "Understanding ASP.NET Services" section, services are objects that provide functionality to other parts of the application. This is a vague description, but that's because services can be used to provide just about any functionality.

Once the services have been created, ASP.NET calls the Configure method. The purpose of the Configure method is to set up the *request pipeline*, which is the set of components—known as *middleware*—that are used to handle incoming HTTP requests and produce responses for them. I explain how the request pipeline works and demonstrate how to create middleware components in the "Understanding ASP.NET Middleware" section. Figure 14-3 shows the way that ASP.NET uses the Startup class.

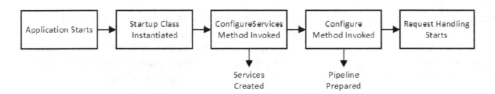

Figure 14-3. *How ASP.NET uses the Startup class to configure an application*

It isn't especially useful to have a Startup class that just returns the same "Hello, World" message for all requests, so before I explain what the methods in the class do in detail, I need to jump ahead a little and enable MVC, as shown in Listing 14-13.

Listing 14-13. Enabling MVC in the Startup.cs File in the ConfiguringApps Folder

```
using System;
using System.Collections.Generic;
using System.Linq;
using System.Threading.Tasks;
using Microsoft.AspNetCore.Builder;
using Microsoft.AspNetCore.Hosting;
using Microsoft.AspNetCore.Http;
using Microsoft.Extensions.DependencyInjection;

namespace ConfiguringApps {
    public class Startup {

        public void ConfigureServices(IServiceCollection services) {
            services.AddMvc();
        }

        public void Configure(IApplicationBuilder app, IHostingEnvironment env) {
            app.UseMvcWithDefaultRoute();
        }
    }
}
```

With these additions—which I explain in the sections that follow—there is enough infrastructure in place to process HTTP requests and generate responses using controllers and views. If you run the application, you will see the output shown in Figure 14-4.

Figure 14-4. *The effect of enabling MVC*

Notice that the content is not styled. The minimal configuration in Listing 14-13 doesn't provide any support for serving up static content, such as CSS stylesheets and JavaScript files, so the `link` element in the HTML rendered by the `Index.cshtml` view produces a request for the Bootstrap CSS style sheet that the application can't process, which prevents the browser from getting the style information it required. I fix this problem in the "Adding the Remaining Middleware Components" section.

Understanding ASP.NET Services

ASP.NET Core calls the `Startup.ConfigureServices` method so that the application can set up the *services* it requires. The term *service* refers to any object that provides functionality to other parts of the application. As noted, this is a vague description because services can do *anything* that your application requires. As an example, I added an `Infrastructure` folder to the project and added to it a class file called `UptimeService.cs`, which I used to define the class shown in Listing 14-14.

Listing 14-14. The Contents of the UptimeService.cs File in the Infrastructure Folder

```
using System.Diagnostics;

namespace ConfiguringApps.Infrastructure {

    public class UptimeService {
        private Stopwatch timer;

        public UptimeService() {
            timer = Stopwatch.StartNew();
        }

        public long Uptime => timer.ElapsedMilliseconds;
    }
}
```

When this class is created, its constructor starts a timer that keeps track of how long the application has been running. This is a nice example of a service because it provides functionality that can be used in the rest of the application and it benefits from being created when the application is started.

ASP.NET services are registered using the `ConfigureServices` method of the `Startup` class, and in Listing 14-15, you can see how I have registered the `UptimeService` class.

Listing 14-15. Registering a Custom Service in the Startup.cs File in the ConfiguringApps Folder

```
using System;
using System.Collections.Generic;
using System.Linq;
using System.Threading.Tasks;
using Microsoft.AspNetCore.Builder;
using Microsoft.AspNetCore.Hosting;
using Microsoft.AspNetCore.Http;
using Microsoft.Extensions.DependencyInjection;
using ConfiguringApps.Infrastructure;

namespace ConfiguringApps {
    public class Startup {

        public void ConfigureServices(IServiceCollection services) {
            services.AddSingleton<UptimeService>();
            services.AddMvc();
        }

        public void Configure(IApplicationBuilder app, IHostingEnvironment env) {
            app.UseMvcWithDefaultRoute();
        }
    }
}
```

As its argument, the ConfigureServices method receives an object that implements the IServiceCollection interface. Services are registered using extension methods called on the IServiceCollection interface that specify different configuration options. I describe the options available for creating services in Chapter 18, but for the moment, I have used the AddSingleton method, which means that a single UptimeService object will be shared throughout the application.

Services are closely related to a feature called *dependency injection*, which allows components such as controllers to easily obtain services and which I describe in depth in Chapter 18. Services registered in Startup.ConfigureServices can be accessed by creating a constructor that accepts an argument of the service type you require. Listing 14-16 shows the constructor I added to the Home controller to receive the shared UptimeService object that I created in Listing 14-15. I have also updated the controller's Index action method so that it includes the value of the service's Update property in the view data it produces.

Listing 14-16. Accessing a Service in the HomeController.cs File in the Controllers Folder

```
using System.Collections.Generic;
using Microsoft.AspNetCore.Mvc;
using ConfiguringApps.Infrastructure;

namespace ConfiguringApps.Controllers {

    public class HomeController : Controller {
        private UptimeService uptime;

        public HomeController(UptimeService up) => uptime = up;
```

```
        public ViewResult Index()
            => View(new Dictionary<string, string> {
                ["Message"] = "This is the Index action",
                ["Uptime"] = $"{uptime.Uptime}ms"
            });
    }
}
```

When MVC needs an instance of the Home controller class to handle an HTTP request, it inspects the HomeController constructor and finds that it requires an UptimeService object. MVC then inspects the set of services that have been configured in the Startup class, finds that UptimeService has been configured so that a single UptimeService object is used for all requests, and passes that object as the constructor argument when the HomeController is created.

Services can be registered and consumed in more complex ways, but this example demonstrates the central idea behind services and shows how defining a service in the Startup class allows you to define functionality or data that be used throughout an application.

If you run the application and request the default URL, you will see a response that includes the number of milliseconds since the application has started, which is obtained from the UptimeService object that was created in the Startup class, as illustrated in Figure 14-5. (Strictly speaking, it is the time since the UptimeService service object was created but this is close enough to the application startup to make no difference for the purpose of this chapter).

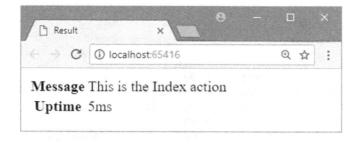

Figure 14-5. *Using a simple service*

Each time a request for the default URL is received, MVC creates a new HomeController object and provides it with the shared UptimeService object as a constructor argument. This allows the Home controller access to the application's uptime without being concerned about how this information is provided or implemented.

Understanding the Built-In MVC Services

A package as complex as MVC uses many services; some are for its internal use, and others offer functionality to developers. Packages define extension methods that set up all the services they require in a single method call. For MVC, this method is called AddMvc, and it is one of the two methods I added to the Startup class to get MVC working.

```
...
public void ConfigureServices(IServiceCollection services) {
    services.AddSingleton<UptimeService>();
    services.AddMvc();
}
...
```

This method sets up every service that MVC needs without filling up the `ConfigureServices` method with an enormous list of individual services.

■ **Note**   The Visual Studio IntelliSense feature will show you a long list of other extension methods that you can call on the `IServiceCollection` object in the `ConfigureServices` method. Some of these methods, such as `AddSingleton` and `AddScoped`, are used to register services in different ways. The other methods, such as `AddRouting` or `AddCors`, add individual services that are already applied by the `AddMvc` method. The result is that for most applications, the `ConfigureServices` method contains a small number of custom services, the call to the `AddMvc` method, and, optionally, some statements to configure the built-in services, which I describe in the "Configuring MVC Services" section.

Understanding ASP.NET Middleware

In ASP.NET Core, *middleware* is the term used for the components that are combined to form the *request pipeline*. The request pipeline is arranged like a chain, and when a new request arrives, it is passed to the first middleware component in the chain. This component inspects the request and decides whether to handle it and generate a response or to pass it to the next component in the chain. Once a request has been handled, the response that will be returned to the client is passed back along the chain, which allows all of the earlier components to inspect or modify it.

The way that middleware components work may seem a little odd, but it allows for a lot of flexibility in the way that applications are put together. Understanding how the use of middleware shapes an application can be important, especially if you are not getting the responses you expect. To explain how the middleware system works, I am going to create some custom components that demonstrate each of the four types of middleware that you will encounter.

Creating Content-Generating Middleware

The most important type of middleware generates content for clients, and it is this category to which MVC belongs. To create a content-generating middleware component without the complexity of MVC, I added a class called `ContentMiddleware.cs` to the `Infrastructure` folder and used it to define the class shown in Listing 14-17.

Listing 14-17. The Contents of the ContentMiddleware.cs File in the Infrastructure Folder

```
using System.Text;
using System.Threading.Tasks;
using Microsoft.AspNetCore.Http;

namespace ConfiguringApps.Infrastructure {

    public class ContentMiddleware {
        private RequestDelegate nextDelegate;

        public ContentMiddleware(RequestDelegate next) => nextDelegate = next;
```

```
        public async Task Invoke(HttpContext httpContext) {
            if (httpContext.Request.Path.ToString().ToLower() == "/middleware") {
                await httpContext.Response.WriteAsync(
                "This is from the content middleware", Encoding.UTF8);
            } else {
                await nextDelegate.Invoke(httpContext);
            }
        }
    }
}
```

Middleware components don't implement an interface or derive from a common base class. Instead, they define a constructor that takes a RequestDelegate object and define an Invoke method. The RequestDelegate object represents the next middleware component in the chain, and the Invoke method is called when ASP.NET receives an HTTP request.

Information about the HTTP request and the response that will be returned to the client is provided through the HttpContext argument to the Invoke method. I describe the HttpContext class and its properties in Chapter 17, but for this chapter, it is enough to know that the Invoke method in Listing 14-17 inspects the HTTP request and checks to see whether the request has been sent to the /middleware URL. If it has, then a simple text response is sent to the client; if a different URL has been used, then the request is forwarded to the next component in the chain.

The request pipeline is set up inside the Configure method of the Startup class. In Listing 14-18, I have removed MVC methods from the example application and used the ContentMiddleware class as the sole component in the pipeline.

Listing 14-18. Using a Custom Middleware in the Startup.cs File in the ConfiguringApps Folder

```
using System;
using System.Collections.Generic;
using System.Linq;
using System.Threading.Tasks;
using Microsoft.AspNetCore.Builder;
using Microsoft.AspNetCore.Hosting;
using Microsoft.AspNetCore.Http;
using Microsoft.Extensions.DependencyInjection;
using ConfiguringApps.Infrastructure;

namespace ConfiguringApps {
    public class Startup {

        public void ConfigureServices(IServiceCollection services) {
            services.AddSingleton<UptimeService>();
            services.AddMvc();
        }

        public void Configure(IApplicationBuilder app, IHostingEnvironment env) {
            app.UseMiddleware<ContentMiddleware>();
        }
    }
}
```

Custom middleware components are registered with the UseMiddleware extension method within the Configure method. The UseMiddleware method uses a type parameter to specify the middleware class. This so that ASP.NET Core can build up a list of all the middleware components that are going to be used and then instantiate them to create the chain. If you run the application and request the /middleware URL, you will see the result shown in Figure 14-6.

Figure 14-6. *Generating content from a custom middleware component*

Figure 14-7 illustrates the middleware pipeline that I created using the ContentMiddleware class. When ASP.NET Core receives an HTTP request, it passes it to the only middleware component registered in the Startup class. If the URL is /middleware, then the component generates a result, which is returned to ASP. NET Core and sent to the client.

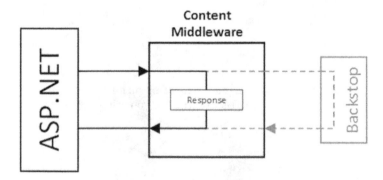

Figure 14-7. *The example middleware pipeline*

If the URL isn't /middleware, then the ContentMiddleware class passes on the request to the next component in the chain. Since there is no other component, the request reaches a backstop handler provided by ASP.NET Core when it creates the pipeline, which sends the request back along the pipeline in the other direction (a process that will make more sense once you see how the other types of middleware work).

Using Services in Middleware

It isn't just controllers that can use services that have been set up in the ConfigureServices method. ASP. NET Core inspects the constructors of middleware classes and uses services to provide values for any arguments that have been defined. In Listing 14-19, I have added an argument to the constructor of the ContentMiddleware class, which tells ASP.NET Core that it requires an UptimeService object.

Listing 14-19. Using a Service in the ContentMiddleware.cs File in the Infrastructure Folder

```
using System.Text;
using System.Threading.Tasks;
using Microsoft.AspNetCore.Http;

namespace ConfiguringApps.Infrastructure {

    public class ContentMiddleware {
        private RequestDelegate nextDelegate;
        private UptimeService uptime;

        public ContentMiddleware(RequestDelegate next, UptimeService up) {
            nextDelegate = next;
            uptime = up;
        }

        public async Task Invoke(HttpContext httpContext) {
            if (httpContext.Request.Path.ToString().ToLower() == "/middleware") {
                await httpContext.Response.WriteAsync(
                    "This is from the content middleware "+
                        $"(uptime: {uptime.Uptime}ms)",  Encoding.UTF8);
            } else {
                await nextDelegate.Invoke(httpContext);
            }
        }
    }
}
```

Being able to use services means that middleware components can share common functionality and avoid code duplication. Run the application and request the /middleware URL and you will see the output shown in Figure 14-8.

Figure 14-8. Using a service in custom middleware

Creating Short-Circuiting Middleware

The next type of middleware intercepts requests before they reach the content generation components in order to *short-circuit* the pipeline process, often for performance purposes. Listing 14-20 shows the contents of a class file called ShortCircuitMiddleware.cs that I added to the Infrastructure folder.

Listing 14-20. The Contents of the ShortCircuitMiddleware.cs File in the Infrastructure Folder

```
using System.Linq;
using System.Threading.Tasks;
using Microsoft.AspNetCore.Http;

namespace ConfiguringApps.Infrastructure {

    public class ShortCircuitMiddleware {
        private RequestDelegate nextDelegate;

        public ShortCircuitMiddleware(RequestDelegate next) => nextDelegate = next;

        public async Task Invoke(HttpContext httpContext) {
            if (httpContext.Request.Headers["User-Agent"]
                    .Any(h => h.ToLower().Contains("edge"))) {
                httpContext.Response.StatusCode = 403;
            } else {
                await nextDelegate.Invoke(httpContext);
            }
        }
    }
}
```

This middleware component inspects the request's User-Agent header, which is used by browsers to identify themselves. Using the User-Agent header to identify specific browsers isn't reliable enough to use in a real application, but it is sufficient for this example.

The term *short-circuiting* is used because this type of middleware doesn't always forward requests to the next component in the chain. In this case, if the User-Agent header contains the term edge, the component sets the status code to 403 – Forbidden and doesn't forward the request to the next component. Since the request is being rejected, there is no point in allowing the request to be handled by other components, which would needlessly consume system resources. Instead, the request handling is terminated early, and the 403 response is sent to the client.

Middleware components receive requests in the order in which they are set up in the Startup class, which means that short-circuiting middleware must be set up before content-generating middleware, as shown in Listing 14-21.

Listing 14-21. Registering Short-Circuiting Middleware in the Startup.cs File in the ConfiguringApps Folder

```
using System;
using System.Collections.Generic;
using System.Linq;
using System.Threading.Tasks;
using Microsoft.AspNetCore.Builder;
using Microsoft.AspNetCore.Hosting;
using Microsoft.AspNetCore.Http;
using Microsoft.Extensions.DependencyInjection;
using ConfiguringApps.Infrastructure;

namespace ConfiguringApps {
    public class Startup {
```

```
    public void ConfigureServices(IServiceCollection services) {
        services.AddSingleton<UptimeService>();
        services.AddMvc();
    }

    public void Configure(IApplicationBuilder app, IHostingEnvironment env) {
        app.UseMiddleware<ShortCircuitMiddleware>();
        app.UseMiddleware<ContentMiddleware>();
    }
  }
}
```

If you run the application and request any URL using the Microsoft Edge browser, then you will see the 403 error. Requests from other browsers are ignored by the ShortCircuitMiddleware component and are passed on to the next component in the chain, which means that a response will be generated when the requested URL is /middleware. Figure 14-9 shows the addition of the short-circuiting component to the middleware pipeline.

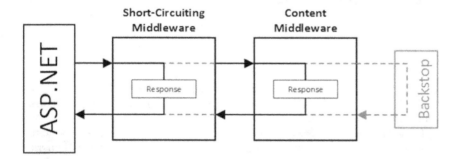

Figure 14-9. *Adding a short-circuiting component to the middleware pipeline*

Creating Request-Editing Middleware

The next type of middleware component examined doesn't generate a response. Instead, it changes requests before they reach other components later in the chain. This kind of middleware is mainly used for platform integration to enrich the ASP.NET Core representation of an HTTP request with platform-specific features. It can also be used to prepare requests so that they are easier to process by subsequent components. As a demonstration, I added the BrowserTypeMiddleware.cs file to the Infrastructure folder and used it to define the middleware component shown in Listing 14-22.

Listing 14-22. The Contents of the BrowserTypeMiddleware.cs File in the Infrastructure Folder

```
using System.Linq;
using System.Threading.Tasks;
using Microsoft.AspNetCore.Http;

namespace ConfiguringApps.Infrastructure {

    public class BrowserTypeMiddleware {
        private RequestDelegate nextDelegate;
```

```
    public BrowserTypeMiddleware(RequestDelegate next) => nextDelegate = next;

    public async Task Invoke(HttpContext httpContext) {
        httpContext.Items["EdgeBrowser"]
            = httpContext.Request.Headers["User-Agent"]
                .Any(v => v.ToLower().Contains("edge"));
        await nextDelegate.Invoke(httpContext);
    }
    }
}
```

This component inspects the User-Agent header of the request and looks for the term edge, which suggests that the request may have been made using the Edge browser. The HttpContext object provides a dictionary through the Items property that is used to pass data between components, and the outcome of the header search is stored with the key EdgeBrowser.

To demonstrate how middleware components can cooperate, Listing 14-23 shows the ShortCircuitMiddleware class, which rejects requests when they are from Edge, making its decision based on the data produced by the BrowserTypeMiddleware component.

Listing 14-23. Cooperating with Another Component in the ShortCircuitMiddleware.cs File

```
using System.Linq;
using System.Threading.Tasks;
using Microsoft.AspNetCore.Http;

namespace ConfiguringApps.Infrastructure {

    public class ShortCircuitMiddleware {
        private RequestDelegate nextDelegate;

        public ShortCircuitMiddleware(RequestDelegate next) => nextDelegate = next;

        public async Task Invoke(HttpContext httpContext) {
            if (httpContext.Items["EdgeBrowser"] as bool? == true) {
                httpContext.Response.StatusCode = 403;
            } else {
                await nextDelegate.Invoke(httpContext);
            }
        }
    }
}
```

By their nature, middleware components that edit requests need to be placed before those components that they cooperate with or that rely on the changes they make. In Listing 14-24, I have registered the BrowserTypeMiddleware class as the first component in the pipeline.

Listing 14-24. Registering a Middleware Component in the Startup.cs File in the ConfiguringApps Folder

```
using System;
using System.Collections.Generic;
using System.Linq;
using System.Threading.Tasks;
```

```csharp
using Microsoft.AspNetCore.Builder;
using Microsoft.AspNetCore.Hosting;
using Microsoft.AspNetCore.Http;
using Microsoft.Extensions.DependencyInjection;
using ConfiguringApps.Infrastructure;

namespace ConfiguringApps {
    public class Startup {

        public void ConfigureServices(IServiceCollection services) {
            services.AddSingleton<UptimeService>();
            services.AddMvc();
        }

        public void Configure(IApplicationBuilder app, IHostingEnvironment env) {
            app.UseMiddleware<BrowserTypeMiddleware>();
            app.UseMiddleware<ShortCircuitMiddleware>();
            app.UseMiddleware<ContentMiddleware>();
        }
    }
}
```

Placing the component at the start of the pipeline ensures that the request has already been modified before it is received by the other components, as shown in Figure 14-10.

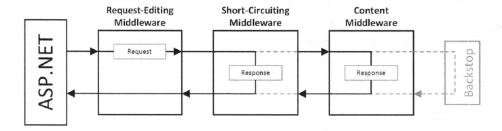

Figure 14-10. *Adding a response-editing component to the middleware pipeline*

Creating Response-Editing Middleware

The final type of middleware operates on the responses generated by other components in the pipeline. This is useful for logging details of requests and their responses or for dealing with errors. Listing 14-25 shows the contents of the ErrorMiddleware.cs file, which I added to the Infrastructure folder to demonstrate this type of middleware component.

Listing 14-25. The Contents of the ErrorMiddleware.cs File in the Infrastructure Folder

```csharp
using System.Text;
using System.Threading.Tasks;
using Microsoft.AspNetCore.Http;
```

```
namespace ConfiguringApps.Infrastructure {

    public class ErrorMiddleware {
        private RequestDelegate nextDelegate;

        public ErrorMiddleware(RequestDelegate next) {
            nextDelegate = next;
        }

        public async Task Invoke(HttpContext httpContext) {
            await nextDelegate.Invoke(httpContext);

            if (httpContext.Response.StatusCode == 403) {
                await httpContext.Response
                    .WriteAsync("Edge not supported", Encoding.UTF8);
            } else if (httpContext.Response.StatusCode == 404) {
                await httpContext.Response
                    .WriteAsync("No content middleware response", Encoding.UTF8);
            }
        }
    }
}
```

The component isn't interested in a request until it has made its way through the middleware pipeline and a response has been generated. If the response status code is 403 or 404, then the component adds a descriptive message to the response. All other responses are ignored. Listing 14-26 shows the registration of the component class in the Startup class.

■ **Tip**   You may be wondering where the 404 – Not Found status code comes from since it isn't set by any of the three middleware components I have created. The answer is that this is how the response is configured by ASP.NET when the request enters the pipeline and is the result returned to the client if no middleware component changes the response.

Listing 14-26. Registering a Response-Editing Middleware Component in the Startup.cs File

```
using System;
using System.Collections.Generic;
using System.Linq;
using System.Threading.Tasks;
using Microsoft.AspNetCore.Builder;
using Microsoft.AspNetCore.Hosting;
using Microsoft.AspNetCore.Http;
using Microsoft.Extensions.DependencyInjection;
using ConfiguringApps.Infrastructure;

namespace ConfiguringApps {
    public class Startup {
```

```
    public void ConfigureServices(IServiceCollection services) {
        services.AddSingleton<UptimeService>();
        services.AddMvc();
    }

    public void Configure(IApplicationBuilder app, IHostingEnvironment env) {
        app.UseMiddleware<ErrorMiddleware>();
        app.UseMiddleware<BrowserTypeMiddleware>();
        app.UseMiddleware<ShortCircuitMiddleware>();
        app.UseMiddleware<ContentMiddleware>();
    }
  }
}
```

I registered the ErrorMiddleware class so that it occupies the first position in the pipeline. This may seem odd for a component that is interested only in responses, but registering the component at the start of the chain ensures that it is able to inspect the responses generated by any other component, as illustrated in Figure 14-11. If this component is placed later in the pipeline, then it will only be able to inspect responses generated by some of the other components.

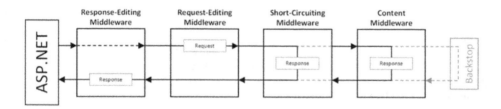

Figure 14-11. *Adding a response-editing component to the middleware pipeline*

You can see the effect of the new middleware by starting the application and requesting any URL except /middleware. The result will be the error message shown in Figure 14-12.

Figure 14-12. *Editing the responses of other middleware components*

Understanding How the Configure Method Is Invoked

The ASP.NET Core platform inspects the Configure method before it is invoked and gets a list of its arguments, which it provides using the services set up in the ConfigureServices method or using the special services shown in Table 14-5.

Table 14-5. *The Special Services Available As Configure Method Arguments*

Type	Description
IApplicationBuilder	This interface defines the functionality required to set up an application's middleware pipeline.
IHostingEnvironment	This interface defines the functionality required to differentiate between different types of environment, such as development and production.

Using the Application Builder

Although you don't have to define any arguments at all for the Configure method, most Startup classes will use at least the IApplicationBuilder interface because it allows the middleware pipeline to be created, as demonstrated earlier in the chapter. For custom middleware components, the UseMiddleware extension method is used to register classes. Complex content-generating middleware packages provide a single method that sets up all of their middleware components in a single step, just like they provide a single method for defining the services they use. In the case of MVC, two extension methods are available, as described in Table 14-6.

Table 14-6. *The MVC IApplicationBuilder Extension Methods*

Name	Description
UseMvcWithDefaultRoute	This method sets up the MVC middleware components with the default route.
UseMvc	This method sets up the MVC middleware components using a custom routing configuration specified using a lambda expression.

Routing is the process by which request URLs are mapped to controllers and actions are defined by the application; I describe routing in detail in Chapters 15 and 16. The UseMvcWithDefaultRoute method is useful for getting started with MVC development, but most applications call the UseMvc method, even if the result is to explicitly define the same routing configuration that would have been created by the UseMvcWithDefaultRoute method, as shown in Listing 14-27. This makes the routing configuration used by the application obvious to other developers and makes it easy to add new routes later (which almost all applications require at some point).

Listing 14-27. Setting Up the MVC Middleware in the Startup.cs File in the ConfiguringApps Folder

```
using System;
using System.Collections.Generic;
using System.Linq;
using System.Threading.Tasks;
using Microsoft.AspNetCore.Builder;
using Microsoft.AspNetCore.Hosting;
using Microsoft.AspNetCore.Http;
using Microsoft.Extensions.DependencyInjection;
using ConfiguringApps.Infrastructure;

namespace ConfiguringApps {
    public class Startup {
```

```
    public void ConfigureServices(IServiceCollection services) {
        services.AddSingleton<UptimeService>();
        services.AddMvc();
    }

    public void Configure(IApplicationBuilder app, IHostingEnvironment env) {
        app.UseMiddleware<ErrorMiddleware>();
        app.UseMiddleware<BrowserTypeMiddleware>();
        app.UseMiddleware<ShortCircuitMiddleware>();
        app.UseMiddleware<ContentMiddleware>();

        app.UseMvc(routes => {
            routes.MapRoute(
                name: "default",
                template: "{controller=Home}/{action=Index}/{id?}");
        });
    }
}
}
```

Since MVC sets up content-generating middleware components, the UseMvc method is called after all the other middleware components have been registered. To prepare the services that MVC depends on, the AddMvc method must be called in the ConfigureServices method.

Using the Hosting Environment

The IHostingEnvironment interface provides some basic—but important—information about the hosting environment in which the application is running using the properties described in Table 14-7.

Table 14-7. The IHostingEnvironment Properties

Name	Description
ApplicationName	This property returns the name of the application, which is set by the hosting platform.
EnvironmentName	This property returns a string that describes the current environment, as described after this table.
ContentRootPath	This property returns the path that contains the application's content files and configuration files.
WebRootPath	This property returns a string that specifies the directory that contains the static content for the application. This is usually the wwwroot folder.
ContentRootFileProvider	This property returns an object that implements the IFileProvider interface and that can be used to read files from the folder specified by the ContentRootPath property.
WebRootFileProvider	This property returns an object that implements the IFileProvider interface and that can be used to read files from the folder specified by the WebRootPath property.

The ContentRootPath and WebRootPath properties are interesting but not needed in most applications because there is a built-in middleware component that can be used to deliver static content, as described in the "Enabling Static Content" section later in this chapter.

The important property is EnvironmentName, which allows the configuration of the application to be modified based on the environment in which it is running. There are three conventional environments (*development, staging,* and *production*), and each represents a commonly used environment.

The current hosting environment is set using an environment variable called ASPNETCORE_ENVIRONMENT. To set the environment variable, select ConfiguringApps Properties from the Visual Studio Project menu and switch to the Debug tab. Double-click the Value field for the environment variable, which is set to Development by default, and change it to Staging, as shown in Figure 14-13. Save your changes to have the new environment name take effect.

■ **Tip**　Environment names are not case-sensitive, so *Staging* and *staging* are treated as the same environment. Although *development, staging,* and *production* are the conventional environments, you can use any name you like. This can be useful if there are multiple developers on a project and each requires different configuration settings, for example. See the "Dealing with Complex Configurations" section later in the chapter for details on how to deal with complex differences between environment configurations.

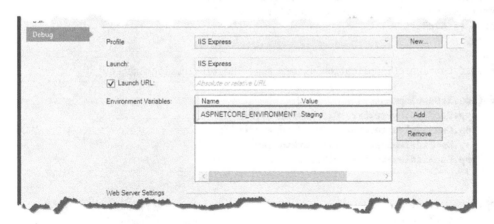

Figure 14-13. *Setting the name of the hosting environment*

Within the Configure method, you can determine which hosting environment is being used by reading the IHostingEnvironment.EnvironmentName property or using one of the extension methods that operate on IHostingEnvironment objects, as described in Table 14-8.

Table 14-8. *IHostingEnvironment Extension Methods*

Name	Description
IsDevelopment()	This method returns true if the hosting environment name is Development.
IsStaging()	This method returns true if the hosting environment name is Staging.
IsProduction()	This method returns true if the hosting environment name is Production.
IsEnvironment(env)	This method returns true if the hosting environment name matches the env argument.

The extension methods are used to alter the set of middleware components in the pipeline to tailor the behavior of the application to different hosting environments. In Listing 14-28, I use one of the extension methods to ensure that the custom middleware components created earlier in the chapter are only present in the pipeline in the Development hosting environment.

Listing 14-28. Using the Hosting Environment in the Startup.cs File in the ConfiguringApps Folder

```
using System;
using System.Collections.Generic;
using System.Linq;
using System.Threading.Tasks;
using Microsoft.AspNetCore.Builder;
using Microsoft.AspNetCore.Hosting;
using Microsoft.AspNetCore.Http;
using Microsoft.Extensions.DependencyInjection;
using ConfiguringApps.Infrastructure;

namespace ConfiguringApps {
    public class Startup {

        public void ConfigureServices(IServiceCollection services) {
            services.AddSingleton<UptimeService>();
            services.AddMvc();
        }

        public void Configure(IApplicationBuilder app, IHostingEnvironment env) {

            if (env.IsDevelopment()) {
                app.UseMiddleware<ErrorMiddleware>();
                app.UseMiddleware<BrowserTypeMiddleware>();
                app.UseMiddleware<ShortCircuitMiddleware>();
                app.UseMiddleware<ContentMiddleware>();
            }

            app.UseMvc(routes => {
                routes.MapRoute(
                    name: "default",
                    template: "{controller=Home}/{action=Index}/{id?}");
            });
        }
    }
}
```

The three custom middleware components won't be added to the pipeline with the current configuration, which has set the hosting environment to Staging. If you run the application and request the /middleware URL, you will receive a 404 - Not Found error because the only middleware components available are the ones set up by the UseMvc method, which have no controllers available that can process this URL.

■ **Note** Once you have tested the effect of changing the hosting environment, be sure to change it back to Development; otherwise, the examples in the rest of the chapter won't work properly.

Adding the Remaining Middleware Components

There are a set of commonly used middleware components that are useful in most MVC projects and that I use in the examples in this book. In the sections that follow, I add these components to the request pipeline and explain how they work.

Enabling Exception Handling

Even the most carefully written application will encounter exceptions, and it is important to handle them appropriately. In Listing 14-29, I have added middleware components that deal with exceptions to the request pipeline to the Startup class. I have also removed the custom middleware components so that I can focus on MVC.

Listing 14-29. Adding Exception-Handling Middleware in the Startup.cs File in the ConfiguringApps Folder

```
using System;
using System.Collections.Generic;
using System.Linq;
using System.Threading.Tasks;
using Microsoft.AspNetCore.Builder;
using Microsoft.AspNetCore.Hosting;
using Microsoft.AspNetCore.Http;
using Microsoft.Extensions.DependencyInjection;
using ConfiguringApps.Infrastructure;

namespace ConfiguringApps {
    public class Startup {

        public void ConfigureServices(IServiceCollection services) {
            services.AddSingleton<UptimeService>();
            services.AddMvc();
        }

        public void Configure(IApplicationBuilder app, IHostingEnvironment env) {

            if (env.IsDevelopment()) {
                app.UseDeveloperExceptionPage();
                app.UseStatusCodePages();
            } else {
                app.UseExceptionHandler("/Home/Error");
            }

            app.UseMvc(routes => {
                routes.MapRoute(
                    name: "default",
                    template: "{controller=Home}/{action=Index}/{id?}");
            });
        }
    }
}
```

The UseStatusCodePages method adds descriptive messages to responses that contain no content, such as 404 - Not Found responses, which can be useful since not all browsers show their own messages to the user.

The UseDeveloperExceptionPage method sets up an error-handling middleware component that displays details of the exception in the response, including the exception trace. This isn't information that should be displayed to users, so the call to UseDeveloperExceptionPage is made only in the development hosting environment, which is detected using the IHostingEnvironmment object.

For the staging or production environment, the UseExceptionHandler method is used instead. This method sets up an error handling that allows a custom error message to be displayed that won't reveal the inner workings of the application. The argument to the UseExceptionHandler method is the URL that the client should be redirected to in order to receive the error message. This can be any URL provided by the application, but the convention is to use /Home/Error.

In Listing 14-30, I have added the ability to generate exceptions on demand to the Index action of the Home controller and have added an Error action so requests generated by the UseExceptionHandler component can be processed.

Listing 14-30. Generating and Handling Exceptions in the HomeController.cs File in the Controllers Folder

```
using System.Collections.Generic;
using Microsoft.AspNetCore.Mvc;
using ConfiguringApps.Infrastructure;

namespace ConfiguringApps.Controllers {

    public class HomeController : Controller {
        private UptimeService uptime;

        public HomeController(UptimeService up) => uptime = up;

        public ViewResult Index(bool throwException = false) {
            if (throwException) {
                throw new System.NullReferenceException();
            }
            return View(new Dictionary<string, string> {
                ["Message"] = "This is the Index action",
                ["Uptime"] = $"{uptime.Uptime}ms"
            });
        }

        public ViewResult Error() => View(nameof(Index),
            new Dictionary<string, string> {
                ["Message"] = "This is the Error action"});
        }
}
```

The changes to the Index action rely on the model binding feature, which I describe in Chapter 26, to obtain a throwException value from the request. The action throws a NullReferenceException if throwException is true and executes normally if it is false.

The Error action uses the Index view to display a simple message. You can see the effect of the different exception-handling middleware components by running the application and requesting the /Home/Index?throwException=true URL. The query string provides the value for the Index action argument, and the response that you see will depend on the hosting environment name. Figure 14-14 shows the output produced by the UseDeveloperExceptionPage (for the Development hosting environment) and UseExceptionHandler middleware (for all other hosting environments).

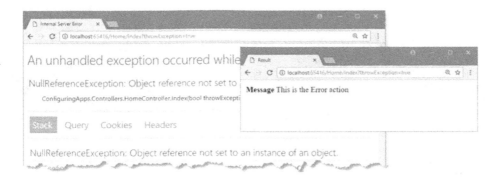

Figure 14-14. *Handling exceptions in development and staging/production*

The developer exception page provides details of the exception and options to explore its stack trace and the request that caused it. By contrast, the user exception page should be used simply to indicate that something has gone wrong.

Enabling Browser Link

I described the Browser Link feature in Chapter 6 and demonstrated how it can be used to manage browsers during development. The server-side part of Browser Link is implemented as a middleware component that must be added to the Startup class as part of the application configuration, without which the Visual Studio integration won't work. Browser Link is useful only during development and should not be used in staging or production because it edits the responses generated by other middleware components to insert JavaScript code that opens HTTP connections back to the server side so that it can receive reload notifications. In Listing 14-31, you can see how the UseBrowserLink method, which registers the middleware component, is called only for the Development hosting environment.

Listing 14-31. Enabling Browser Link in the Startup.cs File in the ConfiguringApps Folder

```
using System;
using System.Collections.Generic;
using System.Linq;
using System.Threading.Tasks;
using Microsoft.AspNetCore.Builder;
using Microsoft.AspNetCore.Hosting;
using Microsoft.AspNetCore.Http;
using Microsoft.Extensions.DependencyInjection;
using ConfiguringApps.Infrastructure;

namespace ConfiguringApps {
    public class Startup {

        public void ConfigureServices(IServiceCollection services) {
            services.AddSingleton<UptimeService>();
            services.AddMvc();
        }
```

```
        public void Configure(IApplicationBuilder app, IHostingEnvironment env) {

            if (env.IsDevelopment()) {
                app.UseDeveloperExceptionPage();
                app.UseStatusCodePages();
                app.UseBrowserLink();
            } else {
                app.UseExceptionHandler("/Home/Error");
            }

            app.UseMvc(routes => {
                routes.MapRoute(
                    name: "default",
                    template: "{controller=Home}/{action=Index}/{id?}");
            });
        }
    }
}
```

Enabling Static Content

The final middleware component that is useful for most projects provides access to the files in the wwwroot folder so that applications can include images, JavaScript files, and CSS stylesheets. The UseStaticFiles method adds a component that short-circuits the request pipeline for static files, as shown in Listing 14-32.

Listing 14-32. Enabling Static Content in the Startup.cs File in the ConfiguringApps Folder

```
using System;
using System.Collections.Generic;
using System.Linq;
using System.Threading.Tasks;
using Microsoft.AspNetCore.Builder;
using Microsoft.AspNetCore.Hosting;
using Microsoft.AspNetCore.Http;
using Microsoft.Extensions.DependencyInjection;
using ConfiguringApps.Infrastructure;

namespace ConfiguringApps {
    public class Startup {

        public void ConfigureServices(IServiceCollection services) {
            services.AddSingleton<UptimeService>();
            services.AddMvc();
        }

        public void Configure(IApplicationBuilder app, IHostingEnvironment env) {

            if (env.IsDevelopment()) {
                app.UseDeveloperExceptionPage();
                app.UseStatusCodePages();
                app.UseBrowserLink();
            } else {
```

```
            app.UseExceptionHandler("/Home/Error");
        }
        app.UseStaticFiles();
        app.UseMvc(routes => {
            routes.MapRoute(
                name: "default",
                template: "{controller=Home}/{action=Index}/{id?}");
        });
    }
  }
}
```

Static content is typically required regardless of the hosting environment, which is why I call the UseStaticFiles section for all environments. This addition means that the link element in the Index view will work properly and allow the browser to load the Bootstrap CSS style sheet. You can see the effect by starting the application, as shown in Figure 14-15.

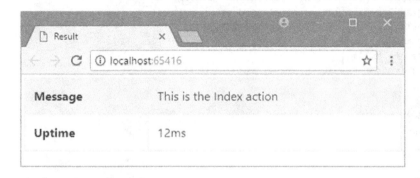

Figure 14-15. *Enabling static content*

Configuring the Application

Some configuration data changes often, such as when the application moves from the development to the production environment and different details are required for database servers. Rather than hard-code this information in the Startup class, ASP.NET Core allows configuration data to be provided from a range of more easily changed sources, such as environment variables, command-line arguments, and files written in the JavaScript Object Notation (JSON) format.

Configuration data is usually handled automatically, but since I have replaced the default settings in the Program class, I need to explicitly add the code that will get the data and make it available for use in the rest of the application, as shown in Listing 14-33.

Listing 14-33. Loading Configuration Data in the Program.cs File in the ConfiguringApps Folder

```
using System;
using System.Collections.Generic;
using System.IO;
using System.Linq;
using System.Threading.Tasks;
using Microsoft.AspNetCore;
using Microsoft.AspNetCore.Hosting;
```

```
using Microsoft.Extensions.Configuration;
using Microsoft.Extensions.Logging;
using System.Reflection;

namespace ConfiguringApps {
    public class Program {

        public static void Main(string[] args) {
            BuildWebHost(args).Run();
        }

        public static IWebHost BuildWebHost(string[] args) {

            return new WebHostBuilder()
                .UseKestrel()
                .UseContentRoot(Directory.GetCurrentDirectory())
                .ConfigureAppConfiguration((hostingContext, config) => {
                    config.AddJsonFile("appsettings.json",
                        optional: true, reloadOnChange: true);
                    config.AddEnvironmentVariables();
                    if (args != null) {
                        config.AddCommandLine(args);
                    }
                })
                .UseIISIntegration()
                .UseStartup<Startup>()
                .Build();
        }
    }
}
```

The ConfigureAppConfiguration method is used to handle the configuration data and its arguments are a WebHostBuilderContext object and an object that implements the IConfigurationBuilder interface. The WebBostBuilderContext class defines the properties described in Table 14-9.

Table 14-9. *The Properties Defined by the WebBostBuilderContext Class*

Name	Description
HostingEnvironment	This property returns an object that implements the IHostingEnvironment interface and provides information about the hosting environment in which the application is running. See the "Using the Hosting Environment" section earlier in the chapter for details.
Configuration	This property returns an object that implements the IConfiguration interface, which provides read-only access to the configuration data in the application.

The IConfigurationBuilder interface is used to prepare the configuration data for the rest of the application, which is typically done using extension methods. The three methods used in Listing 14-33 to add configuration data are described in Table 14-10.

Table 14-10. *The IConfigurationBuilder Extension Methods for Adding Configuration Data*

Name	Description
AddJsonFile	This method is used to load configuration data from a JSON file, such as appsettings.json.
AddEnvironmentVariables	This method is used to load configuration data from environment variables.
AddCommandLine	This method is used to load configuration data from the command-line arguments used to start the application.

Of the three methods that are used to load configuration data in Listing 14-33, it is the AddJsonFile method that is the most interesting. The arguments to the method specify the file name, whether the file is optional, and whether the configuration data should be reloaded if the file changes:

```
...
config.AddJsonFile("appsettings.json", optional: true, reloadOnChange: true);
...
```

The values used for the arguments specify a file called appsettings.json file, which is the conventional name for the JSON configuration file. This file is optional, meaning that an exception will not be thrown if the file doesn't exist, and will be monitored for changes so that the configuration data can be refreshed automatically.

RELOADING CONFIGURATION DATA

The ASP.NET Core configuration system supports reloading data when configuration files change. Some of the built-in middleware components, such as the logging system, support this feature, which means logging levels can be changed at runtime without restarting the application. You can incorporate similar capabilities in custom middleware components as well.

But just because a feature makes something possible doesn't mean it's sensible. Making changes to configuration files on production systems is a recipe for downtime. It is all too easy to mistype the changes you want and create a malfunctioning configuration. There can be unforeseen consequences even if you make the change successfully, such as logging data filling up disks or crippling performance.

My advice is to avoid live edits and make sure all changes are pushed through your standard testing process before being deployed into production. It can be tempting to poke around a live system to diagnose a problem, but it rarely ends well. If you find yourself editing production configuration files, then you should ask yourself whether you are about to make a small problem into a much larger one.

Creating the JSON Configuration File

The most common uses for the appsettings.json file are to store database connection strings and logging settings, but you can store any data that your application requires.

To see how the configuration system works, add a new JSON file called appsettings.json to the root folder of the project with the content shown in Listing 14-34.

Listing 14-34. The Contents of the appsettings.json File in the ConfiguringApps Folder

```
{
  "ShortCircuitMiddleware": {
    "EnableBrowserShortCircuit": true
  }
}
```

The JSON format allows a structure to be defined for configuration settings. The JSON content in the listing defines a configuration category called ShortCircuitMiddleware that contains a configuration property called EnableBrowserShortCircuit, which is set to true.

JSON: QUOTING AND COMMAS

If you are new to working with JSON, then it is worth taking some time to read the specification at www. json.org. The format is simple to work with, and there is good support for generating and parsing JSON data on most platforms, including within MVC applications (see Chapters 20 and 21 for examples) and at the client using a simple JavaScript API. In fact, most MVC developers won't deal directly with JSON at all, and it is only in the configuration files that hand-crafting JSON is required.

There are two pitfalls that many developers new to JSON fall into, and while you should still take the time to read the specification, knowing the most common problems will give you somewhere to start when Visual Studio or ASP.NET Core can't parse your JSON files. Here is an addition to the appsettings.json file to show the two most common problems:

```
{
  "ShortCircuitMiddleware": {
    "EnableBrowserShortCircuit": true
  }
  mysetting : [ fast, slow ]
}
```

First, almost everything in JSON is quoted. It is easy to forget that you are writing C# code and expect property names and values to be accepted without quotes. In JSON, anything other than Boolean values and numbers has to be quoted, like this:

```
{
  "ShortCircuitMiddleware": {
    "EnableBrowserShortCircuit": true
  }
  "mysetting" : [ "fast", "slow"]
}
```

Second, when you add a new property to the JSON description of an object, you must remember to add a comma to the previous brace character, like this:

```
{
  "ShortCircuitMiddleware": {
    "EnableBrowserShortCircuit": true
  },
  "mysetting" : [ "fast", "slow"]
}
```

It can be hard to see the difference even when it is highlighted—which is why it is such a common error—but I have added a comma following the } character that closes the ShortCircuitMiddleware section. Be careful, though, because a trailing comma that has no following section is also illegal. If your JSON changes are causing problems, there are the two errors to check for first.

Using Configuration Data

The Startup class can access the configuration data by defining a constructor with an IConfiguration argument. When the UseStartup method is called in the Program class, the configuration data prepared by the ConfigureAppConfiguration is used to create the Startup object. Listing 14-35 shows the addition of the constructor to the Startup class and shows how the configuration data can be accessed.

Listing 14-35. Receiving and Using Configuration Data in the Startup.cs File in the ConfiguringApps Folder

```
using System;
using System.Collections.Generic;
using System.Linq;
using System.Threading.Tasks;
using Microsoft.AspNetCore.Builder;
using Microsoft.AspNetCore.Hosting;
using Microsoft.AspNetCore.Http;
using Microsoft.Extensions.DependencyInjection;
using ConfiguringApps.Infrastructure;
using Microsoft.Extensions.Configuration;

namespace ConfiguringApps {
    public class Startup {

        public Startup(IConfiguration configuration) {
            Configuration = configuration;
        }

        public IConfiguration Configuration { get; }

        public void ConfigureServices(IServiceCollection services) {
            services.AddSingleton<UptimeService>();
            services.AddMvc();
        }
```

```
    public void Configure(IApplicationBuilder app, IHostingEnvironment env) {

        if ((Configuration.GetSection("ShortCircuitMiddleware")?
                .GetValue<bool>("EnableBrowserShortCircuit")).Value) {
            app.UseMiddleware<BrowserTypeMiddleware>();
            app.UseMiddleware<ShortCircuitMiddleware>();
        }

        if (env.IsDevelopment()) {
            app.UseDeveloperExceptionPage();
            app.UseStatusCodePages();
            app.UseBrowserLink();
        } else {
            app.UseExceptionHandler("/Home/Error");
        }
        app.UseStaticFiles();
        app.UseMvc(routes => {
            routes.MapRoute(
                name: "default",
                template: "{controller=Home}/{action=Index}/{id?}");
        });
    }
}
}
```

The IConfiguration object is received by the constructor and assigned to a property called Configuration, which can then be used to access the configuration data that has been loaded from environment variables, the command line, and the appsettings.json file.

To obtain a value, you navigate through the structure of the data to the configuration section you require, which is represented by another object that implements the IConfiguration interface, which provides a subset of members available for IConfigurationRoot, as shown in Table 14-11.

Table 14-11. *The Members Defined by the IConfiguration Interface*

Name	Description
[key]	The indexer is used to obtain a string value for a specific key.
GetSection(name)	This method returns an IConfiguration object that represents a section of the configuration data.
GetChildren()	This method returns an enumeration of the IConfiguration objects that represent the subsections of the current configuration object.

There are also extension methods that can be used to operate on IConfiguration objects to get values and convert them from strings into other types, as described in Table 14-12.

Table 14-12. *Extension Methods for the IConfiguration Interface*

Name	Description
GetValue<T>(keyName)	This method gets the value associated with the specified key and attempts to convert it to the type T.
GetValue<T>(keyName, defaultValue)	This method gets the value associated with the specified key and attempts to convert it to the type T. The default value will be used if there is no value for the key in the configuration data.

It is important not to assume that a configuration value will be specified. In the listing, I use the null conditional operator to ensure that I have received the ShortCircuitMiddleware section before trying to get the EnableBrowserShortCircuit value. The result is that the custom middleware will be added to the request pipeline only if the ShortCircuitMiddleware/EnableBrowserShortCircuit value has been defined and set to true.

Configuring Logging

ASP.NET Core includes support for capturing and handling logging data, and many of the built-in middleware components have been written to generate logging messages. Logging is set up automatically in most projects, but since I am using individual configuration statements in the Program class, I need to add the statements shown in Listing 14-36 to set up the logging feature.

Listing 14-36. Configuring Logging in the Program.cs File in the ConfiguringApps Folder

```
using System;
using System.Collections.Generic;
using System.IO;
using System.Linq;
using System.Threading.Tasks;
using Microsoft.AspNetCore;
using Microsoft.AspNetCore.Hosting;
using Microsoft.Extensions.Configuration;
using Microsoft.Extensions.Logging;
using System.Reflection;

namespace ConfiguringApps {
    public class Program {

        public static void Main(string[] args) {
            BuildWebHost(args).Run();
        }

        public static IWebHost BuildWebHost(string[] args) {

            return new WebHostBuilder()
                .UseKestrel()
                .UseContentRoot(Directory.GetCurrentDirectory())
                .ConfigureAppConfiguration((hostingContext, config) => {
                    config.AddJsonFile("appsettings.json",
                        optional: true, reloadOnChange: true);
```

415

```
                    config.AddEnvironmentVariables();
                    if (args != null) {
                        config.AddCommandLine(args);
                    }
                })
                .ConfigureLogging((hostingContext, logging) => {
                    logging.AddConfiguration(
                        hostingContext.Configuration.GetSection("Logging"));
                    logging.AddConsole();
                    logging.AddDebug();
                })
                .UseIISIntegration()
                .UseStartup<Startup>()
                .Build();
        }
    }
}
```

The ConfigureLogging method sets up the logging system using a lambda function that receives a WebHostBuilderContext object (described earlier in the chapter) and an object that implements the ILoggingBuilder interface. A set of extension methods operate on the ILoggingBuilder interface to configure the logging system, as described in Table 14-13.

Table 14-13. *Extension Methods for the ILoggingBuilder Interface*

Name	Description
AddConfiguration	This method is used to configure the logging system using the configuration data that has been loaded from the appsettings.json file, from the command line, or from environment variables.
AddConsole	This method sends logging messages to the console, which is useful when starting the application using the dotnet run command.
AddDebug	This method sends logging messages to the debug output window when the Visual Studio debugger is running.
AddEventLog	This method sends logging messages to the Windows Event Log, which is useful if you deploy to Windows Server and want the log messages from the ASP.NET Core MVC application to be incorporated with those from other types of application.

Understanding the Logging Configuration Data

The AddConfiguration method is used to configure the logging system using configuration data that is typically defined in the appsettings.json file. Listing 14-37 adds a configuration section called Logging to the appsettings.json file, which corresponds to the name used for the AddConfiguration method in Listing 14-36.

Listing 14-37. Adding a Configuration Section to the appsettings.json File in the ConfiguringApps Folder

```
{
  "ShortCircuitMiddleware": {
    "EnableBrowserShortCircuit": true
  },
```

```
"Logging": {
  "LogLevel": {
    "Default": "Debug",
    "System": "Information",
    "Microsoft": "Information"
  }
}
}
```

The logging configuration specified the level of message that should be displayed from different sources of logging data. The logging system supports six levels of debugging information, as described in Table 14-14 in order of importance.

Table 14-14. The ASP.NET Debugging Levels

Level	Description
Trace	This level is used for messages that are useful during development but that are not required in production.
Debug	This level is used for detailed messages required by developers to debug problems.
Information	This level is used for messages that describe the general operation of the application.
Warning	This level is used for messages that describe events that are unexpected but that do not interrupt the application.
Error	This level is used for messages that describe errors that interrupt the application.
Critical	This level is used for messages that describe catastrophic failures.
None	This level is used to disable logging messages.

The Default entry in Listing 14-37 sets the threshold for displaying logging messages to Debug, which means that only messages of the Debug level or greater will be displayed. The remaining entries override the default for logging messages from specific namespaces so that logging messages that originate from the System or Microsoft namespaces will be displayed only if they are of the Information level or greater.

To see the effect of enabling logging, start the application using the Visual Studio debugger by selecting Debug ➤ Start Debugging. Look at the Output window and you will see logging messages that show how each HTTP request is handled, like this:

```
info: Microsoft.AspNetCore.Hosting.Internal.WebHost[1]
      Request starting HTTP/1.1 GET http://localhost:65417/
info: Microsoft.AspNetCore.Mvc.Internal.ControllerActionInvoker[1]
      Executing action method ConfiguringApps.Controllers.HomeController.Index
      (ConfiguringApps) with arguments (False) - ModelState is Valid
info: Microsoft.AspNetCore.Mvc.ViewFeatures.Internal.ViewResultExecutor[1]
      Executing ViewResult, running view at path /Views/Home/Index.cshtml.
info: Microsoft.AspNetCore.Mvc.Internal.ControllerActionInvoker[2]
      Executed action ConfiguringApps.Controllers.HomeController.Index
      (ConfiguringApps) in 1597.3535ms
info: Microsoft.AspNetCore.Hosting.Internal.WebHost[2]
      Request finished in 1695.6314ms 200 text/html; charset=utf-8
```

Creating Custom Log Messages

The logging messages in the previous section were generated by the ASP.NET Core and MVC components that handled the HTTP request and generated the response. This kind of message can provide useful information, but you can also generate custom log messages that are specific to your application, as shown in Listing 14-38.

Listing 14-38. Custom Logging in the HomeController.cs File in the Controllers Folder

```
using System.Collections.Generic;
using Microsoft.AspNetCore.Mvc;
using ConfiguringApps.Infrastructure;
using Microsoft.Extensions.Logging;

namespace ConfiguringApps.Controllers {

    public class HomeController : Controller {
        private UptimeService uptime;
        private ILogger<HomeController> logger;

        public HomeController(UptimeService up, ILogger<HomeController> log) {
            uptime = up;
            logger = log;
        }

        public ViewResult Index(bool throwException = false) {
            logger.LogDebug($"Handled {Request.Path} at uptime {uptime.Uptime}");

            if (throwException) {
                throw new System.NullReferenceException();
            }
            return View(new Dictionary<string, string> {
                ["Message"] = "This is the Index action",
                ["Uptime"] = $"{uptime.Uptime}ms"
            });
        }

        public ViewResult Error() => View(nameof(Index),
            new Dictionary<string, string> {
                ["Message"] = "This is the Error action"});
        }
}
```

The ILogger interface defines the functionality required to create log entries and to obtain an object that implements this interface, and the HomeController class has a constructor argument whose type is ILogger<HomeController>. The type parameter allows the logging system to use the name of the class in the log messages, and the value for the constructor argument is provided automatically through the dependency injection feature that I describe in Chapter 18.

Once you have an ILogger, you can create log messages using extension methods defined in the Microsoft.Extensions.Logging namespace. There are methods for each of the logging levels described in Table 14-14. The HomeController class uses the LogDebug method to create a message at the Debug level. To see the effect, run the application using the Visual Studio debugger and examine the Output window for the log message, like this:

```
dbug: ConfiguringApps.Controllers.HomeController[0]
    Handled / at uptime 12
```

There are a lot of messages displayed when the application starts up, which can make it hard to pick out individual messages. It is easier to see single messages if you click the Clear All button at the top of the Output window and then reload the browser—this will ensure that only the log messages that relate to a single request are displayed.

Configuring Dependency Injection

The default configuration for ASP.NET Core applications includes preparing the service provider, which is used by the dependency injection feature that I describe in detail in Chapter 18. Listing 14-39 shows the addition of the configuration statements to the Program class.

Listing 14-39. Configuring Services in the Program.cs File in the ConfiguringApps Folder

```
using System;
using System.Collections.Generic;
using System.IO;
using System.Linq;
using System.Threading.Tasks;
using Microsoft.AspNetCore;
using Microsoft.AspNetCore.Hosting;
using Microsoft.Extensions.Configuration;
using Microsoft.Extensions.Logging;
using System.Reflection;

namespace ConfiguringApps {
    public class Program {

        public static void Main(string[] args) {
            BuildWebHost(args).Run();
        }

        public static IWebHost BuildWebHost(string[] args) {

            return new WebHostBuilder()
                .UseKestrel()
                .UseContentRoot(Directory.GetCurrentDirectory())
                .ConfigureAppConfiguration((hostingContext, config) => {
                    config.AddJsonFile("appsettings.json",
                        optional: true, reloadOnChange: true);
                    config.AddEnvironmentVariables();
                    if (args != null) {
```

```
                    config.AddCommandLine(args);
                }
            })
            .ConfigureLogging((hostingContext, logging) => {
                logging.AddConfiguration(
                    hostingContext.Configuration.GetSection("Logging"));
                logging.AddConsole();
                logging.AddDebug();
            })
            .UseIISIntegration()
            .UseDefaultServiceProvider((context, options) => {
                options.ValidateScopes =
                    context.HostingEnvironment.IsDevelopment();
            })
            .UseStartup<Startup>()
            .Build();
        }
    }
}
```

The UseDefaultServiceProvider method uses the built-in ASP.NET Core service provider. There are alternative service providers available, but the built-in features are acceptable for most projects, and I recommend that you use a third-party component only if you have a specific problem to solve and you have a good understanding of dependency injection, which I describe in Chapter 18.

The UseDefaultServiceProvider accepts a lambda function that receives a WebHostBuilderContext object and a ServiceProviderOptions object, which is used to configure the built-in service provider. The only configuration property is called ValidateScopes, and disabling the feature is required when working with Entity Framework Core, as explained in Chapter 8.

Configuring MVC Services

When you call AddMvc in the ConfigureServices method of the Startup class, it sets up all the services that are required for MVC applications. This has the advantage of convenience because it registers all the MVC services in a single step but does mean that some additional work is required to reconfigure the services to change the default behavior.

The AddMvc method returns an object that implements the IMvcBuilder interface, and MVC provides a set of extension methods that can be used for advanced configuration, the most useful of which are described in Table 14-15. Many of these configuration options relate to features that I describe in detail in later chapters.

Table 14-15. *Useful IMvcBuilder Extension Methods*

Name	Description
AddMvcOptions	This method configures the services used by MVC, as described after the table.
AddFormatterMappings	This method is used to configure a feature that allows clients to specify the data format they receive, as described in Chapter 20.
AddJsonOptions	This method is used to configure the way that JSON data is created, as described in Chapter 20.
AddRazorOptions	This method is used to configure the Razor view engine, as described in Chapter 21.
AddViewOptions	This method is used to configure how MVC handles views, including which view engines are used. See Chapter 21 for details.

The AddMvcOptions method configures the most important MVC services. It accepts a function that receives an MvcOptions object, which provides a set of configuration properties, the most useful of which are described in Table 14-16.

Table 14-16. *Selected MvcOptions Properties*

Name	Description
Conventions	This property returns a list of the model conventions that are used to customize how MVC creates controllers and actions, as described in Chapter 31.
Filters	This property returns a list of the global filters, as described in Chapter 19.
FormatterMappings	This property returns the mappings used to allow clients to specify the data format they receive, as described in Chapter 20.
InputFormatters	This property returns a list of the objects used to parse request data, as described in Chapter 20.
ModelValidatorProviders	This property returns a list of the objects used to validate data, as described in Chapter 27.
OutputFormatters	This property returns a list of the classes that format data sent from API controllers, as described in Chapter 20.
RespectBrowserAcceptHeader	This property specifies whether the Accept header is taken into account when deciding what data format to use for a response, as described in Chapter 20.

These configuration options are used to fine-tune the way that MVC operates, and you will find detailed descriptions of the features they relate to in the chapters specified in the table. As a quick demonstration, however, Listing 14-40 shows how the AddMvcOptions method can be used to change a configuration option.

Listing 14-40. Changing a Configuration Option in the Startup.cs File in the ConfiguringApps Folder

```
...
public void ConfigureServices(IServiceCollection services) {
    services.AddSingleton<UptimeService>();
    services.AddMvc().AddMvcOptions(options => {
        options.RespectBrowserAcceptHeader = true;
    });
}
...
```

The lambda expression passed to the AddMvcOptions method receives an MvcOptions object, which I use to set the RespectBrowserAcceptHeader property to true. This change allows clients to have more influence over the data format selected by the content negotiation process, as described in Chapter 20.

Dealing with Complex Configurations

If you need to support a large number of hosting environments or if there are a lot of differences between your hosting environments, then using if statements to branch configurations in the Startup class can result in a configuration that is hard to read and hard to edit without causing unexpected changes. In the sections that follow, I describe different ways that the Startup class can be used for complex configurations.

Creating Different External Configuration Files

The default configuration for the application performed by the Program class looks for JSON configuration files that are specific to the hosting environment being used to run the application, so a file called appsettings.production.json can be used to store settings that are specific to the production platform. Listing 14-41 restores the statement that loads the JSON file to the Program class, which I removed at the start of the chapter.

Listing 14-41. Loading Environment Files in the Program.cs File in the ConfiguringApps Folder

```
using System;
using System.Collections.Generic;
using System.IO;
using System.Linq;
using System.Threading.Tasks;
using Microsoft.AspNetCore;
using Microsoft.AspNetCore.Hosting;
using Microsoft.Extensions.Configuration;
using Microsoft.Extensions.Logging;
using System.Reflection;

namespace ConfiguringApps {
    public class Program {

        public static void Main(string[] args) {
            BuildWebHost(args).Run();
        }
```

```
        public static IWebHost BuildWebHost(string[] args) {

            return new WebHostBuilder()
                .UseKestrel()
                .UseContentRoot(Directory.GetCurrentDirectory())
                .ConfigureAppConfiguration((hostingContext, config) => {
                    var env = hostingContext.HostingEnvironment;
                    config.AddJsonFile("appsettings.json",
                            optional: true, reloadOnChange: true)
                        .AddJsonFile($"appsettings.{env.EnvironmentName}.json",
                            optional: true, reloadOnChange: true);
                    config.AddEnvironmentVariables();
                    if (args != null) {
                        config.AddCommandLine(args);
                    }
                })
                .ConfigureLogging((hostingContext, logging) => {
                    logging.AddConfiguration(
                        hostingContext.Configuration.GetSection("Logging"));
                    logging.AddConsole();
                    logging.AddDebug();
                })
                .UseIISIntegration()
                .UseDefaultServiceProvider((context, options) => {
                    options.ValidateScopes =
                        context.HostingEnvironment.IsDevelopment();
                })
                .UseStartup<Startup>()
                .Build();
        }
    }
}
```

When you load configuration data from a platform-specific file, the configuration settings it contains override any existing data with the same names. As an example, I used the ASP.NET Configuration File item template to create a file called appsettings.development.json with the configuration data shown in Listing 14-42. The configuration data in this file sets the EnableBrowserShortCircuit value to false.

■ **Tip** The appsettings.development.json file might seem to disappear after you create it. If you extend the arrow to the left of the appsettings.json entry in the Solution Explorer window, you will see that Visual Studio groups items with similar names together.

Listing 14-42. The Contents of the appsettings.development.json File in the ConfiguringApps Folder

```
{
  "ShortCircuitMiddleware": {
    "EnableBrowserShortCircuit": false
  }
}
```

The appsettings.json file will be loaded when the application starts, followed by the appsettings.development.json file the application is running in the development environment. The result is that the EnableBrowserShortCircuit value will be false when the application is running in the development environment and true when in staging and production.

Creating Different Configuration Methods

Selecting different configuration data files can be useful but doesn't provide a complete solution for complex configurations because data files don't contain C# statements. If you want to vary the configuration statements used to create services or register middleware components, then you can use different methods, where the name of the method includes the hosting environment, as shown in Listing 14-43.

Listing 14-43. Using Different Method Names in the Startup.cs File

```
using System;
using System.Collections.Generic;
using System.Linq;
using System.Threading.Tasks;
using Microsoft.AspNetCore.Builder;
using Microsoft.AspNetCore.Hosting;
using Microsoft.AspNetCore.Http;
using Microsoft.Extensions.DependencyInjection;
using ConfiguringApps.Infrastructure;
using Microsoft.Extensions.Configuration;

namespace ConfiguringApps {
    public class Startup {

        public Startup(IConfiguration configuration) {
            Configuration = configuration;
        }

        public IConfiguration Configuration { get; }

        public void ConfigureServices(IServiceCollection services) {
            services.AddSingleton<UptimeService>();
            services.AddMvc().AddMvcOptions(options => {
                options.RespectBrowserAcceptHeader = true;
            });
        }

        public void ConfigureDevelopmentServices(IServiceCollection services) {
            services.AddSingleton<UptimeService>();
            services.AddMvc();
        }

        public void Configure(IApplicationBuilder app, IHostingEnvironment env) {
            app.UseExceptionHandler("/Home/Error");
            app.UseStaticFiles();
            app.UseMvc(routes => {
                routes.MapRoute(
                    name: "default",
```

```
                template: "{controller=Home}/{action=Index}/{id?}");
        });
    }

    public void ConfigureDevelopment(IApplicationBuilder app,
            IHostingEnvironment env) {
        app.UseDeveloperExceptionPage();
        app.UseStatusCodePages();
        app.UseBrowserLink();
        app.UseStaticFiles();
        app.UseMvcWithDefaultRoute();
    }
  }
}
```

When ASP.NET Core looks for the ConfigureServices and Configure methods in the Startup class, it first checks to see whether there are methods that include the name of the hosting environment. In the listing, I added a ConfigureDevelopmentServices method, which will be used instead of the ConfigureServices method in the Development environment, and a ConfigureDevelopment method, which will be used instead of the Configure method. You can define separate methods for each of the environments that you need to support and rely on the default methods being called if there are no environment-specific methods available. In the example, this means the ConfigureServices and Configure methods will be used for the staging and production environments.

■ **Caution**   The default methods are not called if there are environment-specific methods defined. In Listing 14-43, for example, ASP.NET Core will not call the Configure method in the Development environment because there is a ConfigureDevelopment method. This means each method is responsible for the complete configuration required for its environment.

Creating Different Configuration Classes

Using different methods means you don't have to use if statements to check the hosting environment name, but it can result in large classes, which is a problem in itself. For especially complex configurations, the final progression is to create a different configuration class for each hosting environment. When ASP.NET looks for the Startup class, it first checks to see whether there is a class whose name includes the current hosting environment. To this end, I added a class file called StartupDevelopment.cs to the project and used it to define the class shown in Listing 14-44.

Listing 14-44. The Contents of the StartupDevelopment.cs File in the ConfiguringApps Folder

```
using Microsoft.AspNetCore.Builder;
using Microsoft.AspNetCore.Hosting;
using Microsoft.Extensions.DependencyInjection;
using ConfiguringApps.Infrastructure;

namespace ConfiguringApps {
    public class StartupDevelopment {
```

```
        public void ConfigureServices(IServiceCollection services) {
            services.AddSingleton<UptimeService>();
            services.AddMvc();
        }

        public void Configure(IApplicationBuilder app, IHostingEnvironment env) {
            app.UseDeveloperExceptionPage();
            app.UseStatusCodePages();
            app.UseBrowserLink();
            app.UseStaticFiles();
            app.UseMvcWithDefaultRoute();
        }
    }
}
```

This class contains ConfigureServices and Configure methods that are specific to the development hosting environment. To enable ASP.NET to find the environment-specific Startup class, a change is required to the Program class, as shown in Listing 14-45.

Listing 14-45. Enabling Environment-Specific Startup in the Program.cs File

```
using System;
using System.Collections.Generic;
using System.IO;
using System.Linq;
using System.Threading.Tasks;
using Microsoft.AspNetCore;
using Microsoft.AspNetCore.Hosting;
using Microsoft.Extensions.Configuration;
using Microsoft.Extensions.Logging;
using System.Reflection;

namespace ConfiguringApps {
    public class Program {

        public static void Main(string[] args) {
            BuildWebHost(args).Run();
        }

        public static IWebHost BuildWebHost(string[] args) {

            return new WebHostBuilder()
                .UseKestrel()
                .UseContentRoot(Directory.GetCurrentDirectory())
                .ConfigureAppConfiguration((hostingContext, config) => {
                    var env = hostingContext.HostingEnvironment;
                    config.AddJsonFile("appsettings.json",
                        optional: true, reloadOnChange: true)
                    .AddJsonFile($"appsettings.{env.EnvironmentName}.json",
                            optional: true, reloadOnChange: true);
                    config.AddEnvironmentVariables();
                    if (args != null) {
```

```
                    config.AddCommandLine(args);
                }
            })
            .ConfigureLogging((hostingContext, logging) => {
                logging.AddConfiguration(
                    hostingContext.Configuration.GetSection("Logging"));
                logging.AddConsole();
                logging.AddDebug();
            })
            .UseIISIntegration()
            .UseDefaultServiceProvider((context, options) => {
                options.ValidateScopes =
                    context.HostingEnvironment.IsDevelopment();
            })
            .UseStartup(nameof(ConfiguringApps))
            .Build();
        }
    }
}
```

Rather than specifying a class, the UseStartup method is given the name of the assembly that it should use. When the application starts, ASP.NET will look for a class whose name includes the hosting environment, such as StartupDevelopment or StartupProduction, and fall back to using the regular Startup class if one does not exist.

Summary

In this chapter, I explained how MVC applications are configured. I described the role of the Program and Startup classes and the default configuration options they provide. I showed you how requests are processed using a pipeline and how different types of middleware are used to control the flow of requests and the responses they elicit. In the next chapter, I introduce the routing system, which is how MVC deals with mapping request URLs to controllers and actions.

CHAPTER 15

■ ■ ■

URL Routing

Early versions of ASP.NET assumed that there was a direct relationship between requested URLs and the files on the server hard disk. The job of the server was to receive the request from the browser and deliver the output from the corresponding file. This approach worked just fine for Web Forms, where each ASPX page is both a file and a self-contained response to a request.

It *doesn't* make sense for an MVC application, where requests are processed by action methods in controller classes and there is no one-to-one correlation to the files on the disk.

To handle MVC URLs, the ASP.NET platform uses the *routing system*, which has been overhauled for ASP.NET Core. In this chapter, I will show you how to use the routing system to create powerful and flexible URL handling for your projects. As you will see, the routing system lets you create any pattern of URLs you desire and express them in a clear and concise manner. The routing system has two functions.

- Examine an *incoming URL* and select the controller and action to handle the request.

- Generate *outgoing URLs*. These are the URLs that appear in the HTML rendered from views so that a specific action will be invoked when the user clicks the link (at which point it becomes an incoming URL again).

In this chapter, I will focus on defining routes and using them to process incoming URLs so that the user can reach the controllers and actions. There are two ways to create routes in an MVC application: *convention-based routing* and *attribute routing*. I explain both approaches in this chapter.

Then, in the next chapter, I will show you how to use those same routes to generate the outgoing URLs you will need to include in your views, as well as show you how to customize the routing system and use a related feature called *areas*. Table 15-1 puts routing into context.

Table 15-1. *Putting Routing in Context*

Question	Answer
What is it?	The routing system is responsible for processing incoming requests and selecting controllers and action methods to process them. The routing system is also used to generate routes in views, known as *outgoing URLs*.
Why is it useful?	The routing system allows requests to be handled flexibly without URLs being tied to the structure of classes in the Visual Studio project.
How is it used?	The mapping between URLs and the controllers and action methods is defined in the Startup.cs file or by applying the Route attribute to controllers.
Are there any pitfalls or limitations?	The routing configuration for a complex application can become hard to manage.
Are there any alternatives?	No. The routing system is an integral part of ASP.NET Core.

© Adam Freeman 2017
A. Freeman, *Pro ASP.NET Core MVC 2*, https://doi.org/10.1007/978-1-4842-3150-0_15

Table 15-2 summarizes the chapter.

Table 15-2. *Chapter Summary*

Problem	Solution	Listing
Map between URLs and action methods	Define a route	9
Allow URL segments to be omitted	Define default values for route segments	10–12
Match URL segments that don't have corresponding routing variables	Define static segments	13–16
Pass URL segments to action methods	Define custom segment variables	17–19
Allow URL segments for which there are no default values to be omitted	Define optional segments	20–21
Define routes that match any number of URL segments	Use a catchall segment	22–23
Restrict the URLs that a route can match	Apply route constraints	24–33
Define a route within a controller	Use attribute routing	34–38

Preparing the Example Project

For this chapter, I used the ASP.NET Core Web Application (.NET Core) template to create a new Empty project called UrlsAndRoutes. To add support for the MVC Framework, developer error pages, and static files, I add the statements shown in Listing 15-1 to the Startup class.

Listing 15-1. Configuring the Application in the Startup.cs File in the UrlsAndRoutes Folder

```
using System;
using System.Collections.Generic;
using System.Linq;
using System.Threading.Tasks;
using Microsoft.AspNetCore.Builder;
using Microsoft.AspNetCore.Hosting;
using Microsoft.AspNetCore.Http;
using Microsoft.Extensions.DependencyInjection;

namespace UrlsAndRoutes {
    public class Startup {

        public void ConfigureServices(IServiceCollection services) {
            services.AddMvc();
        }

        public void Configure(IApplicationBuilder app, IHostingEnvironment env) {
            app.UseDeveloperExceptionPage();
            app.UseStatusCodePages();
            app.UseStaticFiles();
            app.UseMvc();
        }
    }
}
```

Creating the Model Class

All the effort in this chapter is about matching request URLs to actions. The only model class I need passes details about the controller and action method that has been selected to process a request. I created the Models folder and added a class file called Result.cs, which I used to define the class shown in Listing 15-2.

Listing 15-2. The Contents of the Result.cs File in the Models Folder

```
using System.Collections.Generic;

namespace UrlsAndRoutes.Models {

    public class Result {
        public string Controller { get; set; }

        public string Action { get; set; }

        public IDictionary<string, object> Data { get; }
            = new Dictionary<string, object>();
    }
}
```

The Controller and Action properties will be used to indicate how a request has been processed, and the Data dictionary will be used to store other details about the request produced by the routing system.

Creating the Example Controllers

I need some simple controllers to demonstrate how routing works. I created the Controllers folder and added a class file called HomeController.cs, the contents of which are shown in Listing 15-3.

Listing 15-3. The Contents of the HomeController.cs File in the Controllers Folder

```
using Microsoft.AspNetCore.Mvc;
using UrlsAndRoutes.Models;

namespace UrlsAndRoutes.Controllers {

    public class HomeController : Controller {

        public ViewResult Index() => View("Result",
            new Result {
                Controller = nameof(HomeController),
                Action = nameof(Index)
            });
    }
}
```

The Index action method defined by the Home controller calls the View method to render a view called Result (which I define in the next section) and provides a Result object as the model object. The properties of the model object are set using the nameof function and will be used to indicate which controller and action method have been used to service a request.

I followed the same pattern by adding a `CustomerController.cs` file to the `Controllers` folder and using it to define the `Customer` controller shown in Listing 15-4.

Listing 15-4. The Contents of the CustomerController.cs File in the Controllers Folder

```
using Microsoft.AspNetCore.Mvc;
using UrlsAndRoutes.Models;

namespace UrlsAndRoutes.Controllers {

    public class CustomerController : Controller {

        public ViewResult Index() => View("Result",
            new Result {
                Controller = nameof(CustomerController),
                Action = nameof(Index)
            });

        public ViewResult List() => View("Result",
            new Result {
                Controller = nameof(CustomerController),
                Action = nameof(List)
            });
    }
}
```

The third and final controller is defined in a file called `AdminController.cs`, which I added to the `Controllers` folder, as shown in Listing 15-5. It follows the same pattern as the other controllers.

Listing 15-5. The Contents of the AdminController.cs File in the Controllers Folder

```
using Microsoft.AspNetCore.Mvc;
using UrlsAndRoutes.Models;

namespace UrlsAndRoutes.Controllers {

    public class AdminController : Controller {

        public ViewResult Index() => View("Result",
            new Result {
                Controller = nameof(AdminController),
                Action = nameof(Index)
            });
    }
}
```

Creating the View

I specified the `Result` view in all the action methods defined in the previous section, which allows me to create one view that will be shared by all the controllers. I created the `Views/Shared` folder and added a new view called `Result.cshtml` to it, the contents of which are shown in Listing 15-6.

Listing 15-6. The Contents of the Result.cshtml File in the Views/Shared Folder

```
@model Result
@{ Layout = null; }

<!DOCTYPE html>
<html>
<head>
    <meta name="viewport" content="width=device-width" />
    <title>Routing</title>
    <link rel="stylesheet" asp-href-include="lib/bootstrap/dist/css/*.min.css" />
</head>
<body class="m-1 p-1">
    <table class="table table-bordered table-striped table-sm">
        <tr><th>Controller:</th><td>@Model.Controller</td></tr>
        <tr><th>Action:</th><td>@Model.Action</td></tr>
        @foreach (string key in Model.Data.Keys) {
            <tr><th>@key :</th><td>@Model.Data[key]</td></tr>
        }
    </table>
</body>
</html>
```

The view contains a table that displays the properties from the model object in a table that is styled using Bootstrap. To add Bootstrap to the project, I used the Bower Configuration File item template to create the bower.json file and added the Bootstrap package to the dependencies section, as shown in Listing 15-7.

Listing 15-7. Adding the Bootstrap Package in the bower.json File in the UrlsAndRoutes Folder

```
{
  "name": "asp.net",
  "private": true,
  "dependencies": {
    "bootstrap": "4.0.0-alpha.6"
  }
}
```

The final preparation is to create the _ViewImports.cshtml file in the Views folder, which sets up the built-in tag helpers for use in Razor views and imports the model namespace, as shown in Listing 15-8.

Listing 15-8. The Contents of the _ViewImports.cshtml File in the Views Folder

```
@using UrlsAndRoutes.Models
@addTagHelper *, Microsoft.AspNetCore.Mvc.TagHelpers
```

The configuration in the Startup class doesn't contain any instructions for how MVC should map HTTP requests to controllers and actions. When you start the application, any URL that you request will result in a 404 - Not Found response, as shown in Figure 15-1.

Figure 15-1. *Running the example application*

Introducing URL Patterns

The routing system works its magic using a set of *routes*. These routes collectively comprise the URL *schema* or *scheme* for an application, which is the set of URLs that your application will recognize and respond to.

I do not need to manually type out all of the individual URLs I am willing to support in my application. Instead, each route contains a *URL pattern*, which is compared to incoming URLs. If an incoming URL matches the pattern, then it is used by the routing system to process that URL. Here is a simple URL to get started with:

```
http://mysite.com/Admin/Index
```

URLs can be broken down into *segments*. These are the parts of the URL, excluding the hostname and query string, that are separated by the / character. In the example URL, there are two segments, as shown in Figure 15-2.

http://mysite.com/Admin/Index

↑   ↑

First Segment   Second Segment

Figure 15-2. *The segments in an example URL*

The first segment contains the word Admin, and the second segment contains the word Index. To the human eye, it is obvious that the first segment relates to the controller and the second segment relates to the action. But, of course, I need to express this relationship using a URL pattern that can be understood by the routing system. Here is a URL pattern that matches the example URL:

```
{controller}/{action}
```

When processing an incoming HTTP request, the job of the routing system is to match the URL that has been requested to a pattern and extract values from the URL for the *segment variables* defined in the pattern.

The segment variables are expressed using braces (the { and } characters). The example pattern has two segment variables with the names controller and action, so the value of the controller segment variable will be Admin, and the value of the action segment variable will be Index.

An MVC application will usually have several routes, and the routing system will compare the incoming URL to the URL pattern of each route until it finds a match. By default, a pattern will match any URL that has the correct number of segments. For example, the pattern {controller}/{action} will match any URL that has two segments, as described in Table 15-3.

Table 15-3. *Matching URLs*

Request URL	Segment Variables
http://mysite.com/Admin/Index	controller = Admin action = Index
http://mysite.com/Admin	No match—too few segments
http://mysite.com/Admin/Index/Soccer	No match—too many segments

Table 15-3 highlights two key behaviors of URL patterns.

- URL patterns are *conservative* about the number of segments they match. They will match only URLs that have the same number of segments as the pattern. You can see this in the second and third examples in the table.

- URL patterns are *liberal* about the contents of segments they match. If a URL has the correct number of segments, the pattern will extract the value of each segment for a segment variable, whatever it might be.

These are the default behaviors, which are the keys to understanding how URL patterns function. I show you how to change the defaults later in this chapter.

Creating and Registering a Simple Route

Once you have a URL pattern in mind, you can use it to define a route. Routes are defined in the Startup.cs file and are passed as arguments to the UseMvc method that is used to set up MVC in the Configure method. Listing 15-9 shows a basic route that maps requests to the controllers in the example application.

Listing 15-9. Defining a Basic Route in the Startup.cs File in the UrlsAndRoutes Folder

```
using System;
using System.Collections.Generic;
using System.Linq;
using System.Threading.Tasks;
using Microsoft.AspNetCore.Builder;
using Microsoft.AspNetCore.Hosting;
using Microsoft.AspNetCore.Http;
using Microsoft.Extensions.DependencyInjection;

namespace UrlsAndRoutes {
    public class Startup {

        public void ConfigureServices(IServiceCollection services) {
            services.AddMvc();
        }
```

```
public void Configure(IApplicationBuilder app, IHostingEnvironment env) {
    app.UseDeveloperExceptionPage();
    app.UseStatusCodePages();
    app.UseStaticFiles();
    app.UseMvc(routes => {
        routes.MapRoute(name: "default", template: "{controller}/{action}");
    });
}
}
}
```

Routes are created using a lambda expression passed as an argument to the UseMvc configuration method. The expression receives an object that implements the IRouteBuilder interface from the Microsoft.AspNetCore.Routing namespace, and routes are defined using the MapRoute extension method. To make routes easier to understand, the convention is to specify argument names when calling the MapRoute method, which is why I have explicitly named the name and template arguments in the listing. The name argument specified a name for a route, and the template argument is used to define the pattern.

■ **Tip**   Naming your routes is optional, and there is a philosophical argument that doing so sacrifices some of the clean separation of concerns that otherwise comes from routing. I explain why this can be a problem in the "Generating a URL from a Specific Route" section in Chapter 16.

You can see the effect of the changes I made to the routing by starting the example application. There is no change when the application first starts—you will still see a 404 error—but if you navigate to a URL that matches the {controller}/{action} pattern, you will see a result like the one shown in Figure 15-3, which illustrates the effect of navigating to /Admin/Index.

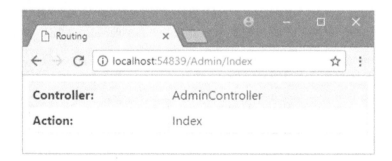

Figure 15-3. *Navigating using a simple route*

The reason that the root URL for the application doesn't work is that the route that I added to the Startup.cs file doesn't tell MVC how to select a controller class and action method when the requested URL has no segments. I'll fix this in the next section.

Defining Default Values

The example application returns a 404 message when the default URL is requested because it didn't match the pattern of the route defined in the Startup class. Since there are no segments in the default URL that can be matched to the controller and action variables defined by the routing pattern, the routing system doesn't make a match.

I explained earlier that URL patterns will match only URLs with the specified number of segments. One way to change this behavior is to use *default values*. A default value is applied when the URL doesn't contain a segment that can be matched by the routing pattern. Listing 15-10 defines a route that uses a default value.

Listing 15-10. Providing a Default Value in the Startup.cs File in the UrlsAndRoutes Folder

```
using System;
using System.Collections.Generic;
using System.Linq;
using System.Threading.Tasks;
using Microsoft.AspNetCore.Builder;
using Microsoft.AspNetCore.Hosting;
using Microsoft.AspNetCore.Http;
using Microsoft.Extensions.DependencyInjection;

namespace UrlsAndRoutes {
    public class Startup {

        public void ConfigureServices(IServiceCollection services) {
            services.AddMvc();
        }

        public void Configure(IApplicationBuilder app, IHostingEnvironment env) {
            app.UseDeveloperExceptionPage();
            app.UseStatusCodePages();
            app.UseStaticFiles();
            app.UseMvc(routes => {
                routes.MapRoute(
                    name: "default",
                    template: "{controller}/{action}",
                    defaults: new { action = "Index" });
            });
        }
    }
}
```

Default values are supplied as properties in an anonymous type, passed to the MapRoute method as the defaults argument. In the listing, I provided a default value of Index for the action variable.

This route will match all two-segment URLs, as it did previously. For example, if the URL http:// mydomain.com/Home/Index is requested, the route will extract Home as the value for the controller and will extract Index as the value for the action.

But now that there is a default value for the action segment, the route will *also* match single-segment URLs. When processing a single-segment URL, the routing system will extract the controller value from the URL and use the default value for the action variable. In this way, the user can request /Home and MVC will invoke the Index action method on the Home controller, as shown in Figure 15-4.

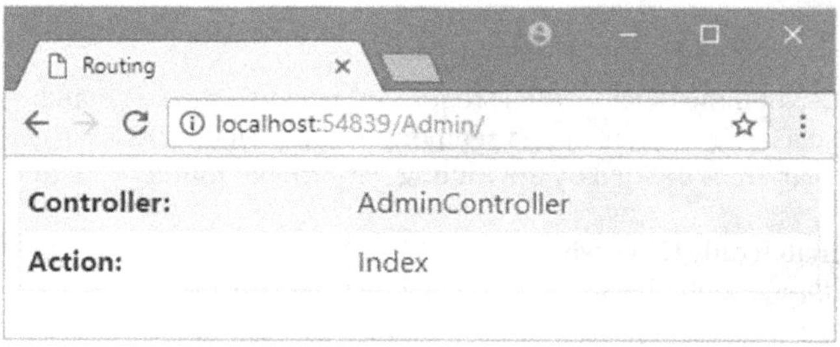

Figure 15-4. *Using a default action*

Defining Inline Default Values

Default values can also be expressed as part of the URL pattern, which is a more concise way to express routes, as shown in Listing 15-11. The inline syntax can be used only to provide defaults for variables that are part of the URL pattern, but, as you will learn, it is often useful to be able to provide defaults outside of that pattern. For this reason, it is useful to understand both ways of expressing defaults.

Listing 15-11. Defining Inline Default Values in the Startup.cs File in the UrlsAndRoutes Folder

```
using System;
using System.Collections.Generic;
using System.Linq;
using System.Threading.Tasks;
using Microsoft.AspNetCore.Builder;
using Microsoft.AspNetCore.Hosting;
using Microsoft.AspNetCore.Http;
using Microsoft.Extensions.DependencyInjection;

namespace UrlsAndRoutes {
    public class Startup {

        public void ConfigureServices(IServiceCollection services) {
            services.AddMvc();
        }

        public void Configure(IApplicationBuilder app, IHostingEnvironment env) {
            app.UseDeveloperExceptionPage();
            app.UseStatusCodePages();
            app.UseStaticFiles();
            app.UseMvc(routes => {
                routes.MapRoute(
                    name: "default",
                    template: "{controller}/{action=Index}");
            });
        }
    }
}
```

I can go further and match URLs that do not contain any segment variables at all, relying on just the default values to identify the action and controller. And as an example, Listing 15-12 shows how I have mapped the root URL for the application by providing default values for both segments.

Listing 15-12. Providing Default Values in the Startup.cs File in the UrlsAndRoutes Folder

```
using System;
using System.Collections.Generic;
using System.Linq;
using System.Threading.Tasks;
using Microsoft.AspNetCore.Builder;
using Microsoft.AspNetCore.Hosting;
using Microsoft.AspNetCore.Http;
using Microsoft.Extensions.DependencyInjection;

namespace UrlsAndRoutes {
    public class Startup {

        public void ConfigureServices(IServiceCollection services) {
            services.AddMvc();
        }

        public void Configure(IApplicationBuilder app, IHostingEnvironment env) {
            app.UseDeveloperExceptionPage();
            app.UseStatusCodePages();
            app.UseStaticFiles();
            app.UseMvc(routes => {
                routes.MapRoute(
                    name: "default",
                    template: "{controller=Home}/{action=Index}");
            });
        }
    }
}
```

By providing default values for both the controller and action variables, the route will match URLs that have zero, one, or two segments, as shown in Table 15-4.

Table 15-4. Matching URLs

Segments	Example	Maps To
0	**/**	controller = Home action = Index
1	**/Customer**	controller = Customer action = Index
2	**/Customer/List**	controller = Customer action = List
3	**/Customer/List/All**	No match—too many segments

The fewer segments received in the incoming URL, the more the route relies on the default values, up until the point where a URL with no segments is matched using only default values.

You can see the effect of the default values by starting the example app. When the browser requests the root URL for the application, the default values for the `controller` and `action` segment variables will be used, which will lead MVC to invoke the Index action method on the Home controller, as shown in Figure 15-5.

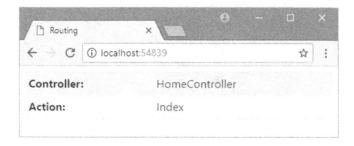

Figure 15-5. *Using default values to broaden the scope of a route*

Using Static URL Segments

Not all the segments in a URL pattern need to be variables. You can also create patterns that have *static segments*. Suppose that the application needs to match URLs that are prefixed with `Public`, like this:

```
http://mydomain.com/Public/Home/Index
```

This can be done by using a URL pattern like the one shown in Listing 15-13.

Listing 15-13. Using Static Segments in the Startup.cs File in the UrlsAndRoutes Folder

```csharp
using System;
using System.Collections.Generic;
using System.Linq;
using System.Threading.Tasks;
using Microsoft.AspNetCore.Builder;
using Microsoft.AspNetCore.Hosting;
using Microsoft.AspNetCore.Http;
using Microsoft.Extensions.DependencyInjection;

namespace UrlsAndRoutes {
    public class Startup {

        public void ConfigureServices(IServiceCollection services) {
            services.AddMvc();
        }

        public void Configure(IApplicationBuilder app, IHostingEnvironment env) {
            app.UseDeveloperExceptionPage();
            app.UseStatusCodePages();
            app.UseStaticFiles();
            app.UseMvc(routes => {
                routes.MapRoute(
```

```
                name: "default",
                template: "{controller=Home}/{action=Index}");

            routes.MapRoute(name: "",
                template: "Public/{controller=Home}/{action=Index}");
        });
    }
  }
}
```

This new pattern will match only URLs that contain three segments, the first of which *must* be Public. The other two segments can contain any value and will be used for the controller and action variables. If the last two segments are omitted, then the default values will be used.

You can also create URL patterns that have segments containing both static and variable elements, such as the one shown in Listing 15-14.

Listing 15-14. Mixing Segments in the Startup.cs File in the UrlsAndRoutes Folder

```
using System;
using System.Collections.Generic;
using System.Linq;
using System.Threading.Tasks;
using Microsoft.AspNetCore.Builder;
using Microsoft.AspNetCore.Hosting;
using Microsoft.AspNetCore.Http;
using Microsoft.Extensions.DependencyInjection;

namespace UrlsAndRoutes {
    public class Startup {

        public void ConfigureServices(IServiceCollection services) {
            services.AddMvc();
        }

        public void Configure(IApplicationBuilder app, IHostingEnvironment env) {
            app.UseDeveloperExceptionPage();
            app.UseStatusCodePages();
            app.UseStaticFiles();
            app.UseMvc(routes => {
                routes.MapRoute("", "X{controller}/{action}");

                routes.MapRoute(
                    name: "default",
                    template: "{controller=Home}/{action=Index}");

                routes.MapRoute(name: "",
                    template: "Public/{controller=Home}/{action=Index}");

            });
        }
    }
}
```

441

The pattern in this route matches any two-segment URL where the first segment starts with the letter X. The value for `controller` is taken from the first segment, excluding the X. The `action` value is taken from the second segment. You can see the effect of this route if you start the application and navigate to /XHome/Index, the result of which is illustrated in Figure 15-6.

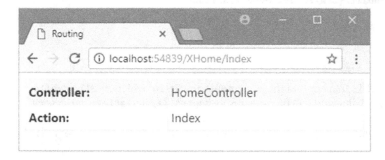

Figure 15-6. *Mixing static and variable elements in a single segment*

ROUTE ORDERING

In Listing 15-14, I defined a new route and placed it before all the others. I did this because routes are applied in the order in which they are defined. The `MapRoute` method adds a route to the end of the routing configuration, which means that routes are generally applied in the order in which they are defined. I say "generally" because there are methods that insert routes in specific locations. I tend not to use these methods because having routes applied in the order in which they are defined makes understanding the routing for an application simpler.

The routing system tries to match an incoming URL against the URL pattern of the route that was defined first and proceeds to the next route only if there is no match. The routes are tried in sequence until a match is found or the set of routes has been exhausted. As a consequence, the most specific routes must be defined first. The route I added in Listing 15-14 is more specific than the route that follows. Suppose that I reversed the order of the routes, like this:

```
...
routes.MapRoute("MyRoute", "{controller=Home}/{action=Index}");
routes.MapRoute("", "X{controller}/{action}");
...
```

Then the first route, which matches *any* URL with zero, one, or two segments, will always be the one that is used. The more specific route, which is now second in the list, will never be reached. The new route excludes the leading X of a URL, but this won't be done by the older route. Therefore, a URL such as this:

```
http://mydomain.com/XHome/Index
```

will be targeted to a controller called XHome, assuming that there is an XHomeController class in the application and it has an action method called Index.

Static URL segments and default values can be combined to create an alias for a specific URL. The URL schema that you use forms a contract with your users when you deploy your application, and if you subsequently refactor an application, you need to preserve the previous URL format so that any URL favorites, macros, or scripts the user has created continue to work.

Imagine that there used to be a controller called Shop, which has now been replaced by the Home controller. Listing 15-15 shows how I can create a route to preserve the old URL schema.

Listing 15-15. Segments and Default Values in the Startup.cs File in the UrlsAndRoutes Folder

```
using System;
using System.Collections.Generic;
using System.Linq;
using System.Threading.Tasks;
using Microsoft.AspNetCore.Builder;
using Microsoft.AspNetCore.Hosting;
using Microsoft.AspNetCore.Http;
using Microsoft.Extensions.DependencyInjection;

namespace UrlsAndRoutes {
    public class Startup {

        public void ConfigureServices(IServiceCollection services) {
            services.AddMvc();
        }

        public void Configure(IApplicationBuilder app, IHostingEnvironment env) {
            app.UseDeveloperExceptionPage();
            app.UseStatusCodePages();
            app.UseStaticFiles();
            app.UseMvc(routes => {
                routes.MapRoute(
                    name: "ShopSchema",
                    template: "Shop/{action}",
                    defaults: new { controller = "Home" });

                routes.MapRoute("", "X{controller}/{action}");

                routes.MapRoute(
                    name: "default",
                    template: "{controller=Home}/{action=Index}");

                routes.MapRoute(name: "",
                    template: "Public/{controller=Home}/{action=Index}");

            });
        }
    }
}
```

The route matches any two-segment URL where the first segment is Shop. The action value is taken from the second URL segment. The URL pattern doesn't contain a variable segment for controller, so the default value is used. The defaults argument provides the controller value because there is no segment to which the value can be applied to as part of the URL pattern.

443

The result is that a request for an action on the Shop controller is translated to a request for the Home controller. You can see the effect of this route by starting the app and navigating to the /Shop/Index URL. As Figure 15-7 shows, the new route causes MVC to target the Index action method in the Home controller.

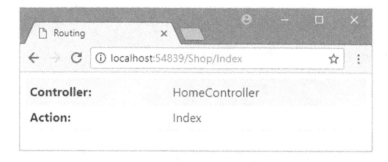

Figure 15-7. *Creating an alias to preserve URL schemas*

I can go one step further and create aliases for action methods that have been refactored away as well and are no longer present in the controller. To do this, I create a static URL and provide the controller and action values as defaults, as shown in Listing 15-16.

Listing 15-16. Aliasing a Controller and an Action in the Startup.cs File in the UrlsAndRoutes Folder

```
using System;
using System.Collections.Generic;
using System.Linq;
using System.Threading.Tasks;
using Microsoft.AspNetCore.Builder;
using Microsoft.AspNetCore.Hosting;
using Microsoft.AspNetCore.Http;
using Microsoft.Extensions.DependencyInjection;

namespace UrlsAndRoutes {
    public class Startup {

        public void ConfigureServices(IServiceCollection services) {
            services.AddMvc();
        }

        public void Configure(IApplicationBuilder app, IHostingEnvironment env) {
            app.UseDeveloperExceptionPage();
            app.UseStatusCodePages();
            app.UseStaticFiles();
            app.UseMvc(routes => {

                routes.MapRoute(
                    name: "ShopSchema2",
                    template: "Shop/OldAction",
                    defaults: new { controller = "Home", action = "Index" });
```

```
            routes.MapRoute(
                name: "ShopSchema",
                template: "Shop/{action}",
                defaults: new { controller = "Home" });

            routes.MapRoute("", "X{controller}/{action}");

            routes.MapRoute(
                name: "default",
                template: "{controller=Home}/{action=Index}");

            routes.MapRoute(name: "",
                template: "Public/{controller=Home}/{action=Index}");

        });
    }
  }
}
```

Notice that the new route is defined first because it is more specific than the routes that follow. If a request for Shop/OldAction were processed by the next defined route, for example, I may get a different result from the one I want if there is a controller with an OldAction action method.

Defining Custom Segment Variables

The controller and action segment variables have special meaning in MVC applications and correspond to the controller and action method that will be used to service the request. These are only the built-in segment variables, and custom segment variables can also be defined, as shown in Listing 15-17. (I have removed the existing routes from the previous section so I can start over).

Listing 15-17. Defining Additional Variables in the Startup.cs File in the UrlsAndRoutes Folder

```
using System;
using System.Collections.Generic;
using System.Linq;
using System.Threading.Tasks;
using Microsoft.AspNetCore.Builder;
using Microsoft.AspNetCore.Hosting;
using Microsoft.AspNetCore.Http;
using Microsoft.Extensions.DependencyInjection;

namespace UrlsAndRoutes {
    public class Startup {

        public void ConfigureServices(IServiceCollection services) {
            services.AddMvc();
        }

        public void Configure(IApplicationBuilder app, IHostingEnvironment env) {
            app.UseDeveloperExceptionPage();
            app.UseStatusCodePages();
```

445

```
        app.UseStaticFiles();
        app.UseMvc(routes => {
            routes.MapRoute(name: "MyRoute",
                template: "{controller=Home}/{action=Index}/{id=DefaultId}");
        });
    }
  }
}
```

The URL pattern defines the standard controller and action variables, as well as a custom variable called id. This route will match any zero-to-three-segment URL. The contents of the third segment will be assigned to the id variable, and if there is no third segment, the default value will be used.

■ **Caution**   Some names are reserved and not available for custom segment variable names. These are controller, action, area, and page. The meaning of the first two is obvious. I explain *areas* in the next chapter, and page is used by the Razor Pages feature.

The Controller class, which is the base for controllers, defines a RouteData property that returns a Microsoft.AspNetCore.Routing.RouteData object that provides details about the routing system and the way that the current request has been routed. Within a controller, I can access any of the segment variables in an action method by using the RouteData.Values property, which returns a dictionary containing the segment variables. To demonstrate, I have added an action method to the Home controller called CustomVariable, as shown in Listing 15-18.

Listing 15-18. Accessing a Segment Variable in the HomeController.cs File in the Controllers Folder

```
using Microsoft.AspNetCore.Mvc;
using UrlsAndRoutes.Models;

namespace UrlsAndRoutes.Controllers {

    public class HomeController : Controller {

        public ViewResult Index() => View("Result",
            new Result {
                Controller = nameof(HomeController),
                Action = nameof(Index)
            });

        public ViewResult CustomVariable() {
            Result r = new Result {
                Controller = nameof(HomeController),
                Action = nameof(CustomVariable),
            };
            r.Data["Id"] = RouteData.Values["id"];
            return View("Result", r);
        }
    }
}
```

This action method obtains the value of the custom `id` variable in the route URL pattern using the `RouteData.Values` property, which returns a dictionary of the variables produced by the routing system. The custom variable is added to the view model object and can be seen by running the application and requesting the following URL:

```
/Home/CustomVariable/Hello
```

The routing template matches the third segment in this URL as the value for the `id` variable, producing the results shown in Figure 15-8.

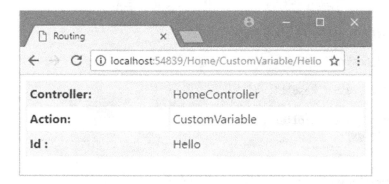

Figure 15-8. *Displaying the value of a custom segment variable*

The URL pattern in Listing 15-17 defines a default value for the `id` segment, which means that the route can also match URLs that have two segments. You can see the use of the default value by requesting this URL:

```
/Home/CustomVariable
```

The routing system uses the default value for the custom variable, as shown in Figure 15-9.

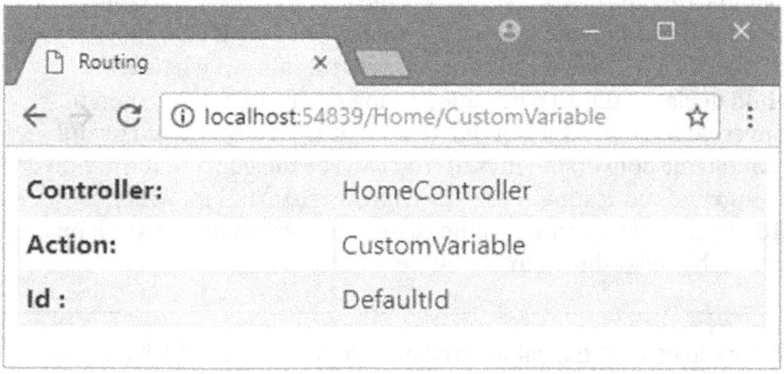

Figure 15-9. *The default value for a custom segment variable*

Using Custom Variables as Action Method Parameters

Using the RouteData.Values collection is only one way to access custom route variables, and the other way can be more elegant. If an action method defines parameters with names that match the URL pattern variables, MVC will automatically pass the values obtained from the URL as arguments to the action method.

The custom variable defined in the route in Listing 15-17 is called id. I can modify the CustomVariable action method in the Home controller so that it has a parameter of the same name, as shown in Listing 15-19.

Listing 15-19. Adding an Action Parameter in the HomeController.cs File in the Controllers Folder

```
using Microsoft.AspNetCore.Mvc;
using UrlsAndRoutes.Models;

namespace UrlsAndRoutes.Controllers {

    public class HomeController : Controller {

        public ViewResult Index() => View("Result",
            new Result {
                Controller = nameof(HomeController),
                Action = nameof(Index)
            });

        public ViewResult CustomVariable(string id) {
            Result r = new Result {
                Controller = nameof(HomeController),
                Action = nameof(CustomVariable),
            };
            r.Data["Id"] = id;
            return View("Result", r);
        }
    }
}
```

When the routing system matches a URL against the route defined in Listing 15-17, the value of the third segment in the URL is assigned to the custom variable id. MVC compares the list of segment variables with the list of action method parameters and, if the names match, passes the values from the URL to the method.

The type of the id parameter is a string, but MVC will try to convert the URL value to whatever parameter type is used. If the action method declared the id parameter as an int or a DateTime, then it would receive the value from the URL converted to an instance of that type. This is an elegant and useful feature that removes the need for me to handle the conversion myself. You can see the effect of the action method parameter by starting the application and requesting /Home/CustomVariable/Hello, which produces the result shown in Figure 15-10. If you omit the third segment, then the action method will be provided with the default segment value, which is also shown in the figure.

■ **Note**   MVC uses the *model binding* feature to convert the values contained in the URL to .NET types, and model binding can handle much more complex situations than shown in this example. I describe model binding in Chapter 26.

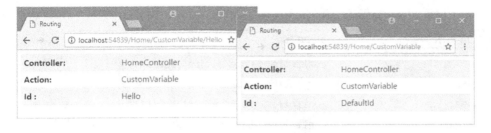

Figure 15-10. *Accessing segment variables using action method parameters*

Defining Optional URL Segments

An *optional* URL segment is one that the user does not need to specify and for which no default value is specified. An optional segment is denoted by a question mark (the ? character) after the segment name, as shown in Listing 15-20.

Listing 15-20. Specifying an Optional Segment in the Startup.cs File in the UrlsAndRoutes Folder

```
using System;
using System.Collections.Generic;
using System.Linq;
using System.Threading.Tasks;
using Microsoft.AspNetCore.Builder;
using Microsoft.AspNetCore.Hosting;
using Microsoft.AspNetCore.Http;
using Microsoft.Extensions.DependencyInjection;

namespace UrlsAndRoutes {
    public class Startup {

        public void ConfigureServices(IServiceCollection services) {
            services.AddMvc();
        }

        public void Configure(IApplicationBuilder app, IHostingEnvironment env) {
            app.UseDeveloperExceptionPage();
            app.UseStatusCodePages();
            app.UseStaticFiles();
            app.UseMvc(routes => {
                routes.MapRoute(name: "MyRoute",
                template: "{controller=Home}/{action=Index}/{id?}");
            });
        }
    }
}
```

This route will match URLs whether or not the id segment has been supplied. Table 15-5 shows how this works for different URLs.

Table 15-5. *Matching URLs with an Optional Segment Variable*

Segments	Example URL	Maps To
0	**/**	controller = Home action = Index
1	**/Customer**	controller = Customer action = Index
2	**/Customer/List**	controller = Customer action = List
3	**/Customer/List/All**	controller = Customer action = List id = All
4	**/Customer/List/All/Delete**	No match—too many segments

As you can see from the table, the id variable is added to the set of variables only when there is a corresponding segment in the incoming URL. This feature is useful if you need to know whether the user supplied a value for a segment variable. When no value has been supplied for an optional segment variable, the value of the corresponding parameter will be null. I have updated the Home controller to respond when no value is provided for the id segment variable in Listing 15-21.

Listing 15-21. Checking for a Segment in the HomeController.cs File in the Controllers Folder

```
using Microsoft.AspNetCore.Mvc;
using UrlsAndRoutes.Models;

namespace UrlsAndRoutes.Controllers {

    public class HomeController : Controller {

        public ViewResult Index() => View("Result",
            new Result {
                Controller = nameof(HomeController),
                Action = nameof(Index)
            });

        public ViewResult CustomVariable(string id) {
            Result r = new Result {
                Controller = nameof(HomeController),
                Action = nameof(CustomVariable),
            };
            r.Data["Id"] = id ?? "<no value>";
            return View("Result", r);
        }
    }
}
```

Figure 15-11 shows the result of starting the application and navigating to the /Home/CustomVariable URL, which doesn't include a value for the id segment variable.

Figure 15-11. *Detecting when a URL doesn't contain a value for an optional segment variable*

UNDERSTANDING THE DEFAULT ROUTING CONFIGURATION

When you add MVC to the Startup class, you can do so using the UseMvcWithDefaultRoute method. This is just a convenience method for setting up the most common routing configuration and is equivalent to the following code:

```
...
app.UseMvc(routes => {
    routes.MapRoute(
        name: "default",
        template: "{controller=Home}/{action=Index}/{id?}");
});
...
```

This default configuration matches URLs that target controller classes and action method by name, with an optional id segment. If the controller or action segments are missing, then default values are used to target the Home controller and the Index action method, respectively.

Defining Variable-Length Routes

Another way of changing the default conservatism of URL patterns is to accept a variable number of URL segments. This allows you to route URLs of arbitrary lengths in a single route. You define support for variable segments by designating one of the segment variables as a *catchall*, done by prefixing it with an asterisk (the * character), as shown in Listing 15-22.

Listing 15-22. Designating a Catchall Variable in the Startup.cs File in the UrlsAndRoutes Folder

```
using Microsoft.AspNetCore.Builder;
using Microsoft.Extensions.DependencyInjection;

namespace UrlsAndRoutes {

    public class Startup {
```

```
        public void ConfigureServices(IServiceCollection services) {
            services.AddMvc();
        }

        public void Configure(IApplicationBuilder app) {
            app.UseStatusCodePages();
            app.UseDeveloperExceptionPage();
            app.UseStaticFiles();
            app.UseMvc(routes => {
                routes.MapRoute(name: "MyRoute",
                template: "{controller=Home}/{action=Index}/{id?}/{*catchall}");
            });
        }
    }
}
```

I have extended the route from the previous example to add a catchall segment variable, which I imaginatively called catchall. This route will now match *any* URL, irrespective of the number of segments it contains or the value of any of those segments. The first three segments are used to set values for the controller, action, and id variables, respectively. If the URL contains additional segments, they are all assigned to the catchall variable, as shown in Table 15-6.

Table 15-6. *Matching URLs with a Catchall Segment Variable*

Segments	Example URL	Maps To
0	/	controller = Home action = Index
1	/Customer	controller = Customer action = Index
2	/Customer/List	controller = Customer action = List
3	/Customer/List/All	controller = Customer action = List id = All
4	/Customer/List/All/Delete	controller = Customer action = List id = All catchall = Delete
5	/Customer/List/All/Delete/Perm	controller = Customer action = List id = All catchall = Delete/Perm

In Listing 15-23, I have updated the Customer controller so that the List action passes the value of the catchall variable to the view via the model object.

Listing 15-23. Updating an Action in the CustomerController.cs File in the Controllers Folder

```
using Microsoft.AspNetCore.Mvc;
using UrlsAndRoutes.Models;

namespace UrlsAndRoutes.Controllers {
    public class CustomerController : Controller {

        public ViewResult Index() => View("Result",
            new Result {
                Controller = nameof(CustomerController),
                Action = nameof(Index)
            });
```

```
    public ViewResult List(string id) {
        Result r = new Result {
            Controller = nameof(HomeController),
            Action = nameof(List),
        };
        r.Data["Id"] = id ?? "<no value>";
        r.Data["catchall"] = RouteData.Values["catchall"];
        return View("Result", r);
    }
}
}
```

To test the catchall segment, run the application and request the following URL:

```
/Customer/List/Hello/1/2/3
```

There is no upper limit to the number of segments that the URL pattern in this route will match. Figure 15-12 shows the effect of the catchall segment. Notice that the segments captured by the catchall are presented in the form *segment/segment/segment* and that I am responsible for processing the string to break out the individual segments.

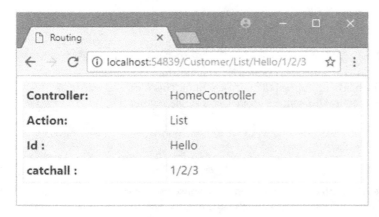

Figure 15-12. *Using a catchall segment*

Constraining Routes

At the start of the chapter, I described how URL patterns are conservative when they match the number of segments in the URL and liberal when they match the content of segments. The previous few sections have explained different techniques for controlling the degree of conservatism: making a route match more or fewer segments using default values, optional variables, and so on.

It is now time to look at how to control the liberalism in matching the *content* of URL segments, namely, how to restrict the set of URLs that a route will match against. Listing 15-24 demonstrates the use of a simple constraint that limits the URLs that a route will match.

Listing 15-24. Constraining a Route in the Startup.cs File in the UrlsAndRoutes Folder

```
using System;
using System.Collections.Generic;
using System.Linq;
```

453

```
using System.Threading.Tasks;
using Microsoft.AspNetCore.Builder;
using Microsoft.AspNetCore.Hosting;
using Microsoft.AspNetCore.Http;
using Microsoft.Extensions.DependencyInjection;

namespace UrlsAndRoutes {
    public class Startup {

        public void ConfigureServices(IServiceCollection services) {
            services.AddMvc();
        }

        public void Configure(IApplicationBuilder app, IHostingEnvironment env) {
            app.UseDeveloperExceptionPage();
            app.UseStatusCodePages();
            app.UseStaticFiles();
            app.UseMvc(routes => {
                routes.MapRoute(name: "MyRoute",
                template: "{controller=Home}/{action=Index}/{id:int?}");
            });
        }
    }
}
```

Constraints are separated from the segment variable name with a colon (the : character). The constraint in the listing is int, and it has been applied to the id segment. This is an example of an *inline constraint*, which is defined as part of the URL pattern applied to a single segment:

```
...
template: "{controller}/{action}/{id:int?}",
...
```

The int constraint only allows the URL pattern to match segments whose value can be parsed to an integer value. The id segment is optional, so the route will match segments that omit the id segment, but if the segment is present, then it must be an integer value, as summarized in Table 15-7.

Table 15-7. *Matching URLs with a Constraint*

Example URL	Maps To
/	controller = Home action = Index id = null
/Home/CustomVariable/Hello	No match—id segment cannot be parsed to an int value.
/Home/CustomVariable/1	controller = Home action = CustomVariable id = 1
/Home/CustomVariable/1/2	No match—too many segments

Constraints can also be specified outside of the URL pattern, using the `constraints` argument to the `MapRoute` method when defining a route. This technique is useful if you prefer to keep the URL pattern separate from its constraints or if you prefer to follow the routing style used by earlier versions of MVC, which did not support inline constraints. Listing 15-25 shows the same `integer` constraint on the `id` segment variable, expressed using a separate constraint. When using this format, the default values are also expressed externally.

Listing 15-25. Expressing a Constraint in the Startup.cs File in the UrlsAndRoutes Folder

```
using System;
using System.Collections.Generic;
using System.Linq;
using System.Threading.Tasks;
using Microsoft.AspNetCore.Builder;
using Microsoft.AspNetCore.Hosting;
using Microsoft.AspNetCore.Http;
using Microsoft.Extensions.DependencyInjection;
using Microsoft.AspNetCore.Routing.Constraints;

namespace UrlsAndRoutes {
    public class Startup {

        public void ConfigureServices(IServiceCollection services) {
            services.AddMvc();
        }

        public void Configure(IApplicationBuilder app, IHostingEnvironment env) {
            app.UseDeveloperExceptionPage();
            app.UseStatusCodePages();
            app.UseStaticFiles();
            app.UseMvc(routes => {
                routes.MapRoute(name: "MyRoute",
                template: "{controller}/{action}/{id?}",
                defaults: new { controller = "Home", action = "Index" },
                constraints: new { id = new IntRouteConstraint() });
            });
        }
    }
}
```

The `constraints` argument to the `MapRoute` method is defined using an anonymous type whose property names correspond to the segment variable being constrained. The `Microsoft.AspNetCore.Routing.Constraints` namespace contains a set of classes that can be used to define individual constraints. In Listing 15-25, the `constraints` argument is configured to use an `IntRouteConstraint` object for the `id` segment, creating the same effect as the inline constraint shown in Listing 15-24.

Table 15-8 describes the complete set of constraint classes in the `Microsoft.AspNetCore.Routing.Constraints` namespace and their inline equivalents for the constraints that can be applied to single segments in the URL pattern, some of which I describe in the sections that follow.

■ **Tip** You can restrict access to action methods to requests made with specific HTTP verbs, such as GET or POST, using a set of attributes provided by MVC, such as the HttpGet and HttpPost attributes. See Chapter 7 for details of using these attributes to handle forms in controllers, and see Chapter 20 for a full list of the attributes available.

Table 15-8. *Segment-Level Route Constraints*

Inline Constraint	Description	Class Name
alpha	Matches alphabet characters, irrespective of case (A–Z, a–z)	AlphaRouteConstraint()
bool	Matches a value that can be parsed into a bool	BoolRouteConstraint()
datetime	Matches a value that can be parsed into a DateTime	DateTimeRouteConstraint()
decimal	Matches a value that can be parsed into a decimal	DecimalRouteConstraint()
double	Matches a value that can be parsed into a double	DoubleRouteConstraint()
float	Matches a value that can be parsed into a float	FloatRouteConstraint()
guid	Matches a value to a globally unique identifier	GuidRouteConstraint()
int	Matches a value that can be parsed into an int	IntRouteConstraint()
length(len) length(min, max)	Matches a value with the specified number of characters or that is between min and max characters in length (inclusive)	LengthRouteConstraint(len) LengthRouteConstraint (min, max)
long	Matches a value that can be parsed into a long	LongRouteConstraint()
maxlength(len)	Matches a string with no more than len characters	MaxLengthRouteConstraint(len)
max(val)	Matches an int value if the value is less than val	MaxRouteConstraint(val)
minlength(len)	Matches a string with at least len characters	MinLengthRouteConstraint(len)
min(val)	Matches an int value if the value is more than val	MinRouteConstraint(val)
range(min, max)	Matches an int value if the value is between min and max (inclusive)	RangeRouteConstraint (min, max)
regex(expr)	Matches a regular expression	RegexRouteConstraint(expr)

Constraining a Route Using a Regular Expression

The constraint that offers the most flexibility is regex, which matches a segment using a regular expression. In Listing 15-26, I have constrained the controller segment to limit the range of URLs that it will match.

Listing 15-26. Using a Regular Expression in the Startup.cs File in the UrlsAndRoutes Folder

```
using System;
using System.Collections.Generic;
using System.Linq;
using System.Threading.Tasks;
using Microsoft.AspNetCore.Builder;
using Microsoft.AspNetCore.Hosting;
using Microsoft.AspNetCore.Http;
using Microsoft.Extensions.DependencyInjection;
using Microsoft.AspNetCore.Routing.Constraints;

namespace UrlsAndRoutes {
    public class Startup {

        public void ConfigureServices(IServiceCollection services) {
            services.AddMvc();
        }

        public void Configure(IApplicationBuilder app, IHostingEnvironment env) {
            app.UseDeveloperExceptionPage();
            app.UseStatusCodePages();
            app.UseStaticFiles();
            app.UseMvc(routes => {
                routes.MapRoute(name: "MyRoute",
                template: "{controller:regex(^H.*)=Home}/{action=Index}/{id?}");
            });
        }
    }
}
```

The constraint I used restricts the route so that it will only match URLs where the controller segment starts with the letter H.

■ **Note**   Default values are applied before constraints are checked. So, for example, if I request the URL /, the default value for controller, which is Home, is applied. The constraints are then checked, and since the controller value begins with H, the default URL will match the route.

Regular expressions can constrain a route so that only specific values for a URL segment will cause a match. This is done using the bar (|) character, as shown in Listing 15-27. (I split the URL pattern into two so that it will fit onto the page, which you won't need to worry about in a real project).

Listing 15-27. Constraining a Route in the Startup.cs File in the UrlsAndRoutes Folder

```
using System;
using System.Collections.Generic;
using System.Linq;
using System.Threading.Tasks;
using Microsoft.AspNetCore.Builder;
using Microsoft.AspNetCore.Hosting;
using Microsoft.AspNetCore.Http;
using Microsoft.Extensions.DependencyInjection;
using Microsoft.AspNetCore.Routing.Constraints;

namespace UrlsAndRoutes {
    public class Startup {

        public void ConfigureServices(IServiceCollection services) {
            services.AddMvc();
        }

        public void Configure(IApplicationBuilder app, IHostingEnvironment env) {
            app.UseDeveloperExceptionPage();
            app.UseStatusCodePages();
            app.UseStaticFiles();
            app.UseMvc(routes => {
                routes.MapRoute(name: "MyRoute",
                    template: "{controller:regex(^H.*)=Home}/"
                    + "{action:regex(^Index$|^About$)=Index}/{id?}");
            });
        }
    }
}
```

This constraint will allow the route to match only URLs where the value of the action segment is Index or About. Constraints are applied together, so the restrictions imposed on the value of the action variable are combined with those imposed on the controller variable. This means that the route in Listing 15-27 will match URLs only when the controller variable begins with the letter H and the action variable is Index or About.

Using Type and Value Constraints

Most of the constraints are used to restrict routes so they only match URLs with segments that can be converted to specified types or have a specific format. The int constraint I used at the start of this section is a good example: it will match routes only when the value of the constrained segment can be parsed to a .NET int value. Listing 15-28 demonstrates the use of the range constraint, which restricts a route so that it matches URLs only when a segment value can be converted to an int and falls between specified values.

Listing 15-28. Constraining Based on Type and Value in the Startup.cs File in the UrlsAndRoutes Folder

```
using System;
using System.Collections.Generic;
using System.Linq;
using System.Threading.Tasks;
using Microsoft.AspNetCore.Builder;
```

```
using Microsoft.AspNetCore.Hosting;
using Microsoft.AspNetCore.Http;
using Microsoft.Extensions.DependencyInjection;
using Microsoft.AspNetCore.Routing.Constraints;

namespace UrlsAndRoutes {
    public class Startup {

        public void ConfigureServices(IServiceCollection services) {
            services.AddMvc();
        }

        public void Configure(IApplicationBuilder app, IHostingEnvironment env) {
            app.UseDeveloperExceptionPage();
            app.UseStatusCodePages();
            app.UseStaticFiles();
            app.UseMvc(routes => {
                routes.MapRoute(name: "MyRoute",
                    template: "{controller=Home}/{action=Index}/{id:range(10,20)?}");
            });
        }
    }
}
```

The constraint in this example has been applied to the optional id segment. The constraint will be ignored if the request URL doesn't have at least three segments. If the id segment is present, the route will match the URL only if the segment value can be converted to an int and the value is between 10 and 20. The range constraint is inclusive, meaning that values of 10 and 20 are considered to be within the range.

Combining Constraints

If you need to apply multiple constraints to a single segment, then you chain them together so that each constraint is separated by a colon, as shown in Listing 15-29.

Listing 15-29. Combining Inline Constraints in the Startup.cs File in the UrlsAndRoutes Folder

```
using System;
using System.Collections.Generic;
using System.Linq;
using System.Threading.Tasks;
using Microsoft.AspNetCore.Builder;
using Microsoft.AspNetCore.Hosting;
using Microsoft.AspNetCore.Http;
using Microsoft.Extensions.DependencyInjection;
using Microsoft.AspNetCore.Routing.Constraints;

namespace UrlsAndRoutes {
    public class Startup {

        public void ConfigureServices(IServiceCollection services) {
            services.AddMvc();
        }
```

```
    public void Configure(IApplicationBuilder app, IHostingEnvironment env) {
        app.UseDeveloperExceptionPage();
        app.UseStatusCodePages();
        app.UseStaticFiles();
        app.UseMvc(routes => {
            routes.MapRoute(name: "MyRoute",
                template: "{controller=Home}/{action=Index}"
                    + "/{id:alpha:minlength(6)?}");
        });
    }
  }
}
```

In this listing, I have applied both the alpha and minlength constraints to the id segment. The question mark that denotes an optional segment is applied after all of the constraints. The effect of combining these constraints is that the route will match URLs only where the id segment is omitted (because it is optional) or when it is present and contains at least six alphabet characters.

If you are not using inline constraints, then you must use the Microsoft.AspNetCore.Routing. CompositeRouteConstraint class, which allows multiple constraints to be associated with a single property in an anonymously typed object. Listing 15-30 shows the combination of constraints that I used in Listing 15-29.

Listing 15-30. Combining Separate Constraints in the Startup.cs File in the UrlsAndRoutes Folder

```
using System;
using System.Collections.Generic;
using System.Linq;
using System.Threading.Tasks;
using Microsoft.AspNetCore.Builder;
using Microsoft.AspNetCore.Hosting;
using Microsoft.AspNetCore.Http;
using Microsoft.Extensions.DependencyInjection;
using Microsoft.AspNetCore.Routing.Constraints;
using Microsoft.AspNetCore.Routing;

namespace UrlsAndRoutes {
    public class Startup {

        public void ConfigureServices(IServiceCollection services) {
            services.AddMvc();
        }

        public void Configure(IApplicationBuilder app, IHostingEnvironment env) {
            app.UseDeveloperExceptionPage();
            app.UseStatusCodePages();
            app.UseStaticFiles();
            app.UseMvc(routes => {
                routes.MapRoute(name: "MyRoute",
                    template: "{controller}/{action}/{id?}",
                    defaults: new { controller = "Home", action = "Index" },
                    constraints: new {
                        id = new CompositeRouteConstraint(
                            new IRouteConstraint[] {
```

```
                        new AlphaRouteConstraint(),
                        new MinLengthRouteConstraint(6)
                    })
                });
            });
        }
    }
}
```

The constructor for the CompositeRouteConstraint class accepts an enumeration of objects that implement the IRouteConstraint objects, which is the interface that defines route constraints. The routing system will allow the route to match a URL only if all the constraints are satisfied.

Defining a Custom Constraint

If the standard constraints are not sufficient for your needs, you can define your own custom constraints by implementing the IRouteConstraint interface, which is defined in the Microsoft.AspNetCore.Routing namespace. To demonstrate this feature, I added an Infrastructure folder to the example project and created a new class file called WeekDayConstraint.cs, the contents of which are shown in Listing 15-31.

Listing 15-31. The Contents of the WeekDayConstraint.cs File in the Infrastructure Folder

```
using Microsoft.AspNetCore.Http;
using Microsoft.AspNetCore.Routing;
using System.Linq;

namespace UrlsAndRoutes.Infrastructure {
    public class WeekDayConstraint : IRouteConstraint {
        private static string[] Days = new[] { "mon", "tue", "wed", "thu",
                                        "fri", "sat", "sun" };

        public bool Match(HttpContext httpContext, IRouter route,
            string routeKey, RouteValueDictionary values,
            RouteDirection routeDirection) {

            return Days.Contains(values[routeKey]?.ToString().ToLowerInvariant());
        }
    }
}
```

The IRouteConstraint interface defines the Match method, which is called to allow a constraint to decide whether a request should be matched by the route. The parameters for the Match method provide access to the request from the client, the route, the name of the segment that is being constrained, the segment variables that have been extracted from the URL, and whether the request is to check for an incoming or outgoing URL (I explain outgoing URLs in Chapter 16).

In the example, I use the routeKey parameter to get the value of the segment variable to which the constraint has been applied from the values parameter, convert it to a lowercase string, and see whether it matches one of the days of the week that are defined in the static Days field. Listing 15-32 applies the new constraint to the example route using the separate technique.

Listing 15-32. Applying a Custom Constraint in the Startup.cs File in the UrlsAndRoutes Folder

```
using System;
using System.Collections.Generic;
using System.Linq;
using System.Threading.Tasks;
using Microsoft.AspNetCore.Builder;
using Microsoft.AspNetCore.Hosting;
using Microsoft.AspNetCore.Http;
using Microsoft.Extensions.DependencyInjection;
using Microsoft.AspNetCore.Routing.Constraints;
using Microsoft.AspNetCore.Routing;
using UrlsAndRoutes.Infrastructure;

namespace UrlsAndRoutes {
    public class Startup {

        public void ConfigureServices(IServiceCollection services) {
            services.AddMvc();
        }

        public void Configure(IApplicationBuilder app, IHostingEnvironment env) {
            app.UseDeveloperExceptionPage();
            app.UseStatusCodePages();
            app.UseStaticFiles();
            app.UseMvc(routes => {
                routes.MapRoute(name: "MyRoute",
                    template: "{controller}/{action}/{id?}",
                    defaults: new { controller = "Home", action = "Index" },
                    constraints: new { id = new WeekDayConstraint() });
            });
        }
    }
}
```

This route will match a URL only if the id segment is absent (such as /Customer/List) or if it matches one of the days of the week defined in the constraint class (such as /Customer/List/Fri).

Defining an Inline Custom Constraint

Setting up a custom constraint so that it can be used inline requires an additional configuration step, as shown in Listing 15-33.

Listing 15-33. Using a Custom Constraint Inline in the Startup.cs File in the UrlsAndRoutes Folder

```
using System;
using System.Collections.Generic;
using System.Linq;
using System.Threading.Tasks;
using Microsoft.AspNetCore.Builder;
using Microsoft.AspNetCore.Hosting;
using Microsoft.AspNetCore.Http;
```

```
using Microsoft.Extensions.DependencyInjection;
using Microsoft.AspNetCore.Routing.Constraints;
using Microsoft.AspNetCore.Routing;
using UrlsAndRoutes.Infrastructure;

namespace UrlsAndRoutes {
    public class Startup {

        public void ConfigureServices(IServiceCollection services) {
            services.Configure<RouteOptions>(options =>
                options.ConstraintMap.Add("weekday", typeof(WeekDayConstraint)));
            services.AddMvc();
        }

        public void Configure(IApplicationBuilder app, IHostingEnvironment env) {
            app.UseDeveloperExceptionPage();
            app.UseStatusCodePages();
            app.UseStaticFiles();
            app.UseMvc(routes => {
                routes.MapRoute(name: "MyRoute",
                template: "{controller=Home}/{action=Index}/{id:weekday?}");
            });
        }
    }
}
```

In the ConfigureService method I configure the RouteOptions object, which controls some of the behaviors of the routing system. The ConstraintMap property returns the dictionary that is used to translate the names of inline constraints to the IRouteConstraint implementation classes that provide the constraint logic. I add a new mapping to the dictionary so that I can refer to the WeekDayConstraint class inline as weekday, like this:

```
...
template: "{controller=Home}/{action=Index}/{id:weekday?}",
...
```

The effect of the constraint is the same, but setting up the mapping allows custom classes to be used inline.

Using Attribute Routing

All the examples so far in this chapter have been defined using a technique known as *convention-based routing*. MVC also supports for a technique known as *attribute routing*, in which routes are defined by C# attributes that are applied directly to the controller classes. In the sections that follow, I show you how to create and configure routes using attributes, which can be mixed freely with the convention-based routes shown in earlier examples.

Preparing for Attribute Routing

Attribute routing is enabled when you call the UseMvc method in the Startup.cs file. MVC examines the controller classes in the application, finds any that have routing attributes, and creates routes for them.

For this section of the chapter, I have returned the example application to the default routing configuration described in the "Understanding the Default Routing Configuration" sidebar, as shown in Listing 15-34.

Listing 15-34. Using the Default Routing Configuration in the Startup.cs File in the UrlsAndRoutes Folder

```
using System;
using System.Collections.Generic;
using System.Linq;
using System.Threading.Tasks;
using Microsoft.AspNetCore.Builder;
using Microsoft.AspNetCore.Hosting;
using Microsoft.AspNetCore.Http;
using Microsoft.Extensions.DependencyInjection;
using Microsoft.AspNetCore.Routing.Constraints;
using Microsoft.AspNetCore.Routing;
using UrlsAndRoutes.Infrastructure;

namespace UrlsAndRoutes {
    public class Startup {

        public void ConfigureServices(IServiceCollection services) {
            services.Configure<RouteOptions>(options =>
                options.ConstraintMap.Add("weekday", typeof(WeekDayConstraint)));
            services.AddMvc();
        }

        public void Configure(IApplicationBuilder app, IHostingEnvironment env) {
            app.UseDeveloperExceptionPage();
            app.UseStatusCodePages();
            app.UseStaticFiles();
            app.UseMvcWithDefaultRoute();
        }
    }
}
```

The default route will match URLs using the following pattern:

```
{controller}/{action}/{id?}
```

Applying Attribute Routing

The Route attribute is used to specify routes for individual controllers and actions. In Listing 15-35, I have applied the Route attribute to the CustomerController class.

Listing 15-35. Applying the Route Attribute in the CustomerController.cs File in the Controllers Folder

```
using Microsoft.AspNetCore.Mvc;
using UrlsAndRoutes.Models;

namespace UrlsAndRoutes.Controllers {
    public class CustomerController : Controller {

        [Route("myroute")]
        public ViewResult Index() => View("Result",
            new Result {
                Controller = nameof(CustomerController),
                Action = nameof(Index)
            });

        public ViewResult List(string id) {
            Result r = new Result {
                Controller = nameof(HomeController),
                Action = nameof(List),
            };
            r.Data["id"] = id ?? "<no value>";
            r.Data["catchall"] = RouteData.Values["catchall"];
            return View("Result", r);
        }
    }
}
```

The Route attribute works by defining a route to the action method or controller it is applied to. In the listing, I applied the attribute to the Index action method and specified myroute as the route that should be used. The effect is to change the set of routes that are used to reach the action methods defined by the Customer controller, as described in Table 15-9.

Table 15-9. The Routes for the Customer Controller

Route	Description
/Customer/List	This URL targets the List action method, relying on the default route in the Startup. cs file.
/myroute	This URL targets the Index action method.

There are two important points to note. The first is that when you use the Route attribute, the value you provide to configure the attribute is used to define a complete route so that myroute becomes the complete URL to reach the Index action method. The second point to note is that using the Route attribute prevents the default routing configuration from being used so that the Index action method can no longer be reached by using the /Customer/Index URL.

Changing the Name of an Action Method

Defining a unique route for a single action method isn't useful in most applications, but the Route attribute can also be used more flexibly. In Listing 15-36, I have used the special [controller] token in the route to refer to the controller and set up the base section of the route.

■ **Tip**   You can also change the name of an action using the `ActionName` attribute, which I describe in Chapter 31.

Listing 15-36. Renaming an Action in the CustomerController.cs File in the Controllers Folder

```
using Microsoft.AspNetCore.Mvc;
using UrlsAndRoutes.Models;

namespace UrlsAndRoutes.Controllers {
    public class CustomerController : Controller {

        [Route("[controller]/MyAction")]
        public ViewResult Index() => View("Result",
            new Result {
                Controller = nameof(CustomerController),
                Action = nameof(Index)
            });

        public ViewResult List(string id) {
            Result r = new Result {
                Controller = nameof(HomeController),
                Action = nameof(List),
            };
            r.Data["id"] = id ?? "<no value>";
            r.Data["catchall"] = RouteData.Values["catchall"];
            return View("Result", r);
        }
    }
}
```

Using the `[controller]` token in the argument for the Route attribute is rather like using a nameof expression and allows for the route to the controller to be specified without hard-coding the class name. Table 15-10 describes the effect of the attribute in Listing 15-36.

Table 15-10. The Routes for the Customer Controller

Route	Description
/Customer/List	This URL targets the List action method.
/Customer/MyAction	This URL targets the Index action method.

Creating a More Complex Route

The Route attribute can also be applied to the controller class, allowing for the structure of the route to be defined, as shown in Listing 15-37.

Listing 15-37. Applying the Route Attribute in the CustomerController.cs File in the Controllers Folder

```
using Microsoft.AspNetCore.Mvc;
using UrlsAndRoutes.Models;

namespace UrlsAndRoutes.Controllers {

    [Route("app/[controller]/actions/[action]/{id?}")]
    public class CustomerController : Controller {

        public ViewResult Index() => View("Result",
            new Result {
                Controller = nameof(CustomerController),
                Action = nameof(Index)
            });

        public ViewResult List(string id) {
            Result r = new Result {
                Controller = nameof(HomeController),
                Action = nameof(List),
            };
            r.Data["id"] = id ?? "<no value>";
            r.Data["catchall"] = RouteData.Values["catchall"];
            return View("Result", r);
        }
    }
}
```

This route defines mixes static segments and variable segments and uses the [controller] and [action] tokens to refer to the names of the controller class and the action methods. Table 15-11 shows the effect of the route.

Table 15-11. *The Routes for the Customer Controller*

Route	Description
app/customer/actions/index	This URL targets the Index action method.
app/customer/actions/index/myid	This URL targets the Index action method with the optional id segment set to myid.
app/customer/actions/list	This URL targets the List action method.
app/customer/actions/list/myid	This URL targets the List action method with the optional id segment set to myid.

Applying Route Constraints

Routes defined using attributes can be constrained just like those defined in the Startup.cs file, using the same inline technique used for convention-based routes. In Listing 15-38, I have applied the custom constraint created earlier in the chapter to the optional id segment defined with the Route attribute.

Listing 15-38. Constraining a Route in the CustomerController.cs File in the Controllers Folder

```
using Microsoft.AspNetCore.Mvc;
using UrlsAndRoutes.Models;

namespace UrlsAndRoutes.Controllers {

    [Route("app/[controller]/actions/[action]/{id:weekday?}")]
    public class CustomerController : Controller {

        public ViewResult Index() => View("Result",
            new Result {
                Controller = nameof(CustomerController),
                Action = nameof(Index)
            });

        public ViewResult List(string id) {
            Result r = new Result {
                Controller = nameof(HomeController),
                Action = nameof(List),
            };
            r.Data["id"] = id ?? "<no value>";
            r.Data["catchall"] = RouteData.Values["catchall"];
            return View("Result", r);
        }
    }
}
```

You can use all the constraints described in Table 15-8 or, as shown in the listing, use custom constraints that have been registered with the RouteOptions service. Multiple constraints can be applied by chaining them together and separating them with colons.

Summary

In this chapter, I took an in-depth look at the routing system. You have seen how routes are defined by convention or with attributes. You have seen how incoming URLs are matched and handled and how to customize routes by changing the way that they match URL segments and by using default values and optional segments. I also showed you how to constrain routes to narrow the range of requests that they will match, both using built-in constraints and using custom constraint classes.

In the next chapter, I show you how to generate outgoing URLs from routes in your views and how to use the areas feature, which relies on the routing system and which can be used to manage large and complex MVC applications.

CHAPTER 16

Advanced Routing Features

In the previous chapter, I showed you how to use the routing system to handle incoming URLs, but this is only part of the story. You also need to be able use your URL schema to generate *outgoing URLs* you can embed in your views so that users can click links and submit forms back to your application in a way that will target the correct controller and action.

In this chapter, I show you different techniques for generating outgoing URLs, how to customize the routing system by replacing the standard MVC routing implementation classes, and how to use the MVC *areas* feature, which allows you to break a large and complex MVC application into manageable chunks. I finish this chapter with some best-practice advice about URL schemas in MVC applications. Table 16-1 puts advanced routing features in context.

Table 16-1. *Putting Advanced Routing Features in Context*

Question	Answer
What is it?	The routing system provides features that go beyond matching the URLs for HTTP requests. There is also support for generating URLs in views, replacing the built-in routing functionality with custom classes, and structuring the application into isolated sections.
Why is it useful?	Each feature is useful for a different reason. Being able to generate URLs makes it easy to change the URL schema without having to update all of your views, being able to use custom classes allows the routing system to be tailored to your needs, and being able to structure the application makes it easier to build complex projects.
How is it used?	See the sections in this chapter for details.
Are there any pitfalls or limitations?	The routing configuration for a complex application can become hard to manage.
Are there any alternatives?	No. The routing system is an integral part of ASP.NET.

Table 16-2 summarizes the chapter.

© Adam Freeman 2017

A. Freeman, *Pro ASP.NET Core MVC 2*, https://doi.org/10.1007/978-1-4842-3150-0_16

Table 16-2. *Chapter Summary*

Problem	Solution	Listing
Generate an anchor element with a URL	Use the asp-action and asp-controller attributes	2–5
Provide values for routing segments	Use attributes with the asp-route- prefix	6–7
Generate fully qualified URLs	Use the asp-procotol, asp-host, and asp-fragment attributes	8
Select a route to generate a URL	Use the asp-route attribute	9–10
Generate a URL without an HTML element	Use the Url.Action helper method in a view or in an action method	11–12
Customize the routing system	Use the Configure method in the Startup class	13
Create a custom routing class	Implement the IRouter interface	14–21
Break an application into functional sections	Create areas and use the Area attribute	22–28

Preparing the Example Project

I am going to continue to use the UrlsAndRoutes project from the previous chapter. The only change required is in the Startup class, where I have replaced the UseMvcWithDefaultRoute method with an explicit route that has the same effect, as shown in Listing 16-1.

Listing 16-1. Changing the Routing Configuration in the Startup.cs File in the UrlsAndRoutes Folder

```
using System;
using System.Collections.Generic;
using System.Linq;
using System.Threading.Tasks;
using Microsoft.AspNetCore.Builder;
using Microsoft.AspNetCore.Hosting;
using Microsoft.AspNetCore.Http;
using Microsoft.Extensions.DependencyInjection;
using Microsoft.AspNetCore.Routing.Constraints;
using Microsoft.AspNetCore.Routing;
using UrlsAndRoutes.Infrastructure;

namespace UrlsAndRoutes {
    public class Startup {

        public void ConfigureServices(IServiceCollection services) {
            services.Configure<RouteOptions>(options =>
                options.ConstraintMap.Add("weekday", typeof(WeekDayConstraint)));
            services.AddMvc();
        }

        public void Configure(IApplicationBuilder app, IHostingEnvironment env) {
            app.UseDeveloperExceptionPage();
            app.UseStatusCodePages();
```

```
        app.UseStaticFiles();
        app.UseMvc(routes => {
            routes.MapRoute(
                name: "default",
                template: "{controller=Home}/{action=Index}/{id?}");
        });
    }
}
}
```

If you start the application, the browser will request the default URL, which will be sent to the Index action on the Home controller, as shown in Figure 16-1.

Figure 16-1. *Running the example application*

Generating Outgoing URLs in Views

In almost every MVC application, you will want to allow the user to navigate from one view to another, which will usually rely on including a link in the first view that targets the action method that generates the second view. It is tempting to just add a static a element (known as an *anchor element*) whose href attribute targets the action method, like this:

```
<a href="/Home/CustomVariable">This is an outgoing URL</a>
```

Assuming that the application is using the default routing configuration, this HTML element creates a link that will target the CustomVariable action method on the Home controller. Manually defined URLs like this one are quick and simple to create. They are also extremely dangerous, and you will break all the URLs you have hard-coded when you change the URL schema for your application. You then must trawl through all the views in your application and update all the references to your controllers and action methods, a process that is tedious, error-prone, and difficult to test. A better alternative is to use the routing system to generate outgoing URLs, which ensures that the URL scheme is used to produce the URLs dynamically and in a way that is guaranteed to reflect the URL schema of the application.

Generating Outgoing Links

The simplest way to generate an outgoing URL in a view is to use the anchor tag helper, which will generate the href attribute for an HTML a element, as illustrated by Listing 16-2, which shows an addition I made to the /Views/Shared/Result.cshtml view.

■ **Tip** I explain how tag helpers work in detail in Chapter 23.

Listing 16-2. Using the Anchor Tag Helper in the Result.cshtml File in the Views/Shared Folder

```
@model Result
@{ Layout = null; }

<!DOCTYPE html>
<html>
<head>
    <meta name="viewport" content="width=device-width" />
    <title>Routing</title>
    <link rel="stylesheet" asp-href-include="lib/bootstrap/dist/css/*.min.css" />
</head>
<body class="m-1 p-1">
    <table class="table table-bordered table-striped table-sm">
        <tr><th>Controller:</th><td>@Model.Controller</td></tr>
        <tr><th>Action:</th><td>@Model.Action</td></tr>
        @foreach (string key in Model.Data.Keys) {
            <tr><th>@key :</th><td>@Model.Data[key]</td></tr>
        }
    </table>
    <a asp-action="CustomVariable">This is an outgoing URL</a>
</body>
</html>
```

The asp-action attribute is used to specify the name of the action method that the URL in the href attribute should target. You can see the result by starting the application, as shown in Figure 16-2.

Figure 16-2. *Using a tag helper to generate a link*

The tag helper sets the href attribute on the a element using the current routing configuration. If you inspect the HTML sent to the browser, you will see that it contains the following element:

```
<a href="/Home/CustomVariable">This is an outgoing URL</a>
```

This may seem like a lot of additional effort to re-create the manually defined URL I showed you earlier, but the benefit of this approach is that it automatically responds to changes in the routing configuration. To demonstrate, I have added a new route to the Startup.cs file, as shown in Listing 16-3.

Listing 16-3. Adding a Route to the Startup.cs File in the UrlsAndRoutes Folder

```
using System;
using System.Collections.Generic;
using System.Linq;
using System.Threading.Tasks;
using Microsoft.AspNetCore.Builder;
using Microsoft.AspNetCore.Hosting;
using Microsoft.AspNetCore.Http;
using Microsoft.Extensions.DependencyInjection;
using Microsoft.AspNetCore.Routing.Constraints;
using Microsoft.AspNetCore.Routing;
using UrlsAndRoutes.Infrastructure;

namespace UrlsAndRoutes {
    public class Startup {

        public void ConfigureServices(IServiceCollection services) {
            services.Configure<RouteOptions>(options =>
                options.ConstraintMap.Add("weekday", typeof(WeekDayConstraint)));
            services.AddMvc();
        }

        public void Configure(IApplicationBuilder app, IHostingEnvironment env) {
            app.UseDeveloperExceptionPage();
            app.UseStatusCodePages();
            app.UseStaticFiles();
            app.UseMvc(routes => {

                routes.MapRoute(
                    name: "NewRoute",
                    template: "App/Do{action}",
                    defaults: new { controller = "Home" });

                routes.MapRoute(
                    name: "default",
                    template: "{controller=Home}/{action=Index}/{id?}");
            });
        }
    }
}
```

The new route changes the URL schema for requests that target the Home controller. If you start the app, you will see that this change is reflected in the HTML that is generated by the ActionLink HTML helper method, as follows:

```
<a href="/App/DoCustomVariable">This is an outgoing URL</a>
```

Generating links using a tag helper addresses an important maintenance issue. I am able to change the routing schema and have the outgoing links in the views reflect the change automatically without having to manually edit the views in the application.

When you click the link, the outgoing URL is used to create an incoming HTTP request, and the same route is then used to target the action method and controller that will handle the request, as shown in Figure 16-3.

Figure 16-3. *The effect of clicking a link is to make an outgoing URL into an incoming request*

UNDERSTANDING OUTBOUND URL ROUTE MATCHING

You have seen how changing the routes that define your URL schema changes the way that outgoing URLs are generated. Applications will usually define several routes, and it is important to understand how they are selected for URL generation. The routing system processes the routes in the order that they were defined, and each route is inspected in turn to see whether it is a match, which requires these three conditions to be met:

- A value must be available for every segment variable defined in the URL pattern. To find values for each segment variable, the routing system looks first at the values you have provided (using the properties of an anonymous type), then at the variable values for the current request, and finally at the default values defined in the route. (I return to the second source of these values later in this chapter).

- None of the values provided for the segment variables may disagree with the default-only variables defined in the route. These are variables for which default values have been provided but which do not occur in the URL pattern. For example, in this route definition, myVar is a default-only variable:

```
routes.MapRoute("MyRoute", "{controller}/{action}",
    new { myVar = "true" });
```

For this route to be a match, I must take care to not supply a value for myVar or to make sure that the value I do supply matches the default value.

- The values for all the segment variables must satisfy the route constraints. See the "Constraining Routes" section in the previous chapter for examples of different kinds of constraints.

To be clear, the routing system doesn't try to find the route that provides the *best* matching route. It finds only the *first* match, at which point it uses the route to generate the URL; any subsequent routes are ignored. For this reason, you should define your most specific routes first. It is important to check your outgoing URL generation. If you try to generate a URL for which no matching route can be found, you will create a link that contains an empty `href` attribute, like this:

```
<a href="">This is an outgoing URL</a>
```

The link will render in the view properly but won't function as intended when the user clicks it. If you are generating just the URL (which I show you how to do later in the chapter), then the result will be `null`, which renders as the empty string in views. You can exert some control over route matching by using named routes. See the "Generating a URL from a Specific Route" section later in this chapter for details.

Targeting Other Controllers

When you specify the `asp-action` attribute on an a element, the tag helper assumes you want to target an action in the same controller that has caused the view to be rendered. To create an outgoing URL that targets a *different* controller, you can use the `asp-controller` attribute, as shown in Listing 16-4.

Listing 16-4. Targeting a Different Controllers in the Result.cshtml File in the Views/Shared Folder

```
@model Result
@{ Layout = null; }

<!DOCTYPE html>
<html>
<head>
    <meta name="viewport" content="width=device-width" />
    <title>Routing</title>
    <link rel="stylesheet" asp-href-include="lib/bootstrap/dist/css/*.min.css" />
</head>
<body class="m-1 p-1">
    <table class="table table-bordered table-striped table-sm">
        <tr><th>Controller:</th><td>@Model.Controller</td></tr>
        <tr><th>Action:</th><td>@Model.Action</td></tr>
        @foreach (string key in Model.Data.Keys) {
            <tr><th>@key :</th><td>@Model.Data[key]</td></tr>
        }
    </table>
    <a asp-controller="Admin" asp-action="Index">
        This targets another controller
    </a>
</body>
</html>
```

When you render the view, you will see the following HTML generated:

```
<a href="/Admin">This targets another controller</a>
```

The request for a URL that targets the Index action method on the Admin controller has been expressed as /Admin by the tag helper. The routing system knows that the route defined in the application will use the Index action method by default, allowing it to omit unneeded segments.

The routing system includes routes that have been defined using the Route attribute when determining how to target a given action method. In Listing 16-5, the asp-controller attribute targets the Index action in the Customer controller, to which the Route attribute was applied in Chapter 15.

Listing 16-5. Targeting an Action in the Result.cshtml File in the Views/Shared Folder

```
@model Result
@{ Layout = null; }

<!DOCTYPE html>
<html>
<head>
    <meta name="viewport" content="width=device-width" />
    <title>Routing</title>
    <link rel="stylesheet" asp-href-include="lib/bootstrap/dist/css/*.min.css" />
</head>
<body class="panel-body">
    <table class="table table-bordered table-striped table-sm">
        <tr><th>Controller:</th><td>@Model.Controller</td></tr>
        <tr><th>Action:</th><td>@Model.Action</td></tr>
        @foreach (string key in Model.Data.Keys) {
            <tr><th>@key :</th><td>@Model.Data[key]</td></tr>
        }
    </table>
    <a asp-controller="Customer" asp-action="Index">This is an outgoing URL</a>
</body>
</html>
```

The link that is generated is as follows:

```
<a href="/app/Customer/actions/Index">This is an outgoing URL</a>
```

This corresponds to the Route attribute I applied to the Customer controller in Chapter 15.

```
...
[Route("app/[controller]/actions/[action]/{id:weekday?}")]
public class CustomerController : Controller {
...
```

Passing Extra Values

You can pass values for segment variables to the routing system by defining attributes whose name starts with asp-route- followed by the segment name so that asp-route-id is used to set the value of the id segment, as shown in Listing 16-6.

Listing 16-6. Supplying Values for Segment Variables in the Result.cshtml File in the Views/Shared Folder

```
@model Result
@{ Layout = null; }

<!DOCTYPE html>
<html>
<head>
    <meta name="viewport" content="width=device-width" />
    <title>Routing</title>
    <link rel="stylesheet" asp-href-include="lib/bootstrap/dist/css/*.min.css" />
</head>
<body class="m-1 p-1">
    <table class="table table-bordered table-striped table-sm">
        <tr><th>Controller:</th><td>@Model.Controller</td></tr>
        <tr><th>Action:</th><td>@Model.Action</td></tr>
        @foreach (string key in Model.Data.Keys) {
            <tr><th>@key :</th><td>@Model.Data[key]</td></tr>
        }
    </table>
    <a asp-controller="Home" asp-action="Index" asp-route-id="Hello">
        This is an outgoing URL
    </a>
</body>
</html>
```

I have supplied a value for a segment variable called id. If the application uses the route shown in Listing 16-6, then the following HTML will be rendered in the view:

```
<a href="/App/DoIndex?id=Hello">This is an outgoing URL</a>
```

Notice that the segment value has been added as part of the query string to fit into the URL pattern described by the route. This is because there is no segment variable that corresponds to id in that route. To address this, I edited the routes in the Startup.cs file to leave only a route that *does* have an id segment, as shown in Listing 16-7.

Listing 16-7. Editing the Routes in the Startup.cs File in the UrlsAndRoutes Folder

```
using System;
using System.Collections.Generic;
using System.Linq;
using System.Threading.Tasks;
using Microsoft.AspNetCore.Builder;
using Microsoft.AspNetCore.Hosting;
using Microsoft.AspNetCore.Http;
```

```
using Microsoft.Extensions.DependencyInjection;
using Microsoft.AspNetCore.Routing.Constraints;
using Microsoft.AspNetCore.Routing;
using UrlsAndRoutes.Infrastructure;

namespace UrlsAndRoutes {
    public class Startup {

        public void ConfigureServices(IServiceCollection services) {
            services.Configure<RouteOptions>(options =>
                options.ConstraintMap.Add("weekday", typeof(WeekDayConstraint)));
            services.AddMvc();
        }

        public void Configure(IApplicationBuilder app, IHostingEnvironment env) {
            app.UseDeveloperExceptionPage();
            app.UseStatusCodePages();
            app.UseStaticFiles();
            app.UseMvc(routes => {

                //routes.MapRoute(
                //    name: "NewRoute",
                //    template: "App/Do{action}",
                //    defaults: new { controller = "Home" });

                routes.MapRoute(
                    name: "default",
                    template: "{controller=Home}/{action=Index}/{id?}");
            });
        }
    }
}
```

Run the application again and you will see that tag helper produces the following HTML element, in which the value of the id property is included as a URL segment:

```
<a href="/Home/Index/Hello">This is an outgoing URL</a>
```

UNDERSTANDING SEGMENT VARIABLE REUSE

When I described the way that routes are matched for outbound URLs, I explained that when trying to find values for each of the segment variables in a route's URL pattern, the routing system will look at the values from the current request. This is a behavior that confuses many programmers and can lead to a lengthy debugging session.

Imagine the application has a single route, as follows:

```
...
app.UseMvc(routes => {
    routes.MapRoute(name: "MyRoute",
        template: "{controller}/{action}/{color}/{page}");

});
...
```

Now imagine that a user is currently at the URL /Home/Index/Red/100, and I render a link as follows:

```
...
<a asp-controller="Home" asp-action="Index" asp-route-page="789">
    This is an outgoing URL
</a>
...
```

You might expect that the routing system would be unable to match the route because I have not supplied a value for the color segment variable and there is no default value defined. You would, however, be wrong. The routing system *will* match against the route I defined. It will generate the following HTML:

```
...
<a href="/Home/Index/Red/789">This is an outgoing URL</a>
...
```

The routing system is keen to make a match against a route, to the extent that it will reuse segment variable values from the *incoming* URL when generating an *outgoing* URL. In this case, I end up with the value Red for the color variable because of the URL from which my imaginary user started.

This is *not* a behavior of last resort. The routing system will apply this technique as part of its regular assessment of routes, even if there is a subsequent route that would match without requiring values from the current request to be reused.

I strongly recommend that you do not rely on this behavior and that you supply values for all of the segment variables in a URL pattern. Relying on this behavior will not only make your code harder to read, but you end up making assumptions about the order in which your users make requests, which is something that will ultimately bite you as your application enters maintenance.

Generating Fully Qualified URLs

All of the links that have been generated so far contained relative URLs, but the anchor element tag helper can also generate fully qualified URLs, as shown in Listing 16-8.

Listing 16-8. Generating a Fully Qualified URL in the Result.cshtml File in the Views/Shared Folder

```
@model Result
@{ Layout = null; }

<!DOCTYPE html>
<html>
<head>
    <meta name="viewport" content="width=device-width" />
    <title>Routing</title>
    <link rel="stylesheet" asp-href-include="lib/bootstrap/dist/css/*.min.css" />
</head>
<body class="m-1 p-1">
    <table class="table table-bordered table-striped table-sm">
        <tr><th>Controller:</th><td>@Model.Controller</td></tr>
        <tr><th>Action:</th><td>@Model.Action</td></tr>
        @foreach (string key in Model.Data.Keys) {
            <tr><th>@key :</th><td>@Model.Data[key]</td></tr>
        }
    </table>
    <a asp-controller="Home" asp-action="Index" asp-route-id="Hello"
        asp-protocol="https" asp-host="myserver.mydomain.com"
        asp-fragment="myFragment">
        This is an outgoing URL
    </a>
</body>
</html>
```

The asp-protocol, asp-host, and asp-fragment attributes are used to specify the protocol (https in the listing), the name of the server (myserver.mydomain.com), and the URL fragment (myFragment). These values are combined with the output from the routing system to create a fully qualified URL, which you can see if you run the application and examine the HTML sent to the browser.

```
<a href="https://myserver.mydomain.com/Home/Index/Hello#myFragment">
    This is an outgoing URL
</a>
```

Be careful when you use fully qualified URLs because they create dependencies on the application infrastructure and, when the infrastructure changes, you will have to remember to make corresponding changes to the MVC views.

Generating a URL from a Specific Route

In the previous examples, the routing system selected the route that will be used to generate a URL. If it is important to generate a URL in a specific format, then you can specify the route that will be used to generate an outgoing URL. To demonstrate how this works, I added a new route to the Startup.cs file so that there are two routes in the example application, as shown in Listing 16-9.

Listing 16-9. Adding a Route in the Startup.cs File in the UrlsAndRoutes Folder

```
using System;
using System.Collections.Generic;
using System.Linq;
using System.Threading.Tasks;
using Microsoft.AspNetCore.Builder;
using Microsoft.AspNetCore.Hosting;
using Microsoft.AspNetCore.Http;
using Microsoft.Extensions.DependencyInjection;
using Microsoft.AspNetCore.Routing.Constraints;
using Microsoft.AspNetCore.Routing;
using UrlsAndRoutes.Infrastructure;

namespace UrlsAndRoutes {
    public class Startup {

        public void ConfigureServices(IServiceCollection services) {
            services.Configure<RouteOptions>(options =>
                options.ConstraintMap.Add("weekday", typeof(WeekDayConstraint)));
            services.AddMvc();
        }

        public void Configure(IApplicationBuilder app, IHostingEnvironment env) {
            app.UseDeveloperExceptionPage();
            app.UseStatusCodePages();
            app.UseStaticFiles();
            app.UseMvc(routes => {

                //routes.MapRoute(
                //    name: "NewRoute",
                //    template: "App/Do{action}",
                //    defaults: new { controller = "Home" });

                routes.MapRoute(
                    name: "default",
                    template: "{controller=Home}/{action=Index}/{id?}");

                routes.MapRoute(
                    name: "out",
                    template: "outbound/{controller=Home}/{action=Index}");
            });
        }
    }
}
```

The view shown in Listing 16-10 contains two anchor elements, each of which specifies the same controller and action. The difference is that the second element uses the asp-route tag helper attribute to specify that the out route should be used to generate the URL for the href attribute.

Listing 16-10. Generating URLs in the Result.cshtml File in the Views/Shared Folder

```
@model Result
@{ Layout = null; }

<!DOCTYPE html>
<html>
<head>
    <meta name="viewport" content="width=device-width" />
    <title>Routing</title>
    <link rel="stylesheet" asp-href-include="lib/bootstrap/dist/css/*.min.css" />
</head>
<body class="m-1 p-1">
    <table class="table table-bordered table-striped table-sm">
        <tr><th>Controller:</th><td>@Model.Controller</td></tr>
        <tr><th>Action:</th><td>@Model.Action</td></tr>
        @foreach (string key in Model.Data.Keys) {
            <tr><th>@key :</th><td>@Model.Data[key]</td></tr>
        }
    </table>
    <a asp-controller="Home" asp-action="CustomVariable">This is an outgoing URL</a>
    <a asp-route="out">This is an outgoing URL</a>
</body>
</html>
```

The asp-route attribute can be used only when the asp-controller and asp-action attributes are absent, which means you can only select a specific route for the controller and action that caused the view to be rendered. If you run the example and request the /Home/CustomVariable URL, you will see the two different URLs that the routes generate.

```
<a href="/Home/CustomVariable">This is an outgoing URL</a>
<a href="/outbound">This is an outgoing URL</a>
```

THE CASE AGAINST NAMED ROUTES

The problem with relying on route names to generate outgoing URLs is that doing so breaks through the separation of concerns that is so central to the MVC design pattern. When generating a link or a URL in a view or action method, I want to focus on the action and controller that the user will be directed to, not the format of the URL that will be used. By bringing knowledge of the different routes into the views or controllers, I am creating dependencies that could be avoided. In my own projects, I tend to avoid naming my routes (by specifying null for the name argument) and prefer to use code comments to remind myself of what each route is intended to do.

Generating URLs (and Not Links)

The limitation of tag helpers is that they transform HTML elements and cannot be readily repurposed if you need to generate a URL for your application without the surrounding HTML.

MVC provides a helper class that can be used to create URLs directly, available through the Url.Action method, as shown in Listing 16-11.

Listing 16-11. Generating a URL in the Result.cshtml File in the Views/Shared Folder

```
@model Result
@{ Layout = null; }

<!DOCTYPE html>
<html>
<head>
    <meta name="viewport" content="width=device-width" />
    <title>Routing</title>
    <link rel="stylesheet" asp-href-include="lib/bootstrap/dist/css/*.min.css" />
</head>
<body class="m-1 p-1">
    <table class="table table-bordered table-striped table-sm">
        <tr><th>Controller:</th><td>@Model.Controller</td></tr>
        <tr><th>Action:</th><td>@Model.Action</td></tr>
        @foreach (string key in Model.Data.Keys) {
            <tr><th>@key :</th><td>@Model.Data[key]</td></tr>
        }
    </table>
    <p>URL: @Url.Action("CustomVariable", "Home", new { id = 100 })</p>
</body>
</html>
```

The arguments to the Url.Action method specify the action method, the controller, and the values for any segment variables. The result of the addition in Listing 16-11 generates the following output:

```
<p>URL: /Home/CustomVariable/100</p>
```

Generating URLs in Action Methods

The Url.Action method can also be used in action methods to create URLs in C# code. In Listing 16-12, I have modified one of the action methods of the Home controller to generate a URL using Url.Action.

Listing 16-12. Generating a URL in an Action Method in the HomeController.cs File in the Controllers Folder

```
using Microsoft.AspNetCore.Mvc;
using UrlsAndRoutes.Models;

namespace UrlsAndRoutes.Controllers {

    public class HomeController : Controller {
```

```
        public ViewResult Index() => View("Result",
            new Result {
                Controller = nameof(HomeController),
                Action = nameof(Index)
            });

        public ViewResult CustomVariable(string id) {
            Result r = new Result {
                Controller = nameof(HomeController),
                Action = nameof(CustomVariable),
            };
            r.Data["Id"] = id ?? "<no value>";
            r.Data["Url"] = Url.Action("CustomVariable", "Home", new { id = 100 });
            return View("Result", r);
        }
    }
}
```

If you run the example and request the /Home/CustomVariable URL, you will see that there is a row in the table that displays the URL, as shown in Figure 16-4.

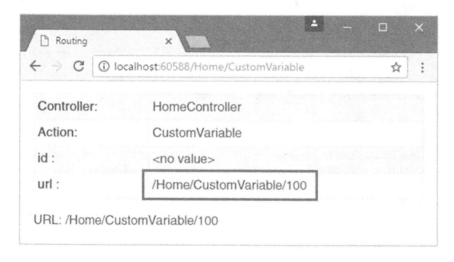

Figure 16-4. *Generating a URL in an action method*

Customizing the Routing System

You have seen how flexible and configurable the routing system is, but if it does not meet your requirements, you can customize the behavior. In this section, I will show you the different ways this can be done.

Changing the Routing System Configuration

In Chapter 15, I showed you how to configure the RouteOptions object in the Startup.cs file to set up a custom route constraint. The RouteOptions object is also used to configure some routing features, using the properties described in Table 16-3.

Table 16-3. *The RouteOptions Configuration Properties*

Name	Description
AppendTrailingSlash	When `true`, this `bool` property appends a trailing slash to the URLs generated by the routing system. The default value is `false`.
LowercaseUrls	When `true`, this `bool` property converts URLs to lowercase when the controller, action, or segment values contain uppercase characters. The default value is `false`.

In Listing 16-13, I have added statements to the `Startup.cs` file to set both of the configuration properties described in Table 16-3.

Listing 16-13. Configuring the Routing System in the Startup.cs File in the UrlsAndRoutes Folder

```csharp
using System;
using System.Collections.Generic;
using System.Linq;
using System.Threading.Tasks;
using Microsoft.AspNetCore.Builder;
using Microsoft.AspNetCore.Hosting;
using Microsoft.AspNetCore.Http;
using Microsoft.Extensions.DependencyInjection;
using Microsoft.AspNetCore.Routing.Constraints;
using Microsoft.AspNetCore.Routing;
using UrlsAndRoutes.Infrastructure;

namespace UrlsAndRoutes {
    public class Startup {

        public void ConfigureServices(IServiceCollection services) {
            services.Configure<RouteOptions>(options => {
                options.ConstraintMap.Add("weekday", typeof(WeekDayConstraint));
                options.LowercaseUrls = true;
                options.AppendTrailingSlash = true;
            });
            services.AddMvc();
        }

        public void Configure(IApplicationBuilder app, IHostingEnvironment env) {
            app.UseDeveloperExceptionPage();
            app.UseStatusCodePages();
            app.UseStaticFiles();
            app.UseMvc(routes => {

                routes.MapRoute(
                    name: "default",
                    template: "{controller=Home}/{action=Index}/{id?}");

                routes.MapRoute(
                    name: "out",
                    template: "outbound/{controller=Home}/{action=Index}");
            });
```

485

```
        }
    }
}
```

If you run the application and examine the URLs that are generated by the routing system, you will see that changing the configuration properties has made the URLs all lowercase and appended a trailing slash, as shown in Figure 16-5.

Figure 16-5. *Configuring the routing system*

Creating a Custom Route Class

If you don't like the way that the routing system matches URLs or you need to implement something specific for your application, you can create your own routing classes and use them to handle URLs. ASP. NET provides the Microsoft.AspNetCore.Routing.IRouter interface, which you can implement to create a custom route. Here is the definition of the IRouter interface:

```
using System.Threading.Tasks;

namespace Microsoft.AspNetCore.Routing {

    public interface IRouter {

        Task RouteAsync(RouteContext context);

        VirtualPathData GetVirtualPath(VirtualPathContext context);
    }
}
```

To create a custom route, you implement the RouteAsync method to handle incoming requests and implement the GetVirtualPath method if you want to generate outgoing URLs.

To demonstrate, I am going to create a custom routing class that will handle legacy URL requests. Imagine that I have migrated an existing application to MVC, but some users have bookmarked the pre-MVC URLs or hard-coded them into scripts. I still want to support those old URLs. I could handle this using the regular routing system, but this problem provides a nice example for this section.

Routing Incoming URLs

To understand how custom routes work, I am going to begin by creating one that handles every aspect of the request itself, without using a controller and view. I created a class file called LegacyRoute.cs in the Infrastructure folder and used it to implement the IRouter interface, as shown in Listing 16-14.

Listing 16-14. The Contents of the LegacyRoute.cs File in the Infrastructure Folder

```
using Microsoft.AspNetCore.Http;
using Microsoft.AspNetCore.Routing;
using System;
using System.Linq;
using System.Text;
using System.Threading.Tasks;

namespace UrlsAndRoutes.Infrastructure {
    public class LegacyRoute : IRouter {
        private string[] urls;

        public LegacyRoute(params string[] targetUrls) {
            this.urls = targetUrls;
        }

        public Task RouteAsync(RouteContext context) {

            string requestedUrl = context.HttpContext.Request.Path
                .Value.TrimEnd('/');

            if (urls.Contains(requestedUrl, StringComparer.OrdinalIgnoreCase)) {
                context.Handler = async ctx => {
                    HttpResponse response = ctx.Response;
                    byte[] bytes = Encoding.ASCII.GetBytes($"URL: {requestedUrl}");
                    await response.Body.WriteAsync(bytes, 0, bytes.Length);
                };
            }
            return Task.CompletedTask;
        }

        public VirtualPathData GetVirtualPath(VirtualPathContext context) {
            return null;
        }
    }
}
```

The LecagyRoute class implements the IRouter interface but only defines code for the RouteAsync method, which is used to handle incoming requests; I add support for outgoing URLs shortly.

There are only a few statements in the RouteAsync method, but they rely on a number of important ASP. NET types to do their work. The best place to start is with the method signature.

```
...
public async Task RouteAsync(RouteContext context) {
...
```

487

The RouteAsync method is responsible for assessing whether a request can be handled and, if it can, managing the process through to generating the response sent back to the client. This process is performed asynchronously, which is why the RouteAsync method returns a Task.

The RouteAsync method is invoked with a RouteContext argument, which provides access to everything that is known about the request and provides the features required to send the response back to the client. The RouteContext class is defined in the Microsoft.AspNetCore.Routing namespace and defines the three properties shown in Table 16-4.

Table 16-4. *The Properties Defined in by the RouteContext Class*

Name	Description
RouteData	This property returns a Microsoft.AspNetCore.Routing.RouteData object. When writing a custom route that relies on MVC features (as described in the next section), this object is used to define the controller, the action method, and the arguments that will be used to handle the request.
HttpContext	This property returns a Microsoft.AspNetCore.Http.HttpContext object, which provides access to details of the HTTP request and the means to produce the HTTP response.
Handler	This property is used to provide the routing system with a RequestDelegate that will handle the request. If the RouteAsync method doesn't set this property, then the routing system will continue working its way through the set of routes in the application configuration.

The routing system calls the RouteAsync method of each of the routes in the application and examines the value of the Handler property after each call. If the property has been set to a RequestDelegate, then the route has provided the routing system with a delegate that can handle the request and the delegate is invoked to generate the response. Here is the signature of the RequestDelegate, which is defined in the Microsoft.AspNetCore.Http namespace:

```
using System.Threading.Tasks;

namespace Microsoft.AspNetCore.Http {
    public delegate Task RequestDelegate(HttpContext context);
}
```

The delegate accepts an HttpContext object and returns a Task that will generate the response. If none of the routes sets the Handler property, then the routing system knows that the application cannot handle the request and will generate a 404 - Not Found response.

With this in mind, the implementation of the RouteAsync method has to establish whether it can handle the request, for which the HttpContext is usually required. In the example, I use the HttpContext.Request property, which returns a Microsoft.AspNetCore.Http.HttpRequest object that describes the request. The HttpRequest object provides access to all the information available about the request, including the headers, the body, and the details of where the request originated, but it is the Path property that I am interested in because it provides details of the URL requested by the client. The Path property returns a PathString object, which provides useful methods for composing and comparing URL paths, but I use the Value property because it gives me the entire path section of the URL as a string, which I can compare with the set of supported URLs that are received by the LegacyRoute constructor.

```
...
string requestedUrl = context.HttpContext.Request.Path.Value.TrimEnd('/');
if (urls.Contains(requestedUrl, StringComparer.OrdinalIgnoreCase)) {
...
```

I use the TrimEnd method on the URL to remove the trailing slash if there is one, which can be added either by the user or by the AppendTrailingSlash configuration option described in the "Changing the Routing System Configuration" section.

If the requested path is one that the LegacyRoute has been configured to support, then I set the Handler property using a lambda function that will generate the response, like this:

```
...
context.Handler = async ctx => {
    HttpResponse response = ctx.Response;
    byte[] bytes = Encoding.ASCII.GetBytes($"URL: {requestedUrl}");
    await response.Body.WriteAsync(bytes, 0, bytes.Length);
};
...
```

The HttpContext.Response property returns an HttpResponse object, which can be used to create the response to the client, providing access to the headers and content that will be sent to the client. I use the HttpResponse.Body.WriteAsync method to asynchronously write a simple ASCII string as the response. This isn't something you would do in a real project, but it allows me to produce a response without having to select and render views (although I show you how to get MVC to do this for you in the next section).

When the Handler property is set, then the routing system knows that its search for a route is complete and that it can invoke the delegate to generate the response to the client.

Applying a Custom Route Class

The MapRoute extension method that I have been using to create routes so far doesn't support the use of custom routing classes. To apply my LegacyRoute class, I have to take a different approach, as shown in Listing 16-15.

Listing 16-15. Applying a Custom Routing Class in the Startup.cs File in the UrlsAndRoutes Folder

```
using System;
using System.Collections.Generic;
using System.Linq;
using System.Threading.Tasks;
using Microsoft.AspNetCore.Builder;
using Microsoft.AspNetCore.Hosting;
using Microsoft.AspNetCore.Http;
using Microsoft.Extensions.DependencyInjection;
using Microsoft.AspNetCore.Routing.Constraints;
using Microsoft.AspNetCore.Routing;
using UrlsAndRoutes.Infrastructure;

namespace UrlsAndRoutes {
    public class Startup {

        public void ConfigureServices(IServiceCollection services) {
            services.Configure<RouteOptions>(options => {
                options.ConstraintMap.Add("weekday", typeof(WeekDayConstraint));
                options.LowercaseUrls = true;
                options.AppendTrailingSlash = true;
            });
```

```
        services.AddMvc();
    }

    public void Configure(IApplicationBuilder app, IHostingEnvironment env) {
        app.UseDeveloperExceptionPage();
        app.UseStatusCodePages();
        app.UseStaticFiles();
        app.UseMvc(routes => {
            routes.Routes.Add(new LegacyRoute(
                "/articles/Windows_3.1_Overview.html",
                "/old/.NET_1.0_Class_Library"));

            routes.MapRoute(
                name: "default",
                template: "{controller=Home}/{action=Index}/{id?}");

            routes.MapRoute(
                name: "out",
                template: "outbound/{controller=Home}/{action=Index}");
        });
    }
}
}
```

When using custom classes, you have to use the Add method on the route collection to register the IRouter implementation class. In the example, the arguments to the LegacyRoute constructor are the legacy URLs that I want the custom route to support. You can see the effect by starting the application and requesting /articles/Windows_3.1_Overview.html. The custom route displays the requested URL, as shown in Figure 16-6.

Figure 16-6. *Using a custom route*

Routing to MVC Controllers

There is a big gap between matching simple URL strings and using the MVC system of controllers, actions, and Razor views. Fortunately, you don't have to implement this functionality yourself when creating custom routes because the class that MVC uses behind the scenes can be used to do all the heavy lifting. To prepare for using the MVC infrastructure, I added a class file called LegacyController.cs in the Controllers folder and used it to define the controller shown in Listing 16-16.

Listing 16-16. The Contents of the LegacyController.cs File in the Controllers Folder

```
using Microsoft.AspNetCore.Mvc;

namespace UrlsAndRoutes.Controllers {

    public class LegacyController : Controller {

        public ViewResult GetLegacyUrl(string legacyUrl)
            => View((object)legacyUrl);
    }
}
```

In this controller, the GetLegacyUrl action method accepts a parameter that contains the legacy URL requested by the client. If I were implementing this controller in a real project, I would use this method to retrieve the files that were requested. But as it is, I am simply going to display the URL in a view.

■ **Tip**   Notice that I cast the argument to the View method in Listing 16-16 to object. One of the overloaded versions of the View method takes a string specifying the name of the view to render, and without the cast, this would be the overload that the C# compiler thinks I want. To avoid this, I cast to object so that I unambiguously call the overload that passes a view model and uses the default view. I could also have solved this by using the overload that takes both the view name and the view model, but I prefer not to make explicit associations between action methods and views if I can help it. See Chapter 17 for more details.

I created the Views/Legacy folder and added a view called GetLegacyUrl.cshtml, as shown in Listing 16-17. The view displays the model value, which will show the URL the client asked for.

Listing 16-17. The Contents of the GetLegacyUrl.cshtml File in the Views/Legacy Folder

```
@model string
@{ Layout = null; }

<!DOCTYPE html>
<html>
<head>
    <meta name="viewport" content="width=device-width" />
    <title>Routing</title>
    <link rel="stylesheet" asp-href-include="lib/bootstrap/dist/css/*.min.css" />
</head>
<body class="m-1 p-1">
    <h2>GetLegacyURL</h2>
    The URL requested was: @Model
</body>
</html>
```

In Listing 16-18, I have updated the LegacyRoute class so that URLs it handles are routed to the GetLegacyUrl action on the Legacy controller.

Listing 16-18. Routing to a Controller in the LegacyRoute.cs File

```csharp
using Microsoft.AspNetCore.Http;
using Microsoft.AspNetCore.Routing;
using System;
using System.Linq;
using System.Text;
using System.Threading.Tasks;
using Microsoft.AspNetCore.Mvc.Internal;
using Microsoft.Extensions.DependencyInjection;

namespace UrlsAndRoutes.Infrastructure {
    public class LegacyRoute : IRouter {
        private string[] urls;
        private IRouter mvcRoute;

        public LegacyRoute(IServiceProvider services, params string[] targetUrls) {
            this.urls = targetUrls;
            mvcRoute = services.GetRequiredService<MvcRouteHandler>();
        }

        public async Task RouteAsync(RouteContext context) {

            string requestedUrl = context.HttpContext.Request.Path
                .Value.TrimEnd('/');

            if (urls.Contains(requestedUrl, StringComparer.OrdinalIgnoreCase)) {
                context.RouteData.Values["controller"] = "Legacy";
                context.RouteData.Values["action"] = "GetLegacyUrl";
                context.RouteData.Values["legacyUrl"] = requestedUrl;
                await mvcRoute.RouteAsync(context);
            }
        }

        public VirtualPathData GetVirtualPath(VirtualPathContext context) {
            return null;
        }
    }
}
```

The Microsoft.AspNetCore.Mvc.Internal.MvcRouteHandler class provides the mechanism by which the controller and action segment variables are used to locate a controller class, execute the action method, and return the result to the client. This class has been written so that it can be called by a custom IRouter implementation that provides the controller and action values, as well as any other values that are required, such as for action method arguments.

In Listing 16-18, I create a new instance of the MvcRouteHandler class, to which the task of locating a controller class is delegated. To do this, I need to provide routing data, as follows:

```csharp
...
context.RouteData.Values["controller"] = "Legacy";
context.RouteData.Values["action"] = "GetLegacyUrl";
context.RouteData.Values["legacyUrl"] = requestedUrl;
...
```

The RouteContext.RouteData.Vales property returns a dictionary that is used to provide data values to the MvcRouteHandler class. In the default routing system, the data values are created by applying the URL pattern to the request, but in my custom route class, I have hard-coded the values so that the GetLegacyUrl action on the Legacy controller is always targeted. The only thing that changes between requests is the legacyUrl data value, which is set to the request URL and which will be used as the argument of the same name received by the action method.

The final change in Listing 16-18 delegates the responsibility of finding and using the controller class to handle the request.

```
...
await mvcRoute.RouteAsync(context);
...
```

The RouteContext object, which now contains the controller, action, and legacyUrl values, is passed to the RouteAsync method of the MvcRouteHandler object, which takes responsibility for any further processing of the request, including setting the Handler property. The result is that the LegacyRoute class can focus on deciding which URLs it will handle without getting bogged down in the detail of working with controllers directly.

The MvcRouteHandler object that is doing the work in this example has to be requested as a service, which I explain in Chapter 18. To provide the LegacyRoute constructor with the IServiceProvider object it needs to create the MvcRouteHandler, I have updated the statement that defines the route to provide it with access to the application's services in the Startup class, as shown in Listing 16-19.

Listing 16-19. Providing Access to Services in the Startup Class in the UrlsAndRoutes Folder

```
using System;
using System.Collections.Generic;
using System.Linq;
using System.Threading.Tasks;
using Microsoft.AspNetCore.Builder;
using Microsoft.AspNetCore.Hosting;
using Microsoft.AspNetCore.Http;
using Microsoft.Extensions.DependencyInjection;
using Microsoft.AspNetCore.Routing.Constraints;
using Microsoft.AspNetCore.Routing;
using UrlsAndRoutes.Infrastructure;

namespace UrlsAndRoutes {
    public class Startup {

        public void ConfigureServices(IServiceCollection services) {
            services.Configure<RouteOptions>(options => {
                options.ConstraintMap.Add("weekday", typeof(WeekDayConstraint));
                options.LowercaseUrls = true;
                options.AppendTrailingSlash = true;
            });
            services.AddMvc();
        }

        public void Configure(IApplicationBuilder app, IHostingEnvironment env) {
            app.UseDeveloperExceptionPage();
            app.UseStatusCodePages();
```

```
        app.UseStaticFiles();
        app.UseMvc(routes => {
            routes.Routes.Add(new LegacyRoute(
                app.ApplicationServices,
                "/articles/Windows_3.1_Overview.html",
                "/old/.NET_1.0_Class_Library"));

            routes.MapRoute(
                name: "default",
                template: "{controller=Home}/{action=Index}/{id?}");

            routes.MapRoute(
                name: "out",
                template: "outbound/{controller=Home}/{action=Index}");
        });
    }
  }
}
```

If you start the application and request /articles/Windows_3.1_Overview.html again, you will see that the simple text response is now replaced with the output from the view, as shown in Figure 16-7.

Figure 16-7. *Delegating dealing with controllers and actions*

Generating Outgoing URLs

To support outgoing URL generation, I need to implement the GetVirtualPath method in the LegacyRoute class, as shown in Listing 16-20.

Listing 16-20. Generating Outgoing URLs in the LegacyRoute.cs File in the Infrastructure Folder

```
using Microsoft.AspNetCore.Http;
using Microsoft.AspNetCore.Routing;
using System;
using System.Linq;
using System.Text;
using System.Threading.Tasks;
using Microsoft.AspNetCore.Mvc.Internal;
using Microsoft.Extensions.DependencyInjection;
```

```
namespace UrlsAndRoutes.Infrastructure {
    public class LegacyRoute : IRouter {
        private string[] urls;
        private IRouter mvcRoute;

        public LegacyRoute(IServiceProvider services, params string[] targetUrls) {
            this.urls = targetUrls;
            mvcRoute = services.GetRequiredService<MvcRouteHandler>();
        }

        public async Task RouteAsync(RouteContext context) {

            string requestedUrl = context.HttpContext.Request.Path
                .Value.TrimEnd('/');

            if (urls.Contains(requestedUrl, StringComparer.OrdinalIgnoreCase)) {
                context.RouteData.Values["controller"] = "Legacy";
                context.RouteData.Values["action"] = "GetLegacyUrl";
                context.RouteData.Values["legacyUrl"] = requestedUrl;
                await mvcRoute.RouteAsync(context);
            }
        }

        public VirtualPathData GetVirtualPath(VirtualPathContext context) {
            if (context.Values.ContainsKey("legacyUrl")) {
                string url = context.Values["legacyUrl"] as string;
                if (urls.Contains(url)) {
                    return new VirtualPathData(this, url);
                }
            }
            return null;
        }
    }
}
```

The routing system calls the GetVirtualPath method of each route that has been defined in the Startup class, giving each a chance to generate the outgoing URL that the application requires. The argument to the GetVirtualPath method is a VirtualPathContext object, which provides information about the URL that is needed. Table 16-5 describes the properties of the VirtualPathContext class.

Table 16-5. *The Properties Defined in by the VirtualPath Context Class*

Name	Description
RouteName	This property returns the name of the route.
Values	This property returns a dictionary of all the values that can be used for segment variables, indexed by name.
AmbientValues	This property returns a dictionary of the values that are helpful for generating the URL but that will not be incorporated into the result. This dictionary is usually empty when you implement your own routing class.
HttpContext	This property returns an HttpContext object that provides information about the request and the response that is being prepared for it.

In the example, I use the Values property to get a value called legacyUrl, and if it matches one of the URLs the route has been configured to support, I return a VirtualPathData object, which provides the routing system with details of the URL. The constructor arguments for the VirtualPathData class are the IRouter that generates the URL and the URL itself.

```
...
return new VirtualPathData(this, url);
...
```

In Listing 16-21, I have changed the Result.cshtml view to require outgoing URLs that target the custom view.

Listing 16-21. Generating Outgoing URLs in the Result.cshtml File in the Views/Shared Folder

```
@model Result
@{ Layout = null; }

<!DOCTYPE html>
<html>
<head>
    <meta name="viewport" content="width=device-width" />
    <title>Routing</title>
    <link rel="stylesheet" asp-href-include="lib/bootstrap/dist/css/*.min.css" />
</head>
<body class="m-1 p-1">
    <table class="table table-bordered table-striped table-sm">
        <tr><th>Controller:</th><td>@Model.Controller</td></tr>
        <tr><th>Action:</th><td>@Model.Action</td></tr>
        @foreach (string key in Model.Data.Keys) {
            <tr><th>@key :</th><td>@Model.Data[key]</td></tr>
        }
    </table>
    <a asp-route-legacyurl="/articles/Windows_3.1_Overview.html"
       class="btn btn-primary">
       This is an outgoing URL
    </a>
    <p>
        URL: @Url.Action(null, null,
            new { legacyurl = "/articles/Windows_3.1_Overview.html" })
    </p>
</body>
</html>
```

In this example, I don't need to specify the controller and action for the outgoing route for the tag helper because they are not used in the URL generation. With that in mind, I have omitted the asp-controller and asp-action tag helper attributes from the a element. When generating just the URL, I set the first two arguments for the Url.Action helper to null for the same reason.

If you run the application and examine the HTML in the response for the default URL, you will see that the custom route class has been used to create the URLs, like this:

```
<a class="btn btn-primary" href="/articles/windows_3.1_overview.html/">
    This is an outgoing URL
</a>
<p>URL: /articles/windows_3.1_overview.html/</p>
```

The trailing slashes that are appended to the URLs are the result of setting the AppendTrailingSlash configuration option to true in the Startup.cs file, and it is important that the incoming route matching is able to match URLs to which the slash character has been added.

■ **Tip**   If the URL that you see in the HTML response has a different format, such as /?legacyurl=%2Fart icles%2FWindows_3.1_Overview.html, then your custom route has not been used to generate the URL, and one of the other routes in the application has been called upon instead. Since there is no controller or action specified, the Index action on the Home controller will be targeted, and the legacyUrl value is added to the URL query string. If this happens, ensure that you have remembered to set the IsBound property to true in the GetVirtualPath method and check that the configuration in the Startup.cs file specifies the correct URLs for the LegacyRoute constructor and that the custom route is defined before any other routes.

Working with Areas

ASP.NET Core MVC supports organizing a web application into *areas*, where each area represents a functional segment of the application, such as administration, billing, customer support, and so on. This is useful in a large project, where having a single set of folders for all of the controllers, views, and models can become difficult to manage.

Each MVC area has its own folder structure, allowing you to keep everything separate. This makes it more obvious which project elements relate to each functional area of the application, helping multiple developers to work on the project without colliding with one another. Areas are supported largely by the routing system, which is why I have described this feature alongside URLs and routes. In this section, I will show you how to set up and use areas in your MVC projects.

Creating an Area

Creating an area requires adding folders to the project. The top-level folder is called Areas and within it is a folder for each of the areas that you require, each of which contains its own Controllers, Views, and Models folders. For this chapter, I am going to create an area called Admin, which means creating the set of folders described in Table 16-6. To prepare the example project, create all the folders shown in the table.

Table 16-6. *Folders Required to Prepare for Areas*

Name	Description
Areas	This folder will contain all the areas in the MVC application.
Areas/Admin	This folder will contain the classes and views for the Admin area.
Areas/Admin/Controllers	This folder will contain the controllers for the Admin area.
Areas/Admin/Views	This folder will contain the views for the Admin area.
Areas/Admin/Views/Home	The folder will contain the views for the Home controller in the Admin area.
Areas/Admin/Models	This folder will contain the models for the Admin area.

Although each area is used separately, many MVC features rely on standard C# or .NET features such as namespaces. To make an area easier to use, the first addition that I made is a view imports file, which allows me to use the models in an area in views without having to include namespaces and to take advantage of tag helpers. I created a view imports file called _ViewImports.cshtml in the Areas/Admin/Views folder and added the statements shown in Listing 16-22.

Listing 16-22. The Contents of the _ViewImports.cshtml File in the Areas/Admin/Views Folder

```
@using UrlsAndRoutes.Areas.Admin.Models
@addTagHelper *, Microsoft.AspNetCore.Mvc.TagHelpers
```

Creating an Area Route

To take advantage of areas, you must add a route to the Startup.cs file that includes an area segment variable, as shown in Listing 16-23.

Listing 16-23. Adding a Route for Areas in the Startup.cs File in the UrlsAndRoutes Folder

```
using System;
using System.Collections.Generic;
using System.Linq;
using System.Threading.Tasks;
using Microsoft.AspNetCore.Builder;
using Microsoft.AspNetCore.Hosting;
using Microsoft.AspNetCore.Http;
using Microsoft.Extensions.DependencyInjection;
using Microsoft.AspNetCore.Routing.Constraints;
using Microsoft.AspNetCore.Routing;
using UrlsAndRoutes.Infrastructure;

namespace UrlsAndRoutes {
    public class Startup {

        public void ConfigureServices(IServiceCollection services) {
            services.Configure<RouteOptions>(options => {
                options.ConstraintMap.Add("weekday", typeof(WeekDayConstraint));
                options.LowercaseUrls = true;
                options.AppendTrailingSlash = true;
            });
```

```
        services.AddMvc();
    }

    public void Configure(IApplicationBuilder app, IHostingEnvironment env) {
        app.UseDeveloperExceptionPage();
        app.UseStatusCodePages();
        app.UseStaticFiles();
        app.UseMvc(routes => {
            routes.MapRoute(
                name: "areas",
                template: "{area:exists}/{controller=Home}/{action=Index}");

            routes.Routes.Add(new LegacyRoute(
                app.ApplicationServices,
                "/articles/Windows_3.1_Overview.html",
                "/old/.NET_1.0_Class_Library"));

            routes.MapRoute(
                name: "default",
                template: "{controller=Home}/{action=Index}/{id?}");

            routes.MapRoute(
                name: "out",
                template: "outbound/{controller=Home}/{action=Index}");
        });
    }
}
```

The area segment variable is used to match URLs that target controllers in specific areas. I have followed the standard URL pattern in the listing, but you can add the area segment to any pattern you require. The route that adds support for areas should appear before less specific routes to ensure that URLs are correctly matched. The exists constraint is used to ensure that requests are matched only to areas that have been defined in the application.

Populating an Area

You can create controllers, views, and models in an area just as you would in the main part of an MVC application. To create a model, I right-clicked the Areas/Admin/Models folder, selected Add ➤ Class from the pop-up menu, and created a class file called Person.cs, the contents of which are shown in Listing 16-24.

Listing 16-24. The Contents of the Person.cs File in the Areas/Admin/Models Folder

```
namespace UrlsAndRoutes.Areas.Admin.Models {
    public class Person {
        public string Name { get; set; }
        public string City { get; set; }
    }
}
```

To create a controller, I right-clicked the Areas/Admin/Controllers folder, selected Add ➤ Class from the pop-up menu, and created a class file called HomeController.cs, which I used to define the controller shown in Listing 16-25.

Listing 16-25. The Contents of the HomeController.cs File in the Areas/Admin/Controllers Folder

```
using Microsoft.AspNetCore.Mvc;
using UrlsAndRoutes.Areas.Admin.Models;

namespace UrlsAndRoutes.Areas.Admin.Controllers {

    [Area("Admin")]
    public class HomeController : Controller {
        private Person[] data = new Person[] {
            new Person { Name = "Alice", City = "London" },
            new Person { Name = "Bob", City = "Paris" },
            new Person { Name = "Joe", City = "New York" }
        };

        public ViewResult Index() => View(data);

    }
}
```

The new controller is entirely standard, except in one regard. To associate a controller with an area, the Area attribute must be applied to the class.

```
...
[Area("Admin")]
public class HomeController : Controller {
...
```

Without the Area attribute, controllers are not part of an area even if they are defined in the main part of the application. Omitting the Area attribute can cause odd results. This is the first thing to check if you are not getting the results you expect when working with areas.

■ **Tip** If you are using attributes to set up routes, as described in Chapter 15, then you can use the [area] token in the argument for the Route attribute to refer to the area specified by the Area attribute: [Route("[area]/app/[controller]/actions/[action]/{id:weekday?}")].

The final item I added was a Razor view called Index.cshtml in the Areas/Admin/Views/Home folder. I used this file to define the view shown in Listing 16-26.

Listing 16-26. The Contents of the Index.cshtml File in the Areas/Admin/Views/Home Folder

```
@model Person[]
@{ Layout = null; }

<!DOCTYPE html>
<html>
```

```
<head>
    <meta name="viewport" content="width=device-width" />
    <title>Areas</title>
    <link rel="stylesheet" asp-href-include="lib/bootstrap/dist/css/*.min.css" />
</head>
<body class="m-1 p-1">
    <table class="table table-bordered table-striped table-sm">
        <tr><th>Name</th><th>City</th></tr>
        @foreach (Person p in Model) {
            <tr><td>@p.Name</td><td>@p.City</td></tr>
        }
    </table>
</body>
</html>
```

The model for this view is an array of Person objects. I am able to refer to the Person type without needing a namespace because of the view imports file that I created in Listing 16-26. Run the application and request the /Admin URL to test the area, which will produce the result shown in Figure 16-8.

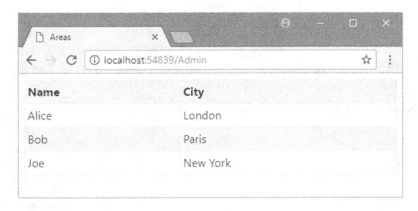

Figure 16-8. *Using an area*

UNDERSTANDING THE EFFECT OF AN AREA ON AN MVC APPLICATION

It is important to understand the effect that areas have on the rest of the application. I created an area called Admin, but there is also an Admin controller in the main part of the application. Before the area was created, a request for /Admin would target the Index action on the Admin controller in the main part of the application; now it will target the Index action on the Home controller in the Admin area (the area root provides default values for the controller and action segment variables). This kind of change can cause unexpected behavior, and the best way to use areas is to incorporate their use into the initial controller naming scheme for the project. If you do have to go back and add areas to an established application, then you must consider the effect on your routes carefully.

Generating Links to Actions in Areas

You do not need to take any special steps to create links that refer to actions in the same MVC area that the current request relates to. MVC detects that a request relates to a particular area and ensures that outbound URL generation will find a match only among routes defined for that area. As an example, Listing 16-27 shows the addition of an a element to the Index.cshtml file in the Areas/Admin/Views/Home folder.

Listing 16-27. Adding an Anchor in the Index.cshtml File in the Areas/Admin/Views/Home Folder

```
@model Person[]
@{ Layout = null; }

<!DOCTYPE html>
<html>
<head>
    <meta name="viewport" content="width=device-width" />
    <title>Areas</title>
    <link rel="stylesheet" asp-href-include="lib/bootstrap/dist/css/*.min.css" />
</head>
<body class="m-1 p-1">
    <table class="table table-bordered table-striped table-sm">
        <tr><th>Name</th><th>City</th></tr>
        @foreach (Person p in Model) {
            <tr><td>@p.Name</td><td>@p.City</td></tr>
        }
    </table>
    <a asp-action="Index" asp-controller="Home">Link</a>
</body>
</html>
```

If you run the application and request the /admin URL, you will see that the response contains the following element:

```
<a href="/admin/">Link</a>
```

The routing system has selected the area route to generate the outgoing link and taken into account the default values that are available for the controller and action segment variables.

You must provide the routing system with a value for the area segment in order to create a link to an action in a *different* area or the main part of the application, as shown in Listing 16-28.

Listing 16-28. Targetting a Different Area in the Index.cshtml File in the Areas/Admin/Views/Home Folder

```
@model Person[]
@{ Layout = null; }

<!DOCTYPE html>
<html>
<head>
    <meta name="viewport" content="width=device-width" />
    <title>Areas</title>
    <link rel="stylesheet" asp-href-include="lib/bootstrap/dist/css/*.min.css" />
```

```
</head>
<body class="m-1 p-1">
    <table class="table table-bordered table-striped table-sm">
        <tr><th>Name</th><th>City</th></tr>
        @foreach (Person p in Model) {
            <tr><td>@p.Name</td><td>@p.City</td></tr>
        }
    </table>
    <a asp-action="Index" asp-controller="Home">Link</a>
    <a asp-action="Index" asp-controller="Home" asp-route-area="">Link</a>
</body>
</html>
```

The `asp-route-area` attribute sets the value for the area segment variable. In this case, the attribute is set to the empty string, which specifies the main part of the application and produces the following HTML element:

```
<a href="/">Link</a>
```

If you have multiple areas in your controllers and want to route to them, then use the area name in place of the empty string.

URL Schema Best Practices

After all of this, you may be left wondering where to start in designing your own URL schema. You could just accept the default schema, but there are benefits in giving your schema some thought. In recent years, the design of an application's URLs has been taken increasingly seriously, and a few important design principles have emerged. If you follow these design patterns, you will improve the usability, compatibility, and search-engine rankings of your applications.

Making Your URLs Clean and Human-Friendly

Users notice the URLs in your applications. Just think back to the last time you tried to send someone an Amazon URL. Here is the URL for an earlier edition of this book:

```
https://www.amazon.com/Pro-ASP-NET-Core-ADAM-FREEMAN/dp/1484203984
```

It is bad enough sending someone such a URL by e-mail but try reading this over the phone. When I needed to do this recently, I ended up quoting the ISBN number and asking the caller to look it up for himself. It would be nice if I could access the book with a URL like this:

```
http://www.amazon.com/books/pro-aspnet-mvc6-framework
```

That is the kind of URL that I *could* read over the phone and it doesn't look like I dropped something on the keyboard while composing an e-mail message.

> **■ Note** To be clear, I have only the highest respect for Amazon, which sells more of my books than everyone else combined. I know for a fact that each and every member of the Amazon team is a strikingly intelligent and beautiful person. Not one of them would be so petty as to stop selling my books over something so minor as criticism of their URL format. I love Amazon. I adore Amazon. I just wish they would fix their URLs.

Here are some simple guidelines to make friendly URLs:

- Design URLs to describe their content, not the implementation details of your application. Use `/Articles/AnnualReport` rather than `/Website_v2/CachedContentServer/FromCache/AnnualReport`.

- Prefer content titles over ID numbers. Use `/Articles/AnnualReport` rather than `/Articles/2392`. If you must use an ID number (to distinguish items with identical titles or to avoid the extra database query needed to find an item by its title), then use both (`/Articles/2392/AnnualReport`). It takes longer to type, but it makes more sense to a human and improves search-engine rankings. Your application can just ignore the title and display the item matching that ID.

- Do *not* use file name extensions for HTML pages (for example, `.aspx` or `.mvc`), but *do* use them for specialized file types (such as `.jpg`, `.pdf`, and `.zip`). Web browsers do not care about file name extensions if you set the MIME type appropriately, but humans still expect PDF files to end with `.pdf`.

- Create a sense of hierarchy (for example, `/Products/Menswear/Shirts/Red`) so your visitor can guess the parent category's URL.

- Be case-insensitive. (Someone might want to type in the URL from a printed page). The ASP.NET Core routing system is case-insensitive by default.

- Avoid symbols, codes, and character sequences. If you want a word separator, use a dash (as in `/my-great-article`). Underscores are unfriendly, and URL-encoded spaces are bizarre (`/my+great+article`) or disgusting (`/my%20great%20article`).

- Do not change URLs. Broken links equal lost business. When you do change URLs, continue to support the old URL schema for as long as possible via redirections.

- Be consistent. Adopt one URL format across your entire application.

URLs should be short, easy to type, hackable (human-editable), and persistent, and they should visualize site structure. Jakob Nielsen, the usability guru, expands on this topic at `www.useit.com/alertbox/990321.html`. Tim Berners-Lee, the inventor of the Web, offers similar advice (see `www.w3.org/Provider/Style/URI`).

GET and POST: Picking the Right One

The rule of thumb is that GET requests should be used for all read-only information retrieval, while POST requests should be used for any operation that changes the application state. In standards-compliance terms, GET requests are for *safe* interactions (having no side effects besides information retrieval), and POST requests are for *unsafe* interactions (making a decision or changing something). These conventions are set by the World Wide Web Consortium (W3C), at `www.w3.org/Protocols/rfc2616/rfc2616-sec9.html`.

GET requests are *addressable*: all the information is contained in the URL, so it's possible to bookmark and link to these addresses.

Do not use GET requests for operations that change state. Many web developers learned this the hard way in 2005 when Google Web Accelerator was released to the public. This application prefetched all the content linked from each page, which is legal within the HTTP because GET requests should be safe. Unfortunately, many web developers had ignored the HTTP conventions and placed simple links to "delete item" or "add to shopping cart" in their applications. Chaos ensued.

One company believed its content management system was the target of repeated hostile attacks because all their content kept getting deleted. The company later discovered that a search-engine crawler had hit upon the URL of an administrative page and was crawling all the delete links. Authentication might protect you from this, but it wouldn't protect you from web accelerators.

Summary

In this chapter, I showed you the advanced features of the routing system, showing you how to generate outgoing links and URLs and how to customize the routing system. Along the way, I introduced the concept of areas and set out my views on how to create a useful and meaningful URL schema. In the next chapter, I turn to controllers and actions, which are the heart of ASP.NET Core MVC. I explain how these work in detail and show you how to use them to get the best results in your application.

CHAPTER 17

Controllers and Actions

Every request that comes to your application is handled by a controller. In ASP.NET Core MVC, controllers are .NET classes that contain the logic required to handle a request. In Chapter 3, I explained that the role of the controller is to encapsulate your application logic. This means controllers are responsible for processing incoming requests, performing operations on the domain model, and selecting views to render to the user.

The controller is free to handle the request any way it sees fit as long as it doesn't stray into the areas of responsibility that belong to the model and view. This means controllers do not contain or store data, nor do they generate user interfaces.

In this chapter, I show you how controllers are implemented and the different ways that you can use controllers to receive and generate output. Table 17-1 puts controllers in context.

Table 17-1. *Putting Controllers in Context*

Question	Answer
What are they?	Controllers contain the logic for receiving requests, updating the application state or model, and selecting the response that will be sent to the client.
Why are they useful?	Controllers are the heart of MVC projects and contain the domain logic for a web application.
How are they used?	Controllers are C# classes whose public methods are invoked to handle an HTTP request. Methods can take responsibility for producing the response to the client directly, but a more common approach is to return an action result, which tells MVC how the response should be prepared.
Are there any pitfalls or limitations?	When you are new to MVC development, it can be easy to create controllers that contain functionality that is better suited to the model or in views. A more specific issue is that any public class whose name ends with `Controller` is assumed to be a controller by MVC; this means it is possible to accidentally handle HTTP requests in classes that are not intended to be controllers.
Are there any alternatives?	No, controllers are a core part of MVC applications.

© Adam Freeman 2017
A. Freeman, *Pro ASP.NET Core MVC 2*, https://doi.org/10.1007/978-1-4842-3150-0_17

Table 17-2 summarizes the chapter.

Table 17-2. *Chapter Summary*

Problem	Solution	Listing
Define a controller	Create a public class whose name ends with `Controller` or derive from the `Controller` class	7–9
Get details of the HTTP request	Use the context objects or define action methods parameters	10–13
Produce a result from an action method	Work directly with the result context object or create an action result object	14–16
Produce an HTML result	Create a view result	17–24
Redirect the client	Create a redirection result	25–30
Return content to the client	Create a content result	31–35
Return an HTTP status code	Create an HTTP result	36–37

Preparing the Example Project

For this chapter, I used the ASP.NET Core Web Application (.NET Core) template to create a new Empty project called ControllersAndActions. In Listing 17-1, I added statements to the `Startup` class to enable the MVC framework and enable other middleware components.

■ **Note** This chapter includes unit tests for key features. For brevity, I have not included the unit test project in the instructions for creating the example project. You can create the test project by following the process described in Chapter 7 or download the project from this book's GitHub repository (`https://github.com/apress/pro-asp.net-core-mvc-2`).

Listing 17-1. Adding MVC and Other Middleware in the Startup.cs File the ControllersAndActions Folder

```
using System;
using System.Collections.Generic;
using System.Linq;
using System.Threading.Tasks;
using Microsoft.AspNetCore.Builder;
using Microsoft.AspNetCore.Hosting;
using Microsoft.AspNetCore.Http;
using Microsoft.Extensions.DependencyInjection;

namespace ControllersAndActions {
    public class Startup {
```

```
    public void ConfigureServices(IServiceCollection services) {
        services.AddMvc();
        services.AddMemoryCache();
        services.AddSession();
    }

    public void Configure(IApplicationBuilder app, IHostingEnvironment env) {
        app.UseStatusCodePages();
        app.UseDeveloperExceptionPage();
        app.UseStaticFiles();
        app.UseSession();
        app.UseMvcWithDefaultRoute();
    }
  }
}
```

The AddMemoryCache and AddSession methods create services that are required for session management. The UseSession method adds a middleware component to the pipeline that associates session data with requests and adds cookies to responses to ensure that future requests can be identified. The UseSession method must be called before the UseMvc method so that the session component can intercept requests before they reach MVC middleware and can modify responses after they have been generated. The other methods set up the standard packages that I described in Chapter 14.

Preparing the Views

The focus of this chapter is controllers and their action methods, and I will be defining controller classes throughout the chapter. To prepare for this, I will define some views that will help me demonstrate how they work. The views I create in this section are defined in the Views/Shared folder so that I can use them from any of the controllers that I create later in the chapter. I created the Views/Shared folder, added to it a Razor view file called Result.cshtml, and applied the markup shown in Listing 17-2.

Listing 17-2. The Contents of the Result.cshtml File in the Views/Shared Folder

```
@model string
@{ Layout = null; }

<!DOCTYPE html>
<html>
<head>
    <meta name="viewport" content="width=device-width" />
    <title>Controllers and Actions</title>
    <link rel="stylesheet" asp-href-include="lib/bootstrap/dist/css/*.min.css" />
</head>
<body class="m-1 p-1">
    Model Data: @Model
</body>
</html>
```

The model for this view is a `string`, which will allow me to display simple messages. Next, I created a file called `DictionaryResult.cshtml`, also in the `Views/Shared` folder, and added the markup shown in Listing 17-3. This model for this view is a dictionary, which displays more complex data than the previous view.

Listing 17-3. The Contents of the DictionaryResult.cshtml File in the Views/Shared Folder

```
@model IDictionary<string, string>
@{ Layout = null; }

<!DOCTYPE html>
<html>
<head>
    <meta name="viewport" content="width=device-width" />
    <title>Controllers and Actions</title>
    <link rel="stylesheet" asp-href-include="lib/bootstrap/dist/css/*.min.css" />
</head>
<body class="m-1 p-1">
    <table class="table table-bordered table-sm table-striped">
        <tr><th>Name</th><th>Value</th></tr>
        @foreach (string key in Model.Keys) {
            <tr><td>@key</td><td>@Model[key]</td></tr>
        }
    </table>
</body>
</html>
```

Next, I created a file called `SimpleForm.cshtml`, also in the `Views/Shared` folder, and used it to define the view shown in Listing 17-4. As its name suggests, this view contains a simple HTML form that will collect data from the user.

Listing 17-4. The Contents of the SimpleForm.cshtml File in the Views/Shared Folder

```
@{ Layout = null; }

<!DOCTYPE html>
<html>
<head>
    <meta name="viewport" content="width=device-width" />
    <title>Controllers and Actions</title>
    <link rel="stylesheet" asp-href-include="lib/bootstrap/dist/css/*.min.css" />
</head>
<body class="m-1 p-1">
    <form method="post" asp-action="ReceiveForm">
        <div class="form-group">
            <label for="name">Name:</label>
            <input class="form-control" name="name" />
        </div>
```

```
        <div class="form-group">
            <label for="name">City:</label>
            <input class="form-control" name="city" />
        </div>
        <button class="btn btn-primary center-block" type="submit">Submit</button>
    </form>
</body>
</html>
```

The views use built-in tag helpers to generate URLs from the routing system. To enable the tag helpers, I created a view imports file called _ViewImports.cshtml in the Views folder and added the expression shown in Listing 17-5.

Listing 17-5. The Contents of the _ViewImports.cshtml File in the Views Folder

```
@addTagHelper *, Microsoft.AspNetCore.Mvc.TagHelpers
```

The views I created in the Views/Shared folder all depend on the Bootstrap CSS package. To add Bootstrap to the project, I used the Bower Configuration File template to create the bower.json file and added the package shown in Listing 17-6.

Listing 17-6. Adding a Package in the bower.json File in the ControllersAndActions Folder

```
{
  "name": "asp.net",
  "private": true,
  "dependencies": {
    "bootstrap": "4.0.0-alpha.6"
  }
}
```

Understanding Controllers

Controllers are C# classes whose public methods (known as *actions* or *action methods*) are responsible for handling an HTTP request and preparing the response that will be returned to the client. MVC uses the routing system, described in Chapters 15 and 16, to work out which controller class and action method it needs to handle a request. MVC creates a new instance of the controller class, invokes the action method, and uses the method's result to produce the response to the client.

MVC provides action methods with *context data* so they can figure out how to handle a request. There is a wide range of context data available, and it describes everything about the current request, the response that is being prepared, the data extracted by the routing system, and details of the user's identity.

When MVC invokes an action method, the method's response describes the response that should be sent to the client. The most common kind of response is created by rendering a Razor view, so the action method uses its response to tell MVC which view to use and what view model data it should be provided with. But there are other kinds of responses available as well, and action methods can do everything from asking MVC to send an HTTP redirection to the client to sending complex data objects.

This means that there are three areas of functionality that are important to understanding controllers. The first is understanding how to define controllers so that MVC can use them to handle requests. Controllers are just C# classes, but there are different ways to create them, and understanding the differences is important. I explain how to controllers are defined in the "Creating Controllers" section.

Second, it is important to understand how MVC provides action methods with context data. Getting the context data that you need is important for effective web application development, but MVC makes it easy by defining a set of classes that are used to describe everything that an action method requires. I explain how MVC describes requests and responses in the "Receiving Context Data" section.

Finally, it is important to understand how action methods produce a response. Action methods rarely need to produce an HTTP response themselves, and you need to know how to instruct MVC to produce the responses you need, which I explain in the "Producing a Response" section.

Creating Controllers

You have seen the use of controllers in almost all the chapters so far. Now it is time to take a step back and look behind the scenes to see how they are defined. In the sections that follow, I describe the different ways that controllers can be created and explain the differences between them.

Creating POCO Controllers

MVC favors convention over configuration, which means the controllers in an MVC application are discovered automatically, rather than being defined in a configuration file. The basic discovery process is simple: any `public` class whose name ends with `Controller` is a controller, and any `public` method it defines is an action. To demonstrate how this works, I added a `Controllers` folder to the project and added to it a class file called `PocoController.cs`, which I used to define the class shown in Listing 17-7.

■ **Tip** Although the convention is to put controllers in the `Controllers` folder, you can put them anywhere in the project and MVC will still find them.

Listing 17-7. The Contents of the PocoController.cs File in the Controllers Folder

```
namespace ControllersAndActions.Controllers {

    public class PocoController {

        public string Index() => "This is a POCO controller";
    }
}
```

The `PocoController` class meets the simple criteria that MVC looks for in a controller. It defines a `public` method called `Index`, which will be used as an action method and which returns a `string`.

The `PocoController` class is an example of a *POCO controller*, where POCO means "plain old CLR object" and refers to the fact the controller is implemented using standard .NET features without any direct dependency on the API provided by the ASP.NET Core MVC.

To test the POCO controller, start the application and request the URL /Poco/Index. The routing system will match the request using the default URL pattern and direct the request to the Index method of the PocoController class, producing the results shown in Figure 17-1.

Figure 17-1. *Using a POCO controller*

USING ATTRIBUTES TO ADJUST CONTROLLER IDENTIFICATION

The support for POCO controllers doesn't always work the way you want. A common problem is that MVC will identify fake classes created for unit testing as controllers. The simplest way to avoid this problem is to pay attention to the names of your classes and avoid names like FakeController. If that isn't possible, then you can apply the NonController attribute, defined in the Microsoft.AspNetCore. Mvc namespace, to a class to tell MVC that it is not a controller. There is also a NonAction attribute that can be applied to methods to stop them from being used as action methods.

In some projects, you might not be able to follow the naming convention on a class that should be used as a POCO controller. You can tell MVC that a class is a controller even when it doesn't meet the POCO selection criteria by applying the Controller attribute, which is also defined in the Microsoft. AspNetCore.Mvc namespace.

Using the MVC Controller API

The PocoController class is a useful demonstration of the way MVC identifies controllers and how simple controllers can be. But *pure* POCO controllers, which have no dependencies on the Microsoft.AspnetCore namespaces, are not especially useful because they don't have access to the features that MVC provides for processing requests.

Some parts of the MVC API can be accessed by creating new instances of classes from the Microsoft. AspnetCore namespaces. As a simple example, a POCO class can ask MVC to render a Razor view by returning a ViewResult object from its action methods, as shown in Listing 17-8. (I come back to the ViewResult class in the "Producing a Response" section.)

Listing 17-8. Using the ASP.NET API in the PocoController.cs File in the Controllers Folder

```
using Microsoft.AspNetCore.Mvc;
using Microsoft.AspNetCore.Mvc.ModelBinding;
using Microsoft.AspNetCore.Mvc.ViewFeatures;
```

```
namespace ControllersAndActions.Controllers {

    public class PocoController {

        public ViewResult Index() => new ViewResult() {
                ViewName = "Result",
                ViewData = new ViewDataDictionary(
                    new EmptyModelMetadataProvider(),
                    new ModelStateDictionary()) {
                        Model = $"This is a POCO controller"
                    }
            };
    }
}
```

This is no longer a pure POCO controller because it has direct dependencies on the MVC API. But purity aside, it is a lot more useful than the previous example because it asks MVC to render a Razor view. Unfortunately, the code is complex. To create a ViewResult object, I need to create ViewDataDictionary, EmptyModelMetadataProvider, and ModelStateDictionary objects, which requires access to three different namespaces. (I describe the features that these types relate to in later chapters.) The point of this example is to demonstrate that the features provided by MVC can be accessed directly, even if the result is a bit of a mess.

The changes in the listing render the Result.cshtml view using a string as the view model. If you run the application and request the /Poco/Index URL, you will see the response shown in Figure 17-2.

Figure 17-2. *Using the MVC API directly*

Using the Controller Base Class

The previous examples show how you can start with a POCO controller and build on it to access MVC features. This approach sheds light on how MVC works, which is useful knowledge if you find yourself inadvertently creating controllers, but POCO controllers are awkward to write, read, and maintain.

An easier way to create controllers is to derive classes from the Microsoft.AspNetCore.Mvc.Controller class, which defines methods and properties that provide access to MVC features in a more concise and useful manner. To demonstrate, I added a class file called DerivedController.cs to the Controllers folder and used it to define the controller shown in Listing 17-9.

Listing 17-9. Deriving from the Controller Class in the DerivedController.cs File in the Controllers Folder

```
using Microsoft.AspNetCore.Mvc;

namespace ControllersAndActions.Controllers {

    public class DerivedController : Controller {

        public ViewResult Index() =>
            View("Result", $"This is a derived controller");
    }
}
```

If you run the application and request the /Derived/Index URL, you will see the results shown in Figure 17-3.

Figure 17-3. *Using the Controller base class*

The controller in Listing 17-9 does the same thing as the one in Listing 17-8 (it asks MVC to render a view with a `string` view model), but using the `Controller` base class means that the result can be achieved more simply.

The key change is that I can create the `ViewResult` object required to render the Razor view using the `View` method, rather than having to instantiate it (and the other types it requires) directly in the action method. The `View` method is inherited from the `Controller` base class, and the `ViewResult` object is still being created in the same way, just without the code cluttering up my action method. Deriving from the `Controller` class doesn't change the way that your controllers work; it just simplifies the code that you write to get common tasks done.

▪ **Note** MVC creates a new instance of a controller class for each request that it is asked to handle. This means you don't need to synchronize access to your action methods or instance properties and fields. Shared objects, including databases and singleton services, which I describe in Chapter 18, can be used concurrently and must be written accordingly.

Receiving Context Data

Regardless of how you define your controllers, they will rarely exist in isolation and usually need to access data from the incoming request, such as query string values, form values, and parameters parsed from the URL by the routing system, collectively known as *context data*. There are three main ways to access context data.

- Extract it from a set of *context objects*
- Receive the data as a *parameter* to an action method
- Explicitly invoke the framework's *model binding* feature

Here, I look at the approaches for getting input for your action methods, focusing on using context objects and action method parameters. I cover model binding in Chapter 26.

Getting Data from Context Objects

One of the main advantages of using the `Controller` base class to create controllers is convenient access to a set of context objects that describe the current request, the response that is being prepared, and the state of the application. In Table 17-3 I have described the most useful `Controller` context properties.

Table 17-3. *Useful Controller Class Properties for Context Data*

Name	Description
Request	This property returns an `HttpRequest` object that describes the request received from the client, as described in Table 17-4.
Response	This property returns an `HttpResponse` object that is used to create the response to the client, as described in Table 17-7.
HttpContext	This property returns an `HttpContext` object, which is the source of many of the objects returned by other properties, such as `Request` and `Response`. It also provides information about the HTTP features available and access to lower-level features like web sockets.
RouteData	This property returns the `RouteData` object produced by the routing system when it matched the request, as described in Chapters 15 and 16.
ModelState	This property returns a `ModelStateDictionary` object, which is used to validate data sent by the client, as described in Chapter 27.
User	This property returns a `ClaimsPrincipal` object that describes the user who has made the request, as described in Chapters 29 and 30.

Many controllers are written without needing to use the properties shown in Table 17-3 because the context data is also available through features that I describe in later chapters, which are more in keeping with the MVC development style. For example, most controllers don't need to use the `Request` property to get details of the HTTP request that is being processed because the same information is available through the model binding process that I describe in Chapter 26.

But it can still be useful to understand and use the context objects, and they are useful for debugging. In Listing 17-10, I have used the `Request` property to access the headers in the HTTP request.

Listing 17-10. Using Context Data in the DerivedController.cs File in the Controllers Folder

```
using Microsoft.AspNetCore.Mvc;
using System.Linq;

namespace ControllersAndActions.Controllers {

    public class DerivedController : Controller {

        public ViewResult Index() =>
            View("Result", $"This is a derived controller");

        public ViewResult Headers() => View("DictionaryResult",
                Request.Headers.ToDictionary(kvp => kvp.Key,
                    kvp => kvp.Value.First()));
    }
}
```

Using the context objects means navigating through a range of different types and namespaces. The Controller.Request property that I used to get context data about the HTTP request in the listing returns an HttpRequest object. Table 17-4 describes the HttpRequest properties that are most useful when writing controllers.

Table 17-4. *Commonly Used HttpRequest Properties*

Name	Description
Path	This property returns the path section of the request URL.
QueryString	This property returns the query string section of the request URL.
Headers	This property returns a dictionary of the request headers, indexed by name.
Body	This property returns a stream that can be used to read the request body.
Form	This property returns a dictionary of the form data in the request, indexed by name.
Cookies	This property returns a dictionary of the request cookies, indexed by name.

I used the Request.Headers property to get a dictionary of the headers, which I processed using LINQ.

```
...
View("DictionaryResult", Request.Headers.ToDictionary(kvp => kvp.Key,
    kvp => kvp.Value.First()));
...
```

The dictionary that is returned by the Request.Headers property stores the value of each header using the StringValues struct, which is used in ASP.NET to represent a sequence of string values. An HTTP client can send several values for HTTP headers, but I want to display only the first value. I used the LINQ ToDictionary method to receive a KeyValuePair<string, StringValues> object for each header and selected the first value. The result is a dictionary containing string values, which can be displayed by the DictionaryResult view. If you run the application and request the /Derived/Headers URL, you will see output similar to that shown in Figure 17-4. (The set of headers and their values will differ based on the browser you use.)

Figure 17-4. *Displaying context data*

Getting Context Data in a POCO Controller

Even if they are not especially useful in regular projects, POCO controllers let us peek behind the curtain to see how MVC does things. Getting context data in a POCO controller is a problem because you can't just instantiate your own HttpRequest or HttpResponse objects; you need the ones that have been created by ASP.NET and updated by all of the middleware components that have populated their data fields as the request has been processed.

To get context data, a POCO controller has to ask MVC to provide it. In Listing 17-11, I have updated the PocoController class to add an action method that displays the HTTP request headers.

Listing 17-11. Displaying Context Data in the PocoController.cs File in the Controllers Folder

```
using Microsoft.AspNetCore.Mvc;
using Microsoft.AspNetCore.Mvc.ModelBinding;
using Microsoft.AspNetCore.Mvc.ViewFeatures;
using System.Linq;

namespace ControllersAndActions.Controllers {

    public class PocoController {

        [ControllerContext]
        public ControllerContext ControllerContext { get; set; }

        public ViewResult Index() => new ViewResult() {
            ViewName = "Result",
            ViewData = new ViewDataDictionary(new EmptyModelMetadataProvider(),
                        new ModelStateDictionary()) {
                Model = $"This is a POCO controller"
            }
        };
```

```
    public ViewResult Headers() =>
        new ViewResult() {
            ViewName = "DictionaryResult",
            ViewData = new ViewDataDictionary(
                new EmptyModelMetadataProvider(),
                new ModelStateDictionary()) {
                    Model = ControllerContext.HttpContext.Request.Headers
                    .ToDictionary(kvp => kvp.Key, kvp => kvp.Value.First())
            }
        };
    }
}
```

To get the context data, I defined a property called ControllerContext whose type is ControllerContext, which has been decorated with an attribute that is also called ControllerContext.

It is worth unpacking these three different uses of the term ControllerContext. First, the ControllerContext class, which is defined in the Microsoft.AspNetCore.Mvc namespace, is a class that brings together all the context objects that are required by a controller's action method, using the properties described in Table 17-5.

Table 17-5. *The Most Important ControllerContext Properties*

Name	Description
ActionDescriptor	This property returns an ActionDescriptor object, which describes the action method.
HttpContext	This property returns an HttpContext object, which provides details of the HTTP request and the HTTP response that will be sent in return. See Table 17-6 for details.
ModelState	This property returns a ModelStateDictionary object, which is used to validate data sent by the client, as described in Chapter 27.
RouteData	This property returns a RouteData object that describes the way that the routing system has processed the request, as described in Chapter 15.

HTTP-related data is accessed through the ControllerContext.HttpContext property, which returns a Microsoft.AspNetCore.Http.HttpContext object. The HttpContext class consolidates several objects that describe different aspects of the request, accessed through the properties shown in Table 17-6.

Table 17-6. *Commonly Used HttpContext Properties*

Name	Description
Connection	This property returns a ConnectionInfo object that describes the low-level connection to the client.
Request	This property returns an HttpRequest object that describes the HTTP request received from the client, as described earlier in this chapter.
Response	This property returns an HttpResponse object that is used to create the response that will be returned to the client, as described in the "Producing a Response" section.
Session	This property returns an ISession object that describes the session with which the request is associated.
User	This property returns a ClaimsPrincipal object that describes the user associated with the request, as described in Chapter 28.

The ControllerContext attribute is used to decorate the property in Listing 17-11 and tells MVC to set the property value with a ControllerContext object that describes the current request. This uses a technique known as *dependency injection*, which I describe in Chapter 18, and MVC will use this property to provide the controller with context data before using an action method to handle a request.

Finally, the third use of the term ControllerContext is the name of the property. You can use any legal C# property name in your own POCO controllers, but I chose this name because it is the one used by the Controller class. Behind the scenes, the Controller class relies on the same ControllerContext class for its context data, which is decorated with the same ControllerContext attribute. All of the Controller properties that I described in Table 17-3 are just more convenient and concise alternatives to using the ControllerContext properties directly, which is exactly what's happening in the properties provided by the Controller class. As an example, here is the definition of the HttpContext property from the Controller class:

```
...
public HttpContext HttpContext {
    get {
        return ControllerContext.HttpContext;
    }
}
...
```

The HttpContext property is just a more convenient way to get the value of the ControllerContext. HttpContext property. There is no magic in the Controller base class: it results in simpler and clearer controllers because it consolidates common tasks into convenience methods and properties, all of which you could re-create yourself in a POCO controller if you needed. A lot of the functionality in ASP.NET Core MVC is surprisingly simple when you dig into the detail, and there is no special sauce—just well-thought-out functionality provided in a carefully designed set of NuGet packages. If you have the time, I recommend you confirm this yourself by downloading the MVC source code from http://github.com/aspnet and exploring.

Using Action Method Parameters

Some context data can also be received through action method parameters, which can produce more natural and elegant code. A common example is when an action method needs to receive form data values submitted by the user. For comparison, I will demonstrate how to get form data through context objects and then through action method parameters.

Form data values are accessed through the Controller class's Request.Form property. To demonstrate, I added a class file called HomeController.cs and used it to define the derived controller shown in Listing 17-12.

Listing 17-12. The Contents of the HomeController.cs File in the Controllers Folder

```
using Microsoft.AspNetCore.Mvc;

namespace ControllersAndActions.Controllers {

    public class HomeController : Controller {

        public ViewResult Index() => View("SimpleForm");

        public ViewResult ReceiveForm() {
            var name = Request.Form["name"];
            var city = Request.Form["city"];
            return View("Result", $"{name} lives in {city}");
        }
    }
}
```

The Index action method in this controller renders the SimpleForm view that I created in the Views/Shared folder at the start of the chapter. It is the ReceiveForm method that is of interest because it uses the HttpRequest context object to get form data values from the request.

As described in Table 17-4, the Form property defined by the HttpRequest class returns a collection containing the form data values, indexed by the name of the associated HTML element. There are two input elements in the SimpleForm view (name and city), and I extract their values from the context object and use them to create a string that is passed to the Result view as its model.

If you run the application and request the /Home URL, you will be presented with a form. If you fill out the fields and click the Submit button, the browser will send the form data as part of an HTTP POST request that will be handled by the ReceiveForm method, producing the result shown in Figure 17-5.

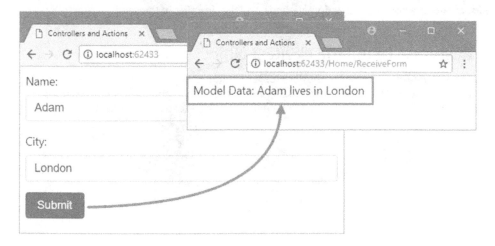

Figure 17-5. *Getting form data from the context objects*

This approach shown in Listing 17-12 works perfectly well, but there is a more elegant alternative. Action methods can define parameters that are used by MVC to pass context data to a controller, including details of the HTTP request. This is neater than extracting it from the context objects directly, and it produces action methods that are easier to read. To receive the form data, declare parameters on the action method whose names correspond to the form data values, as shown in Listing 17-13.

Listing 17-13. Receiving Context Data as Parameters in the HomeController.cs File in the Controllers Folder

```
using Microsoft.AspNetCore.Mvc;

namespace ControllersAndActions.Controllers {

    public class HomeController : Controller {

        public ViewResult Index() => View("SimpleForm");

        public ViewResult ReceiveForm(string name, string city)
            => View("Result", $"{name} lives in {city}");
    }
}
```

The revised action method produces the same result, but the code is easier to read and understand. MVC will provide values for action method parameters by checking context objects automatically, including `Request.QueryString`, `Request.Form`, and `RouteData.Values`. The names of the parameters are treated case-insensitively so that an action method parameter called `city` can be populated by a value from `Request.Form["City"]`, for example. This approach also produces action methods that are easier to unit test because the values that the action method operates on are received as regular C# parameters and don't require context objects to be mocked.

Producing a Response

After an action method has finished processing a request, it needs to generate a response. There are many features available for generating output from action methods, which I describe in the sections that follow.

Producing a Response Using the Context Object

The lowest-level way to generate output is to use the `HttpResponse` context object, which is how ASP. NET Core provides access to the HTTP response that will be sent to the client. Table 17-7 describes the basic features provided by the `HttpResponse` class, which is defined in the `Microsoft.AspNetCore.Http` namespace.

Table 17-7. *Commonly Used HttpResponse Properties*

Name	Description
StatusCode	This property is used to set the HTTP status code for the response.
ContentType	This property is used to set the Content-Type header of the response.
Headers	This property returns a dictionary of the HTTP headers that will be included in the response.
Cookies	This property returns a collection that is used to add cookies to the response.
Body	This property returns a System.IO.Stream object that is used to write the body data for the response.

In Listing 17-14, I have updated the Home controller so that its ReceivedForm action generates a response using the HttpResponse object returned by the Controller.Request property.

Listing 17-14. Producing a Response in the HomeController.cs File in the Controllers Folder

```
using Microsoft.AspNetCore.Mvc;
using System.Text;

namespace ControllersAndActions.Controllers {

    public class HomeController : Controller {

        public ViewResult Index() => View("SimpleForm");

        public void ReceiveForm(string name, string city) {
            Response.StatusCode = 200;
            Response.ContentType = "text/html";
            byte[] content = Encoding.ASCII
                .GetBytes($"<html><body>{name} lives in {city}</body>");
            Response.Body.WriteAsync(content, 0, content.Length);
        }
    }
}
```

This is a terrible way to generate a response because it hard-codes HTML in the action method using C# strings, which is error-prone and hard to unit test. But it does provide a starting point for understanding how responses are created behind the scenes.

There are better alternatives than working directly with the HttpResponse object. MVC builds on the low-level response with a much more useful feature that is at the heart of how controllers work: the *action result*.

Understanding Action Results

MVC uses action results to separate *stating intentions* from *executing intentions*. The concept is simple once you have mastered it, but it can take a while to get your head around the approach at first because there is a bit of indirection going on.

Instead of working directly with the HttpResponse object, action methods return an object that implements the IActionResult interface from the Microsoft.AspNetCore.Mvc namespace. The IActionResult object—known as the *action result*—describes what the response from the controller should be, such as rendering a view or redirecting the client to another URL. But—and this is where the indirection comes in—you don't generate the response directly. Instead, MVC processes the action result to produce the result for you.

■ **Note** The system of action results is an example of the *command pattern*. This pattern describes scenarios where you store and pass around objects that describe operations to be performed. See http://en.wikipedia.org/wiki/Command_pattern for more details.

Here is the definition of the IActionResult interface from MVC source code:

```
using System.Threading.Tasks;

namespace Microsoft.AspNetCore.Mvc {

    public interface IActionResult {
        Task ExecuteResultAsync(ActionContext context);
    }
}
```

This interface may seem simple, but that's because MVC doesn't dictate what kinds of response an action result can produce. When an action method returns an action result, MVC calls its ExecuteResultAsync method, which is responsible generating the response on behalf of the action method. The ActionContext argument provides context data for generating the response, including the HttpResponse object. (The ActionContext class is the superclass of ControllerContext and defines all the properties described in Table 17-5.)

To demonstrate how action results work, I added an Infrastructure folder to the project and added a class file to it called CustomHtmlResult.cs, which I used to define the action result shown in Listing 17-15.

Listing 17-15. The Contents of the CustomHtmlResult.cs File in the Infrastructure Folder

```
using Microsoft.AspNetCore.Mvc;
using System.Text;
using System.Threading.Tasks;

namespace ControllersAndActions.Infrastructure {

    public class CustomHtmlResult : IActionResult {

        public string Content { get; set; }
```

```
        public Task ExecuteResultAsync(ActionContext context) {
            context.HttpContext.Response.StatusCode = 200;
            context.HttpContext.Response.ContentType = "text/html";
            byte[] content = Encoding.ASCII.GetBytes(Content);
            return context.HttpContext.Response.Body.WriteAsync(content,
                0, content.Length);
        }
    }
}
```

The CustomHtmlResult class implements the IActionResult interface, and its ExecuteResultAsync method uses the HttpResponse object to write an HTML response that contains the value of a property called Content. The ExecuteResultAsync method must return a Task so that the response can be produced asynchronously; this fits nicely with the implementation in the CustomHtmlResult class, which relies on the WriteAsync method of the Stream object that represents the response body and which returns a Task method that I can use as the method result.

In Listing 17-16, I have applied the action result class to the Home controller, simplifying the ReceiveForm action method of the Home controller.

Listing 17-16. Using an Action Result in the HomeController.cs File in the Controllers Folder

```
using Microsoft.AspNetCore.Mvc;
using System.Text;
using ControllersAndActions.Infrastructure;

namespace ControllersAndActions.Controllers {

    public class HomeController : Controller {

        public ViewResult Index() => View("SimpleForm");

        public IActionResult ReceiveForm(string name, string city)
            => new CustomHtmlResult {
                Content = $"{name} lives in {city}"
            };
    }
}
```

The code that sends the response is now defined separately from the data that the response contains, which simplifies the action method and allows the same type of response to be produced in other action methods without duplicating the same code.

UNIT TESTING CONTROLLERS AND ACTIONS

Many parts of ASP.NET Core MVC are designed to facilitate unit testing, and this is especially true for actions and controllers. There are a few reasons for this support.

- You can test actions and controllers outside a web server.

- You do not need to parse any HTML to test the result of an action method. You can inspect the IActionResult object that is returned to ensure that you received the expected result.

- You do not need to simulate client requests. The MVC model binding system allows you to write action methods that receive input as method parameters. To test an action method, you simply call the action method directly and provide the parameter values that interest you.

I will show you how to create unit tests for the different kinds of action results throughout this chapter. See Chapter 7 for instructions for setting up a unit test project or download the example projects from this book's GitHub repository (https://github.com/apress/pro-asp.net-core-mvc-2).

Producing an HTML Response

In the previous section, I was able to take the code that generates the response out of the controller class using an action result. ASP.NET Core MVC comes complete with a more flexible approach to producing responses: the ViewResult class.

The ViewResult class is the action result that provides access to the Razor view engine, which processes .cshtml files to incorporate model data and sends the result to the client through the HttpResponse context engine. I explain how view engines work in Chapter 21, but for this chapter, my focus is on the use of the ViewResult class as an action result.

In Listing 17-17, I have replaced the custom action result class with a ViewResult, which is created through the View method provided by the Controller base class.

Listing 17-17. Using the ViewResult Class in the HomeController.cs File in the Controllers Folder

```
using Microsoft.AspNetCore.Mvc;
using System.Text;
using ControllersAndActions.Infrastructure;

namespace ControllersAndActions.Controllers {

    public class HomeController : Controller {

        public ViewResult Index() => View("SimpleForm");

        public ViewResult ReceiveForm(string name, string city)
            => View("Result", $"{name} lives in {city}");
    }
}
```

You can create ViewResult objects directly, as I demonstrated in the POCO controller at the start of the chapter, but using the View method is simpler and more concise. The Controller class provides several different versions of the View method that allow the view that will be rendered to be selected and provided with model data, as described in Table 17-8.

Table 17-8. *The Controller View Methods*

Method	Description
View()	This method creates a ViewResult object for the default view associated with the action method, such that calling View() in a method called MyAction will render a view called MyAction.cshtml. No model data is used.
View(view)	This method creates a ViewResult that will render the specified view, such that calling View("MyView") will render a view called MyView.cshtml. No model data is used.
View(model)	This method creates a ViewResult object for the default view associated with the action method and uses the specified object as the model data.
View(view, model)	This method creates a ViewResult object for the specified view and uses the specified object as the model data.

If you run the application and submit the form, you will see the familiar result shown in Figure 17-6.

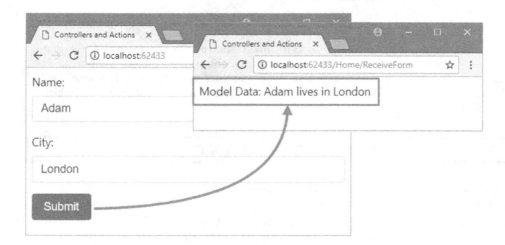

Figure 17-6. *Using a ViewResult to generate an HTML response*

Understanding the Search for a View File

When MVC calls the ExecuteResultAsync method of the ViewResult object, a search will begin for the view that you have specified. The sequence of directories that MVC searches for a view is an example of convention over configuration. You do not need to register your view files with the framework. You just put them in one of a set of known locations and the framework will find them. By default, MVC will look for a view in the following locations:

```
/Views/<ControllerName>/<ViewName>.cshtml
/Views/Shared/<ViewName>.cshtml
```

The search starts with the folder that contains views that are dedicated to the current controller. The name of this folder omits the Controller part of the class name so that the folder for the HomeController class is Views/Home.

If the view name is not specified in the ViewResult object, then the value of the action variable from the routing data will be used. For most controllers, this means that the name of the method will be used so that the default view file associated with the Index method is Index.cshtml. However, if you have used the Route attribute, then the view name associated with an action method may be different.

If your controller is part of an area, as described in Chapter 16, then the search locations are different.

```
/Areas/<AreaName>/Views/<ControllerName>/<ViewName>.cshtml
/Areas/<AreaName>/Views/Shared/<ViewName>.cshtml
/Views/Shared/<ViewName>.cshtml
```

MVC checks to see whether each of these files exists in turn. As soon as it locates a match, it uses that view to render the result of the action method. I am not using areas in the example project, so the action method in Listing 17-17 causes MVC to start its search by looking for the Views/Home/Result.cshtml file. There is no such file, so the search continues, with MVC looking for Views/Shared/Result.cshtml, which does exist and so will be used to render the HTML response.

UNIT TEST: RENDERING A VIEW

To test the view that an action method renders, you can inspect the ViewResult object that it returns. This is not quite the same thing (after all, you are not following the process through to check the final HTML that is generated), but it is close enough, as long as you have reasonable confidence that the MVC view system works properly. I added a new unit test file called ActionTests.cs to the test project to hold the unit tests for this chapter.

The first situation I want to test is when an action method selects a specific view, like this:

```
...
public ViewResult ReceiveForm(string name, string city)
    => View("Result", $"{name} lives in {city}");
...
```

You can determine which view has been selected by reading the ViewName property of the ViewResult object, as shown in this test method:

```
using ControllersAndActions.Controllers;
using Microsoft.AspNetCore.Mvc;
using Xunit;

namespace ControllersAndActions.Tests {

    public class ActionTests {

        [Fact]
        public void ViewSelected() {
            // Arrange
            HomeController controller = new HomeController();

            // Act
            ViewResult result = controller.ReceiveForm("Adam", "London");

            // Assert
            Assert.Equal("Result", result.ViewName);
        }
    }
}
```

A variation arises when you are testing an action method that selects the default view, like this:

```
...
public ViewResult Result() => View();
...
```

In such situations, you need to ensure that the view name is null, like this:

```
...
Assert.Null(result.ViewName);
...
```

A null value is how the ViewResult object signals to MVC that the default view associated with the action method has been selected.

```
┌─────────────────────────────────────────────────────────────────────┐
│                                                                       │
│                   SPECIFYING A VIEW BY ITS PATH                       │
│                                                                       │
└─────────────────────────────────────────────────────────────────────┘
```

The naming convention approach for views is convenient and simple, but it does limit the views you can render. If you want to render a specific view, you can do so by providing an explicit path and bypass the search phase. Here is an example:

```csharp
using Microsoft.AspNetCore.Mvc;

namespace ControllersAndActions.Controllers {

    public class ExampleController : Controller {

        public ViewResult Index() {
            return View("/Views/Admin/Index");
        }
    }
}
```

When you specify a view like this, the path must begin with / or ~/ and can include the file name extension (which is assumed to be .cshtml if unspecified).

If you find yourself using this feature, I suggest that you take a moment and ask yourself what you are trying to achieve. If you are attempting to render a view that belongs to another controller, then you might be better off redirecting the user to an action method in that controller (see the "Redirecting to an Action Method" section later in this chapter for an example). If you are trying to work around the view file naming scheme because it doesn't suit the way you have organized your project, then see Chapter 21, which explains how to implement a custom search sequence.

Passing Data from an Action Method to a View

When you use a ViewResult to select a view, you can pass data from the action method to be used when the HTML content is generated. MVC provides different ways for an action method to pass data to a view, which I describe in the following sections. These features naturally touch on the topic of views, which I describe in depth in Chapter 21. In this chapter, I discuss only enough view functionality to demonstrate the controller features.

Using a View Model Object

You can send an object to the view by passing it as a parameter to the View method, which has the effect of setting the ViewData.Model property of the ViewResult object that is created. I set this property directly earlier in the chapter to explain how POCO controllers work, but the View method takes care of this more concisely. Listing 17-18 shows a new ExampleController class that I added to the Controllers folder and that passes a view model object to the View method.

Listing 17-18. The Contents of the ExampleController.cs File in the Controllers Folder

```csharp
using Microsoft.AspNetCore.Mvc;
using System;
```

530

```
namespace ControllersAndActions.Controllers {

    public class ExampleController : Controller {

        public ViewResult Index() => View(DateTime.Now);
    }
}
```

I passed a DateTime object to the View method to use as the view model. To access the object from within the view, I use the Razor Model keyword. I created the Views/Example folder and added a view called Index.cshtml, which is shown in Listing 17-19.

Listing 17-19. The Contents of the Index.cshtml File in the Views/Example Folder

```
@{ Layout = null; }

<!DOCTYPE html>
<html>
<head>
    <meta name="viewport" content="width=device-width" />
    <title>Controllers and Actions</title>
    <link rel="stylesheet" asp-href-include="lib/bootstrap/dist/css/*.min.css" />
</head>
<body class="m-1 p-1">
    Model: @(((DateTime)Model).DayOfWeek)
</body>
</html>
```

This is an *untyped* or *weakly typed* view. The view does not know anything about the view model object and treats it as an instance of object. To get the value of the DayOfWeek property, I need to cast the object to an instance of DateTime, like this:

```
...
Model: @((((DateTime)Model).DayOfWeek)
...
```

This works but produces messy views. I can tidy this up by creating *strongly typed views*, in which the view includes details of the type of the view model object, as demonstrated in Listing 17-20.

Listing 17-20. Adding Strong Typing to the Index.cshtml File in the Views/Example Folder

```
@model DateTime
@{ Layout = null; }

<!DOCTYPE html>
<html>
<head>
    <meta name="viewport" content="width=device-width" />
    <title>Controllers and Actions</title>
    <link rel="stylesheet" asp-href-include="lib/bootstrap/dist/css/*.min.css" />
</head>
```

```
<body class="m-1 p-1">
    Model: @Model.DayOfWeek
</body>
</html>
```

I specified the view model type using the Razor model keyword. Notice that I use a lowercase m when specifying the model type and an uppercase M when reading the value.

Not only does strong typing help tidy up the view, but Visual Studio supports IntelliSense for strongly typed views, as shown in Figure 17-7.

Figure 17-7. *IntelliSense support for strongly typed views*

UNIT TEST: VIEW MODEL OBJECTS

View model objects are assigned to the ViewResult.ViewData.Model property, which means you can test that an action method sends the expected data when the View method is used. Here is a test method that checks the model type for the action method in Listing 17-20:

```
...
[Fact]
public void ModelObjectType() {
    //Arrange
    ExampleController controller = new ExampleController();

    // Act
    ViewResult result = controller.Index();

    // Assert
    Assert.IsType<System.DateTime>(result.ViewData.Model);
}
...
```

The Assert.IsType method is used to check that the view model object is an instance of DateTime.

There is one wrinkle to be aware of when using the View method, which arises when you want to use the default view associated with an action and provide that view with a string model object, as shown in Listing 17-21.

Listing 17-21. Using the View Method in the ExampleController.cs File in the Controllers Folder

```
using Microsoft.AspNetCore.Mvc;
using System;

namespace ControllersAndActions.Controllers {

    public class ExampleController : Controller {

        public ViewResult Index() => View(DateTime.Now);

        public ViewResult Result() => View("Hello World");
    }
}
```

In the new Result action method, I want to use the View method that renders the default view for the action and specify the model data, which is the third version of the method in Table 17-8. But if you run the application and request the /Example/Result URL, you will see an error like this one:

```
InvalidOperationException: The view 'Hello, World' was not found.
The following locations were searched:
/Views/Example/Hello, World.cshtml
/Views/Shared/Hello, World.cshtml
```

The problem is that my call to the View method with a string was a match to the second version of the View method in Table 17-8, which means that the string argument was interpreted as the name of the view to render, so MVC tries to find a view file called Hello, World.cshtml instead of Result.cshtml. This is a common problem, but it is easy to fix by casting the model data to object, as shown in Listing 17-22.

Listing 17-22. Selecting the Correct View Method in the ExampleController.cs File in the Controllers Folder

```
using Microsoft.AspNetCore.Mvc;
using System;

namespace ControllersAndActions.Controllers {

    public class ExampleController : Controller {

        public ViewResult Index() => View(DateTime.Now);

        public ViewResult Result() => View((object)"Hello World");
    }
}
```

Explicitly casting the model data to object ensures that the call matches the right version of the View method and renders the Result.cshtml file.

Passing Data with the View Bag

I introduced the view bag feature in Chapter 2. This feature allows you to define properties on a dynamic object and access them in a view. The dynamic object is accessed through the ViewBag property provided by the Controller class, as demonstrated in Listing 17-23.

Listing 17-23. Using the View Bag Feature in the ExampleController.cs File in the Controllers Folder

```
using Microsoft.AspNetCore.Mvc;
using System;

namespace ControllersAndActions.Controllers {

    public class ExampleController : Controller {

        public ViewResult Index() {
            ViewBag.Message = "Hello";
            ViewBag.Date = DateTime.Now;
            return View();
        }

        public ViewResult Result() => View((object)"Hello World");
    }
}
```

I have defined view bag properties called Message and Date by assigning values to them. Before this point, no such properties existed, and I made no preparations to create them. To read the data back in the view, I get the same properties that I set in the action method, as shown in Listing 17-24.

Listing 17-24. Reading Data from the ViewBag in the Index.cshtml File in the Views/Example Folder

```
@model DateTime
@{ Layout = null; }

<!DOCTYPE html>
<html>
<head>
    <meta name="viewport" content="width=device-width" />
    <title>Controllers and Actions</title>
    <link rel="stylesheet" asp-href-include="lib/bootstrap/dist/css/*.min.css" />
</head>
<body class="m-1 p-1">
    <p>The day is: @ViewBag.Date.DayOfWeek</p>
    <p>The message is: @ViewBag.Message</p>
</body>
</html>
```

The ViewBag has an advantage over using a view model object in that it is easy to send multiple objects to the view. If MVC only supported view models, then I would need to create a new type that had string and DateTime members in order to get the same effect.

■ **Caution** Visual Studio cannot provide IntelliSense support for any dynamic objects, including the ViewBag, and errors won't be revealed until the view is rendered.

UNIT TEST: VIEWBAG

The ViewResult.ViewData property returns a dictionary whose keys are the names of the view bag properties defined by the action method. Here is a test method for the action method in Listing 17-24:

```
...
[Fact]
public void ModelObjectType() {
    //Arrange
    ExampleController controller = new ExampleController();

    // Act
    ViewResult result = controller.Index();

    // Assert
    Assert.IsType<string>(result.ViewData["Message"]);
    Assert.Equal("Hello", result.ViewData["Message"]);
    Assert.IsType<System.DateTime>(result.ViewData["Date"]);
}
...
```

This test method checks the types for both the Message and Date properties using the Assert.IsType method and checks the value of the Message property using the Assert.Equal method.

Performing Redirections

A common result from an action method is not to produce any output directly but to redirect the client to another URL. Most of the time, this URL is another action method in the application that generates the output you want the users to see. When you perform a redirect, you send one of two HTTP codes to the browser.

HTTP code 302, which is a *temporary* redirection. This is the most frequently used type of redirection, and when using the Post/Redirect/Get pattern, this is the code that you want to send.

HTTP code 301, which indicates a permanent redirection. This should be used with caution because it instructs the recipient of the HTTP code not to request the original URL ever again and to use the new URL that is included alongside the redirection code. If you are in doubt, use temporary redirections; that is, send code 302.

Several different action results can be used to perform a redirection, as described in Table 17-9.

Table 17-9. *The Redirection Action Results*

Name	Controller Method	Description
RedirectResult	Redirect RedirectPermanent	This action result sends a response with the HTTP 301 or 302 status code, redirecting the client to a new URL.
LocalRedirectResult	LocalRedirect LocalRedirectPermanent	This action result redirects the client to a local URL.
RedirectToActionResult	RedirectToAction RedirectionToActionPermanent	This action result redirects the client to a specific action and controller.
RedirectToRouteResult	RedirectToRoute RedirectToRoutePermanent	This action result redirects the client to a URL generated from a specific route.

Redirecting to a Literal URL

The most basic way to redirect a browser is to call the Redirect method provided by the Controller class, which returns an instance of the RedirectResult class, as shown in Listing 17-25.

Listing 17-25. Redirecting to a Literal URL in the ExampleController.cs File in the Controllers Folder

```
using Microsoft.AspNetCore.Mvc;
using System;

namespace ControllersAndActions.Controllers {

    public class ExampleController : Controller {

        public ViewResult Index() {
            ViewBag.Message = "Hello";
            ViewBag.Date = DateTime.Now;
            return View();
        }

        public ViewResult Result() => View((object)"Hello World");

        public RedirectResult Redirect() => Redirect("/Example/Index");
    }
}
```

The redirection URL is expressed as a string argument to the Redirect method, which produces a temporary redirection. You can perform a permanent redirection using the RedirectPermanent method, as shown in Listing 17-26.

■ **Tip**   The LocalRedirectionResult is an alternative action result that will throw an exception if a controller tries to perform a redirection to any URL that is not local. This is useful when you are redirecting to URLs provided by users, where an *open redirection attack* is attempted to redirect another user to an untrusted site. This kind of action result can be created through the LocalRedirect method inherited from the Controller class.

Listing 17-26. Permanently Redirecting in the ExampleController.cs File in the Controllers Folder

```
using Microsoft.AspNetCore.Mvc;
using System;

namespace ControllersAndActions.Controllers {

    public class ExampleController : Controller {

        public ViewResult Index() {
            ViewBag.Message = "Hello";
            ViewBag.Date = DateTime.Now;
            return View();
        }

        public ViewResult Result() => View((object)"Hello World");

        public RedirectResult Redirect() => RedirectPermanent("/Example/Index");
    }
}
```

UNIT TEST: LITERAL REDIRECTIONS

Literal redirections are easy to test. You can read the URL and test whether the redirection is permanent or temporary using the Url and Permanent properties of the RedirectResult class. The following is a test method for the permanent redirection shown in Listing 17-26:

```
...
[Fact]
public void Redirection() {
    // Arrange
    ExampleController controller = new ExampleController();
    // Act
    RedirectResult result = controller.Redirect();
    // Assert
    Assert.Equal("/Example/Index", result.Url);
    Assert.True(result.Permanent);
}
...
```

Notice that I have updated the test to receive a RedirectResult when I call the action method.

Redirecting to a Routing System URL

If you are redirecting the user to a different part of your application, you need to make sure that the URL you send is valid within your URL schema. The problem with using literal URLs for redirection is that any change in your routing schema means that you need to go through your code and update the URLs. Fortunately, you can use the routing system to generate valid URLs with the RedirectToRoute method, which creates an instance of the RedirectToRouteResult, as shown in Listing 17-27.

■ **Tip**   If you are following the examples in this chapter in sequence, then you may have to clear your browser's history for the code in Listing 17-27 to work. This is because the browser remembers the permanent redirection in Listing 17-26 and will translate a request for the /Example/Redirect URL into a request to /Example/Index without contacting the server.

Listing 17-27. Redirecting to a Routing URL in the ExampleController.cs File in the Controllers Folder

```
using Microsoft.AspNetCore.Mvc;
using System;

namespace ControllersAndActions.Controllers {

    public class ExampleController : Controller {

        public ViewResult Index() {
            ViewBag.Message = "Hello";
            ViewBag.Date = DateTime.Now;
            return View();
        }

        public ViewResult Result() => View((object)"Hello World");

        public RedirectToRouteResult Redirect() =>
            RedirectToRoute(new { controller = "Example",
                                  action = "Index",
                                  ID = "MyID" });
    }
}
```

The RedirectToRoute method issues a temporary redirection. Use the RedirectToRoutePermanent method for permanent redirections. Both methods take an anonymous type whose properties are then passed to the routing system to generate a URL, as described in Chapter 16.

```
UNIT TESTING: ROUTED REDIRECTIONS
```

Here is the unit test for the action method in Listing 17-27:

```
...
[Fact]
public void Redirection() {
    // Arrange
    ExampleController controller = new ExampleController();
    // Act
    RedirectToRouteResult result = controller.Redirect();
    // Assert
    Assert.False(result.Permanent);
    Assert.Equal("Example", result.RouteValues["controller"]);
    Assert.Equal("Index", result.RouteValues["action"]);
    Assert.Equal("MyID", result.RouteValues["ID"]);
}
...
```

I have tested the result indirectly by looking at the routing information provided by the
RedirectToRouteResult object, which means that I don't have to parse a URL, which would require
the unit test to make assumptions about the URL schema used by the application.

Redirecting to an Action Method

You can redirect to an action method more elegantly by using the RedirectToAction method (for temporary
redirections) or the RedirectToActionPermanent method (for permanent redirections). These are just
wrappers around the RedirectToRoute method that let you specify values for the action method and the
controller without needing to create an anonymous type, as shown in Listing 17-28.

Listing 17-28. Using the RedirectToAction Method in the ExampleController.cs File in the Controllers
Folder

```
using Microsoft.AspNetCore.Mvc;
using System;

namespace ControllersAndActions.Controllers {

    public class ExampleController : Controller {

        public ViewResult Index() {
            ViewBag.Message = "Hello";
            ViewBag.Date = DateTime.Now;
            return View();
        }

        public RedirectToActionResult Redirect() => RedirectToAction(nameof(Index));
    }
}
```

If you specify just an action method, then it is assumed that you are referring to an action method in the current controller. If you want to redirect to another controller, you need to provide the controller's name as a parameter, like this:

```
...
public RedirectToActionResult Redirect()
    => RedirectToAction(nameof(HomeController), nameof(HomeController.Index));
...
```

There are other overloaded versions that you can use to provide additional values for the URL generation. These are expressed using an anonymous type, which does tend to undermine the purpose of the convenience method but can still make your code easier to read.

■ **Note**   The values that you provide for the action method and controller are not verified before they are passed to the routing system. You are responsible for making sure that the targets you specify actually exist.

UNIT TESTING: ACTION METHOD REDIRECTIONS

Here is the unit test for the action method in Listing 17-28:

```
...
[Fact]
public void Redirection() {
    // Arrange
    ExampleController controller = new ExampleController();
    // Act
    RedirectToActionResult result = controller.Redirect();
    // Assert
    Assert.False(result.Permanent);
    Assert.Equal("Index", result.ActionName);
}
...
```

The RedirectToActionResult class provides ControllerName and ActionName properties that make it easy to inspect the redirection created by the controller without having to parse URLs.

Using the Post/Redirect/Get Pattern

The most frequent use of redirection is in action methods that process HTTP POST requests. As I explained in the previous chapter, POST requests are used when you want to change the state of an application. If you just return an HTML response after you process a POST request, there is a risk that the user will click the browser reload button and resubmit the form a second time, which can have unexpected and undesirable results.

You can see this problem in the Home controller in the example application. The ReceiveForm method accepts parameters whose values are obtained from form data, and it uses the View method to return a ViewResult.

```
...
public ViewResult ReceiveForm(string name, string city)
    => View("Result", $"{name} lives in {city}");
...
```

To see the problem, run the application and request the /Home URL. Submit the form and then click the browser reload button. Use the F12 tools to study the HTTP requests made by the browser and you will see that a new POST request is sent to the server. There is no impact in such a simple application, but this problem can wreak havoc if the POST requests end up repeatedly deleting data, submitting orders, or performing other important tasks that the user didn't intend.

To avoid this problem, you can follow the pattern called Post/Redirect/Get. In this pattern, you receive a POST request, process it, and then redirect the browser so that a GET request is made by the browser for another URL. GET requests should not modify the state of your application, so any inadvertent resubmissions of this request won't cause any problems. In Listing 17-29, I have added a redirection so that the browser is redirected to a different URL with a GET request.

Listing 17-29. The Post/Redirect/Get Pattern in the HomeController.cs File in the Controllers Folder

```
using Microsoft.AspNetCore.Mvc;
using System.Text;
using ControllersAndActions.Infrastructure;

namespace ControllersAndActions.Controllers {

    public class HomeController : Controller {

        public ViewResult Index() => View("SimpleForm");

        [HttpPost]
        public RedirectToActionResult ReceiveForm(string name, string city)
            => RedirectToAction(nameof(Data));

        public ViewResult Data() => View("Result");
    }
}
```

The RedirectToActionResult method receives the data from the user via a POST request and redirects the client to the Data action method. A harmless GET request will be sent to the Data action method if the user reloads the page. The HttpPost attribute, which I describe in Chapter 20, ensures that only POST requests can be sent to the ReceiveForm action.

Using Temp Data

A redirection causes the browser to send an entirely new HTTP request, which means that there is no access to the form data from the original request. This means that the Data method doesn't have any knowledge of the name and city values that should be displayed to the user.

You can use the temp data feature to preserve data from one request to another. Temp data is similar to session data, which I used in Chapter 9, except that temp data values are marked for deletion when they are read and removed from the data store when the request has been processed. This is an ideal arrangement for short-lived data that is needed to make a redirection work in the Post/Redirect/Get pattern. The temp data feature is available through a Controller class property called TempData, as shown in Listing 17-30.

■ **Note** Temp data relies on the session middleware. See the start of this chapter for the middleware components required in the `Startup` class for this feature.

Listing 17-30. Using Temp Data in the HomeController.cs File in the Controllers Folder

```
using Microsoft.AspNetCore.Mvc;
using System.Text;
using ControllersAndActions.Infrastructure;

namespace ControllersAndActions.Controllers {

    public class HomeController : Controller {

        public ViewResult Index() {
            return View("SimpleForm");
        }

        [HttpPost]
        public RedirectToActionResult ReceiveForm(string name, string city) {
            TempData["name"] = name;
            TempData["city"] = city;
            return RedirectToAction(nameof(Data));
        }

        public ViewResult Data() {
            string name = TempData["name"] as string;
            string city = TempData["city"] as string;
            return View("Result", $"{name} lives in {city}");
        }
    }
}
```

The ReceiveForm method uses the TempData property, which returns a dictionary, to store the name and city values before redirecting the client to the Data action. The Data method uses the same TempData property to retrieve the data values and uses them to create the model data that will be displayed by the view.

■ **Tip** The TempData dictionary also provides a Peek method that allows you to get a data value without marking it for deletion and a Keep method, which can be used to prevent a previously read value from being deleted. The Keep method doesn't protect a value forever. If the value is read again, it will be marked for removal once more. Use session data if you want to store items so that they won't be removed when the request is processed.

Returning Different Types of Content

HTML isn't the only kind of response that your action methods can generate, and Table 17-10 shows the built-in action results that can be used for different types of data.

Table 17-10. *The Content Action Results*

Name	Controller Method	Description
JsonResult	Json	This action result serializes an object into JSON and returns it to the client.
ContentResult	Content	This action result sends a response whose body contains a specified object.
ObjectResult	Not Available	This action result will use content negotiation to send an object to the client.
OkObjectResult	Ok	This action result will use content negotiation to send an object to the client with an HTTP 200 status code if the content negotiation is successful.
NotFoundObjectResult	NotFound	This action result will use content negotiation to send an object to the client with an HTTP 404 status code if the content negotiation is successful.

Producing a JSON Response

The JavaScript Object Notation (JSON) format has become the standard way to transfer data between a web application and its clients. JSON has largely replaced XML as a data exchange format because it is simpler to work with, especially when writing client-side JavaScript since JSON is closely related to the syntax that JavaScript uses to define literal data values. I return to the topic of JSON and its role in web applications in Chapter 20, and Listing 17-31 shows the use of the Json method to create a JsonResult object.

Listing 17-31. Generating a JSON Response in the ExampleController.cs File in the Controllers Folder

```
using Microsoft.AspNetCore.Mvc;
using System;

namespace ControllersAndActions.Controllers {

    public class ExampleController : Controller {

        public JsonResult Index() => Json(new[] { "Alice", "Bob", "Joe" });
    }
}
```

Run the example and request the /Example URL and you will see a response that expresses the C# string array from the action method in JSON, like this:

```
["Alice","Bob","Joe"]
```

Most browsers display JSON results inline, but some, including Microsoft Internet Explorer, require you to save the data into a file before you can inspect it.

543

```
┌─────────────────────────────────────────────────────────────────────┐
│              UNIT TESTING: NON-HTML ACTION RESULTS                     │
└─────────────────────────────────────────────────────────────────────┘
```

It is important to remember that your unit tests on an action method should focus on the data that is returned to be formatted and not the formatting itself, which is handled by MVC and which will generally be out of scope for most testing projects. As an example, here is a unit test for the action method in Listing 17-31:

```
...
[Fact]
public void JsonActionMethod() {
    // Arrange
    ExampleController controller = new ExampleController();
    // Act
    JsonResult result = controller.Index();
    // Assert
    Assert.Equal(new[] { "Alice", "Bob", "Joe" }, result.Value);
}
...
```

The JsonResult class provides a Value property that returns the data that will be converted into JSON to produce the response to the client. In the unit test, I compare the Value property with the data that I expect.

Using Objects to Generate Responses

Many applications need just HTML and JSON responses from controllers and rely on support for static files to deliver other types of content, such as images, JavaScript files, and CSS stylesheets. There can be occasions, however, when you need to return a specific content type in a response, and there are action results available to help with this. The simplest is the ContentResult class, created through the Content method, which is used to send a string value with an optional MIME content type. In Listing 17-32, I have used the Content method to manually re-create the JSON result from the previous section.

Listing 17-32. Manually Creating a JSON Result in the ExampleController.cs File in the Controllers Folder

```
using Microsoft.AspNetCore.Mvc;

namespace ControllersAndActions.Controllers {

    public class ExampleController : Controller {

        public ContentResult Index()
            => Content("[\"Alice\",\"Bob\",\"Joe\"]", "application/json");
    }
}
```

This type of action result is useful when you have content that is conveniently in a `string` format and you know that the client is able to accept the MIME type you specify. The danger with this approach is that you send a response to the client in a format that it doesn't know how to process. A more robust approach is to rely on content negotiation, which is performed by the `ObjectResult`, as shown in Listing 17-33.

Listing 17-33. Using Content Negotiation in the ExampleController.cs File in the Controllers Folder

```
using Microsoft.AspNetCore.Mvc;

namespace ControllersAndActions.Controllers {

    public class ExampleController : Controller {

        public ObjectResult Index() => Ok(new string[] { "Alice", "Bob", "Joe" });
    }
}
```

The term *content negotiation* suggests a complex system of figuring out a common format between the browser and the application, but in fact, it is a simple process. When the browser makes an HTTP request, it includes the `Accept` header, which indicates which formats it can handle. Here is the header from the version of Google Chrome I used to test the example:

```
Accept: text/html,application/xhtml+xml,application/xml;q=0.9,image/webp,*/*;q=0.8
```

The supported formats are expressed as MIME types. MVC has a set of formats it can use for data values, and it compares these to the formats that the browser supports. The preferred format used by MVC is JSON, and this will be used most of the time, except when an action returns a `string` value, in which case plain text is used. See Chapter 20 for more details about the content negotiation process and how it is implemented.

Responding with the Contents of Files

Most applications rely on the static files middleware to deliver the contents of files, but there is also a set of action results that can be used to send files to the client, as described in Table 17-11.

■ **Caution**   Be careful when you use these action results and make sure that you do not create an application that allows the contents of arbitrary files to be requested. In particular, do not get the path of the file to send from any part of the request or from any data store that a user can modify through a request.

Table 17-11. *The File Action Results*

Name	Controller Method	Description
FileContentResult	File	This action result sends a byte array to the client with a specified MIME type.
FileStreamResult	File	This action result reads a stream and sends the content to the client.
VirtualFileResult	File	This action result reads a stream from a virtual path (relative to the application on the host).
PhysicalFileResult	PhysicalFile	This action result reads the contents of a file from a specified path and sends the contents to the client.

In Listing 17-34, I have used the File method inherited from the Controller class to return the Bootstrap CSS file as the result of the Index action method on the Example controller.

Listing 17-34. Using a File as a Response in the ExampleController.cs File in the Controllers Folder

```
using Microsoft.AspNetCore.Mvc;

namespace ControllersAndActions.Controllers {

    public class ExampleController : Controller {

        public VirtualFileResult Index()
            => File("/lib/bootstrap/dist/css/bootstrap.css", "text/css");
    }
}
```

To use this action method, I have modified the link element in the SimpleForm.cshtml file so that it uses the Url helper, as shown in Listing 17-35.

Listing 17-35. Targeting an Action Method in the SimplerForm.cshtml File

```
@{ Layout = null; }

<!DOCTYPE html>
<html>
<head>
    <meta name="viewport" content="width=device-width" />
    <title>Controllers and Actions</title>
    <link rel="stylesheet" href="@Url.Action("Index", "Example")" />
</head>
```

```
<body class="m-1 p-1">
    <form method="post" asp-action="ReceiveForm">
        <div class="form-group">
            <label for="name">Name:</label>
            <input class="form-control" name="name" />
        </div>
        <div class="form-group">
            <label for="name">City:</label>
            <input class="form-control" name="city" />
        </div>
        <button class="btn btn-primary center-block" type="submit">Submit</button>
    </form>
</body>
</html>
```

If you run the example and request the /Home URL, the HTML response that is sent to the browser will include the following element:

```
<link rel="stylesheet" href="/Example" />
```

This will cause the browser to send an HTTP request that targets the action method in Listing 17-35, which will send the CSS file required to style the content in the view.

■ **Note**   Tag helpers are a much more useful tool for delivering CSS, as I describe in Chapter 25.

Returning Errors and HTTP Codes

The final set of built-in ActionResult classes can be used to send specific error messages and HTTP result codes to the client, as described in Table 17-12. Most applications do not require these features because ASP. NET Core and MVC will automatically generate these kinds of results. However, they can be useful if you need to take more direct control over the responses sent to the client.

Table 17-12. *The Status Code Action Result*

Name	Controller Method	Description
StatusCodeResult	StatusCode	This action result sends a specified HTTP status code to the client.
OkResult	Ok	This action result sends an HTTP 200 status code to the client.
CreatedResult	Created	This action result sends an HTTP 201 status code to the client.
CreatedAtActionResult	CreatedAtAction	This action result sends an HTTP 201 status code to the client along with a URL in the Location header that targets an action and controller.
CreatedAtRouteResult	CreatedAtRoute	This action result sends an HTTP 201 status code to the client along with a URL in the Location header that is generated from a specific route.
BadRequestResult	BadRequest	This action result sends an HTTP 400 status code to the client.
UnauthorizedResult	Unauthorized	This action result sends an HTTP 401 status code to the client.
NotFoundResult	NotFound	This action result sends an HTTP 404 status code to the client
UnsupportedMediaTypeResult	None	This action result sends an HTTP 415 status code to the client.

Sending a Specific HTTP Result Code

You can send a specific HTTP status code to the browser using the StatusCode method, which creates a StatusCodeResult object, as shown in Listing 17-36.

Listing 17-36. Sending a Specific Status Code in the ExampleController.cs File in the Controllers Folder

```
using Microsoft.AspNetCore.Mvc;
using Microsoft.AspNetCore.Http;

namespace ControllersAndActions.Controllers {

    public class ExampleController : Controller {

        public StatusCodeResult Index()
            => StatusCode(StatusCodes.Status404NotFound);
    }
}
```

The StatusCode method accepts an int value, which you can use to specify a status code directly. The StatusCodes class in the Microsoft.AspNetCore.Http namespace defines fields for all the status codes supported by HTTP. In the listing, I used the Status404NotFound field to return code 404, which signifies that the requested resource does not exist.

Sending a 404 Result Using a Convenience Class

The other action results shown in Table 17-12 extend or rely on the StatusCodeResult class, which provides a more convenient way to send specific status codes. I can achieve the same effect as Listing 17-36 using the more convenient NotFoundResult class, which is derived from StatusCodeResult and can be created using the controller NotFound convenience method, as shown in Listing 17-37.

Listing 17-37. Generating a 404 Result in the ExampleController.cs File in the Controllers Folder

```
using Microsoft.AspNetCore.Mvc;
using Microsoft.AspNetCore.Http;

namespace ControllersAndActions.Controllers {

    public class ExampleController : Controller {

        public StatusCodeResult Index() => NotFound();
    }
}
```

UNIT TEST: HTTP STATUS CODES

The StatusCodeResult class follows the pattern you have seen for the other result types and makes its state available through a set of properties. In this case, the StatusCode property returns the numeric HTTP status code, and the StatusDescription property returns the associated descriptive string. The following test method is for the action method in Listing 17-37:

```
...
[Fact]
public void NotFoundActionMethod() {
    // Arrange
    ExampleController controller = new ExampleController();
    // Act
    StatusCodeResult result = controller.Index();
    // Assert
    Assert.Equal(404, result.StatusCode);
}
...
```

Understanding the Other Action Result Classes

Some additional action result classes are closely linked with MVC features that I describe in other chapters. Table 17-13 lists these classes along with the chapters that describe the feature they relate to.

Table 17-13. *Other Action Result Classes*

Name	Controller Method	Description
PartialViewResult	PartialView	This action result is used to select a partial view, as described in Chapter 21.
ViewComponentResult	ViewComponent	This action result is used to select a view component, as described in Chapter 22.
EmptyResult	None	This action result class does nothing and produces an empty response to the client.
ChallengeResult	None	This action result is used to enforce security policies in requests. See Chapter 30 for details.

Summary

Controllers are one of the key building blocks in the MVC design pattern and are at the heart of MVC development. In this chapter, you have seen how to create POCO controllers using basic C# classes and how to benefit from the convenience offered by the Controller base class. You saw the role that action results play in MVC controllers and how they ease unit testing. I showed you the different ways that you can receive input and generate output from an action method, and I demonstrated the built-in action result that makes this a simple and flexible process. In the next chapter, I describe one of the features that causes the most confusion for ASP.NET Core developers but that is essential for effective MVC development: dependency injection.

CHAPTER 18

■ ■ ■

Dependency Injection

In this chapter, I describe *dependency injection* (DI), a technique that helps create flexible applications and simplifies unit testing. Dependency injection can be a difficult topic to understand, both in terms of why it can be useful and how it is performed. To that end, I build up slowly, starting with the conventional way of building application components and gradually explaining how dependency injection works and why it matters. Table 18-1 puts dependency injection into context.

Table 18-1. *Putting Dependency Injection in Context*

Question	Answer
What is it?	Dependency injection makes it easy to create loosely coupled components, which typically means that components consume functionality defined by interfaces without having any first-hand knowledge of which implementation classes are being used.
Why is it useful?	Dependency injection makes it easier to change the behavior of an application by changing the components that implement the interfaces that define application features. It also results in components that are easier to isolate for unit testing.
How is it used?	The Startup class is used to specify which implementation classes are used to deliver the functionality specified by the interfaces used by the application. When new objects—such as controllers—are created to handle requests, they are automatically provided with instances of the implementation classes they require.
Are there any pitfalls or limitations?	The main limitation is that classes declare their use of services as constructor arguments, which can result in constructors whose only role is to receive dependencies and assign them to instance fields.
Are there any alternatives?	You don't have to use dependency injection in your own code, but it is helpful to know how it works because it is used by MVC to provide features to developers.

© Adam Freeman 2017

A. Freeman, *Pro ASP.NET Core MVC 2*, https://doi.org/10.1007/978-1-4842-3150-0_18

Table 18-2 summarizes the chapter.

Table 18-2. *Chapter Summary*

Problem	Solution	Listing
Create loosely coupled components	Isolate classes through interfaces and connect them together using external mappings	9–16
Declare a dependency in a component, such as a controller	Define a constructor argument of the type that the component requires	17
Configure a service mapping	Add the mapping to the Startup class	18, 20–26
Unit test a component with a dependency	Create a mock implementation of the service interface and pass it as a constructor argument when the component is created in the unit test	19
Specify the way in which implementation objects are created	Create the service mapping using the life-cycle method that suits the service being managed	27–31
Receive dependencies for individual action methods in a controller	Use action injection	32
Manually request an implementation object in a controller	Use the HttpContext.RequestServices property	33

Preparing the Example Project

For this chapter, I used the ASP.NET Core Web Application (.NET Core) template to create a new Empty project called DependencyInjection. Listing 18-1 shows the Startup class, which configures the services and middleware components for the project.

Listing 18-1. The Contents of the Startup.cs File in the DependencyInjection Folder

```
using System;
using System.Collections.Generic;
using System.Linq;
using System.Threading.Tasks;
using Microsoft.AspNetCore.Builder;
using Microsoft.AspNetCore.Hosting;
using Microsoft.AspNetCore.Http;
using Microsoft.Extensions.DependencyInjection;

namespace DependencyInjection {
    public class Startup {

        public void ConfigureServices(IServiceCollection services) {
            services.AddMvc();
        }
```

```
        public void Configure(IApplicationBuilder app, IHostingEnvironment env) {
            app.UseStatusCodePages();
            app.UseDeveloperExceptionPage();
            app.UseStaticFiles();
            app.UseMvcWithDefaultRoute();
        }
    }
}
```

Creating the Model and Repository

The examples in this chapter require a simple model that I created by creating the Models folder and adding a class file called Product.cs, which I used to define the class shown in Listing 18-2.

Listing 18-2. The Contents of the Product.cs File in the Models Folder

```
namespace DependencyInjection.Models {

    public class Product {

        public string Name { get; set; }
        public decimal Price { get; set; }
    }
}
```

To manage the model, I added a class called IRepository.cs to the Models folder and used it to define the interface shown in Listing 18-3.

Listing 18-3. The Contents of the IRepository.cs File in the Models Folder

```
using System.Collections.Generic;

namespace DependencyInjection.Models {

    public interface IRepository {

        IEnumerable<Product> Products { get; }

        Product this[string name] { get; }

        void AddProduct(Product product);
        void DeleteProduct(Product product);
    }
}
```

The interface defines the operations that can be performed on the collection of Product objects. To provide an implementation of the interface, I added a class file called MemoryRepository.cs to the Models folder and defined the class shown in Listing 18-4.

Listing 18-4. The Contents of the MemoryRepository.cs File in the Models Folder

```
using System.Collections.Generic;

namespace DependencyInjection.Models {

    public class MemoryRepository : IRepository {
        private Dictionary<string, Product> products;

        public MemoryRepository() {
            products = new Dictionary<string, Product>();
            new List<Product> {
                new Product { Name = "Kayak", Price = 275M },
                new Product { Name = "Lifejacket", Price = 48.95M },
                new Product { Name = "Soccer ball", Price = 19.50M }
            }.ForEach(p => AddProduct(p));
        }

        public IEnumerable<Product> Products => products.Values;

        public Product this[string name] => products[name];

        public void AddProduct(Product product) =>
            products[product.Name] = product;

        public void DeleteProduct(Product product) =>
            products.Remove(product.Name);
    }
}
```

The MemoryRepository class stores its model objects in memory, using a dictionary. This means that there is no persistent storage and stopping or restarting the application will reset the model to the sample data objects that are created in the constructor. This isn't a sensible approach for a real project, but it will be enough for this chapter, where the focus is on a different aspect of how applications work.

Creating the Controller and View

I created the Controllers folder, added a class file called HomeController.cs, and used it to define the class shown in Listing 18-5.

Listing 18-5. The Contents of the HomeController.cs File in the Controllers Folder

```
using Microsoft.AspNetCore.Mvc;

namespace DependencyInjection.Controllers {

    public class HomeController : Controller {

        public ViewResult Index() => View();
    }
}
```

The controller has only one action method, which uses the `View` method to create a `ViewResult` that will render the default view. To create the view associated with the action method, I created the `Views/Home` folder and added a Razor file called `Index.cshtml`. Listing 18-6 shows the markup I added to the view.

Listing 18-6. The Contents of the Index.cshtml File in the Views/Home Folder

```
@model IEnumerable<Product>
@{ Layout = null; }

<!DOCTYPE html>
<html>
<head>
    <meta name="viewport" content="width=device-width" />
    <title>Dependency Injection</title>
    <link rel="stylesheet" asp-href-include="lib/bootstrap/dist/css/*.min.css" />
</head>
<body class="m-1 p-1">
    @if (ViewData.Count > 0) {
        <table class="table table-bordered table-sm table-striped">
            @foreach (var kvp in ViewData) {
                <tr><td>@kvp.Key</td><td>@kvp.Value</td></tr>
            }
        </table>
    }
    <table class="table table-bordered table-sm table-striped">
        <thead>
            <tr><th>Name</th><th>Price</th></tr>
        </thead>
        <tbody>
            @if (Model == null) {
                <tr><td colspan="3" class="text-center">No Model Data</td></tr>
            } else {
                @foreach (var p in Model) {
                    <tr>
                        <td>@p.Name</td>
                        <td>@string.Format("{0:C2}", p.Price)</td>
                    </tr>
                }
            }
        </tbody>
    </table>
</body>
</html>
```

The view is strongly typed using an enumeration of `Product` objects, and the main content of the view is an HTML table. If the controller doesn't provide any model data, then a message is shown as the only content of the table. If there is model data, then a row is added to the table for each `Product` object in the enumeration. There is also a table that will enumerate the keys and values in the view bag if there are any but is otherwise hidden. I use this table later in the chapter.

The view depends on the Bootstrap CSS package for styling the HTML elements. To add Bootstrap to the project, I used the Bower Configuration File item template to create the `bower.json` file and added the Bootstrap package to the `dependencies` section, as shown in Listing 18-7.

555

Listing 18-7. Adding Bootstrap in the bower.json File in the DependencyInjection Folder

```
{
  "name": "asp.net",
  "private": true,
  "dependencies": {
    "bootstrap": "4.0.0-alpha.6"
  }
}
```

The final preparation is to create the _ViewImports.cshtml file in the Views folder, which sets up the built-in tag helpers for use in Razor views and imports the model namespace, as shown in Listing 18-8.

Listing 18-8. The Contents of the _ViewImports.cshtml File in the Views Folder

```
@using DependencyInjection.Models
@addTagHelper *, Microsoft.AspNetCore.Mvc.TagHelpers
```

Creating the Unit Test Project

I used the xUnit Test Project (.NET Core) template to create a project called DependencyInjection.Tests, following the process described in Chapter 7. I removed the UnitTest1.cs file so there are no tests in the project.

If you run the application, you will see the result shown in Figure 18-1.

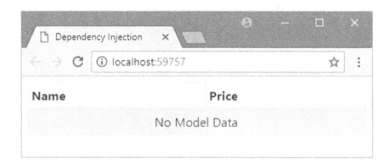

Figure 18-1. *Running the example application*

Creating Loosely Coupled Components

The reason that Figure 18-1 shows no model data is because there is no relationship between the HomeController class, which needs to pass model data to its view, and the MemoryRepository class, which contains the model data. The goal when connecting components together in an MVC application is to able to easily replace a component with an alternative implementation of the same functionality.

Being able to replace components allows effective unit testing, makes it possible to easily change the behavior of the application in different hosting environments (such as development and production servers), and simplifies long-term application maintenance.

In the sections that follow, I start by explaining the alternative approach and the problems it presents. This may seem like an indirect way to explain the dependency injection feature, but one of the challenges with DI is that it solves a problem that isn't always obvious when writing code and that appears only later in the development cycle.

TAKING A VIEW ON DEPENDENCY INJECTION

Dependency injection is one of the topics that readers contact me about most often. About half of the emails complain that I am "forcing" DI upon them. Oddly, the other half are complaints that I did not emphasize the benefits of DI strongly enough and other readers may not have realized how useful it can be.

Dependency injection can be a difficult topic to understand and its value is contentious. DI can be a useful tool, but not everyone likes it—or needs it.

DI offers limited benefit if you are not doing unit testing or if you are working on a small, self-contained and stable project. It is still helpful to understand how DI works because DI is used to access some important MVC features, but you don't always need to embrace DI in the controllers and other classes you write.

I use DI in my own projects, largely because I find that projects often go in unexpected directions and being able to easily replace a component with a new implementation can save me a lot of tedious and error-prone changes. I'd rather put in some effort at the start of the project than have to do a complex set of edits later. I am not dogmatic about dependency injection—it solves a problem that doesn't arise in every project. Only you can determine whether you need DI on your project, and only you can evaluate the benefits and costs.

Examining Closely Coupled Components

For most developers, the natural inclination is to take the most direct path to solve a problem. For the example application, that means using the new keyword to create the repository object that is required by the controller in order to get hold of the model data, as shown in Listing 18-9.

Listing 18-9. Instantiating the Repository in the HomeController.cs File in the Controllers Folder

```
using Microsoft.AspNetCore.Mvc;
using DependencyInjection.Models;

namespace DependencyInjection.Controllers {

    public class HomeController : Controller {

        public ViewResult Index() => View(new MemoryRepository().Products);
    }
}
```

The good news about this code is that it works. If you run the application, you will see the details of the model objects displayed in the browser, as shown in Figure 18-2.

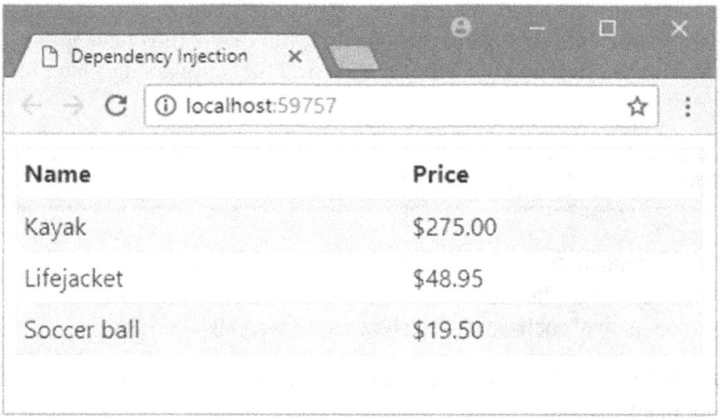

Figure 18-2. *Displaying the model data*

The bad news is that the Home controller and the MemoryRepository class are now *tightly coupled*, which means that I can't replace the repository without altering the HomeController class. As I explained in Chapter 7, performing effective unit tests means being able to isolate a single component, but I can't test the Index action method in Listing 18-9 without also implicitly testing the repository class. If my unit test fails, I won't know whether the problem is in the controller, the repository, or some other component that the repository depends on. For all practical purposes, the Home controller and MemoryRepository form a single individual unit, as illustrated by Figure 18-3.

```
Controller ──→ Repository
```

Figure 18-3. *The effect of tightly coupled components*

Decoupling Components for Unit Testing

In Chapter 7, I used a property to store a reference to the repository class through the interface it implements, which allowed me to create a mock repository for the purposes of unit testing. Listing 18-10 shows this approach applied to the controller in this example application for this chapter.

Listing 18-10. Using a Repository Property in the HomeController.cs File in the Controllers Folder

```
using Microsoft.AspNetCore.Mvc;
using DependencyInjection.Models;

namespace DependencyInjection.Controllers {

    public class HomeController : Controller {

        public IRepository Repository { get; set; } = new MemoryRepository();

        public ViewResult Index() => View(Repository.Products);
    }
}
```

This technique is perfectly serviceable if you want to do unit testing because it lets you isolate the controller class by setting the Repository property before calling the action method in a unit test.

I added a class file called DITests.cs to the DependencyInjection.Tests project and used it to define the unit test shown in Listing 18-11, which uses the Repository property to set up a fake repository before acting on the controller.

Listing 18-11. Testing the Controller in the DITests.cs File in the Unit Test Project

```
using DependencyInjection.Controllers;
using DependencyInjection.Models;
using Microsoft.AspNetCore.Mvc;
using Moq;
using Xunit;

namespace Tests {

    public class DITests {

        [Fact]
        public void ControllerTest() {
            // Arrange
            var data = new[] { new Product { Name = "Test", Price = 100 } };
            var mock = new Mock<IRepository>();
            mock.SetupGet(m => m.Products).Returns(data);
            HomeController controller = new HomeController {
                Repository = mock.Object
            };

            // Act
            ViewResult result = controller.Index();

            // Assert
            Assert.Equal(data, result.ViewData.Model);
        }
    }
}
```

The Repository property allows me to isolate the controller and supply test data that I can inspect in the ViewResult created by the action method. This provides only a partial solution to the tightly coupled component problem because you can't set the Repository property when the application is running. As I explained in Chapter 17, MVC is responsible for instantiating controllers to process requests, and it knows nothing about the special importance attached to the Repository property. The effect that this technique creates is that the controller and repository are loosely coupled for the purposes of unit testing but tightly coupled when the application is running, as shown in Figure 18-4.

Testing

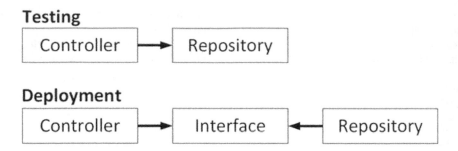

Figure 18-4. *The effect of adding a repository property*

Using a Type Broker

The next logical step is to take the decision about which implementation of the repository interface is used out of the controller class and put it elsewhere in the application. To demonstrate how this can work, I added an Infrastructure folder to the example application and added a class file to it called TypeBroker.cs, the contents of which are shown in Listing 18-12.

Listing 18-12. The Contents of the TypeBroker.cs File in the Infrastructure Folder

```
using DependencyInjection.Models;
using System;

namespace DependencyInjection.Infrastructure {
    public static class TypeBroker {
        private static Type repoType = typeof(MemoryRepository);
        private static IRepository testRepo;

        public static IRepository Repository =>
            testRepo ?? Activator.CreateInstance(repoType) as IRepository;

        public static void SetRepositoryType<T>() where T : IRepository =>
            repoType = typeof(T);

        public static void SetTestObject(IRepository repo) {
            testRepo = repo;
        }

    }
}
```

The TypeBroker class defines a Repository property that returns new objects that implement the IRepository interface. The implementation class used by the Repository property is determined by the value of the repoType field, which defaults to MemoryRepository but which can be changed by calling the SetRepositoryType method.

To support unit testing, the SetTestObject method allows a specific object to be used. In Listing 18-13, I have updated the Home controller so that it obtains the repository object from the broker.

Listing 18-13. Using the Type Broker in the HomeController.cs File in the Controllers Folder

```
using Microsoft.AspNetCore.Mvc;
using DependencyInjection.Models;
using DependencyInjection.Infrastructure;

namespace DependencyInjection.Controllers {

    public class HomeController : Controller {

        public IRepository Repository { get; } = TypeBroker.Repository;

        public ViewResult Index() => View(Repository.Products);
    }
}
```

There is now a more complex set of relationships in the example application, as shown in Figure 18-5. The key point to note is that there is no direct relationship between the controller class and the repository class—everything is mediated through the interface and the broker. This means it is possible to change the repository class without having to make any change to the controller.

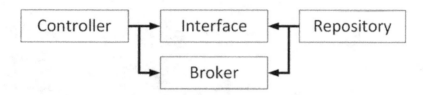

Figure 18-5. *The effect of adding a type broker*

To demonstrate the use of the type broker, I added a class file called AlternateRepository.cs to the Models folder and used it to define another implementation of the IRepository interface, as shown in Listing 18-14.

Listing 18-14. The Contents of the AlternateRepository.cs File in the Models Folder

```
using System.Collections.Generic;

namespace DependencyInjection.Models {
    public class AlternateRepository : IRepository {
        private Dictionary<string, Product> products;

        public AlternateRepository() {
            products = new Dictionary<string, Product>();
            new List<Product> {
                new Product { Name = "Corner Flags", Price = 34.95M },
                new Product { Name = "Stadium", Price = 79500M }
            }.ForEach(p => AddProduct(p));
        }
```

```
        public IEnumerable<Product> Products => products.Values;

        public Product this[string name] => products[name];

        public void AddProduct(Product product) =>
            products[product.Name] = product;

        public void DeleteProduct(Product product) =>
            products.Remove(product.Name);
    }
}
```

In a real application, an alternative repository might store its data in a different format or use a different kind of persistence. In this example, the difference between the AlternateRepository class and the MemoryRepository class is the model data they create when the class is instantiated. To use the AlternateRepository class, I configured the type broker in the ConfigureServices method of the Startup class, as shown in Listing 18-15.

Listing 18-15. Configuring the Broker in the Startup.cs File in the DependencyInjection Folder

```
using System;
using System.Collections.Generic;
using System.Linq;
using System.Threading.Tasks;
using Microsoft.AspNetCore.Builder;
using Microsoft.AspNetCore.Hosting;
using Microsoft.AspNetCore.Http;
using Microsoft.Extensions.DependencyInjection;
using DependencyInjection.Infrastructure;
using DependencyInjection.Models;

namespace DependencyInjection {
    public class Startup {

        public void ConfigureServices(IServiceCollection services) {
            TypeBroker.SetRepositoryType<AlternateRepository>();
            services.AddMvc();
        }

        public void Configure(IApplicationBuilder app, IHostingEnvironment env) {
            app.UseStatusCodePages();
            app.UseDeveloperExceptionPage();
            app.UseStaticFiles();
            app.UseMvcWithDefaultRoute();
        }
    }
}
```

You can see the effect of the change by starting the application, which will show the data provided by the new repository class, as shown in Figure 18-6.

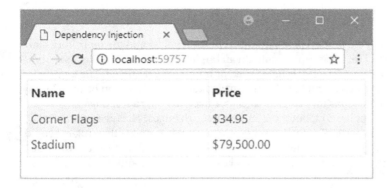

Figure 18-6. *Changing the repository class*

The type broker allows a specific object to be used as the repository, which allows unit tests to be written like the one in Listing 18-16.

Listing 18-16. Testing Through the Broker in the DITests.cs File in the Tests Project

```
using DependencyInjection.Controllers;
using DependencyInjection.Infrastructure;
using DependencyInjection.Models;
using Microsoft.AspNetCore.Mvc;
using Moq;
using Xunit;

namespace Tests {

    public class DITests {

        [Fact]
        public void ControllerTest() {
            // Arrange
            var data = new[] { new Product { Name = "Test", Price = 100 } };
            var mock = new Mock<IRepository>();
            mock.SetupGet(m => m.Products).Returns(data);
            TypeBroker.SetTestObject(mock.Object);
            HomeController controller = new HomeController();

            // Act
            ViewResult result = controller.Index();

            // Assert
            Assert.Equal(data, result.ViewData.Model);
        }
    }
}
```

Introducing ASP.NET Dependency Injection

In the previous section, I walked through the process of separating a controller class and the repository that supplies its model data. The HomeController class can now obtain an implementation of the IRepository interface without having any knowledge of which class is being used or how it is instantiated. The knowledge about which IRepository class is being used is contained in the TypeBroker class, which can be used by any other controller that requires access to the repository and which can be used to apply a test object.

The overall effect is a more flexible application, but there are some rough edges. The biggest drawback is that I have to add new methods and properties for each new type that I want to manage the broker. I could rewrite the TypeBroker class to be more general, but there isn't any need because ASP.NET Core provides a slicker version of the same functionality, packaged in a way that makes it easier to use and doesn't require any special classes.

Preparing for Dependency Injection

The term *dependency injection* (DI) describes an alternative approach to creating loosely coupled components, which is integrated into the ASP.NET Core platform and used automatically by MVC, which means that controllers and other components don't need to have any knowledge of how the types they require are created. Listing 18-17 shows how I have prepared the Home controller for DI.

Listing 18-17. Preparing for DI in the HomeController.cs File in the Controllers Folder

```
using Microsoft.AspNetCore.Mvc;
using DependencyInjection.Models;
using DependencyInjection.Infrastructure;

namespace DependencyInjection.Controllers {

    public class HomeController : Controller {
        private IRepository repository;

        public HomeController(IRepository repo) => repository = repo;

        public ViewResult Index() => View(repository.Products);
    }
}
```

The controller declares its dependencies as constructor arguments. This accounts for the first part of the term: the *dependencies* in dependency injection are the objects that are required to create a new instance of a class. In this case, the controller class has declared a dependency on the IRepository interface.

In ASP.NET Core, a component called the *service provider* is responsible for mapping interfaces to the implementation types that are used to satisfy dependencies.

When a new controller is required, MVC asks the service provider to create a new instance of the HomeController class. The service provider inspects the HomeController constructor to determine its dependencies, creates the service objects that are required, and *injects* them into the HomeController constructor to create a new controller that can be used to handle a request. This is the core process of dependency injection, so I am going to spell it out for clarity.

1. MVC receives an incoming request to an action method on the Home controller.

2. MVC asks the ASP.NET service provider component for a new instance of the HomeController class.

3. The service provider inspects the HomeController constructor and discovers that it has a dependency on the IRepository interface.

4. The service provider consults its mappings to find the implementation class it has been told to use for dependencies on the IRepository interface.

5. The service provider creates a new instance of the implementation class.

6. The service provider creates a new HomeController object, using the implementation object as a constructor argument.

7. The service provider returns the newly created HomeController object to MVC, which uses it to handle the incoming HTTP request.

The overall effect is the same as for the custom type broker class, but an important advantage is that the dependency injection process is integrated into MVC, which means that the service provider component will be used whenever a controller class is created. This allows for controller classes to declare dependencies without needing any knowledge of how they will be resolved. You just write controller classes that declare their dependencies as constructor parameters and let MVC and the service provider component figure out the rest.

■ **Note**   All the examples in this chapter use the built-in dependency injection system that comes as part of ASP.NET Core. There are third-party packages that can be used as drop-in replacements for the built-in functionality and that can offer enhancements and additional features. Popular packages include Autofac and StructureMap, although at the time of writing additional packages are required to integrate them into ASP.NET Core. You can find details at http://github.com/aspnet/DependencyInjection/blob/dev/README.md.

Configuring the Service Provider

Declaring a dependency through the HomeController constructor has broken the application, which you can see if you run the project. When MVC tries to create an instance of the HomeController class to service a request, it encounters the error shown in Figure 18-7.

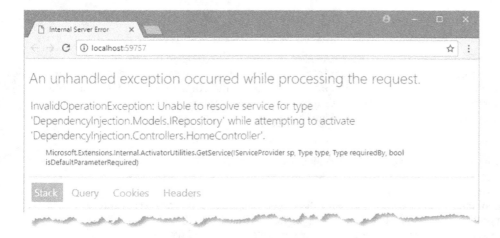

Figure 18-7. Running the example project

To resolve dependencies, the service provider has to be configured so that it knows how to resolve service dependencies. At the moment, the service provider doesn't have that information, and it threw an exception when asked to create a HomeController object because it doesn't know how to resolve the dependency on the IRepository interface.

The configuration for the service provider is defined in the Startup class so that the service is in place before the application starts to receive requests. In Listing 18-18, I have configured the service provider so that it knows how to deal with dependencies on the IRepository interface.

Listing 18-18. Configuring the Service Provider in the Startup.cs File in the DependencyInjection Folder

```
using System;
using System.Collections.Generic;
using System.Linq;
using System.Threading.Tasks;
using Microsoft.AspNetCore.Builder;
using Microsoft.AspNetCore.Hosting;
using Microsoft.AspNetCore.Http;
using Microsoft.Extensions.DependencyInjection;
using DependencyInjection.Infrastructure;
using DependencyInjection.Models;

namespace DependencyInjection {
    public class Startup {

        public void ConfigureServices(IServiceCollection services) {
            services.AddTransient<IRepository, MemoryRepository>();
            services.AddMvc();
        }

        public void Configure(IApplicationBuilder app, IHostingEnvironment env) {
            app.UseStatusCodePages();
            app.UseDeveloperExceptionPage();
            app.UseStaticFiles();
            app.UseMvcWithDefaultRoute();
        }
    }
}
```

Dependency injection is configured using extension methods that are called on the IServiceCollection object received by the ConfigureServices method. The AddTransient extension method that I used in the listing tells the service provider how to handle a dependency (which I describe in more detail later in the chapter). The mapping is expressed using type parameters, with the first type being the interface and the second type being the implementation class.

```
...
services.AddTransient<IRepository, MemoryRepository>();
...
```

This statement tells the service provider to resolve dependencies on the IRepository interface by creating a MemoryRepository object. If you run the application, you will see that the dependency declared by the HomeController constructor is resolved and the controller is provided with access to model data, as shown in Figure 18-8.

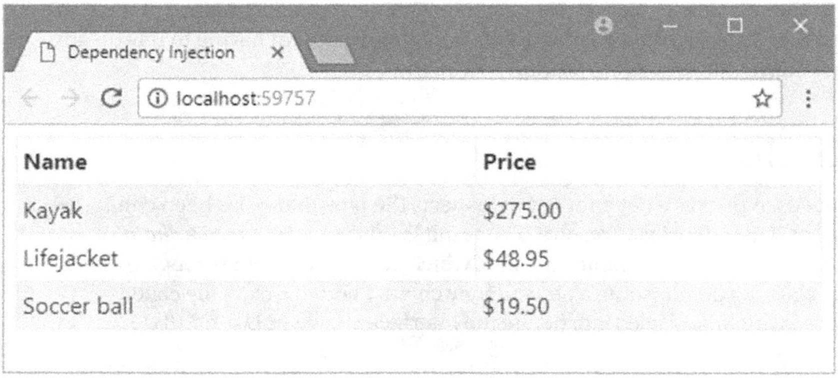

Figure 18-8. *Configuring dependency injection*

Unit Testing a Controller with a Dependency

Using the constructor to receive dependencies makes it easy to unit test controllers. Listing 18-19 shows a unit test for the controller in Listing 18-18.

Listing 18-19. Testing a Controller in the DITests.cs File in the Unit Test Project

```
using DependencyInjection.Controllers;
using DependencyInjection.Models;
using Microsoft.AspNetCore.Mvc;
using Moq;
using Xunit;

namespace Tests {

    public class DITests {

        [Fact]
        public void ControllerTest() {
            // Arrange
            var data = new[] { new Product { Name = "Test", Price = 100 } };
            var mock = new Mock<IRepository>();
            mock.SetupGet(m => m.Products).Returns(data);
            HomeController controller = new HomeController(mock.Object);

            // Act
            ViewResult result = controller.Index();

            // Assert
            Assert.Equal(data, result.ViewData.Model);
        }
    }
}
```

The controller doesn't know—or care—what kind of object is passed to the constructor as long as it implements the correct interface. This allows me to use my fake repository without having to rely on any external class, such as a type broker, that may affect the outcome of the test.

Using Dependency Chains

When the service provider needs to resolve a dependency, it inspects the type that it has been configured to use to see whether it, too, has dependencies to resolve. The result is that you can create a *chain* of dependencies, all of which are resolved at runtime and all of which can be managed through the configuration in the Startup class. To demonstrate a dependency chain, I added a class file called IModelStorage.cs to the Models folder and used it to define the interface shown in Listing 18-20.

Listing 18-20. The Contents of the IModelStorage.cs File in the Models Folder

```
using System.Collections.Generic;

namespace DependencyInjection.Models {

    public interface IModelStorage {
        IEnumerable<Product> Items { get; }
        Product this[string key] { get; set; }
        bool ContainsKey(string key);
        void RemoveItem(string key);
    }
}
```

This interface defines the behavior of a simple storage mechanism for Product objects. To implement this interface, I added a class file called DictionaryStorage.cs to the Models folder and used it to define the class shown in Listing 18-21.

Listing 18-21. The Contents of the DictionaryStorage.cs File in the Models Folder

```
using System.Collections.Generic;

namespace DependencyInjection.Models {
    public class DictionaryStorage : IModelStorage {
        private Dictionary<string, Product> items
            = new Dictionary<string, Product>();

        public Product this[string key] {
            get { return items[key]; }
            set { items[key] = value; }
        }

        public IEnumerable<Product> Items => items.Values;
        public bool ContainsKey(string key) => items.ContainsKey(key);
        public void RemoveItem(string key) => items.Remove(key);
    }
}
```

The DictionaryStorage class implements the IModelStorage interface by using a strongly typed dictionary to store model objects. This is functionality that is currently contained within the MemoryRepository class and there would be little value in separating using an interface in a real project, but it makes for a useful example of how dependency injection can be used without adding too much additional complexity to the example application.

In Listing 18-22, I have updated the MemoryRepository class so that it declares a dependency on the IModelStorage interface but without any knowledge about the implementation class that will be used at runtime.

Listing 18-22. Declaring a Dependency in the MemoryRepository.cs File in the Models Folder

```
using System.Collections.Generic;

namespace DependencyInjection.Models {
    public class MemoryRepository : IRepository {
        private IModelStorage storage;

        public MemoryRepository(IModelStorage modelStore) {
            storage = modelStore;
            new List<Product> {
                new Product { Name = "Kayak", Price = 275M },
                new Product { Name = "Lifejacket", Price = 48.95M },
                new Product { Name = "Soccer ball", Price = 19.50M }
            }.ForEach(p => AddProduct(p));
        }

        public IEnumerable<Product> Products => storage.Items;

        public Product this[string name] => storage[name];

        public void AddProduct(Product product) =>
            storage[product.Name] = product;

        public void DeleteProduct(Product product) =>
            storage.RemoveItem(product.Name);
    }
}
```

If you run the application, you will see that the service provider throws an exception with the following message:

```
InvalidOperationException: Unable to resolve service for type
'DependencyInjection.Models.IModelStorage' while attempting to activate
'DependencyInjection.Models.MemoryRepository'.
```

This demonstrates that the service provider is working its way through the chain of dependencies. When it was asked to create a new controller, it inspected the HomeController constructor and found a dependency on the IRepository interface, which it knows should be resolved with a MemoryRepository object. The service provider then inspected the MemoryRepository constructor, which has a dependency on the IModelStorage interface. The configuration doesn't specify how IModelStorage dependencies should be resolved, which means that the MemoryRepository object cannot be created, and this, in turn, means that the HomeController object can't be created either. The service provider is unable to provide MVC with the object it needs to handle the request, and an exception is thrown.

What I need is a type mapping that tells the service provider how it should resolve dependencies on IModelStorage, which I have added to the application configuration in Listing 18-23.

Listing 18-23. An Additional Type Mapping in the Startup.cs File in the DependencyInjection Folder

```
using System;
using System.Collections.Generic;
using System.Linq;
using System.Threading.Tasks;
using Microsoft.AspNetCore.Builder;
using Microsoft.AspNetCore.Hosting;
using Microsoft.AspNetCore.Http;
using Microsoft.Extensions.DependencyInjection;
using DependencyInjection.Infrastructure;
using DependencyInjection.Models;

namespace DependencyInjection {
    public class Startup {

        public void ConfigureServices(IServiceCollection services) {
            services.AddTransient<IRepository, MemoryRepository>();
            services.AddTransient<IModelStorage, DictionaryStorage>();
            services.AddMvc();
        }

        public void Configure(IApplicationBuilder app, IHostingEnvironment env) {
            app.UseStatusCodePages();
            app.UseDeveloperExceptionPage();
            app.UseStaticFiles();
            app.UseMvcWithDefaultRoute();
        }
    }
}
```

With this addition, the service provider can satisfy both of the dependencies in the chain and is able to create the set of objects required to service the request: a DictionaryStorage object that is injected into the MemoryRepository constructor, which in turn is injected into the HomeController constructor. Dependency chains are not just a clever trick; they allow complex functionality to be composed by combining components that can be easily isolated for testing and that can be easily changed to suit the evolving requirements of a project as it matures.

Using Dependency Injection for Concrete Types

Dependency injection can also be used for concrete types, which are not accessed through interfaces. While this doesn't provide the loose-coupling advantages of using an interface, it is a useful technique in its own right because it allows objects to be accessed anywhere in an application and puts concrete types under life-cycle management, which I describe later in this chapter.

To demonstrate, I added a class file called ProductTotalizer.cs to the Models folder and used it to define the class shown in Listing 18-24.

Listing 18-24. The Contents of the ProductTotalizer.cs File in the Models Folder

```
using System.Linq;

namespace DependencyInjection.Models {
    public class ProductTotalizer {

        public ProductTotalizer(IRepository repo) => Repository = repo;

        public IRepository Repository { get; set; }

        public decimal Total => Repository.Products.Sum(p => p.Price);
    }
}
```

This class doesn't do anything especially useful, but it does have a dependency on the IRepository interface, which means using dependency injection will resolve this dependency using the configuration that applies to the rest of the application as well. In Listing 18-25, I have declared the ProductTotalizer class as a dependency of the HomeController class.

Listing 18-25. Adding a Dependency in the HomeController.cs File in the Controllers Folder

```
using Microsoft.AspNetCore.Mvc;
using DependencyInjection.Models;
using DependencyInjection.Infrastructure;

namespace DependencyInjection.Controllers {

    public class HomeController : Controller {
        private IRepository repository;
        private ProductTotalizer totalizer;

        public HomeController(IRepository repo, ProductTotalizer total) {
            repository = repo;
            totalizer = total;
        }

        public ViewResult Index() {
            ViewBag.Total = totalizer.Total;
            return View(repository.Products);
        }
    }
}
```

The Index action adds a view bag property that contains the total produced by the ProductTotalizer class, which will be displayed in the table for view bag values that I added to the Index.cshtml view at the start of the chapter. The final step is to tell the service provider how to deal with ProductTotalizer requests, as shown in Listing 18-26.

Listing 18-26. Configuring the Service Provider in the Startup.cs File in the DependencyInjection Folder

```
using System;
using System.Collections.Generic;
using System.Linq;
using System.Threading.Tasks;
using Microsoft.AspNetCore.Builder;
using Microsoft.AspNetCore.Hosting;
using Microsoft.AspNetCore.Http;
using Microsoft.Extensions.DependencyInjection;
using DependencyInjection.Infrastructure;
using DependencyInjection.Models;

namespace DependencyInjection {
    public class Startup {

        public void ConfigureServices(IServiceCollection services) {
            services.AddTransient<IRepository, MemoryRepository>();
            services.AddTransient<IModelStorage, DictionaryStorage>();
            services.AddTransient<ProductTotalizer>();
            services.AddMvc();
        }

        public void Configure(IApplicationBuilder app, IHostingEnvironment env) {
            app.UseStatusCodePages();
            app.UseDeveloperExceptionPage();
            app.UseStaticFiles();
            app.UseMvcWithDefaultRoute();
        }
    }
}
```

There is no mapping between a service type and an implementation type in this situation, so there is an override of the AddTransient extension method that accepts a single type parameter that tells the service provider that it should instantiate the ProductTotalizer class to resolve a dependency on this type.

The advantages of this approach—as opposed to simply instantiating the concrete class in the controller—are that the service provider will resolve any dependencies declared by the concrete class and that you can change the configuration so that more specialized subclasses are used to resolve dependencies for a concrete class. Concrete classes are managed by the service provider and are also subject to the life-cycle features that I describe in the next chapter. If you run the application, you will see that the total value of the Product objects in the model is displayed, as shown in Figure 18-9.

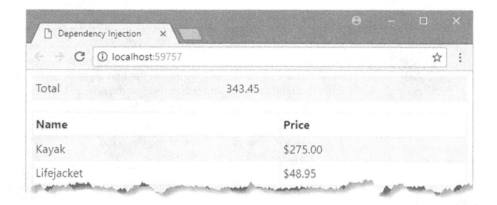

Figure 18-9. *Using dependency injection for classes*

Understanding Service Life Cycles

In the previous section, I used the AddTransient extension method to tell the service provider how it should handle dependencies on the IRepository and IModelStorage interfaces. The AddTransient method is one of four different ways that type mappings can be defined. Table 18-3 describes the extension methods that tell the service provider how to resolve dependencies. The methods shown in Table 18-3 all use type parameters, but there are also extension methods available that accept Type objects as arguments instead, which can be useful if you need to generate mappings at runtime.

Table 18-3. *The Service Provider Dependency Injection Extension Methods*

Name	Description
AddTransient<service, implType>()	This method tells the service provider to create a new instance of the implementation type for every dependency on the service type. See the "Using the Transient Life Cycle" section.
AddTransient<service>()	This method is used to register a single type, which will be instantiated for every dependency, as described in the "Using Dependency Injection for Concrete Types" section.
AddTransient<service>(factoryFunc)	This method is used to register a factory function that will be invoked to create an implementation object for every dependency on the service type, as described in the "Using a Factory Function" section.
AddScoped<service, implType>() AddScoped<service>() AddScoped<service>(factoryFunc)	These methods tell the service provider to reuse instances of the implementation type so that all service requests made by components associated with a common scope, which is usually a single HTTP request, share the same object. These methods follow the same pattern as the corresponding AddTransient methods. See the "Using the Scoped Life Cycle" section.

(continued)

Table 18-3. (*continued*)

Name	Description
AddSingleton<service, implType>() AddSingleton<service>() AddSingleton<service(factoryFunc)	These methods tell the service provider to create a new instance of the implementation type for the first service request and then reuse it for every subsequent service request. See the "Using the Singleton Life Cycle" section.
AddSingleton<service>(instance)	This method provides the service provider with an object that should be used to service all service requests. The service provider will not create any new objects.

Using the Transient Life Cycle

The simplest way to start using dependency injection is to use the AddTransient method, which tells the service provider to create a new instance of the implementation type whenever it needs to resolve a dependency. This is the configuration that is already present in the Startup class, as follows:

```
...
public void ConfigureServices(IServiceCollection services) {
    services.AddTransient<IRepository, MemoryRepository>();
    services.AddTransient<IModelStorage, DictionaryStorage>();
    services.AddTransient<ProductTotalizer>();
    services.AddMvc();
}
...
```

All of the life cycles described in Table 18-3 offer trade-offs. The transient life cycle incurs the cost of creating a new instance of the implementation class every time a dependency is resolved, but the advantage is that you don't have to worry about managing concurrent access or ensure that objects can be safely reused for multiple requests.

To demonstrate the transient life cycle, I have overridden the ToString method in the MemoryRepository class so that it generates a globally unique identifier (GUID), as shown in Listing 18-27.

Listing 18-27. Overriding ToString in the MemoryRepository.cs File in the Models Folder

```
using System.Collections.Generic;

namespace DependencyInjection.Models {
    public class MemoryRepository : IRepository {
        private IModelStorage storage;
        private string guid = System.Guid.NewGuid().ToString();

        public MemoryRepository(IModelStorage modelStore) {
            storage = modelStore;
            new List<Product> {
                new Product { Name = "Kayak", Price = 275M },
                new Product { Name = "Lifejacket", Price = 48.95M },
                new Product { Name = "Soccer ball", Price = 19.50M }
            }.ForEach(p => AddProduct(p));
        }
```

```
    public IEnumerable<Product> Products => storage.Items;

    public Product this[string name] => storage[name];

    public void AddProduct(Product product) =>
        storage[product.Name] = product;

    public void DeleteProduct(Product product) =>
        storage.RemoveItem(product.Name);

    public override string ToString() {
        return guid;
    }
    }
}
```

The GUID will make it easy to identify a specific instance of the MemoryRepository class and see how the different lifecycle methods change the way that the service provider behaves. In Listing 18-28, I updated the Index action method on the Home controller so that it creates a Controller property to the view bag that is set to the GUID from the repository.

Listing 18-28. Using the View Bag in the HomeController.cs File in the Controllers Folder

```
using Microsoft.AspNetCore.Mvc;
using DependencyInjection.Models;
using DependencyInjection.Infrastructure;

namespace DependencyInjection.Controllers {

    public class HomeController : Controller {
        private IRepository repository;
        private ProductTotalizer totalizer;

        public HomeController(IRepository repo, ProductTotalizer total) {
            repository = repo;
            totalizer = total;
        }

        public ViewResult Index() {
            ViewBag.HomeController = repository.ToString();
            ViewBag.Totalizer = totalizer.Repository.ToString();
            return View(repository.Products);
        }
    }
}
```

The Index action method adds values to the view bag that contains the GUIDs for the repository objects received directly to the constructor and through the constructor of the ProductTotalizer class, which you can see if you run the application. The two GUIDs are different because the service provider has been configured with the AddTransient method, which means that it creates a new MemoryRepository object to resolve the dependency of the HomeController and a second one for the ProductTotalizer, as shown in Figure 18-10.

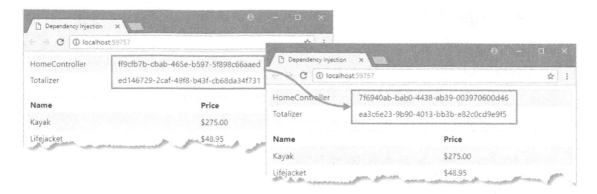

Figure 18-10. *The effect of the transient life cycle*

Each time you reload the web page, the new HTTP request causes MVC to create a new `HomeController`, which leads to the creation of two new `MemoryRepository` objects, each with their own GUIDs.

■ **Tip**   GUIDs are unique—or as close to unique as to make no real difference—and so you will see different values when you run the application on your machine.

Using a Factory Function

One version of the `AddTransient` method accepts a factory function that is invoked every time there is a dependency on the service type. This allows the object that is created to be varied so that different dependencies receive instances of different types or instances that are configured differently. In Listing 18-29, I have used a factory function to select different implementations of the `IRepository` interface based on the hosting environment in which the application is running.

Listing 18-29. Using a Factory in the Startup.cs File in the DependencyInjection Folder

```
using System;
using System.Collections.Generic;
using System.Linq;
using System.Threading.Tasks;
using Microsoft.AspNetCore.Builder;
using Microsoft.AspNetCore.Hosting;
using Microsoft.AspNetCore.Http;
using Microsoft.Extensions.DependencyInjection;
using DependencyInjection.Infrastructure;
using DependencyInjection.Models;

namespace DependencyInjection {
    public class Startup {
        private IHostingEnvironment env;
```

```
public Startup(IHostingEnvironment hostEnv) => env = hostEnv;

public void ConfigureServices(IServiceCollection services) {
    services.AddTransient<IRepository>(provider => {
        if (env.IsDevelopment()) {
            var x = provider.GetService<MemoryRepository>();
            return x;
        } else {
            return new AlternateRepository();
        }
    });
    services.AddTransient<MemoryRepository>();
    services.AddTransient<IModelStorage, DictionaryStorage>();
    services.AddTransient<ProductTotalizer>();
    services.AddMvc();
}

public void Configure(IApplicationBuilder app, IHostingEnvironment env) {
    app.UseStatusCodePages();
    app.UseDeveloperExceptionPage();
    app.UseStaticFiles();
    app.UseMvcWithDefaultRoute();
}
    }
}
```

In Chapter 14, I described how ASP.NET Core provides the Startup class with services to help set up the application, including an implementation of the IHostingEnvironment interface for determining the hosting environment. You can receive these services as arguments to the Configure method but not the ConfigureServices method, so I have added a constructor to the Startup class, which does provide access to an IHostingEnvironment object, and assigned it to a field called env.

Within the ConfigureServices method, I use the AddTransient method to define a factory function using a lambda expression. The expression receives a System.IServiceProvider object, which can be used to create instances of other types that have been registered with the service provider using the methods shown in Table 18-4.

Table 18-4. *The IServiceProvider Methods and Extension Methods*

Name	Description
GetService<service>()	This method uses the service provider to create a new instance of the service type. It returns null if there is no mapping for the requested type.
GetRequiredService<service>()	This method uses the service provider to create a new instance of the service type. It throws an exception if there is no mapping for the requested type.

Within the factory function, I use the IHostingEnvironment to determine whether the application is running in the development environment, and if it is, I use the GetService method to create an instance of the MemoryRepository class and return it from the factory function as the object to use for the IRepository dependency. I use the GetService to create the object because MemoryRepository has its own dependency on the IModelStorage interface and using the service provider to create the object means that detecting and resolving the dependency will be managed automatically—but it does mean I have to specify the life cycle that should be used for MemoryRepository objects, like this:

```
...
services.AddTransient<MemoryRepository>();
...
```

Without this statement, the service provider would not have the information it needs to create and manage MemoryRepository objects.

If the application is not running in the development environment, then the factory function returns a new instance of the AlternateRepository class. This class can be created directly using the new keyword because it doesn't declare any dependencies in its constructor.

Using the Scoped Life Cycle

This life cycle creates a single object from the implementation class that is used to resolve all of the dependencies associated with a single scope, which generally means a single HTTP request. (You can create your own scopes, but this isn't useful in most applications.)

Since the default scope is the HTTP request, this life cycle allows for a single object to be shared by all the components that process a request and is most often used for sharing common context data when writing custom classes, such as routes. The scoped life cycle is created by using the AddScoped extension method to configure the service provider, as shown in Listing 18-30.

■ **Tip**   As described in Table 18-4, there are also versions of the AddScoped method that accept a factory function and that can be used to register a concrete type. These methods work in the same way as the AddTransient method demonstrated in the previous section, with the obvious exception that the life cycle of the objects they create is different.

Listing 18-30. Using the Scoped Life Cycle in the Startup.cs File in the DependencyInjection Folder

```
using System;
using System.Collections.Generic;
using System.Linq;
using System.Threading.Tasks;
using Microsoft.AspNetCore.Builder;
using Microsoft.AspNetCore.Hosting;
using Microsoft.AspNetCore.Http;
using Microsoft.Extensions.DependencyInjection;
using DependencyInjection.Infrastructure;
using DependencyInjection.Models;
```

```
namespace DependencyInjection {
    public class Startup {
        private IHostingEnvironment env;

        public Startup(IHostingEnvironment hostEnv) => env = hostEnv;

        public void ConfigureServices(IServiceCollection services) {
            services.AddScoped<IRepository, MemoryRepository>();
            services.AddTransient<IModelStorage, DictionaryStorage>();
            services.AddTransient<ProductTotalizer>();
            services.AddMvc();
        }

        public void Configure(IApplicationBuilder app, IHostingEnvironment env) {
            app.UseStatusCodePages();
            app.UseDeveloperExceptionPage();
            app.UseStaticFiles();
            app.UseMvcWithDefaultRoute();
        }
    }
}
```

In the example application, the HomeController and ProductTotalizer are instantiated together to handle a request, and both require the service repository to resolve a dependency on the IRepository interface. Using the AddScoped method ensures that both objects' dependencies are resolved with a single MemoryRepository object. You can see the effect by running the example; both of the GUIDs shown by the browser are the same, as shown in Figure 18-11. Reloading the page creates a new HTTP request, which means a new MemoryRepository object is created.

Figure 18-11. *The effect of the scope life cycle*

579

Using the Singleton Life Cycle

The singleton life cycle ensures that a single object is used to resolve all the dependencies for a given service type. When using this life cycle, you must ensure that the implementation classes used to resolve dependencies are safe for concurrent access. In Listing 18-31, I have changed the scope for the IRepository configuration.

Listing 18-31. Using the Scope Life Cycle in the Startup.cs File in the DependencyInjection Folder

```
using System;
using System.Collections.Generic;
using System.Linq;
using System.Threading.Tasks;
using Microsoft.AspNetCore.Builder;
using Microsoft.AspNetCore.Hosting;
using Microsoft.AspNetCore.Http;
using Microsoft.Extensions.DependencyInjection;
using DependencyInjection.Infrastructure;
using DependencyInjection.Models;

namespace DependencyInjection {
    public class Startup {
        private IHostingEnvironment env;

        public Startup(IHostingEnvironment hostEnv) => env = hostEnv;

        public void ConfigureServices(IServiceCollection services) {
            services.AddSingleton<IRepository, MemoryRepository>();
            services.AddTransient<IModelStorage, DictionaryStorage>();
            services.AddTransient<ProductTotalizer>();
            services.AddMvc();
        }

        public void Configure(IApplicationBuilder app, IHostingEnvironment env) {
            app.UseStatusCodePages();
            app.UseDeveloperExceptionPage();
            app.UseStaticFiles();
            app.UseMvcWithDefaultRoute();
        }
    }
}
```

The AddSingleton method creates a new instance of the MemoryRepository class the first time that it has to resolve a dependency on the IRepository interface and then reuses that instance for any subsequent dependencies, even if they are associated with different HTTP requests, as shown in Figure 18-12.

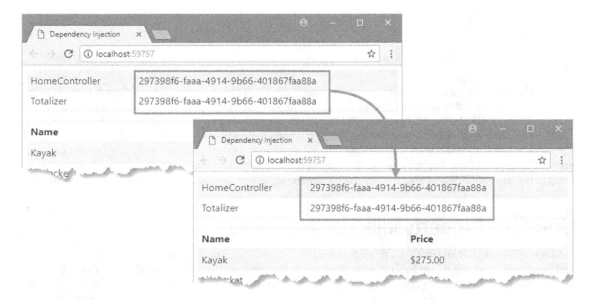

Figure 18-12. *The effect of the singleton life cycle*

Using Action Injection

The standard way to declare a dependency is through a constructor, which is a technique that can be used in any class and that relies on the dependency injection features that are part of the core ASP.NET platform.

MVC supplements the standard functionality with an alternative approach called *action injection*, which allows dependencies to be declared through parameters to action methods. Strictly speaking, action injection is provided by the model binding system that I describe in Chapter 26, but I have described it in this chapter because it allows services to be used in a different way. Action injection is performed using the FromServices attribute, which is applied to an action method parameter, as shown in Listing 18-32.

Listing 18-32. Using Action Injection in the HomeController.cs File in the Controllers Folder

```
using Microsoft.AspNetCore.Mvc;
using DependencyInjection.Models;
using DependencyInjection.Infrastructure;

namespace DependencyInjection.Controllers {

    public class HomeController : Controller {
        private IRepository repository;

        public HomeController(IRepository repo) {
            repository = repo;
        }

        public ViewResult Index([FromServices]ProductTotalizer totalizer) {
            ViewBag.HomeController = repository.ToString();
            ViewBag.Totalizer = totalizer.Repository.ToString();
```

```
            return View(repository.Products);
        }
    }
}
```

MVC uses the service provider to get an instance of the ProductTotalizer class and provides it as an argument when the Index action method is invoked. Using action injection is less common than standard constructor injection, but it can be useful when you have a dependency on an object that is expensive to create and that is required in only one of the action methods defined by a controller. Using constructor injection resolves the dependency for all action methods, even if the one used to handle the request doesn't use the implementation object. Decorating an action method with the FromServices attribute narrows the focus of the dependency and ensures that the implementation type is instantiated only when it is required.

Using the Property Injection Attributes

In Chapter 17, I explained how to receive context data in a POCO controller by declaring a property and decorating it with the ControllerContext attribute. Now that you have read this chapter, you will understand that this was a special form of dependency injection. It is known as *property injection*.

MVC provides a set of specialized attributes that can be used to receive specific types via property injection in controllers and in view components (which I describe in Chapter 22). You won't need to use these attributes if you derive your controllers from the Controller base class because the context information is exposed through convenience properties, but Table 18-5 lists the attributes for use in POCO controllers.

Table 18-5. *The Specialized Property Injection Attributes*

Name	Description
ControllerContext	This attribute sets a ControllerContext property, which provides a superset of the functionality of the ActionContext class, as described in Chapter 31.
ActionContext	This attribute sets an ActionContext property to provide context information to action methods. The Controller classes expose the context information through an ActionContext property, as well as a set of convenience properties described in Chapter 31.
ViewContext	This attribute sets a ViewContext property to provide context data for view operations, including tag helpers (as described in Chapter 23).
ViewComponentContext	This attribute sets a ViewComponentContext property for view components, which I describe in Chapter 22.
ViewDataDictionary	This attribute sets a ViewDataDictionary property to provide access to the model binding data, as described in Chapter 26.

Manually Requesting an Implementation Object

The main ASP.NET dependency injection feature and the additional attributes that MVC provides for property and action injection provide all the support that most applications will require for creating loosely coupled components. There can be occasions, however, when it can be useful to create get an implementation for an interface without relying on injection. In these situations, you can work directly with the service provider, as shown in Listing 18-33.

Listing 18-33. Using the Service Provider Directly in the HomeController.cs File in the Controllers Folder

```
using Microsoft.AspNetCore.Mvc;
using DependencyInjection.Models;
using DependencyInjection.Infrastructure;
using Microsoft.Extensions.DependencyInjection;

namespace DependencyInjection.Controllers {

    public class HomeController : Controller {

        public ViewResult Index([FromServices]ProductTotalizer totalizer) {

            IRepository repository =
                HttpContext.RequestServices.GetService<IRepository>();

            ViewBag.HomeController = repository.ToString();
            ViewBag.Totalizer = totalizer.Repository.ToString();
            return View(repository.Products);
        }
    }
}
```

The HttpContext object returned by the property of the same name defines a RequestServices method that returns an IServiceProvider object, on which the methods described in Table 18-4 can be called. In the listing, I removed the Repository property, which was set using property injection, and used the HttpContext.RequestServices property to obtain an implementation of the IRepository interface.

This is known as the *service locator pattern*, which some developers believe should be avoided. Mark Seemann wrote a good description of the problems it can cause at http://blog.ploeh.dk/2010/02/03/ ServiceLocatorisanAnti-Pattern. My view is more relaxed in that obtaining services in this way is perfectly reasonable when the normal technique of receiving dependencies through the constructor cannot be used for some reason.

Summary

In this chapter, I explained the role that dependency injection plays in an MVC application, helping to create loosely coupled components that can be easily replaced and isolated for testing. I demonstrated the ASP. NET Core dependency injection feature and the attributes that MVC provides for injecting dependencies into properties and action methods. I described the different life-cycle options that are available when configuring the service provider and explained how they affect the way that objects are created. In the next chapter, I introduce filters, which add extra logic into the request-handling process.

CHAPTER 19

Filters

Filters inject extra logic into MVC request processing. They provide a simple and elegant way to implement *crosscutting concerns*—a term that refers to functionality that is used all over an application and doesn't fit neatly into any one place, where it would break the separation of concerns. Classic examples of crosscutting concerns are logging, authorization, and caching. In this chapter, I show you the different categories of filters that MVC supports, how to create and use custom filters, and how to control their execution. Table 19-1 puts filters in context.

Table 19-1. *Putting Filters in Context*

Question	Answer
What are they?	Filters are used to apply logic to action methods without having to add code to the controller class.
Why are they useful?	Filters allow code to be applied that isn't part of the classic MVC pattern definition of an action. The result is simpler controller classes and reusable functionality that can be applied throughout an application.
How are they used?	There are different types of filters that are used by MVC in different ways. The most common way to create a filter is to create a class that subclasses an attribute provided by MVC for the filter type you require.
Are there any pitfalls or limitations?	The functionality provided by the different types of filters overlap, and it can be hard to figure out which type is required.
Are there any alternatives?	No, filters are a core MVC feature and are used to implement commonly required functionality such as authorization.

© Adam Freeman 2017
A. Freeman, *Pro ASP.NET Core MVC 2*, https://doi.org/10.1007/978-1-4842-3150-0_19

Table 19-2 summarizes the chapter.

Table 19-2. *Chapter Summary*

Problem	Solution	Listing
Inject extra logic into request processing	Apply filters to controllers or their action methods	6–9
Restrict access to actions	Use authorization filters	10,11
Inject general-purpose logic into the request-handling process	Use action filters	12–14
Inspect or alter the results produced by action methods	Use result filters	15–19
Handle errors	Use exception filters	20, 21
Use services in filters	Declare dependencies in the filter constructor, register the service in the Startup class, and apply the filter using the TypeFilter attribute	22–26
Put filters under life-cycle management	Use the dependency injection life cycles to register the filters in the Startup class and apply the filters using the ServiceFilter attribute	27–29
Apply filters to every action method in the application	Use a global filter	30–32
Change the order in which filters are executed	Use the Order parameter	33–36

Preparing the Example Project

For this chapter, I followed the same approach to create the example application as in recent chapters. I used the ASP.NET Core Web Application (.NET Core) template to create a new Empty project called Filters. Listing 19-1 shows the changes I made to the Startup class to enable the MVC framework and the other middleware required for development.

Listing 19-1. The Contents of the Startup.cs File in the Filters Folder

```
using System;
using System.Collections.Generic;
using System.Linq;
using System.Threading.Tasks;
using Microsoft.AspNetCore.Builder;
using Microsoft.AspNetCore.Hosting;
using Microsoft.AspNetCore.Http;
using Microsoft.Extensions.DependencyInjection;

namespace Filters {
    public class Startup {
        public void ConfigureServices(IServiceCollection services) {
            services.AddMvc();
        }
```

```
    public void Configure(IApplicationBuilder app, IHostingEnvironment env) {
        app.UseStatusCodePages();
        app.UseDeveloperExceptionPage();
        app.UseStaticFiles();
        app.UseMvcWithDefaultRoute();
    }
  }
}
```

Enabling SSL

Some of the examples in this chapter require the use of SSL, which is disabled by default. To enable SSL, select Filter Properties from the Visual Studio Project menu and check the Enable SSL option in the Debug tab, as shown in Figure 19-1. Make a note of the port that is assigned, which will be different for each project.

Figure 19-1. *Enabling SSL*

Creating the Controller and View

The controllers in this chapter are simple because the focus is on placing logic elsewhere in the application. I created the Controllers folder, added a class file called HomeController.cs, and used it to define the controller shown in Listing 19-2.

Listing 19-2. The Contents of the HomeController.cs File in the Controllers Folder

```
using Microsoft.AspNetCore.Mvc;

namespace Filters.Controllers {

    public class HomeController : Controller {

        public ViewResult Index() => View("Message",
            "This is the Index action on the Home controller");
    }
}
```

The action method renders a view called Message and passes a string as the view data. I created the Views/Shared folder and added a Razor view file called Message.cshtml file with the markup shown in Listing 19-3.

Listing 19-3. The Contents of the Message.cshtml File in the Views/Shared Folder

```
@{ Layout = null; }

<!DOCTYPE html>
<html>
<head>
    <meta name="viewport" content="width=device-width" />
    <title>Filters</title>
    <link asp-href-include="lib/bootstrap/dist/css/*.min.css" rel="stylesheet" />
</head>
<body class="m-1 p-1">
    @if (Model is string) {
        @Model
    } else if (Model is IDictionary<string, string>) {
        var dict = Model as IDictionary<string, string>;
        <table class="table table-sm table-striped table-bordered">
            <thead><tr><th>Name</th><th>Value</th></tr></thead>
            <tbody>
                @foreach (var kvp in dict) {
                    <tr><td>@kvp.Key</td><td>@kvp.Value</td></tr>
                }
            </tbody>
        </table>
    }
</body>
</html>
```

This view is weakly typed and will display either a `string` or a `Dictionary<string, string>`, in which case a table is displayed.

The view depends on the Bootstrap CSS package for styling the HTML elements. To add Bootstrap to the project, I used the Bower Configuration File item template to create the `bower.json` file in the root project folder and added the Bootstrap package to the `dependencies` section, as shown in Listing 19-4.

Listing 19-4. Adding the Bootstrap Package in the bower.json File in the Filters Folder

```
{
  "name": "asp.net",
  "private": true,
  "dependencies": {
    "bootstrap": "4.0.0-alpha.6"
  }
}
```

The final preparation is to create the `_ViewImports.cshtml` file in the `Views` folder, which sets up the built-in tag helpers for use in Razor views, as shown in Listing 19-5.

Listing 19-5. The Contents of the _ViewImports.cshtml File in the Views Folder

```
@addTagHelper *, Microsoft.AspNetCore.Mvc.TagHelpers
```

If you run the application, you will see the output shown in Figure 19-2.

Figure 19-2. *Running the example application*

■ **Tip** You may be prompted to trust a certificate generated by Visual Studio. Accept this option, which is related to the examples in this chapter that rely on SSL.

Using Filters

Filters allow logic that would otherwise be applied in the action method to be removed from the controller and defined in a reusable class. As an example, imagine that I wanted to ensure that action methods could be accessed only using HTTPS and not with regular nonencrypted HTTP. The HttpRequest context object provides the information I need to figure out whether HTTPS is used, as shown in Listing 19-6.

Listing 19-6. Testing for HTTPS in the HomeController.cs File in the Controllers Folder

```
using Microsoft.AspNetCore.Mvc;
using Microsoft.AspNetCore.Http;

namespace Filters.Controllers {

    public class HomeController : Controller {

        public IActionResult Index() {
            if (!Request.IsHttps) {
                return new StatusCodeResult(StatusCodes.Status403Forbidden);
            } else {
                return View("Message",
                    "This is the Index action on the Home controller");
            }
        }
    }
}
```

This is how you would approach the HTTPS issue without filters. If you run the application, your browser will request the non-HTTPs default URL for the project, which the Index action method deals with by returning a StatusCodeResult, which sends the HTTP 403 status code in the response (as described in Chapter 17). If you request the HTTPS default URL, which for me is https://localhost:44318, the Index action method will respond by rendering the Message view (you may need to acknowledge a security warning before the browser will display the result). Figure 19-3 shows both outcomes.

Figure 19-3. *Restricting access to HTTPS requests*

■ **Tip** Clear your browser's history if you don't get the results you expect from the examples in this section. Browsers will often refuse to send requests to servers that have generated SSL errors, which is a good security practice but can be frustrating during development.

The code in Listing 19-6 works but has problems. The first problem is that the action method contains code that is more about implementing a security policy than about handling the request, updating the model, and selecting the response. A more serious problem is that including the HTTP-detecting code within the action method doesn't scale well and must be duplicated in every action method in the controller, as shown in Listing 19-7.

Listing 19-7. Adding an Action Method in the HomeController.cs File in the Controllers Folder

```
using Microsoft.AspNetCore.Http;
using Microsoft.AspNetCore.Mvc;

namespace Filters.Controllers {

    public class HomeController : Controller {

        public IActionResult Index() {
            if (!Request.IsHttps) {
                return new StatusCodeResult(StatusCodes.Status403Forbidden);
            } else {
                return View("Message",
                    "This is the Index action on the Home controller");
            }
        }

        public IActionResult SecondAction() {
            if (!Request.IsHttps) {
                return new StatusCodeResult(StatusCodes.Status403Forbidden);
            } else {
                return View("Message",
                    "This is the SecondAction action on the Home controller");
            }
        }
    }
}
```

I have to remember to implement the same check in every action method in every controller for which I want to require HTTPS. The code to implement the security policy is a substantial part of the—admittedly simple—controller, which makes the controller harder to understand, and it is only a matter of time before I forget to add it to a new action method, creating a hole in my security policy. This is the kind of problems that filters can address, as shown in Listing 19-8.

Listing 19-8. Applying a Filter in the HomeController.cs File in the Controllers Folder

```
using Microsoft.AspNetCore.Http;
using Microsoft.AspNetCore.Mvc;

namespace Filters.Controllers {

    public class HomeController : Controller {

        [RequireHttps]
        public ViewResult Index() => View("Message",
            "This is the Index action on the Home controller");

        [RequireHttps]
        public ViewResult SecondAction() => View("Message",
            "This is the SecondAction action on the Home controller");
    }
}
```

The RequireHttps attribute applies one of the built-in filters to the HomeController class. It restricts access to action methods so that only HTTPS requests are supported and allows me to remove the security code from each method and focus on handling the successful requests.

■ **Note** The RequireHttps filter doesn't work in quite the same way as my custom code in Listing 19-7. For GET requests, the RequireHttps attribute redirects the client to the originally requested URL, but it does so by using the https scheme so that a request to http://localhost/Home/Index will be redirected to https://localhost/Home/Index. This makes sense for most deployed applications but not during development because HTTP and HTTPS are on different local ports. The RequireHttpsAttribute class defines a protected method called HandleNonHttpsRequest that you can override to change the behavior. Alternatively, I re-create the original functionality from scratch in the "Using Authorization Filters" section.

Of course, I still have to remember to apply the RequireHttps attribute to each action method, which means that I might forget. But filters have a useful trick: applying the attribute to a controller class has the same effect as applying it to each individual action method, as shown in Listing 19-9.

Listing 19-9. Applying a Filter to All Action Methods in the HomeController.cs File in the Controllers Folder

```
using Microsoft.AspNetCore.Http;
using Microsoft.AspNetCore.Mvc;

namespace Filters.Controllers {

    [RequireHttps]
    public class HomeController : Controller {

        public ViewResult Index() => View("Message",
            "This is the Index action on the Home controller");

        public ViewResult SecondAction() => View("Message",
            "This is the SecondAction action on the Home controller");
    }
}
```

Filters can be applied with differing levels of granularity. If you want to restrict access to some actions but not others, then you can apply the RequireHttps attribute to just those methods. If you want to protect all the action methods, including any that you add to the controller in the future, then the RequireHttps attribute can be applied to the class. If you want to apply a filter to every action in an application, then you can use *global filters*, which I describe later in this chapter.

Understanding Filters

Now that you have seen how filters are used, it is time to explain what happens behind the scenes. Filters implement the IFilterMetadata interface, which is in the Microsoft.AspNetCore.Mvc.Filters namespace. Here is the definition:

```
namespace Microsoft.AspNetCore.Mvc.Filters {
    public interface IFilterMetadata { }
}
```

The interface is empty and doesn't require a filter class to implement any specific behaviors. This is because there are several distinct types of filter, and each of them works in a different way and is used for a different purpose.

Table 19-3 lists each type of filter, the interfaces that define them, and what they do. (There are some other types of filter supported by MVC, but they are not used directly. Instead, they are integrated into features that I describe in other chapters and applied through specific attributes, including the Produces and Consumes attributes I describe in Chapter 20.)

Table 19-3. *The Different Types of Filter*

Filter	Interfaces	Description
Authorization	IAuthorizationFilter IAsyncAuthorizationFilter	This type of filter is used to apply the application's security policy, including user authorization.
Action	IActionFilter IAsyncActionFilter	This type of filter is used to perform work immediately before or after an action method is performed.
Result	IResultFilter IAsyncResultFilter	This type of filter is used to perform work immediately before or after the result from an action method is processed.
Exception	IExceptionFilter IAsyncExceptionFilter	This type of filter is used to handle exceptions.

The descriptions in the table are vague because you can use filters for a wide range of tasks, limited only by your imagination and the problems you need to solve. This will become clear as I get into the detail of how filters work, but for now, there are two important points to understand.

First, there are two different interfaces for each type of filter in Table 19-3. Filters can do their work synchronously or asynchronously so that a synchronous result filter, for example, implements the IResultFilter interface, while an asynchronous one would implement the IAsyncResultFilter interface.

Second, filters are executed in a specific order. Authorization filters are executed first, followed by action files and then result filters. Exception filters are executed only if an exception is thrown, which disrupts the normal sequence.

Getting Context Data

Filters are provided with context data in the form of a FilterContext object. The FilterContext class is derived from ActionContext, which is also the base class for the ControllerContext class that I described in Chapter 17. For convenience, Table 19-4 lists the properties inherited from the ActionContext class, along with the additional property that FilterContext defines.

Table 19-4. *The FilterContext Properties*

Name	Description
ActionDescriptor	This property returns an ActionDescriptor object, which describes the action method.
HttpContext	This property returns an HttpContext object, which provides details of the HTTP request and the HTTP response that will be sent in return.
ModelState	This property returns a ModelStateDictionary object, which is used to validate data sent by the client, as described in Chapter 27.
RouteData	This property returns a RouteData object that describes the way that the routing system has processed the request, as described in Chapter 15.
Filters	This property returns a list of filters that have been applied to the action method, expressed as an IList<IFilterMetadata>.

Using Authorization Filters

Authorization filters are used to implement an application's security policy. Authorization filters are executed before other types of filter and before the action method is executed. Here is the definition of the IAuthorizationFilter interface:

```
namespace Microsoft.AspNetCore.Mvc.Filters {

    public interface IAuthorizationFilter : IFilterMetadata {

        void OnAuthorization(AuthorizationFilterContext context);
    }
}
```

The OnAuthorization method is called to provide the filter with the opportunity to authorize the request. For asynchronous authorization filters, here is the definition of the IAsyncAuthorizationFilter interface:

```
using System.Threading.Tasks;

namespace Microsoft.AspNetCore.Mvc.Filters {

    public interface IAsyncAuthorizationFilter : IFilterMetadata {

        Task OnAuthorizationAsync(AuthorizationFilterContext context);
    }
}
```

The OnAuthorizationAsync method is called so that the filter can authorize the request. Whichever interface is used, the filter receives context data describing the request through an AuthorizationFilterContext object, which is derived from the FilterContext class and adds one important property, as described in Table 19-5.

Table 19-5. *The AuthorizationFilterContext Property*

Name	Description
Result	This IActionResult property is set by authorization filters when the request doesn't comply with the application's authorization policy. If this property is set, then MVC renders the IActionResult instead of invoking the action method.

Creating an Authorization Filter

To demonstrate how authorization filters work, I created an Infrastructure folder in the example project, added a class file called HttpsOnlyAttribute.cs, and used it to define the filter shown in Listing 19-10.

Listing 19-10. The Contents of the HttpsOnlyAttribute.cs File in the Infrastructure Folder

```
using System;
using Microsoft.AspNetCore.Http;
using Microsoft.AspNetCore.Mvc;
using Microsoft.AspNetCore.Mvc.Filters;
```

```
namespace Filters.Infrastructure {
    public class HttpsOnlyAttribute : Attribute, IAuthorizationFilter {

        public void OnAuthorization(AuthorizationFilterContext context) {
            if (!context.HttpContext.Request.IsHttps) {
                context.Result =
                    new StatusCodeResult(StatusCodes.Status403Forbidden);
            }
        }
    }
}
```

An authorization filter does nothing if a request complies with the authorization policy, and this inaction allows MVC to move on to the next filter and, eventually, to execute the action method.

■ **Note** The Authorize attribute, which can be used to restrict access to specific users and groups, was implemented as a filter, but this is no longer the case in ASP.NET Core MVC. The Authorize attribute is still used, but it works in a different way. Behind the scenes, a global filter (I describe global filters later in this chapter) is used to detect the Authorize attribute and enforce policies defined by ASP.NET Core Identity system, but the Authorize attribute isn't a filter and doesn't implement the IAuthorizationFilter interface. I describe how to use ASP.NET Core Identity and the Authorize attribute in Chapter 29.

If there is a problem, then the filter sets the Result property of the AuthorizationFilterContext object that is passed to the OnAuthorization method. This prevents further execution from happening and provides MVC with a result to return to the client. In the listing, my HttpsOnlyAttribute class inspects the IsHttps property of the HttpRequest context object and sets the Result property to interrupt execution if the request has been made without HTTPS. Listing 19-11 shows the new filter applied to the Home controller.

Listing 19-11. Applying the Custom Filter in the HomeController.cs File in the Controllers Folder

```
using Microsoft.AspNetCore.Mvc;
using Filters.Infrastructure;

namespace Filters.Controllers {

    [HttpsOnly]
    public class HomeController : Controller {

        public ViewResult Index() => View("Message",
            "This is the Index action on the Home controller");

        public ViewResult SecondAction() => View("Message",
            "This is the SecondAction action on the Home controller");
    }
}
```

This filter re-creates the functionality that I included in the action methods in Listing 19-7. This is less useful in real projects than doing a redirection like the built-in RequireHttps filter because users won't understand the meaning of a 403 status code, but it does provide a useful example of how authorization filters work.

UNIT TESTING FILTERS

Most of the work in unit testing a filter is setting up the context object that is passed to the filter's methods. The amount of mocking required depends on the context information used by the filter. As an example, here is a unit test for the HttpsOnly filter from Listing 19-10:

```
using System.Linq;
using Filters.Infrastructure;
using Microsoft.AspNetCore.Http;
using Microsoft.AspNetCore.Mvc;
using Microsoft.AspNetCore.Mvc.Abstractions;
using Microsoft.AspNetCore.Mvc.Filters;
using Moq;
using Xunit;

namespace Tests {

    public class FilterTests {

        [Fact]
        public void TestHttpsFilter() {

            // Arrange
            var httpRequest = new Mock<HttpRequest>();
            httpRequest.SetupSequence(m => m.IsHttps).Returns(true)
                                                     .Returns(false);
            var httpContext = new Mock<HttpContext>();
            httpContext.SetupGet(m => m.Request).Returns(httpRequest.Object);

            var actionContext = new ActionContext(httpContext.Object,
                new Microsoft.AspNetCore.Routing.RouteData(),
                new ActionDescriptor());
            var authContext = new AuthorizationFilterContext(actionContext,
                Enumerable.Empty<IFilterMetadata>().ToList());

            HttpsOnlyAttribute filter = new HttpsOnlyAttribute();

            // Act and Assert
            filter.OnAuthorization(authContext);
            Assert.Null(authContext.Result);

            filter.OnAuthorization(authContext);
            Assert.IsType(typeof(StatusCodeResult), authContext.Result);
```

```
            Assert.Equal(StatusCodes.Status403Forbidden,
                (authContext.Result as StatusCodeResult).StatusCode);
        }
    }
}
```

I start by mocking the HttpRequest and HttpContext context objects, which allows me to present a request with or without HTTPS. I want to test both conditions, which I do like this:

```
...
httpRequest.SetupSequence(m => m.IsHttps).Returns(true).Returns(false);
...
```

This statement sets up the HttpRequest.IsHttps property so that it returns a sequence of values: the property returns true the first time it is read and returns false the second time it is read. Once I have an HttpContext object, I can use it to create an ActionContext object, which allows me to create the AuthorizationContext object I need to do the unit tests. By inspecting the Result property of the AuthorizationFilterContext object, I test how the filter responds to non-HTTPS requests and then test what happens with HTTP requests. There are lots of types required to set up the AuthorizationFilterContext object, and they rely on many ASP.NET Core and MVC namespaces, but once you have the context object, then writing the rest of the test is relatively simple.

Using Action Filters

The best way to understand action filters is to look at the interface that defines them. Here is the IActionFilter interface:

```
namespace Microsoft.AspNetCore.Mvc.Filters {

    public interface IActionFilter : IFilterMetadata {

        void OnActionExecuting(ActionExecutingContext context);

        void OnActionExecuted(ActionExecutedContext context);
    }
}
```

When an action filter has been applied to an action method, the OnActionExecuting method is called just before the action method is invoked, and the OnActionExecuted method is called just after. Action filters are provided with context data through two different context classes: ActionExecutingContext for the OnActionExecuting method and ActionExecutedContext for the OnActionExecuted method. Both of the context classes extend the FilterContext class, which I described in Table 19-4.

The ActionExecutingContext class, which is used to describe an action that is about to be invoked, defines the additional properties described in Table 19-6.

Table 19-6. *The ActionExecutingContext Property*

Name	Description
Controller	This property returns the controller whose action method is about to be invoked. (Details of the action method are available through the ActionDescriptor property inherited from the base classes.)
ActionArguments	This property returns a dictionary of the arguments that will be passed to the action method, indexed by name. The filter can insert, remove, or change the arguments.
Result	If the filter assigns an IActionResult to this property, then the request process will be short-circuited, and the action result will be used to generate the response to the client without invoking the action method.

The ActionExecutedContext class is used to represent an action that has been executed and defines the properties described in Table 19-7.

Table 19-7. *The ActionExecutedContext Properties*

Name	Description
Controller	This property returns the Controller object whose action method will be invoked.
Canceled	This bool property is set to true if another action filter has short-circuited the request-handling process by assigning an action result to the Result property of the ActionExecutingContext object.
Exception	This property contains any Exception that was thrown by the action method.
ExceptionDispatchInfo	This method returns an ExceptionDispatchInfo object that contains the stack trace details of any exception thrown by the action method.
ExceptionHandled	Setting this property to true indicates that the filter has handled the exception, which will not be propagated any further.
Result	This property returns the IActionResult returned by the action method. The filter can change or replace the action result if required.

Creating an Action Filter

Action filters are a general-purpose tool and can be used to implement any crosscutting concern in the application. Action filters can be used to interrupt the request process before an action is invoked and to change the result after an action is performed. The simplest way to create an action filter is to derive a class from the ActionFilterAttribute class, which implements the IActionFilter interface. To demonstrate, I added a class file called ProfileAttribute.cs to the Infrastructure folder and used it to define the filter shown in Listing 19-12.

Listing 19-12. The Contents of the ProfileAttribute.cs File in the Infrastructure Folder

```
using System.Diagnostics;
using System.Text;
using Microsoft.AspNetCore.Mvc.Filters;
```

```
namespace Filters.Infrastructure {

    public class ProfileAttribute : ActionFilterAttribute {
        private Stopwatch timer;

        public override void OnActionExecuting(ActionExecutingContext context) {
            timer = Stopwatch.StartNew();
        }

        public override void OnActionExecuted(ActionExecutedContext context) {
            timer.Stop();
            string result = "<div>Elapsed time: "
                + $"{timer.Elapsed.TotalMilliseconds} ms</div>";
            byte[] bytes = Encoding.ASCII.GetBytes(result);
            context.HttpContext.Response.Body.Write(bytes, 0, bytes.Length);
        }
    }
}
```

In the listing, I use a Stopwatch object to measure the number of milliseconds that it takes for an action method to be executed by starting a timer in the OnActionExecuting method and stop it in the OnActionExecuted method. To note the result, I use the context object to get the HttpResponse and include a simple fragment of HTML in the response.

Listing 19-13 shows the Profile attribute applied to the Home controller. (I also removed the previous filter so that requests over standard HTTP will be accepted.)

▪ **Tip** As an odd quirk, controllers are also action filters. The Controller base class implements the IActionFilter and IAsyncActionFilter interfaces, which means you can override the methods defined by these interfaces to create action filter functionality. For POCO controllers, MVC inspects classes and checks to see whether they implement either of the action filter interfaces and automatically uses them as action filters.

Listing 19-13. Applying a Filter in the HomeController.cs File in the Controllers Folder

```
using Microsoft.AspNetCore.Mvc;
using Filters.Infrastructure;

namespace Filters.Controllers {

    [Profile]
    public class HomeController : Controller {

        public ViewResult Index() => View("Message",
            "This is the Index action on the Home controller");

        public ViewResult SecondAction() => View("Message",
            "This is the SecondAction action on the Home controller");
    }
}
```

If you run the application, you will see a message like the one shown in Figure 19-4. The number of milliseconds you see will vary based on the speed of your development machine.

Figure 19-4. *Using an action filter*

■ **Note** Writing HTML fragments directly to the response relies on the browser being tolerant of badly formed HTML documents: the div element that I generate in the filter appears at the start of the response body, before the DOCTYPE and html elements that indicate the start of the HTML document generated by the Razor view. This technique works and can be useful for producing diagnostic information, but it isn't something you should rely on for production features.

Creating an Asynchronous Action Filter

The IAsyncActionFilter interface is used to define action filters that operate asynchronously. Here is the definition of the interface:

```
using System.Threading.Tasks;

namespace Microsoft.AspNetCore.Mvc.Filters {

    public interface IAsyncActionFilter : IFilterMetadata {

        Task OnActionExecutionAsync(ActionExecutingContext context,
            ActionExecutionDelegate next);
    }
}
```

There is a single method that relies on task continuation to allow the filter to run before and after the action method has been executed. Listing 19-14 shows the use of the OnActionExecutionAsync method in the Profile filter.

Listing 19-14. Creating an Asynchronous Action Filter in the ProfileAttribute.cs File in the Infrastructure Folder

```
using System.Diagnostics;
using System.Text;
using System.Threading.Tasks;
using Microsoft.AspNetCore.Mvc.Filters;
```

```
namespace Filters.Infrastructure {

    public class ProfileAttribute : ActionFilterAttribute {

        public override async Task OnActionExecutionAsync(
                ActionExecutingContext context,
                ActionExecutionDelegate next) {

            Stopwatch timer = Stopwatch.StartNew();

            await next();

            timer.Stop();
            string result = "<div>Elapsed time: "
                + $"{timer.Elapsed.TotalMilliseconds} ms</div>";
            byte[] bytes = Encoding.ASCII.GetBytes(result);
            await context.HttpContext.Response.Body.WriteAsync(bytes,
                0, bytes.Length);
        }
    }
}
```

The ActionExecutingContext object provides context data to the filter, and the ActionExectionDelegate object represents the action method (or the next filter) to execute. The filter does its preparatory work before invoking the delegate and then completes its work when the delegate finishes. The delegate returns a Task, which is why I have used the await keyword in the listing.

Using Result Filters

Result filters are applied before and after MVC processes the action result returned by an action method. Result filters are able to change or replace the action result or cancel the request entirely (even though the action method has already been invoked). Here is the IResultFilter interface that defines result filters:

```
namespace Microsoft.AspNetCore.Mvc.Filters {

    public interface IResultFilter : IFilterMetadata {

        void OnResultExecuting(ResultExecutingContext context);

        void OnResultExecuted(ResultExecutedContext context);
    }
}
```

Result filters follow the same pattern as action filters. The OnResultExecuting method is called before the action result produced by the action method is processed and is provided with context information through a ResultExecutingContext object. The ResultExecutingContext class is derived from FilterContext and defines the additional properties described in Table 19-8.

Table 19-8. *The ResultExecutingContext Properties*

Name	Description
Controller	This property returns the controller whose action method was executed.
Cancel	Setting this bool property to true will stop the action result from being processed to generate a response.
Result	This property returns the IActionResult object returned by the action method.

The OnResultExecuted method is called after MVC has processed the action result and is provided with context data through an instance of the ResultExecutedContext class, which defines the properties shown in Table 19-9 in addition to those inherited from FilterContext.

Table 19-9. *The ResultExecutedContext Properties*

Name	Description
Controller	This property returns the controller whose action method was executed.
Canceled	This bool property indicates whether the request was canceled.
Exception	This property contains any Exception that was thrown by the action method.
ExceptionDispatchInfo	This method returns an ExceptionDispatchInfo object that contains the stack trace details of any exception thrown by the action method.
ExceptionHandled	Setting this property to true indicates that the filter has handled the exception, which will not be propagated any further.
Result	This property returns the IActionResult object that was used to generate the response to the client.

Creating a Result Filter

The ResultFilterAttribute class implements the result filter interfaces and provides the easiest way to create a result filter that can be applied as an attribute. To demonstrate how a result filter works, I added a class file called ViewResultDetailsAttribute.cs to the Infrastructure folder and used it to define the filter shown in Listing 19-15.

Listing 19-15. The Contents of the ViewResultDetailsAttribute.cs File in the Infrastructure Folder

```
using System.Collections.Generic;
using Microsoft.AspNetCore.Mvc;
using Microsoft.AspNetCore.Mvc.Filters;
using Microsoft.AspNetCore.Mvc.ModelBinding;
using Microsoft.AspNetCore.Mvc.ViewFeatures;

namespace Filters.Infrastructure {

    public class ViewResultDetailsAttribute : ResultFilterAttribute {

        public override void OnResultExecuting(ResultExecutingContext context) {
```

```
        Dictionary<string, string> dict = new Dictionary<string, string> {
            ["Result Type"] = context.Result.GetType().Name,
        };

        ViewResult vr;
        if ((vr = context.Result as ViewResult) != null) {
            dict["View Name"] = vr.ViewName;
            dict["Model Type"] = vr.ViewData.Model.GetType().Name;
            dict["Model Data"] = vr.ViewData.Model.ToString();
        }

        context.Result = new ViewResult {
            ViewName = "Message",
            ViewData = new ViewDataDictionary(
                    new EmptyModelMetadataProvider(),
                    new ModelStateDictionary()) { Model = dict }
        };
    }
}
}
```

This class overrides only the OnResultExecuting method and uses the context object to change the action result used to generate a response to the client. The filter creates a ViewResult object that renders the Message view, using a dictionary containing simple diagnostic information as the view model.

The OnResultExecuting method is called after the action method has produced the action result but before it is processed to generate a result, and changing the value of the context object's Result object allows me to supply a different type of result from the action method to which the filter is applied. Listing 19-16 shows the result filter applied to the Home controller.

Listing 19-16. Applying the Result Filter in the HomeController.cs File in the Controllers Folder

```
using Microsoft.AspNetCore.Mvc;
using Filters.Infrastructure;

namespace Filters.Controllers {

    [ViewResultDetails]
    public class HomeController : Controller {

        public ViewResult Index() => View("Message",
            "This is the Index action on the Home controller");

        public ViewResult SecondAction() => View("Message",
            "This is the SecondAction action on the Home controller");
    }
}
```

If you run the application, you will see the effect of the result filter, as shown in Figure 19-5.

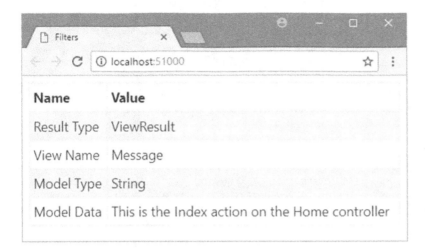

Figure 19-5. *The effect of a result filter*

Creating an Asynchronous Result Filter

The IAsyncResultFilter interface can be used to create asynchronous result filters. Here is the definition of the interface:

```
using System.Threading.Tasks;

namespace Microsoft.AspNetCore.Mvc.Filters {

    public interface IAsyncResultFilter : IFilterMetadata {

        Task OnResultExecutionAsync(ResultExecutingContext context,
            ResultExecutionDelegate next);
    }
}
```

This interface is similar to the one for asynchronous action filters. In Listing 19-17, I have rewritten the ViewResultDetailsAttribute class to implement the IAsyncResultFilter interface.

Listing 19-17. Creating an Asynchronous Filter in the ViewResultDetailsAttribute.cs File in the Infrastructure Folder

```
using System.Collections.Generic;
using System.Threading.Tasks;
using Microsoft.AspNetCore.Mvc;
using Microsoft.AspNetCore.Mvc.Filters;
using Microsoft.AspNetCore.Mvc.ModelBinding;
using Microsoft.AspNetCore.Mvc.ViewFeatures;

namespace Filters.Infrastructure {
```

```
public class ViewResultDetailsAttribute : ResultFilterAttribute {

    public override async Task OnResultExecutionAsync(
            ResultExecutingContext context,
            ResultExecutionDelegate next) {

        Dictionary<string, string> dict = new Dictionary<string, string> {
            ["Result Type"] = context.Result.GetType().Name,
        };

        ViewResult vr;
        if ((vr = context.Result as ViewResult) != null) {
            dict["View Name"] = vr.ViewName;
            dict["Model Type"] = vr.ViewData.Model.GetType().Name;
            dict["Model Data"] = vr.ViewData.Model.ToString();
        }

        context.Result = new ViewResult {
            ViewName = "Message",
            ViewData = new ViewDataDictionary(
                    new EmptyModelMetadataProvider(),
                    new ModelStateDictionary()) {
                        Model = dict
                    }
        };

        await next();
    }
}
```

Notice that I am responsible for invoking the delegate received as an argument to the
OnResultExecutionAsync method. If don't invoke the delegate, the request processing pipeline won't
complete and the action result won't be rendered.

Creating a Hybrid Action/Result Filter

It isn't always helpful to distinguish between the action and the result stages of request processing. This can
be because you want to treat both stages as a single step or because your filter responds to the way that an
action is executed but does so by interfering with the result. It can be useful to be able to create a filter that is
both an action filter and a result filter and is able to perform work at each stage.

This is such a common requirement that the ActionFilterAttribute class implements the interfaces
for both kinds of filter, which means you can mix and match filter types in a single attribute. To demonstrate
how this works, I have revised the ProfileAttribute class in Listing 19-18 so that it combines an action filter
with a result filter.

Listing 19-18. Creating a Hybrid Filter in the ProfileAttribute.cs File in the Infrastructure Folder

```
using System.Diagnostics;
using System.Text;
using System.Threading.Tasks;
using Microsoft.AspNetCore.Mvc.Filters;
```

```
namespace Filters.Infrastructure {

    public class ProfileAttribute : ActionFilterAttribute {
        private Stopwatch timer;
        private double actionTime;

        public override async Task OnActionExecutionAsync(
                ActionExecutingContext context,
                ActionExecutionDelegate next) {

            timer = Stopwatch.StartNew();

            await next();

            actionTime = timer.Elapsed.TotalMilliseconds;
        }

        public override async Task OnResultExecutionAsync(
                ResultExecutingContext context,
                ResultExecutionDelegate next) {

            await next();

            timer.Stop();
            string result = "<div>Action time: "
                + $"{actionTime} ms</div><div>Total time: "
                + $"{timer.Elapsed.TotalMilliseconds} ms</div>";
            byte[] bytes = Encoding.ASCII.GetBytes(result);

            await context.HttpContext.Response.Body.WriteAsync(bytes,
                0, bytes.Length);
        }
    }
}
```

I have used the asynchronous methods for both types of filter, but you can mix and match to get the functionality you require because the default implementations of these methods call their synchronous counterparts. Within the filter, I use the Stopwatch to measure how long it takes the action to be processed and what the total elapsed time is and write the results to the response. In Listing 19-19, I have applied the combined filter to the Home controller.

Listing 19-19. Applying a Hybrid Filter in the HomeController.cs File in the Controllers Folder

```
using Microsoft.AspNetCore.Mvc;
using Filters.Infrastructure;

namespace Filters.Controllers {

    [Profile]
    [ViewResultDetails]
    public class HomeController : Controller {
```

```
    public ViewResult Index() => View("Message",
        "This is the Index action on the Home controller");

    public ViewResult SecondAction() => View("Message",
        "This is the SecondAction action on the Home controller");
    }
}
```

If you run the application, you will see output similar to that shown in Figure 19-6. The output appears after the content provided by ViewResultDetails because it is written in the post-processed stage of the result filter, rather than from the action filter method used in the previous version.

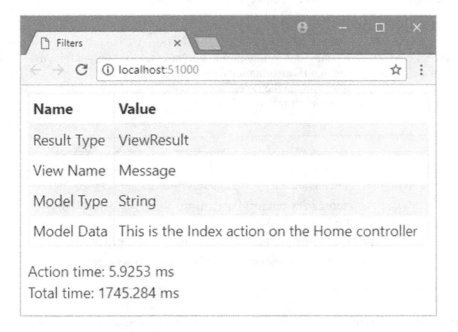

Figure 19-6. *Output from a hybrid action/result filter*

Using Exception Filters

Exception filters allow you to respond to exceptions without having to write try...catch blocks in every action method. Exception filters can be applied to controller classes or action methods. They are invoked when an exception is not handled by the action method or by the action or result filters that have been applied to the action method. (Action and result filters can deal with an unhandled exception by setting the ExceptionHandled property of their context objects to true.) Exception filters implement the IExceptionFilter interface, which is defined as follows:

```
namespace Microsoft.AspNetCore.Mvc.Filters {

    public interface IExceptionFilter : IFilterMetadata {

        void OnException(ExceptionContext context);
    }
}
```

The OnException method is called if an unhandled exception is encountered. The IAsyncExceptionFilter interface can be used to create asynchronous exception filters, which is useful if you need to respond to exceptions using an asynchronous API. Here is the definition of the asynchronous interface:

```
using System.Threading.Tasks;

namespace Microsoft.AspNetCore.Mvc.Filters {

    public interface IAsyncExceptionFilter : IFilterMetadata {

        Task OnExceptionAsync(ExceptionContext context);
    }
}
```

The OnExceptionAsync method is the asynchronous counterpart to the OnException method from the IExceptionFilter interface and is called when there is an unhandled exception.

For both interfaces, context data is provided through the ExceptionContext class, which is derived from FilterContext and defines the additional properties shown in Table 19-10.

Table 19-10. *The ExceptionContext Properties*

Name	Description
Exception	This property contains any Exception that was thrown.
ExceptionDispatchInfo	This method returns an ExceptionDispatchInfo object that contains the stack trace details for the exception.
ExceptionHandled	This bool property is used to indicate if the exception has been handled.
Result	This property sets the IActionResult that will be used to generate the response.

Creating an Exception Filter

The ExceptionFilterAttribute class implements both of the exception filter interfaces and is the easiest way to create a filter so that it can be applied as an attribute. The most common use for an exception filter is to present a custom error page for a specific exception type in order to provide the user with more useful information than the standard error-handling capabilities can provide. As a demonstration, I added a class file called RangeExceptionAttribute.cs to the Infrastructure folder and used it to define the filter shown in Listing 19-20.

Listing 19-20. The Contents of the RangeExceptionAttribute.cs File in the Infrastructure Folder

```
using System;
using Microsoft.AspNetCore.Mvc;
using Microsoft.AspNetCore.Mvc.Filters;
using Microsoft.AspNetCore.Mvc.ModelBinding;
using Microsoft.AspNetCore.Mvc.ViewFeatures;

namespace Filters.Infrastructure {
```

```
public class RangeExceptionAttribute : ExceptionFilterAttribute {

    public override void OnException(ExceptionContext context) {
        if (context.Exception is ArgumentOutOfRangeException) {
            context.Result = new ViewResult() {
                ViewName = "Message",
                ViewData = new ViewDataDictionary(
                    new EmptyModelMetadataProvider(),
                    new ModelStateDictionary()) {
                        Model = @"The data received by the
                                application cannot be processed"
                    }
            };
        }
    }
}
```

This filter uses the ExceptionContext object to get the type of the unhandled exception and, if the type is ArgumentOutOfRangeException, creates an action result that displays a message to the user. In Listing 19-21, I have added an action method to the Home controller and applied the exception filter to it.

Listing 19-21. Applying an Exception Filter in the HomeController.cs File in the Controllers Folder

```
using Filters.Infrastructure;
using Microsoft.AspNetCore.Mvc;
using System;

namespace Filters.Controllers {

    [Profile]
    [ViewResultDetails]
    [RangeException]
    public class HomeController : Controller {

        public ViewResult Index() => View("Message",
            "This is the Index action on the Home controller");

        public ViewResult SecondAction() => View("Message",
            "This is the SecondAction action on the Home controller");

        public ViewResult GenerateException(int? id) {
            if (id == null) {
                throw new ArgumentNullException(nameof(id));
            } else if (id > 10) {
                throw new ArgumentOutOfRangeException(nameof(id));
            } else {
                return View("Message", $"The value is {id}");
            }
        }
    }
}
```

The GenerateException action method relies on the default routing pattern to receive a nullable int value from the request URL. The action method throws an ArgumentNullException if there is no matching URL segment and throws an ArgumentOutOfRangeException if its value is greater than 50. If there is a value and it is in range, then the action method returns a ViewResult.

You can test the exception filter by running the application and requesting the /Home/ GenerateException/100 URL. The final segment will exceed the range expected by the action method, which will throw the exception type that is handled by the filter, producing the result shown in Figure 19-7. If you request /Home/GenerateException, then the exception thrown by the action method won't be handled by the filter, and the default error handling will be used.

Figure 19-7. *Using an exception filter*

Using Dependency Injection for Filters

When you derive a filter from one of the convenience attribute classes, such as ExceptionFilterAttribute, MVC creates a new instance of the filter class to handle every request. This is a reasonable approach because it avoids any possible reuse or concurrency problems and it suits the needs of most filter classes that developers require.

An alternative approach is to use the dependency injection system to select a different life cycle for filters. There are two different approaches to using dependency injection in filters, which I describe in the following sections.

Resolving Filter Dependencies

The first approach is to use dependency injection to manage context data for filters, which allows different types of filters to share data or for a single filter to share data with instances of itself used to process other requests. To demonstrate how this works, I added a class file called FilterDiagnostics.cs to the Infrastructure folder and used it to define the interface and implementation class shown in Listing 19-22.

Listing 19-22. The Contents of the FilterDiagnostics.cs File in the Infrastructure Folder

```
using System.Collections.Generic;

namespace Filters.Infrastructure {

    public interface IFilterDiagnostics {
        IEnumerable<string> Messages { get; }
        void AddMessage(string message);
    }
```

```
public class DefaultFilterDiagnostics : IFilterDiagnostics {
    private List<string> messages = new List<string>();

    public IEnumerable<string> Messages => messages;

    public void AddMessage(string message) =>
        messages.Add(message);
    }
}
```

The IFilterDiagnostics interface defines a simple model for collecting diagnostic messages during filter execution. The DefaultFilterDiagnostics class is the implementation I will use. In Listing 19-23, I have updated the Startup class to configure the service provider with the new interface and its implementation.

Listing 19-23. Configuring the Service Provider in the Startup.cs File in the Filters Folder

```
using System;
using System.Collections.Generic;
using System.Linq;
using System.Threading.Tasks;
using Microsoft.AspNetCore.Builder;
using Microsoft.AspNetCore.Hosting;
using Microsoft.AspNetCore.Http;
using Microsoft.Extensions.DependencyInjection;
using Filters.Infrastructure;

namespace Filters {
    public class Startup {
        public void ConfigureServices(IServiceCollection services) {
            services.AddScoped<IFilterDiagnostics, DefaultFilterDiagnostics>();
            services.AddMvc();
        }

        public void Configure(IApplicationBuilder app, IHostingEnvironment env) {
            app.UseStatusCodePages();
            app.UseDeveloperExceptionPage();
            app.UseStaticFiles();
            app.UseMvcWithDefaultRoute();
        }
    }
}
```

I used the AddScoped extension method to configure the service provider, which means that all the filters instantiated to deal with a single request will receive the same DefaultFilterDiagnostics object. This is the basis for sharing custom context data between filters.

Creating Filters with Dependencies

The next step is to create filters that declare dependencies on the IFilterDiagnostics interface. I created a class file called TimeFilter.cs in the Infrastructure folder and used it to define the class shown in Listing 19-24.

Listing 19-24. The Contents of the TimeFilter.cs File in the Infrastructure Folder

```
using System.Diagnostics;
using System.Threading.Tasks;
using Microsoft.AspNetCore.Mvc.Filters;

namespace Filters.Infrastructure {

    public class TimeFilter : IAsyncActionFilter, IAsyncResultFilter {
        private Stopwatch timer;
        private IFilterDiagnostics diagnostics;

        public TimeFilter(IFilterDiagnostics diags) {
            diagnostics = diags;
        }

        public async Task OnActionExecutionAsync(
                ActionExecutingContext context,
                ActionExecutionDelegate next) {

            timer = Stopwatch.StartNew();
            await next();
            diagnostics.AddMessage($@"Action time:
                {timer.Elapsed.TotalMilliseconds}");
        }

        public async Task OnResultExecutionAsync(
                ResultExecutingContext context,
                ResultExecutionDelegate next) {

            await next();
            timer.Stop();
            diagnostics.AddMessage($@"Result time:
                {timer.Elapsed.TotalMilliseconds}");
        }
    }
}
```

The TimeFilter is a hybrid action/result filter that re-creates the timer functionality from a previous example but stores its timing information using an implementation of the IFilterDiagnostics interface, which is declared as a constructor argument and will be provided by the dependency injection system when the filter is created.

Notice that the TimeFilter class implements the filter interfaces directly, rather than deriving from the convenience attribute class. As you will see, filters that rely on dependency injection are applied through a different attribute and are not used to decorate controllers or actions directly.

To demonstrate how filters can use dependency injection to share context data, I added a class file called `DiagnosticsFilter.cs` to the `Infrastructure` folder and used it to create the filter shown in Listing 19-25.

Listing 19-25. The Contents of the DiagnosticsFilter.cs File in the Infrastructure Folder

```
using System.Text;
using System.Threading.Tasks;
using Microsoft.AspNetCore.Mvc.Filters;

namespace Filters.Infrastructure {

    public class DiagnosticsFilter : IAsyncResultFilter {
        private IFilterDiagnostics diagnostics;

        public DiagnosticsFilter(IFilterDiagnostics diags) {
            diagnostics = diags;
        }

        public async Task OnResultExecutionAsync(
                ResultExecutingContext context,
                ResultExecutionDelegate next) {

            await next();

            foreach (string message in diagnostics?.Messages) {
                byte[] bytes = Encoding.ASCII
                    .GetBytes($"<div>{message}</div>");
                await context.HttpContext.Response.Body
                    .WriteAsync(bytes, 0, bytes.Length);
            }
        }
    }
}
```

The `DiagnosticsFilter` class is a result filter that receives an implementation of the `IFilterDiagnostics` interface as a constructor argument and writes out the messages it contains to the response.

Applying the Filters

The final step is to apply the filters to the controller class. Standard C# attributes don't have integral support for resolving constructor dependencies, which is why the filters in the previous sections are not attributes. Instead, the `TypeFilter` attribute is applied and is configured with the type of the filter that is needed, as shown in Listing 19-26.

■ **Tip** The order in which I applied the filters in Listing 19-26 is important, as I explain in the "Understanding and Changing Filter Order" section later in the chapter.

Listing 19-26. Applying Filters with Dependencies in the HomeController.cs File in the Controllers Folder

```
using Microsoft.AspNetCore.Mvc;
using Filters.Infrastructure;
using System;

namespace Filters.Controllers {

    [TypeFilter(typeof(DiagnosticsFilter))]
    [TypeFilter(typeof(TimeFilter))]
    public class HomeController : Controller {

        public ViewResult Index() => View("Message",
            "This is the Index action on the Home controller");

        public ViewResult SecondAction() => View("Message",
            "This is the SecondAction action on the Home controller");

        public ViewResult GenerateException(int? id) {
            if (id == null) {
                throw new ArgumentNullException(nameof(id));
            } else if (id > 10) {
                throw new ArgumentOutOfRangeException(nameof(id));
            } else {
                return View("Message", $"The value is {id}");
            }
        }
    }
}
```

The TypeFilter attribute creates a new instance of the filter class for each request but does so using the dependency injection feature, which allows for loosely coupled components to be created and puts the objects used to resolve dependencies under life-cycle management.

In the example, this means that both of the filters applied in Listing 19-26 will receive the same IFilterDiagnostics implementation object and so the messages written by the TimeFilter class will be written out to the response by the DiagnosticsFilter class. Figure 19-8 shows the effect, which you can see by starting the application and requesting the default URL for the application.

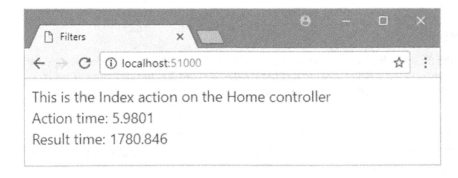

Figure 19-8. Using filters with dependencies

Managing Filter Life Cycles

When using the TypeFilter attribute, a new instance of the filter class is created for every request. This is the same behavior as applying a filter directly as an attribute, except that the TypeFilter attribute allows a filter class to declare dependencies that are resolved through the service provider.

The ServiceFilter attribute goes a step further and uses the service provider to create the filter object. This allows filter objects to be placed under life-cycle management as well. As a demonstration, in Listing 19-27, I have modified the TimeFilter class so that it keeps a simple average of the times it records.

Listing 19-27. Keeping Averages in the TimeFilter.cs File in the Infrastructure Folder

```
using System.Collections.Concurrent;
using System.Diagnostics;
using System.Linq;
using System.Threading.Tasks;
using Microsoft.AspNetCore.Mvc.Filters;

namespace Filters.Infrastructure {

    public class TimeFilter : IAsyncActionFilter, IAsyncResultFilter {
        private ConcurrentQueue<double> actionTimes = new ConcurrentQueue<double>();
        private ConcurrentQueue<double> resultTimes = new ConcurrentQueue<double>();
        private IFilterDiagnostics diagnostics;

        public TimeFilter(IFilterDiagnostics diags) {
            diagnostics = diags;
        }

        public async Task OnActionExecutionAsync(
                ActionExecutingContext context, ActionExecutionDelegate next) {

            Stopwatch timer = Stopwatch.StartNew();
            await next();
            timer.Stop();
            actionTimes.Enqueue(timer.Elapsed.TotalMilliseconds);
            diagnostics.AddMessage($@"Action time:
                {timer.Elapsed.TotalMilliseconds}
                Average: {actionTimes.Average():F2}");
        }

        public async Task OnResultExecutionAsync(
                ResultExecutingContext context, ResultExecutionDelegate next) {

            Stopwatch timer = Stopwatch.StartNew();
            await next();
            timer.Stop();
            resultTimes.Enqueue(timer.Elapsed.TotalMilliseconds);
            diagnostics.AddMessage($@"Result time:
                {timer.Elapsed.TotalMilliseconds}
                Average: {resultTimes.Average():F2}");
        }
    }
}
```

615

The filter now uses a thread-safe collection to store the times it records for the action and result phases of request processing and uses a separate Stopwatch each time it is asked to process a request. In Listing 19-28, I have registered the TimeFilter class as a singleton with the service provider in the Startup class.

Listing 19-28. Configuring the Service Provider in the Startup.cs File in the Filters Folder

```
using System;
using System.Collections.Generic;
using System.Linq;
using System.Threading.Tasks;
using Microsoft.AspNetCore.Builder;
using Microsoft.AspNetCore.Hosting;
using Microsoft.AspNetCore.Http;
using Microsoft.Extensions.DependencyInjection;
using Filters.Infrastructure;

namespace Filters {
    public class Startup {
        public void ConfigureServices(IServiceCollection services) {
            services.AddSingleton<IFilterDiagnostics, DefaultFilterDiagnostics>();
            services.AddSingleton<TimeFilter>();
            services.AddMvc();
        }

        public void Configure(IApplicationBuilder app, IHostingEnvironment env) {
            app.UseStatusCodePages();
            app.UseDeveloperExceptionPage();
            app.UseStaticFiles();
            app.UseMvcWithDefaultRoute();
        }
    }
}
```

Notice that I also changed the life cycle for IFilterDiagnostics so that is a singleton. If I had continued to create a new instance for each request, then the singleton TimeFilter would receive a different IFilterDiagnostics object from the DiagnosticsFilter, which continues to be instantiated through the TypeFilter attribute and will be created for each request.

Applying the Filter

The final step is to apply the filter to the controller using the ServiceType attribute, as shown in Listing 19-29.

Listing 19-29. Applying a Filter in the HomeController.cs File in the Controllers Folder

```
using Microsoft.AspNetCore.Mvc;
using Filters.Infrastructure;
using System;

namespace Filters.Controllers {
```

```
[TypeFilter(typeof(DiagnosticsFilter))]
[ServiceFilter(typeof(TimeFilter))]
public class HomeController : Controller {

    public ViewResult Index() => View("Message",
        "This is the Index action on the Home controller");

    public ViewResult SecondAction() => View("Message",
        "This is the SecondAction action on the Home controller");

    public ViewResult GenerateException(int? id) {
        if (id == null) {
            throw new ArgumentNullException(nameof(id));
        } else if (id > 10) {
            throw new ArgumentOutOfRangeException(nameof(id));
        } else {
            return View("Message", $"The value is {id}");
        }
    }
}
}
```

You can see the effect by running the application and requesting the default URL. Since a single implementation object for the IFilterDiagnostics interface is used to resolve all dependencies, the set of messages displayed builds up with each request, as shown in Figure 19-9.

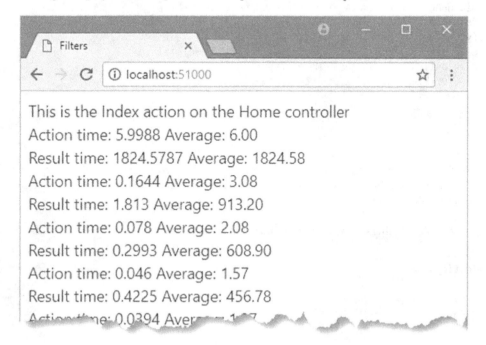

Figure 19-9. *Using the service provider to manage the filter life cycle*

Creating Global Filters

At the start of the chapter, I explained that you can apply filters to a controller class so that you don't have to apply them to individual action methods. *Global filters* go a step further and are applied once in the Startup class and, as their name suggests, are automatically applied to every action method in every controller in the application. Any filter can be used as a global filter; to demonstrate, I created a class file called ViewResultDiagnostics.cs to the Infrastructure folder and used it to define the filter shown in Listing 19-30.

Listing 19-30. The Contents of the ViewResultDiagnostics.cs File in the Infrastructure Folder

```
using Microsoft.AspNetCore.Mvc;
using Microsoft.AspNetCore.Mvc.Filters;

namespace Filters.Infrastructure {
    public class ViewResultDiagnostics : IActionFilter {
        private IFilterDiagnostics diagnostics;

        public ViewResultDiagnostics(IFilterDiagnostics diags) {
            diagnostics = diags;
        }

        public void OnActionExecuting(ActionExecutingContext context) {
            // do nothing - not used in this filter
        }

        public void OnActionExecuted(ActionExecutedContext context) {
            ViewResult vr;
            if ((vr = context.Result as ViewResult) != null) {
                diagnostics.AddMessage($"View name: {vr.ViewName}");
                diagnostics.AddMessage($@"Model type:
                    {vr.ViewData.Model.GetType().Name}");
            }
        }
    }
}
```

The filter uses an IFilterDiagnostics object to store messages about the view name and model type of ViewResult action results. In Listing 19-31, I applied this filter globally, along with the DiagnosticsFilter class that it depends on to write out the diagnostics messages.

Listing 19-31. Registering Global Filters in the Startup.cs File in the Filters Folder

```
using System;
using System.Collections.Generic;
using System.Linq;
using System.Threading.Tasks;
using Microsoft.AspNetCore.Builder;
using Microsoft.AspNetCore.Hosting;
using Microsoft.AspNetCore.Http;
using Microsoft.Extensions.DependencyInjection;
using Filters.Infrastructure;
```

```
namespace Filters {
    public class Startup {
        public void ConfigureServices(IServiceCollection services) {
            services.AddScoped<IFilterDiagnostics, DefaultFilterDiagnostics>();
            services.AddScoped<TimeFilter>();
            services.AddScoped<ViewResultDiagnostics>();
            services.AddScoped<DiagnosticsFilter>();
            services.AddMvc().AddMvcOptions(options => {
                options.Filters.AddService(typeof(ViewResultDiagnostics));
                options.Filters.AddService(typeof(DiagnosticsFilter));
            });
        }

        public void Configure(IApplicationBuilder app, IHostingEnvironment env) {
            app.UseStatusCodePages();
            app.UseDeveloperExceptionPage();
            app.UseStaticFiles();
            app.UseMvcWithDefaultRoute();
        }
    }
}
```

Global filters are set up by configuring the MVC services package. In the example, I used the
MvcOptions.Filters.AddService method to register filters globally. The AddService method accepts a
.NET type that will be instantiated using the life-cycle rules specified elsewhere in the ConfigureServices
method. I changed the life cycle of the other filter types to scoped so that new instances are created for each
request. The result is that new instances of the ViewResultDiagnostics and DiagnosticsFilter filters will
be created and applied for every request to every controller.

■ **Tip** You can also add global filters using an Add method instead of the AddService method, which allows a
filter object to be registered as a global filter without relying on dependency injection and the service provider. I
use the Add method in the next section.

I added a class file called GlobalController.cs to the Controllers folder and used it to define the
controller shown in Listing 19-32.

Listing 19-32. The Contents of the GlobalController.cs File in the Controllers Folder

```
using Microsoft.AspNetCore.Mvc;

namespace Filters.Controllers {

    public class GlobalController : Controller {

        public ViewResult Index() => View("Message",
            "This is the global controller");
    }
}
```

No filters have been applied to the Global controller, but if you start the application and request the /global URL, you will see the output from the two global filters, as shown in Figure 19-10.

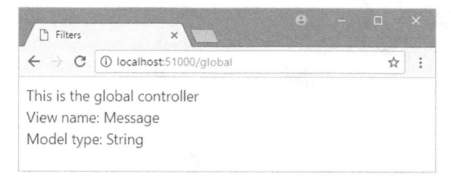

Figure 19-10. *Using global filters*

Understanding and Changing Filter Order

Filters run in a specific sequence: authorization, action, and then result. But if there are multiple filters of a given type, then the order in which they are applied is driven by the scope through which the filters have been applied. To demonstrate how this works, I added a class file called MessageAttribute.cs to the Infrastructure folder and used it to define the filter shown in Listing 19-33.

Listing 19-33. The Contents of the MessageAttribute.cs File in the Infrastructure Folder

```
using System.Text;
using Microsoft.AspNetCore.Mvc.Filters;

namespace Filters.Infrastructure {

    public class MessageAttribute : ResultFilterAttribute {
        private string message;

        public MessageAttribute(string msg) {
            message = msg;
        }

        public override void OnResultExecuting(ResultExecutingContext context) {
            WriteMessage(context, $"<div>Before Result:{message}</div>");
        }

        public override void OnResultExecuted(ResultExecutedContext context) {
            WriteMessage(context, $"<div>After Result:{message}</div>");
        }

        private void WriteMessage(FilterContext context, string msg) {
            byte[] bytes = Encoding.ASCII
                .GetBytes($"<div>{msg}</div>");
```

```
            context.HttpContext.Response
                .Body.Write(bytes, 0, bytes.Length);
        }
    }
}
```

This is a result filter that writes out fragments of HTML to the response before and after the action result is processed. The message written by the filter is configured through a constructor argument that can be used when applied as an attribute. In Listing 19-34, I have simplified the Home controller and replaced the filters from previous examples with multiple instances of the Message filter.

Listing 19-34. Applying a Filter in the HomeController.cs File in the Controllers Folder

```
using Microsoft.AspNetCore.Mvc;
using Filters.Infrastructure;

namespace Filters.Controllers {

    [Message("This is the Controller-Scoped Filter")]
    public class HomeController : Controller {

        [Message("This is the First Action-Scoped Filter")]
        [Message("This is the Second Action-Scoped Filter")]
        public ViewResult Index() => View("Message",
            "This is the Index action on the Home controller");
    }
}
```

I have changed the set of global filters so that the Message filter is used there as well, as shown Listing 19-35.

Listing 19-35. Creating a Global Filter in the Startup.cs File in the Filters Folder

```
using System;
using System.Collections.Generic;
using System.Linq;
using System.Threading.Tasks;
using Microsoft.AspNetCore.Builder;
using Microsoft.AspNetCore.Hosting;
using Microsoft.AspNetCore.Http;
using Microsoft.Extensions.DependencyInjection;
using Filters.Infrastructure;

namespace Filters {
    public class Startup {
        public void ConfigureServices(IServiceCollection services) {
            services.AddScoped<IFilterDiagnostics, DefaultFilterDiagnostics>();
            services.AddScoped<TimeFilter>();
            services.AddScoped<ViewResultDiagnostics>();
            services.AddScoped<DiagnosticsFilter>();
            services.AddMvc().AddMvcOptions(options => {
```

```
        options.Filters.Add(new
            MessageAttribute("This is the Globally-Scoped Filter"));
    });
}

public void Configure(IApplicationBuilder app, IHostingEnvironment env) {
    app.UseStatusCodePages();
    app.UseDeveloperExceptionPage();
    app.UseStaticFiles();
    app.UseMvcWithDefaultRoute();
}
```

Four instances of the filter will be used when the Index method responds to a request. If you run the application and request the default URL, you will see the following output displayed in the browser:

```
Before Result:This is the Globally-Scoped Filter
Before Result:This is the Controller-Scoped Filter
Before Result:This is the First Action-Scoped Filter
Before Result:This is the Second Action-Scoped Filter
After Result:This is the Second Action-Scoped Filter
After Result:This is the First Action-Scoped Filter
After Result:This is the Controller-Scoped Filter
After Result:This is the Globally-Scoped Filter
```

By default, MVC runs global filters, then filters applied to controller filter, and finally filters applied to action methods. Once the action method has been invoked or the action result has been processed, the stack of filters is unwound, which is why the After Result messages in the output are shown in reverse order.

Changing Filter Order

The default order can be changed by implementing the IOrderedFilter interface, which MVC looks for when it is working out how to stack filters in sequence. Here is the definition of the interface:

```
namespace Microsoft.AspNetCore.Mvc.Filters {

    public interface IOrderedFilter : IFilterMetadata {
        int Order { get; }
    }
}
```

The Order property returns an int value; a low value tells MVC to apply a filter before those with higher Order values. The convenience attributes already implement the IOrder value, and in Listing 19-36, I have set the Order property for the filters applied to the Home controller.

░ **Tip** The TypeFilter and ServiceFilter attributes also implement the IOrderedFilter interface, which means you can change the filter order when using dependency injection as well.

Listing 19-36. Setting Filter Order in the HomeController.cs File in the Controllers Folder

```csharp
using Filters.Infrastructure;
using Microsoft.AspNetCore.Mvc;

namespace Filters.Controllers {

    [Message("This is the Controller-Scoped Filter", Order = 10)]
    public class HomeController : Controller {

        [Message("This is the First Action-Scoped Filter", Order = 1)]
        [Message("This is the Second Action-Scoped Filter", Order = -1)]
        public ViewResult Index() => View("Message",
            "This is the Index action on the Home controller");
    }
}
```

Order values can also be negative, which is a helpful way of ensuring that a filter is applied before any global filters with the default order (although you can also set the order when creating global filters, too). If you run the example, you will see that the order of the output messages has changed to reflect the new priorities.

```
Before Result:This is the Second Action-Scoped Filter
Before Result:This is the Globally-Scoped Filter
Before Result:This is the First Action-Scoped Filter
Before Result:This is the Controller-Scoped Filter
After Result:This is the Controller-Scoped Filter
After Result:This is the First Action-Scoped Filter
After Result:This is the Globally-Scoped Filter
After Result:This is the Second Action-Scoped Filter
```

Summary

In this chapter, you saw how to encapsulate the logic that addresses crosscutting concerns as filters. I showed you the different kinds of filters available and how to implement them. You saw how filters can be applied as attributes to controllers and action methods and how they can be applied as global filters. In the next chapter, I show you how to use controllers to create web services.

CHAPTER 20

■ ■ ■

API Controllers

Not all controllers are used to send HTML documents to clients. There are also API controllers, which are used to provide access to an application's data. This is a feature that was previously provided through the separate Web API framework but has now been integrated into ASP.NET Core MVC. In this chapter, I explain the role that API controllers play in a web application, describe the problems they solve, and demonstrate how they are created, tested, and used. Table 20-1 puts API controllers in context.

Table 20-1. *Putting API Controllers in Context*

Question	Answer
What are they?	API controllers are like regular controllers, except that the responses produced by their action methods are data objects that are sent to the client without HTML markup.
Why are they useful?	API controllers allow clients to access the data in an application without also receiving the HTML markup that is required to present that content to the user. Not all clients are browsers, and not all clients present data to a user. An API controller makes an application open for supporting new types of clients or clients developed by a third-party.
How are they used?	API controllers are used like regular HTML controllers.
Are there any pitfalls or limitations?	The most common problems relate to the way that data objects are serialized so they can be sent to the client. See the "Understanding Content Formatting" section for details.
Are there any alternatives?	You don't have to use API controllers in your project, but doing so can increase the value of your platform to your clients.

© Adam Freeman 2017
A. Freeman, *Pro ASP.NET Core MVC 2*, https://doi.org/10.1007/978-1-4842-3150-0_20

Table 20-2 summarizes the chapter.

Table 20-2. *Chapter Summary*

Problem	Solution	Listing
Provide access to the data in an application	Create an API controller	10
Request data from an API controller	Use an Ajax query, either directly using the browser's API or through a library like jQuery	11–13
Override the content negotiation process	Use the `Produces` attribute	14-16
Allow clients to override the `Accept` header by specifying the data format in the URL	Add formatter mappings in the `Startup` class, add a segment variable that captures the data format, and, optionally, apply the `FormatFilter` attribute	17–18
Provide full support for the content negotiation process	Enable the `HttpNotAcceptableOutputFormatter` formatter and set the `RespectBrowserAcceptHeader` configuration property	19–20
Receive data in different formats using different action methods	Apply the `Consumes` attribute	21

Preparing the Example Project

For this chapter, I used the ASP.NET Core Web Application (.NET Core) template to create a new Empty project called ApiControllers.

Creating the Model and Repository

I started by creating the `Models` folder, adding a class file called `Reservation.cs`, and using it to define the model class shown in Listing 20-1.

Listing 20-1. The Contents of the Reservation.cs File in the Models Folder

```
namespace ApiControllers.Models {

    public class Reservation {
        public int ReservationId { get; set; }
        public string ClientName { get; set; }
        public string Location { get; set; }
    }
}
```

I also added a file called IRepository.cs to the Models folder and used it to define the interface for a model repository, as shown in Listing 20-2.

Listing 20-2. The Contents of the IRepository.cs File in the Models Folder

```
using System.Collections.Generic;

namespace ApiControllers.Models {

    public interface IRepository {

        IEnumerable<Reservation> Reservations { get; }
        Reservation this[int id] { get; }

        Reservation AddReservation(Reservation reservation);
        Reservation UpdateReservation(Reservation reservation);
        void DeleteReservation(int id);
    }
}
```

I added a class file called MemoryRepository.cs to the Models folder and used it to define a nonpersistent implementation of the IRepository interface, as shown in Listing 20-3.

Listing 20-3. The Contents of the MemoryRepository.cs File in the Models Folder

```
using System.Collections.Generic;

namespace ApiControllers.Models {

    public class MemoryRepository : IRepository {
        private Dictionary<int, Reservation> items;

        public MemoryRepository() {
            items = new Dictionary<int, Reservation>();
            new List<Reservation> {
                new Reservation { ClientName = "Alice", Location = "Board Room" },
                new Reservation { ClientName = "Bob", Location = "Lecture Hall" },
                new Reservation { ClientName = "Joe", Location = "Meeting Room 1" }
            }.ForEach(r => AddReservation(r));
        }

        public Reservation this[int id] => items.ContainsKey(id) ? items[id] : null;

        public IEnumerable<Reservation> Reservations => items.Values;

        public Reservation AddReservation(Reservation reservation) {
            if (reservation.ReservationId == 0) {
                int key = items.Count;
                while (items.ContainsKey(key)) { key++; };
                reservation.ReservationId = key;
            }
```

```
        items[reservation.ReservationId] = reservation;
        return reservation;
    }

    public void DeleteReservation(int id) => items.Remove(id);

    public Reservation UpdateReservation(Reservation reservation)
        => AddReservation(reservation);

    }
}
```

The repository creates a simple set of model objects when it is instantiated, and since there is no persistent storage, any changes will be lost when the application is stopped or restarted. (See Chapter 8 for an example of how to create a persistent repository as part of the SportsStore example application.)

Creating the Controller and Views

Later in the chapter, I will be creating RESTful controllers, but in preparation, I need to create a regular controller to provide a foundation for later examples. I created the Controllers folder, added a file called HomeController.cs, and used it to define the controller shown in Listing 20-4.

Listing 20-4. The Contents of the HomeController.cs File in the Controllers Folder

```
using Microsoft.AspNetCore.Mvc;
using ApiControllers.Models;

namespace ApiControllers.Controllers {

    public class HomeController : Controller {
        private IRepository repository { get; set; }

        public HomeController(IRepository repo) => repository = repo;

        public ViewResult Index() => View(repository.Reservations);

        [HttpPost]
        public IActionResult AddReservation(Reservation reservation) {
            repository.AddReservation(reservation);
            return RedirectToAction("Index");
        }
    }
}
```

This controller defines the Index action, which is the default for the application and renders the data model. It also defines an AddReservation action, which is accessible only for HTTP POST requests and will be used to receive form data from the user. These actions follow the Post/Redirect/Get pattern described in Chapter 17 so that reloading the web page won't create a duplicate form submission.

I created a layout so that I can separate the HTML content from the document header, which will simplify some changes I make later in the chapter. I created the Views/Shared folder, added a layout called the _Layout.cshtml file, and added the markup shown in Listing 20-5.

Listing 20-5. The Contents of the _Layout.cshtml File in the Views/Shared Folder

```
<!DOCTYPE html>
<html>
<head>
    <meta name="viewport" content="width=device-width" />
    <title>RESTful Controllers</title>
    <link asp-href-include="lib/bootstrap/dist/css/*.min.css" rel="stylesheet" />
</head>
<body class="m-1 p-1">
    @RenderBody()
</body>
</html>
```

Next, I created the Views/Home folder, added a view file called Index.cshtml, and added the content shown in Listing 20-6.

Listing 20-6. The Contents of the Index.cshtml File in the Views/Home Folder

```
@model IEnumerable<Reservation>
@{  Layout = "_Layout"; }

<form id="addform" asp-action="AddReservation" method="post">
    <div class="form-group">
        <label for="ClientName">Name:</label>
        <input class="form-control" name="ClientName" />
    </div>
    <div class="form-group">
        <label for="Location">Location:</label>
        <input class="form-control" name="Location" />
    </div>
    <div class="text-center panel-body">
        <button type="submit" class="btn btn-sm btn-primary">Add</button>
    </div>
</form>

<table class="table table-sm table-striped table-bordered m-2">
    <thead><tr><th>ID</th><th>Client</th><th>Location</th></tr></thead>
    <tbody>
        @foreach (var r in Model) {
            <tr>
                <td>@r.ReservationId</td>
                <td>@r.ClientName</td>
                <td>@r.Location</td>
            </tr>
        }
    </tbody>
</table>
```

This strongly typed view receives a sequence of Reservation objects as its model and uses a Razor foreach loop to populate a table with them. There is also a form that has been configured to send POST requests to the AddReservation action.

The examples in this chapter depend on the Bootstrap CSS package. To add Bootstrap to the project, I used the Bower Configuration File item template to create the bower.json file in the root of the project and added the package to the dependencies section, as shown in Listing 20-7.

Listing 20-7. Adding a Package in the bower.json File

```
{
  "name": "asp.net",
  "private": true,
  "dependencies": {
    "bootstrap": "4.0.0-alpha.6"
  }
}
```

Next, I created a _ViewImports.cshtml file in the Views folder and used it to set up the built-in tag helpers for use in Razor views and to import the model namespace, as shown in Listing 20-8.

Listing 20-8. The Contents of the _ViewImports.cshtml File in the Views Folder

```
@using ApiControllers.Models
@addTagHelper *, Microsoft.AspNetCore.Mvc.TagHelpers
```

To enable the MVC Framework and the middleware components required for development, I made the changes shown in Listing 20-9 to the Startup class. I also used the AddSingleton method to set up the service mapping for the model repository.

Listing 20-9. Enabling Middleware in the Startup.cs File in the ApiControllers Folder

```
using System;
using System.Collections.Generic;
using System.Linq;
using System.Threading.Tasks;
using Microsoft.AspNetCore.Builder;
using Microsoft.AspNetCore.Hosting;
using Microsoft.AspNetCore.Http;
using Microsoft.Extensions.DependencyInjection;
using ApiControllers.Models;

namespace ApiControllers {
    public class Startup {

        public void ConfigureServices(IServiceCollection services) {
            services.AddSingleton<IRepository, MemoryRepository>();
            services.AddMvc();
        }

        public void Configure(IApplicationBuilder app, IHostingEnvironment env) {
            app.UseStatusCodePages();
            app.UseDeveloperExceptionPage();
            app.UseStaticFiles();
            app.UseMvcWithDefaultRoute();
        }
    }
}
```

Setting the HTTP Port

Some of the examples in this chapter are tested by manually typing URLs. To make this easier to describe, I will set the port that will be used to receive HTTP requests. Select ApiControllers Properties from the Visual Studio Project menu, display the Debug tab, and change the value of the App URL field to http://localhost:7000/, as shown in Figure 20-1. Make sure you save the changes after you have set the port number.

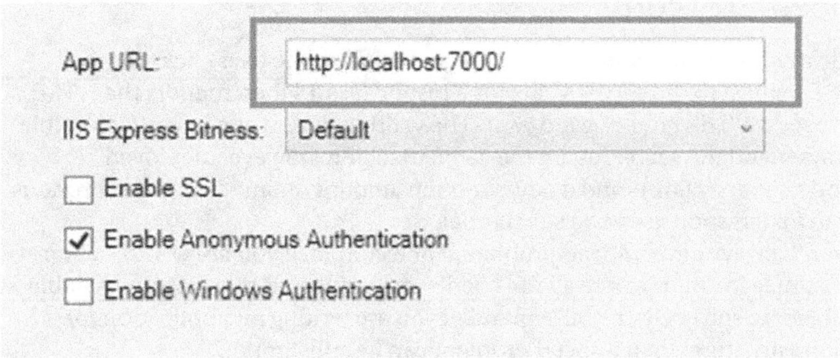

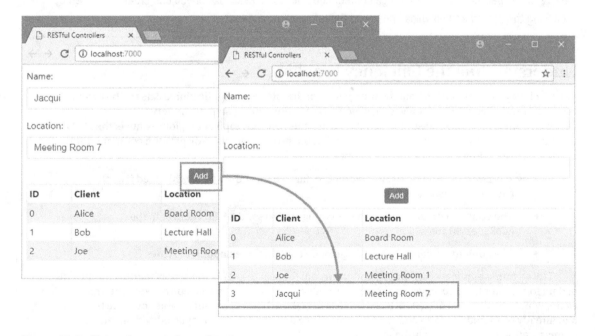

Figure 20-1. *Setting the application URL*

Start the application, fill out the form, and click the Add button; the application will add a new Reservation to the model, as shown in Figure 20-2. The changes you make to the repository are not persistent and will be lost when the application is stopped or restarted.

Figure 20-2. *Using the example application*

Understanding the Role of RESTful Controllers

The example application is an example of a classic web application. All of the logic in the application exists at the server, contained in C# classes, which makes them easy to manage, test, and maintain. But an application designed in this way can have serious deficiencies with regard to speed, efficiency, and openness.

Understanding the Speed Problem

At the moment, the example application is a *synchronous* web application. When the user clicks the Add button, the browser sends the POST request to the server, waits for a response, and then renders the HTML it receives. During this period, the user can't do anything but wait. The waiting period can be imperceptible during development when the browser and the server are on the same machine; however, deployed applications are subject to real-world capacity limits and delays, and the amount of time that a synchronous application requires the user to wait for a response can be substantial.

A synchronous application won't always have a speed problem. For example, if you are writing a line-of-business application for use in a single location where all the clients are connected by a fast and reliable LAN, then you may not have a problem to solve. On the other hand, if you are writing an application for mobile clients in areas with poor infrastructure, then a speed problem can be substantial.

■ **Tip**   Some browsers let you simulate different types of network, which can be a useful tool for seeing whether your users are likely to accept working with a synchronous application for a range of scenarios. Google Chrome, for example, offers a feature called *network throttling*, which is available in the Network section of the F12 developer tools. There is a range of predefined networks available, or you can create your own by specifying the upload and download rates and the latency.

Understanding the Efficiency Problem

The efficiency problem arises from the way that a synchronous web application treats the browser as an HTML rendering engine used only to display the HTML documents sent by the server.

When the user first requests the default URL for the example application, for instance, the HTML document that is sent back contains everything that the browser needs to display the content for the application, including the following information:

- The content relies on the Bootstrap CSS file, which should be downloaded if a cached copy isn't available.

- The content contains a form that is configured to send a POST request to the AddReservation action.

- The content contains a table whose body contains three populated rows.

The example application is simple, and the initial request results in the server sending about 1.3KB of data to the client. However, when the user submits the form, the client is redirected to the Index action again, which results in another 1.3KB of data to reflect the addition of a single table row. The browser had already rendered the form and the table, but these are discarded and replaced with an entirely new representation of what is largely the same content.

You may think that 1.3KB of data isn't much and, of course, you would be right. But if you consider the ratio of useful content to duplicate content, you will see that the vast majority of the data sent to the browser is wasted. And the example application is deliberately simple; few real applications require so little HTML, and the amount of duplicated content will be substantially increased as the complexity of the application rises.

Understanding the Openness Problem

The final problem presented by traditional web applications is that the design is closed, meaning that the data in the model can be accessed only through the actions provided by the Home controller. Closed applications become a problem when there is a need to use the underlying data in another application, especially when that application is being developed by a different team or even a different organization. Developers often believe that the value in an application is in the user interactions that it offers users, largely because those are the parts that we spend time thinking about and writing. But once an application is established and has an active user base, it is often the data that the application contains that becomes important.

Introducing REST and API Controllers

An *API controller* is an MVC controller that is responsible for providing access to the data in an application without encapsulating it in HTML. This allows the data in the model to be retrieved or modified without having to use the actions provided by the regular controllers, such as the Home controller in the example application.

The most common approach for delivering data from an application is to use the *Representational State Transfer* pattern, known as REST. There is no detailed specification for REST, which leads to a lot of different approaches that fall under the RESTful banner. There are, however, some unifying ideas that are useful in client-side web application development.

The core premise of a RESTful web service is to embrace the characteristics of HTTP so that request methods—also known as *verbs*—specify an operation for the server to perform, and the request URL specifies one or more data objects to which the operation will be applied.

As an example, here is a URL that might refer to a specific Reservation in the example application:

```
/api/reservations/1
```

The first part of the URL—api—is used to separate out the data part of the application from the standard controllers that generate HTML. The next part—reservations—indicates the collection of objects that will be operated on. The final part—1—specifies an individual object within the reservations collection. In the example application, it is the value of the ReservationId property that uniquely identifies an object and that would be used in the URL.

URLs that identify an object are combined with HTTP methods to specify operations. In Table 20-3, I have listed the most common HTTP methods and what they represent when combined with an example URL. I have also included details of what data—the *payload*—is included in the request and response for each method and URL combination. The API controller that processes these requests uses the response status code to report on the outcome of the request.

Table 20-3. *Combining HTTP Methods with URLs to Specify a RESTful Web Service*

Verb	URL	Description	Payloads
GET	/api/reservations	This combination retrieves all the objects.	This response contains the complete collection of Reservation objects.
GET	/api/reservations/1	This combination retrieves the reservation object whose ReservationId is 1.	The response contains the specified Reservation object.
POST	/api/reservation	This combination creates a new Reservation.	The request contains the values for the other properties required to create a Reservation object. The response contains the object that was stored, ensuring that the client receives the saved data.
PUT	/api/reservation	This combination replaces an existing Reservation.	The request contains the values required to change the properties of the specified Reservation. The response contains the object that was stored, ensuring that the client receives the saved data.
PATCH	/api/reservation/1	This combination modifies the existing Reservation object whose ReservationId is 1.	This request contains a set of modifications that should be applied to the specified Reservation object. This response is a confirmation that the changes have been applied.
DELETE	/api/reservation/1	This combination deletes the Reservation object whose ReservationId is 1.	There is no payload in the request or response.

Following the RESTful convention isn't a requirement, but it does help make your application easier to work with because the same broad approach has been adopted by many established web applications.

Creating an API Controller

The process for creating an API controller builds on the approach used for standard controllers, with some additional features to help specify the API that is presented to clients. To demonstrate, I added a class file called ReservationController.cs to the Controllers folder and used it to define the class shown in Listing 20-10. I break down the functionality provided by this controller in the sections that follow.

■ **Tip** Remember that controller classes can be defined anywhere in the project and not just in the Controllers folder. For large and complex projects, it can be helpful to define the API controllers separately from the regular HTML controllers and place them in a subfolder or even separate folder entirely.

Listing 20-10. The Contents of the ReservationController.cs File in the Controllers Folder

```
using System.Collections.Generic;
using Microsoft.AspNetCore.Mvc;
using ApiControllers.Models;
using Microsoft.AspNetCore.JsonPatch;

namespace ApiControllers.Controllers {

    [Route("api/[controller]")]
    public class ReservationController : Controller {
        private IRepository repository;

        public ReservationController(IRepository repo) => repository = repo;

        [HttpGet]
        public IEnumerable<Reservation> Get() => repository.Reservations;

        [HttpGet("{id}")]
        public Reservation Get(int id) => repository[id];

        [HttpPost]
        public Reservation Post([FromBody] Reservation res) =>
            repository.AddReservation(new Reservation {
                ClientName = res.ClientName,
                Location = res.Location
            });

        [HttpPut]
        public Reservation Put([FromBody] Reservation res) =>
            repository.UpdateReservation(res);

        [HttpPatch("{id}")]
        public StatusCodeResult Patch(int id,
                [FromBody]JsonPatchDocument<Reservation> patch) {
            Reservation res = Get(id);
            if (res != null) {
                patch.ApplyTo(res);
                return Ok();
            }
            return NotFound();
        }

        [HttpDelete("{id}")]
        public void Delete(int id) => repository.DeleteReservation(id);
    }
}
```

API controllers work in the same basic way as regular controllers, which means that you can create a POCO controller or derive a class from the Controller base class, which provides more convenient access to the request context data.

ADAPTING THE RESTFUL PATTERN

REST has encouraged a certain amount of dogmatism about how web application APIs should be presented to clients. REST isn't a standard or even a well-defined pattern, and there are some helpful approaches that make REST easier to adopt with an ASP.NET Core MVC application but that have a tendency to upset those programmers who have fixed views about what counts as RESTful.

In Table 20-3, the URLs that I listed for the POST and PUT operations do not uniquely identify a resource, which some people consider an essential REST characteristic. In the case of the POST operation, the unique identifier of a Reservation object is assigned by the model, which means that the client is unable to provide it as part of the URL. In the case of the PUT operation, the MVC model binding feature—which I describe in Chapter 26 and is the reason I applied the FromBody attribute in Listing 20-10—makes it easier to receive details of the Reservation object that is to be modified from the request body. So, that's where the Reservation controller expects to find the ReservationId value that identifies the model object that is to be modified.

In common with all patterns, REST is a starting point that contains helpful and useful ideas. It is not a rigid standard that must be followed at all costs, and the only important thing is to write code that can be understood, tested, and maintained. Accommodating the nature of MVC applications and the design of the repository makes for a simpler application while still providing a useful API for clients to consume. My advice is to consider patterns to be a guiding principle that you adapt to your own needs—something that is as true for REST as it is for MVC itself.

Defining the Route

The route by which API controllers are reached can be defined only using the Route attribute and cannot be defined in the application configuration in the Startup class. The convention for API controllers is to use a route prefixed with api, followed by the name of the controller, so that the ReservationController controller shown in Listing 20-10 is reached through the URL /api/reservation, like this:

```
...
[Route("api/[controller]")]
public class ReservationController : Controller {
...
```

Declaring Dependencies

API controllers are instantiated in the same way as regular controllers, which means that they can declare dependencies that will be resolved using the service provider. The ReservationController class declares a constructor dependency on the IRepository interface, which will be resolved to provide access to the data in the model.

```
...
public ReservationController(IRepository repo) => repository = repo;
...
```

Defining the Action Methods

Each action method is decorated with an attribute that specifies the HTTP method that it accepts, like this:

```
...
[HttpGet]
public IEnumerable<Reservation> Get() => repository.Reservations;
...
```

The HttpGet attribute is one of a set that is used to restrict access to action methods to requests that have a specific HTTP method or verb. The complete set of attributes is described in Table 20-4.

Table 20-4. The HTTP Method Attributes

Name	Description
HttpGet	This attribute specifies that the action can be invoked only by HTTP requests that use the GET verb.
HttpPost	This attribute specifies that the action can be invoked only by HTTP requests that use the POST verb.
HttpDelete	This attribute specifies that the action can be invoked only by HTTP requests that use the DELETE verb.
HttpPut	This attribute specifies that the action can be invoked only by HTTP requests that use the PUT verb.
HttpPatch	This attribute specifies that the action can be invoked only by HTTP requests that use the PATCH verb.
HttpHead	This attribute specifies that the action can be invoked only by HTTP requests that use the HEAD verb.
AcceptVerbs	This attribute is used to specify multiple HTTP verbs.

Routes are further refined by including a routing fragment as the argument to the HTTP method attribute, like this:

```
...
[HttpGet("{id}")]
public Reservation Get(int id) => repository[id];
...
```

The routing fragment, {id}, is combined with the route defined by the Route attribute applied to the controller and a constraint based on the HTTP method. In this case, it means that this action can be reached by sending a GET request whose URL matches the /api/reservations/{id} routing pattern, where the id segment is then used to identify the reservation object that should be retrieved.

Notice that the routes generated for an API controller don't include an {action} segment variable, which means that the name of the action method isn't part of the URL required to target a specific method. All the actions in an API controller are reached through the same base URL (/api/reservation for the example), and the HTTP method and optional segments are used to differentiate between them.

Defining the Action Results

Action methods for API controllers don't rely on ViewResult objects to present their results since there are no views required when delivering data. Instead, API controller action methods return data objects, like this:

```
...
[HttpGet]
public IEnumerable<Reservation> Get() => repository.Reservations;
...
```

This action returns a sequence of Reservation objects and leaves MVC to take responsibility for serializing them into a format that can be processed by the client. I explain this process in more detail in the "Understanding Content Formatting" section.

CUSTOMIZING API RESULTS

One of the most appealing aspects of API controllers is that you can just return C# objects from action methods and let MVC figure out what to do with them. MVC is pretty good at working out what to do. For example, if you return null from an API controller action method, then the client will be sent a 204 - No Content response.

But API controllers are able to use the features available to regular controllers, too, and that means you can override the default behavior by returning an IActionResult from your action methods that specifies what kind of result you want to send. As an example, here is an implementation of an action method from the example controller that sends a 404 - Not Found response for queries that don't correspond to an object in the model:

```
...
[HttpGet("{id}")]
public IActionResult Get(int id) {
    Reservation result = repository[id];
    if (result == null) {
        return NotFound();
    } else {
        return Ok(result);
    }
}
...
```

If there is no object in the repository for the specified ID, then I call the NotFound method, which creates a NotFoundResult object that, in turn, leads to a 404 - Not Found response being sent to the client. If there is an object in the repository, then I call the Ok method to create an ObjectResult object. The Ok method allows me to send an object to the client within an action that returns an IActionResult, as described in Chapter 17. You won't often need to override the default API controller responses, but the full range of action results are available if the need does arise.

Testing an API Controller

There are lots of tools available to help test web application APIs. Good examples include Fiddler (www.telerik.com/fiddler), which is a stand-alone HTTP debugging tool, and Swashbuckle (http://github.com/domaindrivendev/Swashbuckle), which is a NuGet package that adds a summary page to an application that describes its API operations and allows them to be tested.

But the simplest way to make sure that an API controller is to use PowerShell, which makes it easy to create HTTP requests from the command line and which lets you focus on the results of API operations without needing to dig into the details. PowerShell originated on Windows but is now available for Linux and macOS as well.

In the sections that follow, I show you how to use PowerShell to test each of the operations provided by the Reservation controller. You can open a new PowerShell window to run the test commands or use the Visual Studio Package Manager Console window, which uses PowerShell.

Testing the GET Operations

To test the GET operation provided by the Reservation API controller, start the application by selecting Start Without Debugging from the Visual Studio Debug menu and wait until you see the synchronous response provided by the Home controller. Once the application is running, open a PowerShell window and type the following command:

```
Invoke-RestMethod http://localhost:7000/api/reservation -Method GET
```

This command uses the Invoke-RestMethod PowerShell cmdlet to send a GET request to the /api/reservation URL. The result is parsed and formatted to make the data easy to read, as follows:

```
reservationId clientName location
------------- ---------- --------
            0 Alice      Board Room
            1 Bob        Lecture Hall
            2 Joe        Meeting Room 1
```

The server responds to the GET request with a JSON representation of the Reservation objects contained in the model, which the Invoke-RestMethod cmdlet presents in a table format.

UNDERSTANDING JSON

The *JavaScript Object Notation* (JSON) has become the standard data format for web applications. JSON has become popular because it is simple, concise, and easy to work with. It is especially easy to process JSON data in JavaScript code because the JSON format is similar to the way that literal objects are expressed in JavaScript code. Modern browsers include built-in support for generating and parsing JSON data, and popular JavaScript libraries, such as jQuery, will automatically convert to and from JSON.

Although JSON has evolved from JavaScript, its structure is easy for C# developers to read and understand. As an example, here is a response from the API controller in the example application:

```
...
[{"reservationId":0,"clientName":"Alice","location":"Board Room"},
 {"reservationId":1,"clientName":"Bob","location":"Lecture Hall"},
 {"reservationId":2,"clientName":"Joe","location":"Meeting Room 1"}]
...
```

This JSON string describes an array of objects. The array is denoted by the [and] characters, and each object is denoted using the { and } characters. The objects are a collection of key/value pairs, where each key is separated from its value with a colon (the : character) and pairs are separated with commas (the , character). This is loosely similar to the C# literal syntax that I used in the MemoryRepository class to define the data in Listing 20-3.

```
...
new List<Reservation> {
    new Reservation { ClientName = "Alice", Location = "Board Room" },
    new Reservation { ClientName = "Bob", Location = "Lecture Hall" },
    new Reservation { ClientName = "Joe", Location = "Meeting Room 1" }
...
```

Notice, however, that MVC changes the capitalization of property names from the C# convention (ClientName, with an initial uppercase letter) to the JavaScript convention (clientName, with an initial lowercase letter).

Even though the formats are not identical, there is sufficient similarity that a C# developer can read and understand JSON data with little effort. You don't need to get into the detail of JSON for most web applications because MVC does all the heavy lifting, but you can learn more about JSON at www.json.org.

There are two GET operations provided by the Reservation controller. When a GET request is sent to /api/reservation, then a response containing all the objects is returned. To retrieve a single object, its ReservationId value is specified as the final segment in the URL, like this:

```
Invoke-RestMethod http://localhost:7000/api/reservation/1 -Method GET
```

This command requests the Reservation object whose ReservationId value is 1 and produces the following result:

```
reservationId clientName location
------------- ---------- --------
            1 Bob        Lecture Hall
```

Testing the POST Operation

All the operations provided by the API controller can be tested using PowerShell, although the format of the commands can be a little awkward. Here is a command that sends a POST request to the API controller to create a new Reservation object in the repository and writes out the data sent back in the response:

```
Invoke-RestMethod http://localhost:7000/api/reservation -Method POST -Body
(@{clientName="Anne"; location="Meeting Room 4"} | ConvertTo-Json) -ContentType
"application/json"
```

This command uses the -Body argument to specify the body for the request, which is encoded as JSON. The -ContentType argument is used to set the Content-Type header for the request. The command will produce the following result:

```
reservationId clientName location
------------- ---------- --------
            3 Anne       Meeting Room 4
```

The POST operation uses the clientName and location values to create a Reservation object and returns a JSON representation of the new object to the client, which includes the ReservationId value that has been assigned to the new object. This may seem like the client is simply receiving data values that it has sent to the server in the request, but this approach ensures that the client is working with the same data that the server is using and caters for any formatting or translations that the server performs on the data it receives from the client. To see the effect of the POST request, send another GET request to the /api/reservation API, like this:

```
Invoke-RestMethod http://localhost:7000/api/reservation -Method GET
```

The data that is returned by the client reflects the addition of the new Reservation object.

```
reservationId clientName location
------------- ---------- --------
            0 Alice      Board Room
            1 Bob        Lecture Hall
            2 Joe        Meeting Room 1
            3 Anne       Meeting Room 4
```

Testing the PUT Operation

The PUT method is used to replace existing objects in the model. The ReservationId value of the object is specified as part of the request URL, and the clientName and location values are provided in the request body. Here is a PowerShell command that sends a PUT request to modify a Reservation object:

```
Invoke-RestMethod http://localhost:7000/api/reservation -Method PUT -Body
(@{reservationId="1"; clientName="Bob"; location="Media Room"} | ConvertTo-Json)
-ContentType "application/json"
```

This request changes the `Reservation` object whose `ReservationId` value is 1 and specifies a new value for the `Location` property. If you run the command, you will see the following response, which indicates that the change has been made:

```
reservationId clientName location
------------- ---------- --------
            1 Bob        Media Room
```

To see the effect of the PUT request, send a GET request to the `/api/reservation` API, like this:

```
Invoke-RestMethod http://localhost:7000/api/reservation -Method GET
```

The data that is returned by the client reflects the addition of the new `Reservation` object.

```
reservationId clientName location
------------- ---------- --------
            0 Alice      Board Room
            1 Bob        Media Room
            2 Joe        Meeting Room 1
            3 Anne       Meeting Room 4
```

Testing the Patch Operation

The PATCH method is used to modify an existing object in the model. Many applications use PUT requests and ignore PATCH entirely, which is a reasonable approach if your clients have access to all the properties defined by the objects in the model. But in complex applications, clients may receive a specific set of property values for security reasons, which prevents them from sending a complete object as part of a PUT request. PATCH requests are more selective and allow clients to specify a set of granular changes to an object.

ASP.NET Core MVC has support for working with the JSON Patch standard, which allows changes to be specified in a uniform way. I am not going to go into the detail of the JSON Patch standard, which you can read at `https://tools.ietf.org/html/rfc6902`, but for the example application, the client is going to send the API controller JSON data like this in its HTTP PATCH request:

```
[
{ "op": "replace", "path": "clientName", "value": "Bob"},
{ "op": "replace", "path": "location", "value": "Lecture Hall"}
]
```

A JSON Patch document is expressed as an array of operations. Each operation has an op property, which specifies the type of operation, and a path property, which specifies where the operation will be applied.

For the example application—and, in fact, for most applications—only the `replace` operation is required, which is used to change the value of a property. This JSON Patch data sets new values for the `clientName` and `location` properties, while the object that is to be modified will be identified by the request URL. ASP.NET Core MVC will automatically process the JSON data and present it to the action method as a `JsonPatchDocument<T>` object, where T is the type of the model object to be modified. The `JsonPatchDocument<T>` object can then be used to modify an object from the repository using the `ApplyTo` method. Here is a PowerShell command that sends a PATCH request:

```
Invoke-RestMethod http://localhost:7000/api/reservation/2 -Method PATCH -Body (@
{ op="replace"; path="clientName"; value="Bob"},@{ op="replace"; path="location";
value="Lecture Hall"} | ConvertTo-Json)  -ContentType "application/json"
```

This request asks the server to modify the clientName and location properties of the Reservation object whose ReservationId is 2. To see the effect of the PUT request, send a get request to the /api/reservation API, like this:

```
Invoke-RestMethod http://localhost:7000/api/reservation -Method GET
```

The data that is returned by the client reflects the addition of the new Reservation object.

```
reservationId clientName location
------------- ---------- --------
            0 Alice      Board Room
            1 Bob        Media Room
            2 Bob        Lecture Hall
            3 Anne       Meeting Room 4
```

Testing the Delete Operation

The final test is to send a DELETE request, which will remove a Reservation object from the repository, as follows:

```
Invoke-RestMethod http://localhost:7000/api/reservation/2 -Method DELETE
```

The action that accepts DELETE requests in the Reservation controller doesn't return a result, so no data is displayed when the command has completed. To see the effect of the deletion, request the contents of the repository using the following command:

```
Invoke-RestMethod http://localhost:7000/api/reservation -Method GET
```

The Reservation object whose ReservationId value is 2 was removed from the repository.

```
reservationId clientName location
------------- ---------- --------
            0 Alice      Board Room
            1 Bob        Media Room
            3 Anne       Meeting Room 4
```

Using the API Controller in the Browser

Defining an API controller has addressed the openness issue for my application, but it hasn't done anything for my speed or efficiency issues. For this, I need to update the HTML part of the application so that it relies on JavaScript to make HTTP requests to the API controller to perform data operations.

In the browser, asynchronous HTTP requests are typically known as *Ajax requests*, where Ajax used to be an acronym for *Asynchronous JavaScript and XML*. The XML data format has lost popularity in recent years, but the name Ajax is still used to refer to asynchronous HTTP requests, even when they return JSON data. More broadly, the technique described in this section is the foundation for single-page applications, where JavaScript in a single HTML page is used to pull in the data for multiple sections of the application, generating the content to display dynamically.

■ **Note** Client-side development is a topic in its own right and outside the scope of this book. In this section, I create only a basic asynchronous HTTP request without detailed explanations, just to give a sense of how it is done. See my *Pro Angular and Essential Angular for ASP.NET Core MVC books, also published by Apress,* for detailed coverage of client-side development with the Angular framework and supporting Angular clients using ASP.NET Core MVC.

There is a JavaScript API provided by browsers for making Ajax requests, but it is a little awkward to deal with, and there are some differences in the way that browsers implement some optional features. The simplest way to make Ajax requests is to use the jQuery library, which is an endlessly useful tool for client-side development. In Listing 20-11, I added the jQuery package to the bower.json file.

Listing 20-11. Adding jQuery in the bower.json File in the ApiControllers Folder

```
{
  "name": "asp.net",
  "private": true,
  "dependencies": {
    "bootstrap": "4.0.0-alpha.6",
    "jquery": "3.2.1"
  }
}
```

In fact, since some Bootstrap features depend on jQuery, Bower will have already installed the package in the wwwroot/lib folder. The addition in Listing 20-11 has the effect of making the dependency explicit. To use the features provided by jQuery, I created the wwwroot/js folder and added a JavaScript file called client.js, the contents of which are shown in Listing 20-12.

Listing 20-12. The Contents of the client.js File in the wwwroot/js Folder

```
$(document).ready(function () {

    $("form").submit(function (e) {
        e.preventDefault();
        $.ajax({
            url: "api/reservation",
            contentType: "application/json",
            method: "POST",
            data: JSON.stringify({
                clientName: this.elements["ClientName"].value,
                location: this.elements["Location"].value
            }),
```

```
            success: function(data) {
                addTableRow(data);
            }
        })
    });
});

var addTableRow = function (reservation) {
    $("table tbody").append("<tr><td>" + reservation.reservationId + "</td><td>"
        + reservation.clientName + "</td><td>"
        + reservation.location + "</td></tr>");
}
```

The JavaScript file in this file responds when the user submits the form in the browser, encodes the form data as JSON, and sends it to the server using an HTTP POST request. The JSON data that is returned by the server is automatically parsed by jQuery and then used to add a row to the HTML table. In Listing 20-13, I have updated the layout to include script elements for the jQuery library for the client.js file.

Listing 20-13. Adding JavaScript References in the _Layout.cshtml File

```
<!DOCTYPE html>
<html>
<head>
    <meta name="viewport" content="width=device-width" />
    <title>RESTful Controllers</title>
    <link asp-href-include="lib/bootstrap/dist/css/*.min.css" rel="stylesheet" />
    <script src="lib/jquery/dist/jquery.js"></script>
    <script src="js/client.js"></script>
</head>
<body class="m-1 p-1">
    @RenderBody()
</body>
</html>
```

The first script element tells the browser to load the jQuery library, and the second specifies the file that will contain my custom code. There is no obvious visual difference if you run the application and use the HTML form to create a Reservation in the application repository, but if you examine the HTTP request that is sent by the browser, you will see that it requires much less data than the synchronous version of the application did. In my simple testing, the asynchronous request required 440 bytes of data, which is about 40 percent of what the synchronous request required. The improvement is more substantial in real applications where the size of data tends to be much less than the size of the HTML document that is used to display it.

Understanding Content Formatting

When an action method returns a C# object as its result, MVC has to work out which data format should be used to encode the object and send it to the client. In this section, I explain what the default process is and how it is influenced by the request sent by the client and the configuration of the application. To help explain how the process works, I added a class file called ContentController.cs to the Controllers folder and used it to define the API controller shown in Listing 20-14.

Listing 20-14. The Contents of the ContentController.cs File in the Controllers Folder

```
using Microsoft.AspNetCore.Mvc;
using ApiControllers.Models;

namespace ApiControllers.Controllers {

    [Route("api/[controller]")]
    public class ContentController : Controller {

        [HttpGet("string")]
        public string GetString() => "This is a string response";

        [HttpGet("object")]
        public Reservation GetObject() => new Reservation {
            ReservationId = 100,
            ClientName = "Joe",
            Location = "Board Room"
        };
    }
}
```

I specified static segment variables as the arguments to the HttpGet attribute for two of the actions in this controller, which means that they can be reached by the /api/controller/string and /api/controller/object URLs. The Content controller doesn't follow the REST pattern even loosely, but it will make it easy to understand how content negotiation works.

The content format selected by MVC depends on four factors: the formats that the client will accept, the formats that MVC can produce, the content policy specified by the action, and the type returned by the action method. Figuring out how everything fits together can be daunting, but the good news is that the default policy works just fine for most applications, and you only need to understand what happens behind the scenes when you need to make a change or when you are not getting results in the format that you expect.

Understanding the Default Content Policy

The starting point is the standard application configuration that is used when neither the client nor the action method applies any restrictions to the formats that can be used. In this situation, the outcome is simple and predictable.

- If the action method returns a string, the string is sent unmodified to the client, and the Content-Type header of the response is set to text/plain.

- For all other data types, including other simple types such as int, the data is formatted as JSON, and the Content-Type header of the response is set to application/json.

The reason that strings get special treatment is that they cause problems when they are encoded as JSON. When you encode other simple types, such as the C# int value 2, then the result is a quoted string, such as "2". When you encode a string, you end up with two sets of quotes so that "Hello" becomes ""Hello"". Not all clients cope well with this double encoding, so it is more reliable to use the text/plain format and sidestep the issue entirely. This is rarely an issue because few applications send string values;

it is more common to send objects in the JSON format. You can see both outcomes by using PowerShell. Here is a command that invokes the GetString method, which returns a string:

```
Invoke-WebRequest http://localhost:7000/api/content/string | select
@{n='Content-Type';e={ $_.Headers."Content-Type" }}, Content
```

This command sends a GET request to the /api/content/string URL and processes the response to display the Content-Type header and the content from the response.

■ **Tip** You may receive an error when you use the Invoke-WebRequest cmdlet if you have not performed the initial setup for Internet Explorer. This is especially likely on a Windows 10 machine where Edge has replaced it. The problem can be fixed by running IE and selecting the initial configurations you require.

The command produces the following output:

```
Content-Type            Content
------------            -------
text/plain; charset=utf-8 This is a string response
```

The same command can also be used to show the JSON format by changing just the URL that is requested, like this:

```
Invoke-WebRequest http://localhost:7000/api/content/object | select
@{n='Content-Type';e={ $_.Headers."Content-Type" }}, Content
```

This command produces output, formatted for clarity, that shows that the response has been encoded as JSON:

```
Content-Type                    Content
------------                    -------
application/json; charset=utf-8 {"reservationId":100,
                                 "clientName":"Joe",
                                 "location":"Board Room"}
```

Understanding Content Negotiation

Most clients will include an Accept header in a request, which specifies the set of formats that they are willing to receive in the response, expressed as a set of MIME types. Here is the Accept header that Google Chrome sends in requests:

```
Accept: text/html,application/xhtml+xml,application/xml;q=0.9,image/webp,*/*;q=0.8
```

This header indicates that Chrome can handle the HTML and XHTML formats (XHTML is an XML-compliant dialect of HTML), XML, and the WEBP image format. The q values in the header specify relative preference, where the value is 1.0 by default. Specifying a q value for 0.9 for application/xml tells the server that Chrome will accept XML data but prefers to deal with HTML or XHTML. The final item, */*, tells the server that Chrome will accept any format, but its q value specifies that it is the lowest preference of the specified types. Putting all of this together means that the Accept header sent by Chrome provides the server with the following information:

1. Chrome prefers to receive HTML or XHTML data or WEBP images.

2. If those formats are not available, then the next most preferred format is XML.

3. If none of the preferred formats is available, then Chrome will accept any format.

You might assume from this that you can change the format a request receives from an MVC application by setting the Accept header, but it doesn't work that way—or, rather, it doesn't work that way just yet because there is some preparation required. First, here is a PowerShell command that sends a GET request to the GetObject method with an Accept header that specifies the client will only accept XML data:

```
Invoke-WebRequest http://localhost:7000/api/content/object -Headers @{Accept="application/
xml"} | select @{n='Content-Type';e={ $_.Headers."Content-Type" }}, Content
```

Here are the results, which show that the server has sent an application/json response:

```
Content-Type                    Content
------------                    -------
application/json; charset=utf-8 {"reservationId":100,
                                 "clientName":"Joe",
                                 "location":"Board Room"}
```

Including the Accept header has no effect on the format, even though the server has sent the client a format that it hasn't specified. The problem is that, by default, MVC is configured to support JSON only, so it has no other formats it can use. Rather than return an error, MVC sends JSON data in the hope that the client can process it, even though it was not one of the formats specified by the request Accept header.

CONFIGURING THE JSON SERIALIZER

ASP.NET Core MVC uses a popular third-party JSON package called Json.Net to serialize objects into JSON. The default configuration is suitable for most projects but can be changed if you need to create JSON in a specific way. The AddMvc().AddJsonOptions extension method is used in the Startup class and provides access to a MvcJsonOptions object, through which the Json.Net package is configured. See www.newtonsoft.com/json for details of the configuration options available.

Enabling XML Formatting

To see content negotiation at work, you have to give MVC some choice in the formats it uses to encode response data. Although JSON has become the default format for web applications, MVC can also support encoding data as XML, as shown in Listing 20-15.

■ **Tip** You can create your own content format by deriving from the `Microsoft.AspNetCore.Mvc.` `Formatters.OutputFormatter` class. This is rarely used because creating a custom data format isn't a useful way of exposing the data in your application and because the most common formats—JSON and XML—are already implemented.

Listing 20-15. Enabling XML Formatting in the Startup.cs File in the ApiControllers Folder

```
using System;
using System.Collections.Generic;
using System.Linq;
using System.Threading.Tasks;
using Microsoft.AspNetCore.Builder;
using Microsoft.AspNetCore.Hosting;
using Microsoft.AspNetCore.Http;
using Microsoft.Extensions.DependencyInjection;
using ApiControllers.Models;

namespace ApiControllers {
    public class Startup {

        public void ConfigureServices(IServiceCollection services) {
            services.AddSingleton<IRepository, MemoryRepository>();
            services.AddMvc().AddXmlDataContractSerializerFormatters();
        }

        public void Configure(IApplicationBuilder app, IHostingEnvironment env) {
            app.UseStatusCodePages();
            app.UseDeveloperExceptionPage();
            app.UseStaticFiles();
            app.UseMvcWithDefaultRoute();
        }
    }
}
```

When MVC had only the JSON format available, It had no choice but to encode responses as JSON. Now that there is a choice, you can see the content negotiation process working more fully.

■ **Tip** I used the `AddXmlDataContractSerializerFormatters` extension method in Listing 20-15, but you can also use the `AddXmlSerializerFormatters` extension method, which provides access to an older serialization class. The difference can be helpful if you are generating XML content for older .NET clients.

Here is the PowerShell command that requests XML data again:

```
Invoke-WebRequest http://localhost:7000/api/content/object -Headers @{Accept="application/
xml"} | select @{n='Content-Type';e={ $_.Headers."Content-Type" }}, Content
```

Run this command and you will see that now the server returns XML data, rather than JSON, as follows (I have omitted the XML namespace attributes for brevity):

```
Content-Type                         Content
------------                         -------
application/xml; charset=utf-8 <Reservation>
                                        <ClientName>Joe</ClientName>
                                        <Location>Board Room</Location>
                                        <ReservationId>100</ReservationId>
                                    </Reservation>
```

Specifying an Action Data Format

You can override the content negotiation system and specify a data format directly on an action method by applying the Produces attribute, as shown in Listing 20-16.

Listing 20-16. Specifying a Data Format in the ContentController.cs File in the Controllers Folder

```
using Microsoft.AspNetCore.Mvc;
using ApiControllers.Models;

namespace ApiControllers.Controllers {

    [Route("api/[controller]")]
    public class ContentController : Controller {

        [HttpGet("string")]
        public string GetString() => "This is a string response";

        [HttpGet("object")]
        [Produces("application/json")]
        public Reservation GetObject() => new Reservation {
            ReservationId = 100,
            ClientName = "Joe",
            Location = "Board Room"
        };
    }
}
```

The Produces attribute is a filter that changes the content type of ObjectResult objects, which are used behind the scenes by MVC to represent action results in API controllers. The argument for the attribute specifies the format that will be used for the result from the action, and additional allowed types can also be specified. The Produces attribute forces the format used by the response, which can be seen by running the following PowerShell command:

```
(Invoke-WebRequest http://localhost:7000/api/content/object -Headers
@{Accept="application/xml"}).Headers."Content-Type"
```

This command displays the value of the Content-Type header from the response to a GET request to the /api/content/object URL. Running the command shows that JSON is used, as specified by the Produces attribute, even though the Accept header of the request specifies that XML should be used.

Getting the Data Format from the Route or Query String

The Accept header isn't always under the control of the programmer who is writing the client, especially if development is being done using an old browser or toolkit. For such situations, it can be helpful to allow the data format for the response to be requested through the route used to target an action method or in the query string section of the request URL. The first step is to define shorthand values in the Startup class that can be used to refer to formats in the route or the query string. There is one mapping by default, in which json is used as shorthand for application/json. In Listing 20-17, I have added an additional mapping for XML.

Listing 20-17. Adding a Format Shorthand in the Startup.cs File in the ApiControllers Folder

```
using System;
using System.Collections.Generic;
using System.Linq;
using System.Threading.Tasks;
using Microsoft.AspNetCore.Builder;
using Microsoft.AspNetCore.Hosting;
using Microsoft.AspNetCore.Http;
using Microsoft.Extensions.DependencyInjection;
using ApiControllers.Models;
using Microsoft.Net.Http.Headers;

namespace ApiControllers {
    public class Startup {

        public void ConfigureServices(IServiceCollection services) {
            services.AddSingleton<IRepository, MemoryRepository>();
            services.AddMvc()
                .AddXmlDataContractSerializerFormatters()
                .AddMvcOptions(opts => {
                    opts.FormatterMappings.SetMediaTypeMappingForFormat("xml",
                        new MediaTypeHeaderValue("application/xml"));
                });
        }

        public void Configure(IApplicationBuilder app, IHostingEnvironment env) {
            app.UseStatusCodePages();
            app.UseDeveloperExceptionPage();
            app.UseStaticFiles();
            app.UseMvcWithDefaultRoute();
        }
    }
}
```

The MvcOptions.FormatterMappings property is used to set and manage the mappings. In the listing, I used the SetMediaTypeMappingForFormat method to create a new mapping so that the shorthand xml will refer to the application/xml format. The next step is to apply the FormatFilter attribute to an action method and, optionally, adjust the route for the action so that it includes a format segment variable, as shown in Listing 20-18.

Listing 20-18. Applying the FormatFilter Attribute in the ContentController.cs File in the Controllers Folder

```
using Microsoft.AspNetCore.Mvc;
using ApiControllers.Models;

namespace ApiControllers.Controllers {

    [Route("api/[controller]")]
    public class ContentController : Controller {

        [HttpGet("string")]
        public string GetString() => "This is a string response";

        [HttpGet("object/{format?}")]
        [FormatFilter]
        [Produces("application/json", "application/xml")]
        public Reservation GetObject() => new Reservation {
            ReservationId = 100,
            ClientName = "Joe",
            Location = "Board Room"
        };
    }
}
```

I have applied the FormatFilter attribute to the GetObject method and modified the route for the action so that it includes an optional format segment. You don't have to use the Produces attribute in conjunction with the FormatFilter attribute, but if you do, only requests that specify formats for which the Produces attribute has been configured will work. Requests that specify a format for which the Produces attribute has not been configured will receive a 404 - Not Found response. If you don't apply the Produces attribute, then the request can specify any format that MVC has been configured to use.

I also added the application/xml format to the Produces attribute so that the action method will support requests for both JSON and XML.

This PowerShell command specifies the xml format as part of the request URL:

```
(Invoke-WebRequest http://localhost:7000/api/content/object/xml).Headers."Content-Type"
```

Running this command shows the content type of the response, as follows:

```
application/xml; charset=utf-8
```

The FormatFilter attribute looks for a routing segment variable called format, gets the shorthand value that it contains, and retrieves the associated data format from the application configuration. This format is then used for the response. If there is no routing data available, then the query string is inspected as well. Here is a PowerShell command that requests XML using the query string:

```
(Invoke-WebRequest http://localhost:7000/api/content/object?format=xml).Headers.
"Content-Type"
```

The format found by the FormatFilter attribute overrides any formats specified by the Accept header, which puts the format selection in the hands of the client developer, even when working with toolkits and browsers that don't allow the Accept header to be set.

Enabling Full Content Negotiation

For most applications, sending JSON data when there is no other format available is a sensible policy since a web application client is more likely to have incorrectly set its Accept header than be unable to process JSON. That said, some applications will have to deal with clients that cause problems if JSON is returned regardless of what the Accept headers say. Getting content negotiation working requires two configuration changes in the Startup class, as shown in Listing 20-19.

Listing 20-19. Enabling Full Content Negotiation in the Startup.cs File in the ApiControllers Folder

```
using System;
using System.Collections.Generic;
using System.Linq;
using System.Threading.Tasks;
using Microsoft.AspNetCore.Builder;
using Microsoft.AspNetCore.Hosting;
using Microsoft.AspNetCore.Http;
using Microsoft.Extensions.DependencyInjection;
using ApiControllers.Models;
using Microsoft.Net.Http.Headers;

namespace ApiControllers {
    public class Startup {

        public void ConfigureServices(IServiceCollection services) {
            services.AddSingleton<IRepository, MemoryRepository>();
            services.AddMvc()
                .AddXmlDataContractSerializerFormatters()
                .AddMvcOptions(opts => {
                    opts.FormatterMappings.SetMediaTypeMappingForFormat("xml",
                        new MediaTypeHeaderValue("application/xml"));
                    opts.RespectBrowserAcceptHeader = true;
                    opts.ReturnHttpNotAcceptable = true;
                });
        }

        public void Configure(IApplicationBuilder app, IHostingEnvironment env) {
            app.UseStatusCodePages();
            app.UseDeveloperExceptionPage();
            app.UseStaticFiles();
            app.UseMvcWithDefaultRoute();
        }
    }
}
```

The RespectBrowserAcceptHeader option is used to control whether the Accept header is fully respected. The ReturnHttpNotAcceptable option is used to control whether a 406 - Not Acceptable response will be sent to the client if there is no suitable format available.

I also have to remove the Produces attribute from the action method so that the content negotiation process isn't overridden, as shown in Listing 20-20.

Listing 20-20. Removing the Produces Attribute in the ContentController.cs File in the Controllers Folder

```
using Microsoft.AspNetCore.Mvc;
using ApiControllers.Models;

namespace ApiControllers.Controllers {

    [Route("api/[controller]")]
    public class ContentController : Controller {

        [HttpGet("string")]
        public string GetString() => "This is a string response";

        [HttpGet("object/{format?}")]
        [FormatFilter]
        //[Produces("application/json", "application/xml")]
        public Reservation GetObject() => new Reservation {
            ReservationId = 100,
            ClientName = "Joe",
            Location = "Board Room"
        };
    }
}
```

Here is a PowerShell command that sends a GET request to the /api/content/object URL with an Accept header that specifies a content type that the application cannot provide:

```
Invoke-WebRequest http://localhost:7000/api/content/object -Headers
@{Accept="application/custom"}
```

If you run this command, you will see that the 406 error message is displayed, indicating to the client that the server has been unable to provide the requested format.

Receiving Different Data Formats

When the client sends data to the controller, such as in a POST request, you can specify different action methods to handle specific data formats using the Consumes attribute, as shown in Listing 20-21.

Listing 20-21. Handling Different Data Formats in the ContentController.cs File in the Controllers Folder

```
using Microsoft.AspNetCore.Mvc;
using ApiControllers.Models;

namespace ApiControllers.Controllers {
```

```
[Route("api/[controller]")]
public class ContentController : Controller {

    [HttpGet("string")]
    public string GetString() => "This is a string response";

    [HttpGet("object/{format?}")]
    [FormatFilter]
    //[Produces("application/json", "application/xml")]
    public Reservation GetObject() => new Reservation {
        ReservationId = 100,
        ClientName = "Joe",
        Location = "Board Room"
    };

    [HttpPost]
    [Consumes("application/json")]
    public Reservation ReceiveJson([FromBody] Reservation reservation) {
        reservation.ClientName = "Json";
        return reservation;
    }

    [HttpPost]
    [Consumes("application/xml")]
    public Reservation ReceiveXml([FromBody] Reservation reservation) {
        reservation.ClientName = "Xml";
        return reservation;
    }
}
}
```

The ReceiveJson and ReceiveXml actions both accept POST requests, and the difference between them is the data format that is specified with the Consumes attribute, which examines the Content-Type header to work out whether the action method can process the request. The result is that when there is a request whose Content-Type is set to application/json, the ReceiveJson method will be used, but if the Content-Type header is set to application/xml, then the ReceiveXml method will be used.

Summary

In this chapter, I explained the role that an API controller plays in an MVC application. I demonstrated how to create and test an API controller, briefly demonstrated how to make asynchronous HTTP requests using jQuery, and explained the content formatting process. In the next chapter, I explain how views and view engines work in more detail.

CHAPTER 21

Views

In Chapter 17, you saw how action methods can return ViewResult objects, which tells MVC to render a view and return an HTML response to the client.

Throughout this book, you have seen views being used in many examples already, so you know roughly what they do, but I dig into the details in this chapter.

I begin by showing you how MVC handles ViewResult objects using view engines, including demonstrating how to create a custom view engine. I also describe techniques for working effectively with the built-in Razor view engine, including the use of partial views and layout sections, which are essential topics for effective MVC development. Table 21-1 puts views into context.

Table 21-1. *Putting Views in Context*

Question	Answer
What are they?	Views are the part of the MVC pattern used to display content to the user. In an ASP.NET Core MVC application, a view is a file that contains HTML elements and C# code, which is processed to generate a response.
Why are they useful?	Views allow the presentation of data to be separated from the logic that processes requests. Views also allow the same presentation to be applied throughout the application since many controllers can use the same view.
How are they used?	Most MVC applications use the Razor view engine, which makes it easy to mix HTML and C# content. Views are selected by returning a ViewResult object as the result of an action method, as described in Chapter 17.
Are there any pitfalls or limitations?	It can take a while to get used to using Razor and its mix of HTML and C#. In this chapter, I explain how Razor works, which helps demystify some of its operations.
Are there any alternatives?	There are a number of third-party view engines available for MVC, but their use is limited.

Table 21-2 summarizes the chapter.

Table 21-2. *Chapter Summary*

Problem	Solution	Listing
Create a custom view engine	Implement the IViewEngine and IView interfaces	3–6
Easily create responses that mix HTML and C# code	Use the Razor view engine	7–11
Define regions of content for use in a layout	Use Razor sections	12–18
Create reusable fragments of markup	Use partial views	19–22
Add JSON content to views	Use the @Json.Serialze expression	23–25
Change the locations that Razor searches for views	Create a view location expander	26–30

Preparing the Example Project

For this chapter, I used the ASP.NET Core Web Application (.NET Core) template to create a new Empty project called Views. To enable the MVC Framework and the other middleware components useful for developments, I made the changes shown in Listing 21-1 to the Startup class.

Listing 21-1. The Contents of the Startup.cs File

```
using System;
using System.Collections.Generic;
using System.Linq;
using System.Threading.Tasks;
using Microsoft.AspNetCore.Builder;
using Microsoft.AspNetCore.Hosting;
using Microsoft.AspNetCore.Http;
using Microsoft.Extensions.DependencyInjection;

namespace Views {
    public class Startup {
        public void ConfigureServices(IServiceCollection services) {
            services.AddMvc();
        }

        public void Configure(IApplicationBuilder app, IHostingEnvironment env) {
            app.UseStatusCodePages();
            app.UseDeveloperExceptionPage();
            app.UseStaticFiles();
            app.UseMvcWithDefaultRoute();
        }
    }
}
```

I created the Controllers folder, added a class file called HomeController.cs, and used it to define the controller shown in Listing 21-2.

Listing 21-2. The Contents of the HomeController.cs File in the Controllers Folder

```
using System;
using Microsoft.AspNetCore.Mvc;

namespace Views.Controllers {

    public class HomeController : Controller {

        public ViewResult Index() {
            ViewBag.Message = "Hello, World";
            ViewBag.Time = DateTime.Now.ToString("HH:mm:ss");
            return View("DebugData");
        }

        public ViewResult List() => View();
    }
}
```

Creating a Custom View Engine

I am going to dive in at the deep end and create a custom view engine. You do not need to do this for most projects because MVC includes the Razor view engine, whose syntax I described in Chapter 5 and which I have been using for all the examples so far in this book (and will continue to use again shortly).

The value in creating a custom view engine is to see what happens behind the scenes and expand your knowledge of how MVC works, including understanding just how much freedom view engines have in translating a ViewResult into a response to the client.

View engines are classes that implement the IViewEngine interface, which is defined in the Microsoft. AspNetCore.Mvc.ViewEngines namespace. Here is the definition of the IViewEngine interface:

```
namespace Microsoft.AspNetCore.Mvc.ViewEngines {
    public interface IViewEngine {

        ViewEngineResult GetView(string executingFilePath, string viewPath,
            bool isMainPage);

        ViewEngineResult FindView(ActionContext context, string viewName,
            bool isMainPage);
    }
}
```

The role of a view engine is to translate requests for views into ViewEngineResult objects. When MVC needs a view, it starts by calling the GetView method, which gives the view engine the opportunity to provide the view just using its name.

If the GetView method cannot provide the view, then the FindView method is called so that the view engine has a chance to search for the view using the ActionContext object, which provides information about the action method that created the ViewResult object.

The job of the view engine is to provide MVC with `ViewEngineResult` objects that can be used to generate responses. The `ViewEngineResult` class cannot be instantiated directly but provides static methods that are used to create instances, as described in Table 21-3.

Table 21-3. *The Static Methods of the ViewEngineResult Class*

Name	Description
`Found(name, view)`	Calling this method provides MVC with the requested view, which is set using the `view` parameter. Views implement the `IView` interface.
`NotFound(name, locations)`	Calling this method creates a `ViewEngineResult` object that tells MVC that the requested view could not be found. The `locations` parameter is an enumeration of `string` values that describe where the view engine has looked for the view.

When writing a view engine, you choose one of the methods described in Table 21-3 to indicate the outcome of a request for a view. The `Found` method creates a `ViewEngineResult` that indicates a successful request and provides MVC with a view to process. The `NotFound` method creates a `ViewEngineResult` that indicates an unsuccessful request and provides MVC with a list of locations that the view engine searched when looking for the view (and which will be displayed to the developer as part of an error message).

The other building block of the view engine system is the `IView` interface, which is used to describe the functionality provided by views, regardless of the view engine that created them. Here is the `IView` interface:

```
using Microsoft.AspNetCore.Mvc.Rendering;
using System.Threading.Tasks;

namespace Microsoft.AspNetCore.Mvc.ViewEngines {

    public interface IView {

        string Path { get; }
        Task RenderAsync(ViewContext context);
    }
}
```

The `Path` property returns the path of the view, which assumes that views are defined as files on disk. The `RenderAsync` method is called by MVC to generate the response to the client. Context data is provided to the view through an instance of the `ViewContext` class, which is derived from `ActionContext`. In addition to the context properties inherited from its parent (which provide access to the request, the routing data, the controller, and so on), the `ViewContext` class provides properties that are useful in rendering responses, the most useful of which I have described in Table 21-4.

Table 21-4. *Useful ViewContext Properties*

Name	Description
`ViewData`	This property returns a `ViewDataDictionary` object that contains the view data provided by the controller.
`TempData`	This property returns a dictionary containing the temp data (as described in Chapter 17).
`Writer`	This property returns a `TextWriter` that should be used to write the output from the view.

The most interesting of these properties is ViewData, which returns a ViewDataDictionary object. The ViewDataDictionary class defines a number of useful properties that give access to the view model, the view bag, and the view model metadata. I have described the most useful of these properties in Table 21-5.

Table 21-5. *Useful ViewDataDictionary Properties*

Name	Description
Model	This object property returns the model data provided by the controller.
ModelMetadata	This property returns a ModelMetadata object that can be used to reflect on the type of the model data.
ModelState	This property returns the state of the model, which I describe in Chapter 27.
Keys	This property returns an enumeration of key values that can be used to access ViewBag data.

The simplest way to see how this works—how IViewEngine, ViewEngineResult, and IView fit together—is to create a view engine. I am going to create a simple view engine that returns one kind of view. This view will render a result that contains information about the request and the view data produced by the action method. This approach lets me demonstrate the way that view engines operate without getting bogged down in parsing view templates and re-creating other features that Razor provides.

Creating a Custom IView

I am going to start by creating an implementation of the IView interface. I added an Infrastructure folder to the example project and created a new class file called DebugDataView.cs, which is shown in Listing 21-3.

Listing 21-3. The Contents of the DebugDataView.cs in the Infrastructure Folder

```
using System;
using System.Text;
using System.Threading.Tasks;
using Microsoft.AspNetCore.Mvc.Rendering;
using Microsoft.AspNetCore.Mvc.ViewEngines;

namespace Views.Infrastructure {

    public class DebugDataView : IView {
        public string Path => String.Empty;

        public async Task RenderAsync(ViewContext context) {
            context.HttpContext.Response.ContentType = "text/plain";

            StringBuilder sb = new StringBuilder();

            sb.AppendLine("---Routing Data---");
            foreach (var kvp in context.RouteData.Values) {
                sb.AppendLine($"Key: {kvp.Key}, Value: {kvp.Value}");
            }
```

```
            sb.AppendLine("---View Data---");
            foreach (var kvp in context.ViewData) {
                sb.AppendLine($"Key: {kvp.Key}, Value: {kvp.Value}");
            }

            await context.Writer.WriteAsync(sb.ToString());
        }
    }
}
```

When this view is rendered, it writes out details of the routing data and the view data, obtained using the ViewContext argument to the RenderAsync method. The response is simple text, so I have used the context objects to set the Content-Type header on the response to text/plain. Without this, ASP.NET defaults to using text/html, which will cause the browser to display the data as a single unbroken line of characters.

Creating an IViewEngine Implementation

The purpose of the view engine is to produce a ViewEngineResult object that contains either an IView or a list of the places that searched for a suitable view. Now that I have an IView implementation to work with, I can create the view engine. I added a class file called DebugDataViewEngine.cs in the Infrastructure folder, the contents of which are shown in Listing 21-4.

Listing 21-4. The Contents of the DebugDataViewEngine.cs File in the Infrastructure Folder

```
using Microsoft.AspNetCore.Mvc;
using Microsoft.AspNetCore.Mvc.ViewEngines;

namespace Views.Infrastructure {

    public class DebugDataViewEngine : IViewEngine {

        public ViewEngineResult GetView(string executingFilePath, string viewPath,
                bool isMainPage) {
            return ViewEngineResult.NotFound(viewPath,
                new string[] { "(Debug View Engine - GetView)" });
        }

        public ViewEngineResult FindView(ActionContext context, string viewName,
                bool isMainPage) {
            if (viewName == "DebugData") {
                return ViewEngineResult.Found(viewName, new DebugDataView());
            } else {
                return ViewEngineResult.NotFound(viewName,
                    new string[] { "(Debug View Engine - FindView)" });
            }
        }
    }
}
```

The GetView method in this view engine always returns a NotFound response. The FindView method supports only a single view, which is called DebugData. When it receives a request for a view with that name, it returns a new instance of the DebugDataView class, like this:

```
...
if (viewName == "DebugData") {
    return ViewEngineResult.Found(viewName, new DebugDataView());
}
...
```

If I were implementing a complete view engine, I would use this opportunity to search for templates. As it is, this simple example only requires a new instance of the DebugDataView class. If I receive a request for a view other than DebugData, I create a NotFound response, like this:

```
...
return ViewEngineResult.NotFound(viewName,
    new string[] { "(Debug View Engine - FindView)" });
...
```

The ViewEngineResult.NotFound method assumes that the view engine has places it needs to look to find views. This is a reasonable assumption because views are typically template files that are stored as files in the project. In this case, I do not have anywhere to look, so I just return a dummy location, which will indicate which method was invoked to locate the view.

Registering a Custom View Engine

View engines are registered in the Startup class by configuring the MvcViewOptions object, as shown in Listing 21-5.

Listing 21-5. Registering a Custom View Engine in the Startup.cs File

```
using System;
using System.Collections.Generic;
using System.Linq;
using System.Threading.Tasks;
using Microsoft.AspNetCore.Builder;
using Microsoft.AspNetCore.Hosting;
using Microsoft.AspNetCore.Http;
using Microsoft.Extensions.DependencyInjection;
using Microsoft.AspNetCore.Mvc;
using Views.Infrastructure;

namespace Views {
    public class Startup {
        public void ConfigureServices(IServiceCollection services) {
            services.AddMvc();
            services.Configure<MvcViewOptions>(options => {
                options.ViewEngines.Insert(0, new DebugDataViewEngine());
            });

        }
```

```
        public void Configure(IApplicationBuilder app, IHostingEnvironment env) {
            app.UseStatusCodePages();
            app.UseDeveloperExceptionPage();
            app.UseStaticFiles();
            app.UseMvcWithDefaultRoute();
        }
    }
}
```

The MvcViewOptions class defines a ViewEngines property, which is a collection of IViewEngine objects. Razor is added to the ViewEngine collection by the AddMvc method, and I supplemented the default view engine with my custom class.

When MVC receives a ViewResult from an action method, it calls the FindView methods of each view engine contained in the MvcViewOptions.ViewEngines collection until it receives a ViewEngineResult that has been created using the Found method.

The order in which engines are added to the ViewEngines.Engines collection is significant if two or more engines are able to service a request for the same view name. If you want your view to take precedence, then it should be inserted at the start of view engines collection, as shown in Listing 21-5.

Testing the View Engine

When the application is started, the browser will automatically navigate to the root URL for the project, which will be mapped to the Index action in the Home controller. The action method uses the View method to return a ViewResult that specifies the DebugData view.

MVC will turn to the collection of view engines and start calling their FindView methods. Since the requested view is the one that the custom view engine is set up to handle, it provides MVC with a view that produces the results shown in Figure 21-1.

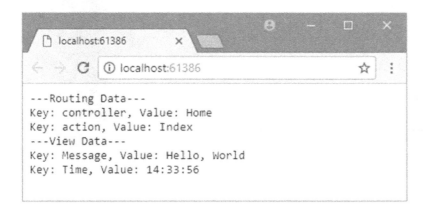

Figure 21-1. Using a custom view engine

To see what happens when no view engine can provide a view, request the /Home/List URL. This will create a ViewResult that specifies a view called List, which neither Razor nor the custom view engine can provide. You will see the error shown in Figure 21-2.

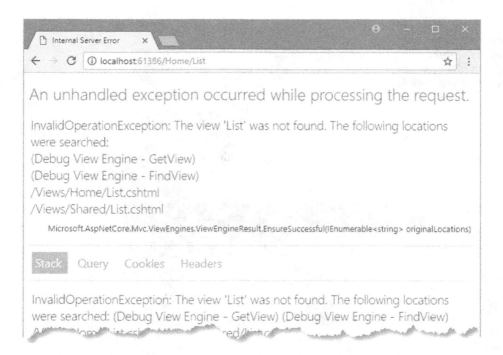

Figure 21-2. *Requesting a view that cannot be provided*

You can see that the messages produced by the custom view engine are reported in the list of locations that have been searched for the List view, alongside the locations that Razor has checked.

If I want to ensure that only my view engine is used, then I have to call the Clear method on the collection of view engines to remove Razor, as shown in Listing 21-6.

Listing 21-6. Removing Other View Engines in the Startup.cs File in the Views Project

```
using System;
using System.Collections.Generic;
using System.Linq;
using System.Threading.Tasks;
using Microsoft.AspNetCore.Builder;
using Microsoft.AspNetCore.Hosting;
using Microsoft.AspNetCore.Http;
using Microsoft.Extensions.DependencyInjection;
using Microsoft.AspNetCore.Mvc;
using Views.Infrastructure;

namespace Views {
    public class Startup {
        public void ConfigureServices(IServiceCollection services) {
            services.AddMvc();
            services.Configure<MvcViewOptions>(options => {
                options.ViewEngines.Clear();
                options.ViewEngines.Insert(0, new DebugDataViewEngine());
            });
        }
```

```
    public void Configure(IApplicationBuilder app, IHostingEnvironment env) {
        app.UseStatusCodePages();
        app.UseDeveloperExceptionPage();
        app.UseStaticFiles();
        app.UseMvcWithDefaultRoute();
    }
  }
}
```

If you start the application and navigate to /Home/List again, only the custom view engine will be used, as shown in Figure 21-3.

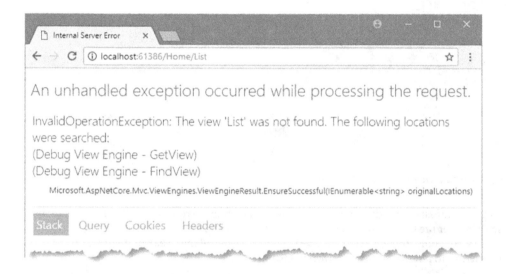

Figure 21-3. *Using only the custom view engine in the example application*

Working with the Razor Engine

In the previous section, I was able to create a custom view engine by implementing just two interfaces. Admittedly, I ended up with something simple that generated ugly content, but you saw how easy MVC makes it to add or replace core functionality.

The complexity in a view engine comes from the system of view templates that includes code fragments, support layouts, and performance optimization. I did not do any of these things in the simple custom view engine—and there isn't much need to—because the built-in Razor engine provides all of these features and more. In fact, the functionality that almost all MVC applications require is available in Razor. Only a vanishingly small number of projects need to go to the trouble of creating a custom view engine.

I gave you a primer on the Razor syntax in Chapter 5, and in this section, I show you how to use other features to create and render Razor views. You will also learn how to customize the Razor engine.

Preparing the Example Project

Some changes are required to prepare the example project to take advantage of Razor. First, I changed the Index action of the Home controller so that it selects the default view and provides some model data, as shown in Listing 21-7.

Listing 21-7. Changing the Index Action in the HomeController.cs File in the Controllers Folder

```
using System;
using Microsoft.AspNetCore.Mvc;

namespace Views.Controllers {

    public class HomeController : Controller {

        public ViewResult Index() =>
            View(new string[] { "Apple", "Orange", "Pear" });

        public ViewResult List() => View();
    }
}
```

To provide the Index action method with a view, I created the Views/Home folder and added a view file called Index.cshtml with the content shown in Listing 21-8.

Listing 21-8. The Contents of the Index.cshtml File in the Views/Home Folder

```
@model string[]
@{ Layout = null; }

<!DOCTYPE html>
<html>
<head>
    <meta name="viewport" content="width=device-width" />
    <title>Razor</title>
    <link asp-href-include="lib/bootstrap/dist/css/*.min.css" rel="stylesheet" />
</head>
<body class="m-1 p-1">
    This is a list of fruit names:
    @foreach (string name in Model) {
        <span><b>@name</b></span>
    }
</body>
</html>
```

The view relies on the Bootstrap CSS library. To add Bootstrap to the example project, I used the Bower Configuration File template to create the bower.json file in the root folder of the project, with the addition shown in Listing 21-9.

Listing 21-9. The Contents of the bower.json File

```
{
  "name": "asp.net",
  "private": true,
  "dependencies": {
    "bootstrap": "4.0.0-alpha.6"
  }
}
```

I created a view imports file called _ViewImports.cshtml in the Views folder, with the expression shown in Listing 21-10 to enable the built-in tag helpers.

Listing 21-10. The Contents of the _ViewImports.cshtml File in the Views Folder

```
@addTagHelper *, Microsoft.AspNetCore.Mvc.TagHelpers
```

The final preparatory step is to reset the view engines in the Startup class to remove the custom engine and remove the call to the Clear method that disabled Razor, as shown in Listing 21-11.

Listing 21-11. Resetting the View Engines in the Startup.cs File

```
using System;
using System.Collections.Generic;
using System.Linq;
using System.Threading.Tasks;
using Microsoft.AspNetCore.Builder;
using Microsoft.AspNetCore.Hosting;
using Microsoft.AspNetCore.Http;
using Microsoft.Extensions.DependencyInjection;
using Microsoft.AspNetCore.Mvc;
using Views.Infrastructure;

namespace Views {
    public class Startup {
        public void ConfigureServices(IServiceCollection services) {
            services.AddMvc();
            //services.Configure<MvcViewOptions>(options => {
            //    options.ViewEngines.Clear();
            //    options.ViewEngines.Insert(0, new DebugDataViewEngine());
            //});
        }

        public void Configure(IApplicationBuilder app, IHostingEnvironment env) {
            app.UseStatusCodePages();
            app.UseDeveloperExceptionPage();
            app.UseStaticFiles();
            app.UseMvcWithDefaultRoute();
        }
    }
}
```

If you run the project, you will see the result shown in Figure 21-4.

Figure 21-4. *Running the example application*

Demystifying Razor Views

Understanding a little of how Razor works can help put a lot of functionality into context and take the mystery out of how CSHTML files are processed.

So, how does Razor take the mix of HTML elements and C# statements and produce content for an HTTP response? The answer is simple and clever and builds on MVC functionality that you have already learned about in earlier chapters. Razor converts CSHTML files into C# classes, compiles them, and then creates new instances each time a view is required to generate a result. Here is the C# class that Razor creates for the Index.cshtml view shown in Listing 21-8:

```
using System.Threading.Tasks;
using Microsoft.AspNetCore.Mvc;
using Microsoft.AspNetCore.Mvc.Razor;
using Microsoft.AspNetCore.Mvc.Razor.Internal;
using Microsoft.AspNetCore.Mvc.Rendering;

namespace Asp {

    public class ASPV_Views_Home_Index_cshtml : RazorPage<string[]> {

        public IUrlHelper Url { get; private set; }

        public IViewComponentHelper Component { get; private set; }

        public IJsonHelper Json { get; private set; }

        public IHtmlHelper<string[]> Html { get; private set; }

        public override async Task ExecuteAsync() {
            Layout = null;

            WriteLiteral(@"<!DOCTYPE html><html><head>
                <meta name=""viewport"" content=""width=device-width"" />
                <title>Razor</title>
                <link asp-href-include=""lib/bootstrap/dist/css/*.min.css""
                    rel=""stylesheet"" />
                </head><body class=""m-1 p-1"">This is a list of fruit names:");
```

```
        foreach (string name in Model) {
            WriteLiteral("<span><b>");
            Write(name);
            WriteLiteral("</b></span>");
        }
        WriteLiteral("</body></html>");
      }
    }
}
```

I have tidied up the code in the class to make it easier to read and removed some C# statements that Razor adds for instrumentation when it generates the class. I'll break down the class in the sections that follow and explain how compiled views work.

▪ **Note**   It used to be easy to look at the classes created by earlier versions of Razor because each view produced a C# file on disk that was then compiled for use in the application. Inspecting the class was just a matter of finding the right file. The current version of Razor relies on advances in the C# compiler that allow code to be generated and compiled in memory, which offers performance enhancements but makes it more difficult to see what's happening. To get the class shown previously, I had to repurpose some of the unit tests included with the ASP.NET Core MVC source code, which provided me with fake implementations of the classes that Razor relies on to locate and process view files. This isn't something you need to do in day-to-day development, but it is a process that reveals much about how views work.

Understanding the Class Name

The best place to start is the name of the class that Razor creates.

```
...
public class ASPV_Views_Home_Index_cshtml : RazorPage<string[]> {
...
```

Razor needs some way to translate the name and path of a CSHTML file into the class that it creates when it parses the file, and it does this by encoding the information in the class name. Razor prefixes the class name with ASPV, followed by the project name, the controller name, and finally the view file name; this combination makes it easy to check to see whether a class is available when MVC requests a view through the IViewEngine described earlier in the chapter.

Understanding the Base Class

A lot of the core features of Razor, such as being able to refer to the view model as @Model are possible because of the base class that the generated classes are derived from.

```
...
public class ASPV_Views_Home_Index_cshtml : RazorPage<string[]> {
...
```

View classes inherit from the RazorPage class or the RazorPage<T> class if the @model directive has been used to specify a model type. The RazorPage class provides methods and properties that can be used in CSHTML files to access MVC features, the most useful of which are described in Table 21-6.

Table 21-6. *Useful RazorPage<T> Properties for View Development*

Name	Description
Model	This property returns the model data provided by the action method.
ViewData	This property returns a ViewDataDictionary object that provides access to other view data features.
ViewContext	This property returns a ViewContext object, which is described in Table 21-4.
Layout	This property is used to specify a layout, as described in Chapter 5 and revisited in the "Using Layout Sections" section of this chapter.
ViewBag	This property provides access to the view bag object, as described in Chapter 17.
TempData	This property provides access to the temp data, as described in Chapter 17.
Context	This property returns an HttpContext object that describes the current request and the response that is being prepared.
User	This property returns the profile of the user associated with this request. See Chapter 28 for details of user authentication and authorization.
RenderSection()	This method is used to insert a section of content from the view into a layout, as described in the "Using Layout Sections" section of this chapter.
RenderBody()	This method inserts all the content in a view that is not contained in a section into a layout. See "Using Layout Sections" for details.
IsSectionDefined()	This method is used to determine whether a view defines a section.

UNDERSTANDING RAZOR PAGES

With ASP.NET Core 2, Microsoft has added support for Razor Pages, which breaks the MVC model and associates the code required to support a view in a file that is associated with a Razor view. This is similar to how ASP.NET Web Forms was structured, and it is a design approach that Microsoft returns to periodically to try recapture the simplicity of the old Web Pages platforms without the drawbacks, which were described in Chapter 1.

Don't confuse the RazorPage base class described in this section with the Razor Pages feature. Although they share a similar name, the RazorPage base class provides the foundation for the Razor view engine as used by the MVC Framework. I don't describe the Razor Pages feature in this book because it doesn't conform to the MVC model and isn't part of the MVC platform.

Razor also provides some helper properties that can be used in views to generate content, as described in Table 21-7.

Table 21-7. *The Razor Helper Properties*

Name	Description
HtmlEncoder	This property returns an HtmlEncoder object that can be used to safely encode HTML content in a view.
Component	This property returns a view component helper, as described in Chapter 22.
Json	This property returns a JSON helper, as described in the "Adding JSON Content to Views" section.
Url	This property returns a URL helper that can be used to generate URLs using the routing configuration, as described in Chapter 16.
Html	This property returns an HTML helper, which can be used to generate dynamic content. This feature has been largely superseded by tag helpers but is still used for partial views, as described in the "Using Partial Views" section of this chapter.

The properties described in Table 21-6 and Table 21-7 are the ones that you will use in everyday MVC development to access model data, configure views, and perform other important tasks. These properties take the mystery out of using Razor and put it firmly back into the well-understood world of C#. When you access the view model object using the @Model directive or retrieve a temp data value using @TempData, for example, you are referring to the properties that are defined by the RazorPage class.

Understanding the View Rendering

In addition to the properties and methods that provide features to developers, the RazorPage class is also responsible for generating response content through its ExecuteAsyc method. This method shows how Razor processed the Index.cshtml file into a set of C# statements:

```
...
public override async Task ExecuteAsync() {
    Layout = null;
    WriteLiteral(@"<!DOCTYPE html><html><head>
            <meta name=""viewport"" content=""width=device-width"" />
            <title>Razor</title>
            <link asp-href-include=""lib/bootstrap/dist/css/*.min.css""
                rel=""stylesheet"" />
            </head><body class=""m-1 p-1"">This is a list of fruit names:");
    foreach (string name in Model) {
        WriteLiteral("<span><b>");
        Write(name);
        WriteLiteral("</b></span>");
    }
    WriteLiteral("</body></html>");
}
...
```

Data values, such as the values from the Model property, are sent to the client using the Write method, which escapes strings so that they won't be interpreted as HTML elements by the browser. This is important because it prevents malicious data values from adding content to the output of your application.

The WriteLiteral method doesn't escape strings and is used for the static content in the Index.cshtml file, which, of course, the browser should interpret as HTML elements. The result is that the static and dynamic content of a CSHTML file is contained in a regular C# class and emitted through a simple method call.

Adding Dynamic Content to a Razor View

The whole purpose of views is to allow you to render parts of your domain model to the user. To do that, you need to be able to add *dynamic content* to views. Dynamic content is generated at runtime and can be different for every request. This is opposed to *static content*, such as HTML, which you create when you are writing the application and is the same for each and every request. You can add dynamic content to views in the different ways described in Table 21-8.

Table 21-8. *Adding Dynamic Content to a View*

Technique	When to Use
Inline code	Use for small, self-contained pieces of view logic, such as if and foreach statements. This is the fundamental tool for creating dynamic content in views, and some of the other approaches are built on it. I introduced this technique in Chapter 5, and you have seen countless examples in the chapters since.
Tag helpers	Used to generate attributes on HTML elements. I describe tag helpers in Chapters 23, 24, and 25.
Sections	Use for creating sections of content that will be inserted into layout at specific locations, as described later in this section.
Partial views	Use for sharing subsections of view markup between views. Partial views can contain inline code, HTML helper methods, and references to other partial views. Partial views do not invoke an action method, so they cannot be used to perform business logic. Partial views are described later in this section.
View components	Use for creating reusable UI controls or widgets that need to contain business logic. I describe view components in Chapter 22.

Using Layout Sections

The Razor view engine supports the concept of *sections*, which allow you to provide regions of content within a layout. Razor sections give greater control over which parts of the view are inserted into the layout and where they are placed. To demonstrate the sections feature, I have edited the /Views/Home/Index.cshtml file, as shown in Listing 21-12.

Listing 21-12. Defining Sections in the Index.cshtml File in the Views/Home Folder

```
@model string[]
@{ Layout = "_Layout"; }

@section Header {
    <div class="bg-success">
        @foreach (string str in new [] {"Home", "List", "Edit"}) {
            <a class="btn btn-sm btn-primary" asp-action="str">@str</a>
        }
    </div>
}
```

```
This is a list of fruit names:
@foreach (string name in Model) {
    <span><b>@name</b></span>
}


@section Footer {
    <div class="bg-success">
        This is the footer
    </div>
}
```

I have removed some of the HTML elements from the view and set the Layout property to specify that a layout file called _Layout.cshtml should be used to render the content.

I have also added some sections to the view. Sections are defined using the Razor @section expression followed by a name for the section. I created sections called Header and Footer. The content of a section contains the usual mix of HTML markup and Razor expressions that you have seen outside sections in other examples.

Sections are defined in the view but applied in a layout with the @RenderSection expression. To demonstrate how this works, I created the Views/Shared folder and added a layout called _Layout.cshtml file with the content shown in Listing 21-13.

Listing 21-13. The Contents of the _Layout.cshtml File in the Views/Shared Folder

```
<!DOCTYPE html>
<html>
<head>
    <meta name="viewport" content="width=device-width" />
    <title>@ViewBag.Title</title>
    <link asp-href-include="lib/bootstrap/dist/css/*.min.css" rel="stylesheet" />
</head>
<body class="m-1 p-1">
    @RenderSection("Header")

    <div class="bg-info">
        This is part of the layout
    </div>

    @RenderBody()

    <div class="bg-info">
        This is part of the layout
    </div>

    @RenderSection("Footer")

    <div class="bg-info">
        This is part of the layout
    </div>
</body>
</html>
```

When Razor parses the layout, the RenderSection helper method is replaced with the contents of the section in the view with the specified name. The parts of the view that are not contained within a section are inserted into the layout using the RenderBody helper.

You can see the effect of the sections by starting the application, as shown in Figure 21-5. I used some Bootstrap styles to help make it clear which sections of the output are from the view and which are from the layout. This result is not pretty, but it neatly demonstrates how you can put regions of content from the view into specific locations in the layout.

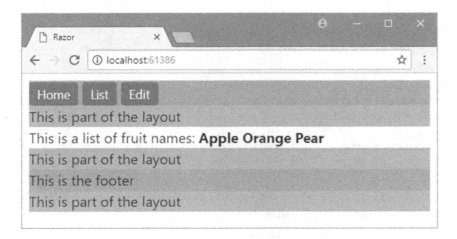

Figure 21-5. *Using sections in a view to locate content in a layout*

■ **Note** A view can define only the sections that are referred to in the layout. MVC will throw an exception if you attempt to define sections in the view for which there is no corresponding @RenderSection expression in the layout.

Mixing the sections in with the rest of the view is unusual. The convention is to define the sections at either the start or the end of the view to make it easier to see which regions of content will be treated as sections and which will be captured by the RenderBody helper. Another approach is to define the view solely in terms of sections, including one for the body, as shown in Listing 21-14.

Listing 21-14. Defining a View Using Razor Sections in the Index.cshtml File in the Views/Home Folder

```
@model string[]
@{ Layout = "_Layout"; }

@section Header {
    <div class="bg-success">
        @foreach (string str in new [] {"Home", "List", "Edit"}) {
            <a class="btn btn-sm btn-primary" asp-action="str">@str</a>
        }
    </div>
}
```

```
@section Body {
    This is a list of fruit names:
    @foreach (string name in Model) {
        <span><b>@name</b></span>
    }
}

@section Footer {
    <div class="bg-success">
        This is the footer
    </div>
}
```

I find this makes for clearer views and reduces the chances of extraneous content being captured by RenderBody. To use this approach, I have to replace the call to the RenderBody helper with RenderSection("Body"), as shown in Listing 21-15.

Listing 21-15. Rendering the Body as a Section in the _Layout.cshtml File in the Views/Shared Folder

```
<!DOCTYPE html>
<html>
<head>
    <meta name="viewport" content="width=device-width" />
    <title>@ViewBag.Title</title>
    <link asp-href-include="lib/bootstrap/dist/css/*.min.css" rel="stylesheet" />
</head>
<body class="m-1 p-1">
    @RenderSection("Header")

    <div class="bg-info">
        This is part of the layout
    </div>

    @RenderSection("Body")

    <div class="bg-info">
        This is part of the layout
    </div>

    @RenderSection("Footer")

    <div class="bg-info">
        This is part of the layout
    </div>
</body>
</html>
```

Testing for Sections

You can check to see whether a view has defined a specific section from the layout. This is a useful way to provide default content for a section when a view does not need or want to provide specific content. I have modified the _Layout.cshtml file to check to see whether a Footer section is defined, as shown in Listing 21-16.

Listing 21-16. Checking Whether a Section Is Defined in the _Layout.cshtml File in the Views/Shared Folder

```
<!DOCTYPE html>
<html>
<head>
    <meta name="viewport" content="width=device-width" />
    <title>@ViewBag.Title</title>
    <link asp-href-include="lib/bootstrap/dist/css/*.min.css" rel="stylesheet" />
</head>
<body class="m-1 p-1">
    @RenderSection("Header")

    <div class="bg-info">
        This is part of the layout
    </div>

    @RenderSection("Body")

    <div class="bg-info">
        This is part of the layout
    </div>

    @if (IsSectionDefined("Footer")) {
        @RenderSection("Footer")
    } else {
        <h4>This is the default footer</h4>
    }

    <div class="bg-info">
        This is part of the layout
    </div>
</body>
</html>
```

The IsSectionDefined helper takes the name of the section you want to check and returns true if the view you are rendering defines that section. In the example, I used this helper to determine whether I should render some default content when the view does not define the Footer section.

Rendering Optional Sections

By default, a view has to contain all the sections for which there are RenderSection calls in the layout. If sections are missing, then MVC will report an exception to the user. To demonstrate, I added a new RenderSection call to the _Layout.cshtml file for a section called scripts, as shown in Listing 21-17.

Listing 21-17. Rendering a Nonexistent Section in the _Layout.cshtml File in the Views/Shared Folder

```
<!DOCTYPE html>
<html>
<head>
    <meta name="viewport" content="width=device-width" />
    <title>@ViewBag.Title</title>
    <link asp-href-include="lib/bootstrap/dist/css/*.min.css" rel="stylesheet" />
</head>
<body class="m-1 p-1">
    @RenderSection("Header")

    <div class="bg-info">
        This is part of the layout
    </div>

    @RenderSection("Body")

    <div class="bg-info">
        This is part of the layout
    </div>

    @if (IsSectionDefined("Footer")) {
        @RenderSection("Footer")
    } else {
        <h4>This is the default footer</h4>
    }

    @RenderSection("scripts")

    <div class="bg-info">
        This is part of the layout
    </div>
</body>
</html>
```

When you start the application and the Razor engine attempts to render the layout and the view, you will see the error shown in Figure 21-6.

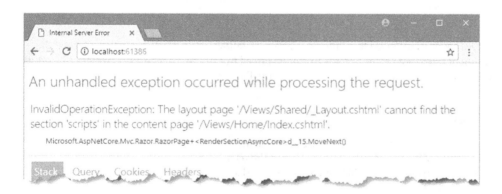

Figure 21-6. *The error shown when there is a missing section*

You can use the IsSectionDefined method to avoid making RenderSection calls for sections that the view does not define, but a more elegant approach is to use optional sections, which you do by passing an additional false argument to the RenderSection method, as shown in Listing 21-18.

Listing 21-18. Making a Section Optional

```
...
@RenderSection("scripts", false)
...
```

This creates an optional section, the contents of which will be inserted into the result if the view defines it and which will not throw an exception otherwise.

Using Partial Views

You will often need to use the same fragments of Razor tags and HTML markup in several different places in the application. Rather than duplicate the content, you can use *partial views*, which are separate view files that contain fragments of tags and markup that can be included in other views. In this section, I show you how to create and use partial views, explain how they work, and demonstrate the techniques available for passing view data to a partial view.

Creating a Partial View

Partial views are just regular CSHTML files, and it is their use that differentiates them from regular Razor views. Visual Studio provides some tooling support for creating prepopulated partial views, but the simplest way to create a partial view is to create a regular view using the MVC View Page item template. To demonstrate, I added a file called MyPartial.cshtml to the Views/Home folder and added the content shown in Listing 21-19.

Listing 21-19. The Contents of the MyPartial.cshtml File in the Views/Home Folder

```
<div class="bg-info">
    <div>This is the message from the partial view.</div>
    <a asp-action="Index">This is a link to the Index action</a>
</div>
```

I want to demonstrate that you can mix static and dynamic content in a partial view, so I have defined a simple message and added an anchor element that uses a tag helper.

Applying a Partial View

A partial view is consumed by calling the @Html.Partial expression from within another view. To demonstrate, I created a new file called List.cshtml in the Views/Home folder and added the content shown in Listing 21-20.

Listing 21-20. The Contents of the List.cshtml File in the Views/Home Folder

```
@{ Layout = null; }

<!DOCTYPE html>
<html>
<head>
    <meta name="viewport" content="width=device-width" />
    <title>Razor</title>
    <link asp-href-include="lib/bootstrap/dist/css/*.min.css" rel="stylesheet" />
</head>
<body class="m-1 p-1">
    This is the List View
    @Html.Partial("MyPartial")
</body>
</html>
```

The Partial method is an extension method that is applied to the Html property added to the class that Razor generates from the view file. This is an example of an HTML helper, which used to be the way that dynamic content was generated in views in earlier versions of MVC but which has largely been replaced by tag helpers. The argument passed to the Partial method is the name of the partial view, the contents of which are inserted into the output sent to the client.

■ **Tip**   Razor looks for partial views in the same way that it looks for regular views (in the Views/<controller> and Views/Shared folders). This means you can create specialized versions of partial views that are controller-specific and override partial views of the same name in the Shared folder.

You can see the effect of consuming the partial view by starting the application and navigating to the /Home/List URL, as shown in Figure 21-7.

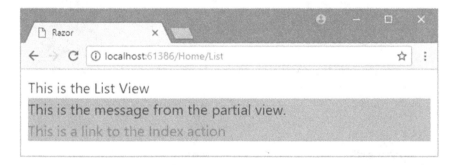

Figure 21-7. Using a partial view

Using Strongly Typed Partial Views

You can create strongly typed partial views and provide them with view model objects to be used when the partial view is rendered. To demonstrate this feature, I created a new view file called MyStronglyTypedPartial.cshtml in the Views/Home folder and added the content shown in Listing 21-21.

Listing 21-21. The Contents of the MyStronglyTypedPartial.cshtml File in the Views/Home Folder

```
@model IEnumerable<string>

<div class="bg-info">
    This is the message from the partial view.
    <ul>
        @foreach (string str in Model) {
            <li>@str</li>
        }
    </ul>
</div>
```

The view model type is defined using the standard @model expression, and I used a @foreach loop to display the contents of the view model object as items in an HTML list. To demonstrate the use of this partial view, I updated the /Views/Common/List.cshtml file, as shown in Listing 21-22.

Listing 21-22. Using a Strongly Typed Partial View in the List.cshtml File in the Views/Common Folder

```
@{ Layout = null; }

<!DOCTYPE html>
<html>
<head>
    <meta name="viewport" content="width=device-width" />
    <title>Razor</title>
    <link asp-href-include="lib/bootstrap/dist/css/*.min.css" rel="stylesheet" />
</head>
<body class="m-1 p-1">
    This is the List View
    @Html.Partial("MyStronglyTypedPartial",
        new string[] { "Apple", "Orange", "Pear" })
</body>
</html>
```

The difference from the previous example is that I pass an additional argument to the Partial helper method that supplies the view model. You can see the strongly typed partial view in use by starting the application and navigating to the /Home/List URL, as shown in Figure 21-8.

Figure 21-8. *Using a strongly typed partial view*

Adding JSON Content to Views

JSON is often included in views to provide client-side JavaScript code with data that can be used to generate content dynamically. To prepare for this example, I added the jQuery package to the application by editing the bower.json file, as shown in Listing 21-23. This will make it easy to process the JSON data when it is received by the browser as part of the HTML document.

Listing 21-23. Adding jQuery in the bower.json File

```
{
    "name": "asp.net",
    "private": true,
    "dependencies": {
        "bootstrap": "4.0.0-alpha.6",
        "jquery": "3.2.1"
    }
}
```

Listing 21-24 shows additions to the List.cshtml view that uses Razor to include JSON data in the response sent to the browser.

Listing 21-24. Working with JSON Data in the List.cshtml File in the Views/Common Folder

```
@{ Layout = null; }

<!DOCTYPE html>
<html>
<head>
    <meta name="viewport" content="width=device-width" />
    <title>Razor</title>
    <link asp-href-include="lib/bootstrap/dist/css/*.min.css" rel="stylesheet" />
    <script id="jsonData" type="application/json">
        @Json.Serialize(new string[] { "Apple", "Orange", "Pear" })
    </script>
</head>
```

```
<body class="m-1 p-1">
    This is the List View
    <ul id="list"></ul>
</body>
</html>
```

The `@Json.Serialize` expression accepts an object and serializes it into the JSON format. In the listing, I have added a `script` element to the view that contains the JSON data. When the view is rendered and sent to the browser, it includes an element like this:

```
...
<script id="jsonData" type="application/json">["Apple","Orange","Pear"]</script>
...
```

To make use of the JSON data, Listing 21-25 shows the addition of the jQuery library and some inline JavaScript code that uses jQuery to parse the JSON data and creates some HTML elements dynamically.

Listing 21-25. Using the JSON Data in the List.cshtml File in the Views/Common Folder

```
@{ Layout = null; }

<!DOCTYPE html>
<html>
<head>
    <meta name="viewport" content="width=device-width" />
    <title>Razor</title>
    <link asp-href-include="lib/bootstrap/dist/css/*.min.css" rel="stylesheet" />
    <script id="jsonData" type="application/json">
        @Json.Serialize(new string[] { "Apple", "Orange", "Pear" })
    </script>
    <script asp-src-include="lib/jquery/dist/*.min.js"></script>
    <script type="text/javascript">
        $(document).ready(function () {
            var list = $("#list")
            JSON.parse($("#jsonData").text()).forEach(function (val) {
                console.log("Val: " + val);
                list.append($("<li>").text(val));
            });
        });
    </script>
</head>
<body class="m-1 p-1">
    This is the List View
    <ul id="list"></ul>
</body>
</html>
```

If you run the example application and request the /Home/List URL, you will see the content shown in Figure 21-9. This isn't the most exciting use of JSON data, but it does demonstrate how it can be included in views.

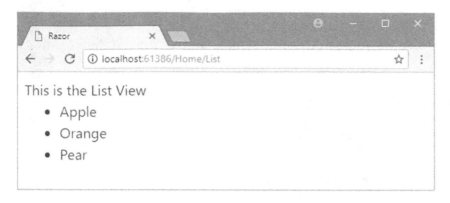

Figure 21-9. *Using JSON data in a view*

Configuring Razor

Razor can be configured using the RazorViewEngineOptions class, which is defined in the Microsoft. AspNetCore.Mvc.Razor namespace. This class defines two configuration properties, which are described in Table 21-9.

Table 21-9. *The RazorViewEngineOptions Properties*

Name	Description
FileProvider	This property is used to set the object that provides Razor with the contents of files and directories. The functionality is defined by the Microsoft. AspNetCore.FileProviders.IFileProvider interface, and the default implementation is PhysicalFileProvider, which reads files from a disk.
ViewLocationExpanders	The property is used to configure the view expanders, which are used to change how Razor locates a view.

■ **Tip** If you really want to dig deep, then you can replace the internal Razor components by creating classes that implement interfaces in the Microsoft.AspNetCore.Mvc.Razor namespace and registering them with the service provider in the Startup class. This is something that most developers will never need to do and shouldn't be undertaken lightly, but it is a useful option if you want to get complete control of how the content in your application is handled. Download the Razor source code from http://github.com/aspnet to get started.

The FileProvider property isn't one that many applications will need to change because reading view files from disk is exactly what most projects require, and Razor only uses the provider to load the views so they can be compiled when the application first runs. The ViewLocationExpanders property is more useful, however, because it allows applications to apply custom logic to the way that Razor locates views.

Understanding View Location Expanders

Razor uses view location expanders to build up a list of locations that should be searched for a view. View location expanders implement the IViewLocationExpander interface, which is defined as follows:

```
using System.Collections.Generic;

namespace Microsoft.AspNetCore.Mvc.Razor {

    public interface IViewLocationExpander {

        void PopulateValues(ViewLocationExpanderContext context);

        IEnumerable<string> ExpandViewLocations(ViewLocationExpanderContext context,
            IEnumerable<string> viewLocations);
    }
}
```

In the sections that follow, I explain how view location expanders work and create a custom implementation of the IViewLocationExpander interface. To prepare for creating view location expanders, in Listing 21-26 I have changed the Index action method of the Home controller so that it requests a nonexistent view. The error message that this causes will show the locations that Razor searches for the view and the effect on them that the view location expanders have.

Listing 21-26. Requesting a Nonexistent View in the HomeController.cs File in the Controllers Folder

```
using System;
using Microsoft.AspNetCore.Mvc;

namespace Views.Controllers {

    public class HomeController : Controller {

        public ViewResult Index() =>
            View("MyView", new string[] { "Apple", "Orange", "Pear" });

        public ViewResult List() => View();
    }
}
```

If you start the application and request the default URL, you will see the default view search locations displayed in the error message, as follows:

```
/Views/Home/MyView.cshtml
/Views/Shared/MyView.cshtml
```

685

Creating a Simple View Location Expander

The simplest view location expanders simply change the set of locations where Razor looks for all views. This is done by implementing the ExpandViewLocations method and returning the list of locations that you want to support. To demonstrate, I added a class file called SimpleExpander.cs to the Infrastructure folder and created the class shown in Listing 21-27.

Listing 21-27. The Contents of the SimpleExpander.cs File in the Infrastructure Folder

```
using System.Collections.Generic;
using Microsoft.AspNetCore.Mvc.Razor;

namespace Views.Infrastructure {

    public class SimpleExpander : IViewLocationExpander {

        public void PopulateValues(ViewLocationExpanderContext context) {
            // do nothing - not required
        }

        public IEnumerable<string> ExpandViewLocations(
                ViewLocationExpanderContext context,
                IEnumerable<string> viewLocations) {

            foreach (string location in viewLocations) {
                yield return location.Replace("Shared", "Common");
            }
            yield return "/Views/Legacy/{1}/{0}/View.cshtml";
        }
    }
}
```

Razor calls the ExpandViewLocations method when it requires the list of search locations, and it provides the default locations as a sequence of strings in the viewLocations parameter. Locations are expressed as templates with placeholders for the name of the action and controller. Here are the location templates that are used by default in an application that doesn't use routing areas:

```
"/Views/{1}/{0}.cshtml"
"/Views/Shared/{0}.cshtml"
```

The placeholder {0} is used to refer to the name of the action method, and {1} is the placeholder for the controller name. The job of the view location expander is to return the set of locations that should be searched, and in the listing, I use the string.Replace method to change Shared with Common in the default locations as well as adding my own location that follows a different file and folder structure.

Applying the View Location Expander

In Listing 21-28, I set up my view location expander by configuring Razor in the Startup class. The ViewLocationExpanders property returns a List<IViewLocationExpander> object on which I call the Add method.

Listing 21-28. Configuring Razor in the Startup.cs File

```
using System;
using System.Collections.Generic;
using System.Linq;
using System.Threading.Tasks;
using Microsoft.AspNetCore.Builder;
using Microsoft.AspNetCore.Hosting;
using Microsoft.AspNetCore.Http;
using Microsoft.Extensions.DependencyInjection;
using Microsoft.AspNetCore.Mvc;
using Views.Infrastructure;
using Microsoft.AspNetCore.Mvc.Razor;

namespace Views {
    public class Startup {
        public void ConfigureServices(IServiceCollection services) {
            services.AddMvc();
            services.Configure<RazorViewEngineOptions>(options => {
                options.ViewLocationExpanders.Add(new SimpleExpander());
            });
        }

        public void Configure(IApplicationBuilder app, IHostingEnvironment env) {
            app.UseStatusCodePages();
            app.UseDeveloperExceptionPage();
            app.UseStaticFiles();
            app.UseMvcWithDefaultRoute();
        }
    }
}
```

If you run the example, the error message will show the set of locations that the custom view location expander has provided to Razor.

```
/Views/Home/MyView.cshtml
/Views/Common/MyView.cshtml
/Views/Legacy/Home/MyView/View.cshtml
```

Selecting Specific Views for Requests

View location expanders make it easy to change the search locations for all requests but can also change the search locations for individual requests. I implemented only the ExpandViewLocations method in the previous example, but the real power comes through the PopulateValues method, which is the other method in the IViewLocationExpander interface.

Each time that Razor requires a view, it calls the PopulateValues method of its view location expanders, providing a ViewLocationExpanderContext object for context data. The ViewLocationExpanderContext class defines the properties shown in Table 21-10.

Table 21-10. *The ViewLocationExpanderContext Properties*

Name	Description
ActionContext	This property returns an ActionContext object that describes the action method that has requested a view and also includes details about the request and response.
ViewName	This property returns the name of the view that the action method has requested.
ControllerName	This property returns the name of the controller that contains the action method.
AreaName	This property returns the name of the area that contains the controller if areas have been defined.
IsMainPage	This property returns false if Razor is looking for a partial view and true otherwise.
Values	This property returns an IDictionary<string, string> to which the view location expander adds key/value pairs that uniquely identify the category of request, as explained in the following text.

The purpose of the PopulateValues method is to categorize the request by adding key/value pairs to the dictionary returned by the Values property of the context object. Razor doesn't care how the request is categorized, and the method used to populate the dictionary is left entirely to the view location expander. This is most readily explained by an example, so I added a class file called ColorExpander.cs to the Infrastructure folder and used it to define the class shown in Listing 21-29.

Listing 21-29. The Contents of the ColorExpander.cs File in the Infrastructure Folder

```
using System.Collections.Generic;
using Microsoft.AspNetCore.Mvc.Razor;

namespace Views.Infrastructure {

    public class ColorExpander : IViewLocationExpander {
        private static Dictionary<string, string> Colors
            = new Dictionary<string, string> {
                ["red"] = "Red", ["green"] = "Green", ["blue"] = "Blue"
            };

        public void PopulateValues(ViewLocationExpanderContext context) {

            var routeValues = context.ActionContext.RouteData.Values;
            string color;

            if (routeValues.ContainsKey("id")
                    && Colors.TryGetValue(routeValues["id"] as string, out color)
                    && !string.IsNullOrEmpty(color)) {
                context.Values["color"] = color;
            }
        }

        public IEnumerable<string> ExpandViewLocations(
                ViewLocationExpanderContext context,
                IEnumerable<string> viewLocations) {
```

```
            string color;
            context.Values.TryGetValue("color", out color);
            foreach (string location in viewLocations) {
                if (!string.IsNullOrEmpty(color)) {
                    yield return location.Replace("{0}", color);
                } else {
                    yield return location;
                }
            }
        }
    }
}
```

The PopulateValues method uses ActionContext to get the routing data and looks for the value of the id URL segment. If there is an id segment and its value is red, green, or blue, then the view location expander adds a color property to the Values dictionary. This is the categorization process: requests whose id segment matches a color are categorized with a color key whose value is derived from the segment value.

Next, Razor calls the ExpandViewLocations method and provides the same context object that was used for the PopulateValues method. This allows the view location expander to look at the categorization performed previously and generate the set of locations that Razor should look in for views. In the example, I using the string.Replace method to swap the {0} placeholder with the color name.

■ **Tip**   Razor calls the PopulateValues method for every view request but caches the set of search locations returned by the ExpandViewLocations method. This means that subsequent requests for which the PopulateValues method generates the same set of categorization keys, and values won't require the ExpandViewLocations method to be called.

In Listing 21-30, I have configured Razor to use the ColorExpander class.

Listing 21-30. Adding a View Location Expander in the Startup.cs File in the Views Folder

```
using System;
using System.Collections.Generic;
using System.Linq;
using System.Threading.Tasks;
using Microsoft.AspNetCore.Builder;
using Microsoft.AspNetCore.Hosting;
using Microsoft.AspNetCore.Http;
using Microsoft.Extensions.DependencyInjection;
using Microsoft.AspNetCore.Mvc;
using Views.Infrastructure;
using Microsoft.AspNetCore.Mvc.Razor;

namespace Views {
    public class Startup {
        public void ConfigureServices(IServiceCollection services) {
            services.AddMvc();
            services.Configure<RazorViewEngineOptions>(options => {
                options.ViewLocationExpanders.Add(new SimpleExpander());
```

```
        options.ViewLocationExpanders.Add(new ColorExpander());
    });
}

public void Configure(IApplicationBuilder app, IHostingEnvironment env) {
    app.UseStatusCodePages();
    app.UseDeveloperExceptionPage();
    app.UseStaticFiles();
    app.UseMvcWithDefaultRoute();
}
}
}
```

You can see the effect of the new view location expander by starting the application and requesting the /Home/Index/red URL, which will cause Razor to search in the following locations:

```
/Views/Home/Red.cshtml
/Views/Common/Red.cshtml
/Views/Legacy/Home/Red/View.cshtml
```

Similarly, a request for the /Home/Index/green URL will cause Razor to search in these locations:

```
/Views/Home/Green.cshtml
/Views/Common/Green.cshtml
/Views/Legacy/Home/Green/View.cshtml
```

The order in which view location expanders are registered is important because the set of locations generated by the ExpandViewLocations method of one expander is used as the viewLocations argument for the next expander in the list. You can see this in the locations shown previously, where Views/Common and Views/Legacy locations are generated by the SimpleExpander class, which appears before ColorExpander in the Startup class.

Summary

In this chapter, I demonstrated how to create a custom view engine and explained how Razor works by translating CSHTML files into C# classes. I showed you how to use layout sections and partial views and demonstrated how to change the locations that Razor uses to locate view files. In the next chapter, I describe view components, which are used to provide logic to support partial views.

CHAPTER 22

View Components

I describe *view components* in this chapter, which are a new addition in ASP.NET Core MVC and replace the child action feature from previous versions. View components are classes that provide action-style logic to support partial views, which means complex content can be embedded in views while allowing the C# code that supports it to be easily maintained and unit tested. Table 22-1 puts view components in context.

Table 22-1. *Putting View Components in Context*

Question	Answer
What are they?	View components are classes that provide application logic to support partial views or to inject small fragments of HTML or JSON data into a parent view.
Why are they useful?	Without view components, it is hard to create embedded functionality such as shopping baskets or login panels in a way that is easy to maintain and unit test.
How are they used?	View components are typically derived from the ViewComponent class and are applied in a parent view using the @await Component.InvokeAsync expression.
Are there any pitfalls or limitations?	No, view components are a simple and predictable feature. The main pitfall is not using them and trying to include application logic within views where it is difficult to test and maintain.
Are there any alternatives?	You could put the data access and processing logic directly in a partial view, but the result is difficult to work with and hard to test effectively.

© Adam Freeman 2017
A. Freeman, *Pro ASP.NET Core MVC 2*, https://doi.org/10.1007/978-1-4842-3150-0_22

Table 22-2 summarizes the chapter.

Table 22-2. *Chapter Summary*

Problem	Solution	Listing
Provide a partial view with its own logic and data	Use a view component	12
Invoke a view component	Use the `@await Component.InvokeAsync` expression in a view	13
Simplify access to context data and results	Derive from the `ViewComponent` class	14–16
Select a partial view	Use the `View` method to create and return a `ViewViewComponentResult` object	17–19
Create a fragment of HTML	Return the `Content` method to create a `ContentViewComponentResult` object or explicitly create an `HtmlContentViewComponentResult` object if you don't want the fragment to be encoded	20, 21
Use details of the request to generate the result	Use the view component context data	22
Provide context data when invoking a view component	Provide arguments to the `InvokeAsync` method	23–25
Create an asynchronous view component	Implement the `InvokeAsync` method and return a `Task` that yields the result you require	26–29
Create a hybrid controller/view component	Apply the `ViewComponent` attribute to a controller class	30–33

Preparing the Example Project

For this chapter, I used the ASP.NET Core Web Application (.NET Core) template to create a new Empty project called UsingViewComponents.

Creating the Models and Repositories

I need two different sources of data to demonstrate how view components work. Part of the application will operate on a set of product descriptions; to prepare for this, I created the Models folder and added a file called Product.cs, which I used to define the class shown in Listing 22-1.

Listing 22-1. The Contents of the Product.cs File in the Models Folder

```
namespace UsingViewComponents.Models {

    public class Product {
        public string Name { get; set; }
        public decimal Price { get; set; }
    }
}
```

To create a repository for the Product objects, I added a file called ProductRepository.cs to the Models folder and defined the interface and implementation class shown in Listing 22-2.

Listing 22-2. The Contents of the ProductRepository.cs File in the Models Folder

```
using System.Collections.Generic;

namespace UsingViewComponents.Models {

    public interface IProductRepository {
        IEnumerable<Product> Products { get; }
        void AddProduct(Product newProduct);
    }

    public class MemoryProductRepository : IProductRepository {
        private List<Product> products = new List<Product> {
                new Product { Name = "Kayak", Price = 275M },
                new Product { Name = "Lifejacket", Price = 48.95M },
                new Product { Name = "Soccer ball", Price = 19.50M }
        };

        public IEnumerable<Product> Products => products;

        public void AddProduct(Product newProduct) {
            products.Add(newProduct);
        }
    }
}
```

The IProductRepository interface defines a limited set of repository features, and the MemoryProductRepository class implements the interface using an in-memory List.

The other part of the application will operate on descriptions of cities. To that end, I added a class file called City.cs to the Models folder and used it to define the class shown in Listing 22-3.

Listing 22-3. The Contents of the City.cs File in the Models Folder

```
namespace UsingViewComponents.Models {

    public class City {
        public string Name { get; set; }
        public string Country { get; set; }
        public int Population { get; set; }
    }
}
```

For the repository of City objects, I created a class file called CityRepository.cs and used it to define the interface and implementation class shown in Listing 22-4.

Listing 22-4. The Contents of the CityRepository.cs File in the Models Folder

```
using System.Collections.Generic;

namespace UsingViewComponents.Models {

    public interface ICityRepository {
        IEnumerable<City> Cities { get; }

        void AddCity(City newCity);
    }

    public class MemoryCityRepository : ICityRepository {

        private List<City> cities = new List<City> {
            new City { Name = "London", Country = "UK", Population = 8539000},
            new City { Name = "New York", Country = "USA", Population = 8406000 },
            new City { Name = "San Jose", Country = "USA", Population = 998537 },
            new City { Name = "Paris", Country = "France", Population = 2244000 }
        };

        public IEnumerable<City> Cities => cities;

        public void AddCity(City newCity) {
            cities.Add(newCity);
        }
    }
}
```

The ICityRepository interface provides a limited set of repository features, and the MemoryCityRepository class implements the interface using an in-memory list.

Creating the Controller and Views

I need only one controller to get started, so I created the Controllers folder, added a file called HomeController.cs to the Controllers folder, and used it to define the class shown in Listing 22-5.

Listing 22-5. The Contents of the HomeController.cs File in the Controllers Folder

```
using Microsoft.AspNetCore.Mvc;
using UsingViewComponents.Models;

namespace UsingViewComponents.Controllers {

    public class HomeController : Controller {
        private IProductRepository repository;

        public HomeController(IProductRepository repo) {
            repository = repo;
        }
```

```
public ViewResult Index() => View(repository.Products);

public ViewResult Create() => View();

[HttpPost]
public IActionResult Create(Product newProduct) {
    repository.AddProduct(newProduct);
    return RedirectToAction("Index");
}
}
}
```

The Home controller uses its constructor to declare a dependency on the IProductRepository interface, which will be resolved by the service provider when the controller is used to handle requests. The Index action retrieves all the Product objects from the repository and renders them using the default view. The two Create methods use the Post/Redirect/Get pattern to add new objects to the repository using form data provided by the client.

The views for this example will share a common layout. I created the Views/Shared folder, and I added a file called _Layout.cshtml with the markup shown in Listing 22-6.

Listing 22-6. The Contents of the _Layout.cshtml File in the Views/Shared Folder

```
<!DOCTYPE html>
<html>
<head>
    <meta name="viewport" content="width=device-width" />
    <title>@ViewBag.Title</title>
    <link asp-href-include="lib/bootstrap/dist/css/*.min.css" rel="stylesheet" />
</head>
<body class="m-1 p-1">
    <div class="bg-primary m-1 p-1">
        <div class="row text-white">
            <div class="col-7"><h1>Products</h1></div>
            <div class="col-5">
                <div class="bg-info text-center m-1 p-1">City Placeholder</div>
            </div>
        </div>
    </div>
    <div class="m-1 p-1">@RenderBody()</div>
</body>
</html>
```

The layout defines a header that includes a placeholder for content that I will create later in the chapter using the city repository. Next, I created the Views/Home folder and added a file called Index.cshtml with the markup shown in Listing 22-7, which lists the details of Product objects in a table.

Listing 22-7. The Contents of the Index.cshtml File in the Views/Home Folder

```
@model IEnumerable<Product>
@{
    ViewData["Title"] = "Products";
    Layout = "_Layout";
}
```

```
<table class="table table-sm table-striped table-bordered">
    <thead>
        <tr><th>Name</th><th>Price</th></tr>
    </thead>
    <tbody>
        @foreach (var product in Model) {
            <tr>
                <td>@product.Name</td>
                <td>@product.Price</td>
            </tr>
        }
    </tbody>
</table>
<a asp-action="Create" class="btn btn-primary">Create</a>
```

The final element in the Index view is an a element that I have styled as a button and that targets the Create action so the user can create a new Product object in the repository. To provide the form that the user fills in, I added a Create.cshtml file to the Views/Home folder and added the markup shown in Listing 22-8.

Listing 22-8. The Contents of the Create.cshtml File in the Views/Home Folder

```
@model Product
@{
    ViewData["Title"] = "Create Product";
    Layout = "_Layout";
}

<form method="post" asp-action="Create">
    <div class="form-group">
        <label asp-for="Name">Name:</label>
        <input class="form-control" asp-for="Name" />
    </div>
    <div class="form-group">
        <label asp-for="Price">Price:</label>
        <input class="form-control" asp-for="Price" />
    </div>
    <button type="submit" class="btn btn-primary">Create</button>
    <a class="btn btn-secondary" asp-action="Index">Cancel</a>
</form>
```

The views use the built-in tag helpers, which I enabled by creating the _ViewImports.cshtml file in the Views folder and adding the expressions shown in Listing 22-9, which also make the classes in the Models folder available without namespaces.

Listing 22-9. The Contents of the _ViewImports.cshtml File in the Views Folder

```
@using UsingViewComponents.Models
@addTagHelper *, Microsoft.AspNetCore.Mvc.TagHelpers
```

The views also rely on the Bootstrap CSS package to style content. I used the Bower Configuration File item template to create the bower.json file in the root folder of the project and added the Bootstrap package to the dependencies section, as shown in Listing 22-10.

Listing 22-10. Adding Bootstrap to the bower.json File in the UsingViewComponents Folder

```
{
  "name": "asp.net",
  "private": true,
  "dependencies": {
    "bootstrap": "4.0.0-alpha.6"
  }
}
```

Configuring the Application

The final preparatory step is to configure the application, as shown in Listing 22-11. In addition to setting up the MVC services and middleware, I have created singleton services for the two data repositories.

Listing 22-11. The Contents of the Startup.cs File in the UsingViewComponents Folder

```
using System;
using System.Collections.Generic;
using System.Linq;
using System.Threading.Tasks;
using Microsoft.AspNetCore.Builder;
using Microsoft.AspNetCore.Hosting;
using Microsoft.AspNetCore.Http;
using Microsoft.Extensions.DependencyInjection;
using UsingViewComponents.Models;

namespace UsingViewComponents {

    public class Startup {

        public void ConfigureServices(IServiceCollection services) {
            services.AddSingleton<IProductRepository, MemoryProductRepository>();
            services.AddSingleton<ICityRepository, MemoryCityRepository>();
            services.AddMvc();
        }

        public void Configure(IApplicationBuilder app, IHostingEnvironment env) {
            app.UseStatusCodePages();
            app.UseDeveloperExceptionPage();
            app.UseStaticFiles();
            app.UseMvcWithDefaultRoute();
        }
    }
}
```

If you run the application, you will see a list of the Product objects in the product repository. You can add new products by clicking the Create button, filling in the form, and submitting it to the server, which will then redirect the browser back to the list, as shown in Figure 22-1. Since the views in the application share a common layout, there is a placeholder for city data shown throughout this process.

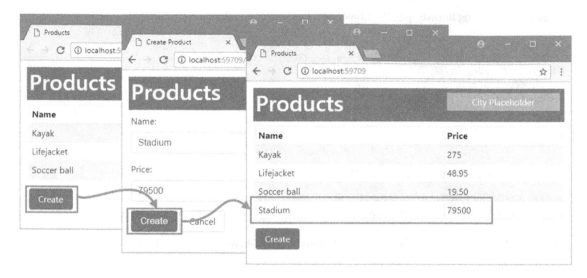

Figure 22-1. *Running the example application*

Understanding View Components

Applications commonly need to embed content in views that isn't related to the main purpose of the application. Common examples include site navigation tools and authentication panels that let the user log in without visiting a separate page.

The common thread that all these examples have is that the data required to display the embedded content isn't part of the model data passed from the action to the view. It is for this reason that I have created two repositories in the example application: I am going to display some content generated using the `City` repository, which isn't easily done in a view that receives data from the `Product` repository from its actions.

In Chapter 21, I described how partial views are used to create reusable markup that is required in views, avoiding the need to duplicate the same content in multiple places in the application. Partial views are a useful feature, but they just contain fragments of HTML and Razor directives, and the data they operate on is received from the parent view. If you need to display different data, then you run into a problem. You could access the data you need directly from the partial view, but this breaks the separation of concerns that underpins the MVC pattern and results in data retrieval and processing logic being placed in a view file where it cannot be unit tested. Alternatively, you could extend the view models used by the application so that it includes the data you require, but this means you have to change every action method and it is hard to isolate the functionality of action methods for effective testing.

This is where view components come in. A view component is a C# class that provides a partial view with the data that it needs, independently from the parent view and the action that renders it. In this regard, a view component can be thought of as a specialized action, but one that is used only to provide a partial view with data; it cannot receive HTTP requests, and the content that it provides will always be included in the parent view.

Creating a View Component

View components can be created in three different ways: by defining a POCO view component, by deriving from the `ViewComponent` base class, and by using the `ViewComponent` attribute. I describe the POCO and base class techniques in the sections that follow and explain the use of the attribute in the "Creating Hybrid Controller/View Component Classes" section, later in the chapter.

Creating POCO View Components

A *POCO view component* is a class that provides view component functionality without relying on any of the MVC APIs. As with POCO controllers, this kind of view component is awkward to work with but can be helpful in understanding how they work. A POCO view component is any class whose name ends with ViewComponent and that defines an Invoke method. View component classes can be defined anywhere in an application, but the convention is to group them together in a folder called Components at the root level of the project. I created this folder and added a class file called PocoViewComponent.cs, which I used to define the class shown in Listing 22-12.

Listing 22-12. The Contents of the PocoViewComponent.cs File in the Components Folder

```
using System.Linq;
using UsingViewComponents.Models;

namespace UsingViewComponents.ViewComponents {

    public class PocoViewComponent {
        private ICityRepository repository;

        public PocoViewComponent(ICityRepository repo) {
            repository = repo;
        }

        public string Invoke() {
            return $"{repository.Cities.Count()} cities, "
                + $"{repository.Cities.Sum(c => c.Population)} people";
        }
    }
}
```

View components can take advantage of dependency injection to receive the services they require. In this example, the POCO view component declares a dependency on the ICityRepository interface, which is then used in the Invoke method to create a string that describes the number of cities and the population total.

To use a view component, the Razor @await Component.Invoke expression is required. The view component is selected by providing the name of the class, without the ViewComponent ending, as an argument. In Listing 22-13, I have removed the placeholder in the shared layout and applied the POCO view component instead.

Listing 22-13. Applying a View Component in the _Layout.cshtml File in the Views/Shared Folder

```
<!DOCTYPE html>
<html>
<head>
    <meta name="viewport" content="width=device-width" />
    <title>@ViewBag.Title</title>
    <link asp-href-include="lib/bootstrap/dist/css/*.min.css" rel="stylesheet" />
</head>
<body class="m-1 p-1">
    <div class="bg-primary m-1 p-1">
        <div class="row text-white">
            <div class="col-7"><h1>Products</h1></div>
```

```
        <div class="col-5">
            @await Component.InvokeAsync("Poco")
        </div>
    </div>
</div>
<div class="m-1 p-1">@RenderBody()</div>
</body>
</html>
```

To apply the view component, I specified Poco as the argument to the Invoke method. When the layout is used by a view, it locates the PocoViewComponent class, calls its Invoke method, and inserts the result into the parent view's output, as shown in Figure 22-2.

Figure 22-2. *Using a simple view component*

This is a simple example, but it illustrates some important characteristics of view components. First, the PocoViewComponent class was able to get access to the data it required without depending on the action handling the HTTP request or its parent view. Second, defining the logic required to obtain and process the City summary in a C# class means that it can be readily unit tested (see the "Unit Testing View Components" sidebar later in the chapter for an example). Third, the application hasn't been twisted out of shape trying to include City objects in view models that are focused on Product objects. In short, a view component is a self-contained chunk of reusable functionality that can be applied throughout the application and can be developed and tested in isolation.

■ **Caution**   You must include the await keyword when you apply a view component in a view. You won't see an error if you just call @Component.Invoke but a string representation of a Task will be displayed, similar to this: System.Threading.Tasks.Task`1[Microsoft.AspNetCore.Html.IHtmlContent].

Deriving from the ViewComponent Base Class

POCO view components are limited in functionality unless they take advantage of the MVC API, which is possible but requires a lot more effort than the more common approach, which is to derive from the ViewComponent class. The ViewComponent class, which is defined in the Microsoft.AspNetCore.Mvc namespace, provides convenient access to context data and makes it easier to generate results. Listing 22-14 shows the contents of the CitySummary.cs file, which I added to the Components folder.

Listing 22-14. The Contents of the CitySummary.cs File in the Components Folder

```
using System.Linq;
using Microsoft.AspNetCore.Mvc;
using UsingViewComponents.Models;

namespace UsingViewComponents.Components {

    public class CitySummary : ViewComponent {
        private ICityRepository repository;

        public CitySummary(ICityRepository repo) {
            repository = repo;
        }

        public string Invoke() {
            return $"{repository.Cities.Count()} cities, "
            + $"{repository.Cities.Sum(c => c.Population)} people";
        }
    }
}
```

You don't need to include ViewComponent in the class name when you derive from the base class. Aside from using the base class, this view component is functionally identical to the POCO. In the sections that follow, I'll show you how to use the convenience features provided by the base class to use different view component features.

■ **Tip** Notice that the Invoke method isn't overridden in Listing 22-14. The ViewComponent class doesn't provide a default implementation of the Invoke method, which must be defined explicitly.

In preparation for demonstrating the view component features, I changed the component used in the shared layout, as shown in Listing 22-15. Instead of using a literal string to specify the view component name, I used nameof, as described in Chapter 4, which reduces the chances of mistyping the class name.

Listing 22-15. Changing the View Component in the _Layout.cshtml File in the Views/Shared Folder

```
<!DOCTYPE html>
<html>
<head>
    <meta name="viewport" content="width=device-width" />
    <title>@ViewBag.Title</title>
    <link asp-href-include="lib/bootstrap/dist/css/*.min.css" rel="stylesheet" />
</head>
<body class="m-1 p-1">
    <div class="bg-primary m-1 p-1">
        <div class="row text-white">
            <div class="col-7"><h1>Products</h1></div>
```

```
        <div class="col-5">
            @await Component.InvokeAsync(nameof(CitySummary))
        </div>
    </div>
</div>
<div class="m-1 p-1">@RenderBody()</div>
</body>
</html>
```

So that I can refer to the CitySummary class in the nameof expression without a namespace, I make the change shown in Listing 22-16 to the view imports file.

Listing 22-16. Adding a Namespace in the _ViewImports.cshtml File in the Views Folder

```
@using UsingViewComponents.Models
@using UsingViewComponents.Components
@addTagHelper *, Microsoft.AspNetCore.Mvc.TagHelpers
```

Understanding View Component Results

The ability to insert simple string values into a parent view isn't especially useful, but fortunately, view components are capable of much more. More complex effects can be achieved by having the Invoke method return an object that implements the IViewComponentResult interface. Three built-in classes implement the IViewComponentResult interface, and they are described in Table 22-3, along with the convenience methods for creating them provided by the ViewComponent base class. I describe the use of each result type in the sections that follow.

■ **Note**　If you are using POCO view components, you can create instances of these classes directly, although they can be awkward to work with because they have complex constructor arguments that the convenience methods provided by the ViewComponent class provide.

Table 22-3. *The Built-in IViewComponentResult Implementation Classes*

Name	Description
ViewViewComponentResult	This class is used to specify a Razor view, with optional view model data. Instances of this class are created using the View method.
ContentViewComponentResult	This class is used to specify a text result that will be safely encoded for inclusion in an HTML document. Instances of this class are created using the Content method.
HtmlContentViewComponentResult	This class is used to specify a fragment of HTML that will be included in the HTML document without further encoding. There is no ViewComponent method to create this type of result.

There is special handling for two result types. If a view component returns a string, then it is used to create a ContentViewComponentResult object, which is what I relied on in earlier examples. If a view component returns an IHtmlContent object, then it is used to create an HtmlContentViewComponentResult object.

Returning a Partial View

The most useful response is the awkwardly named ViewViewComponentResult object, which tells Razor to render a partial view and include the result in the parent view. The ViewComponent base class provides the View method for creating ViewViewComponentResult objects, and there are four versions of the method available, as described in Table 22-4.

Table 22-4. *The ViewComponent.View Methods*

Name	Description
View()	Using this method selects the default view for the view component and does not provide a view model.
View(model)	Using the method selects the default view and uses the specified object as the view model.
View(viewName)	Using this method selects the specified view and does not provide a view model.
View(viewName, model)	Using this method selects the specified view and uses the specified object as the view model.

These methods correspond to those provided by the Controller base class and are used in much the same way. I added a class file called CityViewModel.cs to the Models folder and used it to define the view model shown in Listing 22-17.

Listing 22-17. The Contents of the CityViewModel.cs File in the Models Folder

```
namespace UsingViewComponents.Models {

    public class CityViewModel {
        public int Cities { get; set; }
        public int Population { get; set; }
    }
}
```

In Listing 22-18, I have modified the Invoke method of the CitySummary view component so that it uses the View method to select a partial view and provides view data using a CityViewModel object.

Listing 22-18. Selecting a Partial View in the CitySummary.cs File in the Components Folder

```
using System.Linq;
using Microsoft.AspNetCore.Mvc;
using UsingViewComponents.Models;
```

```
namespace UsingViewComponents.Components {

    public class CitySummary : ViewComponent {
        private ICityRepository repository;

        public CitySummary(ICityRepository repo) {
            repository = repo;
        }

        public IViewComponentResult Invoke() {
            return View(new CityViewModel{
                Cities = repository.Cities.Count(),
                Population = repository.Cities.Sum(c => c.Population)
            });
        }
    }
}
```

Selecting a partial view in a view component is similar to selecting a view in a controller but with two important differences: Razor looks for views in different locations and uses a different default view name if one isn't specified.

Since I have not created a partial view for the view component, you will see an error message when you run the application that reveals the files that Razor is looking for.

- /Views/Home/Components/CitySummary/Default.cshtml

- /Views/Shared/Components/CitySummary/Default.cshtml

If no name is specified, then Razor looks for a file called Default.cshtml. Razor looks in two locations for the partial view. The first location takes into account the name of the controller handling the HTTP request, which allows each controller to have its own custom view. The second location is shared between all controllers.

■ **Tip** Notice that shared partial views are still distinguished by view component, which means that view components do not share partial views. You can override this behavior by including a path in the name of the view when you call the View method, such that calling View("Views/Shared/Components/Common/Default.html") will override the normal search locations.

To complete the example, I created the Views/Home/Components/CitySummary folder and added to it a new file called Default.cshtml, to which I added the markup shown in Listing 22-19.

Listing 22-19. The Content of the Default.cshtml File in the Views/Home/Components/CitySummary Folder

```
@model CityViewModel

<table class="table table-sm table-bordered">
    <tr>
        <td>Cities:</td>
        <td class="text-right">
```

```
        @Model.Cities
    </td>
</tr>
<tr>
    <td>Population:</td>
    <td class="text-right">
        @Model.Population.ToString("#,###")
    </td>
</tr>
</table>
```

Partial views for view components work in the same way as they do for controllers. In this case, I have created a strongly typed view that expects a CityViewModel object and displays its Cities and Population values in a table, as shown in Figure 22-3.

Figure 22-3. *Rendering a view using a view component*

Returning HTML Fragments

The ContentViewComponentResult class is used to include fragments of HTML in the parent view without using a view. Instances of the ContentViewComponentResult class are created using the Content method inherited from the ViewComponent base class, which accepts a string value. Listing 22-20 demonstrates the use of the Content method. In addition to the Content method, the Invoke method can return a string, and MVC will automatically convert to a ContentViewComponentResult.

Listing 22-20. Using the Content Method in the CitySummary.cs File in the Components Folder

```
using System.Linq;
using Microsoft.AspNetCore.Mvc;
using UsingViewComponents.Models;

namespace UsingViewComponents.Components {

    public class CitySummary : ViewComponent {
        private ICityRepository repository;
```

```
        public CitySummary(ICityRepository repo) {
            repository = repo;
        }

        public IViewComponentResult Invoke() {
            return Content("This is a <h3><i>string</i></h3>");
        }
    }
}
```

The string received by the Content method is encoded to make it safe to include in an HTML document. This is particularly important when dealing with content that has been provided by users or external systems because it prevents JavaScript content from being embedded into the HTML generated by the application. In this example, the string that I passed to the Content method contains some basic HTML tags, and if you run the application, you will see that they have been encoded safely, as shown in Figure 22-4.

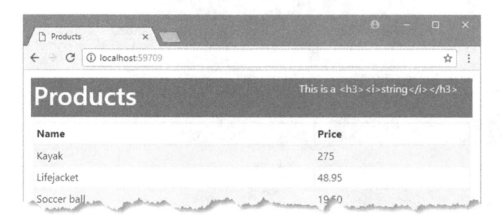

Figure 22-4. *Returning an encoded HTML fragment using a view component*

If you look at the HTML that the view component produced, you will see that the angle brackets have been replaced so that the browser doesn't interpret the content as HTML elements, as follows:

```
...
<div class="col-5">This is a &lt;h3&gt;&lt;i&gt;string&lt;/i&gt;&lt;/h3&gt;</div>
...
```

You don't need to encode content if you trust its source and want it to be interpreted as HTML. The Content method always encodes its argument, so you must create the HtmlContentViewComponentResult object directly and provide its constructor with an HtmlString object, which represents a string that you know is safe to display, either because it comes from a source that you trust or because you are confident that it has already been encoded, as shown in Listing 22-21.

Listing 22-21. Returning a Trusted HTML Fragment in the CitySummary.cs File in the Components Folder

```
using System.Linq;
using Microsoft.AspNetCore.Mvc;
using UsingViewComponents.Models;
using Microsoft.AspNetCore.Mvc.ViewComponents;
using Microsoft.AspNetCore.Html;

namespace UsingViewComponents.Components {

    public class CitySummary : ViewComponent {
        private ICityRepository repository;

        public CitySummary(ICityRepository repo) {
            repository = repo;
        }

        public IViewComponentResult Invoke() {
            return new HtmlContentViewComponentResult(
                new HtmlString("This is a <h3><i>string</i></h3>"));
        }
    }
}
```

This technique should be used with caution and only with sources of content that cannot be tampered with and that perform their own encoding. If you run the application, you will see that the angle brackets have been included in the parent view without modification, which allows the browser to interpret the output of the view component as HTML elements, illustrated in Figure 22-5.

Figure 22-5. Returning an unencoded HTML fragment using a view component

Getting Context Data

Details about the current request and the parent view are provided to a view component through properties of the ViewComponentContext class; Table 22-5 describes the most useful properties it provides.

Table 22-5. *The ViewComponentContext Properties*

Name	Description
Arguments	This property returns a dictionary of the arguments provided by the view, which can also be received via the Invoke method.
HtmlEncoder	This property returns an HtmlEncoder object that can be used to safely encode HTML fragments.
ViewComponentDescriptor	This property returns a ViewComponentDescriptor, which provides a description of the view component.
ViewContext	This property returns the ViewContext object from the parent view. See Chapter 21 for details of the features this class provides.
ViewData	This property returns a ViewDataDictionary, which provides access to the view data provided for the view component.

The ViewComponent base class provides a set of convenience properties that make it easier to access specific context information, as described in Table 22-6.

Table 22-6. *The ViewComponent Convenience Properties*

Name	Description
ViewComponentContext	This property returns the ViewComponentContext object.
HttpContext	This property returns an HttpContext object that describes the current request and the response that is being prepared.
Request	This property returns an HttpRequest object that describes the current HTTP request.
User	This property returns an IPrincipal object that describes the current user, as described in Chapter 28.
RouteData	This property returns a RouteData object that describes the routing data for the current request, as described in Chapter 15.
ViewBag	This property returns the dynamic view bag object, which can be used to pass data between the view component and the view.
ModelState	This property returns a ModelStateDictionary, which provides details of the model binding process, as described in Chapter 26.
ViewContext	This property returns the ViewContext object that was provided to the parent view, as described in Chapter 21.
ViewData	This property returns a ViewDataDictionary, which provides access to the view data provided for the view component.
Url	This property returns an IUrlHelper object that can be used to generate URLs, as described in Chapter 15.

The context data can be used in whatever way helps the view component do its work, including varying the way that data is selected or rendering different content or views. In Listing 22-22, I have used the routing data to narrow the selection of City objects.

Listing 22-22. Using Context Data in the CitySummary.cs File in the Components Folder

```
using System.Linq;
using Microsoft.AspNetCore.Mvc;
using UsingViewComponents.Models;
using Microsoft.AspNetCore.Mvc.ViewComponents;
using Microsoft.AspNetCore.Mvc.Rendering;

namespace UsingViewComponents.Components {

    public class CitySummary : ViewComponent {
        private ICityRepository repository;

        public CitySummary(ICityRepository repo) {
            repository = repo;
        }

        public IViewComponentResult Invoke() {
            string target = RouteData.Values["id"] as string;
            var cities = repository.Cities
                .Where(city => target == null ||
                    string.Compare(city.Country, target, true) == 0);
            return View(new CityViewModel{
                Cities = cities.Count(),
                Population = cities.Sum(c => c.Population)
            });
        }
    }
}
```

The browser uses the `id` segment from the route to specify the country that is used by LINQ to filter the objects in the repository. All the cities are displayed if you start the application and request the default URL. You can narrow the selection by requesting a URL such as /Home/Index/USA, which will narrow the selection to cities in the United States, as shown in Figure 22-6.

Figure 22-6. Using context data in a view component

709

Providing Context from the Parent View Using Arguments

Parent views can provide additional context data as arguments to the @await Component.Invoke expression. This feature can be used to provide data from the parent view model or to give guidance about the type of content that the view component should produce. To demonstrate this feature, I created a view file called CityList.cshtml in the Views/Home/Component/CitySummary folder and added the markup shown in Listing 22-23.

Listing 22-23. The Contents of the CityList.cshtml File in the Views/Home/Component/CitySummary Folder

```
@model IEnumerable<City>

<table class="table table-sm table-bordered">
    @foreach (var city in Model) {
        <tr>
            <td>@city.Name</td>
            <td class="text-right">
                @city.Population.ToString("#,###")
            </td>
        </tr>
    }
    <tr>
        <th>Total:</th>
        <td class="text-right">
            @Model.Sum(p => p.Population).ToString("#,###")
        </td>
    </tr>
</table>
```

Adding a second view allows the view component to choose between them, which it does based on an argument added to the Invoke method, as shown in Listing 22-24.

Listing 22-24. Selecting Views in the CitySummary.cs File in the Components Folder

```
using System.Linq;
using Microsoft.AspNetCore.Mvc;
using UsingViewComponents.Models;
using Microsoft.AspNetCore.Mvc.ViewComponents;
using Microsoft.AspNetCore.Mvc.Rendering;

namespace UsingViewComponents.Components {

    public class CitySummary : ViewComponent {
        private ICityRepository repository;

        public CitySummary(ICityRepository repo) {
            repository = repo;
        }
```

```
    public IViewComponentResult Invoke(bool showList) {
        if (showList) {
            return View("CityList", repository.Cities);
        } else {
            return View(new CityViewModel {
                Cities = repository.Cities.Count(),
                Population = repository.Cities.Sum(c => c.Population)
            });
        }
    }
}
}
```

If the showList argument to the Invoke method is true, then the view component selects the CityList and passes all the City objects in the repository as the view model. If the showList argument is false, then the default view is selected and provided with a CitySummary object for the view model.

The final step is to provide context data when applying the view component in the parent view, which is done by passing an anonymous object to the Invoke method, as shown in Listing 22-25.

Listing 22-25. Providing Context Data in the _Layout.cshtml File in the Views/Shared Folder

```
<!DOCTYPE html>
<html>
<head>
    <meta name="viewport" content="width=device-width" />
    <title>@ViewBag.Title</title>
    <link asp-href-include="lib/bootstrap/dist/css/*.min.css" rel="stylesheet" />
</head>
<body class="m-1 p-1">
    <div class="bg-primary m-1 p-1">
        <div class="row text-white">
            <div class="col-7"><h1>Products</h1></div>
            <div class="col-5">
                @await Component.InvokeAsync("CitySummary", new { showList = true })
            </div>
        </div>
    </div>
    <div class="m-1 p-1">@RenderBody()</div>
</body>
</html>
```

If you run the application, the view component will receive the value specified by the parent view and respond accordingly, as shown in Figure 22-7.

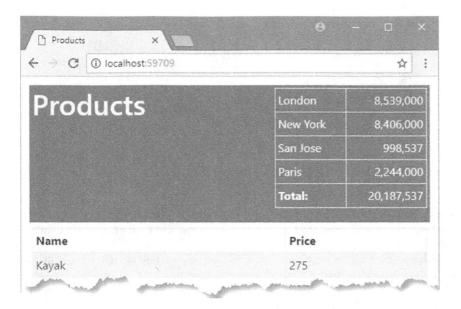

Figure 22-7. *Providing context data to a view component*

UNIT TESTING VIEW COMPONENTS

View components follow the general MVC approach of separating out the logic that selects and processes the model data from the view markup that formats and presents it, which makes it easy to perform unit tests. Here is an example unit test for CitySummary from the example application:

```
using System.Collections.Generic;
using Microsoft.AspNetCore.Mvc.ViewComponents;
using Moq;
using UsingViewComponents.Models;
using UsingViewComponents.Components;
using Xunit;

namespace UsingViewComponents.Tests {

    public class SummaryViewComponentTests {

        [Fact]
        public void TestSummary() {

            // Arrange
            var mockRepository = new Mock<ICityRepository>();
            mockRepository.SetupGet(m => m.Cities).Returns(new List<City> {
                new City { Population = 100 },
                new City { Population = 20000 },
                new City { Population = 1000000 },
                new City { Population = 500000 }
            });
```

```
            var viewComponent
                = new CitySummary(mockRepository.Object);

            // Act
            ViewViewComponentResult result
                = viewComponent.Invoke(false) as ViewViewComponentResult;

            // Assert
            Assert.IsType(typeof(CityViewModel), result.ViewData.Model);
            Assert.Equal(4, ((CityViewModel)result.ViewData.Model).Cities);
            Assert.Equal(1520100,
                ((CityViewModel)result.ViewData.Model).Population);
        }
    }
}
```

To arrange the test, I created a fake repository and passed it to the constructor of the CitySummary class to create a new instance of the view component. For the act section of the test, I called the Invoke method, which provided me with a result object. The view component selects a Razor view, so I cast the result to a ViewViewComponentResult and access the view model object through the ViewData.Model property it provides. For the assert section of the test, I check the type of the view model data and the values it contains.

Creating Asynchronous View Components

All of the examples so far in this chapter have been synchronous view components, which can be recognized because they define the Invoke method. If your view component relies on asynchronous APIs, then you can create an asynchronous view component by defining an InvokeAsync method that returns a Task. When Razor receives the Task from the InvokeAsync method, it will wait for it to complete and then insert the result into the main view. To prepare for this example, right-click the UsingViewComponents project item in the Solution Explorer, select Edit UsingViewComponents.csproj, and make the change shown in Listing 22-26 to add a new package to the project.

Listing 22-26. Adding a Package in the UsingViewComponents.csproj File

```
<Project Sdk="Microsoft.NET.Sdk.Web">

  <PropertyGroup>
    <TargetFramework>netcoreapp2.0</TargetFramework>
  </PropertyGroup>

  <ItemGroup>
    <Folder Include="wwwroot\" />
  </ItemGroup>

  <ItemGroup>
    <PackageReference Include="Microsoft.AspNetCore.All" Version="2.0.0 " />
    <PackageReference Include="System.Net.Http" Version="4.3.2" />
  </ItemGroup>

</Project>
```

The System.Net.Http package provides an API for making asynchronous HTTP requests, which I will use to query the Apress.com web site. Listing 22-27 shows the contents of a class file called PageSize.cs, which I added to the Components folder and used to create an asynchronous view component.

Listing 22-27. The Contents of the PageSize.cs File in the Components Folder

```
using System.Net.Http;
using System.Threading.Tasks;
using Microsoft.AspNetCore.Mvc;

namespace UsingViewComponents.Components {

    public class PageSize : ViewComponent {

        public async Task<IViewComponentResult> InvokeAsync() {
            HttpClient client = new HttpClient();
            HttpResponseMessage response
                = await client.GetAsync("http://apress.com");
            return View(response.Content.Headers.ContentLength);
        }
    }
}
```

The InvokeAsync method uses the async and await keywords, described in Chapter 4, to consume the asynchronous API provided by the HttpClient class and get the length of the content returned by sending a GET request to Apress.com. The length is passed to the View method, which selects the default partial view associated with the view component.

To create the view, I added the Views/Shared/Components/PageSize folder to the project and added a view file called Default.cshtml, with the content shown in Listing 22-28.

Listing 22-28. The Contents of the Default.cshtml File in the Views/Shared/Components/PageSize Folder

```
@model long
<div class="m-1 p-1 bg-info text-white">Page size: @Model</div>
```

The final step is to use the component, which I have done in the _Layout.cshtml file, as shown in Listing 22-29.

Listing 22-29. Using an Asynchronous Component in the _Layout.cshtml File in the Views/Shared Folder

```
<!DOCTYPE html>
<html>
<head>
    <meta name="viewport" content="width=device-width" />
    <title>@ViewBag.Title</title>
    <link asp-href-include="lib/bootstrap/dist/css/*.min.css" rel="stylesheet" />
</head>
<body class="m-1 p-1">
    <div class="bg-primary m-1 p-1">
        <div class="row text-white">
            <div class="col-7"><h1>Products</h1></div>
            <div class="col-5">
                @await Component.InvokeAsync("CitySummary",
```

```
                    new { showList = true })
            </div>
        </div>
    </div>
    <div class="m-1 p-1">@RenderBody()</div>
    @await Component.InvokeAsync("PageSize")
</body>
</html>
```

If you start the application, you will see a new addition in the content presented by the browser, as shown in Figure 22-8. The number displayed may change when you run the example, since Apress updates its web site often.

Figure 22-8. *Creating an asynchronous view component*

Creating Hybrid Controller/View Component Classes

View components often provide a summary or snapshot of functionality that is handled in-depth by a controller. For a view component that summarizes a shopping basket, for example, there will often be a link that targets a controller that provides a detailed list of the products in the basket and that can be used to check out and complete the purchase.

In this situation, you can create a class that is a controller and a view component, which allows for related functionality to be grouped together and reduces code duplication. To demonstrate, I added a class file called CityController.cs to the Controllers folder and used it to define the controller shown in Listing 22-30.

Listing 22-30. The Contents of the CityController.cs File in the Controllers Folder

```
using System.Collections.Generic;
using Microsoft.AspNetCore.Mvc;
using Microsoft.AspNetCore.Mvc.ViewComponents;
using Microsoft.AspNetCore.Mvc.ViewFeatures;
using UsingViewComponents.Models;

namespace UsingViewComponents.Controllers {

    [ViewComponent(Name = "ComboComponent")]
    public class CityController : Controller {
        private ICityRepository repository;

        public CityController(ICityRepository repo) {
            repository = repo;
        }
```

715

```
    public ViewResult Create() => View();

    [HttpPost]
    public IActionResult Create(City newCity) {
        repository.AddCity(newCity);
        return RedirectToAction("Index", "Home");
    }

    public IViewComponentResult Invoke() => new ViewViewComponentResult() {
        ViewData = new ViewDataDictionary<IEnumerable<City>>(ViewData,
            repository.Cities)
    };
  }
}
```

The ViewComponent attribute is applied to classes that don't inherit from the ViewComponent base class and whose name doesn't end with ViewComponent, meaning that the normal discovery process wouldn't normally categorize the class as a view component. The Name property sets the name by which the class can be referred to when applying the class using the @Component.Invoke expression in the parent view. In this example, I used the Name property to set the name of the view component part of the class to ComboComponent. This name will be used to invoke the view component and used to locate its views.

Since hybrid classes don't inherit from the ViewComponent base class, they don't have access to the convenience methods for creating IViewComponentResult objects, which means that I have to create the ViewViewComponentResult object directly, just as would be required in a POCO view component.

Creating the Hybrid Views

A hybrid class requires two sets of views: those that are rendered when the class is used as a controller and those that are rendered when the class is used as a view component. First, I created the Views/City folder and added a view file called Create.cshtml, the contents of which are shown in Listing 22-31.

Listing 22-31. The Contents of the Create.cshtml File in the Views/City Folder

```
@model City
@{
    ViewData["Title"] = "Create City";
    Layout = "_Layout";
}

<form method="post" asp-action="Create">
    <div class="form-group">
        <label asp-for="Name">Name:</label>
        <input class="form-control" asp-for="Name" />
    </div>
    <div class="form-group">
        <label asp-for="Country">Country:</label>
        <input class="form-control" asp-for="Country" />
    </div>
    <div class="form-group">
        <label asp-for="Population">Population:</label>
        <input class="form-control" asp-for="Population" />
    </div>
```

```
<button type="submit" class="btn btn-primary">Create</button>
<a class="btn btn-secondary" asp-controller="Home"
    asp-action="Index">
    Cancel
</a>
</form>
```

This view presents a simple form for creating new City objects. The Create button sends a POST request to the Create action on the City controller, while the Cancel button sends a GET request to the Index action on the Home controller.

Next, I created the Views/Shared/Components/ComboComponent folder and added a view file called Default.cshtml with the content shown in Listing 22-32. I placed the partial view in the Views/Shared folder because it will be the controller whose view uses the view component whose name will be included in the path used to locate the view.

Listing 22-32. The Default.cshtml File in the Views/Shared/Components/ComboComponent Folder

```
@model IEnumerable<City>

<table class="table table-sm table-bordered">
    <tr>
        <td>Biggest City:</td>
        <td>
            @Model.OrderByDescending(c => c.Population).First().Name
        </td>
    </tr>
</table>
<a class="btn btn-sm btn-info" asp-controller="City" asp-action="Create">
    Create City
</a>
```

This partial view receives a sequence of City objects that it sorts using LINQ to select the one with the largest Population value. There is also an anchor element, formatted to appear as a button, which targets the Create action on the City controller.

■ **Tip**   Notice that I explicitly specified the City controller for the a element in Listing 22-32. URLs are generated using the context data provided by the parent view, which means that the default controller is the one that is handling the request, not the one that is also a view component. If I had omitted the asp-controller attribute, the link would have targeted the Create method on the Home controller.

Applying the Hybrid Class

The final step is to apply the hybrid class as a view component in the shared layout using the name specified by the ViewComponent attribute, as shown in Listing 22-33.

Listing 22-33. Applying a Hybrid Class in the _Layout.cshtml File in the Views/Shared Folder

```
<!DOCTYPE html>
<html>
<head>
    <meta name="viewport" content="width=device-width" />
    <title>@ViewBag.Title</title>
    <link asp-href-include="lib/bootstrap/dist/css/*.min.css" rel="stylesheet" />
</head>
<body class="m-1 p-1">
    <div class="bg-primary m-1 p-1">
        <div class="row text-white">
            <div class="col-7"><h1>Products</h1></div>
            <div class="col-5">
                @await Component.InvokeAsync("ComboComponent")
            </div>
        </div>
    </div>
    <div class="m-1 p-1">@RenderBody()</div>
    @await Component.InvokeAsync("PageSize")
</body>
</html>
```

The result is a view component that is backed up by its own integrated controller (or, if you prefer, a controller that has its own integrated view component). If you run the application, you will see that London is listed as the most populous city. Click the Create City button and you will be presented with a form that lets you add a new City to the application. Fill in and submit the form, and the controller will receive the data, update the repository, and redirect the browser to the default URL for the application. If you have added a City whose population exceeds the others in the repository, then the output from the view component will change, as shown in Figure 22-9.

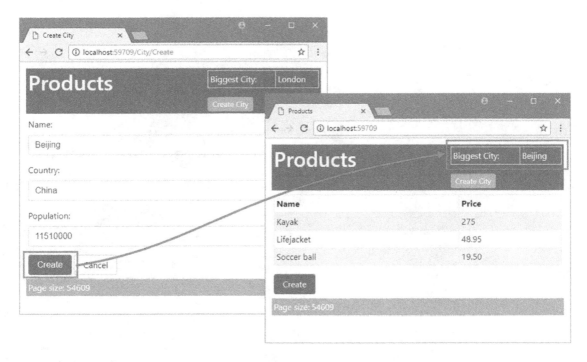

Figure 22-9. Using a hybrid controller/view component class

Summary

I introduced view components in this chapter, which is a new feature in ASP.NET Core MVC that replaces the child actions feature from previous MVC versions. I demonstrated how to create POCO view components and how to use the ViewComponent base class, and I showed you the three different types of result that view components can produce, including the selection of partial views for including in the parent view. I finished the chapter by demonstrating how to add view component functionality to a controller class to reduce code duplication and simplify an application. In the next chapter, I introduce tag helpers, which are used to transform HTML elements in views.

CHAPTER 23

■ ■ ■

Understanding Tag Helpers

Tag helpers are a new feature that has been introduced in ASP.NET Core MVC and are C# classes that transform HTML elements in a view. Common uses for tag helpers include generating URLs for forms using the application's routing configuration, ensuring that elements of a specific type are styled consistently, and replacing custom shorthand elements with commonly used fragments of content. In this chapter, I describe how tag helpers work and how custom tag helpers are created and applied. In Chapter 24, I describe the built-in tag helpers that support HTML forms, and in Chapter 25 I describe the other built-in tag helpers that are provided by MVC. Table 23-1 puts tag helpers in context.

TAG HELPER COMPONENTS

The ASP.NET Core 2 platform introduces *tag helper components*, which are classes that modify a specific piece of HTML in the responses sent to clients and that can be used by tag helpers. I don't describe this feature because the implementation is awkward and of little use to most MVC developers. If you want to transform content in the responses sent to clients, then use the tag helper features described in this chapter.

Table 23-1. *Putting Tag Helpers in Context*

Question	Answer
What are they?	Tag helpers are classes that manipulate HTML elements, either to change them in some way, to supplement them with additional content, or to replace them entirely with new content.
Why are they useful?	Tag helpers allow view content to be generated or transformed using C# logic, ensuring that the HTML sent to the client reflects the state of the application.
How are they used?	The HTML elements to which tag helpers are applied are selected based on the name of the class or through the use of the HTMLTargetElement attribute. When a view is rendered, elements are transformed by tag helpers and included in the HTML sent to the client.
Are there any pitfalls or limitations?	It can be easy to get carried away and generate complex sections of HTML content using tag helpers, which is something that is more readily achieved using view components, as described in Chapter 22.
Are there any alternatives?	You don't have to use tag helpers, but they make it easy to generate complex HTML in MVC applications.

© Adam Freeman 2017
A. Freeman, *Pro ASP.NET Core MVC 2*, https://doi.org/10.1007/978-1-4842-3150-0_23

Table 23-2 summarizes the chapter.

Table 23-2. *Chapter Summary*

Problem	Solution	Listing
Transform an HTML element	Create a tag helper and register it using the @ addTagHelper expression in a view or in a view imports file	10–12
Manage the scope of a tag helper	Use the HtmlTargetElement attribute	13–17
Support a shorthand element	Use the TagHelperOutput object to generate replacements elements	18, 19
Insert content around or inside the target element	Use the Pre- and Post- properties provided by the TagHelperOutput class	22–23
Receive context data in a tag helper	Decorate a property with the ViewContext and HtmlAttributeNotBound attributes	24, 25
Access the view model	Use a ModelExpression property	26, 27
Coordinate tag helpers	Use the TagHelperContext.Items property	28, 29
Suppress an element	Use the SuppressOutput method	30, 31

Preparing the Example Project

For this chapter, I used the ASP.NET Core Web Application (.NET Core) template to create a new Empty project called Cities.

Creating the Model and Repository

I created the Models folder, added a file called City.cs, and used it to define the class shown in Listing 23-1.

Listing 23-1. The Contents of the City.cs File in the Models Folder

```
namespace Cities.Models {

    public class City {
        public string Name { get; set; }
        public string Country { get; set; }
        public int? Population { get; set; }
    }
}
```

To create a repository for the City objects, I added a class file called Repository.cs to the Models folder and used it to define the interface and implementation class shown in Listing 23-2.

Listing 23-2. The Contents of the Repository.cs File in the Models Folder

```
using System.Collections.Generic;

namespace Cities.Models {

    public interface IRepository {

        IEnumerable<City> Cities { get; }
        void AddCity(City newCity);
    }

    public class MemoryRepository : IRepository {

        private List<City> cities = new List<City> {
            new City { Name = "London", Country = "UK", Population = 8539000},
            new City { Name = "New York", Country = "USA", Population = 8406000 },
            new City { Name = "San Jose", Country = "USA", Population = 998537 },
            new City { Name = "Paris", Country = "France", Population = 2244000 }
        };

        public IEnumerable<City> Cities => cities;

        public void AddCity(City newCity) {
            cities.Add(newCity);
        }
    }
}
```

Creating the Controller, Layout, and Views

Only one controller is required for the examples in this chapter. I created the Controllers folder, added a class file called HomeController.cs, and used it to define the controller shown in Listing 23-3.

Listing 23-3. The Contents of the HomeController.cs File in the Controllers Folder

```
using Microsoft.AspNetCore.Mvc;
using Cities.Models;

namespace Cities.Controllers {

    public class HomeController : Controller {
        private IRepository repository;

        public HomeController(IRepository repo) {
            repository = repo;
        }
```

```
        public ViewResult Index() => View(repository.Cities);

        public ViewResult Create() => View();

        [HttpPost]
        public IActionResult Create(City city) {
            repository.AddCity(city);
            return RedirectToAction("Index");
        }
    }
}
```

The controller provides an Index action that lists the objects in the repository and a pair of Create methods that will allow the user to use a form to create new City objects, following the same pattern as examples in earlier chapters.

The views in this application will use a shared layout. I created the Views/Shared folder, added a layout a file called _Layout.cshtml in the Views/Shared folder, and added the markup shown in Listing 23-4.

■ **Note**   Since the purpose of this chapter is to demonstrate how tag helpers work, the layout and the views for the example application are written using standard HTML elements only, which will be replaced as different tag helpers are introduced.

Listing 23-4. The Contents of the _Layout.cshtml File in the Views/Shared Folder

```
<!DOCTYPE html>
<html>
<head>
    <meta name="viewport" content="width=device-width" />
    <title>Cities</title>
    <link href="/lib/bootstrap/dist/css/bootstrap.css" rel="stylesheet" />
</head>
<body class="m-1 p-1">
    <div>@RenderBody()</div>
</body>
</html>
```

Next, I created the Views/Home folder and added a file called Index.cshtml with the markup shown in Listing 23-5.

Listing 23-5. The Contents of the Index.cshtml File in the Views/Home Folder

```
@model IEnumerable<City>

@{ Layout = "_Layout"; }

<table class="table table-sm table-bordered">
    <thead class="bg-primary text-white">
        <tr>
```

```
            <th>Name</th>
            <th>Country</th>
            <th class="text-right">Population</th>
        </tr>
    </thead>
    <tbody>
        @foreach (var city in Model) {
            <tr>
                <td>@city.Name</td>
                <td>@city.Country</td>
                <td class="text-right">@city.Population?.ToString("#,###")</td>
            </tr>
        }
    </tbody>
</table>
<a href="/Home/Create" class="btn btn-primary">Create</a>
```

This view uses the sequence of City objects to populate a table and includes an a element that targets the /Home/Create URL, styled as a button using Bootstrap. For the second view, I added a file called Create.cshtml to the Views/Home folder, with the markup shown in Listing 23-6.

Listing 23-6. The Contents of the Create.cshtml File in the Views/Home Folder

```
@model City

@{ Layout = "_Layout"; }

<form method="post" action="/Home/Create">
    <div class="form-group">
        <label for="Name">Name:</label>
        <input class="form-control" name="Name" />
    </div>
    <div class="form-group">
        <label for="Country">Country:</label>
        <input class="form-control" name="Country" />
    </div>
    <div class="form-group">
        <label for="Population">Population:</label>
        <input class="form-control" name="Population" />
    </div>

    <button type="submit" class="btn btn-primary">Add</button>
    <a class="btn btn-primary" href="/Home/Index">Cancel</a>
</form>
```

I created a view imports file called _ViewImports.cshtml in the Views folder and added the expression shown in Listing 23-7. This allows me to refer to the classes in the Models folder without using namespaces.

Listing 23-7. The Contents of the _ViewImports.cshtml File in the Views Folder

```
@using Cities.Models
```

The views in this example rely on the Bootstrap CSS package. To add Bootstrap to the example project, I used the Bower Configuration File item template to create a file called bower.json in the root folder of the project and added the package shown in Listing 23-8 to the dependencies section.

Listing 23-8. Adding Bootstrap in the bower.json File in the Cities Folder

```
{
  "name": "asp.net",
  "private": true,
  "dependencies": {
    "bootstrap": "4.0.0-alpha.6"
  }
}
```

Configuring the Application

The final preparatory step is to configure the application, as shown in Listing 23-9. This is the same basic configuration that I have been using in all the example projects in this part of the book, with an additional statement that registers the repository as a service using the singleton life cycle.

Listing 23-9. The Contents of the Startup.cs File in the Cities Folder

```
using System;
using System.Collections.Generic;
using System.Linq;
using System.Threading.Tasks;
using Microsoft.AspNetCore.Builder;
using Microsoft.AspNetCore.Hosting;
using Microsoft.AspNetCore.Http;
using Microsoft.Extensions.DependencyInjection;
using Cities.Models;

namespace Cities {
    public class Startup {

        public void ConfigureServices(IServiceCollection services) {
            services.AddSingleton<IRepository, MemoryRepository>();
            services.AddMvc();
        }
```

```
    public void Configure(IApplicationBuilder app, IHostingEnvironment env) {
        app.UseStatusCodePages();
        app.UseDeveloperExceptionPage();
        app.UseStaticFiles();
        app.UseMvcWithDefaultRoute();
    }
  }
}
```

If you run the application, you will see the list of the City objects that the repository creates by default. Click the Create button, fill out the form, and click the Add button; a new object will be added to the repository, as shown in Figure 23-1.

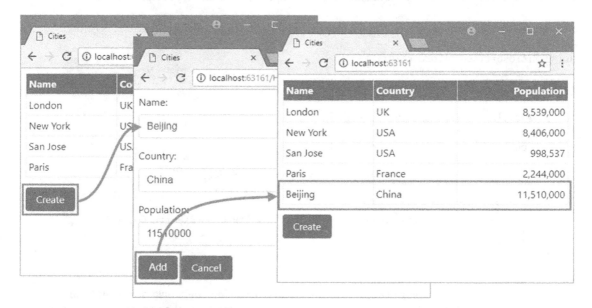

Figure 23-1. *Running the application*

Creating a Tag Helper

As with many MVC features, the best way to understand tag helpers is to create one, which reveals how they operate and how they fit into an application. In the sections that follow, I go through the process of creating and applying a tag helper that will apply the Bootstrap CSS classes for a button element so that an element like this:

```
...
<button type="submit" bs-button-color="danger">Add</button>
...
```

will be transformed into this:

```
...
<button type="submit" class="btn btn-danger">Add</button>
...
```

727

The tag helper will recognize the bs-button-color attribute and use its value to set the class attribute on the element sent to the browser. This isn't the most dramatic—or useful—transformation, but it provides a foundation for explaining how tag helpers work.

Defining the Tag Helper Class

Tag helpers can be defined anywhere in the project, but it helps to keep them together because, unlike most MVC components, they need to be registered before they can be used. I am going to create the tag helpers in the Infrastructure/TagHelpers folder, which I added to the project.

Tag helpers are derived from the TagHelper class, which is defined in the Microsoft.AspNetCore. Razor.TagHelpers namespace. To create a tag helper, I added a file called ButtonTagHelper.cs file to the Infrastructure/TagHelpers folder and used it to define the class shown in Listing 23-10.

Listing 23-10. The Contents of the ButtonTagHelper.cs File in the Infrastructure/TagHelpers Folder

```
using Microsoft.AspNetCore.Razor.TagHelpers;

namespace Cities.Infrastructure.TagHelpers {

    public class ButtonTagHelper : TagHelper {

        public string BsButtonColor { get; set; }

        public override void Process(TagHelperContext context,
                                     TagHelperOutput output) {

            output.Attributes.SetAttribute("class", $"btn btn-{BsButtonColor}");
        }
    }
}
```

The TagHelper class defines a Process method, which is overridden by subclasses to implement the behavior that transforms elements. The name of the tag helper combines the name of the element it transforms followed by TagHelper. In the case of the example, the class name ButtonTagHelper tells MVC that this is a tag helper that operates on button elements. The scope of a tag helper can be broadened or narrowed using attributes, which I describe in the "Managing the Scope of a Tag Helper" section, but this is the default behavior.

■ **Tip**   Asynchronous tag helpers can be created by overriding the ProcessAsync method instead of the Process method, but this isn't required for most helpers, which tend to make small and focused changes to HTML elements. The default implementation of ProcessAsync calls the Process method anyway. You can see an example of an asynchronous tag helper in Chapter 24.

Receiving Context Data

Tag helpers receive information about the element they are transforming through an instance of the TagHelperContext class, which is received as an argument to the Process method and which defines the properties described in Table 23-3.

Table 23-3. *The TagHelperContext Properties*

Name	Description
AllAttributes	This property returns a read-only dictionary of the attributes applied to the element being transformed, indexed by name and by index.
Items	This property returns a dictionary that is used to coordinate between tag helpers, as described in the "Coordinating Between Tag Helpers" section.
UniqueId	This property returns a unique identifier for the element being transformed.

Although you can access details of the element's attributes through the AllAttributes dictionary, a more convenient approach is to define a property whose name corresponds to the attribute you are interested in, like this:

```
...
public string BsButtonColor { get; set; }
...
```

When a tag helper is being used, MVC inspects the properties it defines and sets the value of any whose name matches attributes applied to the HTML element. As part of this process, MVC will try to convert an attribute value to match the type of the C# property so that bool properties can be used to receive true and false attribute values and int properties can be used to receive numeric attribute values such as 1 and 2.

WHAT HAPPENED TO HTML HELPERS?

Earlier versions of ASP.NET MVC used HTML helpers to generate form elements. HTML helpers were methods accessed through Razor expressions that begin with @Html so that creating an input element for the Population property would be done like this:

```
...
@Html.TextBoxFor(m => m.Population)
...
```

The problem with HTML helper expressions is that they don't fit with the structure of HTML elements, which leads to awkward expressions like this one, which adds Bootstrap styles to the element that is produced:

```
...
@Html.TextBoxFor(m => m.Population, new { @class = "form-control" })
...
```

Attributes have to be expressed in a dynamic object and have to be prefixed with @ if they are reserved C# words, such as class. As the HTML elements that are required become more complex, the HTML helper expression becomes more awkward. Tag helpers remove the awkwardness by using HTML attributes, like this:

```
...
<input class="form-control" asp-for="Population" />
...
```

The result is a more natural fit with the nature of HTML and produces views that are easier to read and understand. MVC still supports HTML helpers (and, in fact, tag helpers use HTML helpers behind the scenes), so you can use them for backward compatibility in views originally developed for MVC 5, but new views should take advantage of the more natural approach that tag helpers provide.

The name of the attribute is automatically converted from the default HTML style, bs-button-color, to the C# style, BsButtonColor. You can use any attribute prefix except asp- (which Microsoft uses) and data- (which is reserved for custom attributes that are sent to the client). In the example, I use this attribute to receive the color scheme to apply to the button element in the Process method, as follows:

```
...
output.Attributes.SetAttribute("class", $"btn btn-{BsButtonColor}");
...
```

Properties for which there are no corresponding HTML element attributes are not set, which means you should check to ensure that you are not dealing with null or default values. See the "Managing the Scope of Tag Helper" section for details of changing the scope of a tag helper so that it is used only on elements that define the attributes you depend on.

■ **Tip**　Using the HTML attribute name for tag helper properties doesn't always lead to readable or understandable classes. You can break the link between the name of the property and the attribute it represents using the HtmlAttributeName attribute, which can be used to specify the HTML attribute that the property will represent.

Producing Output

The Process method transforms an element by configuring the TagHelperOutput object that is received as an argument. The TagHelperOuput starts out describing the HTML element as it appears in the Razor view and is modified through the properties and methods described in Table 23-4.

Table 23-4. *The TagHelperOutput Properties and Methods*

Name	Description
TagName	This property is used to get or set the tag name for the output element.
Attributes	This property returns a dictionary containing the attributes for the output element.
Content	This property returns a TagHelperContent object that is used to set the content of the element.
PreElement	This property returns a TagHelperContext object that is used to insert content in the view before the output element. See the "Prepending and Appending Content and Elements" section.
PostElement	This property returns a TagHelperContext object that is used to insert content in the view after the output element. See the "Prepending and Appending Content and Elements" section.
PreContent	This property returns a TagHelperContext object that is used to insert content before the output element's content. See the "Prepending and Appending Content and Elements" section.
PostContent	This property returns a TagHelperContext object that is used to insert content after the output element's content. See the "Prepending and Appending Content and Elements" section.
TagMode	This property specifies how the output element will be written, using a value from the TagMode enumeration. See the "Creating Shorthand Elements" section.
SupressOuput()	Calling this method excludes an element from the view. See the "Suppressing the Output Element" section.

In the ButtonTagHelper class, I used the Attributes dictionary to add a class attribute to the HTML element that specifies the Bootstrap styles for a button, including the value of the BsButtonColor property, which means that different colors can be specified using the Bootstrap names such as primary, info, and danger.

Registering Tag Helpers

Tag helper classes can be used only once they have been registered using the Razor @addTagHelper expression. The set of views to which a tag helper will be applied depends on where the @addTagHelper expression is used. For a single view, the expression appears in the view itself. For a subset of the views in an application, the expression appears in a _ViewImports.cshtml file in the folder that contains the views or a parent folder, such that the @addTagHelper expression in the /Views/Home/_ViewImports.cshtml file registers tag helpers for all of the views associated with the Home controller. I want the tag helpers that I create in this chapter to be available in all the views in the application, so I used the final option, which is to add the @addTagHelper expression to the Views/_ViewImports.cshtml file, as shown in Listing 23-11.

Listing 23-11. Registering Tag Helpers in the _ViewImports.cshtml File in the Views Folder

```
@using Cities.Models
@addTagHelper Cities.Infrastructure.TagHelpers.*, Cities
```

The first part of the argument specifies the names of the tag helper classes, with support for wildcards, and the second part specifies the name of the assembly in which they are defined. In the listing, I have registered any tag helper in the `Cities.Infrastructure.TagHelpers` namespace from the `Cities` assembly.

Using a Tag Helper

The final step is to use the tag helper to transform an element. In Listing 23-12, I have removed the `class` attribute from the `button` element in the `Create.cshtml` view and replaced it with the attribute that the `ButtonTagHelper` class looks for.

Listing 23-12. Using a Tag Helper in the Create.cshtml File in the Views/Home Folder

```
@model City

@{  Layout = "_Layout"; }

<form method="post" action="/Home/Create">
    <div class="form-group">
        <label for="Name">Name:</label>
        <input class="form-control" name="Name" />
    </div>
    <div class="form-group">
        <label for="Country">Country:</label>
        <input class="form-control" name="Country" />
    </div>
    <div class="form-group">
        <label for="Population">Population:</label>
        <input class="form-control" name="Population" />
    </div>

    <button type="submit" bs-button-color="danger">Add</button>
    <a class="btn btn-primary" href="/Home/Index">Cancel</a>
</form>
```

If you run the application and click the Create button, the browser will request the `/Home/Create` URL, and you will see that the style and color of the Add button has changed, as shown in Figure 23-2.

Figure 23-2. *Using a tag helper to style a button*

```
┌─────────────────────────────────────────────────────────────────────┐
│                     UNIT TESTING A TAG HELPER                         │
└─────────────────────────────────────────────────────────────────────┘
```

Unit testing a tag helper class is a relatively simple process that hinges on providing the `Process` method with meaningful content to work with. Here is an example unit test for the tag helper in Listing 23-12:

```csharp
using System.Collections.Generic;
using System.Linq;
using System.Threading.Tasks;
using Cities.Infrastructure.TagHelpers;
using Microsoft.AspNetCore.Razor.TagHelpers;
using Xunit;

namespace Cities.Tests {

    public class TagHelperTests {

        [Fact]
        public void TestTagHelper() {
            // Arrange
            var context = new TagHelperContext(
                new TagHelperAttributeList(),
                new Dictionary<object, object>(),
                "myuniqueid");

            var output = new TagHelperOutput("button",
                new TagHelperAttributeList(), (cache, encoder) =>
                    Task.FromResult<TagHelperContent>
                        (new DefaultTagHelperContent()));

            // Act
            var tagHelper = new ButtonTagHelper {
                BsButtonColor = "testValue"
            };
            tagHelper.Process(context, output);

            // Assert
            Assert.Equal($"btn btn-{tagHelper.BsButtonColor}",
                output.Attributes["class"].Value);
        }
    }
}
```

Most of the work in this unit test sets up the `TagHelperContext` and `TagHelperOutput` objects so they can be passed to the `Process` method of the tag helper and inspected to ensure that the HTML element has been transformed correctly. The amount of effort required to prepare a tag helper for testing depends, naturally enough, on the complexity of the HTML it operates on and the degree by which it is transformed. Most tag helpers are relatively simple, however, and can be tested by following the basic pattern shown earlier.

Managing the Scope of a Tag Helper

Tag helpers are applied to all the elements of a given type, which means that the Process method of the ButtonTagHelper class created in the previous section will be invoked for every button element in every view in the application. This isn't always useful. To give an example of the problem, I added another button element to the Create.cshtml view, as shown in Listing 23-13.

Listing 23-13. Adding a Button Element in the Create.cshtml File in the Views/Home Folder

```
@model City

@{ Layout = "_Layout"; }

<form method="post" action="/Home/Create">
    <div class="form-group">
        <label for="Name">Name:</label>
        <input class="form-control" name="Name" />
    </div>
    <div class="form-group">
        <label for="Country">Country:</label>
        <input class="form-control" name="Country" />
    </div>
    <div class="form-group">
        <label for="Population">Population:</label>
        <input class="form-control" name="Population" />
    </div>

    <button type="submit" bs-button-color="danger">Add</button>
    <button type="reset" class="btn btn-primary" >Reset</button>
    <a class="btn btn-primary" href="/Home/Index">Cancel</a>
</form>
```

The new button element already has a class attribute and doesn't require the transformation performed by the ButtonTagHelper class. But if you run the application and request the /Home/Create URL, you will see that a problem has arisen, as illustrated by Figure 23-3.

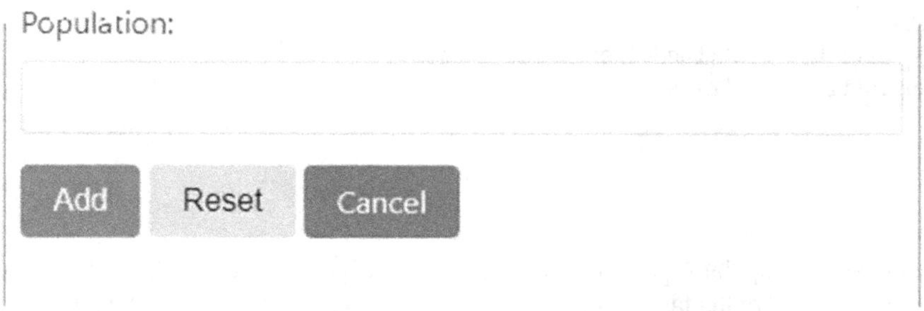

Figure 23-3. *The effect of the default scope of a tag helper*

You can see the cause of the poor formatting by looking at the HTML sent to the browser, which reveals a problem with the class attribute, as follows:

```
<button type="reset" class="btn btn-">Reset</button>
```

MVC applied the ButtonTagHelper to the new button element but doesn't set a value for the BsButtonColor property because there is no corresponding bs-button-color attribute on the HTML element. As a consequence, the tag helper replaces the class attribute with one that doesn't correctly specify Bootstrap styles and produces a poorly formatted element.

Narrowing the Scope of a Tag Helper

There are two possible approaches to solving this problem. The first is to modify the ButtonTagHelper class so that it is sensitive to the different button elements it might encounter. For the example application, this would invoke checking to see whether there is a bs-button-color attribute and making sure not to replace a class attribute if one has been defined. The problem with this approach is that the tag helper class gets more and more complicated as views that contain button elements are added to the application, and all of the new additional complexity describes the conditions under which the ButtonTagHelper class won't perform its transformation.

The second approach is to allow a tag helper to describe restrictions on how it is used, narrowing the scope in which it will be applied. Tag helper restrictions are applied using the HtmlTargetElement attribute, as shown in Listing 23-14.

Listing 23-14. Narrowing Scope in the ButtonTagHelper.cs File in the Infrastructure/TagHelpers Folder

```
using Microsoft.AspNetCore.Razor.TagHelpers;

namespace Cities.Infrastructure.TagHelpers {

    [HtmlTargetElement("button", Attributes = "bs-button-color", ParentTag = "form")]
    public class ButtonTagHelper : TagHelper {

        public string BsButtonColor { get; set; }

        public override void Process(TagHelperContext context,
                                     TagHelperOutput output) {

            output.Attributes.SetAttribute("class", $"btn btn-{BsButtonColor}");
        }
    }
}
```

The HtmlTargetElement attribute describes the elements to which the tag helper applies. The first argument specifies the element type and supports the additional named properties described in Table 23-5.

Table 23-5. *The HtmlTargetElement Properties*

Name	Description
Attributes	This property is used to specify that a tag helper should be applied only to elements that have a given set of attributes, supplied as a comma-separated list. An element must have all of the specified attributes. An attribute name that ends with an asterisk will be treated like a prefix so that bs-button-* will match bs-button-color, bs-button-size, and so on.
ParentTag	This property is used to specify that a tag helper should be applied only to elements that are contained within an element of a given type.
TagStructure	This property is used to specify that a tag helper should be applied only to elements whose tag structure corresponds to the given value from the TagStructure enumeration, which defines Unspecified, NormalOrSelfClosing, and WithoutEndTag.

In Listing 23-14, I restricted the ButtonTagHelper class so that it is applied only to button elements that have the bs-button-color attribute and whose parent is a form element. If you run the application and request the /Home/Create URL, you will see that the Reset button is no longer transformed since it lacks the required attribute, as shown in Figure 23-4.

Figure 23-4. *Narrowing the scope of a tag helper*

Widening the Scope of a Tag Helper

The HtmlTargetElement attribute can also be used to widen the scope of a tag helper so that it matches a broader range of elements. This is useful when you need to perform the same transformation on multiple element types, which goes against the premise of matching elements based on the tag helper class name, as shown in Listing 23-15.

Listing 23-15. Widening Scope in the ButtonTagHelper.cs File in the Infrastructure/TagHelpers Folder

```
using Microsoft.AspNetCore.Razor.TagHelpers;

namespace Cities.Infrastructure.TagHelpers {

    [HtmlTargetElement(Attributes = "bs-button-color", ParentTag = "form")]
    public class ButtonTagHelper : TagHelper {

        public string BsButtonColor { get; set; }

        public override void Process(TagHelperContext context,
                                    TagHelperOutput output) {

            output.Attributes.SetAttribute("class", $"btn btn-{BsButtonColor}");
        }
    }
}
```

This listing omits the element type for `HtmlTargetElement`, which means that the tag helper will be applied to any element that has a `bs-button-color` attribute, regardless of the element type. In Listing 23-16, I have modified the a element in the form, which uses the same set of Bootstrap styles as `button` elements so that it will be transformed by the tag helper.

Listing 23-16. Modifying an Anchor Element in the Create.cshtml File in the Views/Home Folder

```
@model City

@{ Layout = "_Layout"; }

<form method="post" action="/Home/Create">
    <div class="form-group">
        <label for="Name">Name:</label>
        <input class="form-control" name="Name" />
    </div>
    <div class="form-group">
        <label for="Country">Country:</label>
        <input class="form-control" name="Country" />
    </div>
    <div class="form-group">
        <label for="Population">Population:</label>
        <input class="form-control" name="Population" />
    </div>

    <button type="submit" bs-button-color="danger">Add</button>
    <button type="reset" class="btn btn-primary" >Reset</button>
    <a bs-button-color="primary" href="/Home/Index">Cancel</a>
</form>
```

Broadening the scope of a tag helper means you don't have to create tag helpers that repeat the same operation on different element types. Some care is required, however, because it is easy to create a tag helper that will start matching elements too broadly in the future as the contents of the views in the application evolves. A more balanced approach is to apply the HtmlTargetElement attribute multiple times, specifying the complete set of elements that will be transformed as a combination of narrowly defined matches, as shown in Listing 23-17.

Listing 23-17. Balancing Scope in the ButtonTagHelper.cs File in the Infrastructure/TagHelpers Folder

```
using Microsoft.AspNetCore.Razor.TagHelpers;

namespace Cities.Infrastructure.TagHelpers {

    [HtmlTargetElement("button", Attributes = "bs-button-color", ParentTag = "form")]
    [HtmlTargetElement("a", Attributes = "bs-button-color", ParentTag = "form")]
    public class ButtonTagHelper : TagHelper {

        public string BsButtonColor { get; set; }

        public override void Process(TagHelperContext context,
                                TagHelperOutput output) {

            output.Attributes.SetAttribute("class", $"btn btn-{BsButtonColor}");
        }
    }
}
```

This configuration has the same effect on the application but ensures that the tag helper doesn't cause problems if I start adding bs-button-color attributes to different element types for a different reason later in the development process.

ORDERING TAG HELPER EXECUTION

As a general rule, it is a good idea to use only one tag helper on any given HTML element. That's because it is easy to create a situation where one tag helper tramples on the transformation applied by another, overwriting attribute values or content. If you do need to apply multiple tag helpers, then you can control the sequence in which they execute by setting the Order property, which is inherited from the TagHelper base class. Managing the sequence can help minimize the conflicts between tag helpers, although it is still easy to encounter problems.

Advanced Tag Helper Features

The previous section demonstrated how to create a basic tag helper, but that just scratches the surface of what's possible. In the sections that follow, I show more advanced uses for tag helpers and the features they provide.

Creating Shorthand Elements

Tag helpers are not restricted to transforming the standard HTML elements and can also be used to replace custom elements with commonly used content. This can be a useful feature for making views more concise and making their intent more obvious. To demonstrate, I replaced the `button` elements in the `Create.cshtml` view with the custom elements shown in Listing 23-18.

Listing 23-18. Adding Custom HTML Elements in the Create.cshtml File

```
@model City

@{ Layout = "_Layout"; }

<form method="post" action="/Home/Create">
    <div class="form-group">
        <label for="Name">Name:</label>
        <input class="form-control" name="Name" />
    </div>
    <div class="form-group">
        <label for="Country">Country:</label>
        <input class="form-control" name="Country" />
    </div>
    <div class="form-group">
        <label for="Population">Population:</label>
        <input class="form-control" name="Population" />
    </div>
    <formbutton type="submit" bg-color="danger" />
    <formbutton type="reset" />
    <a bs-button-color="primary" href="/Home/Index">Cancel</a>
</form>
```

The `formbutton` element isn't part of the HTML specification and won't be understood by browsers. Instead, I am going to use these elements as a shorthand for generating the button elements that the form requires. I added a class file called `FormButtonTagHelper.cs` to the `Infrastructure/TagHelper` folder and defined the class shown in Listing 23-19.

▓ **Tip** When dealing with custom elements that are not part of the HTML specification, you must apply the `HtmlTargetElement` attribute and specify the element name, as shown in Listing 23-19. The convention of applying tag helpers to elements based on the class name works only for standard element names.

739

Listing 23-19. The FormButtonTagHelper.cs File in the Infrastructure/TagHelpers Folder

```
using Microsoft.AspNetCore.Razor.TagHelpers;

namespace Cities.Infrastructure.TagHelpers {

    [HtmlTargetElement("formbutton")]
    public class FormButtonTagHelper : TagHelper {

        public string Type { get; set; } = "Submit";

        public string BgColor { get; set; } = "primary";

        public override void Process(TagHelperContext context,
                                     TagHelperOutput output) {

            output.TagName = "button";
            output.TagMode = TagMode.StartTagAndEndTag;
            output.Attributes.SetAttribute("class", $"btn btn-{BgColor}");
            output.Attributes.SetAttribute("type", Type);
            output.Content.SetContent(Type == "submit" ? "Add" : "Reset");
        }
    }
}
```

The Process method uses the properties of the TagHelperOuput object to generate a completely different element: the TagName property is used to specify a button element, the TagMode property is used to specify that the element is written using start and end tags, the Attributes.SetAttribute method is used to define a class attribute with Bootstrap styles, and the Content property is used to set the element content.

■ **Tip**   Notice that I set the type attribute on the output element in Listing 23-19. This is because any attribute for which there is a property defined by a tag helper is omitted from the output element. This is usually a good idea because it stops the attributes used to configure tag helpers from appearing in the HTML sent to the browser. However, in this case, I used the type attribute to configure the tag helper, and I want it to be present in the output element as well.

Setting the TagName property is important because the output element is written in the same style as the custom element by default. In Listing 23-18, I used a self-closing tag, like this:

```
...
<formbutton type="submit" bg-color="danger" />
...
```

Since I want the output element to contain content, I have to explicitly specify the TagMode.Start TagAndEndTag enumeration value so that separate start and end tags are used.

The Content property returns an instance of the TagHelperContent class, which is used to set the content of elements. Table 23-6 describes the most important TagHelperContent methods.

Table 23-6. *Useful TagHelperContent Methods*

Name	Description
SetContent(text)	This method sets the content of the output element. The string argument is encoded so that it is safe for inclusion in an HTML element.
SetHtmlContent(html)	This method sets the content of the output element. The string argument is assumed to be safely encoded. Use with caution.
Append(text)	This method safely encodes the specified string and adds it to the content of the output element.
AppendHtml(html)	This method adds the specified string to the content of the output element without performing any encoding. Use with caution.
Clear()	This method removes the content of the output element.

In Listing 23-19, the tag helper uses the SetContent method to set the content of the output element based on the value of the type attribute, which is provided through the Type property. If you run the application and request the /Home/Create URL, you will see that the custom formbutton elements have been replaced with standard HTML elements so that these elements:

```
...
<formbutton type="submit" bg-color="danger" />
<formbutton type="reset" />
...
```

are transformed into these elements:

```
<button class="btn btn-danger" type="submit">Add</button>
<button class="btn btn-primary" type="reset">Reset</button>
```

Prepending and Appending Content and Elements

The TagHelperOutput class provides four properties that make it easy to inject new content into a view so that it surrounds an element or the element's content, as described in Table 23-7. In the sections that follow, I explain how you can insert content around and inside the target element.

Table 23-7. *The TagHelperOutput Properties for Appending Context and Elements*

Name	Description
PreElement	This property is used to insert elements into the view before the target element.
PostElement	This property is used to insert elements into the view after the target element.
PreContent	This property is used to insert content into the target element, before any existing content.
PostContent	This property is used to insert content into the target element, after any existing content.

Inserting Content Around the Output Element

The first TagHelperOuput properties are PreElement and PostElement, which are used to insert elements into the view before and after the output element. As a demonstration, I added a class file called ContentWrapperTagHelper.cs and used it to create the tag helper class shown in Listing 23-20.

Listing 23-20. The ContentWrapperTagHelper.cs File in the Infrastructure/TagHelpers Folder

```
using Microsoft.AspNetCore.Mvc.Rendering;
using Microsoft.AspNetCore.Razor.TagHelpers;

namespace Cities.Infrastructure.TagHelpers {

    [HtmlTargetElement("div", Attributes = "title")]
    public class ContentWrapperTagHelper : TagHelper {

        public bool IncludeHeader { get; set; } = true;
        public bool IncludeFooter { get; set; } = true;

        public string Title { get; set; }

        public override void Process(TagHelperContext context,
                                    TagHelperOutput output) {

            output.Attributes.SetAttribute("class", "m-1 p-1");

            TagBuilder title = new TagBuilder("h1");
            title.InnerHtml.Append(Title);

            TagBuilder container = new TagBuilder("div");
            container.Attributes["class"] = "bg-info m-1 p-1";

            container.InnerHtml.AppendHtml(title);

            if (IncludeHeader) {
                output.PreElement.SetHtmlContent(container);
            }

            if (IncludeFooter) {
                output.PostElement.SetHtmlContent(container);
            }
        }
    }
}
```

This tag helper transforms div elements that have a title attribute, and it works by using the PreElement and PostElement properties to add a header and a footer element that will surround the output element.

When generating new HTML elements, you can use standard C# string formatting to create the content you require, but this is an awkward and error-prone process for all but the simplest elements. A more robust approach is to use the TagBuilder class, which is defined in the Microsoft.AspNetCore.Mvc.Rendering namespace and which allows elements to be created in a more structured manner. The TagHelperContent class defines methods that accept TagBuilder objects, which makes it easy to create HTML content in tag helpers.

CHAPTER 23 ■ UNDERSTANDING TAG HELPERS

This tag helper uses the TagBuilder class to create an h1 element that is contained in a div element that has been styled with Bootstrap classes. There are optional bool include-header and include-footer attributes used to specify where the content is injected, and the default is to add elements before and after the output element. In Listing 23-21, I have updated the shared layout so that it contains an element that will be transformed by the tag helper.

Listing 23-21. Enabling a Tag Helper in the _Layout.cshtml File in the Views/Shared Folder

```
<!DOCTYPE html>
<html>
<head>
    <meta name="viewport" content="width=device-width" />
    <title>Cities</title>
    <link href="/lib/bootstrap/dist/css/bootstrap.css" rel="stylesheet" />
</head>
<body class="m-1 p-1">
    <div title="Cities">@RenderBody()</div>
</body>
</html>
```

If you run the application, you will see that the tag helper is applied throughout the application and adds a header and footer to every page, as illustrated by Figure 23-5.

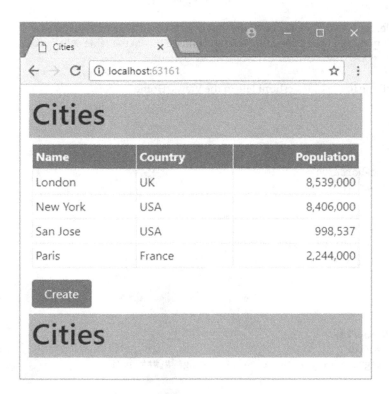

Figure 23-5. Inserting HTML elements with a tag helper

Inserting Content Inside the Output Element

The PreContent and PostContent properties are used to insert content inside the output element, surrounding the original contents. As a demonstration, I added a class called TableCellTagHelper.cs to the Infrastructure/TagHelpers folder and used it to define the class shown in Listing 23-22.

Listing 23-22. The TableCellTagHelper.cs File in the Infrastructure/TagHelpers Folder

```
using Microsoft.AspNetCore.Razor.TagHelpers;

namespace Cities.Infrastructure.TagHelpers {

    [HtmlTargetElement("td", Attributes = "wrap")]
    public class TableCellTagHelper : TagHelper {

        public override void Process(TagHelperContext context,
                                     TagHelperOutput output) {

            output.PreContent.SetHtmlContent("<b><i>");
            output.PostContent.SetHtmlContent("</i></b>");
        }
    }
}
```

This tag helper operates on td elements with the wrap attribute and inserts b and i elements around the output element's content. In Listing 23-23, I have added the wrap attribute to one of the table cells in the Index.cshtml view file.

Listing 23-23. Adding an HTML Attribute in the Index.cshtml File in the Views/Home Folder

```
@model IEnumerable<City>

@{ Layout = "_Layout"; }

<table class="table table-sm table-bordered">
    <thead class="bg-primary text-white">
        <tr>
            <th>Name</th>
            <th>Country</th>
            <th class="text-right">Population</th>
        </tr>
    </thead>
    <tbody>
        @foreach (var city in Model) {
            <tr>
                <td wrap>@city.Name</td>
                <td>@city.Country</td>
                <td class="text-right">@city.Population?.ToString("#,###")</td>
            </tr>
        }
    </tbody>
</table>
<a href="/Home/Create" class="btn btn-primary">Create</a>
```

744

If you run the application, you will see that the first column of cells in the table that lists the City objects is shown in bold, italic text. Examine the HTML sent to the browser and you will see how the content added through PreContent and PostContent properties appears on both sides of the element's original content, as follows:

```
...
<tr>
    <td wrap><b><i>London</i></b></td>
    <td>UK</td>
    <td class="text-right">8,539,000</td>
</tr>
...
```

■ **Tip** Notice that the wrap attribute has been left on the output element. This is because I didn't define a property in the tag helper class that corresponds to this attribute. If you want to prevent attributes from being included in the output, then define a property for them in the tag helper class, even if you don't need to use the attribute value.

Getting View Context Data and Using Dependency Injection

One of the most common uses for tag helpers—including the built-in helpers that I described in Chapters 24 and 25—is to transform elements so they contain details of the current request or the current view model. As an example, I added a class file called FormTagHelper.cs to the Infrastructure/TagHelpers folder and defined the class shown in Listing 23-24.

Listing 23-24. The Contents of the FormTagHelper.cs File in the Infrastructure/TagHelpers Folder

```
using Microsoft.AspNetCore.Mvc;
using Microsoft.AspNetCore.Mvc.Rendering;
using Microsoft.AspNetCore.Mvc.Routing;
using Microsoft.AspNetCore.Mvc.ViewFeatures;
using Microsoft.AspNetCore.Razor.TagHelpers;

namespace Cities.Infrastructure.TagHelpers {

    public class FormTagHelper : TagHelper {
        private IUrlHelperFactory urlHelperFactory;

        public FormTagHelper(IUrlHelperFactory factory) {
            urlHelperFactory = factory;
        }

        [ViewContext]
        [HtmlAttributeNotBound]
        public ViewContext ViewContextData { get; set; }
```

```
        public string Controller { get; set; }
        public string Action { get; set; }

        public override void Process(TagHelperContext context,
                                     TagHelperOutput output) {

            IUrlHelper urlHelper = urlHelperFactory.GetUrlHelper(ViewContextData);

            output.Attributes.SetAttribute("action", urlHelper.Action(
                Action ??
                    ViewContextData.RouteData.Values["action"].ToString(),
                Controller ??
                    ViewContextData.RouteData.Values["controller"].ToString()));
        }
    }
}
```

As its name suggests, the FormTagHelper class operates on form elements, setting their action attributes to specify where form data will be sent. If the form element has controller and action attributes, then these values will be used to generate the target URL; otherwise, the controller and action values from the routing data for the current request will be used.

To get context data, I added a property called ViewContextData and decorated it with two attributes, like this:

```
...
[ViewContext]
[HtmlAttributeNotBound]
public ViewContext ViewContextData { get; set; }
...
```

The ViewContext attribute denotes that the value of this property should be assigned a ViewContext object when a new instance of the FormTagHelper class is created, as described in Chapter 18. The ViewContext class provides details of the view that is being rendered, the routing data, and the current HTTP request, as described in Chapter 21.

The HtmlAttributeNotBound attribute prevents MVC from assigning a value to this property if there is a view-context attribute on the input HTML element. This is good practice, especially if you are writing tag helpers for other developers to use.

■ **Tip** There is a built-in tag helper for the form class that can be used to target action methods and that you should use in real projects. The helper in this section is just to demonstrate how context data can be used. See Chapter 24 for details of the built-in tag helper.

Tag helpers can declare dependencies on services in their constructor, which are resolved using the dependency injection feature. In this example, I declared a dependency on the IUrlHelperFactory service, which allows outgoing URLs to be created from routing data (and is the service behind the Url property provided by the Controller class that I described in Chapter 16). Within the Process method, the tag helper uses the IUrlHelperFactory.GetUrlHelper method to get an IUrlHelper object that is configured using the ViewContext object and that is then used to create a URL for the action attribute on the output element. Listing 23-25 shows the preparation of the view, in which I have removed the action attribute so that it can be set by the tag helper.

Listing 23-25. Removing a Form Element Attribute in the Create.cshtml File

```
@model City

@{ Layout = "_Layout"; }

<form method="post">
    <div class="form-group">
        <label for="Name">Name:</label>
        <input class="form-control" name="Name" />
    </div>
    <div class="form-group">
        <label for="Country">Country:</label>
        <input class="form-control" name="Country" />
    </div>
    <div class="form-group">
        <label for="Population">Population:</label>
        <input class="form-control" name="Population" />
    </div>
    <formbutton type="submit" bg-color="danger" />
    <formbutton type="reset" />
    <a bs-button-color="primary" href="/Home/Index">Cancel</a>
</form>
```

If you run the application, request the /Home/Create URL, and examine the HTML that is sent to the browser, you will see that the form element has an action attribute whose value is obtained using context data, as follows:

```
...
<form method="post" action="/Home/Create">
...
```

Working with the View Model

Tag helpers can operate on the view model, tailoring the transformations they perform or the output they create. To demonstrate, I added a file called LabelAndInputTagHelper.cs to the Infrastructure/TagHelpers folder and used it to define the class shown in Listing 23-26.

Listing 23-26. The LabelAndInputTagHelper.cs File in the Infrastructure/TagHelpers Folder

```
using Microsoft.AspNetCore.Mvc.ViewFeatures;
using Microsoft.AspNetCore.Razor.TagHelpers;

namespace Cities.Infrastructure.TagHelpers {

    [HtmlTargetElement("label", Attributes = "helper-for")]
    [HtmlTargetElement("input", Attributes = "helper-for")]
    public class LabelAndInputTagHelper : TagHelper {

        public ModelExpression HelperFor { get; set; }
```

```
    public override void Process(TagHelperContext context,
                                 TagHelperOutput output) {

        if (output.TagName == "label") {
            output.TagMode = TagMode.StartTagAndEndTag;
            output.Content.Append(HelperFor.Name);
            output.Attributes.SetAttribute("for", HelperFor.Name);

        } else if (output.TagName == "input") {
            output.TagMode = TagMode.SelfClosing;
            output.Attributes.SetAttribute("name", HelperFor.Name);
            output.Attributes.SetAttribute("class", "form-control");
            if (HelperFor.Metadata.ModelType == typeof(int?)) {
                output.Attributes.SetAttribute("type", "number");
            }
        }
    }
}
```

This tag helper transforms label and input elements that have a helper-for attribute. The important part of this tag helper is the type of the HelperFor property, which is used to receive the value of the helper-for attribute.

```
...
public ModelExpression HelperFor { get; set; }
...
```

The ModelExpression class is used when you want to operate on part of the view model, which is most easily explained by jumping forward and showing how the tag helper is applied in the view, as shown in Listing 23-27.

Listing 23-27. Applying a Tag Helper in the Create.cshtml File in the Views/Home Folder

```
@model Cities.Models.City

@{ Layout = "_Layout"; }

<form method="post">
    <div class="form-group">
        <label helper-for="Name" />
        <input helper-for="Name" />
    </div>
    <div class="form-group">
        <label helper-for="Country" />
        <input helper-for="Country" />
    </div>
    <div class="form-group">
        <label helper-for="Population"/>
        <input helper-for="Population" />
    </div>
```

```
    <formbutton type="submit" bg-color="danger" />
    <formbutton type="reset" />
    <a bs-button-color="primary" href="/Home/Index">Cancel</a>
</form>
```

The value of the helper-for attribute is a property from the Model class, which is detected by MVC and presented to the tag helper as a ModelExpression object.

I am not going to describe the ModelExpression class in any detail because any introspection on types leads to endless lists of classes and properties. Further, MVC comes with a useful set of built-in tag helpers that use the view model to transform elements, as described in Chapter 24, and which means that you don't need to create your own.

For the example tag helper, I use two basic features that are worth describing. The first is to get the name of the model property so that I can include it in the output element, like this:

```
...
output.Content.Append(HelperFor.Name);
output.Attributes.SetAttribute("for", HelperFor.Name);
...
```

The Name property returns the name of the model property. The second feature is to get the type of the model property so that I can change the value of the type attribute on input elements, like this:

```
...
if (HelperFor.Metadata.ModelType == typeof(int?)) {
    output.Attributes.SetAttribute("type", "number");
}
...
```

If you run the example, request the /Home/Create URL, and examine the HTML sent to the browser, you will see that the following elements:

```
<div class="form-group">
    <label for="Name">Name</label>
    <input name="Name" class="form-control" />
</div>
<div class="form-group">
    <label for="Country">Country</label>
    <input name="Country" class="form-control" />
</div>
<div class="form-group">
    <label for="Population">Population</label>
    <input name="Population" class="form-control" type="number" />
</div>
```

The type attribute for the Population input element has been set to number to reflect the fact that the City.Population property in the C# class is an int, showing how the HTML produced by a tag helper can reflect different characteristics of the model. Depending on which browser you use, this input element will only allow numbers to be entered.

Coordinating Between Tag Helpers

The TagHelperContext.Items property provides a dictionary that is used to coordinate between tag helpers that operate on elements and those that operate on their descendants. To demonstrate the use of the Items collection, I added a class file called CoordinatingTagHelpers.cs to the Infrastructure/TagHelpers folder and used it to define the pair of tag helpers shown in Listing 23-28.

Listing 23-28. The CoordinatingTagHelpers.cs File in the Infrastructure/TagHelpers Folder

```
using Microsoft.AspNetCore.Razor.TagHelpers;

namespace Cities.Infrastructure.TagHelpers {

    [HtmlTargetElement("div", Attributes = "theme")]
    public class ButtonGroupThemeTagHelper : TagHelper {

        public string Theme { get; set; }

        public override void Process(TagHelperContext context,
                                        TagHelperOutput output) {
            context.Items["theme"] = Theme;
        }
    }

    [HtmlTargetElement("button", ParentTag = "div")]
    [HtmlTargetElement("a", ParentTag = "div")]
    public class ButtonThemeTagHelper : TagHelper {

        public override void Process(TagHelperContext context,
                                        TagHelperOutput output) {

            if (context.Items.ContainsKey("theme")) {
                output.Attributes.SetAttribute("class",
                    $"btn btn-{context.Items["theme"]}");
            }
        }
    }
}
```

The first tag helper is the ButtonGroupThemeTagHelper class, which operates on div elements that have a theme attribute. Coordinating tag helpers can transform their own elements, but this example simply adds the value of the theme attribute to the Items dictionary so that it is available to tag helpers that operate on elements contained within the div element.

The second tag helper is the ButtonThemeTagHelper class, which operates on button and a elements that are contained within a div element. This helper uses the theme value from the Items dictionary to set the Bootstrap style for its output elements. Listing 23-29 shows a set of elements to which these helpers will be applied.

Listing 23-29. Applying Coordinating Tag Helpers in the Create.cshtml File in the Views/Home Folder

```
@model Cities.Models.City

@{ Layout = "_Layout"; }

<form method="post">
    <div class="form-group">
        <label helper-for="Name" />
        <input helper-for="Name" />
    </div>
    <div class="form-group">
        <label helper-for="Country" />
        <input helper-for="Country" />
    </div>
    <div class="form-group">
        <label helper-for="Population" />
        <input helper-for="Population" />
    </div>
    <div theme="primary">
        <button type="submit">Add</button>
        <button type="reset">Reset</button>
        <a href="/Home/Index">Cancel</a>
    </div>
</form>
```

If you run the application and request the /Home/Create URL, you will see that the group of buttons are all styled in the same way. If you change the value of the theme attribute on the div element to another Bootstrap theme setting, such as info or danger, and reload the page, you will see the change reflected in the styles of the buttons, as shown in Figure 23-6.

Figure 23-6. *Coordinating tag helpers*

Suppressing the Output Element

Tag helpers can be used to prevent an element from being included in the HTML sent to the browser by calling the SuppressOuput method on the TagHelperOutput object that is received as an argument to the Process method. In Listing 23-30, I have added an element to the shared layout that displays a highly visible message but that I only want to be shown for requests to a given action.

Listing 23-30. Adding a Visible Message in the _Layout.cshtml File in the Views/Shared Folder

```
<!DOCTYPE html>
<html>
<head>
    <meta name="viewport" content="width=device-width" />
    <title>Cities</title>
    <link href="/lib/bootstrap/dist/css/bootstrap.css" rel="stylesheet" />
</head>
<body class="m-1 p-1">
    <div show-for-action="Index" class="m-1 p-1 bg-danger">
        <h2>Important Message</h2>
    </div>
    <div title="Cities">@RenderBody()</div>
</body>
</html>
```

The show-for-action attribute specifies the name of the action for which I want to display the warning. This wouldn't be a useful way of controlling the inclusion of content in a real application, but it is sufficient for an example application with only one controller and two action names. Listing 23-31 shows the contents of the SelectiveTagHelper.cs class file, which I added to the Infrastructure/TagHelpers folder.

Listing 23-31. The SelectiveTagHelper.cs File in the Infrastructure/TagHelpers Folder

```
using System;
using Microsoft.AspNetCore.Mvc.Rendering;
using Microsoft.AspNetCore.Mvc.ViewFeatures;
using Microsoft.AspNetCore.Razor.TagHelpers;

namespace Cities.Infrastructure.TagHelpers {

    [HtmlTargetElement(Attributes = "show-for-action")]
    public class SelectiveTagHelper : TagHelper {

        public string ShowForAction { get; set; }

        [ViewContext]
        [HtmlAttributeNotBound]
        public ViewContext ViewContext { get; set; }
```

```
public override void Process(TagHelperContext context,
                             TagHelperOutput output) {

    if (!ViewContext.RouteData.Values["action"].ToString()
            .Equals(ShowForAction, StringComparison.OrdinalIgnoreCase)) {
        output.SuppressOutput();
    }
  }
 }
}
```

This tag helper uses the ViewContext to get the action value from the routing data and compares it to the value of the show-for-action attribute on the HTML element. If they don't match, then the SuppressOutput method is called. To see the effect, start the application and request the /Home/Index and /Home/Create URLs. As Figure 23-7 shows, the message is displayed only when the Index action is targeted.

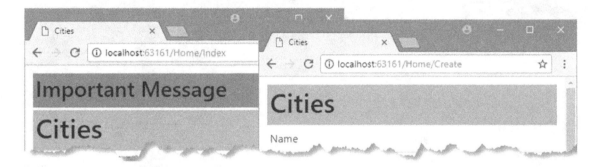

Figure 23-7. *Suppressing elements using a tag helper*

Summary

In this chapter, I described the use of tag helpers, which are a new addition to ASP.NET Core MVC. I explained the role they play in a Razor view and demonstrated how custom tag helpers are created, registered, and applied. I showed you how to control the scope of a tag helper and described the different ways that tag helpers can transform HTML elements. In the next chapter, I describe the tag helpers that are used to work with HTML form elements.

■ ■ ■

CHAPTER 24

Using the Form Tag Helpers

MVC provides a set of built-in tag helpers that are used to perform commonly required transformations on HTML elements. In this chapter, I describe the tag helpers that operate on HTML forms, which include the form, input, label, select, option, and textarea elements. In Chapter 25, I describe the other built-in tag helpers, which provide features that are not related to forms. Table 24-1 puts the form tag helpers in context.

Table 24-1. *Putting the Form Tag Helpers in Context*

Question	Answer
What are they?	The form tag helpers are used to transform HTML form elements so that you don't have to write custom tag helpers to solve the most common problems.
Why are they useful?	The form tag helpers ensure that HTML form elements, which include the elements inside forms, such as label and input, are generated consistently. For the most part, the tag helpers ensure that important attributes such as id, name, and for are set directly using view model classes, but some of the tag helpers can generate content as well, such as populating select elements with option elements.
How are they used?	The built-in tag helpers look for attributes prefixed with asp-, such as asp-for.
Are there any pitfalls or limitations?	The only limitation is the way that model data has to be provided to the tag helper that generates option elements inside of select elements. In the "Working with Select and Option Elements" section, I describe the problem and provide a custom tag helper that solves it.
Are there any alternatives?	You can write HTML forms in views without using the tag helper attributes at all. You could also write your own tag helpers, using the techniques that I described Chapter 23.

Table 24-2 summarizes the chapter.

Table 24-2. *Chapter Summary*

Problem	Solution	Listing
Set the action attribute on a form element	Use the form element tag helper	5
Prevent cross-site request forgery	Apply the ValidateAntiForgeryToken attribute to the action method and, optionally, set the asp-antiforgery attribute to true on the form element	6, 7
Set the id, name, and value attributes on an input element	Apply the asp-for attribute	8
Format a value displayed by an input element	Apply the asp-format attribute to the input element or apply the DisplayFormat attribute in the model class	9–12
Set the for attribute and content of a label element	Apply the asp-for attribute	13
Change the content of label elements to which the asp-for attribute has been applied	Apply the Display attribute to the model class property and use the Name property to specify the content	14
Set the id and name attributes on a select element	Apply the asp-for attribute	15
Generate option elements	Apply the asp-items attribute	16–21
Set the id and name attributes on a textarea element	Apply the asp-for attribute	22, 23

Preparing the Example Project

In this chapter, I continue using the Cities project that I created in Chapter 23. For this chapter, I want to enable the built-in tag helpers that come with MVC and disable the custom helpers that I created in Chapter 23. Listing 24-1 shows the changes that I made to the view imports file, in which I replaced the @ addTagHelper expression for the helper classes in the Cities assembly with one that sets up the MVC tag helpers instead, which are defined in an assembly called Microsoft.AspNetCore.Mvc.TagHelpers.

Listing 24-1. Changing the Tag Helpers in the _ViewImports.cshtml File in the Views Folder

```
@using Cities.Models
@addTagHelper *, Microsoft.AspNetCore.Mvc.TagHelpers
```

Resetting the Views and Layout

Listing 24-2 shows the contents of the Index.cshtml view, in which I have removed the attributes that are used by the custom tag helper classes.

Listing 24-2. The Contents of the Index.cshtml File in the Views/Home Folder

```
@model IEnumerable<City>

@{ Layout = "_Layout"; }

<table class="table table-sm table-bordered">
    <thead class="bg-primary text-white">
        <tr>
            <th>Name</th>
            <th>Country</th>
            <th class="text-right">Population</th>
        </tr>
    </thead>
    <tbody>
        @foreach (var city in Model) {
            <tr>
                <td>@city.Name</td>
                <td>@city.Country</td>
                <td class="text-right">@city.Population?.ToString("#,###")</td>
            </tr>
        }
    </tbody>
</table>
<a href="/Home/Create" class="btn btn-primary">Create</a>
```

Listing 24-3 shows the corresponding changes to the Create.cshtml file, which I have returned to using standard HTML elements without the attributes used in Chapter 23.

Listing 24-3. The Contents of the Create.cshtml File in the Views/Home Folder

```
@model City

@{ Layout = "_Layout"; }

<form method="post" action="/Home/Create">
    <div class="form-group">
        <label for="Name">Name:</label>
        <input class="form-control" name="Name" />
    </div>
    <div class="form-group">
        <label for="Country">Country:</label>
        <input class="form-control" name="Country" />
    </div>
    <div class="form-group">
        <label for="Population">Population:</label>
        <input class="form-control" name="Population" />
    </div>
    <button type="submit" class="btn btn-primary">Add</button>
    <a class="btn btn-primary" href="/Home/Index">Cancel</a>
</form>
```

The final change is to the shared layout, as shown in Listing 24-4.

Listing 24-4. The Contents of the _Layout.cshtml File in the Views/Shared Folder

```
<!DOCTYPE html>
<html>
<head>
    <meta name="viewport" content="width=device-width" />
    <title>Cities</title>
    <link href="/lib/bootstrap/dist/css/bootstrap.css" rel="stylesheet" />
</head>
<body class="m-1 p-1">
    <div>@RenderBody()</div>
</body>
</html>
```

If you run the application, you will see the list of cities, and you can click the Create button and fill in the form to submit new data to the server, as shown in Figure 24-1.

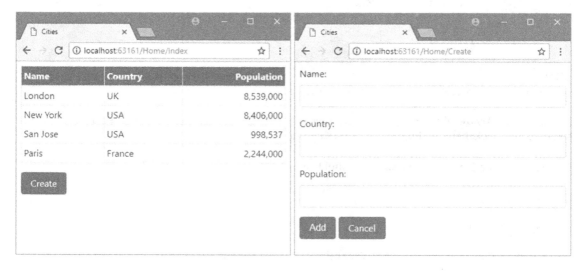

Figure 24-1. *Running the example application*

Working with Form Elements

The FormTagHelper class is the built-in tag helper for form elements and is used to manage the configuration of HTML forms so that they target the right action method based on the application's routing configuration. This tag helper supports the attributes described in Table 24-3.

Table 24-3. *The Built-In Tag Helper Attributes for Form Elements*

Name	Description
asp-controller	This attribute is used to specify the controller value to the routing system for the action attribute URL. If omitted, then the controller rendering the view will be used.
asp-action	This attribute is used to specify the action method for the action value to the routing system for the action attribute URL. If omitted, then the action rendering the view will be used.
asp-route-*	Attributes whose names begin with asp-route- are used to specify additional values for the action attribute URL so that the asp-route-id attribute is used to provide a value for the id segment to the routing system.
asp-route	This attribute is used to specify the name of the route that will be used to generate the URL for the action attribute.
asp-area	This attribute is used to specify the name of the area that will be used to generate the URL for the action attribute.
asp-antiforgery	This attribute controls whether anti-forgery information is added to the view, as described in the "Using the Anti-forgery Feature" section.

Setting the Form Target

The main purpose of the FormTagHelper class is to set the action attribute of the form element using the application's routing configuration, ensuring that the form data is always sent to the correct URL, even when the routing scheme changes. In Listing 24-5, I have used the asp-action and asp-controller attributes to target the Create action method on the Home controller.

■ **Note**   The tag helper doesn't set the method attribute, and if you omit it from the form element, then the browser will use a GET request to send the form data to the client. As I explained in Chapter 17, this can cause problems if the form data is used to modify the data in the application. It is good practice to set the method attribute, even if you do want GET requests so that it is obvious that you have not forgotten to select a method type.

Listing 24-5. Setting the Form Target in the Create.cshtml File in the Views/Home Folder

```
@model City

@{  Layout = "_Layout"; }

<form method="post" asp-controller="Home" asp-action="Create">
    <div class="form-group">
        <label for="Name">Name:</label>
        <input class="form-control" name="Name" />
    </div>
    <div class="form-group">
        <label for="Country">Country:</label>
        <input class="form-control" name="Country" />
    </div>
    <div class="form-group">
        <label for="Population">Population:</label>
        <input class="form-control" name="Population" />
    </div>
    <button type="submit" class="btn btn-primary">Add</button>
    <a class="btn btn-primary" href="/Home/Index">Cancel</a>
</form>
```

If you run the application, request the /Home/Create URL, and examine the HTML that is sent to the client, you will see that the tag helper adds an action attribute to the form element and sets its value using the routing system, as follows:

```
<form method="post" action="/Home/Create">
```

Using the Anti-forgery Feature

Cross-site request forgery (CSRF) is a way to exploit a web application to take advantage of the way that user requests are authenticated. Most web applications—including those created using ASP.NET Core—use cookies to identify which requests are related to a specific session, with which a user identity is usually associated.

CSRF—also known as *session riding*—is described in detail at http://en.wikipedia.org/wiki/Cross-site_request_forgery but relies on the user visiting a malicious web site after using your web application and without explicitly ending their sessions by clicking a Logout button. The application still regards the user's session as being active, and the cookie that the browser has stored has not yet expired. The malicious site contains some JavaScript code that sends a form request to your application that performs an operation without the user's consent, where the nature of the operation will depend on the application being attacked. Since the JavaScript code is executed by the user's browser, the request to the application includes the session cookie, and the application performs the operation without the user's knowledge or consent.

If a form element doesn't contain an action attribute—because it is being generated from the routing system with the asp-controller and asp-acton attributes—then the FormTagHelper class automatically enables the anti-CSRF feature, whereby a security token is added to the form in a hidden input element to the HTML sent to the client along with a cookie. The application will process the request only if it contains both the cookie and the hidden value from the form, which the malicious site cannot access. Each request for the form generates a new and unique set of security tokens.

If you run the application, request the /Home/Create URL, and look at the HTML sent to the browser, you will see a hidden input element like this one:

```
<input name="__RequestVerificationToken" type="hidden" value="CfDJ8KuVkH8hFlRApe
    FBxTrhCFTKZeOB9BKwnWDJqLRUDk__PrEwaeCJmiBbGkwW1ZI816c_TrM5XQkJBeqNI5IL8FhuO
    RvjZuYIL-GZvnWZ62OThsZYTO2HNX_Lu5LWDNWDdVoS5O5hZtzaoHLeY5lNto" />
```

If you use the browser's F12 tools, you can also see the corresponding cookie that is added to the response. Adding the security tokens to HTML responses is only part of the process; they must also be validated by the controller, as shown in Listing 24-6.

Listing 24-6. Validating Anti-forgery Tokens in the HomeController.cs File in the Controllers Folder

```
using Microsoft.AspNetCore.Mvc;
using Cities.Models;

namespace Cities.Controllers {

    public class HomeController : Controller {
        private IRepository repository;

        public HomeController(IRepository repo) {
            repository = repo;
        }

        public ViewResult Index() => View(repository.Cities);

        public ViewResult Create() => View();

        [HttpPost]
        [ValidateAntiForgeryToken]
        public IActionResult Create(City city) {
            repository.AddCity(city);
            return RedirectToAction("Index");
        }
    }
}
```

The ValidateAntoForgeryToken attribute ensures that a request contains valid anti-CSRF tokens and will throw an exception if they are absent or do not contain the expected values.

The FormTagHelper class provides the asp-antiforgery attribute to override the default anti-CSRF behavior. If the value of the attribute is true, then the security tokens will be included in responses, even if the form element has an action attribute. If the value of the attribute is false, then the security tokens will be disabled. In Listing 24-7, I have explicitly enabled the feature, even though the security tokens would have been added anyway because there is no action attribute defined on the form element.

Listing 24-7. Enabling the Anti-CSRF Feature in the Create.cshtml File in the Views/Home Folder

```
@model City

@{ Layout = "_Layout"; }

<form method="post" asp-controller="Home" asp-action="Create"
                      asp-antiforgery="true">
    <div class="form-group">
        <label for="Name">Name:</label>
        <input class="form-control" name="Name" />
    </div>
    <div class="form-group">
        <label for="Country">Country:</label>
        <input class="form-control" name="Country" />
    </div>
    <div class="form-group">
        <label for="Population">Population:</label>
        <input class="form-control" name="Population" />
    </div>
    <button type="submit" class="btn btn-primary">Add</button>
    <a class="btn btn-primary" href="/Home/Index">Cancel</a>
</form>
```

■ **Tip**   Testing the anti-CSRF feature is a little tricky. I do it by requesting the URL that contains the form (/Home/Create for the example) and then using the browser's F12 developer tools to locate and remove the hidden input element from the form (or change the element's value). When I populate the form and send it to the application, the browser doesn't have one part of the required data, and the request should fail and show an error page.

Working with Input Elements

The input element is the backbone of HTML forms and provides the main means by which a user can provide an application with unstructured data. The InputTagHelper class is used to transform input elements so they reflect the data type and format of the view model property they are used to gather, using the attributes described in Table 24-4.

Table 24-4. The Built-in Tag Helper Attributes for Input Elements

Name	Description
asp-for	This attribute is used to specify the view model property that the input element represents.
asp-format	This attribute is used to specify a format for the value of the view model property that the input element represents.

Configuring Input Elements

The asp-for attribute is set to the name of a view model property, which is then used to set the name, id, type, and value attributes of the input element. In Listing 24-8, I have applied the asp-for attribute to the input elements in the Create.cshtml view.

Listing 24-8. Configuring Input Elements in the Create.cshtml File in the Views/Home Folder

```
@model City

@{  Layout = "_Layout"; }

<form method="post" asp-controller="Home" asp-action="Create"
                     asp-antiforgery="true">
    <div class="form-group">
        <label for="Name">Name:</label>
        <input class="form-control" asp-for="Name" />
    </div>
    <div class="form-group">
        <label for="Country">Country:</label>
        <input class="form-control" asp-for="Country" />
    </div>
    <div class="form-group">
        <label for="Population">Population:</label>
        <input class="form-control" asp-for="Population" />
    </div>
    <button type="submit" class="btn btn-primary">Add</button>
    <a class="btn btn-primary" href="/Home/Index">Cancel</a>
</form>
```

If you run the application and request the /Home/Create URL, you will see that the tag helper has used the property specified by the asp-for attribute to tailor each input element, like this fragment (which omits the anti-CSRF security token):

```
<form method="post" action="/Home/Create">
    <div class="form-group">
        <label for="Name">Name:</label>
        <input class="form-control" type="text" id="Name" name="Name" value="" />
    </div>
    <div class="form-group">
        <label for="Country">Country:</label>
        <input class="form-control" type="text" id="Country"
               name="Country" value="" />
    </div>
    <div class="form-group">
        <label for="Population">Population:</label>
        <input class="form-control" type="number" id="Population"
               name="Population" value="" />
    </div>
    <button type="submit" class="btn btn-primary">Add</button>
    <a class="btn btn-primary" href="/Home/Index">Cancel</a>
</form>
```

The type attribute of the input element tells the browser how to display the element in a form. You can see a simple outcome of this process in the input element for the Population property, for which the type attribute has been set to number. This has been done because the C# type of the Population property is int? and so the tag helper used the type attribute to indicate to the browser that only numeric values will be accepted.

■ **Note** The way that the type attribute is interpreted is left to the browser. Not all browsers respond to all the type values that are defined in the HTML5 specification, and even when they do, there are differences in how they are implemented. The type attribute can be a useful hint for the kind of data you are expecting in a form, but you should use the model validation feature to ensure that users provide usable data, as described in Chapter 27.

Table 24-5 describes the way that different C# property types are used to set the type attribute of input elements.

Table 24-5. *C# Property Types and the Input Type Elements They Generate*

C# Type	Input Element Type Attribute
byte, sbyte, int, uint, short, ushort, long, ulong	number
float, double, decimal	text, with additional attributes for model validation, as described in the following text
bool	checkbox
string	text
DateTime	datetime

The float, double, and decimal types produce input elements whose type is text because not all browsers allow the full range of characters that can be used to express legal values of this type. To provide assistance to the user, the tag helper adds attributes to the input element that are used with the model validation feature, which I describe in Chapter 27.

You can override the default mappings shown in Table 24-5 by defining the type attribute on the input element. The tag helper won't override the value you define, which allows you to take advantage of the different input element types available, such as password or hidden, or the new types added in HTML5 such as number.

One drawback of this approach is that you have to remember to set the type attribute in all the views where input elements are generated for a given model property. If you need to override the default mapping in multiple views, then you can apply the UIHint attribute to the property in the C# model class, specifying one of the values shown in Table 24-6 as the attribute argument.

■ **Tip** The tag helper will set the type attribute of input elements to text if the model property isn't one of the types in Table 24-5 and has not been decorated with the UIHint attribute.

Table 24-6. *The UIHint Arguments and the Input Type Elements They Generate*

Value	Input Element Type Attribute
HiddenInput	hidden
Password	password
Text	text
PhoneNumber	tel
Url	url
EmailAddress	email
Time	time (this value is used to display the time component of a DateTime object)
Date	date (this value is used to display the date component of a DateTime object)
DateTime-local	datetime-local (this value is used to display a DateTime object without providing time zone information)

Formatting Data Values

When the action method provides the view with a view model object, the tag helper uses the value of the property given to the asp-for attribute to set the input element's value attribute. The asp-format attribute is used to specify how that data value is formatted.

To demonstrate, I added a new action method to the Home controller, as shown in Listing 24-9. The action method selects the first City object from the repository and uses it as the view model for the Create view.

Listing 24-9. Adding an Action Method in the HomeController.cs File in the Controllers Folder

```
using Microsoft.AspNetCore.Mvc;
using Cities.Models;
using System.Linq;

namespace Cities.Controllers {

    public class HomeController : Controller {
        private IRepository repository;

        public HomeController(IRepository repo) {
            repository = repo;
        }

        public ViewResult Index() => View(repository.Cities);

        public ViewResult Edit() => View("Create", repository.Cities.First());
```

```
        public ViewResult Create() => View();

        [HttpPost]
        [ValidateAntiForgeryToken]
        public IActionResult Create(City city) {
            repository.AddCity(city);
            return RedirectToAction("Index");
        }
    }
}
```

If you run the application, request the /Home/Edit URL, and examine the HTML that has been sent to the browser, you will see that the value attributes have been populated using the view model object, like this:

```
<input class="form-control" type="number" id="Population"
       name="Population" value="8539000" />
```

The asp-format attribute accepts a value that will be passed to the standard C# string formatting system, as shown in Listing 24-10.

Listing 24-10. Formatting a Data Value in the Create.cshtml File in the Views/Home Folder

```
@model City

@{  Layout = "_Layout"; }

<form method="post" asp-controller="Home" asp-action="Create"
                    asp-antiforgery="true">
    <div class="form-group">
        <label for="Name">Name:</label>
        <input class="form-control" asp-for="Name" />
    </div>
    <div class="form-group">
        <label for="Country">Country:</label>
        <input class="form-control" asp-for="Country" />
    </div>
    <div class="form-group">
        <label for="Population">Population:</label>
        <input class="form-control" asp-for="Population" asp-format="{0:#,###}" />
    </div>
    <button type="submit" class="btn btn-primary">Add</button>
    <a class="btn btn-primary" href="/Home/Index">Cancel</a>
</form>
```

The attribute value is used verbatim, which means you have to include the curly brace characters and the 0: reference, as well as the format you require. If you run the application and request the /Home/Edit URL, you will see that the Population value has been formatted like this:

```
<input class="form-control" type="number" id="Population"
       name="Population" value="8,539,000" />
```

This feature should be used with caution because you must ensure that the rest of the application is configured to support the format you use. In this case, I have created a problem by formatting the Population value. The tag helper has set the type attribute of the input element to number, using the default mappings described in Table 24-5 for the Population property, but the format string I have specified has generated a value attribute that contains non-numeric characters. The result is that browsers that respect the number element type (not all do, remember) may not display any value in the element.

You must also ensure that the application is able to parse values in the format you use. The example application expects to receive a Population value that can be parsed into an int, and values that contain non-numeric characters will cause validation errors, as described in Chapter 27.

Applying Formatting via the Model Class

If you always want to use the same formatting for a model property, then you can decorate the C# class with the DisplayFormat attribute, which is defined in the System.ComponentModel.DataAnnotations namespace. The DisplayFormat attribute requires two arguments to format a data value: the DataFormatString argument specifies the formatting string, and the ApplyFormatInEditMode argument specifies that formatting should be used when values are being edited. In Listing 24-11, I have decorated the Population attribute with the DisplayFormat attribute, using a format that can be processed by both the application and the browser as a number.

Listing 24-11. Applying a Formatting Attribute to the Model Class in the City.cs File in the Models Folder

```
using System.ComponentModel.DataAnnotations;

namespace Cities.Models {

    public class City {

        public string Name { get; set; }
        public string Country { get; set; }

        [DisplayFormat(DataFormatString = "{0:F2}", ApplyFormatInEditMode = true)]
        public int? Population { get; set; }
    }
}
```

The `asp-format` attribute takes precedence over the `DisplayFormat` attribute, so I have removed the attribute from the view, as shown in Listing 24-12.

Listing 24-12. Removing the Formatting Attribute in the Create.cshtml File in the Views/Home Folder

```
@model City

@{ Layout = "_Layout"; }

<form method="post" asp-controller="Home" asp-action="Create"
    asp-antiforgery="true">
    <div class="form-group">
        <label for="Name">Name:</label>
        <input class="form-control" asp-for="Name" />
    </div>
    <div class="form-group">
        <label for="Country">Country:</label>
        <input class="form-control" asp-for="Country" />
    </div>
    <div class="form-group">
        <label for="Population">Population:</label>
        <input class="form-control" asp-for="Population" />
        </div>
    <button type="submit" class="btn btn-primary">Add</button>
    <a class="btn btn-primary" href="/Home/Index">Cancel</a>
</form>
```

If you run the application and request the /Home/Edit URL, you will see that the `Population` value has been formatted with two decimal fractions, like this:

```
<input class="form-control" type="number" id="Population"
    name="Population" value="8539000.00" />
```

Working with Label Elements

The `label` element is transformed by the `LabelTagHelper` class, which uses the view model class to ensure that labels are typo-free and consistent. There is only one supported attribute, which is described in Table 24-7.

Table 24-7. The Built-in Tag Helper Attribute for Label Elements

Name	Description
asp-for	This attribute is used to specify the view model property that the label element represents.

The tag helper will use the name of the view model property to set the value of the `for` attribute and the contents of the `label` element. In Listing 24-13, I have applied the `asp-for` attribute to the `label` elements in the form they will be transformed by the tag helper.

Listing 24-13. Applying the Label Tag Helper in the Create.cshtml File in the Views/Home Folder

```
@model City

@{ Layout = "_Layout"; }

<form method="post" asp-controller="Home" asp-action="Create"
        asp-antiforgery="true">
    <div class="form-group">
        <label asp-for="Name"></label>
        <input class="form-control" asp-for="Name" />
    </div>
    <div class="form-group">
        <label asp-for="Country"></label>
        <input class="form-control" asp-for="Country" />
    </div>
    <div class="form-group">
        <label asp-for="Population"></label>
        <input class="form-control" asp-for="Population" />
    </div>
    <button type="submit" class="btn btn-primary">Add</button>
    <a class="btn btn-primary" href="/Home/Index">Cancel</a>
</form>
```

Since the label elements are empty, the tag helper will use the model property names as the elements'
content and set the for attribute, which tells the browser which input element each label is associated
with. If you run the example, request the /Home/Create or /Home/Edit URL, and inspect the HTML sent to
the browser, you will see the following output elements:

```
<form method="post" action="/Home/Create">
    <div class="form-group">
        <label for="Name">Name</label>
        <input class="form-control" type="text" id="Name"
                name="Name" value="London" />
    </div>
    <div class="form-group">
        <label for="Country">Country</label>
        <input class="form-control" type="text" id="Country"
                name="Country" value="UK" />
    </div>
    <div class="form-group">
        <label for="Population">Population</label>
        <input class="form-control" type="number" id="Population"
                name="Population" value="8539000.00" />
    </div>
    <button type="submit" class="btn btn-primary">Add</button>
    <a class="btn btn-primary" href="/Home/Index">Cancel</a>
</form>
```

You can override the value used as the label element's content by applying the Display attribute to the
model class property, as shown in Listing 24-14.

Listing 24-14. Changing the Description for a Model Property in the City.cs File in the Models Folder

```
using System.ComponentModel.DataAnnotations;

namespace Cities.Models {

    public class City {

        [Display(Name = "City")]
        public string Name { get; set; }

        public string Country { get; set; }

        [DisplayFormat(DataFormatString = "{0:F2}", ApplyFormatInEditMode = true)]
        public int? Population { get; set; }
    }
}
```

The Name argument specifies the value to use instead of the property name. If you run the example, request the /Home/Create URL, and examine the HTML sent to the browser, you will see that the content of the label element has changed, like this:

```
<div class="form-group">
    <label for="Name">City</label>
    <input class="form-control" type="text" id="Name" name="Name" value="London" />
</div>
```

Notice that the value of the for attribute has not changed, so the browser knows that the label element is associated with a specific input element, which is not affected by the Display attribute.

■ **Tip**   You can prevent the tag helper from setting the content of a label element by defining it yourself. This is useful if you want your label elements to contain more than just the name of a property, which is all that the built-in tag helper can provide.

Working with Select and Option Elements

The select and option elements are used to provide the user with a fixed set of choices, rather than the open data entry that is possible with an input element. The SelectTagHelper is responsible for transforming select elements and supports the attributes described in Table 24-8.

Table 24-8. *The Built-in Tag Helper Attributes for select Elements*

Name	Description
asp-for	This attribute is used to specify the view model property that the select element represents.
asp-items	This attribute is used to specify a source of values for the option elements contained within the select element.

The `asp-for` attribute sets the value of the `for` and `id` attributes to reflect the model property that it receives. In Listing 24-15, I have replaced the `input` element for the `Country` property with a `select` element that defines the `asp-for` attribute.

Listing 24-15. Using a select Element in the Create.cshtml File in the Views/Home Folder

```
@model City

@{ Layout = "_Layout"; }

<form method="post" asp-controller="Home" asp-action="Create"
        asp-antiforgery="true">
    <div class="form-group">
        <label asp-for="Name"></label>
        <input class="form-control" asp-for="Name" />
    </div>
    <div class="form-group">
        <label asp-for="Country"></label>
        <select class="form-control" asp-for="Country">
            <option disabled selected value="">Select a Country</option>
            <option>UK</option>
            <option>USA</option>
            <option>France</option>
            <option>China</option>
        </select>
    </div>
    <div class="form-group">
        <label asp-for="Population"></label>
        <input class="form-control" asp-for="Population" />
    </div>
    <button type="submit" class="btn btn-primary">Add</button>
    <a class="btn btn-primary" href="/Home/Index">Cancel</a>
</form>
```

I have manually populated the `select` element with `option` elements that provide a range of countries for the user to choose from. If you run the application and request the /Home/Create URL, you will see that the HTML sent to the browser contains the following `select` element:

```
<select class="form-control" id="Country" name="Country">
    <option disabled selected value="">Select a Country</option>
    <option>UK</option>
    <option>USA</option>
    <option>France</option>
    <option>China</option>
</select>
```

If you request the /Home/Edit URL and examine the HTML sent to the browser, you will see that the value of the Country property of the view model object has been used to change the selected option element, like this:

```
<select class="form-control" id="Country" name="Country">
    <option disabled selected value="">Select a Country</option>
    <option selected="selected">UK</option>
    <option>USA</option>
    <option>France</option>
    <option>China</option>
</select>
```

The task of selecting an option element is performed by the OptionTagHelper class, which receives instructions from the SelectTagHelper through the TagHelperContext.Items collection. As I explained in Chapter 23, this collection is used by tag helpers that need to work together, and I take advantage of the data that the SelectTagHelper adds to the Items collection in the next section when I create a custom tag helper to work around a limitation of the built-in one.

Using a Data Source to Populate a select Element

Explicitly defining the option elements for a select element is a useful approach for choices that always have the same possible values but doesn't help when you need to provide options that are taken from the data model or where you need the same set of options in multiple views and don't want to manually maintain duplicated content.

Generating Option Elements from an enum

If you have a fixed set of options to present to the user and don't want to duplicate them in views throughout the application, then you can use an enum. I added a class file called CountryNames.cs to the Models folder and used it to define the enum shown in Listing 24-16.

Listing 24-16. The Contents of the CountryNames.cs File in the Models Folder

```
namespace Cities.Models {

    public enum CountryNames {
        UK,
        USA,
        France,
        China
    }
}
```

You can't use an enum directly in the asp-items attribute because the tag helper expects to work with a sequence of SelectListItem objects. However, there is a convenient helper method available that performs the conversion that is required, as shown in Listing 24-17.

Listing 24-17. Using an enum in the Create.cshtml File in the Views/Home Folder

```
@model City

@{ Layout = "_Layout"; }

<form method="post" asp-controller="Home" asp-action="Create"
        asp-antiforgery="true">
    <div class="form-group">
        <label asp-for="Name"></label>
        <input class="form-control" asp-for="Name" />
    </div>
    <div class="form-group">
        <label asp-for="Country"></label>
        <select class="form-control" asp-for="Country"
                asp-items="@new SelectList(Enum.GetNames(typeof(CountryNames)))">
            <option disabled selected value="">Select a Country</option>
        </select>
    </div>
    <div class="form-group">
        <label asp-for="Population"></label>
        <input class="form-control" asp-for="Population" />
    </div>
    <button type="submit" class="btn btn-primary">Add</button>
    <a class="btn btn-primary" href="/Home/Index">Cancel</a>
</form>
```

When using an enumeration, the best way to generate the option elements is to provide the asp-items attribute with a SelectList object that is populated with the enum value names. Behind the scenes, the SelectTagHelper class generates option elements from an IEnumerable<SelectListItem>, and the SelectList class implements this interface.

If you run the application and request the /Home/Create or /Home/Edit URL, you will see that the HTML sent to the browser includes a set of option elements that correspond to the values in the enum, as follows:

```
<select class="form-control" id="Country" name="Country">
    <option disabled selected value="">Select a Country</option>
    <option>UK</option>
    <option>USA</option>
    <option>France</option>
    <option>China</option>
</select>
```

Notice that the tag helper has left the placeholder option element alone. Any option elements you define explicitly remain in place, which means that you don't have to mix placeholders with your data values.

Generating Option Elements from the Model

If you need to generate option elements to reflect the data in the model, then the simplest approach is to provide the data required to generate the elements through the view bag, as shown in Listing 24-18.

Listing 24-18. Providing Data via the View Bag in the HomeController.cs File in the Controllers Folder

```
using Microsoft.AspNetCore.Mvc;
using Cities.Models;
using System.Linq;
using Microsoft.AspNetCore.Mvc.Rendering;

namespace Cities.Controllers {

    public class HomeController : Controller {
        private IRepository repository;

        public HomeController(IRepository repo) {
            repository = repo;
        }

        public ViewResult Index() => View(repository.Cities);

        public ViewResult Edit() {
            ViewBag.Countries = new SelectList(repository.Cities
                .Select(c => c.Country).Distinct());
            return View("Create", repository.Cities.First());
        }

        public ViewResult Create() {
            ViewBag.Countries = new SelectList(repository.Cities
                .Select(c => c.Country).Distinct());
            return View();
        }

        [HttpPost]
        [ValidateAntiForgeryToken]
        public IActionResult Create(City city) {
            repository.AddCity(city);
            return RedirectToAction("Index");
        }
    }
}
```

The Edit and Create action methods set the ViewBag.Countries property to a SelectList object that is populated with the unique values for the City.Country property in the repository. In Listing 24-19, I have used the asp-items attribute to tell the tag helper to obtain the data for the option elements from this view bag property.

Listing 24-19. Using the View Bag for option Elements in the Create.cshtml File in the Views/Home Folder

```
@model City

@{ Layout = "_Layout"; }

<form method="post" asp-controller="Home" asp-action="Create"
        asp-antiforgery="true">
    <div class="form-group">
        <label asp-for="Name"></label>
        <input class="form-control" asp-for="Name" />
    </div>
    <div class="form-group">
        <label asp-for="Country"></label>
        <select class="form-control" asp-for="Country" asp-items="ViewBag.Countries">
            <option disabled selected value="">Select a Country</option>
        </select>
    </div>
    <div class="form-group">
        <label asp-for="Population"></label>
        <input class="form-control" asp-for="Population" />
    </div>
    <button type="submit" class="btn btn-primary">Add</button>
    <a class="btn btn-primary" href="/Home/Index">Cancel</a>
</form>
```

If you run the application and request the /Home/Create or /Home/Edit URL, you will see that option elements are created as follows:

```
<select class="form-control" id="Country" name="Country">
    <option disabled selected value="">Select a Country</option>
    <option selected>UK</option>
    <option>USA</option>
    <option>France</option>
</select>
```

Using a Custom Tag Helper to Generate Option Elements from the Model

The problem with passing the data required for option elements through the view bag is that you must remember to generate the data in every action method that renders the view that uses the tag helper. This leads to code duplication, which you can get a sense of in Listing 24-18, and makes it harder to test and maintain a controller properly.

A better approach is to create a custom tag helper that supplements the built-in SelectTagHelper class. I added a class file called SelectOptionTagHelper.cs to the Infrastructure/TagHelper folder and defined the class shown in Listing 24-20.

Listing 24-20. The SelectOptionTagHelper.cs File in the Infrastructure/TagHelper Folder

```
using System;
using System.Linq;
using System.Reflection;
using System.Threading.Tasks;
using Cities.Models;
using Microsoft.AspNetCore.Mvc.ViewFeatures;
using Microsoft.AspNetCore.Razor.TagHelpers;

namespace Cities.Infrastructure.TagHelpers {

    [HtmlTargetElement("select", Attributes = "model-for")]
    public class SelectOptionTagHelper : TagHelper {
        private IRepository repository;

        public SelectOptionTagHelper(IRepository repo) {
            repository = repo;
        }

        public ModelExpression ModelFor { get; set; }

        public override async Task ProcessAsync(TagHelperContext context,
                TagHelperOutput output) {

            output.Content.AppendHtml(
                (await output.GetChildContentAsync(false)).GetContent());

            string selected = ModelFor.Model as string;

            PropertyInfo property = typeof(City)
                .GetTypeInfo().GetDeclaredProperty(ModelFor.Name);
            foreach (string country in repository.Cities
                    .Select(c => property.GetValue(c)).Distinct()) {
                if (selected != null && selected.Equals(country,
                        StringComparison.OrdinalIgnoreCase)) {
                    output.Content
                        .AppendHtml($"<option selected>{country}</option>");
                } else {
                    output.Content.AppendHtml($"<option>{country}</option>");
                }
            }
            output.Attributes.SetAttribute("Name", ModelFor.Name);
            output.Attributes.SetAttribute("Id", ModelFor.Name);
        }
    }
}
```

This tag helper operates on select elements with a model-for attribute and uses the dependency injection to receive a repository object that it can use to access model data independently from the controller that is rendering the view. This tag helper defines the asynchronous ProcessAsync method because it simplifies the process of obtaining and preserving any existing content of the select element, which is done through the GetChildContentAsync method.

The SelectTagHelper indicates the names of the option elements that should be selected through an entry in the Items collection using its own type as the key. The tag helper gets a list of the selected items and uses it in combination with the results of a LINQ query to generate option elements for each unique value in the repository. In Listing 24-21, I have updated the select element so that the asp-items attribute is replaced with the model-for attribute, and I've added an @addTagHelper expression that enables the custom tag helper just for this view.

Listing 24-21. Enabling the Custom Tag Helper in the Create.cshtml File in the Views/Home Folder

```
@model City
@addTagHelper Cities.Infrastructure.TagHelpers.SelectOptionTagHelper, Cities

@{ Layout = "_Layout"; }

<form method="post" asp-controller="Home" asp-action="Create"
    asp-antiforgery="true">
    <div class="form-group">
        <label asp-for="Name"></label>
        <input class="form-control" asp-for="Name" />
    </div>
    <div class="form-group">
        <label asp-for="Country"></label>
        <select class="form-control" model-for="Country">
            <option disabled selected value="">Select a Country</option>
        </select>
    </div>
    <div class="form-group">
        <label asp-for="Population"></label>
        <input class="form-control" asp-for="Population" />
    </div>
    <button type="submit" class="btn btn-primary">Add</button>
    <a class="btn btn-primary" href="/Home/Index">Cancel</a>
</form>
```

The new tag helper generates the same output but does so without needing the view bag data that the built-in helper requires. I like this approach because it keeps the action methods focused on their specific tasks and preserves the overall shape of the application.

Working with Text Areas

The textarea element is used to solicit a larger amount of text from the user and is typically used for unstructured data, such as notes or observations. The TextAreaTagHelper is responsible for transforming textarea elements and supports the single attribute described in Table 24-9.

Table 24-9. The Built-in Tag Helper Attributes for TextArea Elements

Name	Description
asp-for	This attribute is used to specify the view model property that the textarea element represents.

The TextAreaTagHelper is relatively simple, and the value provided for the asp-for attribute is used to set the id and name attributes on the textarea element. To demonstrate this tag helper, I added a new property to the City model class, as shown in Listing 24-22.

Listing 24-22. Adding a Property in the City.cs File in the Models Folder

```
using System.ComponentModel.DataAnnotations;

namespace Cities.Models {

    public class City {

        [Display(Name = "City")]
        public string Name { get; set; }

        public string Country { get; set; }

        [DisplayFormat(DataFormatString = "{0:F2}", ApplyFormatInEditMode = true)]
        public int? Population { get; set; }

        public string Notes { get; set; }
    }
}
```

In Listing 24-23, I added a textarea element to the Create.cshtml view, using the asp-for attribute to associate the element with the Notes property of the City class.

Listing 24-23. Adding a Text Area in the Create.cshtml File in the Views/Home Folder

```
@model City
@addTagHelper Cities.Infrastructure.TagHelpers.SelectOptionTagHelper, Cities

@{ Layout = "_Layout"; }

<form method="post" asp-controller="Home" asp-action="Create"
      asp-antiforgery="true">
    <div class="form-group">
        <label asp-for="Name"></label>
        <input class="form-control" asp-for="Name" />
    </div>
    <div class="form-group">
        <label asp-for="Country"></label>
        <select class="form-control" asp-for="Country" asp-items="ViewBag.Countries">
            <option disabled selected value="">Select a Country</option>
        </select>
    </div>
```

```
    <div class="form-group">
        <label asp-for="Population"></label>
        <input class="form-control" asp-for="Population" />
    </div>
    <div class="form-group">
        <label asp-for="Notes"></label>
        <textarea class="form-control" asp-for="Notes"></textarea>
    </div>
    <button type="submit" class="btn btn-primary">Add</button>
    <a class="btn btn-primary" href="/Home/Index">Cancel</a>
</form>
```

If you run the application and request the /Home/Create or /Home/Edit URL, you will see that the HTML sent to the browser includes a textarea element like this:

```
<div class="form-group">
    <label for="Notes">Notes</label>
    <textarea id="Notes" name="Notes"></textarea>
</div>
```

The TextAreaTagHelper is relatively simple, but it provides consistency with the rest of the form element tag helpers that I have described in this chapter.

Understanding the Validation Form Tag Helpers

There are two other tag helpers that relate to HTML forms, which I have described in Table 24-10 for completeness but which I describe in more detail in Chapter 27. These helpers are used to provide the user with feedback when the data the user provides doesn't meet the expectations of the application.

Table 24-10. The Validation Tag Helper Classes

Name	Description
ValidationMessage	This tag helper is used to provide validation feedback about a single form element.
ValidationSummary	This tag helper is used to provide validation feedback about all the elements in a form.

Summary

In this chapter, I described the built-in tag helpers that are used to transform the HTML form elements. These tag helpers ensure that forms are generated directly from the model class, which reduces the potential for errors and provides a consistent approach for writing Razor views. In the next chapter, I describe the remaining built-in tag helpers, which operate on a range of HTML elements.

CHAPTER 25

■ ■ ■

Using the Other Built-in Tag Helpers

The tag helpers that I described in Chapter 24 are focused on producing HTML forms, but they are not the only built-in tag helpers that are provided by ASP.NET Core MVC. In this chapter, I describe tag helpers that manage JavaScript and CSS stylesheets, create URLs for anchor elements, provide cache busting for image elements, and support data caching. I also describe the tag helper that provides support for application-relative URLs, which help ensure that browsers can access static content when an application is deployed into an environment shared with other applications. Table 25-1 summarizes the chapter.

Table 25-1. *Chapter Summary*

Problem	Solution	Listing
Include content based on the hosting environment	Use the environment element	2, 8
Select JavaScript files	Apply the asp-src-include and asp-src-exclude attributes to a script element	3–7
Use a CDN for JavaScript files	Apply the asp-fallback attributes to a script element	9, 10
Select CSS files	Apply the asp-href-include and asp-href-exclude attributes to a link element	11
Use a CDN for CSS files	Apply the asp-fallback attributes to a link element	12
Generate a URL for an anchor element	Use the AnchorTagHelper helper	13
Ensure that changes to images are detected	Apply the asp-append-version attribute to an img element	14
Cache data	Use the cache element	15–23
Create application relative URLs	Prefix URLs with a ~ character	24–26

© Adam Freeman 2017
A. Freeman, *Pro ASP.NET Core MVC 2*, https://doi.org/10.1007/978-1-4842-3150-0_25

Preparing the Example Project

I am going to continue using the Cities project from Chapter 24. To prepare for this chapter, I created the wwwroot/images folder and added an image file called city.png. This is a public domain panorama of the New York City skyline, as shown in Figure 25-1.

Figure 25-1. *Adding an image to the project*

This image file is included in the source code for this chapter, which is available in the GitHub repository for this book (https://github.com/apress/pro-asp.net-core-mvc-2). You can substitute your own image if you don't want to download the example project.

The other change required for this chapter is to add jQuery to the project using Bower, as shown in Listing 25-1.

Listing 25-1. Add jQuery to the bower.json File in the Cities Folder

```
{
  "name": "asp.net",
  "private": true,
  "dependencies": {
    "bootstrap": "4.0.0-alpha.6",
    "jquery": "3.2.1"
  }
}
```

If you run the application, you will be able to list the objects in the repository and create new ones, as illustrated in Figure 25-2.

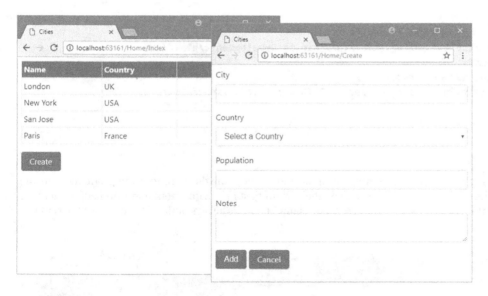

Figure 25-2. *Running the example application*

Using the Hosting Environment Tag Helper

The EnvironmentTagHelper class is applied to the custom environment element and determines whether a region of content is included in the HTML sent to the browser based on the hosting environment, which I described in Chapter 14. This may not seem like the most exciting place to start, but this tag helper is needed to make the best use of some related features that I describe later. The environment element relies on the names attribute, which I have described in Table 25-2 for future quick reference.

Table 25-2. *The Built-in Tag Helper Attribute for environment Elements*

Name	Description
names	This attribute is used to specify a comma-separated list of hosting environment names for which the content contained within the environment element will be included in the HTML sent to the client.

In Listing 25-2, I have added environment elements to the shared layout including different content in the view for the development and production hosting environments.

Listing 25-2. Using the environment Element in the _Layout.cshtml File in the Views/Shared Folder

```
<!DOCTYPE html>
<html>
<head>
    <meta name="viewport" content="width=device-width" />
    <title>Cities</title>
    <link href="/lib/bootstrap/dist/css/bootstrap.css" rel="stylesheet" />
</head>
```

```
<body class="m-1 p-1">
    <environment names="development">
        <div class="m-1 p-1 bg-info"><h2>This is Development</h2></div>
    </environment>
    <environment names="production">
        <div class="m-1 p-1 bg-danger"><h2>This is Production</h2></div>
    </environment>
    <div>@RenderBody()</div>
</body>
</html>
```

Figure 25-3 shows the effect of running the application in both the development and production hosting environments. The environment element checks the current hosting environment name and either includes the content it contains or omits it (the environment element itself is always omitted from the HTML sent to the client).

Figure 25-3. *Managing content using the hosting environment*

Using the JavaScript and CSS Tag Helpers

The next category of built-in tag helpers is used to manage JavaScript files and CSS stylesheets through the script and link elements, which are usually included in a shared layout. As you will see in the sections that follow, these tag helpers are powerful and flexible but require close attention to avoid creating unexpected results.

Managing JavaScript Files

The ScriptTagHelper class is the built-in tag helper for script elements and is used to manage the inclusion of JavaScript files in views using the attributes described in Table 25-3, which I describe in the sections that follow.

Table 25-3. *The Built-in Tag Helper Attributes for script Elements*

Name	Description
asp-src-include	This attribute is used to specify JavaScript files that will be included in the view.
asp-src-exclude	This attribute is used to specify JavaScript files that will be excluded from the view.
asp-append-version	This attribute is used for cache busting, as described in the "Understanding Cache Busting" sidebar.
asp-fallback-src	This attribute is used to specify a fallback JavaScript file to use if there is a problem with a content delivery network.
asp-fallback-src-include	This attribute is used to select JavaScript files that will be used if there is a content delivery network problem.
asp-fallback-src-exclude	This attribute is used to exclude JavaScript files to present their use when there is a content delivery network problem.
asp-fallback-test	This attribute is used to specify a fragment of JavaScript that will be used to determine whether JavaScript code has been correctly loaded from a content delivery network.

Selecting JavaScript Files

The asp-src-include attribute is used to include JavaScript files in a view using globbing patterns. Globbing patterns support a set of wildcards that are used to match files and Table 25-4 describes the most common globbing patterns.

Table 25-4. *Common Globbing Patterns*

Pattern	Example	Description
?	js/src?.js	This pattern matches any single character except /. The example matches any file contained in the js directory whose name is src, followed by any character, followed by .js, such as js/src1.js and js/srcX.js but not js/src123.js or js/mydir/src1.js.
*	js/*.js	This pattern matches any number of characters except /. The example matches any file contained in the js directory with the .js file extension, such as js/src1.js and js/src123.js but not js/mydir/src1.js.
**	js/**/*.js	This pattern matches any number of characters including /. The example matches any file with the .js extension that is contained within the js directory or any subdirectory, such as /js/src1.js and /js/mydir/src1.js.

Using a globbing pattern with the asp-src-include attribute means that a view will always include the JavaScript files in the application, even if the name or path of the files changes or files are added or removed. In Listing 25-3, I have selected the JavaScript files for the jQuery package, which Bower installs into the wwwroot/lib/jquery/dist folder.

Listing 25-3. Selecting JavaScript Files in the _Layout.cshtml File in the Views/Shared Folder

```
<!DOCTYPE html>
<html>
<head>
    <meta name="viewport" content="width=device-width" />
    <title>Cities</title>
    <script asp-src-include="/lib/jquery/dist/**/*.js"></script>
    <link href="/lib/bootstrap/dist/css/bootstrap.css" rel="stylesheet" />
</head>
<body class="m-1 p-1">
    <div>@RenderBody()</div>
</body>
</html>
```

The pattern that I used in this example is a common one. Patterns are evaluated within the wwwroot folder, and the jQuery library is delivered as a single JavaScript file called jquery.js.

The globbing pattern tries to select the jQuery file while accommodating any future changes in the way that jQuery is distributed, such as changing the JavaScript file name. If you run the example and examine the HTML sent to the client, you will see that it contains a problem, as follows:

```
<head>
    <meta name="viewport" content="width=device-width" />
    <title>Cities</title>
    <script src="/lib/jquery/dist/core.js"></script>
    <script src="/lib/jquery/dist/jquery.js"></script>
    <script src="/lib/jquery/dist/jquery.min.js"></script>
    <script src="/lib/jquery/dist/jquery.slim.js"></script>
    <script src="/lib/jquery/dist/jquery.slim.min.js"></script>
    <link href="/lib/bootstrap/dist/css/bootstrap.css" rel="stylesheet" />
</head>
```

The ScriptTagHelper class generates a script element for every file that matches the pattern passed to the asp-src-include attribute. Rather than just selecting the jquery.js file, there are also elements for the jquery.min.js file, which is the minified version of the jquery.js file, as well as regular and minified version of the core and slim versions of the jQuery library.

You might not have realized that the jQuery distribution contains so many files because Visual Studio hides them by default. To reveal the full contents of the wwwroot/lib/jquery/dist folder, you have to expand the jquery.js item in the Solution Explorer and then do the same again to the items it contains, as shown in Figure 25-4.

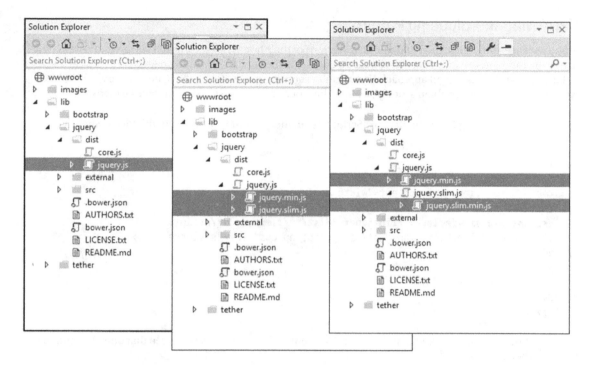

Figure 25-4. *Revealing the full contents of a directory in the Solution Explorer*

The pattern that I used in Listing 25-3 has sent the jQuery code to the browser several times, which wastes bandwidth and slows the application down. For some libraries, it can also result in errors or unexpected behavior. There are three ways to solve this problem, which I describe in the following sections.

USING SOURCE MAPS

JavaScript files are minified to make them smaller, which means they can be delivered to the client faster and using less bandwidth. The minification process removes all the whitespace from the file and renames functions and variables so that meaningful names such as `myHelpfullyNamedFunction` will be represented by a smaller number of characters, such as `x1`. When using the browser's JavaScript debugger to track down problems in your minified code, names like `x1` make it almost impossible to follow progress through the code.

The `jquery.min.map` file is a *source map*, which some browsers can use to help debug minified code by providing a map between the minified code and the developer-readable, un-minified source file.

As I write this, source maps are not a universally supported feature, but you can use them on the most recent versions of Chrome and Edge. In the case of Chrome, for example, the browser will automatically request the source map file if the developer tools window is open, which means that you don't can always send the minified version of your JavaScript files to the browser and still be able to debug them easily.

Narrowing the Globbing Pattern

Many packages provide regular and minified versions of their JavaScript files, and if you are only ever going to use the minified version, then you can restrict the set of files that the globbing pattern matches, as shown in Listing 25-4. This is a good approach if you don't expect to have to debug the jQuery library, which is well-written and causes few problems, or if you know that your target browsers support source maps.

Listing 25-4. Selecting Only Minified JavaScript Files in the _Layout.cshtml File in the Views/Shared Folder

```
<!DOCTYPE html>
<html>
<head>
    <meta name="viewport" content="width=device-width" />
    <title>Cities</title>
    <script asp-src-include="/lib/jquery/dist/**/*.min.js"></script>
    <link href="/lib/bootstrap/dist/css/bootstrap.css" rel="stylesheet" />
</head>
<body class="m-1 p-1">
    <div>@RenderBody()</div>
</body>
</html>
```

If you run the example and examine the HTML sent to the browser, you will see that only the minified files have been included:

```
<head>
    <meta name="viewport" content="width=device-width" />
    <title>Cities</title>
    <script src="/lib/jquery/dist/jquery.min.js">
    </script><script src="/lib/jquery/dist/jquery.slim.min.js"></script>
    <link href="/lib/bootstrap/dist/css/bootstrap.css" rel="stylesheet" />
</head>
```

Narrowing the pattern for the JavaScript files has helped but the browser will still end up with the normal and slim versions of the jQuery library (the slim version omits some less commonly- used functions - see jquery.com for details). To narrow the selection further, I can include slim in the globbing pattern, as shown in Listing 25-5.

Listing 25-5. Narrowing the Focus in the _Layout.cshtml File in the Views/Shared Folder

```
<!DOCTYPE html>
<html>
<head>
    <meta name="viewport" content="width=device-width" />
    <title>Cities</title>
    <script asp-src-include="/lib/jquery/dist/**/*.slim.min.js"></script>
    <link href="/lib/bootstrap/dist/css/bootstrap.css" rel="stylesheet" />
</head>
<body class="m-1 p-1">
    <div>@RenderBody()</div>
</body>
</html>
```

The result is that only one version of the jQuery file will be sent to the browser, while still preserving the flexibility for the location of the file:

```
<head>
    <meta name="viewport" content="width=device-width" />
    <title>Cities</title>
    <script src="/lib/jquery/dist/jquery.slim.min.js"></script>
    <link href="/lib/bootstrap/dist/css/bootstrap.css" rel="stylesheet" />
</head>
```

Excluding Files

Narrowing the pattern for the JavaScript files helps when you want to select a file whose name contains a specific term, such as slim. It isn't helpful when the file you want doesn't have that term, such as when you want the full version of the minified file. Fortunately, you can use the asp-src-exclude attribute to remove files from the list matched by the asp-src-include attribute, as shown in Listing 25-6.

Listing 25-6. Excluding Files in the _Layout.cshtml File in the Views/Shared Folder

```
<!DOCTYPE html>
<html>
<head>
    <meta name="viewport" content="width=device-width" />
    <title>Cities</title>
    <script asp-src-include="/lib/jquery/dist/**/*.min.js"
        asp-src-exclude="**.slim.**">
    </script>
    <link href="/lib/bootstrap/dist/css/bootstrap.css" rel="stylesheet" />
</head>
<body class="m-1 p-1">
    <div>@RenderBody()</div>
</body>
</html>
```

Run the application and examine the HTML sent to the browser and you will see that only the full minified version of the jQuery library has been included:

```
<head>
    <meta name="viewport" content="width=device-width" />
    <title>Cities</title>
    <script src="/lib/jquery/dist/jquery.min.js"></script>
    <link href="/lib/bootstrap/dist/css/bootstrap.css" rel="stylesheet" />
</head>
```

The same technique can be used when you want the non-minified versions of the file, which can be useful during development, as shown in Listing 25-7.

Listing 25-7. Selecting a Non-Minified File in the _Layout.cshtml File in the Views/Shared Folder

```
<!DOCTYPE html>
<html>
<head>
    <meta name="viewport" content="width=device-width" />
    <title>Cities</title>
    <script asp-src-include="/lib/jquery/dist/**/j*.js"
            asp-src-exclude="**.slim.**,**.min.**">
    </script>
    <link href="/lib/bootstrap/dist/css/bootstrap.css" rel="stylesheet" />
</head>
<body class="m-1 p-1">
    <div>@RenderBody()</div>
</body>
</html>
```

Notice that I am able to specify multiple terms by separating them with a comma. If you run the application and examine the HTML sent to the browser, you will see that only the un-minified version of the JavaScript file has been included:

```
<head>
    <meta name="viewport" content="width=device-width" />
    <title>Cities</title>
    <script src="/lib/jquery/dist/jquery.js"></script>
    <link href="/lib/bootstrap/dist/css/bootstrap.css" rel="stylesheet" />
</head>
```

Using the Hosting Environment to Select Files

A common approach is to work with the regular JavaScript files during development, which makes debugging easy, and use the minified files in production, which reduces bandwidth. This can be achieved by using the environment element to selectively include script elements based on the hosting environment, as shown in Listing 25-8.

Listing 25-8. Selecting Files in the _Layout.cshtml File in the Views/Shared Folder

```
<!DOCTYPE html>
<html>
<head>
    <meta name="viewport" content="width=device-width" />
    <title>Cities</title>
    <environment names="development">
        <script asp-src-include="/lib/jquery/dist/**/j*.js"
                asp-src-exclude="**.slim.**,**.min.**">
        </script>
    </environment>
    <environment names="staging, production">
        <script asp-src-include="/lib/jquery/dist/**/*.min.js"
                asp-src-exclude="**.slim.**">
        </script>
    </environment>
```

```
    <link href="/lib/bootstrap/dist/css/bootstrap.css" rel="stylesheet" />
</head>
<body class="m-1 p-1">
    <div>@RenderBody()</div>
</body>
</html>
```

This approach has the advantage of adapting the application to the hosting environment but does mean that you have to write and maintain multiple sets of script elements.

UNDERSTANDING CACHE BUSTING

Static content, such as images, CSS stylesheets, and JavaScript files, is often cached to stop requests for content that rarely changes from reaching the application servers. Caching can be done in different ways: the browser can be told to cache content by the server, the application can use cache servers to supplement the application servers, or the content can be distributed using a content delivery network. Not all caching will be under your control. Large corporations, for example, often install caches to reduce their bandwidth demands since a substantial percentage of requests tend to go to the same sites or applications.

One problem with caching is that clients don't immediately receive new versions of static files when you deploy them because their requests are still being serviced by previously cached content. Eventually, the cached content will expire and the new content will be used, but that leaves a period where the dynamic content generated by the application's controllers is out of step with the static content being delivered by the caches. This can lead to layout problems or unexpected application behavior, depending on the content that has been updated.

Addressing this problem is called *cache busting*. The idea is to allow caches to handle static content but immediately reflect any changes that are made at the server. The tag helper classes support cache busting by adding a query string to the URLs for static content that includes a checksum that acts as a version number. For JavaScript files, for example, the ScriptTagHelper class supports cache busting through the asp-append-version attribute, like this:

```
...
<script asp-src-include="/lib/jquery/dist/**/j*.js"
        asp-src-exclude="**.slim.**,**.min.**"
        asp-append-version="true">
</script>
...
```

Enabling the cache busting feature produces an element like this in the HTML sent to the browser:

```
...
<script src="/lib/jquery/dist/jquery.min.js?v=3zRSQ1HF-ocUiVcdv9yKTXqM">
</script>
...
```

The same version number will be used by the tag helper until you change the contents of the file, such as by updating a JavaScript library, at which point a different checksum will be calculated. The addition of the version number means that each time you change the file, the client will request a different URL, which caches treat as a request for new content that cannot be satisfied with the previously cached content and pass on to the application server. The content is then cached as normal until the next update, which produces another URL with a different version.

Working with Content Delivery Networks

Content delivery networks (CDNs) are used to offload requests for application content to servers that are closer to the user. Rather than requesting a JavaScript file from your servers, the browser requests it from a host name that resolves to a geographically local server, which reduces the amount of time required to load files and reduces the amount of bandwidth you have to provision for your application. If you have a large, geographically disbursed set of users, then it can make commercial sense to sign up to a CDN, but even the smallest and simplest application can benefit from using the free CDNs operated by major technology companies to deliver common JavaScript packages, such as jQuery.

For this chapter, I am going to use the Microsoft CDN, which provides free access to popular packages, a list of which can be found at `www.asp.net/ajax/cdn`. I am using jQuery 3.2.1, and there are six URLs for this release of Microsoft CDN:

- `http://ajax.aspnetcdn.com/ajax/jQuery/jquery-3.2.1.js`

- `http://ajax.aspnetcdn.com/ajax/jQuery/jquery-3.2.1.min.js`

- `http://ajax.aspnetcdn.com/ajax/jQuery/jquery-3.2.1.min.map`

- `http://ajax.aspnetcdn.com/ajax/jQuery/jquery-3.2.1.slim.js`

- `http://ajax.aspnetcdn.com/ajax/jQuery/jquery-3.2.1.slim.min.js`

- `http://ajax.aspnetcdn.com/ajax/jQuery/jquery-3.2.1.slim.min.map`

These URLs provide the regular JavaScript file, the minified JavaScript file, and the source map for the minified file for both the full and slim versions of jQuery. In Listing 25-9, I have modified the layout in the example application to replace the local files with files obtained from the CDN.

Listing 25-9. Using a CDN in the _Layout.cshtml File in the Views/Shared Folder

```
<!DOCTYPE html>
<html>
<head>
    <meta name="viewport" content="width=device-width" />
    <title>Cities</title>
    <script src="http://ajax.aspnetcdn.com/ajax/jQuery/jquery-3.2.1.min.js"></script>
    <link href="/lib/bootstrap/dist/css/bootstrap.css" rel="stylesheet" />
</head>
<body class="m-1 p-1">
    <div>@RenderBody()</div>
</body>
</html>
```

Specifying the CDN means that no request for jQuery will reach the application's servers. The problem with CDNs is that they are not under your organization's control, and that means they can fail, leaving your application running but unable to work as expected because the CDN content isn't available. To help work around this, the `ScriptTagHelper` class provides the ability to fall back to local files when the CDN content cannot be loaded by the client, as shown in Listing 25-10.

Listing 25-10. Using CDN Fallback in the _Layout.cshtml File in the Views/Shared Folder

```
<!DOCTYPE html>
<html>
<head>
    <meta name="viewport" content="width=device-width" />
    <title>Cities</title>
    <script src="http://ajax.aspnetcdn.com/ajax/jQuery/jquery-3.2.1.min.js"
            asp-fallback-src-include="/lib/jquery/dist/**/*.min.js"
            asp-fallback-src-exclude="**.slim.**"
            asp-fallback-test="window.jQuery">
    </script>
    <link href="/lib/bootstrap/dist/css/bootstrap.css" rel="stylesheet" />
</head>
<body class="m-1 p-1">
    <div>@RenderBody()</div>
</body>
</html>
```

The `asp-fallback-src-include` and `asp-fallback-src-exclude` attributes are used to select and exclude local files that will be used if the CDN is unable to deliver the file specified by the regular `src` attribute. To figure out whether the CDN is working, the `asp-fallback-test` attribute is used to define a fragment of JavaScript that will be evaluated at the browser. If the fragment evaluates as `false`, then the fallback files will be requested.

To see how this works, run the application and examine the HTML that is sent to the client. You will see that the `ScriptTagHelper` class has taken the fragment from the `asp-fallback-test` attribute and used it to create another `script` element like this:

```
<head>
    <meta name="viewport" content="width=device-width" />
    <title>Cities</title>
    <script src="http://ajax.aspnetcdn.com/ajax/jQuery/jquery-3.2.1.min.js">
    </script>
    <script>
        (window.jQuery||document.write("\u003Cscript
            src=\u0022\/lib\/jquery\/dist\/jquery.min.js
            \u0022\u003E\u003C\/script\u003E"));
    </script>
    <link href="/lib/bootstrap/dist/css/bootstrap.css" rel="stylesheet" />
</head>
```

The fragment of JavaScript that you specify in the `asp-fallback-test` attribute must return `true` if the file from the CDN has loaded and `false` otherwise. The simplest approach is usually to check for the entry point into the functionality provided by the JavaScript code. The jQuery library creates a function called jQuery on the global `window` object, and that is what I test for in Listing 25-10. You will need to find an equivalent test for each file that you load from a CDN.

793

It is important to test your fallback settings because you won't find out if they fail until the CDN has stopped working and your users cannot access your application. The simplest way to check the fallback is to change the name of the file specified by the src attribute to something that you know doesn't exist (I append the word FAIL to the file name) and then look at the network requests that the browser makes using the F12 developer tools. You should see an error for the CDN file followed by a request for the fallback file.

■ **Caution**   The CDN fallback feature relies on browsers loading and executing the contents of script elements synchronously and in the order in which they are defined. There are a number of techniques in use to speed up JavaScript loading and execution by making the process asynchronous, but these can lead to the fallback test being performed before the browser has retrieved a file from the CDN and executed its contents, resulting in requests for the fallback files even when the CDN is working perfectly and defeating the use of a CDN in the first place. Do not mix asynchronous script loading with the CDN fallback feature.

Managing CSS Stylesheets

The LinkTagHelper class is the built-in tag helper for link elements and is used to manage the inclusion of CSS style sheets in a view. This tag helper supports the attributes described in Table 25-5, which I demonstrate in the following sections.

Table 25-5. *The Built-in Tag Helper Attributes for link Elements*

Name	Description
asp-href-include	This attribute is used to select files for the href attribute of the output element.
asp-href-exclude	This attribute is used to exclude files from the href attribute of the output element.
asp-append-version	This attribute is used to enable cache busting, as described in the "Understanding Cache Busting" sidebar.
asp-fallback-href	This attribute is used to specify a fallback file if there is a problem with a CDN.
asp-fallback-href-include	This attribute is used to select files that will be used if there is a CDN problem.
asp-fallback-href-exclude	This attribute is used to exclude files from the set that will be used when there is a CDN problem.
asp-fallback-href-test-class	This attribute is used to specify the CSS class that will be used to test the CDN.
asp-fallback-href-test-property	This attribute is used to specify the CSS property that will be used to test the CDN.
asp-fallback-href-test-value	This attribute is used to specify the CSS value that will be used to test the CDN.

Selecting Stylesheets

The LinkTagHelper shares many features with the ScriptTagHelper, including support for globbing patterns to select or exclude CSS files so they do not have to be specified individually. Being able to accurately select CSS files is as important as it is for JavaScript files because stylesheets come in regular and minified versions, too, and also support source maps. The popular Bootstrap package, which I have been using to style HTML elements throughout this book, includes its CSS stylesheets in the wwwroot/lib/bootstrap/dist/css folder, and if you expand all the items in the Solution Explorer, you will see that there are several files available, as shown in Figure 25-5.

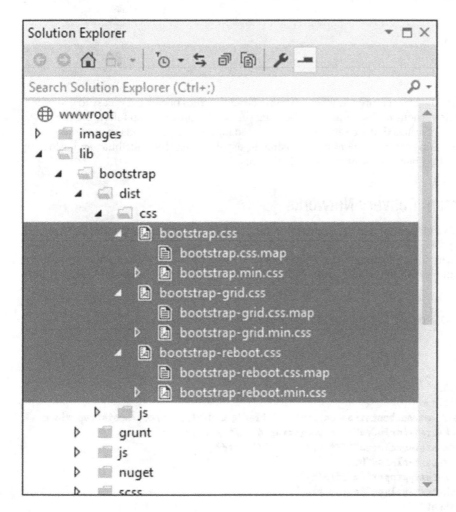

Figure 25-5. *The Bootstrap distribution files*

The bootstrap.css file is the regular stylesheet, the bootstrap.min.css file is the minified version, and the bootstrap.css.map file is a source map. The other files provide specified features that are described that are not of interest for this chapter. In Listing 25-11, I have used the asp-href-include attribute on a link element to select the minified stylesheet. (I have also removed the script element that loads jQuery, which is no longer required.)

Listing 25-11. Selecting a Stylesheet in the _Layout.cshtml File in the Views/Shared Folder

```
<!DOCTYPE html>
<html>
<head>
    <meta name="viewport" content="width=device-width" />
    <title>Cities</title>
    <link rel="stylesheet"
          asp-href-include="/lib/bootstrap/dist/**/*.min.css"
          asp-href-exclude="**/*-reboot*,**/*-grid*"/>
</head>
<body class="m-1 p-1">
    <div>@RenderBody()</div>
</body>
</html>
```

The same attention to detail is required as when selecting JavaScript files because it is easy to generate link elements for multiple versions of the same file or files that you don't want. You can follow the same three approaches to control the files that are selected as I described for JavaScript files in the previous section: narrowing the globbing pattern, excluding files using the asp-href-exclude attribute, and using the environment element to select between duplicate sets of elements.

Working with Content Delivery Networks

The LinkTag helper class provides a set of attributes for falling back to local content when a CDN isn't available, although the process for testing to see whether a stylesheet has loaded is a little more complex than testing for a JavaScript file. In Listing 25-12, I have used the MaxCDN URL for the Bootstrap library just to show an alternative to the Microsoft platform (MaxCDN is the CDN recommended by the Bootstrap project).

Listing 25-12. Using a CDN to Load CSS in the _Layout.cshtml File in the Views/Shared Folder

```
<!DOCTYPE html>
<html>
<head>
    <meta name="viewport" content="width=device-width" />
    <title>Cities</title>
    <link href="https://maxcdn.bootstrapcdn.com/bootstrap/4.0.0-alpha.6/css/bootstrap.min.css"
          asp-fallback-href-include="/lib/bootstrap/dist/**/*.min.css"
          asp-fallback-href-exclude="**/*-reboot*,**/*-grid*"
          asp-fallback-test-class="btn"
          asp-fallback-test-property="display"
          asp-fallback-test-value="inline-block"
          rel="stylesheet" />
</head>
<body class="m-1 p-1">
    <div>@RenderBody()</div>
</body>
</html>
```

The href attribute is used to specify the CDN URL, and I have used the asp-fallback-href-include and asp-fallback-href-exclude attributes to select the file that will be used if the CDN is unavailable. Testing whether the CDN works, however, requires the use of three different attributes and an understanding of the CSS classes defined by the CSS stylesheet that is being used.

The CSS fallback feature works by adding a meta element to the document that has been added to the class defined by the asp-fallback-test-class attribute. I specified the btn class in the listing, which means that an element like this will be added to the HTML sent to the browser:

```
<meta name="x-stylesheet-fallback-test" class="btn" />
```

The CSS class that you specify must be defined in the stylesheet that is to be loaded from the CDN. The btn class that I specified provides the basic formatting for Bootstrap button elements.

The asp-fallback-test-property attribute is used to specify a CSS property that is set by the CSS class, and the asp-fallback-test-value attribute is used to specify the value that it will be set to. The tag helper adds JavaScript to the view that tests the value of the CSS property on the meta element to figure out whether the stylesheet has been loaded and, if not, adds link elements for the fallback files. The Bootstrap btn class sets the display property to inline-block, and this provides the test to see whether the browser has been able to load the Bootstrap stylesheet from the CDN.

■ **Tip**   The easiest way to figure out how to test for third-party packages like Bootstrap is to use the browser's F12 developer tools. To determine the test in Listing 25-12, I assigned an element to the btn class and then inspected it in the browser, looking at the individual CSS properties that the class changes. I find this easier than trying to read through long and complex stylesheets.

Working with Anchor Elements

The a element is the basic tool for navigating an application and sending GET requests to the application to request different content. The AnchorTagHelper class is used to transform the href attribute of a elements so they target URLs generated using the routing system, using the attributes described in Table 25-6.

Table 25-6. *The Built-in Tag Helper Attributes for Anchor Elements*

Name	Description
asp-action	This attribute specifies the action method that the URL will target.
asp-controller	This attribute specifies the controller that the URL will target.
asp-area	This attribute specifies the area that the UTR will target.
asp-fragment	This attribute is used to specify the URL fragment (which appears after the # character).
asp-host	This attribute specifies the name of the host that the URL will target.
asp-protocol	This attribute specifies the protocol that the URL will use.
asp-route	This attribute specifies the name of the route that will be used to generate the URL.
asp-route-*	Attributes whose names begin with asp-route- are used to specify additional values for the URL so that the asp-route-id attribute is used to provide a value for the id segment to the routing system.

The AnchorTagHelper is simple and predictable and makes it easy to generate URLs in a elements that use the application's routing configuration. In Listing 25-13, I have updated the a element in the Index. cshtml view so that its href attribute is produced by the tag helper.

Listing 25-13. Transforming an Anchor Element in the Index.cshtml File in the Views/Home Folder

```
@model IEnumerable<City>

@{  Layout = "_Layout"; }

<table class="table table-sm table-bordered">
    <thead class="bg-primary text-white">
        <tr>
            <th>Name</th>
            <th>Country</th>
            <th class="text-right">Population</th>
        </tr>
    </thead>
    <tbody>
        @foreach (var city in Model) {
            <tr>
                <td>@city.Name</td>
                <td>@city.Country</td>
                <td class="text-right">@city.Population?.ToString("#,###")</td>
            </tr>
        }
    </tbody>
</table>
<a asp-action="Create" class="btn btn-primary">Create</a>
```

If you run the application and request the /Home/Index URL, you will see that the tag helper has transformed the a element like this:

```
<a class="btn btn-primary" href="/Home/Create">Create</a>
```

Working with Image Elements

The ImageTagHelper class is used to provide cache busting for images through the src attribute of img elements, allowing an application to take advantage of caching while ensuring that modifications to images are reflected immediately. The ImageTagHelper class operates in img elements that define the asp-append-version attribute, which is described in Table 25-7 for quick reference.

Table 25-7. The Built-in Tag Helper Attribute for Image Elements

Name	Description
asp-append-version	This attribute is used to enable cache busting, as described in the "Understanding Cache Busting" sidebar.

In Listing 25-14, I have added an img element to the shared layout for the city skyline image that I added to the project at the start of the chapter. (I have also reset the style element for brevity so that it uses local files.)

Listing 25-14. Adding an Image in the _Layout.cshtml File in the Views/Shared Folder

```
<!DOCTYPE html>
<html>
<head>
    <meta name="viewport" content="width=device-width" />
    <title>Cities</title>
    <link href="https://maxcdn.bootstrapcdn.com/bootstrap/4.0.0-alpha.6/css/bootstrap.min.css"
          asp-fallback-href-include="/lib/bootstrap/dist/**/*.min.css"
          asp-fallback-href-exclude="**/*-reboot*,**/*-grid*"
          asp-fallback-test-class="btn"
          asp-fallback-test-property="display"
          asp-fallback-test-value="inline-block"
          rel="stylesheet" />
</head>
<body class="m-1 p-1">
    <img src="/images/city.png" asp-append-version="true" />
    <div>@RenderBody()</div>
</body>
</html>
```

If you run the application, you will see that the image is displayed at the top of every page. If you examine the HTML that has been sent to the browser, you will see that the URL used to request the image file includes a version checksum, like this:

```
<img src="/images/city.png?v=KaMNDSZFbzNpE8Pkb3oEXcAJufRcRDpKhoK_IIPNc7E" />
```

As with the cache busting features for JavaScript files and CSS stylesheets, the checksum included in the URL will remain constant until the file is modified.

Using the Data Cache

MVC includes an in-memory cache that can be used to cache fragments of content in order to speed up view rendering. The content that is to be cached is denoted using the cache element in the view file, which is processed by the CacheTagHelper class using the attributes described in Table 25-8.

■ **Note** Caching is a useful tool for reusing sections of content so they don't have to be generated for every request. But using caching effectively requires careful thought and planning. While caching can improve the performance of an application, it can also create odd effects, such as users receiving stale content, multiple caches containing different versions of content, and update deployments that are broken because content cached from the previous version of the application is mixed with content from the new version. Don't enable caching unless you have a clearly defined performance problem to resolve, and make sure you understand the impact that caching will have.

Table 25-8. *The Built-in Tag Helper Attributes for cache Elements*

Name	Description
enabled	This bool attribute is used to control whether the contents of the cache element are cached. Omitting this attribute enables caching.
expires-on	This attribute is used to specify an absolute time at which the cached content will expire, expressed as a DateTime value.
expires-after	This attribute used to specify a relative time at which the cached content will expire, expressed as a TimeSpan value.
expires-sliding	This attribute is used to specify the period since it was last used when the cached content will expire, expressed as a TimeSpan value.
vary-by-header	This attribute is used to specify the name of a request header that will be used to manage different versions of the cached content.
vary-by-query	This attribute is used to specify the name of a query string key that will be used to manage different versions of the cached content.
vary-by-route	This attribute is used to specify the name of a routing variable that will be used to manage different versions of the cached content.
vary-by-cookie	This attribute is used to specify the name of a cookie that will be used to manage different versions of the cached content.
vary-by-user	This bool attribute is used to specify whether the name of the authenticated user will be used to manage different versions of the cached content.
vary-by	This attribute is evaluated to provide a key used to manage different versions of the content.
priority	This attribute is used to specify a relative priority that will be taken into account when the memory cache runs out of space and purges unexpired cached content.

To demonstrate the way that the cache attribute operates, I created the Components folder, added a class file called TimeViewComponent.cs, and used it to define the view component shown in Listing 25-15.

Listing 25-15. The Contents of the TimeViewComponent.cs File in the Components Folder

```
using System;
using Microsoft.AspNetCore.Mvc;

namespace Cities.Components {

    public class TimeViewComponent : ViewComponent {

        public IViewComponentResult Invoke() {
            return View(DateTime.Now);
        }
    }
}
```

The Invoke method selects the default view and provides a DateTime object as the view model. To provide a view for the view component, I created the Views/Home/Components/Time folder and added a view file called Default.cshtml with the markup shown in Listing 25-16.

Listing 25-16. The Default.cshtml File in the Views/Home/Components/Time Folder

```
@model DateTime

<div class="m-1 p-1 bg-info text-white">
    Rendered at @Model.ToString("HH:mm:ss")
</div>
```

The DateTime model object is used to display the current time, accurate to the second. In Listing 25-17, I have replaced the img element from the previous section with an @await Component.InvokeAsync expression that calls the view component.

Listing 25-17. Using a View Components in the _Layout.cshtml File in the Views/Shared Folder

```
<!DOCTYPE html>
<html>
<head>
    <meta name="viewport" content="width=device-width" />
    <title>Cities</title>
    <link href="https://maxcdn.bootstrapcdn.com/bootstrap/4.0.0-alpha.6/css/bootstrap.min.css"
          asp-fallback-href-include="/lib/bootstrap/dist/**/*.min.css"
          asp-fallback-href-exclude="**/*-reboot*,**/*-grid*"
          asp-fallback-test-class="btn"
          asp-fallback-test-property="display"
          asp-fallback-test-value="inline-block"
          rel="stylesheet" />
</head>
<body class="m-1 p-1">
    @await Component.InvokeAsync("Time")
    <div>@RenderBody()</div>
</body>
</html>
```

If you run the application, you will see the banner displaying the time that the content was rendered. Wait a few seconds and reload the page and you will see that the time displayed has changed, as shown in Figure 25-6.

Figure 25-6. Displaying the time in the example application

The cache element is used to surround content that should be added to the cache. In Listing 25-18, I have used the cache attribute to add the output from the view component to the cache.

Listing 25-18. Caching Content in the _Layout.cshtml File in the Views/Shared Folder

```
<!DOCTYPE html>
<html>
<head>
    <meta name="viewport" content="width=device-width" />
    <title>Cities</title>
    <link href="https://maxcdn.bootstrapcdn.com/bootstrap/4.0.0-alpha.6/css/bootstrap.min.css"
        asp-fallback-href-include="/lib/bootstrap/dist/**/*.min.css"
        asp-fallback-href-exclude="**/*-reboot*,**/*-grid*"
        asp-fallback-test-class="btn"
        asp-fallback-test-property="display"
        asp-fallback-test-value="inline-block"
        rel="stylesheet" />
</head>
<body class="m-1 p-1">
    <cache>
        @await Component.InvokeAsync("Time")
    </cache>
    <div>@RenderBody()</div>
</body>
</html>
```

Applying the cache element without any attributes tells MVC to reuse the content to satisfy all future requests. If you start the application, the content generated by the view component is cached so that the same time is shown even when the page is reloaded.

■ **Tip**   The cache used by the CacheTagHelper class is memory-based, which means that its capacity is limited by the available RAM. Content will be ejected from the cache when there is a shortage of capacity available, and the entire contents are lost when the application is stopped or restarted.

Setting Cache Expiry

The expires-* attributes allow you to specify when cached content will expire, expressed as an absolute time, relative to the current time, or a period of time that the cached content isn't requested. In Listing 25-19, I have used the expires-after attribute to specify that the content should be cached for 15 seconds.

Listing 25-19. Setting Cache Expiry in the _Layout.cshtml File in the Views/Shared Folder

```
<!DOCTYPE html>
<html>
<head>
    <meta name="viewport" content="width=device-width" />
    <title>Cities</title>
    <link href="https://maxcdn.bootstrapcdn.com/bootstrap/4.0.0-alpha.6/css/bootstrap.min.css"
        asp-fallback-href-include="/lib/bootstrap/dist/**/*.min.css"
```

```
            asp-fallback-href-exclude="**/*-reboot*,**/*-grid*"
            asp-fallback-test-class="btn"
            asp-fallback-test-property="display"
            asp-fallback-test-value="inline-block"
            rel="stylesheet" />
</head>
<body class="m-1 p-1">
    <cache expires-after="@TimeSpan.FromSeconds(15)">
        @await Component.InvokeAsync("Time")
    </cache>
    <div>@RenderBody()</div>
</body>
</html>
```

If you run the application, you will see that the cached data expires after 15 seconds, after which reloading the page will invoke the view component and create a new cached entry that will last another 15 seconds.

Setting a Fixed Expiry Point

You can specify a fixed time at which cached content will expire using the expires-on attribute, which accepts a DateTime value, as shown in Listing 25-20.

Listing 25-20. Specifying a Fixed Cache Expiry Point in the _Layout.cshtml File in the Views/Shared Folder

```
<!DOCTYPE html>
<html>
<head>
    <meta name="viewport" content="width=device-width" />
    <title>Cities</title>
    <link href="https://maxcdn.bootstrapcdn.com/bootstrap/4.0.0-alpha.6/css/bootstrap.min.css"
          asp-fallback-href-include="/lib/bootstrap/dist/**/*.min.css"
          asp-fallback-href-exclude="**/*-reboot*,**/*-grid*"
          asp-fallback-test-class="btn"
          asp-fallback-test-property="display"
          asp-fallback-test-value="inline-block"
          rel="stylesheet" />
</head>
<body class="m-1 p-1">
    <cache expires-on="@DateTime.Parse("2100-01-01")">
        @await Component.InvokeAsync("Time")
    </cache>
    <div>@RenderBody()</div>
</body>
</html>
```

I have specified that the data should be cached until the year 2100. This isn't a useful caching strategy since the application is likely to be restarted before the next century starts, but it does illustrate how you can specify a fixed point in the future rather than expressing the expiry point relative to the moment when the content is cached.

Setting a Last-Used Expiry Period

The expires-sliding attribute is used to specify a period after which content is expired if it hasn't been retrieved from the cache. In Listing 25-21, I have specified a sliding expiry of ten seconds.

Listing 25-21. Specifying a Last-Used Expiry Period in the _Layout.cshtml File in the Views/Shared Folder

```
<!DOCTYPE html>
<html>
<head>
    <meta name="viewport" content="width=device-width" />
    <title>Cities</title>
    <link href="https://maxcdn.bootstrapcdn.com/bootstrap/4.0.0-alpha.6/css/bootstrap.min.css"
        asp-fallback-href-include="/lib/bootstrap/dist/**/*.min.css"
        asp-fallback-href-exclude="**/*-reboot*,**/*-grid*"
        asp-fallback-test-class="btn"
        asp-fallback-test-property="display"
        asp-fallback-test-value="inline-block"
        rel="stylesheet" />
</head>
<body class="m-1 p-1">
    <cache expires-sliding="@TimeSpan.FromSeconds(10)">
        @await Component.InvokeAsync("Time")
    </cache>
    <div>@RenderBody()</div>
</body>
</html>
```

You can see the effect of the express-sliding attribute by running the application and periodically reloading the page. As long as you reload the page within ten seconds, the cached content will be used. If you wait longer than ten seconds to reload the page, then the cached content will be discarded, the view component will be used to generate new content, and the process will begin anew.

Using Cache Variations

By default, all requests receive the same cached content. The CacheTagHelper class can maintain different versions of cached content and use them to satisfy different types of HTTP requests, specified using one of the attributes whose name begins with vary-by. Listing 25-22 shows the use of the vary-by-route attribute to create cache variations based on the action value matched by the routing system.

Listing 25-22. Creating a Cache Variation in the _Layout.cshtml File in the Views/Shared Folder

```
<!DOCTYPE html>
<html>
<head>
    <meta name="viewport" content="width=device-width" />
    <title>Cities</title>
    <link href="https://maxcdn.bootstrapcdn.com/bootstrap/4.0.0-alpha.6/css/bootstrap.min.css"
        asp-fallback-href-include="/lib/bootstrap/dist/**/*.min.css"
        asp-fallback-href-exclude="**/*-reboot*,**/*-grid*"
        asp-fallback-test-class="btn"
```

```
            asp-fallback-test-property="display"
            asp-fallback-test-value="inline-block"
            rel="stylesheet" />
</head>
<body class="m-1 p-1">
    <cache expires-sliding="@TimeSpan.FromSeconds(10)" vary-by-route="action">
        @await Component.InvokeAsync("Time")
    </cache>
    <div>@RenderBody()</div>
</body>
</html>
```

If you run the application and use two browser tabs or windows to request the /Home/Index and /Home/Create URLs, you will see that each window receives its own cached content with its own expiration, since each request produces a different action routing value. The CacheTagHelper class supports a range of attributes that define different variations, including caching content for individual users.

There is also a vary-by header that allows you to define arbitrary cache variations using any data value. In Listing 25-23, I have re-created the effect of the vary-by-route attribute by specifying a value obtained directly from the route data.

Listing 25-23. Specifying a Custom Cache Variation in the _Layout.cshtml File in the Views/Shared Folder

```
<!DOCTYPE html>
<html>
<head>
    <meta name="viewport" content="width=device-width" />
    <title>Cities</title>
    <link href="https://maxcdn.bootstrapcdn.com/bootstrap/4.0.0-alpha.6/css/bootstrap.min.css"
        asp-fallback-href-include="/lib/bootstrap/dist/**/*.min.css"
        asp-fallback-href-exclude="**/*-reboot*,**/*-grid*"
        asp-fallback-test-class="btn"
        asp-fallback-test-property="display"
        asp-fallback-test-value="inline-block"
        rel="stylesheet" />
</head>
<body class="m-1 p-1">
    <cache expires-sliding="@TimeSpan.FromSeconds(10)"
            vary-by="@ViewContext.RouteData.Values["action"]">
        @await Component.InvokeAsync("Time")
    </cache>
    <div>@RenderBody()</div>
</body>
</html>
```

The vary-by attribute can be used to create more complex caching variations, although care should be taken because it is easy to get carried away and end up creating variations that are so specific that the content in the cache is never reused before it expires.

Using Application-Relative URLs

The final built-in tag helper is the UrlResolutionTagHelper class, and it is used to provide support for application-relative URLs, which are URLs that are prefixed with a tilde (the ~ character). In Listing 25-24, I have changed the link element in the shared layout so that it uses an explicitly defined URL, rather than using tag helpers to generate the URL from the routing system.

Listing 25-24. Using an Explicit URL in the _Layout.cshtml File in the Views/Shared Folder

```
<!DOCTYPE html>
<html>
<head>
    <meta name="viewport" content="width=device-width" />
    <title>Cities</title>
    <link href="/lib/bootstrap/dist/css/bootstrap.min.css" rel="stylesheet" />
</head>
<body class="m-1 p-1">
    <cache expires-sliding="@TimeSpan.FromSeconds(10)"
            vary-by="@ViewContext.RouteData.Values["action"]">
        @await Component.InvokeAsync("Time")
    </cache>
    <div>@RenderBody()</div>
</body>
</html>
```

Explicit URLs are perfectly acceptable as long as you understand that you will have to update them if you change the application's URL schema. And for many applications, that's the only consideration you have to make.

However, some applications will be deployed into a shared environment, where a single server supports multiple applications that are differentiated by adding a prefix to the URL. In Listing 25-25, I have changed the configuration of the application so that the request pipeline is set up to handle requests with a prefix of mvcapp, simulating a shared environment.

Listing 25-25. Adding a URL Prefix in the Startup.cs File in the Cities Folder

```
using System;
using System.Collections.Generic;
using System.Linq;
using System.Threading.Tasks;
using Microsoft.AspNetCore.Builder;
using Microsoft.AspNetCore.Hosting;
using Microsoft.AspNetCore.Http;
using Microsoft.Extensions.DependencyInjection;
using Cities.Models;

namespace Cities {
    public class Startup {

        public void ConfigureServices(IServiceCollection services) {
            services.AddSingleton<IRepository, MemoryRepository>();
            services.AddMvc();
        }
```

```
public void Configure(IApplicationBuilder app, IHostingEnvironment env) {
    app.Map("/mvcapp", appBuilder => {
        appBuilder.UseStatusCodePages();
        appBuilder.UseDeveloperExceptionPage();
        appBuilder.UseStaticFiles();
        appBuilder.UseMvcWithDefaultRoute();
    });
}
}
}
```

The Map method allows multiple request pipelines to be set up with different prefixes. This isn't an especially useful feature in day-to-day MVC development because you can create URLs prefixes within the MVC application using the routing system. But for this chapter, it is a useful feature because it means that every URL is requested by clients, including requests for static content.

You can see the problem that has arisen by starting the application and requesting the /mvcapp URL, which is now the default URL for the application and targets the Index action on the Home controller. Now that all URLs have to start with /mvcapp, the explicit URL for the stylesheet in the link element doesn't work, which means that the content in the application can't be styled, as shown in Figure 25-7. (You may have to clear your browser's cache to see the problem.)

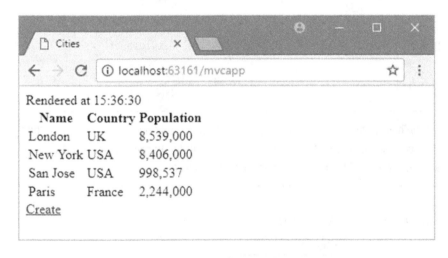

Figure 25-7. *The effect of an explicitly defined URL*

I could fix this problem by updating the explicit URL to include the prefix, but that isn't always possible because the prefix may change in deployment or may not be known at development time. A better solution is to use an application-relative URL, in which the path to the static content is expressed relative to any prefix that may have been configured, as shown in Listing 25-26.

Listing 25-26. Using an Application-Relative URL in the _Layout.cshtml File in the Views/Shared Folder

```
<!DOCTYPE html>
<html>
<head>
    <meta name="viewport" content="width=device-width" />
    <title>Cities</title>
    <link href="~/lib/bootstrap/dist/css/bootstrap.min.css" rel="stylesheet" />
</head>
<body class="m-1 p-1">
    <cache expires-sliding="@TimeSpan.FromSeconds(10)"
            vary-by="@ViewContext.RouteData.Values["action"]">
        @await Component.InvokeAsync("Time")
    </cache>
    <div>@RenderBody()</div>
</body>
</html>
```

The tilde is detected by the UrlResolutionTagHelper class, which replaces the tilde with the path required to reach the contents of the wwwroot folder. If you run the application, you will see that the content is styled, and examining the HTML sent to the browser will show that the link element contains a URL that includes the mvcapp prefix.

```
<link href="/mvcapp/lib/bootstrap/dist/css/bootstrap.min.css" rel="stylesheet" />
```

The UrlResolutionTag helper looks for URLs in a wide range of elements, as described in Table 25-9.

▪ **Tip** If you use another of the built-in tag helpers to generate URLs from the routing system, the HTML they generate will automatically include any required prefix, which is obtained from the HttpRequest.PathBase context property and whose value is provided by the server that hosts the application.

Table 25-9. *The Elements and Attributes Transformed by the UrlResolutionTagHelper*

Element	Attributes
a	href
applet	archive
area	href
audio	src
base	href
blockquote	cite
button	formaction
del	cite

(*continued*)

Table 25-9. (*continued*)

Element	Attributes
embed	src
form	action
html	manifest
iframe	src
img	src, srcset
input	src, formaction
ins	cite
link	href
menuitem	icon
object	archive, data
q	cite
script	src
source	src, srcset
track	src
video	src, poster

Summary

In this chapter, I described the built-in tag helpers that are not related to HTML forms. These tag helpers help manage access to JavaScript files and CSS stylesheets, creating URLs for anchor elements, performing cache busting for images, caching data, and transforming application-relative URLs. In the next chapter, I introduce the model binding system, which is used to process the data in HTTP requests so that it can be easily consumed within an MVC application.

CHAPTER 26

■ ■ ■

Model Binding

Model binding is the process of creating .NET objects using the data from the HTTP request in order to provide action methods with the arguments they need. In this chapter, I describe the way the model binding system works; show how it binds simple types, complex types, and collections; and demonstrate how you can take control of the process to specify which part of the request provides the data values your action methods require. Table 26-1 puts model binding in context.

Table 26-1. *Putting Model Binding in Context*

Question	Answer
What is it?	Model binding is the process of creating the objects that action methods require as arguments using data values obtained from the HTTP request.
Why is it useful?	Model binding lets action methods declare parameters using C# types and automatically receive data from the request without having to inspect, parse, and process the data directly.
How is it used?	In its simplest form, action methods declare parameters whose names are used to retrieve data values from the HTTP request. The part of the request used to obtain the data can be configured by applying attributes to the action method parameters.
Are there any pitfalls or limitations?	The main pitfall is getting data from the wrong part of the request. I explain the way that requests are searched for data in the "Understanding Model Binding" section, and the search locations can be specified explicitly using the attributes that I describe in the "Specifying a Model Binding Source" section.
Are there any alternatives?	Action methods don't have to declare parameters at all and can use the context objects that I described in Chapter 17 to get data directly from the HTTP request. However, the result is more complicated code that is hard to read and maintain.

© Adam Freeman 2017
A. Freeman, *Pro ASP.NET Core MVC 2*, https://doi.org/10.1007/978-1-4842-3150-0_26

Table 26-2 summarizes the chapter.

Table 26-2. *Chapter Summary*

Problem	Solution	Listing
Bind to a simple type or collection	Add a parameter to an action method	1–10, 23–29
Bind to a complex type	Ensure that the HTML generated by a view is well-structured	11–19
Selectively bind properties	Specify the names of data values using the Bind attribute or use the BindNever attribute to exclude model properties from the binding process	20–22
Specify the source of a data binding value	Apply an attribute to the action method argument or model property that identifies where the binding value should come from	30–38

Preparing the Example Project

For this chapter, I used the ASP.NET Core Web Application (.NET Core) template to create a new Empty project called MvcModels.

Creating the Model and Repository

I created the Models folder and added a class file called Person.cs, which I used to define the classes and enum shown in Listing 26-1.

Listing 26-1. The Contents of the Person.cs File in the Models Folder

```
using System;

namespace MvcModels.Models {

    public class Person {
        public int PersonId { get; set; }
        public string FirstName { get; set; }
        public string LastName { get; set; }
        public DateTime BirthDate { get; set; }
        public Address HomeAddress { get; set; }
        public bool IsApproved { get; set; }
        public Role Role { get; set; }
    }

    public class Address {
        public string Line1 { get; set; }
        public string Line2 { get; set; }
        public string City { get; set; }
        public string PostalCode { get; set; }
        public string Country { get; set; }
    }
```

```
    public enum Role {
        Admin,
        User,
        Guest
    }
}
```

Next, I added a class file called Repository.cs to the Models folder and defined the interface and implementation class shown in Listing 26-2.

Listing 26-2. The Contents of the Repository.cs File in the Models Folder

```
using System.Collections.Generic;

namespace MvcModels.Models {

    public interface IRepository {
        IEnumerable<Person> People { get; }

        Person this[int id] { get; set; }
    }

    public class MemoryRepository : IRepository {
        private Dictionary<int, Person> people
                    = new Dictionary<int, Person> {
            [1] = new Person {PersonId = 1, FirstName = "Bob",
                LastName = "Smith", Role = Role.Admin},
            [2] = new Person {PersonId = 2, FirstName = "Anne",
                LastName = "Douglas", Role = Role.User},
            [3] = new Person {PersonId = 3, FirstName = "Joe",
                LastName = "Able", Role = Role.User},
            [4] = new Person {PersonId = 4, FirstName = "Mary",
                LastName = "Peters", Role = Role.Guest}
        };

        public IEnumerable<Person> People => people.Values;

        public Person this[int id] {
            get {
                return people.ContainsKey(id) ? people[id] : null;
            }
            set {
                people[id] = value;
            }
        }
    }
}
```

The IRepository interface defines a People property to retrieve all the objects in the model and an indexer that allows individual Person objects to be retrieved or stored. The MemoryRepository class implements the interface using a dictionary with some default content. The repository implementation is not persistent, so the state of the application will revert to the default content when it is stopped or restarted.

Creating the Controller and View

I created the Controllers folder, added a class file called HomeController.cs, and used it to define the controller shown in Listing 26-3. The controller relies on dependency injection to receive a repository, which it uses in the Index method to select a single Person object from the repository using the value of its PersonId property.

Listing 26-3. The Contents of the HomeController.cs File in the Controllers Folder

```
using Microsoft.AspNetCore.Mvc;
using MvcModels.Models;

namespace MvcModels.Controllers {

    public class HomeController : Controller {
        private IRepository repository;

        public HomeController(IRepository repo) {
            repository = repo;
        }

        public ViewResult Index(int id) => View(repository[id]);
    }
}
```

To provide the action method with a view, I created the Views/Home folder and added a Razor file called Index.cshtml with the markup shown in Listing 26-4, which presents some of the properties from the model object in a table.

Listing 26-4. The Contents of the Index.cshtml File in the Views/Home Folder

```
@model Person
@{ Layout = "_Layout"; }

<div class="bg-primary m-1 p-1 text-white"><h2>Person</h2></div>

<table class="table table-sm table-bordered table-striped">
    <tr><th>PersonId:</th><td>@Model.PersonId</td></tr>
    <tr><th>First Name:</th><td>@Model.FirstName</td></tr>
    <tr><th>Last Name:</th><td>@Model.LastName</td></tr>
    <tr><th>Role:</th><td>@Model.Role</td></tr>
</table>
```

The Index.cshtml view relies on a shared layout. I created the Views/Shared folder and added a layout called _Layout.cshtml to it, the contents of which can be seen in Listing 26-5.

Listing 26-5. The Contents of the _Layout.cshtml File in the Views/Shared Folder

```
<!DOCTYPE html>
<html>
<head>
    <meta name="viewport" content="width=device-width" />
    <title>@ViewBag.Title</title>
```

```html
    <link asp-href-include="/lib/bootstrap/dist/**/*.min.css" rel="stylesheet" />
    @RenderSection("scripts", false)
</head>
<body class="m-1 p-1">
    @RenderBody()
</body>
</html>
```

The layout includes a `link` element for the Bootstrap stylesheet and renders the contents of the view. There is also an optional `scripts` section, which I will use later in the chapter. To simplify the views used in this chapter, I added the namespace that contains the model classes to the _ViewImports.cshtml file in the Views folder, as shown in Listing 26-6.

Listing 26-6. Importing Namespaces in the _ViewImports.cshtml File in the Views Folder

```
@using MvcModels.Models
@addTagHelper *, Microsoft.AspNetCore.Mvc.TagHelpers
```

The views rely on the Bootstrap CSS framework, which I added to the project by using the Bower Configuration File item template to create the bower.json file in the root folder of the project and by adding the package shown in Listing 26-7.

Listing 26-7. Adding a Package in the bower.json File in the MvcModels Folder

```
{
  "name": "asp.net",
  "private": true,
  "dependencies": {
    "bootstrap": "4.0.0-alpha.6"
  }
}
```

Configuring the Application

To complete the initial setup of the example application, I enabled the MVC framework and the other middleware useful for development in the `Startup` class, as shown in Listing 26-8. I also created a service for the repository so that the controller can gain access to the data model.

Listing 26-8. The Contents of the Startup.cs File in the MvcModels Folder

```
using System;
using System.Collections.Generic;
using System.Linq;
using System.Threading.Tasks;
using Microsoft.AspNetCore.Builder;
using Microsoft.AspNetCore.Hosting;
using Microsoft.AspNetCore.Http;
using Microsoft.Extensions.DependencyInjection;
using MvcModels.Models;
```

```
namespace MvcModels {

    public class Startup {

        public void ConfigureServices(IServiceCollection services) {
            services.AddSingleton<IRepository, MemoryRepository>();
            services.AddMvc();
        }

        public void Configure(IApplicationBuilder app, IHostingEnvironment env) {
            app.UseStatusCodePages();
            app.UseDeveloperExceptionPage();
            app.UseStaticFiles();
            app.UseMvc(routes => {
                routes.MapRoute(
                    name: "default",
                    template: "{controller=Home}/{action=Index}/{id?}");
            });
        }
    }
}
```

Start the application and request the /Home/Index/1 URL to produce the result shown in Figure 26-1. (The default URL will produce an error at the moment.)

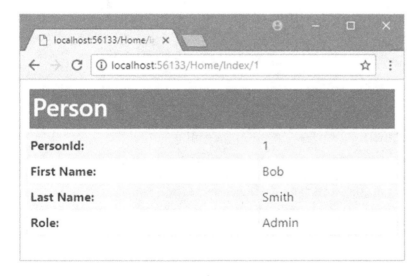

Figure 26-1. *Running the example application*

Understanding Model Binding

Model binding is an elegant bridge between the HTTP request and C# action methods. Most MVC applications rely on model binding to some extent, including the example application for this chapter. Model binding was used when I tested the example application in the previous section. The URL I requested contained the value of the PersonId property of the Person object I wanted to view, like this:

```
/Home/Index/1
```

MVC translated that part of the URL and used it as the argument when it called the Index method in the Home controller class to service the request.

```
...
public ViewResult Index(int id) => View(repository[id]);
...
```

To be able to invoke the Index method, MVC needs a value for the id argument, and providing that value is the responsibility of the model binding system, which is responsible for providing data values that can be used to invoke action methods.

The model binding system relies on *model binders*, which are components responsible for providing data values from one part of the request or application. The default model binders look for data values in these three places:

- Form data values
- Routing variables
- Query strings

Each source of data is inspected in order until a value for the argument is found. There is no form data in the example application, so no value will be found there. But there is a routing segment called id in the application configuration I used in Listing 26-8, and that allows the model binding system to provide MVC with a value that can be used to invoke the Index method. The search stops after a suitable data value has been found, which means that the query string isn't searched for a data value.

■ **Tip** In the "Specifying a Model Binding Source" section, I explain how you can specify the source of model binding data using attributes. This allows you to specify that a data value is obtained from, for example, the query string, even if there is also suitable data in the form or routing data.

Knowing the order in which data values are sought is important because a request can contain multiple values, like this URL:

```
/Home/Index/3?id=1
```

The routing system will process the request and match the id segment in the URL template to the value 3, and the query string contains an id value of 1. Since the routing data is searched for data before the query string, the Index action method will receive the value 3, and the query string value will be ignored.

On the other hand, if you request a URL that doesn't have an id segment, then the query string will be examined, which means that a URL like this one will also allow the model binding system to provide MVC with a value for the id argument so that it can invoke the Index method:

```
/Home/Index?id=1
```

You can see the effect of both of these URLs in Figure 26-2.

Figure 26-2. *The effect of model binding data source ordering*

Understanding Default Binding Values

Model binding is a best-effort feature, which means that MVC will use model binding to try to get the values it needs to invoke an action method but will still invoke the method even if data values cannot be provided. This can cause some unexpected behavior. As an example, requesting the URL /Home/Index produces the exception shown in Figure 26-3.

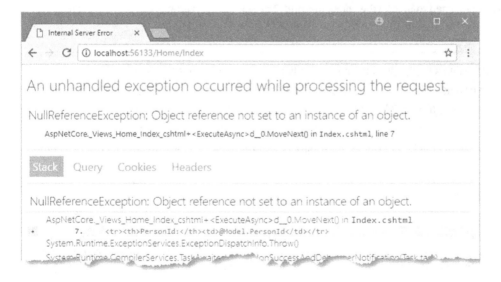

Figure 26-3. *An error processing a model property*

This exception isn't reported by the model binding system. Instead, it occurred when the Index view selected by the Index action method was processed. To invoke the Index method, MVC had to provide a value for the id argument, so it asked each of the model binders to inspect their part of the request and provide a value.

There is no form data in the example, no value for the id routing segment, and no query string in the URL, which means that the model binding system is unable to provide a data value. MVC has to provide *some* value for the id argument in order to invoke the Index method, so it uses a default value and hopes for the best. For int arguments, the default value is 0, and this is what leads to the exception. The definition of the Index method uses the value of the id argument to retrieve a model object from the repository.

```
...
public ViewResult Index(int id) => View(repository[id]);
...
```

When MVC uses the default value, the action method tries to retrieve a data model object with the id of 0. There is no such object, and the repository returns null, which is then passed on to the controller's View method to provide view model data to the Index.cshtml view. When the Razor expressions in the Index.cshtml file try to access the properties of the view model object, they cause the NullReferenceException shown in Figure 26-3.

This means that action methods have to be written to cope with default values provided by the model binding system, which can be done in several ways. You can add default values to the routing URL patterns (as described in Chapter 15), assign default values to the action method parameters, or ensure that the action method doesn't pass on bad data values as part of its response. The best approach will depend on what the action method is doing; in Listing 26-9, I have taken the last approach, which is to modify the action method so that it ensures that a Person object is always passed to the View method, even when the id argument doesn't correspond to an object in the data model.

Listing 26-9. Guarding Against Default Values in the HomeController.cs File in the Controllers Folder

```
using Microsoft.AspNetCore.Mvc;
using MvcModels.Models;
using System.Linq;

namespace MvcModels.Controllers {

    public class HomeController : Controller {
        private IRepository repository;

        public HomeController(IRepository repo) {
            repository = repo;
        }

        public ViewResult Index(int id) =>
            View(repository[id] ?? repository.People.First());
    }
}
```

The action method uses the LINQ and the null coalescing operator to return the first object in the repository when the value of the id parameter doesn't retrieve an object.

Binding Simple Types

When there is a suitable value available, it has to be converted into a C# value so that it can be used to invoke an action method. Simple types are values that originate from one item of data in the request that can be parsed from a string. This includes numeric values, bool values, dates, and, of course, string values.

The id argument of the Index action method is an int, so the model binding process provides MVC with a value by parsing the id segment variable into an int value.

If the request value cannot be converted (for example, if I supplied a value of apple for a parameter that requires an int value), then model binding process won't be able to provide a value for the application, and the default value will be used.

This presents a problem because it means that there are two situations in which the action method will receive the default value, zero. The first is when the request contains a value that cannot be parsed into the argument type, such as for the URL /Home/Index/Apple. The second is when the request does contain a value that can be parsed and it happens to be zero, such as for the URL /Home/Index/0.

Most applications need to be able to tell the difference between these situations, and the easiest way to do this is to use a nullable type for the action method argument, as shown in Listing 26-10.

Listing 26-10. Using a Nullable Type in the HomeController.cs File in the Controllers Folder

```
using Microsoft.AspNetCore.Mvc;
using MvcModels.Models;

namespace MvcModels.Controllers {

    public class HomeController : Controller {
        private IRepository repository;

        public HomeController(IRepository repo) {
            repository = repo;
        }

        public IActionResult Index(int? id) {
            Person person;
            if (id.HasValue && (person = repository[id.Value]) != null) {
                return View(person);
            } else {
                return NotFound();
            }
        }
    }
}
```

The default value for nullable types is null, which allows me to differentiate between requests where the request doesn't contain a value that can be parsed into an int and requests that do, and the int value happens to be zero. The implementation of the Index method in this example uses the NotFound method to return a 404 error if the nullable argument doesn't have a value or if the value doesn't correspond to an object in the model, which is a more robust approach than simply hoping that the first object in the model is suitable, which is the approach I took in the previous section.

Binding Complex Types

When the action method parameter is a complex type (in other words, any type that cannot be parsed from a single string value), then the model binding process uses reflection to get a set of the target type's public properties and performs the binding process on each of them in turn. To demonstrate how this works, I added two action methods to the Home controller, as shown in Listing 26-11.

Listing 26-11. Adding Action Methods in the HomeController.cs File in the Controllers Folder

```
using Microsoft.AspNetCore.Mvc;
using MvcModels.Models;

namespace MvcModels.Controllers {

    public class HomeController : Controller {
        private IRepository repository;

        public HomeController(IRepository repo) {
            repository = repo;
        }

        public IActionResult Index(int? id) {
            Person person;
            if (id.HasValue && (person = repository[id.Value]) != null) {
                return View(person);
            } else {
                return NotFound();
            }
        }

        public ViewResult Create() => View(new Person());

        [HttpPost]
        public ViewResult Create(Person model) => View("Index", model);
    }
}
```

The version of the Create method without parameters creates a new Person object and passes it to the View method, which has the effect of selecting the default view associated with the action. I added a view file called Create.cshtml to the Views/Home folder and added the markup shown in Listing 26-12.

Listing 26-12. The Contents of the Create.cshtml File in the Views/Home Folder

```
@model Person
@{
    ViewBag.Title = "Create Person";
    Layout = "_Layout";
}

<form asp-action="Create" method="post">
    <div class="form-group">
        <label asp-for="PersonId"></label>
```

```
        <input asp-for="PersonId" class="form-control" />
    </div>
    <div class="form-group">
        <label asp-for="FirstName"></label>
        <input asp-for="FirstName" class="form-control" />
    </div>
    <div class="form-group">
        <label asp-for="LastName"></label>
        <input asp-for="LastName" class="form-control" />
    </div>
    <div class="form-group">
        <label asp-for="Role"></label>
        <select asp-for="Role" class="form-control"
                asp-items="@new SelectList(Enum.GetNames(typeof(Role)))"></select>
    </div>
    <button type="submit" class="btn btn-primary">Submit</button>
</form>
```

This view contains a form that allows values for some of the properties of a Person object to be provided and contains a form element that posts the data back to the version of the Create method in the Home controller that has been decorated with the HttpPost attribute.

The action method that receives the form data uses the /Views/Home/Index.cshtml view to display it. You can see how this works work by starting the application, navigating to /Home/Create, filling out the form, and clicking the Submit button, as shown in Figure 26-4.

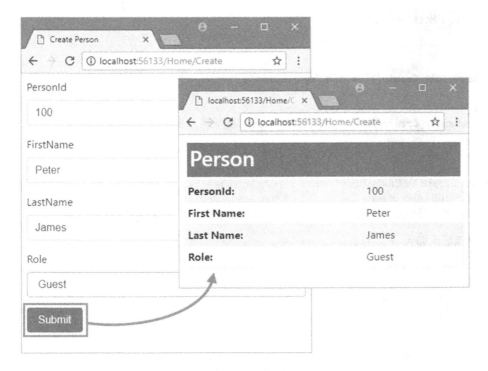

Figure 26-4. *Using the CreatePerson action methods*

When the form data is sent to the server, the model binding process discovers that the action method requires a complex type: a `Person` object. The `Person` class is examined to discover its public properties. For each public property that returns a simple property type, the model binder tries to locate a request value, just as it did in the previous example.

So, for example, the model binder finds the `PersonId` property and looks for a `PersonId` value in the same locations that were searched for an `id` value in the previous section. Since the form data contains a suitable value, which is set up using the `asp-for` tag helper on an `input` element, this is the value that will be used.

If a property requires another complex type, then the process is repeated for the new type. The set of public properties is obtained, and the binder tries to find values for all the properties. The difference is that the property names are nested. For example, the `HomeAddress` property of the `Person` class is of the `Address` type, as highlighted here:

```
using System;

namespace MvcModels.Models {

    public class Person {
        public int PersonId { get; set; }
        public string FirstName { get; set; }
        public string LastName { get; set; }
        public DateTime BirthDate { get; set; }
        public Address HomeAddress { get; set; }
        public bool IsApproved { get; set; }
        public Role Role { get; set; }
    }

    public class Address {
        public string Line1 { get; set; }
        public string Line2 { get; set; }
        public string City { get; set; }
        public string PostalCode { get; set; }
        public string Country { get; set; }
    }

    public enum Role {
        Admin,
        User,
        Guest
    }
}
```

When looking for a value for the `Line1` property, the model binder looks for a value for `HomeAddress.Line1`, as in the name of the property in the model object combined with the name of the property in the nested model type.

Creating Easily Bound HTML

The use of prefixes means that views have to include the information that the model binder looks for. This is easily done using tag helpers, which automatically add the required prefixes to the elements they transform. In Listing 26-13, I have extended the form so that it takes address data.

Listing 26-13. Updating the Form in the Create.cshtml File in the Views/Home Folder

```
@model Person
@{
    ViewBag.Title = "Create Person";
    Layout = "_Layout";
}

<form asp-action="Create" method="post">
    <div class="form-group">
        <label asp-for="PersonId"></label>
        <input asp-for="PersonId" class="form-control" />
    </div>
    <div class="form-group">
        <label asp-for="FirstName"></label>
        <input asp-for="FirstName" class="form-control" />
    </div>
    <div class="form-group">
        <label asp-for="LastName"></label>
        <input asp-for="LastName" class="form-control" />
    </div>
    <div class="form-group">
        <label asp-for="Role"></label>
        <select asp-for="Role" class="form-control"
                asp-items="@new SelectList(Enum.GetNames(typeof(Role)))"></select>
    </div>
    <div class="form-group">
        <label asp-for="HomeAddress.City"></label>
        <input asp-for="HomeAddress.City" class="form-control" />
    </div>
    <div class="form-group">
        <label asp-for="HomeAddress.Country"></label>
        <input asp-for="HomeAddress.Country" class="form-control" />
    </div>
    <button type="submit" class="btn btn-primary">Submit</button>
</form>
```

When using a tag helper, the nested property name is specified using C# conventions so that the outer and nested property names are separated by a period: HomeAddress.Country. If you run the application, request the /Home/Create URL, and examine the HTML sent to the browser, you will see that a different convention is used for some attributes.

```
<div class="form-group">
    <label for="HomeAddress_City">City</label>
    <input class="form-control" type="text" id="HomeAddress_City"
        name="HomeAddress.City" value="" />
</div>
```

```
<div class="form-group">
    <label for="HomeAddress_Country">Country</label>
    <input class="form-control" type="text" id="HomeAddress_Country"
        name="HomeAddress.Country" value="" />
</div>
```

The name attributes on the input elements follow the C# style, but the for attributes on the label elements and the id attributes on the input elements separate the property names with underscores. If you prefer to define the HTML elements without tag helpers, then you should ensure that you use the same naming scheme.

As a consequence of this feature, I don't have to take any special action to ensure that the model binder can create the Address object for the HomeAddress property. I can demonstrate this by editing the Index.cshtml view to display the HomeAddress properties when they are submitted from the form, as shown in Listing 26-14.

Listing 26-14. Displaying the HomeAddress Properties in the Index.cshtml File in the Views/Home Folder

```
@model Person
@{ Layout = "_Layout"; }

<div class="bg-primary m-1 p-1 text-white"><h2>Person</h2></div>

<table class="table table-sm table-bordered table-striped">
    <tr><th>PersonId:</th><td>@Model.PersonId</td></tr>
    <tr><th>First Name:</th><td>@Model.FirstName</td></tr>
    <tr><th>Last Name:</th><td>@Model.LastName</td></tr>
    <tr><th>Role:</th><td>@Model.Role</td></tr>
    <tr><th>City:</th><td>@Model.HomeAddress?.City</td></tr>
    <tr><th>Country:</th><td>@Model.HomeAddress?.Country</td></tr>
</table>
```

If you start the application and navigate to the /Home/Create URL, you can enter values for the City and Country properties and check that they are being bound to the model object by submitting the form, as shown in Figure 26-5.

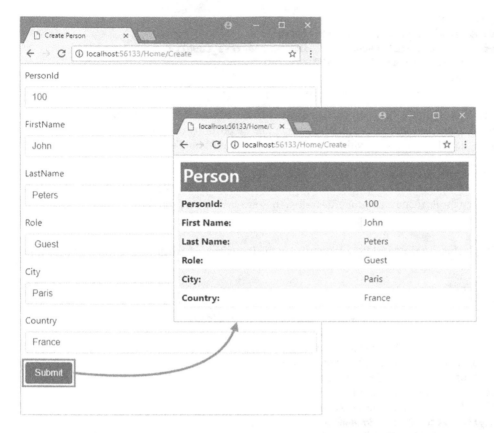

Figure 26-5. *Binding to properties in complex objects*

Specifying Custom Prefixes

There are occasions when the HTML you generate relates to one type of object but you want to bind it to another. This means that the prefixes containing the view won't correspond to the structure that the model binder is expecting, and your data won't be properly processed. To demonstrate this problem, I added a file called AddressSummary.cs to the Models folder and used it to define the class shown in Listing 26-15.

Listing 26-15. The Contents of the AddressSummary.cs File in the Models Folder

```
namespace MvcModels.Models {

    public class AddressSummary {
        public string City { get; set; }
        public string Country { get; set; }
    }
}
```

I added a new action method in the Home controller that uses the AddressSummary class, as shown in Listing 26-16.

Listing 26-16. Adding an Action Method in the HomeController.cs File in the Controllers Folder

```
using Microsoft.AspNetCore.Mvc;
using MvcModels.Models;

namespace MvcModels.Controllers {

    public class HomeController : Controller {
        private IRepository repository;

        public HomeController(IRepository repo) {
            repository = repo;
        }

        public IActionResult Index(int? id) {
            Person person;
            if (id.HasValue && (person = repository[id.Value]) != null) {
                return View(person);
            } else {
                return NotFound();
            }
        }

        public ViewResult Create() => View(new Person());

        [HttpPost]
        public ViewResult Create(Person model) => View("Index", model);

        public ViewResult DisplaySummary(AddressSummary summary) => View(summary);
    }
}
```

The new action method is called DisplaySummary. It has an AddressSummary parameter, which it passes to the View method so that it can be displayed by the default view. I created the DisplaySummary.cshtml file in the /Views/Home folder and added the markup shown in Listing 26-17.

Listing 26-17. The Contents of the DisplaySummary.cshtml File in the Views/Home Folder

```
@model AddressSummary
@{
    ViewBag.Title = "DisplaySummary";
    Layout = "_Layout";
}

<div class="bg-primary m-1 p-1 text-white"><h2>Address</h2></div>

<table class="table table-sm table-bordered table-striped">
    <tr><th>City:</th><td>@Model.City</td></tr>
    <tr><th>Country:</th><td>@Model.Country</td></tr>
</table>
```

This view displays the values of the two properties defined by the AddressSummary class. To demonstrate the problem with prefixes when binding to different model types, I changed the form element in the Create. cshtml view so that it sends its data to the DisplaySummary action, as shown in Listing 26-18.

Listing 26-18. Changing the Form Target Action in the Create.cshtml File in the Views/Home Folder

```
@model Person
@{
    ViewBag.Title = "Create Person";
    Layout = "_Layout";
}

<form asp-action="DisplaySummary" method="post">

    <!-- HTML elements omitted for brevity -->

</form>
```

You can see what happens by starting the application and navigating to the /Home/Create URL. When you submit the form, the values that you entered for the City and Country properties are not displayed in the HTML generated by the DisplaySummary view.

The problem is that the name attributes in the form have the HomeAddress prefix, which is not what the model binder is looking for when it tries to bind the AddressSummary type.

To fix the problem, the Bind attribute can be applied to the action method parameter, which specifies the prefix that should be used during model binding, as shown in Listing 26-19.

Listing 26-19. Changing the Model Binding Prefix in the HomeController.cs File in the Controllers Folder

```
using Microsoft.AspNetCore.Mvc;
using MvcModels.Models;

namespace MvcModels.Controllers {

    public class HomeController : Controller {
        private IRepository repository;

        public HomeController(IRepository repo) {
            repository = repo;
        }

        public IActionResult Index(int? id) {
            Person person;
            if (id.HasValue && (person = repository[id.Value]) != null) {
                return View(person);
            } else {
                return NotFound();
            }
        }

        public ViewResult Create() => View(new Person());
```

```
    [HttpPost]
    public ViewResult Create(Person model) => View("Index", model);

    public ViewResult DisplaySummary(
        [Bind(Prefix = nameof(Person.HomeAddress))] AddressSummary summary)
            => View(summary);
    }
}
```

The syntax is awkward, but the effect is useful. When populating the properties of the AddressSummary object, the model binder will look for HomeAddress.City and HomeAddress.Country data values in the request. If you run the application and submit the form again, you will see that the values you enter into the City and Country fields are now correctly displayed, as shown in Figure 26-6. This may seem like a long setup for a simple problem, but the need to bind to a different kind of object is surprisingly common, and this is a technique worth knowing.

Figure 26-6. Binding to the properties of a different object type

Selectively Binding Properties

Imagine that the Country property of the AddressSummary class is especially sensitive and that the user should not be able to specify values for it. The first thing I can do is prevent the user from seeing or editing the property by making sure that I don't include any HTML elements in the application's views that refer to the property.

However, a nefarious user could simply edit the form data sent to the server when submitting the form data and pick the value for the Country property that suits them. What I really want to do is tell the model binder not to bind a value for the Country property from the request, which I can do by configuring the Bind attribute on the action method parameter, specifying the names of only the properties that I want to bind, as shown in Listing 26-20.

Listing 26-20. Specifying the Properties in the HomeController.cs File in the Controllers Folder

```
using Microsoft.AspNetCore.Mvc;
using MvcModels.Models;

namespace MvcModels.Controllers {

    public class HomeController : Controller {
        private IRepository repository;

        public HomeController(IRepository repo) {
            repository = repo;
        }

        public IActionResult Index(int? id) {
            Person person;
            if (id.HasValue && (person = repository[id.Value]) != null) {
                return View(person);
            } else {
                return NotFound();
            }
        }

        public ViewResult Create() => View(new Person());

        [HttpPost]
        public ViewResult Create(Person model) => View("Index", model);

        public ViewResult DisplaySummary(
            [Bind(nameof(AddressSummary.City), Prefix = nameof(Person.HomeAddress))]
                AddressSummary summary) => View(summary);
    }
}
```

The first argument to the Bind attribute is a comma-separated list of the names of the properties that should be included in the model binding process. In the listing, I have specified that the City property should be included in the process, and since it is not listed, this means that the Country property will be excluded.

If you run the application, request the /Home/Create URL, and fill in and send the form, you will see that there is no value displayed for the Country property, even though one was sent by the browser as part of the HTTP POST request, as illustrated in Figure 26-7.

Figure 26-7. *Excluding a property from the model binding process*

When the Bind attribute is applied to an action method parameter, it only affects instances of that class that are bound for that action method; all other action methods will continue to try to bind all the properties defined by the parameter type. If you want to create a more widespread effect, then you can apply the Bind attribute to the model class itself, as shown in Listing 26-21.

Listing 26-21. Applying the Bind Attribute in the AddressSummary.cs File in the Models Folder

```
using Microsoft.AspNetCore.Mvc;

namespace MvcModels.Models {

    [Bind(nameof(City))]
    public class AddressSummary {
        public string City { get; set; }

        public string Country { get; set; }
    }
}
```

You can also exclude properties explicitly by decorating them with the BindNever attribute, as shown in Listing 26-22, although this does mean that new properties added to the model class will be included in the model binding process unless you remember to apply the attribute to them.

Listing 26-22. Applying the NeverBind Attribute in the AddressSummary.cs File in the Models Folder

```
using Microsoft.AspNetCore.Mvc;
using Microsoft.AspNetCore.Mvc.ModelBinding;

namespace MvcModels.Models {

    public class AddressSummary {
```

```
        public string City { get; set; }

        [BindNever]
        public string Country { get; set; }
    }
}
```

■ **Tip**   There is also a `BindRequired` attribute that tells the model binding process that a request must include a value for a property. If the request doesn't have a required value, then a model validation error is produced, as described in Chapter 27.

Binding to Arrays and Collections

The model binding process has some nice features for binding request data to arrays and collections, which I demonstrate in the following sections.

Binding to Arrays

One elegant feature of the default model binder is how it supports action method parameters that are arrays. To demonstrate this, I have added a new method to the Home controller called Names, which you can see in Listing 26-23.

Listing 26-23. Adding an Action Method in the HomeController.cs File in the Controllers Folder

```
using Microsoft.AspNetCore.Mvc;
using MvcModels.Models;

namespace MvcModels.Controllers {

    public class HomeController : Controller {
        private IRepository repository;

        public HomeController(IRepository repo) {
            repository = repo;
        }

        public IActionResult Index(int? id) {
            Person person;
            if (id.HasValue && (person = repository[id.Value]) != null) {
                return View(person);
            } else {
                return NotFound();
            }
        }

        public ViewResult Create() => View(new Person());
```

```
        [HttpPost]
        public ViewResult Create(Person model) => View("Index", model);

        public ViewResult DisplaySummary(
            [Bind(nameof(AddressSummary.City), Prefix = nameof(Person.HomeAddress))]
                AddressSummary summary) => View(summary);

        public ViewResult Names(string[] names) => View(names ?? new string[0]);
    }
}
```

The Names action method has a string array parameter called names. The model binder will look for any data item that is called names and create an array that contains those values. To provide the action method with a view, I created a Razor file called Names.cshtml in the Views/Home folder and added the markup shown in Listing 26-24.

Listing 26-24. The Contents of the Names.cshtml File in the Views/Home Folder

```
@model string[]
@{
    ViewBag.Title = "Names";
    Layout = "_Layout";
}

@if (Model.Length == 0) {
    <form asp-action="Names" method="post">
        @for (int i = 0; i < 3; 1++) {
            <div class="form-group">
                <label>Name @(i + 1):</label>
                <input id="names" name="names" class="form-control" />
            </div>
        }
        <button type="submit" class="btn btn-primary">Submit</button>
    </form>
} else {
    <table class="table table-sm table-bordered table-striped">
        @foreach (string name in Model) {
            <tr><th>Name:</th><td>@name</td></tr>
        }
    </table>
    <a asp-action="Names" class="btn btn-primary">Back</a>
}
```

This view displays different content based on the number of items there are in the view model. If there are no items, then the view displays a form that contains three identical input elements, like this:

```
...
<form method="post" action="/Home/Names">
    <div class="form-group">
        <label>Name 1:</label>
        <input id="names" name="names" class="form-control" />
    </div>
```

```
    <div class="form-group">
        <label>Name 2:</label>
        <input id="names" name="names" class="form-control" />
    </div>
    <div class="form-group">
        <label>Name 3:</label>
        <input id="names" name="names" class="form-control" />
    </div>
    <button type="submit" class="btn btn-primary">Submit</button>
</form>
...
```

When the form is submitted, the model binding process sees that the target action method takes an array and looks for data items that have the same name as the action method parameter. For this example, this means that all the values from the input elements whose name attribute is names will be gathered together to create an array and used as the argument to invoke the action method. To see the effect, start the application, navigate to the /Home/Names URL, and fill out the form. When you submit the form, you will see that all the values you entered are displayed, as shown in Figure 26-8.

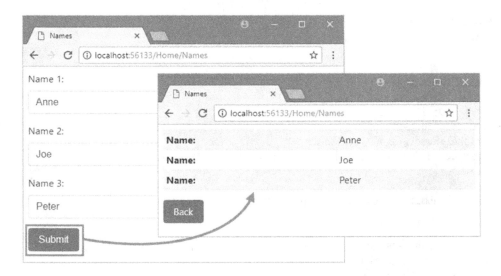

Figure 26-8. *Model binding for arrays*

Binding to Collections

It isn't just arrays that the model binding process can create. It also supports collection classes. In Listing 26-25 I changed the type of the Names action method parameter to be a strongly typed list.

Listing 26-25. Using a Strongly Typed Collection in the HomeController.cs File in the Controllers Folder

```
using Microsoft.AspNetCore.Mvc;
using MvcModels.Models;
using System.Collections.Generic;

namespace MvcModels.Controllers {
```

```
public class HomeController : Controller {
    private IRepository repository;

    public HomeController(IRepository repo) {
        repository = repo;
    }

    // ...other action methods omitted for brevity...

    public ViewResult Names(IList<string> names) =>
        View(names ?? new List<string>());
}
}
```

I used the IList<T> interface. I don't need to specify a concrete implementation class, although I could have if I preferred. In Listing 26-26, I modified the Names.cshtml view file to use the new model type.

Listing 26-26. Using a Collection As the Model Type in the Names.cshtml File in the Views/Home Folder

```
@model IList<string>
@{
    ViewBag.Title = "Names";
    Layout = "_Layout";
}

@if (Model.Count == 0) {
    <form asp-action="Names" method="post">
        @for (int i = 0; i < 3; i++) {
            <div class="form-group">
                <label>Name @(i + 1):</label>
                <input id="names" name="names" class="form-control" />
            </div>
        }
        <button type="submit" class="btn btn-primary">Submit</button>
    </form>
} else {
    <table class="table table-sm table-bordered table-striped">
        @foreach (string name in Model) {
            <tr><th>Name:</th><td>@name</td></tr>
        }
    </table>
    <a asp-action="Names" class="btn btn-primary">Back</a>
}
```

The functionality of the Names action is unchanged, but I am now able to work with a collection class rather than an array.

Binding to Collections of Complex Types

You can also bind individual data values to an array of complex types, which allows multiple objects (such as the AddressSummary model class in the example) to be collected from a single request. In Listing 26-27, I added an action method to the Home controller called Address, whose parameter is a list of AddressSummary objects.

Listing 26-27. Defining an Action Method in the HomeController.cs File in the Controllers Folder

```
using Microsoft.AspNetCore.Mvc;
using MvcModels.Models;
using System.Collections.Generic;

namespace MvcModels.Controllers {

    public class HomeController : Controller {
        private IRepository repository;

        public HomeController(IRepository repo) {
            repository = repo;
        }

        public IActionResult Index(int? id) {
            Person person;
            if (id.HasValue && (person = repository[id.Value]) != null) {
                return View(person);
            } else {
                return NotFound();
            }
        }

        public ViewResult Create() => View(new Person());

        [HttpPost]
        public ViewResult Create(Person model) => View("Index", model);

        public ViewResult DisplaySummary(
            [Bind(nameof(AddressSummary.City), Prefix = nameof(Person.HomeAddress))]
                AddressSummary summary) => View(summary);

        public ViewResult Names(IList<string> names) =>
            View(names ?? new List<string>());

        public ViewResult Address(IList<AddressSummary> addresses) =>
            View(addresses ?? new List<AddressSummary>());
    }
}
```

To provide the new action method with a view, I added a file called Address.cshtml to the Views/Home folder and added the markup shown in Listing 26-28.

Listing 26-28. The Contents of the Address.cshtml File in the Views/Home Folder

```
@model IList<AddressSummary>
@{
    ViewBag.Title = "Address";
    Layout = "_Layout";
}

@if (Model.Count() == 0) {
    <form asp-action="Address" method="post">
        @for (int i = 0; i < 3; i++) {
            <fieldset class="form-group">
                <legend>Address @(i + 1)</legend>
                <div class="form-group">
                    <label>City:</label>
                    <input name="[@i].City" class="form-control" />
                </div>
                <div class="form-group">
                    <label>Country:</label>
                    <input name="[@i].Country" class="form-control" />
                </div>
            </fieldset>
        }
        <button type="submit" class="btn btn-primary">Submit</button>
    </form>
} else {
    <table class="table table-sm table-bordered table-striped">
        <tr><th>City</th><th>Country</th></tr>
        @foreach (var address in Model) {
            <tr><td>@address.City</td><td>@address.Country</td></tr>
        }
    </table>
    <a asp-action="Address" class="btn btn-primary">Back</a>
}
```

This view renders a form element if there are no items in the model collection. The form consists of pairs of input elements whose name attributes are prefixed with an array index, like this:

```
...
<form method="post" action="/Home/Address">
    <fieldset class="form-group">
        <legend>Address 1</legend>
        <div class="form-group">
            <label>City:</label>
            <input name="[0].City" class="form-control" />
        </div>
        <div class="form-group">
            <label>Country:</label>
            <input name="[0].Country" class="form-control" />
        </div>
    </fieldset>
    <fieldset class="form-group">
```

```
            <legend>Address 2</legend>
            <div class="form-group">
                <label>City:</label>
                <input name="[1].City" class="form-control" />
            </div>
            <div class="form-group">
                <label>Country:</label>
                <input name="[1].Country" class="form-control" />
            </div>
        </fieldset>
        <fieldset class="form-group">
            <legend>Address 3</legend>
            <div class="form-group">
                <label>City:</label>
                <input name="[2].City" class="form-control" />
            </div>
            <div class="form-group">
                <label>Country:</label>
                <input name="[2].Country" class="form-control" />
            </div>
        </fieldset>
        <button type="submit" class="btn btn-primary">Submit</button>
</form>
...
```

When the form is submitted, the model binder realizes that it needs to create a collection of AddressSummary objects and uses the array index prefixes in the name attributes to obtain values for the object properties. The properties prefixed with [0] are used for the first AddressSummary object, those prefixed with [1] are used for the second object, and so on.

The Address.cshtml view defines input elements for three such indexed objects and displays them when the model collection contains items. Before I can demonstrate this, I need to remove the BindNever attribute from the AddressSummary model class, as shown in Listing 26-29; otherwise, the model binder will ignore the Country property.

Listing 26-29. Removing the BindNever Attribute from the AddressSummary.cs File in the Models Folder

```
using Microsoft.AspNetCore.Mvc;
using Microsoft.AspNetCore.Mvc.ModelBinding;

namespace MvcModels.Models {

    public class AddressSummary {

        public string City { get; set; }

        //[BindNever]
        public string Country { get; set; }
    }
}
```

You can see how the binding process for custom object collections works by starting the application and navigating to the /Home/Address URL. Enter some cities and countries and then click the Submit button to post the form to the server.

The model binding process will find and process the indexed data values and use them to create the collection of AddressSummary objects that are provided to the action method, which then uses the View convenience method to pass them back to the view so they can be displayed, as illustrated in Figure 26-9.

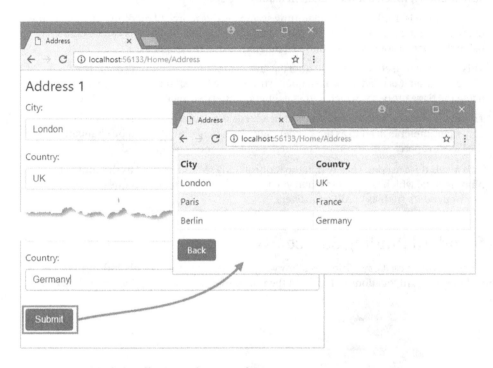

Figure 26-9. *Binding collections of custom objects*

Specifying a Model Binding Source

As I explained at the start of the chapter, the default model binding process looks for data in three places: the form's data values, the routing data, and the request query string.

The default search sequence isn't always helpful, either because you always want data to come from a specific part of the request or because you want to use a data source that isn't searched by default. The model binding feature includes a set of attributes that are used to override the default search behavior, as described in Table 26-3.

Table 26-3. *The Model Binding Source Attributes*

Name	Description
FromForm	This attribute is used to select form data as the source of binding data. The name of the parameter is used to locate a form value by default, but this can be changed using the Name property, which allows a different name to be specified.
FromRoute	This attribute is used to select the routing system as the source of binding data. The name of the parameter is used to locate a route data value by default, but this can be changed using the Name property, which allows a different name to be specified.
FromQuery	This attribute is used to select the query string as the source of binding data. The name of the parameter is used to locate a query string value by default, but this can be changed using the Name property, which allows a different query string key to be specified.
FromHeader	This attribute is used to select a request header as the source of binding data. The name of the parameter is used to as the header name by default, but this can be changed using the Name property, which allows a different header name to be specified.
FromBody	This attribute is used to specify that the request body should be used as the source of binding data, which is required when you want to receive data from requests that are not form-encoded, such as in API controllers.

Selecting a Standard Binding Source

The FromForm, FromRoute, and FromQuery attributes allow you to specify that the model binding data will be obtained from one of the standard locations but without the normal search sequence. Earlier in the chapter, I used this URL:

```
/Home/Index/3?id=1
```

This URL contains two possible values that can be used for the id parameter of the Index action method on the Home controller. The routing system will assign the final segment of the URL to a variable called id, which is defined in the URL pattern in the Startup class, and the query string contains also contains an id value. The default search pattern means that the model binding data will be taken from the route data and the query string will be ignored.

To change this behavior, in Listing 26-30, I have applied the FromQuery attribute to the action method. To keep the example simple, I have also removed all the other action method that I defined in previous examples.

Listing 26-30. Selecting the Query String in the HomeController.cs File in the Controllers Folder

```
using Microsoft.AspNetCore.Mvc;
using MvcModels.Models;

namespace MvcModels.Controllers {

    public class HomeController : Controller {
        private IRepository repository;

        public HomeController(IRepository repo) {
            repository = repo;
        }
```

```
public IActionResult Index([FromQuery] int? id) {
    Person person;
    if (id.HasValue && (person = repository[id.Value]) != null) {
        return View(person);
    } else {
        return NotFound();
    }
}
    }
  }
}
```

I have applied the FromQuery attribute to the id parameter, which means that only the query string will be used when the model binding process is looking for an id data value.

■ **Tip** You can still bind complex types when specifying a model binding source such as the query string. For each simple property in the parameter type, the model binding process will look for a query string key with the same name.

Using Headers As Binding Sources

The FromHeader attribute allows HTTP request headers to be used as the source for binding data. In Listing 26-31, I have added a simple action method to the Home controller that receives a parameter bound using data from a standard HTTP request header.

Listing 26-31. Model Binding from a Header in the HomeController.cs Filein the Controllers Folder

```
using Microsoft.AspNetCore.Mvc;
using MvcModels.Models;

namespace MvcModels.Controllers {

    public class HomeController : Controller {
        private IRepository repository;

        public HomeController(IRepository repo) {
            repository = repo;
        }

        public IActionResult Index([FromQuery] int? id) {
            Person person;
            if (id.HasValue && (person = repository[id.Value]) != null) {
                return View(person);
            } else {
                return NotFound();
            }
        }

        public string Header([FromHeader]string accept) => $"Header: {accept}";
    }
}
```

The Header action method defines an accept parameter, the value for which will be taken from the Accept header in the current request and returned as the method result. If you run the application and request the /Home/Header URL, you will see a result like this (although the exact result may differ based on the browser you use):

```
Header: text/html,application/xhtml+xml,application/xml;q=0.9,image/webp,*/*;q=0.8
```

Not all HTTP header names can be easily selected by relying on the name of the action method parameter because the model binding system doesn't convert from C# naming conventions to those used by HTTP headers. In these situations, you must configure the FromHeader attribute using the Name property to specify the name of the header, as shown in Listing 26-32.

Listing 26-32. Specifying the Name of the Header in the HomeController.cs File in the Controllers Folder

```
using Microsoft.AspNetCore.Mvc;
using MvcModels.Models;

namespace MvcModels.Controllers {

    public class HomeController : Controller {
        private IRepository repository;

        public HomeController(IRepository repo) {
            repository = repo;
        }

        public IActionResult Index([FromQuery] int? id) {
            Person person;
            if (id.HasValue && (person = repository[id.Value]) != null) {
                return View(person);
            } else {
                return NotFound();
            }
        }

        public string Header([FromHeader(Name = "Accept-Language")] string accept)
            => $"Header: {accept}";
    }
}
```

I can't use Accept-Language as the name of a C# parameter, and the model binder won't automatically convert a name like AcceptLanguage into Accept-Language so that it matches the header. Instead, I used the Name property to configure the attribute so that it matches the right header. If you start the application and request the /Home/Header URL, you will see a response like this one, which will vary based on your locale settings:

```
Header: en-US,en;q=0.8
```

Binding Complex Types from Headers

Although it is a rare requirement, you can bind complex types using header values by applying the FromHeader attribute to the properties of a model class. As an example, I added a file called HeaderModel.cs to the Models folder and defined the class shown in Listing 26-33.

Listing 26-33. The Contents of the HeaderModel.cs File in the Models Folder

```
using Microsoft.AspNetCore.Mvc;

namespace MvcModels.Models {

    public class HeaderModel {

        [FromHeader]
        public string Accept { get; set; }

        [FromHeader(Name = "Accept-Language")]
        public string AcceptLanguage { get; set; }

        [FromHeader(Name = "Accept-Encoding")]
        public string AcceptEncoding { get; set; }
    }
}
```

This class defines three properties, each of which has been decorated with the FromHeader attribute. I have used the Name property on two of the attributes to specify header names that cannot be expressed as C# parameter names. In Listing 26-34, I have updated the Header action method in the Home controller to receive a HeaderModel object.

Listing 26-34. Using the Header Model Class in the HomeController.cs File in the Controllers Folder

```
using Microsoft.AspNetCore.Mvc;
using MvcModels.Models;

namespace MvcModels.Controllers {

    public class HomeController : Controller {
        private IRepository repository;

        public HomeController(IRepository repo) {
            repository = repo;
        }

        public IActionResult Index([FromQuery] int? id) {
            Person person;
```

```
                if (id.HasValue && (person = repository[id.Value]) != null) {
                    return View(person);
                } else {
                    return NotFound();
                }
            }

        public ViewResult Header(HeaderModel model) => View(model);
    }
}
```

To complete the example, I added a view file called Header.cshtml to the Views/Home folder and added the markup shown in Listing 26-35.

Listing 26-35. The Contents of the Header.cshtml File in the Views/Home Folder

```
@model HeaderModel
@{
    ViewBag.Title = "Headers";
    Layout = "_Layout";
}

<table class="table table-sm table-bordered table-striped">
    <tr><th>Accept:</th><td>@Model.Accept</td></tr>
    <tr><th>Accept-Encoding:</th><td>@Model.AcceptEncoding</td></tr>
    <tr><th>Accept-Language:</th><td>@Model.AcceptLanguage</td></tr>
</table>
```

The model binding process will examine the properties of complex types looking for the attributes described in Table 26-3. This allows me to use the FromHeader attribute to define a complex type whose properties are model bound from headers, which you can see if you run the application and request the /Home/Header URL, which produces the result shown in Figure 26-10.

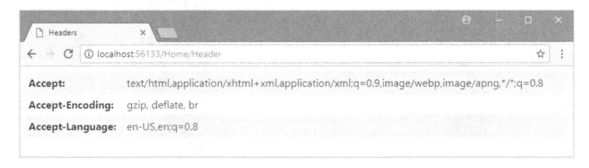

Figure 26-10. *Model binding a complex type from request headers*

Using Request Bodies as Binding Sources

Not all data sent by clients is sent as form data, such as when a JavaScript client sends JSON data to an API controller. The FromBody attribute specifies that the request body should be decoded and used as a source of model binding data. In Listing 26-36, I have added new Body action methods that demonstrate how this works.

Listing 26-36. Adding Action Methods in the HomeController.cs File in the Controllers Folder

```
using Microsoft.AspNetCore.Mvc;
using MvcModels.Models;

namespace MvcModels.Controllers {

    public class HomeController : Controller {
        private IRepository repository;

        public HomeController(IRepository repo) {
            repository = repo;
        }

        public IActionResult Index([FromQuery] int? id) {
            Person person;
            if (id.HasValue && (person = repository[id.Value]) != null) {
                return View(person);
            } else {
                return NotFound();
            }
        }

        public ViewResult Header(HeaderModel model) => View(model);

        public ViewResult Body() => View();

        [HttpPost]
        public Person Body([FromBody]Person model) => model;
    }
}
```

I have decorated the parameter for the Body method that accepts POST requests with the FromBody attribute, which means that request body content will be decoded and used for model binding. As I explained in Chapter 20, MVC has an extensible system for working with data formats but is set up to deal only with JSON data by default.

Next, I edited the bower.json file to add jQuery to the application, as shown in Listing 26-37.

Listing 26-37. Adding jQuery to the bower.json File in the MvcModels Folder

```
{
  "name": "asp.net",
  "private": true,
  "dependencies": {
    "bootstrap": "4.0.0-alpha.6",
```

```
    "jquery": "3.2.1"
  }
}
```

To provide the action method with the data it requires, I added a file called Body.cshtml to the Views/Home folder and added the content shown in Listing 26-38.

Listing 26-38. The Contents of the Body.cshtml File in the Views/Home Folder

```
@{
    ViewBag.Title = "Address";
    Layout = "_Layout";
}

@section scripts {
    <script src="/lib/jquery/dist/jquery.min.js"></script>
    <script type="text/javascript">
        $(document).ready(function () {
            $("button").click(function (e) {
                $.ajax("/Home/Body", {
                    method: "post",
                    contentType: "application/json",
                    data: JSON.stringify({
                        firstName: "Bob",
                        lastName: "Smith"
                    }),
                    success: function (data) {
                        $("#firstName").text(data.firstName);
                        $("#lastName").text(data.lastName);
                    }
                });
            });
        });
    </script>
}

<table class="table table-sm table-bordered table-striped">
    <tr><th>First Name:</th><td id="firstName"></td></tr>
    <tr><th>Last Name:</th><td id="lastName"></td></tr>
</table>
<button class="btn btn-primary">Submit</button>
```

For simplicity, this view contains some inline JavaScript code that uses jQuery to send an HTTP POST request containing JSON data to the /Home/Body URL when a button element is clicked. The server encodes the object created using model binding and sends it back to the client, encoded as JSON. You can see the effect by running the application, requesting the /Home/Body URL, and clicking the Submit button, as illustrated in Figure 26-11.

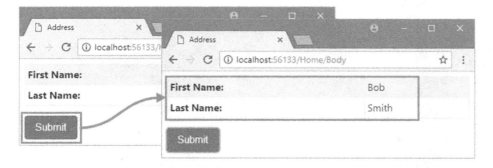

Figure 26-11. *Using the request body for model binding*

■ **Tip**   Not all JavaScript client code requires the use of the FromBody attribute. I had to avoid using the jQuery convenience method for sending Ajax POST requests in this example because it encodes data as form data. Instead, I had to use a different method that allows me to send JSON data.

The FromBody attribute can be used to model bind only one action method parameter, and an exception will be thrown if the attribute is used more than once for a single method. If you need to create multiple model objects from a request body, then you will have to create a simple data transfer class that has all the properties you need and use the data it contains to create the objects you require inside the action method.

Summary

In this chapter, I described the model binding process, which is used to provide action methods with the arguments they require using data values from the HTTP request that is being processed. I explained how simple and complex types are model bound, how arrays and collections are dealt with, and the ways in which the model binding process can be controlled by applying attributes to action method parameters or model class properties. In the next chapter, I describe the model validation feature.

CHAPTER 27

■ ■ ■

Model Validation

In the previous chapter, I showed you how MVC creates model objects from HTTP requests through the model binding process. Throughout that chapter, I worked on the basis that the data the user supplied was valid. The reality is that users will often enter data that isn't valid and cannot be used, which leads me to the topic of this chapter: model validation.

Model validation is the process of ensuring the data received by the application is suitable for binding to the model and, when this is not the case, providing useful information to the user that will help explain the problem.

The first part of the process, checking the data received, is one of the key ways to preserve the integrity of the domain model. Rejecting data that doesn't make sense in the context of the domain can prevent odd and unwanted states from arising in the application. The second part, helping the user correct the problem, is equally important. Without the information and feedback they need to interact with the application, users become frustrated and confused. In public-facing applications, this means users will simply stop using the application. In corporate applications, this means the user's workflow will be hindered. Neither outcome is desirable, but fortunately MVC provides extensive support for model validation. Table 27-1 puts model validation in context.

Table 27-1. Putting Model Validation in Context

Question	Answer
What is it?	Model validation is the process of ensuring that the data provided in a request is valid for use in the application.
Why is it useful?	Users do not always enter valid data, and using it in the application can produce unexpected and undesirable errors.
How is it used?	Controllers check the outcome of the validation process, and tag helpers are used to include validation feedback in views displayed to the user. Validation is performed automatically during the model binding process and is usually supplemented with custom validation in a controller class or by using validation attributes.
Are there any pitfalls or limitations?	It is important to test the efficacy of your validation code to ensure that it prevents against the full range of values that the application can receive.
Are there any alternatives?	No, model validation is tightly integrated into ASP.NET Core MVC.

© Adam Freeman 2017
A. Freeman, *Pro ASP.NET Core MVC 2*, https://doi.org/10.1007/978-1-4842-3150-0_27

Table 27-2 summarizes the chapter.

Table 27-2. *Chapter Summary*

Problem	Solution	Listing
Explicitly validate a model	Use the ModelState to record validation errors	9–10
Generate a summary of validation errors	Apply the asp-validation-summary attribute to a div element	11
Change the default model binding messages	Redefine the message functions in the model binding message provider	12
Generate property-level validation errors	Apply the asp-validation-for attribute to a span element	13
Generate model-level validation errors	Use the ModelState to record validation errors that are not associated with a specific property and use the ModelOnly value for the asp-validation-summary attribute in the div element	14, 15
Define a self-validating model	Apply data validation attributes to the model properties	16, 17
Create a custom validation attribute	Implement the IModelValidator interface	18–19
Perform client-side validation	Use the jQuery validation and jQuery unobtrusive validation packages	20, 21
Perform remove validation	Define an action method to perform the validation and apply the Remote attribute to the model property	22, 23

Preparing the Example Project

For this chapter, I used the ASP.NET Core Web Application (.NET Core) template to create a new Empty project called ModelValidation. Listing 27-1 shows the Startup class, in which I added the MVC Framework and enabled the middleware components that are useful for development.

Listing 27-1. The Contents of the Startup.cs File in the ModelValidation Folder

```
using System;
using System.Collections.Generic;
using System.Linq;
using System.Threading.Tasks;
using Microsoft.AspNetCore.Builder;
using Microsoft.AspNetCore.Hosting;
using Microsoft.AspNetCore.Http;
using Microsoft.Extensions.DependencyInjection;

namespace ModelValidation {

    public class Startup {

        public void ConfigureServices(IServiceCollection services) {
```

```
        services.AddMvc();
    }

    public void Configure(IApplicationBuilder app, IHostingEnvironment env) {
        app.UseStatusCodePages();
        app.UseDeveloperExceptionPage();
        app.UseStaticFiles();
        app.UseMvcWithDefaultRoute();
    }
  }
}
```

Creating the Model

I created the Models folder, added a class file called Appointment.cs, and used it to define the class shown in Listing 27-2.

Listing 27-2. The Contents of the Appointment.cs File in the Models Folder

```
using System;
using System.ComponentModel.DataAnnotations;

namespace ModelValidation.Models {
    public class Appointment {

        public string ClientName { get; set; }

        [UIHint("Date")]
        public DateTime Date { get; set; }

        public bool TermsAccepted { get; set; }
    }
}
```

The Appointment model class defines three properties, and I have used the UIHint attribute to indicate that the Date property should be expressed as a date without a time component.

Creating the Controller

I created the Controllers folder, added a class file called HomeController.cs, and used it to define the controller shown in Listing 27-3, which operates on the Appointment model class.

Listing 27-3. The Contents of the HomeController.cs File in the Controllers Folder

```
using System;
using Microsoft.AspNetCore.Mvc;
using ModelValidation.Models;

namespace ModelValidation.Controllers {

    public class HomeController : Controller {
```

```
    public IActionResult Index() =>
        View("MakeBooking", new Appointment { Date = DateTime.Now });

    [HttpPost]
    public ViewResult MakeBooking(Appointment appt) =>
        View("Completed", appt);

    }
}
```

The Index action renders the MakeBooking view with a new Appointment object as the view model. The MakeBooking action method is more interesting in this chapter since this is the method in which model validation will be performed.

■ **Note**   The example application is so simple that I have not defined a repository and do not need to add any code to store the Appointment objects that are produced by the model binding process. That said, it is important to bear in mind that the main reason to validate a model is to prevent bad or meaningless data from being placed in the repository and causing problems (either when trying to store the data or when trying to process the data later).

Creating the Layout and Views

I will need a simple layout for some of the examples in this chapter. I created the Views/Shared folder and added the _Layout.cshtml file to it, the contents of which you can see in Listing 27-4.

Listing 27-4. The Contents of the _Layout.cshtml File in the Views/Shared Folder

```
<!DOCTYPE html>
<html>
<head>
    <meta charset="utf-8" />
    <meta name="viewport" content="width=device-width" />
    <title>Model Validation</title>
    <link asp-href-include="/lib/bootstrap/dist/css/bootstrap.min.css" rel="stylesheet" />
    @RenderSection("scripts", false)
</head>
<body class="m-1 p-1">
    @RenderBody()
</body>
</html>
```

To provide the action methods with views, I created the Views/Home folder and added a file called MakeBooking.cshtml with the markup shown in Listing 27-5.

Listing 27-5. The Contents of the MakeBooking.cshtml File in the Views/Home Folder

```
@model Appointment

@{ Layout = "_Layout"; }

<div class="bg-primary m-1 p-1 text-white"><h2>Book an Appointment</h2></div>

<form class="m-1 p-1" asp-action="MakeBooking" method="post">
    <div class="form-group">
        <label asp-for="ClientName">Your name:</label>
        <input asp-for="ClientName" class="form-control" />
    </div>
    <div class="form-group">
        <label asp-for="Date">Appointment Date:</label>
        <input asp-for="Date" type="text" asp-format="{0:d}" class="form-control" />
    </div>
    <div class="radio form-group">
        <input asp-for="TermsAccepted" />
        <label asp-for="TermsAccepted" class="form-check-label">
            I accept the terms & conditions
        </label>
    </div>
    <button type="submit" class="btn btn-primary">Make Booking</button>
</form>
```

When the form contained in the Index.cshtml file is posted back to the application, the MakeBooking action method displays the details of the appointment that the user has created using the Completed.cshtml view in the Views/Home folder, which is shown in Listing 27-6.

Listing 27-6. The Contents of the Completed.cshtml File in the Views/Home Folder

```
@model Appointment
@{ Layout = "_Layout"; }

<div class="bg-success m-1 p-1 text-white"><h2>Your Appointment</h2></div>

<table class="table table-bordered">
    <tr>
        <th>Your name is:</th>
        <td>@Model.ClientName</td>
    </tr>
    <tr>
        <th>Your appontment date is:</th>
        <td>@Model.Date.ToString("d")</td>
    </tr>
</table>
<a class="btn btn-success" asp-action="Index">Make Another Appointment</a>
```

The views depend on the Bootstrap CSS package for styling the HTML elements. To add Bootstrap to the project, I used the Bower Configuration File item template to create the bower.json file and added the Bootstrap package to the dependencies section, as shown in Listing 27-7. I have also added jQuery to the project, which I use later in the chapter.

Listing 27-7. Adding the Bootstrap Package in the bower.json File

```json
{
  "name": "asp.net",
  "private": true,
  "dependencies": {
    "bootstrap": "4.0.0-alpha.6",
    "jquery": "3.2.1"
  }
}
```

The final preparation is to create the _ViewImports.cshtml file in the Views folder, which sets up the built-in tag helpers for use in Razor views and imports the model namespace, as shown in Listing 27-8.

Listing 27-8. The Contents of the _ViewImports.cshtml File in the Views Folder

```
@using ModelValidation.Models
@addTagHelper *, Microsoft.AspNetCore.Mvc.TagHelpers
```

As you may have gathered, the example for this chapter is based around creating appointments. You can see how it works by starting the application and requesting the default URL. Entering details into the form and clicking the Make Booking button will send the data to the server, which performs the model-binding process to create an Appointment object, the details of which are then rendered using the Completed.cshtml view, as shown in Figure 27-1.

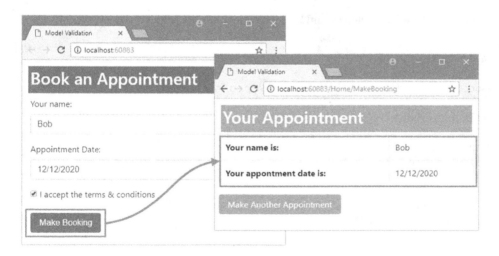

Figure 27-1. Using the example application

Understanding the Need for Model Validation

Model validation is the process of enforcing the requirements that an application has for the data it receives from clients. Without validation, an application will try to operate on any data it receives, which can lead to exceptions and unexpected behaviors that appear immediately or long-term problems that appear gradually as the repository is populated with bad, incomplete, or malicious data.

At the moment, the example application will accept any data that the user submits. To preserve the integrity of the application and domain model, I need the following three things to be true before I know that the user has provided an acceptable Appointment object:

- The user must provide a name.

- The user must provide a date that is in the future.

- The user must have selected the check box to accept the terms and conditions.

In the sections that follow, I demonstrate how model validation can be used to enforce these requirements by checking the data that the application receives and providing feedback to the user when the application cannot use the data the user has submitted.

Explicitly Validating a Model

The most direct way of validating a model is to do so in the action method. In Listing 27-9, I have added explicit checks for each property defined by the Appointment class in the MakeBooking action method.

Listing 27-9. Explicitly Validating a Model in the HomeController.cs File in the Controllers Folder

```
using System;
using Microsoft.AspNetCore.Mvc;
using ModelValidation.Models;
using Microsoft.AspNetCore.Mvc.ModelBinding;

namespace ModelValidation.Controllers {

    public class HomeController : Controller {

        public IActionResult Index() =>
            View("MakeBooking", new Appointment { Date = DateTime.Now });

        [HttpPost]
        public ViewResult MakeBooking(Appointment appt) {
            if (string.IsNullOrEmpty(appt.ClientName)) {
                ModelState.AddModelError(nameof(appt.ClientName),
                    "Please enter your name");
            }

            if (ModelState.GetValidationState("Date")
                    == ModelValidationState.Valid && DateTime.Now > appt.Date) {
                ModelState.AddModelError(nameof(appt.Date),
                    "Please enter a date in the future");
            }
```

```
        if (!appt.TermsAccepted) {
            ModelState.AddModelError(nameof(appt.TermsAccepted),
                "You must accept the terms");
        }

        if (ModelState.IsValid) {
            return View("Completed", appt);
        } else {
            return View();
        }
    }
  }
}
```

I check the values that the model binder has assigned to the properties of the parameter object and register any errors I find using the ModelStateDictionary object that is returned by the ModelState property inherited from the Controller base class.

As its name suggests, the ModelStateDictionary class is a dictionary that is used to track details of the state of the model object, with an emphasis on validation errors. Table 27-3 describes the most important ModelStateDictionary members.

Table 27-3. *Selected ModelStateDictionary Members*

Name	Description
AddModelError(property, message)	This method is used to record a model validation error for the specified property.
GetValidationState(property)	This method is used to determine whether there are model validation errors for a specific property, expressed as a value from the ModelValidationState enumeration.
IsValid	This property returns true if all the model properties are valid and returns false otherwise.

As an example of using the ModelStateDictionary, consider how the ClientName property was validated.

```
...
if (string.IsNullOrEmpty(appt.ClientName)) {
    ModelState.AddModelError(nameof(appt.ClientName), "Please enter your name");
}
...
```

One of the example validation goals is to ensure that the user provides a value for this property, so I use the static string.IsNullOrEmpty method to test the property value that the model binding process has extracted from the request. If the ClientName property is null or an empty string, then I know that my validation goal has not been met, and I use the ModelState.AddModelError method to register a validation error, specifying the name of the property (ClientName) and a message that will be displayed to the user to explain the nature of the problem (Please enter your name).

The model binding system also uses the ModelStateDictionary to record any problems with finding and assigning values to model properties. The GetValidationState method is used to see whether there have been any errors recorded for a model property, either from the model binding process or because the AddModelError method has been called during explicit validation in the action method. The GetValidationState method returned a value from the ModelValidationState enumeration, which defines the values described in Table 27-4.

Table 27-4. *The ModelValidationState Values*

Name	Description
Unvalidated	This value means that no validation has been performed on the model property, usually because there was no value in the request that corresponded to the property name.
Valid	This value means that the request value associated with the property is valid.
Invalid	This value means that the request value associated with the property is invalid and should not be used.
Skipped	This value means that the model property has not been processed, which usually means that there have been so many validation errors that there is no point continuing to perform validation checks.

For the Date property, I check to see whether the model binding process has reported a problem parsing the value sent by the browser into a DateTime object, like this:

```
...
if (ModelState.GetValidationState("Date") == ModelValidationState.Valid
        && DateTime.Now > appt.Date) {
    ModelState.AddModelError(nameof(appt.Date), "Please enter a date in the future");
}
...
```

My validation goal for the Date property is to ensure that the user provides a valid future date. I use the GetValidationState method to see whether the model binding process was able to parse the request value into a DateTime object by checking for the ModelValidationState.Valid value. If there is a valid date, then I check to make sure it is in the future and use the AddModelError method to record a validation problem if it is not.

After I have validated all the properties in the model object, I check the ModelState.IsValid property to see whether there were errors. This method returns true if the Model.State.AddModelError method was called during the checks or if the model binder had any problems creating the Appointment object.

```
...
if (ModelState.IsValid) {
    return View("Completed", appt);
} else {
    return View();
}
...
```

The Appointment object is valid if the IsValid property returns true, in which case the action method renders the Completed.cshtml view. There is a validation problem if the IsValue property returns false, which is dealt with by calling the View method to render the default view.

Displaying Validation Errors to the User

It may seem odd to deal with a validation error by calling the View method, but the context data that MVC provides to the view contains details of the model validation errors, which is automatically detected and used by the tag helper that is used to transform the input elements.

To see how this works, start the application and click the Make Booking button without filling in any of the form details. There won't be any visible change shown in the browser window, but if you inspect the HTML that MVC returns from the POST request, you will see that the class attribute of the form element changes. Here is what the ClientName element looks like before the form is submitted:

```
<input class="form-control" type="text" id="ClientName" name="ClientName" value="">
```

Here is the input element that is sent when the empty form has been submitted:

```
<input class="form-control input-validation-error" type="text" id="ClientName"
    name="ClientName" value="">
```

The tag helper adds elements whose values have failed validation to the input-validation-error class, which can then be styled to highlight the problem to the user.

You can do this by defining custom CSS styles in a stylesheet, but a little extra work is required if you want to use the built-in validation styles that CSS libraries like Bootstrap provides. The name of the class added to the form elements cannot be changed, which means that some JavaScript code is required to map between the name used by MVC and the CSS error classes provided by Bootstrap.

■ **Tip**   Using JavaScript code like this can be awkward, and it can be tempting to use custom CSS styles, even when working with a CSS library like Bootstrap. However, the colors used for validation classes in Bootstrap can be overridden by using themes or by customizing the package and defining your own styles, which means you have to ensure that any changes to the theme are matched by corresponding changes to any custom styles you define. Ideally, Microsoft will make the validation class names configurable in a future release of ASP.NET Core MVC, but until then, using JavaScript to apply Bootstrap styles is a more robust approach than creating custom stylesheets.

In Listing 27-10, I have added jQuery code to the MakeBooking view to find the elements in the input-validation-error class, locate the closest parent that has been assigned to the form-group class, and add that element to the has-danger class (which Bootstrap uses to set the error color for form elements).

Listing 27-10. Assigning Validation Classes in the MakeBooking.cshtml File in the Views/Home Folder

```
@model Appointment

@{ Layout = "_Layout"; }

@section scripts {
    <script src="/lib/jquery/dist/jquery.min.js"></script>
    <script type="text/javascript">
        $(document).ready(function () {
            $("input.input-validation-error")
                .closest(".form-group").addClass("has-danger");
        });
    </script>
}

<div class="bg-primary m-1 p-1 text-white"><h2>Book an Appointment</h2></div>

<form class="m-1 p-1" asp-action="MakeBooking" method="post">
    <div class="form-group">
        <label asp-for="ClientName">Your name:</label>
        <input asp-for="ClientName" class="form-control" />
    </div>
    <div class="form-group">
        <label asp-for="Date">Appointment Date:</label>
        <input asp-for="Date" type="text" asp-format="{0:d}" class="form-control" />
    </div>
    <div class="radio form-group">
        <input asp-for="TermsAccepted" />
        <label asp-for="TermsAccepted" class="form-check-label">
            I accept the terms & conditions
        </label>
    </div>
    <button type="submit" class="btn btn-primary">Make Booking</button>
</form>
```

The jQuery code runs when the browser has finished parsing all the elements in the HTML document, and the effect is to highlight the input elements that have been assigned to the input-validaton-error class. You can see the effect by running the application and submitting the form without filling in any of the fields, producing the result shown in Figure 27-2.

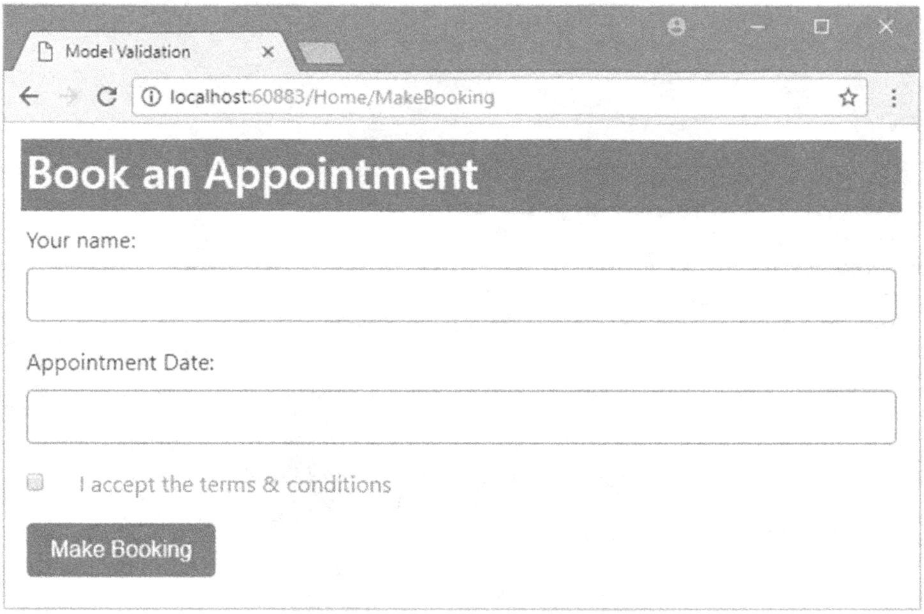

Figure 27-2. *Highlighting validation errors*

When you submit the form without entering any data, errors are highlighted for all three properties. The user will not be shown the Completed.cshtml view until the form is submitted with data that can be parsed by the model browser and that passes the explicit validation checks in the MakeBooking action method. Until that happens, submitting the form will cause the MakeBooking.cshtml view to be rendered with the current validation errors.

Displaying Validation Messages

The CSS classes that the tag helpers apply to input elements indicate that there are problems with a form field, but they do not tell the user what the problem is. Providing the user with more information requires the use of a different tag helper, which adds a summary of the problems to the view, as shown in Listing 27-11.

Listing 27-11. Displaying a Summary in the MakeBooking.cshtml File in the Views/Home Folder

```
@model Appointment

@{ Layout = "_Layout"; }

@section scripts {
<script src="/lib/jquery/dist/jquery.min.js"></script>
<script type="text/javascript">
    $(document).ready(function () {
        $("input.input-validation-error")
            .closest(".form-group").addClass("has-danger");
    });
</script>
}
```

```
<div class="bg-primary m-1 p-1 text-white"><h2>Book an Appointment</h2></div>

<form class="m-1 p-1" asp-action="MakeBooking" method="post">
    <div asp-validation-summary="All" class="text-danger"></div>
    <div class="form-group">
        <label asp-for="ClientName">Your name:</label>
        <input asp-for="ClientName" class="form-control" />
    </div>
    <div class="form-group">
        <label asp-for="Date">Appointment Date:</label>
        <input asp-for="Date" type="text" asp-format="{0:d}" class="form-control" />
    </div>
    <div class="radio form-group">
        <input asp-for="TermsAccepted" />
        <label asp-for="TermsAccepted" class="form-check-label">
            I accept the terms & conditions
        </label>
    </div>
    <button type="submit" class="btn btn-primary">Make Booking</button>
</form>
```

The `ValidationSummaryTagHelper` class detects the `asp-validation-summary` attribute on `div` elements and responds by adding messages that describe any validation errors that have been detected by the action method. The value of the `asp-validation-summary` attribute is a value from the `ValidationSummary` enumeration, which defines the values shown in Table 27-5 and which I demonstrate shortly.

Table 27-5. *The ValidationSummary Values*

Name	Description
All	This value is used to display all the validation errors that have been recorded.
ModelOnly	This value is used to display only the validation errors for the entire model, excluding those that have been recorded for individual properties, as described in the "Displaying Model-Level Messages" section.
None	This value is used to disable the tag helper so that it does not transform the HTML element.

If you run the application and submit the form without making any changes, you can see the summary that the tag helper generates. The text color for this example is defined by the `text-danger` Bootstrap class, which ensures that the text matches the color used to highlight the text fields, as shown in Figure 27-3.

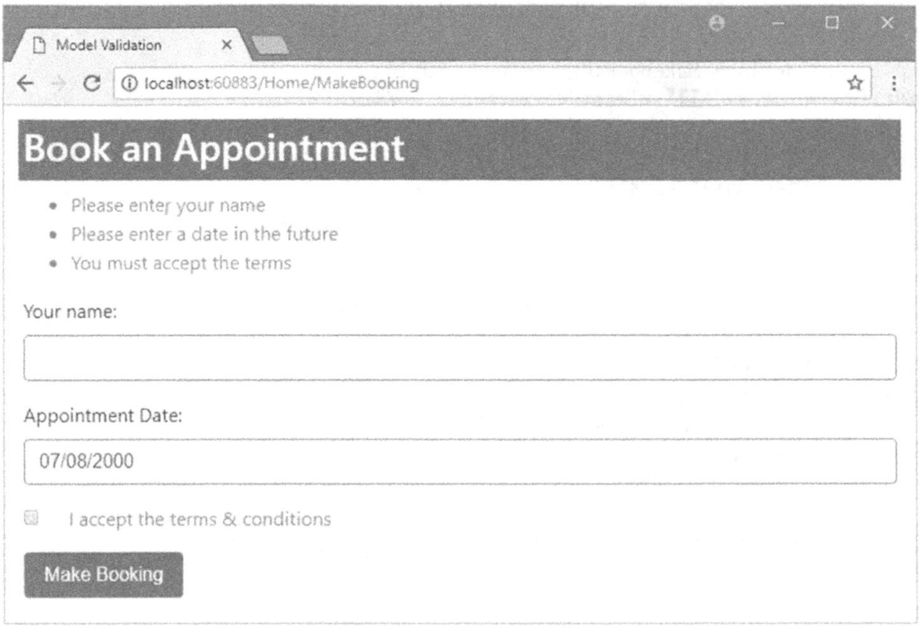

Figure 27-3. *Showing a validation summary to the user*

If you look HTML that has been received by the browser, you will see that the validation messages have been sent as a list, like this:

```
<div class="text-danger validation-summary-errors" data-valmsg-summary="true">
  <ul>
    <li>Please enter your name</li>
    <li>Please enter a date in the future</li>
    <li>You must accept the terms</li>
  </ul>
</div>
```

Configuring the Default Validation Error Messages

The model binding process that I described in Chapter 26 performs its own validation when it tries to provide the data values required to invoke an action method. To see how this works, start the application, clear the contents of the Appointment Date field, and submit the form. You will see that one of the validation error messages shown has changed and does not match any of the strings passed to the AddModelError method in the action method.

```
The value '' is invalid
```

This message is added to the ModelStateDictionary by the model binding process when it can't find a value for a property or does find a value but can't parse it. In this case, the error has arisen because the empty string sent in the form data can't be parsed into a DateTime object for the Date property of the Appointment class.

The model binder has a set of predefined messages that it uses for validation errors. These can be replaced with custom messages using the methods defined by the DefaultModelBindingMessageProvider class, as described in Table 27-6.

Table 27-6. *The DefaultModelBindingMessageProvider Methods*

Name	Description
SetValueMustNotBeNullAccessor	The function assigned to this property is used to generate a validation error message when a value is null for a model property that is non-nullable.
SetMissingBindRequiredValueAccessor	The function assigned to this property is used to generate a validation error message when the request does not contain a value for a required property.
SetMissingKeyOrValueAccessor	The function assigned to this property is used to generate a validation error message when the data required for dictionary model object contains null keys or values.
SetAttemptedValueIsInvalidAccessor	The function assigned to this property is used to generate a validation error message when the model binding system cannot convert the data value into the required C# type.
SetUnknownValueIsInvalidAccessor	The function assigned to this property is used to generate a validation error message when the model binding system cannot convert the data value into the required C# type.
SetValueMustBeANumberAccessor	The function assigned to this property is used to generate a validation error message when the data value cannot be parsed into a C# numeric type.
SetValueIsInvalidAccessor	The function assigned to this property is used to generate a fallback validation error message that is used as a last resort.

Each of the methods described in the table accepts a function that is invoked in order to get the validation message to display to the user. These methods are used in the Startup class to configure the application, as shown in Listing 27-12 in which I have replaced the default message that is displayed when a value is null.

Listing 27-12. Replacing a Binding Message in the Startup.cs File in the ModelValidation Folder

```
using System;
using System.Collections.Generic;
using System.Linq;
using System.Threading.Tasks;
using Microsoft.AspNetCore.Builder;
using Microsoft.AspNetCore.Hosting;
using Microsoft.AspNetCore.Http;
using Microsoft.Extensions.DependencyInjection;
```

```
namespace ModelValidation {

    public class Startup {

        public void ConfigureServices(IServiceCollection services) {
            services.AddMvc().AddMvcOptions(opts =>
                opts.ModelBindingMessageProvider
                    .SetValueMustNotBeNullAccessor(value => "Please enter a value")
            );
        }

        public void Configure(IApplicationBuilder app, IHostingEnvironment env) {
            app.UseStatusCodePages();
            app.UseDeveloperExceptionPage();
            app.UseStaticFiles();
            app.UseMvcWithDefaultRoute();
        }
    }
}
```

The function that you specify receives the value that the user has supplied, although that is not especially useful when dealing with null values. To see the custom message, restart the application and submit the form after clearing the Appointment Date field, as shown in Figure 27-4.

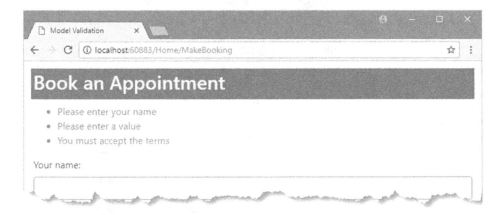

Figure 27-4. *Changing the model binding error messages*

Displaying Property-Level Validation Messages

Although the custom error message is more meaningful than the default one, it still isn't that helpful because it doesn't clearly indicate the problem to the user. For this kind of error, it is more useful to display the validation error messages alongside the HTML elements that contain the problem data. This can be done using the ValidationMessageTag tag helper, which looks for span elements that have the asp-validation-for attribute, which is used to specify the model property for which error messages should be displayed.

In Listing 27-13, I have added property-level validation message elements for each of the input elements in the form. I also removed the scripts section because the individual validation messages will provide enough highlighting to indicate which elements have validation errors.

Listing 27-13. Adding Property-Level Messages in the MakeBooking.cshtml File in the Views/Home Folder

```
@model Appointment

@{ Layout = "_Layout"; }

@section scripts {
<script src="/lib/jquery/dist/jquery.min.js"></script>
<script type="text/javascript">
    $(document).ready(function () {
        $("input.input-validation-error")
            .closest(".form-group").addClass("has-danger");
    });
</script>
}

<div class="bg-primary m-1 p-1 text-white"><h2>Book an Appointment</h2></div>

<form class="m-1 p-1" asp-action="MakeBooking" method="post">
    <div asp-validation-summary="All" class="text-danger"></div>
    <div class="form-group">
        <label asp-for="ClientName">Your name:</label>
        <div><span asp-validation-for="ClientName" class="text-danger"></span></div>
        <input asp-for="ClientName" class="form-control" />
    </div>
    <div class="form-group">
        <label asp-for="Date">Appointment Date:</label>
        <div><span asp-validation-for="Date" class="text-danger"></span></div>
        <input asp-for="Date" type="text" asp-format="{0:d}" class="form-control" />
    </div>
    <span asp-validation-for="TermsAccepted" class="text-danger"></span>
    <div class="radio form-group">
        <input asp-for="TermsAccepted" />
        <label asp-for="TermsAccepted" class="form-check-label">
            I accept the terms & conditions
        </label>
    </div>
    <button type="submit" class="btn btn-primary">Make Booking</button>
</form>
```

Since span elements are displayed inline, some care has to be taken to present the validation messages so it is obvious to which element the message relates. You can see the effect of the new validation messages by running the application and submitting the form without entering any data, as shown in Figure 27-5.

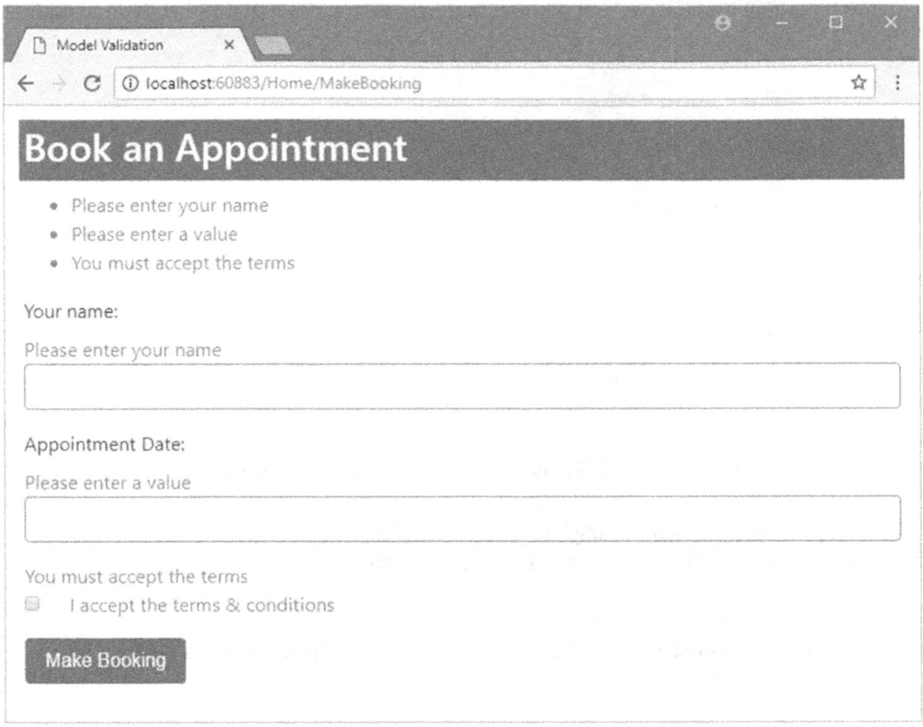

Figure 27-5. *Using property-level validation messages*

Displaying Model-Level Messages

It may seem that the validation summary message is superfluous because it just duplicates the property-level messages, which are generally more helpful to the user because they appear next to the form element where the problem has to be resolved. But the summary has a useful trick, which is the ability to display messages that apply to the entire model and not just individual properties. This means you can report errors that arise from a combination of individual properties, such as when a given date is valid only when combined with a specific name, for example.

In Listing 27-14, I have added a validation check that prevents clients called Joe from booking appointments on Mondays.

Listing 27-14. Performing Model-Level Validation in the HomeController.cs File in the Controllers Folder

```
using System;
using Microsoft.AspNetCore.Mvc;
using ModelValidation.Models;
using Microsoft.AspNetCore.Mvc.ModelBinding;

namespace ModelValidation.Controllers {

    public class HomeController : Controller {

        public IActionResult Index() =>
            View("MakeBooking", new Appointment() { Date = DateTime.Now });
```

866

```
    [HttpPost]
    public ViewResult MakeBooking(Appointment appt) {
        if (string.IsNullOrEmpty(appt.ClientName)) {
            ModelState.AddModelError(nameof(appt.ClientName),
                "Please enter your name");
        }

        if (ModelState.GetValidationState("Date")
                == ModelValidationState.Valid && DateTime.Now > appt.Date) {
            ModelState.AddModelError(nameof(appt.Date),
                "Please enter a date in the future");
        }

        if (!appt.TermsAccepted) {
            ModelState.AddModelError(nameof(appt.TermsAccepted),
                "You must accept the terms");
        }

        if (ModelState.GetValidationState(nameof(appt.Date))
                == ModelValidationState.Valid
            && ModelState.GetValidationState(nameof(appt.ClientName))
                == ModelValidationState.Valid
            && appt.ClientName.Equals("Joe", StringComparison.OrdinalIgnoreCase)
            && appt.Date.DayOfWeek == DayOfWeek.Monday) {
                ModelState.AddModelError("",
                    "Joe cannot book appointments on Mondays");
        }

        if (ModelState.IsValid) {
            return View("Completed", appt);
        } else {
            return View();
        }
    }
}
}
```

This code looks more convoluted than it really is, which is the nature of data validation. I make sure that I have received valid ClientName and Date values by inspecting the model state before checking to see whether the specified date is a Monday and whether the ClientName property is Joe. If Joe is trying to book a Monday appointment, then I call the AddModelError method using the empty string ("") as the first argument, which indicates that the error applies to the entire model and not just to an individual property.

In Listing 27-15, I have changed the value of the asp-validation-summary attribute to ModelOnly, which excludes property-level errors, meaning that the summary will display only those errors that apply to the entire model.

Listing 27-15. Displaying Model-Level Errors in the MakeBooking.cshtml File in the Views/Home Folder

```
@model Appointment

@{ Layout = "_Layout"; }

@section scripts {
<script src="/lib/jquery/dist/jquery.min.js"></script>
<script type="text/javascript">
    $(document).ready(function () {
        $("input.input-validation-error")
            .closest(".form-group").addClass("has-danger");
    });
</script>
}

<div class="bg-primary m-1 p-1 text-white"><h2>Book an Appointment</h2></div>

<form class="m-1 p-1" asp-action="MakeBooking" method="post">
    <div asp-validation-summary="ModelOnly" class="text-danger"></div>
    <div class="form-group">
        <label asp-for="ClientName">Your name:</label>
        <div><span asp-validation-for="ClientName" class="text-danger"></span></div>
        <input asp-for="ClientName" class="form-control" />
    </div>
    <div class="form-group">
        <label asp-for="Date">Appointment Date:</label>
        <div><span asp-validation-for="Date" class="text-danger"></span></div>
        <input asp-for="Date" type="text" asp-format="{0:d}" class="form-control" />
    </div>
    <span asp-validation-for="TermsAccepted" class="text-danger"></span>
    <div class="radio form-group">
        <input asp-for="TermsAccepted" />
        <label asp-for="TermsAccepted" class="form-check-label">
            I accept the terms & conditions
        </label>
    </div>
    <button type="submit" class="btn btn-primary">Make Booking</button>
</form>
```

You can see the effect by running the application, entering Joe into the ClientName field, and selecting a date that you know to be a Monday, such as 01/18/2027. When you submit the form, you will see the response shown in Figure 27-6.

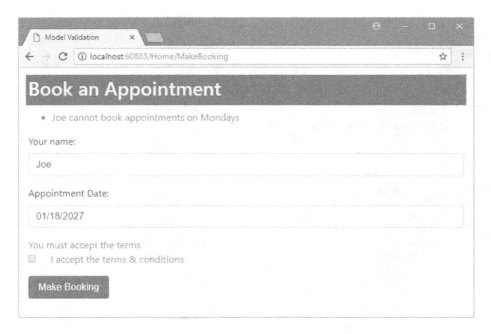

Figure 27-6. *Using model- and property-level validation messages*

Specifying Validation Rules Using Metadata

One problem with putting validation logic into an action method is that it ends up being duplicated in every action method that receives data from the user. To help reduce duplication, the validation process supports the use of attributes to express model validation rules directly in the model class, ensuring that the same set of validation rules will be applied regardless of which action method is used to process a request.

In Listing 27-16, I have applied attributes to the Appointment class to enforce the same set of property-level validation rules I used in the previous section.

Listing 27-16. Applying Validation Attributes in the Appointment.cs File in the Models Folder

```
using System;
using System.ComponentModel.DataAnnotations;

namespace ModelValidation.Models {

    public class Appointment {

        [Required]
        [Display(Name = "name")]
        public string ClientName { get; set; }

        [UIHint("Date")]
        [Required(ErrorMessage = "Please enter a date")]
        public DateTime Date { get; set; }
```

```
    [Range(typeof(bool), "true", "true",          ErrorMessage = "You must accept
      the terms")]
    public bool TermsAccepted { get; set; }
  }
}
```

I used two validation attributes in the listing: Required and Range. The Required attribute specifies that it is a validation error if the user doesn't submit a value for a property. The Range attribute specifies a subset of acceptable values. Table 27-7 shows the set of built-in validation attributes available in an MVC application.

Table 27-7. The Built-in Validation Attributes

Attribute	Example	Description
Compare	[Compare ("OtherProperty")]	This attribute ensures that properties must have the same value, which is useful when you ask the user to provide the same information twice, such as an e-mail address or a password.
Range	[Range(10, 20)]	This attribute ensures that a numeric value (or any property type that implements IComparable) does not lie beyond the specified minimum and maximum values. To specify a boundary on only one side, use a MinValue or MaxValue constant—for example, [Range(int.MinValue, 50)].
RegularExpression	[RegularExpression ("pattern")]	This attribute ensures that a string value matches the specified regular expression pattern. Note that the pattern has to match the *entire* user-supplied value, not just a substring within it. By default, it matches case sensitively, but you can make it case insensitive by applying the (?i) modifier—that is, [RegularExpression("(?i)mypattern")].
Required	[Required]	This attribute ensures that the value is not empty or a string consisting only of spaces. If you want to treat whitespace as valid, use [Required(AllowEmptyStrings = true)].
StringLength	[StringLength(10)]	This attribute ensures that a string value is no longer than a specified maximum length. You can also specify a minimum length: [StringLength(10, MinimumLength=2)].

All the validation attributes support specifying a custom error message by setting a value for the ErrorMessage property, like this:

```
...
[UIHint("Date")]
[Required(ErrorMessage = "Please enter a date")]
public DateTime Date { get; set; }
...
```

If there is no custom error message, then default messages will be used, but they tend to reveal details of the model class that will make no sense to the user unless you also use the `Display` attribute, which is the combination I applied to the `ClientName` property.

```
...
[Required]
[Display(Name = "name")]
public string ClientName { get; set; }
...
```

The default message generated by the `Required` attribute reflects the name specified with the `Display` attribute and so doesn't reveal the name of the property to the user.

Some care is required to get this kind of validation to work consistently. As an example, consider this attribute applied to the `TermsAccepted` property:

```
...
[Range(typeof(bool), "true", "true", ErrorMessage="You must accept the terms")]
public bool TermsAccepted { get; set; }
...
```

I want to make sure that the user selects the box to accept the terms. I cannot use the `Required` attribute because the browser will send a `false` value for this property if the user has not selected the radio button. To work around this, I use a feature of the `Range` attribute that lets me provide a `Type` and specify the upper and lower bounds as string values. By setting both bounds to `true`, I create the equivalent of the `Required` attribute for `bool` properties that are edited using check boxes. Some experimentation can be required to ensure that the validation attributes and the data sent by the browser work together.

The use of the validation attributes on the model class means that the action method in the controller can be simplified, as shown in Listing 27-17.

Listing 27-17. Removing Property-Level Validation in the HomeController.cs File in the Controllers Folder

```
using System;
using Microsoft.AspNetCore.Mvc;
using ModelValidation.Models;
using Microsoft.AspNetCore.Mvc.ModelBinding;

namespace ModelValidation.Controllers {

    public class HomeController : Controller {

        public IActionResult Index() =>
            View("MakeBooking", new Appointment() { Date = DateTime.Now });

        [HttpPost]
        public ViewResult MakeBooking(Appointment appt) {

            if (ModelState.GetValidationState(nameof(appt.Date))
                    == ModelValidationState.Valid
                && ModelState.GetValidationState(nameof(appt.ClientName))
                    == ModelValidationState.Valid
                && appt.ClientName.Equals("Joe", StringComparison.OrdinalIgnoreCase)
                && appt.Date.DayOfWeek == DayOfWeek.Monday) {
```

```
        ModelState.AddModelError("",
            "Joe cannot book appointments on Mondays");
    }

    if (ModelState.IsValid) {
        return View("Completed", appt);
    } else {
        return View();
    }
  }
 }
}
```

The validation attributes are applied before the action method is called, which means that I can still rely on the model state to determine whether individual properties are valid when performing model-level validation. To see the validation attributes in action, start the application and submit the form without entering any data, as shown in Figure 27-7.

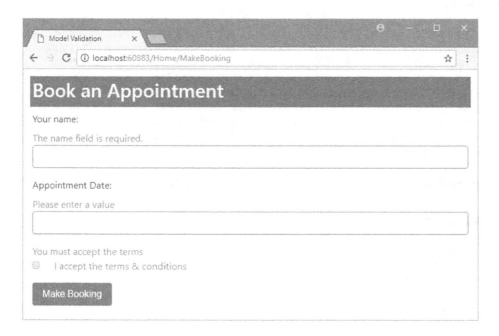

Figure 27-7. *Using validation attributes*

Creating a Custom Property Validation Attribute

The validation process can be extended by creating an attribute that implements the IModelValidator interface. To demonstrate, I created an Infrastructure folder and added a class file called MustBeTrueAttribute.cs to it, in which I defined the class shown in Listing 27-18.

Listing 27-18. The Contents of the MustBeTrueAttribute.cs File in the Infrastructure Folder

```
using System;
using System.Collections.Generic;
using System.Linq;
using Microsoft.AspNetCore.Mvc.ModelBinding.Validation;

namespace ModelValidation.Infrastructure {
    public class MustBeTrueAttribute : Attribute, IModelValidator {

        public bool IsRequired => true;

        public string ErrorMessage { get; set; } = "This value must be true";

        public IEnumerable<ModelValidationResult> Validate(
                ModelValidationContext context) {
            bool? value = context.Model as bool?;
            if (!value.HasValue || value.Value == false) {
                return new List<ModelValidationResult> {
                    new ModelValidationResult("", ErrorMessage)
                };
            } else {
                return Enumerable.Empty<ModelValidationResult>();
            }
        }
    }
}
```

The IModelValidator interface defines an IsRequired property, which is used to indicate whether validation by this class is required (which is a little misleading because the value returned by this property is simply used to order validation attributes so that the required ones are executed first). The Validate method is used to perform validation and receives information through an instance of the ModelValidationContext class, whose most useful properties are described in Table 27-8.

Table 27-8. *Useful ModelValidationContext Class*

Name	Description
Model	This property returns the property value that is to be validated, which would be the value of the TermsAccepted property in the example.
Container	This property returns the object that contains the property, which would be the Appointment object in the example.
ActionContext	This property returns an ActionContext object that provides context data and describes the action method that will process the request.
ModelMetadata	This property returns a ModelMetadata object that describes the model class that is being validated in detail.

The Validate method returns a sequence of ModelValidationResult objects, each of which describes a single validation error. In the example attribute, I create a ModelValidationResult if the model value isn't true. The first argument to the ModelValidationResult constructor is the name of the property to which the error is associated and is specified as the empty string when validating individual properties. The second argument is the error message that will be displayed to the user. In Listing 27-19, I have replaced the Range attribute with the custom attribute.

Listing 27-19. Applying a Custom Validation Attribute in the Appointment.cs File in the Models Folder

```
using System;
using System.ComponentModel.DataAnnotations;
using ModelValidation.Infrastructure;

namespace ModelValidation.Models {

    public class Appointment {

        [Required]
        [Display(Name = "name")]
        public string ClientName { get; set; }

        [UIHint("Date")]
        [Required(ErrorMessage = "Please enter a date")]
        public DateTime Date { get; set; }

        [MustBeTrue(ErrorMessage = "You must accept the terms")]
        public bool TermsAccepted { get; set; }
    }
}
```

The result of using the custom validation attribute is just the same as using the Range attribute, but the purpose of the custom attribute is more obvious when reading the code.

Performing Client-Side Validation

The validation techniques I have demonstrated so far have all been examples of server-side validation. This means the user submits their data to the server, and the server validates the data and sends back the results of the validation (either success in processing the data or a list of errors that need to be corrected).

In web applications, users typically expect immediate validation feedback—without having to submit anything to the server. This is known as *client-side validation* and is implemented using JavaScript. The data that the user has entered is validated before being sent to the server, providing the user with immediate feedback and an opportunity to correct any problems.

MVC supports *unobtrusive client-side validation*. The term *unobtrusive* means that validation rules are expressed using attributes added to the HTML elements that views generate. These attributes are interpreted by a JavaScript library that is included as part of MVC that, in turn, configures the jQuery Validation library, which does the actual validation work. In the following sections, I will show you how the built-in validation support works and demonstrate how I can extend the functionality to provide custom client-side validation.

■ **Tip** Client-side validation is focused on validating individual properties. In fact, it is hard to set up model-level client-side validation using the built-in support that comes with MVC. To that end, most MVC applications use client-side validation for property-level issues and rely on server-side validation for the overall model.

The first step is to add new JavaScript packages to the application using Bower, as shown in Listing 27-20.

Listing 27-20. Adding Packages in the bower.json File in the ModelValidation Folder

```
{
  "name": "asp.net",
  "private": true,
  "dependencies": {
    "bootstrap": "4.0.0-alpha.6",
    "jquery": "3.2.1",
    "jquery-validation": "1.17.0",
    "jquery-validation-unobtrusive": "3.2.6"
  }
}
```

Using client-side validation means adding three JavaScript files to the view: the jQuery library, the jQuery validation library, and the Microsoft unobtrusive validation library, all of which are shown in Listing 27-21.

■ **Tip** The Bower tool doesn't always perform the installation of the validation packages correctly. If you find that your wwwroot/lib folder doesn't contain the files that are required, then remove wwwroot/lib and its contents. Open a new PowerShell window, navigate to the project folder and run bower cache clean followed by bower install to download fresh copies of the validation packages.

Listing 27-21. Adding the JavaScript Elements in the MakeBooking.cshtml File in the Views/Home Folder

```
@model Appointment

@{ Layout = "_Layout"; }

@section scripts {
    <script src="/lib/jquery/dist/jquery.min.js"></script>
    <script src="/lib/jquery-validation/dist/jquery.validate.min.js"></script>
    <script
        src="/lib/jquery-validation-unobtrusive/jquery.validate.unobtrusive.min.js">
    </script>
}

<div class="bg-primary m-1 p-1 text-white"><h2>Book an Appointment</h2></div>

<form class="m-1 p-1" asp-action="MakeBooking" method="post">
    <div asp-validation-summary="ModelOnly" class="text-danger"></div>
    <div class="form-group">
```

```
        <label asp-for="ClientName">Your name:</label>
        <div><span asp-validation-for="ClientName" class="text-danger"></span></div>
        <input asp-for="ClientName" class="form-control" />
    </div>
    <div class="form-group">
        <label asp-for="Date">Appointment Date:</label>
        <div><span asp-validation-for="Date" class="text-danger"></span></div>
        <input asp-for="Date" type="text" asp-format="{0:d}" class="form-control" />
    </div>
    <span asp-validation-for="TermsAccepted" class="text-danger"></span>
    <div class="radio form-group">
        <input asp-for="TermsAccepted" />
        <label asp-for="TermsAccepted" class="form-check-label">
            I accept the terms & conditions
        </label>
    </div>
    <button type="submit" class="btn btn-primary">Make Booking</button>
</form>
```

The files must be added in the order in which they are shown. When the tag helpers transform the input elements, they inspect the validation attributes applied to the model class property and add attributes to the output element. If you run the application and inspect the HTML sent to the browser, you will see an element like this one:

```
<input class="form-control" type="text" data-val="true"
    data-val-required="The name field is required." id="ClientName"
    name="ClientName" value="" />
```

The JavaScript code looks for elements with the data-val attribute and performs local validation in the browser when the user submits the form, without sending an HTTP request to the server. You can see the effect by running the application and submitting the form while using the F12 tools to note that validation error messages are displayed even though no HTTP request is sent to the server.

AVOIDING CONFLICTS WITH BROWSER VALIDATION

Some HTML5 browsers support simple client-side validation based on the attributes applied to input elements. The general idea is that, say, an input element to which the required attribute has been applied, for example, will cause the browser to display a validation error when the user tries to submit the form without providing a value.

If you are generating form elements from models, as I have been doing in this chapter, then you won't have any problems with browser validation because MVC generates and uses data attributes to denote validation rules (so that, for example, an input element that must have a value is denoted with the data-val-required attribute, which browsers do not recognize).

However, you may run into problems if you are unable to completely control the markup in your application, something that often happens when you are passing on content generated elsewhere. The result is that the jQuery validation and the browser validation can both operate on the form, which is just confusing to the user. To avoid this problem, you can add the novalidate attribute to the form element.

One of the nice features about MVC client-side validation is that the same attributes used to specify validation rules are applied at the client *and* at the server. This means that data from browsers that do not support JavaScript are subject to the same validation as those that do, without requiring any additional effort. It does mean, however, that custom validation attributes are not supported for client-side validation because the JavaScript code has no way to implement the custom logic at the client. Put another way, if you want to use client-side validation, you need to stick to the built-in attributes described in Table 27-7.

MVC CLIENT VALIDATION VERSUS JQUERY VALIDATION

The MVC client-validation features are built on top of the jQuery Validation library. If you prefer, you can use the Validation library directly and ignore the MVC features. The Validation library is flexible and feature-rich. It is well worth exploring if only to understand how to customize the MVC features to take the best advantage of the available validation options. I cover the jQuery Validation library in depth in my *Pro jQuery 2.0* book, also published by Apress.

Performing Remote Validation

The last validation feature described in this chapter is *remote validation*. This is a client-side validation technique that invokes an action method on the server to perform validation.

A common example of remote validation is to check whether a username is available in applications where such names must be unique, when the user submits the data, and the client-side validation is performed. As part of this process, an Ajax request is made to the server to validate the username that has been requested. If the username has been taken, a validation error is displayed so that the user can enter another value.

This may seem like regular server-side validation, but there are some benefits to this approach. First, only some properties will be remotely validated; the client-side validation benefits still apply to all the other data values that the user has entered. Second, the request is relatively lightweight and is focused on validation, rather than processing an entire model object.

The third difference is that the remote validation is performed in the background. The user doesn't have to click the submit button and then wait for a new view to be rendered and returned. It makes for a more responsive user experience, especially when there is a slow network between the browser and the server.

That said, remote validation is a compromise. It strikes a balance between client-side and server-side validation, but it does require requests to the application server, and it is not as quick to validate as normal client-side validation.

The first step toward using remote validation is to create an action method that can validate one of the model properties. I am going to validate the Date property of the Appointment model to ensure that the requested appointment is in the future. (This is one of the original validation rules I used at the start of the chapter but that isn't possible to validate using the standard client-side validation features.) Listing 27-22 shows the addition of a ValidateDate action method to the Home controller.

Listing 27-22. Adding an Action to the HomeController.cs File in the Controllers Folder

```
using System;
using Microsoft.AspNetCore.Mvc;
using ModelValidation.Models;
using Microsoft.AspNetCore.Mvc.ModelBinding;
```

```csharp
namespace ModelValidation.Controllers {

    public class HomeController : Controller {

        public IActionResult Index() =>
            View("MakeBooking", new Appointment() { Date = DateTime.Now });

        [HttpPost]
        public ViewResult MakeBooking(Appointment appt) {

            if (ModelState.GetValidationState(nameof(appt.Date))
                    == ModelValidationState.Valid
                && ModelState.GetValidationState(nameof(appt.ClientName))
                    == ModelValidationState.Valid
                && appt.ClientName.Equals("Joe", StringComparison.OrdinalIgnoreCase)
                && appt.Date.DayOfWeek == DayOfWeek.Monday) {
                ModelState.AddModelError("",
                    "Joe cannot book appointments on Mondays");
            }

            if (ModelState.IsValid) {
                return View("Completed", appt);
            } else {
                return View();
            }
        }

        public JsonResult ValidateDate(string Date) {
            DateTime parsedDate;

            if (!DateTime.TryParse(Date, out parsedDate)) {
                return Json("Please enter a valid date (mm/dd/yyyy)");
            } else if (DateTime.Now > parsedDate) {
                return Json("Please enter a date in the future");
            } else {
                return Json(true);
            }
        }
    }
}
```

Actions methods that support remote validation must return the JsonResult type, which tells MVC that I am working with JSON data, as explained in Chapter 20. In addition to the result, validation action methods must define a parameter that has the same name as the data field being validated; this is Date for the example. Within the action method, validation is performed by parsing the value into a DateTime object and checking to see that it is in the future.

■ **Tip**   I could have taken advantage of model binding so that the parameter to my action method would be a DateTime object, but doing so would mean that the validation method wouldn't be called if the user entered a nonsense value like apple, for example. This is because the model binder wouldn't have been able to create a DateTime object from apple and throws an exception when it tries. The remote validation feature doesn't have a way to express that exception and so it is quietly discarded. This has the unfortunate effect of *not* highlighting the data field and so creating the impression that the value that the user has entered is valid. As a general rule, the best approach to remote validation is to accept a string parameter in the action method and perform any type conversion, parsing, or model binding explicitly.

I express validation results using the Json method, which creates a JSON-formatted result that the client-side remote validation script can parse and process. If the value is valid, then I pass true as the parameter to the Json method, like this:

```
...
return Json(true);
...
```

If there is a problem, I pass the validation error message that the user should see as the parameter, like this:

```
...
return Json("Please enter a date in the future");
...
```

To use the remote validation method, I apply the Remote attribute to a property in the model class, as shown in Listing 27-23.

Listing 27-23.   Using the Remote Attribute in the Appointment.cs File in the Models Folder

```
using System;
using System.ComponentModel.DataAnnotations;
using ModelValidation.Infrastructure;
using Microsoft.AspNetCore.Mvc;

namespace ModelValidation.Models {

    public class Appointment {

        [Required]
        [Display(Name = "name")]
        public string ClientName { get; set; }

        [UIHint("Date")]
        [Required(ErrorMessage = "Please enter a date")]
        [Remote("ValidateDate", "Home")]
        public DateTime Date { get; set; }
```

```
        [MustBeTrue(ErrorMessage = "You must accept the terms")]
        public bool TermsAccepted { get; set; }
    }
}
```

The arguments for the attribute are the name of the action and the controller that should be used to generate the URL that the JavaScript validation library will call to perform the validation—in this case, the ValidateDate action on the Home controller.

You can see how the remote validation works by starting the application, navigating to the /Home URL, and entering a date that is in the past. When you select a value and the focus moves to another element, the validation message will appear, as shown in Figure 27-8.

■ **Caution**   The validation action method will be called when the user first submits the form and then again each time the data is edited. For text input elements, every keystroke will lead to a call to the server. For some applications, this can be a significant number of requests and must be taken into account when specifying the server capacity and bandwidth that an application requires in production. Also, you might choose *not* to use remote validation for properties that are expensive to validate (for example, if you have to query a slow server to determine whether a username is unique).

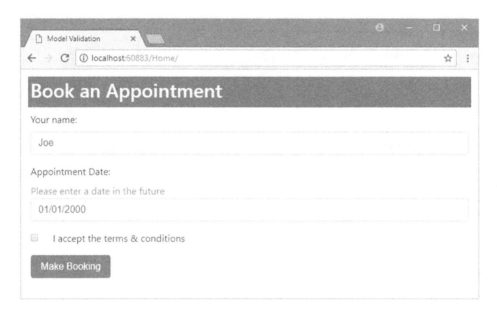

Figure 27-8. Performing remote validation

Summary

In this chapter, I examined the wide range of techniques available to perform model validation, ensuring that the data that the user has provided is consistent with the constraints imposed on the data model. Model validation is an important topic, and getting the right validation in place for an application is essential to ensure that the users have a good and frustration-free experience. In the next chapter, I explain how to secure an MVC application using ASP.NET Core Identity.

CHAPTER 28

■ ■ ■

Getting Started with Identity

ASP.NET Core Identity is an API from Microsoft to manage users in ASP.NET applications. In this chapter, I demonstrate the process of setting up ASP.NET Core Identity and creating a simple user administration tool that manages individual user accounts that are stored in a database.

ASP.NET Core Identity supports other kinds of user accounts, such as those stored using Active Directory, but I don't describe them since they are not used that often outside corporations (where Active Directive implementations tend to be so convoluted that it would be difficult for me to provide useful general examples).

■ **Note** This chapter requires the SQL Server LocalDB feature to be installed for Visual Studio. You can add LocalDB by running the Visual Studio installer and installing the SQL Server Express 2016 LocalDB option from the Individual Components section.

In Chapter 29, I show you how to perform authentication and authorization using those user accounts, and in Chapter 30, I show you how to move beyond the basics and apply some advanced techniques. Table 28-1 puts ASP.NET Core Identity in context.

Table 28-1. *Putting ASP.NET Core Identity in Context*

Question	Answer
What is it?	ASP.NET Core Identity is an API for managing users and storing user data in repositories such as relational databases through Entity Framework Core.
Why is it useful?	User management is an important feature for most applications, and ASP.NET Core Identity provides a ready-made and well-tested platform that doesn't require you to create custom versions of commonly demanded functions.
How is it used?	Identity is used through services and middleware added to the Startup class and through classes that act as bridges between the application and the Identity functionality.
Are there any pitfalls or limitations?	Microsoft has compensated for the inflexibility of earlier ASP.NET user management APIs by making Identity so flexible and so configurable that it can be a challenge figuring out what is possible and what you need. I only scratch the surface of the deep and complex system in this book.
Are there any alternatives?	You could implement your own APIs, but that can be a lot of work and tends to create security vulnerabilities unless done carefully.

Table 28-2 summarizes the chapter.

Table 28-2. *Chapter Summary*

Problem	Solution	Listing
Add Identity to a project	Add the middleware for ASP.NET Identity Core and Entity Framework Core, create a user class and a database context class, and create a database migration	1–13
Read user data	Query the Identity database using the context class	14–15
Create a user account	Call the UserManager.CreateAsync method	16–18
Change the default password policy	Set the password options in the Startup class	19
Implement custom password validation	Implement the IPasswordValidator interface or subclass from the PasswordValidator class	20–22
Change the account validation policy	Set the user options in the Startup class	23
Implement custom account validation	Implement the IUserValidator interface or subclass from the UserValidator class	24–26
Delete a user account	Call the UserManager.DeleteAsync method	27, 28
Edit a user account	Call the UserManager.UpdateAsync method	29–31

Preparing the Example Project

For this chapter, I used the ASP.NET Core Web Application (.NET Core) template to create a new Empty project called Users. The example application requires the Entity Framework Core command-line tools, which must be added to the project by manually editing the csproj file. Right-click the Users project item in the Solution Explorer, select Edit Users.csproj file and add the element shown in Listing 28-1.

Listing 28-1. Adding a Package in the Users.csproj File in the Users Folder

```
<Project Sdk="Microsoft.NET.Sdk.Web">

  <PropertyGroup>
    <TargetFramework>netcoreapp2.0</TargetFramework>
  </PropertyGroup>

  <ItemGroup>
    <Folder Include="wwwroot\" />
  </ItemGroup>

  <ItemGroup>
    <PackageReference Include="Microsoft.AspNetCore.All" Version="2.0.0" />
    <DotNetCliToolReference Include="Microsoft.EntityFrameworkCore.Tools.DotNet"
        Version="2.0.0" />
  </ItemGroup>

</Project>
```

Listing 28-2 shows the Startup class, which sets up the MVC Framework and enables middleware components useful for development, as described in Chapter 14.

Listing 28-2. The Contents of the Startup.cs File in the Users Folder

```
using Microsoft.AspNetCore.Builder;
using Microsoft.Extensions.DependencyInjection;

namespace Users {

    public class Startup {

        public void ConfigureServices(IServiceCollection services) {
            services.AddMvc();
        }

        public void Configure(IApplicationBuilder app) {
            app.UseStatusCodePages();
            app.UseDeveloperExceptionPage();
            app.UseStaticFiles();
            app.UseMvcWithDefaultRoute();
        }
    }
}
```

Creating the Controller and View

I created the Controllers folder, added a class file called HomeController.cs, and defined the controller shown in Listing 28-3. I'll be using this controller to describe details of user accounts and data, and the Index action method passes a dictionary of values to the default view via the View method.

Listing 28-3. The Contents of the HomeController.cs File in the Controllers Folder

```
using System.Collections.Generic;
using Microsoft.AspNetCore.Mvc;

namespace Users.Controllers {

    public class HomeController : Controller {

        public ViewResult Index() =>
            View(new Dictionary<string, object>
                {["Placeholder"] = "Placeholder" });
    }
}
```

To provide the controller with a view, I created the Views/Home folder and added a view file called Index.cshtml with the markup shown in Listing 28-4.

Listing 28-4. The Contents of the Index.cshtml File in the Views/Home Folder

```
@model Dictionary<string, object>

<div class="bg-primary m-1 p-1 text-white"><h4>User Details</h4></div>

<table class="table table-sm table-bordered m-1 p-1">
    @foreach (var kvp in Model) {
        <tr><th>@kvp.Key</th><td>@kvp.Value</td></tr>
    }
</table>
```

The view displays the contents of the model dictionary in a table. To support the view, I created the Views/Shared folder, adding a view file called _Layout.cshtml with the markup shown in Listing 28-5.

Listing 28-5. The Contents of the _Layout.cshtml File in the Views/Shared Folder

```
<!DOCTYPE html>
<html>
<head>
    <title>Users</title>
    <meta name="viewport" content="width=device-width" />
    <link href="/lib/bootstrap/dist/css/bootstrap.css" rel="stylesheet" />
</head>
<body class="m-1 p-1">
    @RenderBody()
</body>
</html>
```

The view depends on the Bootstrap CSS package to style the HTML elements. To add Bootstrap to the project, I used the Bower Configuration File item template to create the bower.json file and added the Bootstrap package to the dependencies section, as shown in Listing 28-6.

Listing 28-6. Adding the Bootstrap Package in the bower.json File in the Users Folder

```
{
  "name": "asp.net",
  "private": true,
  "dependencies": {
    "bootstrap": "4.0.0-alpha.6"
  }
}
```

The final preparation is to create the _ViewImports.cshtml file in the Views folder, which sets up the built-in tag helpers for use in the views, as shown in Listing 28-7.

Listing 28-7. The Contents of the _ViewImports.cshtml File in the Views Folder

```
@addTagHelper *, Microsoft.AspNetCore.Mvc.TagHelpers
```

The final addition I made was to create a view start file called _ViewStart.cshtml in the Views folder with the content shown in Listing 28-8. This ensures that the layout I created in Listing 28-7 will be used by all the views in the application.

Listing 28-8. The Contents of the _ViewStart.cshtml File in the Views Folder

```
@{
    Layout = "_Layout";
}
```

Start the application and you will see the output shown in Figure 28-1.

Figure 28-1. *Running the example application*

Setting Up ASP.NET Core Identity

The process for setting up Identity touches on almost every part of an application, requiring new model classes, configuration changes, and controllers and actions to support authentication and authorization operations. In the sections that follow, I walk through the process of setting up Identity in a basic configuration to show the different steps that are involved. There are lots of different ways of using Identity in an application, and the configuration I use in this chapter follows the simplest and most commonly used options.

Creating the User Class

The first step is to define a class to represent a user in the application, which is known as the *user class*. The user class is derived from IdentityUser, which is defined in the Microsoft.AspNetCore.Identity namespace. IdentityUser provides the basic user representation, which can be extended by adding properties to the derived class, which I describe in Chapter 30. Table 28-3 shows the most useful built-in properties that IdentityUser defines, including the ones I use in this chapter.

Table 28-3. *The Properties Defined by the IdentityUser Class*

Name	Description
Id	This property contains the unique ID for the user.
UserName	This property returns the user's username.
Claims	This property returns the collection of claims for the user, which I describe in Chapter 30.
Email	This property contains the user's e-mail address.
Logins	This property returns a collection of logins for the user, which is used for third-party authentication, as described in Chapter 30.
PasswordHash	This property returns a hashed form of the user password, which I use in the "Implementing the Edit Feature" section.
Roles	This property returns the collection of roles that the user belongs to, which I describe in Chapter 29.
PhoneNumber	This property returns the user's phone number.
SecurityStamp	This property returns a value that is changed when the user identity is altered, such as by a password change.

The individual properties don't matter at the moment. What's important is that the IdentityUser class provides access to basic information about a user: the user's name, e-mail, phone number, password hash, role memberships, and so on. If I want to store any additional information about the user, I have to add properties to the class that I derive from IdentityUser and that will be used to represent users in my application.

To create the user class for my application, I created the Models folder and added a class file called AppUserModels.cs that I used to create the AppUser class, which is shown in Listing 28-9.

Listing 28-9. The Contents of the AppUser.cs File in the Models Folder

```
using Microsoft.AspNetCore.Identity;

namespace Users.Models {

    public class AppUser : IdentityUser {
        // no additional members are required
        // for basic Identity installation
    }
}
```

That's all I have to do at the moment, although I'll return to this class in Chapter 30, when I show you how to add application-specific user data properties.

Configuring the View Imports

Although not directly related to setting up ASP.NET Core Identity, I will be working with AppUser objects in views in the next section. To make writing the views simpler, I added the Users.Models namespace to the view imports file, as shown in Listing 28-10.

Listing 28-10. Adding a Namespace in the _ViewImports.cshtml File in the Views Folder

```
@using Users.Models
@addTagHelper *, Microsoft.AspNetCore.Mvc.TagHelpers
```

Creating the Database Context Class

The next step is to create an Entity Framework Core database context class that operates on the AppUser class. The context class is derived from IdentityDbContext<T>, where T is the user class (AppUser in the example project). I added a class file called AppIdentityDbContext.cs to the Models folder and defined the class shown in Listing 28-11.

Listing 28-11. The Contents of the AppIdentityDbContext.cs File in the Models Folder

```
using Microsoft.AspNetCore.Identity.EntityFrameworkCore;
using Microsoft.EntityFrameworkCore;

namespace Users.Models {

    public class AppIdentityDbContext : IdentityDbContext<AppUser> {

        public AppIdentityDbContext(DbContextOptions<AppIdentityDbContext> options)
            : base(options) { }
    }
}
```

The database context class can be extended to customize the way that the database is set up and used, but for a basic ASP.NET Core Identity application, just defining the class is enough to get started and to provide a placeholder for any future customization.

■ **Note** Don't worry if the role of these classes doesn't make sense. If you are unfamiliar with Entity Framework Core, then I suggest you treat it as something of a black box. Once the basic building blocks are in place—and you can copy the ones into your project to get things working—then you will rarely need to edit them.

Configuring the Database Connection String Setting

The first configuration step for ASP.NET Core Identity is to define the connection string that will be used for the database. The convention is to put the connection string in the appsettings.json file, which is then loaded when the application starts and can be accessed in the Startup class, as explained in Chapter 14. I used the ASP.NET Configuration File item template to create the appsettings.json file in the root folder of the project and added the configuration settings shown in Listing 28-12.

Listing 28-12. The Contents of the appsettings.json File in the Users Folder

```
{
  "Data": {
    "SportStoreIdentity": {
      "ConnectionString":
```

```
"Server=(localdb)\\MSSQLLocalDB;Database=IdentityUsers;Trusted_Connection=True;
MultipleActiveResultSets=true"
    }
  }
}
```

In the connection string, I have specified the localdb option, which provides convenient database support for developers. For the database itself, I have specified the name IdentityUsers.

■ **Note**   The width of the printed page doesn't allow for sensible formatting of the connection string, which must appear in a single unbroken line. That works well in the Visual Studio editor but means that it has to wrap multiple lines in the listing. When you add the connection string to your own project, make sure that it is on a single line.

With the database connection string in place, I can update the Startup class to receive the configuration data, as shown in Listing 28-13.

Listing 28-13. Reading the Application Settings in the Startup.cs File in the Users Folder

```
using Microsoft.AspNetCore.Builder;
using Microsoft.Extensions.DependencyInjection;
using Microsoft.Extensions.Configuration;
using Microsoft.AspNetCore.Identity;
using Microsoft.EntityFrameworkCore;
using Users.Models;

namespace Users {

    public class Startup {

        public Startup(IConfiguration configuration) =>
            Configuration = configuration;

        public IConfiguration Configuration { get; }

        public void ConfigureServices(IServiceCollection services) {
            services.AddDbContext<AppIdentityDbContext>(options =>
                options.UseSqlServer(
                    Configuration["Data:SportStoreIdentity:ConnectionString"]));

            services.AddIdentity<AppUser, IdentityRole>()
                .AddEntityFrameworkStores<AppIdentityDbContext>()
                .AddDefaultTokenProviders();

            services.AddMvc();
        }
```

```
        public void Configure(IApplicationBuilder app) {
            app.UseStatusCodePages();
            app.UseDeveloperExceptionPage();
            app.UseStaticFiles();
            app.UseAuthentication();
            app.UseMvcWithDefaultRoute();
        }
    }
}
```

There are three sets of changes required to create a basic ASP.NET Core Identity installation. The first step is to set up Entity Framework (EF) Core, which provides data access services to MVC applications.

```
...
services.AddDbContext<AppIdentityDbContext>(options =>
    options.UseSqlServer(Configuration["Data:SportStoreIdentity:ConnectionString"]));
...
```

The AddDbContext method adds the services required for Entity Framework Core, and the UseSqlServer method sets up the support required for storing data using Microsoft SQL Server. The AddDbContext method allows me to apply the database context class that I created earlier and specify that it will be backed up with a SQL Server database whose connection string is obtained from the application's configuration (which, for the example application, means the appsettings.json file).

I also need to set up the services for ASP.NET Core Identity, which is done like this:

```
...
services.AddIdentity<AppUser, IdentityRole>()
    .AddEntityFrameworkStores<AppIdentityDbContext>()
    .AddDefaultTokenProviders();
...
```

The AddIdentity method has type parameters that specify the class used to represent users and the class used to represent roles. I have specified the AppUser class for users and the built-in IdentityRole class for roles. The AddEntityFrameworkStores method specifies that Identity should use Entity Framework Core to store and retrieve its data, using the database context class I created earlier. The AddDefaultTokenProviders method uses the default configuration to support operations that require a token, such as changing a password.

The final change to the Startup class adds ASP.NET Core Identity to the request-handing pipeline, which allows user credentials to be associated with requests based on cookies or URL rewriting, meaning that details of user accounts are not directly included in the HTTP requests sent to the application or the responses it generates.

```
...
app.UseAuthentication();
...
```

Creating the Identity Database

Almost everything is in place, and the only remaining step is to actually create the database that will be used to store the Identity data. Open a new command prompt or PowerShell window, navigate to the Users project folder (the one that contains the Startup.cs file), and run the following command:

```
dotnet ef migrations add Initial
```

As I explained when I set up the database for the SportsStore application, Entity Framework Core manages changes to database schemas through a feature called *migrations*. When you modify the model classes that are used to generate the schema, you can produce a migration file that contains the SQL commands required to update the database. The command creates the migration files that will set up the database for Identity.

When the dotnet ef command completes, you will see a Migrations folder in the Solution Explorer. If you examine the contents of the files, you can see the SQL commands that will be used to create the initial database. To use the migration files to create the database, run this command:

```
dotnet ef database update
```

It can take a moment for the process to complete, but once the command has finished, the database will have been created and prepared for use.

Using ASP.NET Core Identity

Now that the basic setup is out of the way, I can start to use ASP.NET Core Identity to add support for managing users to the example application. In the sections that follow, I demonstrate how the Identity API can be used to create administration tools that allow for centralized management of users.

Centralized user administration tools are useful in just about all applications, even those that allow users to create and manage their own accounts. There will always be some customers who require bulk account creation, for example, and support issues that require inspection and adjustment of user data. From the perspective of this chapter, administration tools are useful because they consolidate a lot of basic user management functions into a small number of classes, making them useful examples to demonstrate the fundamental features of ASP.NET Core Identity.

Enumerating User Accounts

The starting point for this section is to enumerate all the user accounts in the database, which will allow me to see the effect of code that I add to the application later. I started by adding a class file called AdminController.cs to the Controllers folder and using it to define the controller shown in Listing 28-14, which I will use to define my user administration functionality.

Listing 28-14. The Contents of the AdminController.cs File in the Controllers Folder

```
using Microsoft.AspNetCore.Identity;
using Microsoft.AspNetCore.Mvc;
using Users.Models;

namespace Users.Controllers {
```

```
public class AdminController : Controller {
    private UserManager<AppUser> userManager;

    public AdminController(UserManager<AppUser> usrMgr) {
        userManager = usrMgr;
    }

    public ViewResult Index() => View(userManager.Users);
}
}
```

The Index action method enumerates the users managed by the Identity system; there aren't any users at the moment, of course, but there will be soon. Access to the user data is through the UserManager<AppUser> object that is received by the controller constructor and provided through dependency injection.

With a UserManager<AppUser> object, I can start to query the data store. The Users property returns an enumeration of user objects—instances of the AppUser class in this application—which can be queried and manipulated using LINQ. In the action method, I pass the value of the Users property, which will enumerate all the users in the database, to the View method so I can display the account details. To provide the action method with a view, I created the Views/Admin folder, added a file called Index.cshtml to it, and applied the markup shown in Listing 28-15.

Listing 28-15. The Contents of the Index.cshtml File in the Views/Admin Folder

```
@model IEnumerable<AppUser>

<div class="bg-primary m-1 p-1 text-white"><h4>User Accounts</h4></div>

<table class="table table-sm table-bordered">
    <tr><th>ID</th><th>Name</th><th>Email</th></tr>
    @if (Model.Count() == 0) {
        <tr><td colspan="3" class="text-center">No User Accounts</td></tr>
    } else {
        foreach (AppUser user in Model) {
            <tr>
                <td>@user.Id</td>
                <td>@user.UserName</td>
                <td>@user.Email</td>
            </tr>
        }
    }
</table>

<a class="btn btn-primary" asp-action="Create">Create</a>
```

This view contains a table that has rows for each user, with columns for the unique ID, username, and e-mail address. If there are no users in the database, then a message is displayed, as shown in Figure 28-2, which you can see if you start the application and request the /Admin URL.

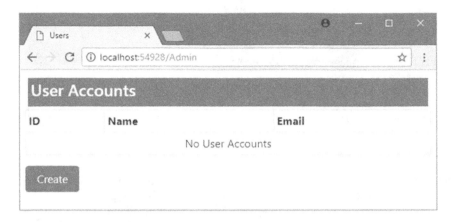

Figure 28-2. *Displaying the (empty) list of users*

I included a Create anchor element link in the view (styled as a button) that targets the Create action on the Admin controller. This will be the action that supports adding users.

RESETTING THE DATABASE

You can see the database that is created for Identity by opening the Visual Studio SQL Server Object Explorer window. If this is the first time that you have used SQL Server Object Explorer window, then you will need to select Connect to Database from the Tools menu to tell Visual Studio about the database you are working with. For the data source, select Microsoft SQL Server, use (localdb)\mssqllocaldb as the server name, leave Use Windows Authentication selected, and click the drop-down arrow for the Select Or Enter a Database Name field. After a few seconds, you will see a list of the LocalDB databases that are available, and you should be able to select IdentityUsers, which is the database for the example application. Click OK, and a new entry will appear in the SQL Server Object Explorer window. Visual Studio will remember the database, so you should need to perform this process only once.

You can explore the database by expanding the (localdb)\mssqllocaldb ➤ Databases ➤ IdentityUsers item in the SQL Server Object Explorer window. You will be able to see the tables that were created by the migrations file, with names like AspNetUsers and AspNetRoles. You can query the database to see the contents of the table once you have added users to the database, which I demonstrate in the next section.

To delete the database, right-click the IdentityUsers item in the SQL Server Object Explorer window and select Delete from the pop-up menu. Check both of the options in the Delete Database dialog and click the OK button to delete the database.

To re-create the database, open the Package Manager Console window and run the following command:

```
dotnet ef database update
```

The database will be re-created and will be ready for use when you next start the application.

Creating Users

I am going to use MVC model validation for the input the application receives, and the easiest way to do this is to create simple view models for each of the operations that the controller supports. I added a class file called UserViewModels.cs to the Models folder and used it to define the class shown in Listing 28-16.

Listing 28-16. The Contents of the UserViewModels.cs File in the Models Folder

```
using System.ComponentModel.DataAnnotations;

namespace Users.Models {

    public class CreateModel {
        [Required]
        public string Name { get; set; }
        [Required]
        public string Email { get; set; }
        [Required]
        public string Password { get; set; }
    }
}
```

The initial model I have defined is called CreateModel, and it defines the basic properties that I require to create a user account: a username, an e-mail address, and a password. I used the Required attribute from the System.ComponentModel.DataAnnotations namespace to denote that values are required for all three properties defined in the model.

In Listing 28-17, I added a pair of Create action methods to the Admin controller; they are targeted by the link in the Index view from the previous section and use the standard controller pattern to present a view to the user for a GET request and process form data for a POST request.

Listing 28-17. Defining the Create Actions in the AdminController.cs File in the Controllers Folder

```
using Microsoft.AspNetCore.Identity;
using Microsoft.AspNetCore.Mvc;
using Users.Models;
using System.Threading.Tasks;

namespace Users.Controllers {

    public class AdminController : Controller {
        private UserManager<AppUser> userManager;

        public AdminController(UserManager<AppUser> usrMgr) {
            userManager = usrMgr;
        }

        public ViewResult Index() => View(userManager.Users);

        public ViewResult Create() => View();

        [HttpPost]
```

```
public async Task<IActionResult> Create(CreateModel model) {
    if (ModelState.IsValid) {
        AppUser user = new AppUser {
            UserName = model.Name,
            Email = model.Email
        };
        IdentityResult result
            = await userManager.CreateAsync(user, model.Password);

        if (result.Succeeded) {
            return RedirectToAction("Index");
        } else {
            foreach (IdentityError error in result.Errors) {
                ModelState.AddModelError("", error.Description);
            }
        }
    }
    return View(model);
}
}
}
```

The important part of this listing is the Create action method that accepts a CreateModel argument and that will be invoked when the administrator submits the form data. The ModelState.IsValid property is used to check that the data contains the required values, and if it does, a new instance of the AppUser class is created and passed to the asynchronous UserManager.CreateAsync method, like this:

```
...
AppUser user = new AppUser { UserName = model.Name, Email = model.Email };
IdentityResult result = await userManager.CreateAsync(user, model.Password);
...
```

The result from the CreateAsync method is an IdentityResult object, which describes the outcome of the operation through the properties listed in Table 28-4.

Table 28-4. *The Properties Defined by the IdentityResult Class*

Name	Description
Succeeded	Returns true if the operation succeeded.
Errors	Returns a sequence of IdentityError objects describing the errors encountered while attempting the operation. The IdentityError class provides a Description property that summarizes the problem.

I inspect the Succeeded property in the Create action method to determine whether a new user record has been created in the database. If the Succeeded property is true, then the client is redirected to the Index action so that list of users is displayed.

```
...
if (result.Succeeded) {
    return RedirectToAction("Index");
} else {
```

```
    foreach (IdentityError error in result.Errors) {
        ModelState.AddModelError("", error.Description);
    }
}
...
```

If the Succeeded property is false, then the sequence of IdentityError objects provided by the Errors property is enumerated, with the Description property used to create a model-level validation error using the ModelState.AddModelError method, as described in Chapter 27.

To provide the new action methods with a view, I created a view file called Create.cshtml in the Views/Admin folder and added the markup shown in Listing 28-18.

Listing 28-18. The Contents of the Create.cshtml File in the Views/Admin Folder

```
@model CreateModel

<div class="bg-primary m-1 p-1 text-white"><h4>Create User</h4></div>
<div asp-validation-summary=" All" class="text-danger"></div>
<form asp-action="Create" method="post">
    <div class="form-group">
        <label asp-for="Name"></label>
        <input asp-for="Name" class="form-control" />
    </div>
    <div class="form-group">
        <label asp-for="Email"></label>
        <input asp-for="Email" class="form-control" />
    </div>
    <div class="form-group">
        <label asp-for="Password"></label>
        <input asp-for="Password" class="form-control" />
    </div>
    <button type="submit" class="btn btn-primary">Create</button>
    <a asp-action="Index" class="btn btn-secondary">Cancel</a>
</form>
```

There is nothing special about this view—it is a simple form that gathers values that MVC will bind to the properties of the model class that is passed to the Create action method and that contains a summary for when there are validation errors.

Testing the Create Functionality

To test the ability to create a new user account, start the application, navigate to the /Admin URL, and click the Create button. Fill in the form with the values shown in Table 28-5.

■ **Tip**   There are domains reserved for testing, including example.com. You can see a complete list at https://tools.ietf.org/html/rfc2606.

Table 28-5. *The Values for Creating an Example User*

Name	Value
Name	Joe
Email	joe@example.com
Password	Secret123$

Once you have entered the values, click the Create button. ASP.NET Core Identity will create the user account, which will be displayed when your browser is redirected to the Index action method, as shown in Figure 28-3. (You will see a different ID value because IDs are randomly generated for each user account.)

Figure 28-3. *Adding a new user account*

Click the Create button again and enter the same details into the form, using the values in Table 28-5. This time when you submit the form, you will see an error reported through the model validation summary, as shown in Figure 28-4.

Figure 28-4. *An error trying to create a new user*

Validating Passwords

One of the most common requirements, especially for corporate applications, is to enforce a password policy. You can see the default policy by running the application, requesting the /Admin/Create URL, and populating the form with the data shown in Table 28-6, where the important difference from the data in the previous section is the value entered into the password field.

Table 28-6. *The Values for Creating an Example User*

Name	Value
Name	Alice
Email	alice@example.com
Password	secret

When you submit the form to the server, the Identity system checks the candidate password and generates errors if it doesn't match the requirements, generating the errors shown in Figure 28-5.

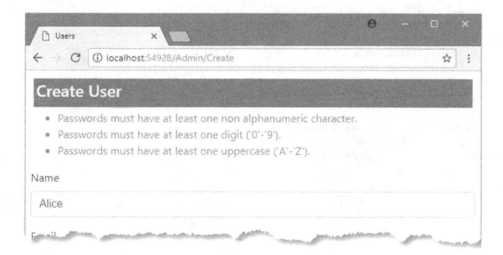

Figure 28-5. *Password validation errors*

You can configure the password validation rules in the Startup class, as shown in Listing 28-19.

Listing 28-19. Configuring Password Validation in the Startup.cs File in the Users Folder

```
using Microsoft.AspNetCore.Builder;
using Microsoft.Extensions.DependencyInjection;
using Microsoft.Extensions.Configuration;
using Microsoft.AspNetCore.Identity;
using Microsoft.EntityFrameworkCore;
using Users.Models;
```

```
namespace Users {

    public class Startup {

        public Startup(IConfiguration configuration) =>
            Configuration = configuration;

        public IConfiguration Configuration { get; }

        public void ConfigureServices(IServiceCollection services) {

            services.AddDbContext<AppIdentityDbContext>(options =>
                options.UseSqlServer(
                    Configuration["Data:SportStoreIdentity:ConnectionString"]));

            services.AddIdentity<AppUser, IdentityRole>(opts => {
                opts.Password.RequiredLength = 6;
                opts.Password.RequireNonAlphanumeric = false;
                opts.Password.RequireLowercase = false;
                opts.Password.RequireUppercase = false;
                opts.Password.RequireDigit = false;
            }).AddEntityFrameworkStores<AppIdentityDbContext>()
                .AddDefaultTokenProviders();

            services.AddMvc();
        }

        public void Configure(IApplicationBuilder app) {
            app.UseStatusCodePages();
            app.UseDeveloperExceptionPage();
            app.UseStaticFiles();
            app.UseAuthentication();
            app.UseMvcWithDefaultRoute();
        }
    }
}
```

The AddIdentity method can be used with a function that accepts an IdentityOptions object, whose Password property returns an instance of the PasswordOptions class, which provides the properties described in Table 28-7 for managing the password policy.

Table 28-7. *The PasswordOptions Properties*

Name	Description
RequiredLength	This int property is used to specify the minimum length for passwords.
RequireNonAlphanumeric	Setting this bool property to true requires passwords to contain at least one character that is not a letter or a digit.
RequireLowercase	Setting this bool property to true requires passwords to contain at least one lowercase character.
RequireUppercase	Setting this bool property to true requires passwords to contain at least one uppercase character.
RequireDigit	Setting this bool property to true requires passwords to contain at least numeric character.

In the listing, I specified that passwords must have a minimum length of six characters and disabled the other constraints. This isn't something that you should do lightly in a real project, but it allows for an effective demonstration. If you start the application, navigate to the /Admin/Create URL, and repeat the form submission, you will see that the password secret is now accepted and a new account, for Alice, has been created, as shown in Figure 28-6.

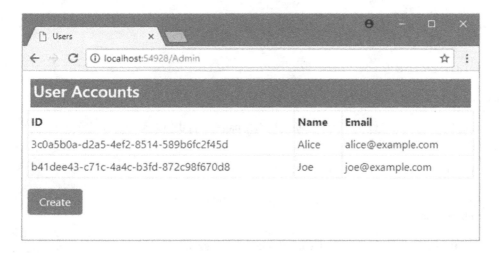

Figure 28-6. *Changing the password validation policy*

Implementing a Custom Password Validator

The built-in password validation is sufficient for most applications, but you may need to implement a custom policy, especially if you are implementing a corporate line-of-business application where complex password policies are common. The password validation functionality is defined by the IPasswordValidator<T> interface in the Microsoft.AspNetCore.Identity namespace, where T is the application-specific user class (AppUser in the example application).

```
using System.Threading.Tasks;

namespace Microsoft.AspNetCore.Identity {

    public interface IPasswordValidator<TUser> where TUser : class {

        Task<IdentityResult> ValidateAsync(UserManager<TUser> manager,
            TUser user, string password);
    }
}
```

The ValidateAsync method is called to validate a password and is provided with context data through a UserManager object (which allows for the Identity database to be queried), the object that represents the user, and the candidate password. The result is an IdentityResult object, which is created using the static Success property if there are no validation issues, or the static Failed method, which is passed an array of IdentityError objects, each of which describes a validation problem.

To demonstrate the use of a custom validation policy, I created the Infrastructure folder, added a class file called CustomPasswordValidator.cs to it, and used the file to define the class shown in Listing 28-20.

Listing 28-20. The Contents of the CustomPasswordValidator.cs File in the Infrastructure Folder

```
using System.Collections.Generic;
using System.Threading.Tasks;
using Microsoft.AspNetCore.Identity;
using Users.Models;

namespace Users.Infrastructure {

    public class CustomPasswordValidator : IPasswordValidator<AppUser> {

        public Task<IdentityResult> ValidateAsync(UserManager<AppUser> manager,
                AppUser user, string password) {

            List<IdentityError> errors = new List<IdentityError>();

            if (password.ToLower().Contains(user.UserName.ToLower())) {
                errors.Add(new IdentityError {
                    Code = "PasswordContainsUserName",
                    Description = "Password cannot contain username"
                });
            }
            if (password.Contains("12345")) {
                errors.Add(new IdentityError {
                    Code = "PasswordContainsSequence",
                    Description = "Password cannot contain numeric sequence"
                });
            }

            return Task.FromResult(errors.Count == 0 ?
                IdentityResult.Success : IdentityResult.Failed(errors.ToArray()));
        }
    }
}
```

900

The validator class checks to see that the password does not contain the username and that the password does not contain the sequence 12345. In Listing 28-21, I have registered the CustomPasswordValidator class as the password validator for AppUser objects.

Listing 28-21. Registering a Custom Password Validator in the Startup.cs File

```
using Microsoft.AspNetCore.Builder;
using Microsoft.Extensions.DependencyInjection;
using Microsoft.Extensions.Configuration;
using Microsoft.AspNetCore.Identity;
using Microsoft.EntityFrameworkCore;
using Users.Models;
using Users.Infrastructure;

namespace Users {

    public class Startup {

        public Startup(IConfiguration configuration) =>
            Configuration = configuration;

        public IConfiguration Configuration { get; }

        public void ConfigureServices(IServiceCollection services) {

            services.AddTransient<IPasswordValidator<AppUser>,
                CustomPasswordValidator>();

            services.AddDbContext<AppIdentityDbContext>(options =>
                options.UseSqlServer(
                    Configuration["Data:SportStoreIdentity:ConnectionString"]));

            services.AddIdentity<AppUser, IdentityRole>(opts => {
                opts.Password.RequiredLength = 6;
                opts.Password.RequireNonAlphanumeric = false;
                opts.Password.RequireLowercase = false;
                opts.Password.RequireUppercase = false;
                opts.Password.RequireDigit = false;
            }).AddEntityFrameworkStores<AppIdentityDbContext>()
                .AddDefaultTokenProviders();

            services.AddMvc();
        }

        public void Configure(IApplicationBuilder app) {
            app.UseStatusCodePages();
            app.UseDeveloperExceptionPage();
            app.UseStaticFiles();
            app.UseAuthentication();
            app.UseMvcWithDefaultRoute();
        }
    }
}
```

To test the custom policy, start the application, request the /Admin/Create URL, and fill out the form using the data values in Table 28-8.

Table 28-8. *The Values for Creating an Example User*

Name	Value
Name	Bob
Email	bob@example.com
Password	bob12345

The password in the table breaks both of the validation rules enforced by the custom class and results in the error messages shown in Figure 28-7.

Figure 28-7. *Using a custom password validator*

You can also implement a custom validation policy that builds on the foundation provided by the built-in class that is used by default. The default class is called PasswordValidator and is defined in the Microsoft.AspNetCore.Identity namespace. In Listing 28-22, I have changed the custom validator class so that it is derived from PasswordValidator and builds on the basic checks it provides.

Listing 28-22. Deriving from the Built-in Validator in the CustomPasswordValidator.cs File

```
using System.Collections.Generic;
using System.Threading.Tasks;
using Microsoft.AspNetCore.Identity;
using Users.Models;
using System.Linq;

namespace Users.Infrastructure {

    public class CustomPasswordValidator : PasswordValidator<AppUser> {
```

```
    public override async Task<IdentityResult> ValidateAsync(
            UserManager<AppUser> manager, AppUser user, string password) {

        IdentityResult result = await base.ValidateAsync(manager,
            user, password);

        List<IdentityError> errors = result.Succeeded ?
            new List<IdentityError>() : result.Errors.ToList();

        if (password.ToLower().Contains(user.UserName.ToLower())) {
            errors.Add(new IdentityError {
                Code = "PasswordContainsUserName",
                Description = "Password cannot contain username"
            });
        }
        if (password.Contains("12345")) {
            errors.Add(new IdentityError {
                Code = "PasswordContainsSequence",
                Description = "Password cannot contain numeric sequence"
            });
        }

        return errors.Count == 0 ? IdentityResult.Success
            : IdentityResult.Failed(errors.ToArray());
    }
  }
}
```

To test the combined validation, run the application and populate the form returned for the /Admin/ Create URL with the data in Table 28-9.

Table 28-9. *The Values for Creating an Example User*

Name	Value
Name	Bob
Email	bob@example.com
Password	12345

When you submit the form, you will see a combination of custom and built-in validation errors, as shown in Figure 28-8.

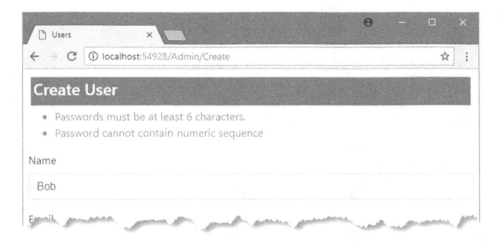

Figure 28-8. *Combining custom and built-in password validation*

Validating User Details

Validation is also performed on usernames and e-mail addresses when accounts are created. To see the built-in validation, start the application and fill out the /Admin/Create form with the data shown in Table 28-10.

Table 28-10. *The Values for Creating an Example User*

Name	Value
Name	Bob!
Email	alice@example.com
Password	secret

When you submit the form, you will see the validation error shown in Figure 28-9.

Figure 28-9. *User account validation errors*

904

Validation can be configured in the Startup class using the IdentityOptions.User property, which returns an instance of the UserOptions class. Table 28-11 describes the UserOptions properties.

Table 28-11. *The UserOptions Properties*

Name	Description
AllowedUserNameCharacters	This string property contains all the legal characters that can be used in a username. The default value specifies a–z, A–Z, and 0–9 and the hyphen, period, underscore, and @ characters. This property is not a regular expression, and every legal character must be specified explicitly in the string.
RequireUniqueEmail	Setting this bool property to true requires new accounts to specify e-mail addresses that have not been used previously.

In Listing 28-23, I have changed the configuration of the application so that unique e-mail addresses are required and only lowercase alphabetic characters are allowed in usernames.

Listing 28-23. Changing the User Account Validation Settings in the Startup.cs File

```
using Microsoft.AspNetCore.Builder;
using Microsoft.Extensions.DependencyInjection;
using Microsoft.Extensions.Configuration;
using Microsoft.AspNetCore.Identity;
using Microsoft.EntityFrameworkCore;
using Users.Models;
using Users.Infrastructure;

namespace Users {

    public class Startup {

        public Startup(IConfiguration configuration) =>
            Configuration = configuration;

        public IConfiguration Configuration { get; }

        public void ConfigureServices(IServiceCollection services) {

            services.AddTransient<IPasswordValidator<AppUser>,
                CustomPasswordValidator>();

            services.AddDbContext<AppIdentityDbContext>(options =>
                options.UseSqlServer(
                    Configuration["Data:SportStoreIdentity:ConnectionString"]));

            services.AddIdentity<AppUser, IdentityRole>(opts => {
                opts.User.RequireUniqueEmail = true;
                opts.User.AllowedUserNameCharacters = "abcdefghijklmnopqrstuvwxyz";
                opts.Password.RequiredLength = 6;
                opts.Password.RequireNonAlphanumeric = false;
```

```
                opts.Password.RequireLowercase = false;
                opts.Password.RequireUppercase = false;
                opts.Password.RequireDigit = false;
            }).AddEntityFrameworkStores<AppIdentityDbContext>()
                .AddDefaultTokenProviders();

            services.AddMvc();
        }

        public void Configure(IApplicationBuilder app) {
            app.UseStatusCodePages();
            app.UseDeveloperExceptionPage();
            app.UseStaticFiles();
            app.UseAuthentication();
            app.UseMvcWithDefaultRoute();
        }
    }
}
```

If you resubmit the data from the previous test, you will see that the e-mail address now causes an error and that the characters used in the name are still rejected, as shown in Figure 28-10.

Figure 28-10. *Changing the account validation settings*

Implementing Custom User Validation

The validation functionality is specified by the IUserValidator<T> interface, which is defined in the Microsoft.AspNetCore.Identity namespace.

```
using System.Threading.Tasks;

namespace Microsoft.AspNetCore.Identity {

    public interface IUserValidator<TUser> where TUser : class {
        Task<IdentityResult> ValidateAsync(UserManager<TUser> manager, TUser user);
    }
}
```

The ValidateAsync method is called to perform the validation, and the outcome is returned using an IdentityResult object, which is the same class used to validate passwords. To demonstrate a custom validator, I added a class called CustomUserValidator.cs to the Infrastructure folder and used it to define the class shown in Listing 28-24.

Listing 28-24. The Contents of the CustomUserValidator.cs File in the Infrastructure Folder

```
using System.Threading.Tasks;
using Microsoft.AspNetCore.Identity;
using Users.Models;

namespace Users.Infrastructure {

    public class CustomUserValidator : IUserValidator<AppUser> {

        public Task<IdentityResult> ValidateAsync(UserManager<AppUser> manager,
                AppUser user) {

            if (user.Email.ToLower().EndsWith("@example.com")) {
                return Task.FromResult(IdentityResult.Success);
            } else {
                return Task.FromResult(IdentityResult.Failed(new IdentityError {
                    Code = "EmailDomainError",
                    Description = "Only example.com email addresses are allowed"
                }));
            }
        }
    }
}
```

This validator checks the domain of the e-mail address to make sure that it is part of the example.com domain. In Listing 28-25, I have registered the custom class as the validator for AppUser objects.

Listing 28-25. Registering a Customer User Validator in the Startup.cs File

```
...
public void ConfigureServices(IServiceCollection services) {

    services.AddTransient<IPasswordValidator<AppUser>,
        CustomPasswordValidator>();
    services.AddTransient<IUserValidator<AppUser>,
        CustomUserValidator>();

    services.AddDbContext<AppIdentityDbContext>(options =>
        options.UseSqlServer(
            Configuration["Data:SportStoreIdentity:ConnectionString"]));

    services.AddIdentity<AppUser, IdentityRole>(opts => {
        opts.User.RequireUniqueEmail = true;
        opts.User.AllowedUserNameCharacters = "abcdefghijklmnopqrstuvwxyz";
        opts.Password.RequiredLength = 6;
        opts.Password.RequireNonAlphanumeric = false;
        opts.Password.RequireLowercase = false;
        opts.Password.RequireUppercase = false;
        opts.Password.RequireDigit = false;
    }).AddEntityFrameworkStores<AppIdentityDbContext>()
        .AddDefaultTokenProviders();

    services.AddMvc();
}
...
```

To test the custom validator, run the application and fill out the /Admin/Create form using the data shown in Table 28-12.

Table 28-12. *The Values for Creating an Example User*

Name	Value
Name	bob
Email	bob@invalid.com
Password	secret

The user's name and password pass validation, but the e-mail address is not in the correct domain. When you submit the form, you will see the validation error shown in Figure 28-11.

Figure 28-11. *Performing custom user validation*

The process for combining the built-in validation, which is provided by the UserValidator<T> class, with custom validation follows the same pattern as for validating passwords, as shown in Listing 28-26.

Listing 28-26. Extending the Built-in User Validation in the CustomUserValidator.cs File

```
using System.Collections.Generic;
using System.Linq;
using System.Threading.Tasks;
using Microsoft.AspNetCore.Identity;
using Users.Models;

namespace Users.Infrastructure {

    public class CustomUserValidator : UserValidator<AppUser> {

        public override async Task<IdentityResult> ValidateAsync(
                UserManager<AppUser> manager,
                AppUser user) {

            IdentityResult result = await base.ValidateAsync(manager, user);

            List<IdentityError> errors = result.Succeeded ?
                new List<IdentityError>() : result.Errors.ToList();

            if (!user.Email.ToLower().EndsWith("@example.com")) {
                errors.Add(new IdentityError {
                    Code = "EmailDomainError",
                    Description = "Only example.com email addresses are allowed"
                });
            }

            return errors.Count == 0 ? IdentityResult.Success
                : IdentityResult.Failed(errors.ToArray());
        }
    }
}
```

909

Completing the Administration Features

I only have to implement the features for editing and deleting users to complete my administration tool. In Listing 28-27, you can see the changes I made to the Views/Admin/Index.cshtml file to target Edit and Delete actions in the Admin controller.

Listing 28-27. Adding Edit and Delete Buttons to the Index.cshtml File in the Views/Admin Folder

```
@model IEnumerable<AppUser>

<div class="bg-primary m-1 p-1 text-white"><h4>User Accounts</h4></div>

<div class="text-danger" asp-validation-summary="ModelOnly"></div>

<table class="table table-sm table-bordered">
    <tr><th>ID</th><th>Name</th><th>Email</th></tr>
    @if (Model.Count() == 0) {
        <tr><td colspan="3" class="text-center">No User Accounts</td></tr>
    } else {
        foreach (AppUser user in Model) {
            <tr>
                <td>@user.Id</td><td>@user.UserName</td><td>@user.Email</td>
                <td>
                    <form asp-action="Delete" asp-route-id="@user.Id" method="post">
                        <a class="btn btn-sm btn-primary" asp-action="Edit"
                            asp-route-id="@user.Id">Edit</a>
                        <button type="submit"
                            class="btn btn-sm btn-danger">Delete</button>
                    </form>
                </td>
            </tr>
        }
    }
</table>
<a class="btn btn-primary" asp-action="Create">Create</a>
```

The Delete button posts a form to the Delete action on the Admin controller, which is important because a POST request is required when changing the application state. The Edit button is an anchor element that will send a GET request because the first step in the edit process is to display the current data. The Edit button is contained in the form element so that the Bootstrap CSS styles don't stack them vertically. I also added a model validation summary to the view so that I can easily display any errors that arise from the remaining administration features.

Implementing the Delete Feature

The UserManager<T> class defines a DeleteAsync method that takes an instance of the user class and removes it from the database. In Listing 28-28, you can see how I have used the DeleteAsync method to implement the delete feature of the Admin controller.

Listing 28-28. Deleting Users in the AdminController.cs File in the Controllers Folder

```
using Microsoft.AspNetCore.Identity;
using Microsoft.AspNetCore.Mvc;
using Users.Models;
using System.Threading.Tasks;

namespace Users.Controllers {

    public class AdminController : Controller {
        private UserManager<AppUser> userManager;

        public AdminController(UserManager<AppUser> usrMgr) {
            userManager = usrMgr;
        }

        // ...other actions omitted for brevity...

        [HttpPost]
        public async Task<IActionResult> Delete(string id) {
            AppUser user = await userManager.FindByIdAsync(id);
            if (user != null) {
                IdentityResult result = await userManager.DeleteAsync(user);
                if (result.Succeeded) {
                    return RedirectToAction("Index");
                } else {
                    AddErrorsFromResult(result);
                }
            } else {
                ModelState.AddModelError("", "User Not Found");
            }
            return View("Index", userManager.Users);
        }

        private void AddErrorsFromResult(IdentityResult result) {
            foreach (IdentityError error in result.Errors) {
                ModelState.AddModelError("", error.Description);
            }
        }
    }
}
```

My action method receives the unique ID for the user as an argument, and I use the FindByIdAsync method to locate the corresponding user object so that I can pass it to DeleteAsync method. The result of the DeleteAsync method is an IdentityResult, which I process in the same way I did in earlier examples to ensure that any errors are displayed to the user. You can test the delete functionality by creating a new user and then clicking the Delete button that appears alongside it in the Index view, as shown in Figure 28-12.

Figure 28-12. *Deleting user accounts*

Implementing the Edit Feature

To complete the administration tool, I need to add support for editing the e-mail address and password for a user account. These are the only properties defined by users at the moment, but I'll show you how to extend the schema with custom properties in Chapter 30. Listing 28-29 shows the Edit action methods that I added to the Admin controller.

Listing 28-29. Adding the Edit Actions in the AdminController.cs File in the Controllers Folder

```
using Microsoft.AspNetCore.Identity;
using Microsoft.AspNetCore.Mvc;
using Users.Models;
using System.Threading.Tasks;

namespace Users.Controllers {

    public class AdminController : Controller {
        private UserManager<AppUser> userManager;
        private IUserValidator<AppUser> userValidator;
        private IPasswordValidator<AppUser> passwordValidator;
        private IPasswordHasher<AppUser> passwordHasher;

        public AdminController(UserManager<AppUser> usrMgr,
                IUserValidator<AppUser> userValid,
                IPasswordValidator<AppUser> passValid,
                IPasswordHasher<AppUser> passwordHash) {
            userManager = usrMgr;
            userValidator = userValid;
            passwordValidator = passValid;
            passwordHasher = passwordHash;
        }
```

```csharp
// ...other action methods omitted for brevity...

public async Task<IActionResult> Edit(string id) {
    AppUser user = await userManager.FindByIdAsync(id);
    if (user != null) {
        return View(user);
    } else {
        return RedirectToAction("Index");
    }
}


[HttpPost]
public async Task<IActionResult> Edit(string id, string email,
        string password) {
    AppUser user = await userManager.FindByIdAsync(id);
    if (user != null) {
        user.Email = email;
        IdentityResult validEmail
            = await userValidator.ValidateAsync(userManager, user);
        if (!validEmail.Succeeded) {
            AddErrorsFromResult(validEmail);
        }
        IdentityResult validPass = null;
        if (!string.IsNullOrEmpty(password)) {
            validPass = await passwordValidator.ValidateAsync(userManager,
                user, password);
            if (validPass.Succeeded) {
                user.PasswordHash = passwordHasher.HashPassword(user,
                    password);
            } else {
                AddErrorsFromResult(validPass);
            }
        }
        if ((validEmail.Succeeded && validPass == null)
                || (validEmail.Succeeded
                && password != string.Empty && validPass.Succeeded)) {
            IdentityResult result = await userManager.UpdateAsync(user);
            if (result.Succeeded) {
                return RedirectToAction("Index");
            } else {
                AddErrorsFromResult(result);
            }
        }
    } else {
        ModelState.AddModelError("", "User Not Found");
    }
    return View(user);
}
```

```
        private void AddErrorsFromResult(IdentityResult result) {
            foreach (IdentityError error in result.Errors) {
                ModelState.AddModelError("", error.Description);
            }
        }
    }
}
}
```

The Edit action targeted by GET requests uses the ID string embedded in the Index view to call the FindByIdAsync method to get an AppUser object that represents the user.

The more complex implementation receives the POST request, with arguments for the user ID, the new e-mail address, and the password. I have to perform several tasks to complete the editing operation.

The first task is to validate the values I have received. I am working with a simple user object at the moment—although I'll show you how to customize the data stored for users in Chapter 30—but even so, I need to validate the user data to ensure that I don't violate the custom policies defined in the "Validating User Details" and "Validating Passwords" sections. I start by validating the e-mail address, which I do like this:

```
...
user.Email = email;
IdentityResult validEmail = await userValidator.ValidateAsync(userManager, user);
if (!validEmail.Succeeded) {
    AddErrorsFromResult(validEmail);
}
...
```

I added a dependency to the controller constructor for an IUserValidator<AppUser> object so that I could validate the new e-mail address. Notice that I have to change the value of the Email property before I perform the validation because the ValidateAsync method only accepts instances of the user class.

The next step is to change the password, if one has been supplied. ASP.NET Core Identity stores hashes of passwords, rather than the passwords themselves. This is intended to prevent passwords from being stolen. My next step is to take the validated password and generate the hash code that will be stored in the database so that the user can be authenticated, which I demonstrate in Chapter 29.

Passwords are converted to hashes through an implementation of the IPasswordHasher<AppUser> interface, which is obtained by declaring a constructor argument that will be resolved through dependency injection. The IPasswordHasher interface defines the HashPassword method, which takes a string argument and returns its hashed value, like this:

```
...
if (!string.IsNullOrEmpty(password)) {
    validPass = await passwordValidator.ValidateAsync(userManager, user, password);
    if (validPass.Succeeded) {
        user.PasswordHash = passwordHasher.HashPassword(user, password);
    } else {
        AddErrorsFromResult(validPass);
    }
}
...
```

Changes to the user class are not stored in the database until the UpdateAsync method is called, like this:

```
...
if ((validEmail.Succeeded && validPass == null) || (validEmail.Succeeded
        && password != string.Empty && validPass.Succeeded)) {
    IdentityResult result = await userManager.UpdateAsync(user);
    if (result.Succeeded) {
        return RedirectToAction("Index");
    } else {
        AddErrorsFromResult(result);
    }
}
...
```

Creating the View

The final component is the view that will display the current values for a user and allow new values to be submitted to the controller. Listing 28-30 shows the contents of the Edit.cshtml file, which I created in the Views/Admin folder.

Listing 28-30. The Contents of the Edit.cshtml File in the Views/Admin Folder

```
@model AppUser

<div class="bg-primary m-1 p-1"><h4>Edit User</h4></div>

<div asp-validation-summary="All" class="text-danger"></div>

<form asp-action="Edit" method="post">
    <div class="form-group">
        <label asp-for="Id"></label>
        <input asp-for="Id" class="form-control" disabled />
    </div>
    <div class="form-group">
        <label asp-for="Email"></label>
        <input asp-for="Email" class="form-control" />
    </div>
    <div class="form-group">
        <label for="password">Password</label>
        <input name="password" class="form-control" />
    </div>
    <button type="submit" class="btn btn-primary">Save</button>
    <a asp-action="Index" class="btn btn-secondary">Cancel</a>
</form>
```

This view displays the user ID, which cannot be changed, as static text and provides a form for editing the e-mail address and password, as shown in Figure 28-13. Notice that I don't use a tag helper for the password elements because the user class doesn't contain password information, since only hashed values are stored in the database.

The final change is to comment out the user validation settings from the Startup class so that the default characters for usernames are used, as shown in Listing 28-31. Since some of the accounts in the database were created before I changed the validation setting, you won't be able to edit them because the usernames won't pass validation. And since validation is applied to the entire user object when the e-mail address is validated, the result is a user account that cannot be changed.

Listing 28-31. Disabling the Custom Validation Settings in the Startup.cs File in the Users Folder

```
...
public void ConfigureServices(IServiceCollection services) {

    services.AddTransient<IPasswordValidator<AppUser>,
        CustomPasswordValidator>();
    services.AddTransient<IUserValidator<AppUser>,
        CustomUserValidator>();

    services.AddDbContext<AppIdentityDbContext>(options =>
        options.UseSqlServer(
            Configuration["Data:SportStoreIdentity:ConnectionString"]));

    services.AddIdentity<AppUser, IdentityRole>(opts => {
        opts.User.RequireUniqueEmail = true;
        //opts.User.AllowedUserNameCharacters = "abcdefghijklmnopqrstuvwxyz";
        opts.Password.RequiredLength = 6;
        opts.Password.RequireNonAlphanumeric = false;
        opts.Password.RequireLowercase = false;
        opts.Password.RequireUppercase = false;
        opts.Password.RequireDigit = false;
    }).AddEntityFrameworkStores<AppIdentityDbContext>()
        .AddDefaultTokenProviders();

    services.AddMvc();
}
...
```

To test the edit feature, run the application, request the /Admin URL, and click one of the Edit buttons. Change the e-mail address or enter a new password (or both) and click the Save button to update the database and return to the /Admin URL.

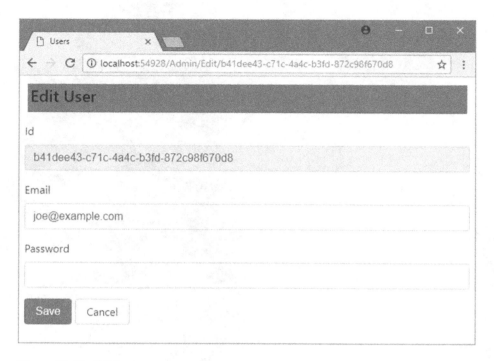

Figure 28-13. Editing a user account

Summary

In this chapter, I showed you how to create the configuration and classes required to use ASP.NET Core Identity and demonstrated how they can be applied to create a user administration tool. In the next chapter, I show you how to perform authentication and authorization with ASP.NET Core Identity.

CHAPTER 29

■ ■ ■

Applying ASP.NET Core Identity

In this chapter, I show you how to apply ASP.NET Core Identity to authenticate and authorize the user accounts created in the previous chapter. Table 29-1 summarizes this chapter.

Table 29-1. *Chapter Summary*

Problem	Solution	Listing
Restrict access to an action method	Apply the Authorize attribute	1
Authenticate users	Create an Account controller that receives user credentials and check them using the UserManager class	2–5
Create and manage roles	Use the RoleManager class	6–10
Authorize access to an action method using roles	Add user accounts to roles and use the Authorize attribute to specify which roles can access action methods	11–18
Ensure that there is an administration account	Seed the database to create an account automatically	19–24

Preparing the Example Project

In this chapter, I am going to continue working on the Users project I created in Chapter 28. To prepare for this chapter, run the application, navigate to the /Admin URL, and use the Create button to ensure that the user accounts in Table 29-2 are in the database.

Table 29-2. *The User Accounts Required For This Chapter*

Username	Email	Password
Joe	joe@example.com	secret123
Alice	alice@example.com	secret123
Bob	bob@example.com	secret123

© Adam Freeman 2017
A. Freeman, *Pro ASP.NET Core MVC 2*, https://doi.org/10.1007/978-1-4842-3150-0_29

When you have finished, requesting the /Admin URL should show you a list of users, including the ones described in Table 29-2 (it doesn't matter if you have created additional users, just as long as the ones in the table are present), as shown in Figure 29-1.

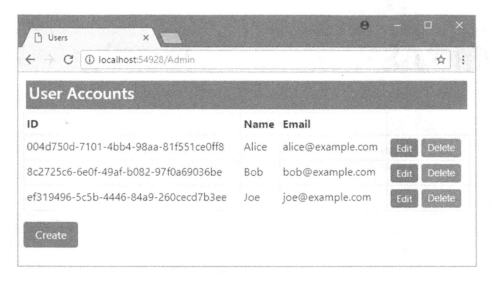

Figure 29-1. *Running the example application*

Authenticating Users

The most fundamental activity for ASP.NET Core Identity is to authenticate users. The key tool for restricting access to action methods is the Authorize attribute, which tells MVC that only requests from authenticated users should be processed. In Listing 29-1, I applied the Authorize attribute to the Index action of the Home controller.

Listing 29-1. Restricting Access in the HomeController.cs File in the Controllers Folder

```
using System.Collections.Generic;
using Microsoft.AspNetCore.Mvc;
using Microsoft.AspNetCore.Authorization;

namespace Users.Controllers {

    public class HomeController : Controller {

        [Authorize]
        public ViewResult Index() =>
            View(new Dictionary<string, object> { ["Placeholder"] = "Placeholder" });
    }
}
```

If you start the application, the browser will send a request to the default URL, which will target the action method that has been decorated with the Authorize attribute. There is no way for users to authenticate themselves at the moment, and the result is the error shown in Figure 29-2.

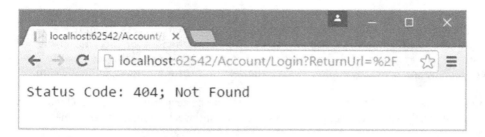

Figure 29-2. *Targeting a protected action method*

The Authorize attribute doesn't specify how the user should be authenticated and has no direct link to ASP.NET Core Identity. The Identity services and middleware work across the ASP.NET Core platform, which makes integration into MVC applications simple and seamless and works by modifying the context objects that describe HTTP requests, providing MVC with details of the outcome of the authentication process without needing to provide it with any details.

The ASP.NET Core platform provides information about the user through the HttpContext object, which is used by the Authorize attribute to check the status of the current request and see whether the user has been authenticated. The HttpContext.User property returns an implementation of the IPrincipal interface, which is defined in the System.Security.Principal namespace. The IPrincipal interface defines the property and method shown in Table 29-3.

Table 29-3. *Selected Members Defined by the IPrincipal Interface*

Name	Description
Identity	Returns an implementation of the IIdentity interface that describes the user associated with the request.
IsInRole(role)	Returns true if the user is a member of the specified role. See the "Authorizing Users with Roles" section for details of managing authorizations with roles.

The implementation of the IIdentity interface returned by the IPrincipal.Identity property provides some basic, but useful, information about the current user through the properties I have described in Table 29-4.

Table 29-4. *Selected Properties Defined by the IIdentity Interface*

Name	Description
AuthenticationType	Returns a string that describes the mechanism used to authenticate the user
IsAuthenticated	Returns true if the user has been authenticated
Name	Returns the name of the current user

■ **Tip**   In Chapter 30, I describe the implementation class that ASP.NET Core Identity uses for the IIdentity interface.

921

The ASP.NET Core Identity middleware uses cookies sent by the browser to determine whether the user has been authenticated. If the user has been authenticated, then the IIdentity.IsAuthenticated property is set to true. Since the example application doesn't yet have an authentication mechanism, the IsAuthenticated property always returns false, which causes an authentication error that leads to the client being redirected to the /Account/Login URL, which is the default URL for providing authentication credentials.

The browser requests the /Account/Login URL, but since it doesn't correspond to any controller or action in the example project, the server returns a 404 – Not Found response, leading to the error message shown in Figure 29-2.

CHANGING THE LOGIN URL

Although /Account/Login is the default URL that clients are redirected to when authorization is required, you can specify your own URL in the ConfigureServices method of the Startup class by changing a configuration option when setting up the ASP.NET Core Identity services, like this:

```
...
services.ConfigureApplicationCookie(opts => opts.LoginPath = "/Users/Login");
...
```

The Identity system cannot rely on the routing system being present to generate its URLs and so the redirection target has to be specified literally. If you change the routing scheme used by your application, you must also ensure that you change the Identity setting so that the URL will still reach your target controller.

Preparing to Implement Authentication

Even though the request ends in an error message, the request in the previous section illustrates how the ASP.NET Core Identity system fits into the standard ASP.NET request life cycle. The next step is to implement a controller that will receive requests for the /Account/Login URL and authenticate the user. I started by adding a new model class to the UserViewModels.cs file, as shown in Listing 29-2.

Listing 29-2. Adding a New Model Class to the UserViewModels.cs File in the Models Folder

```
using System.ComponentModel.DataAnnotations;

namespace Users.Models {

    public class CreateModel {
        [Required]
        public string Name { get; set; }
        [Required]
        public string Email { get; set; }
        [Required]
        public string Password { get; set; }
    }
```

```
public class LoginModel {
    [Required]
    [UIHint("email")]
    public string Email { get; set; }

    [Required]
    [UIHint("password")]
    public string Password { get; set; }
}
}
```

The new model has Email and Password properties, both of which are decorated with the Required attribute so that I can use model validation to check that the user has provided values. I have decorated the properties with the UIHint attribute, which ensures that the input elements rendered by the tag helper in the view will have their type attributes set appropriately.

▪ **Tip** In a real project, client-side validation could be used to check that the user has provided name and password values before submitting the form to the server. See Chapter 27 for details of client-side validation.

I added a class file called AccountController.cs to the Controllers folder and used it to define the controller shown in Listing 29-3.

Listing 29-3. The Contents of the AccountController.cs File in the Controllers Folder

```
using System.Threading.Tasks;
using Microsoft.AspNetCore.Authorization;
using Microsoft.AspNetCore.Mvc;
using Users.Models;

namespace Users.Controllers {

    [Authorize]
    public class AccountController : Controller {

        [AllowAnonymous]
        public IActionResult Login(string returnUrl) {
            ViewBag.returnUrl = returnUrl;
            return View();
        }

        [HttpPost]
        [AllowAnonymous]
        [ValidateAntiForgeryToken]
        public async Task<IActionResult> Login(LoginModel details, string returnUrl) {
            return View(details);
        }
    }
}
```

I have not implemented the authentication logic in the listing because I am going to define the view and then walk through the process of validating user credentials and signing users into the application.

Even though it doesn't authenticate users yet, the Account controller contains some useful infrastructure that I want to explain separately from the ASP.NET Core Identity code that I'll add to the Login action method shortly.

First, notice that both versions of the Login action method take an argument called returnUrl. When a user requests a restricted URL, they are redirected to the /Account/Login URL with a query string that specifies the URL that the user should be sent back to once they have been authenticated. You can see this if you start the application and request the /Home/Index URL. Your browser will be redirected, like this:

```
/Account/Login?ReturnUrl=%2FHome%2FIndex
```

The value of the ReturnUrl query string parameter allows me to redirect the user so that navigating between open and secured parts of the application is a smooth and seamless process.

Next, notice the attributes that I have applied to the Account controller. Controllers that manage user accounts contain functionality that should be available only to authenticated users, such as password reset, for example. To that end, I have applied the Authorize attribute to the controller class and then used the AllowAnonymous attribute on the individual action methods. This restricts action methods to authenticated users by default but allows unauthenticated users to log into the application. I applied the ValidateAntiForgeryToken attribute, which I described in Chapter 24 and which works in conjunction with the form element tag helper to protect against cross-site request forgery.

The last preparatory step is to create the view that will be rendered to gather credentials from the user. I created the Views/Account folder and added a view called Login.cshtml with the markup shown in Listing 29-4.

Listing 29-4. The Contents of the Login.cshtml File in the Views/Account Folder

```
@model LoginModel

<div class="bg-primary m-1 p-1 text-white"><h4>Log In</h4></div>

<div class="text-danger" asp-validation-summary="All"></div>

<form asp-action="Login" method="post">
    <input type="hidden" name="returnUrl" value="@ViewBag.returnUrl" />
    <div class="form-group">
        <label asp-for="Email"></label>
        <input asp-for="Email" class="form-control" />
    </div>
    <div class="form-group">
        <label asp-for="Password"></label>
        <input asp-for="Password" class="form-control" />
    </div>
    <button class="btn btn-primary" type="submit">Log In</button>
</form>
```

The only notable aspect of this view is the hidden input element, which preserves the returnUrl argument. In all other respects, this is a standard Razor view, but it completes the preparations for authentication and demonstrates the way that unauthenticated requests are intercepted and redirected. To test the new controller, start the application. When the browser requests the default URL for the application, it will be redirected to the /Account/Login URL, which produces the content shown in Figure 29-3.

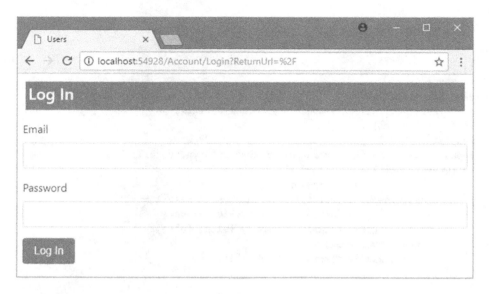

Figure 29-3. *Prompting the user for credentials*

Adding User Authentication

Requests for protected action methods are being correctly redirected to the Account controller, but the credentials provided by the user are not yet used for authentication. In Listing 29-5, I have completed the implementation of the Login action, using ASP.NET Core Identity services to authenticate the user against the details held in the database.

Listing 29-5. Adding Authentication in the AccountController.cs File in the Controllers Folder

```
using System.Threading.Tasks;
using Microsoft.AspNetCore.Authorization;
using Microsoft.AspNetCore.Mvc;
using Users.Models;
using Microsoft.AspNetCore.Identity;

namespace Users.Controllers {

    [Authorize]
    public class AccountController : Controller {
        private UserManager<AppUser> userManager;
        private SignInManager<AppUser> signInManager;

        public AccountController(UserManager<AppUser> userMgr,
                SignInManager<AppUser> signinMgr) {
            userManager = userMgr;
            signInManager = signinMgr;
        }

        [AllowAnonymous]
        public IActionResult Login(string returnUrl) {
            ViewBag.returnUrl = returnUrl;
```

925

```
            return View();
        }

        [HttpPost]
        [AllowAnonymous]
        [ValidateAntiForgeryToken]
        public async Task<IActionResult> Login(LoginModel details,
                string returnUrl) {
            if (ModelState.IsValid) {
                AppUser user = await userManager.FindByEmailAsync(details.Email);
                if (user != null) {
                    await signInManager.SignOutAsync();
                    Microsoft.AspNetCore.Identity.SignInResult result =
                            await signInManager.PasswordSignInAsync(
                                user, details.Password, false, false);
                    if (result.Succeeded) {
                        return Redirect(returnUrl ?? "/");
                    }
                }
                ModelState.AddModelError(nameof(LoginModel.Email),
                    "Invalid user or password");
            }
            return View(details);
        }
    }
}
```

The simplest part is getting the AppUser object that represents the user, which I do through the FindByEmailAsync method of the UserManager<AppUser> class.

```
...
AppUser user = await userManager.FindByEmailAsync(details.Email);
...
```

This method locates a user account using the e-mail address that was used to create it. There are alternative methods for locating users by ID, by name, and by login. I have used the e-mail address for login because it is the approach taken by most Internet-facing web applications and has also become popular in corporate applications.

If there is an account with the e-mail address that the user has specified, then the next step is to perform the authentication step, which is done using the SignInManager<AppUser> class, for which I added a constructor argument that will be resolved using dependency injection. I use the SignInManager class to perform two authentication steps.

```
...
await signInManager.SignOutAsync();
Microsoft.AspNetCore.Identity.SignInResult result =
    await signInManager.PasswordSignInAsync(user, details.Password, false, false);
...
```

The SignOutAsync method cancels any existing session that the user has, and the PasswordSignIn method performs the authentication. The arguments for the PasswordSignInAsync method are the user object, the password that the user has provided, a bool argument that controls whether the authentication cookie is persistent (which I disabled) and whether the account should be locked out if the password is correct (which I also disabled).

The result of the PasswordSignInAsync method is a SignInResult object, which defines a bool Succeeded property that indicates if the authentication process has been successful.

In the example, I check the Succeeded property and redirect the user to the returnUrl location if it is true and add a validation error and redisplay the Login view to the user so they can try again.

As part of the authentication process, Identity adds a cookie to the response, which the browser then includes in any subsequent request and which is used to identify the user's session and the account that is associated with it. You don't have to create or manage the cookie directly, as it is handled automatically by the Identity middleware.

CONSIDERING TWO-FACTOR AUTHENTICATION

I have performed single-factor authentication in this chapter, which is where the user is able to authenticate using a single piece of information known to them in advance: the password.

ASP.NET Core Identity also supports two-factor authentication, where the user needs something extra, usually something that is given to the user at the moment they want to authenticate. The most common examples are a value from a SecureID token or an authentication code that is sent as an e-mail or text message (strictly speaking, the two factors can be anything, including fingerprints, iris scans, and voice recognition, although these are options that are rarely required for most web applications).

Security is increased because an attacker needs to know the user's password *and* have access to whatever provides the second factor, such an e-mail account or cell phone.

I don't show two-factor authentication in the book for two reasons. The first is that it requires a lot of preparatory work, such as setting up the infrastructure that distributes the second-factor e-mails and texts and implementing the validation logic, all of which is beyond the scope of this book.

The second reason is that two-factor authentication forces the user to remember to jump through an additional hoop to authenticate, such as remembering their phone or keeping a security token nearby, something that isn't always appropriate for web applications. I carried a SecureID token of one sort or another for more than a decade in various jobs, and I lost count of the number of times that I couldn't log in to an employer's system because I left the token at home.

If you are interested in two-factor security, then I recommend relying on a third-party provider such as Google for authentication, which allows the user to choose whether they want the additional security (and inconvenience) that two-factor authentication provides. I demonstrate third-party authentication in Chapter 30.

Testing Authentication

To test user authentication, start the application and request the /Home/Index URL. When redirected to the /Account/Login URL, enter the details of one of the users I listed at the start of the chapter (for instance, the e-mail address joe@example.com and the password secret123). Click the Log In button, and your browser will be redirected back to the /Home/Index URL, but this time it will submit the authentication cookie that grants it access to the action method, as shown in Figure 29-4.

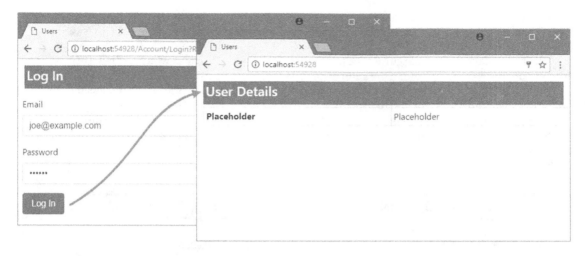

Figure 29-4. *Authenticating a user*

■ **Tip**   You can use the browser's developer tools to see the cookies that are used to identify authenticated requests.

Authorizing Users with Roles

In the previous section, the Authorize attribute was used in its most basic form, which allows any authenticated user to execute the action method. It can also be used to refine authorization to give fine-grained control over which users can perform which actions, based on a user's membership of a *role*.

A role is just an arbitrary label that you define to represent permission to perform a set of activities within an application. Almost every application differentiates between users who can perform administration functions and those who cannot. In the world of roles, this is done by creating an Administrators role and assigning users to it. Users can belong to many roles, and the permissions associated with roles can be as coarse or as granular as you like, so you can use separate roles to differentiate between administrators who can perform basic tasks, such as creating new accounts, and those who can perform more sensitive operations, such as accessing payment data.

ASP.NET Core Identity takes responsibility for managing the set of roles defined in the application and keeping track of which users are members of each one. But it has no knowledge of what each role means; that information is contained within the MVC part of the application, where access to action methods is restricted based on role membership.

ASP.NET Core Identity provides a strongly typed base class for accessing and managing roles called RoleManager<T>, where T is the class that represents roles in the storage mechanism. Entity Framework Core uses a class called IdentityRole to represent roles, which defines the properties described in Table 29-5.

Table 29-5. *Selected IdentityRole Properties*

Name	Description
Id	Defines the unique identifier for the role
Name	Defines the name of the role
Users	Returns a collection of IdentityUserRole objects that represent the members of the role

You can create an application-specific role class if you want to extend the built-in functionality, which I describe for user objects in Chapter 30, but I am going to use the IdentityRole class since it does everything that most applications need. I already told ASP.NET Core Identity to use IdentityRole to represent roles when I configured the application in Chapter 28, as this statement from the ConfigureServices method of Startup class shows:

```
...
services.AddIdentity<AppUser, IdentityRole>(opts => {
    opts.User.RequireUniqueEmail = true;
    //opts.User.AllowedUserNameCharacters = "abcdefghijklmnopqrstuvwxyz";
    opts.Password.RequiredLength = 6;
    opts.Password.RequireNonAlphanumeric = false;
    opts.Password.RequireLowercase = false;
    opts.Password.RequireUppercase = false;
    opts.Password.RequireDigit = false;
}).AddEntityFrameworkStores<AppIdentityDbContext>()
    .AddDefaultTokenProviders();
...
```

The type parameters for the AddIdentity method specify the classes that will be used to represent users and roles. In the example application, the AppUser class is used to represent users, and the built-in IdentityRole class is used for roles.

Creating and Deleting Roles

To demonstrate how roles are used, I am going to create an administration tool for managing them, starting by creating action methods that can create and delete roles. I added a class file called RoleAdminController.cs to the Controllers folder and used it to define the controller shown in Listing 29-6.

Listing 29-6. The Contents of the RoleAdminController.cs File in the Controllers Folder

```
using System.ComponentModel.DataAnnotations;
using System.Threading.Tasks;
using Microsoft.AspNetCore.Identity;
using Microsoft.AspNetCore.Identity.EntityFrameworkCore;
using Microsoft.AspNetCore.Mvc;

namespace Users.Controllers {

    public class RoleAdminController : Controller {
        private RoleManager<IdentityRole> roleManager;
```

```
        public RoleAdminController(RoleManager<IdentityRole> roleMgr) {
            roleManager = roleMgr;
        }

        public ViewResult Index() => View(roleManager.Roles);

        public IActionResult Create() => View();

        [HttpPost]
        public async Task<IActionResult> Create([Required]string name) {
            if (ModelState.IsValid) {
                IdentityResult result
                    = await roleManager.CreateAsync(new IdentityRole(name));
                if (result.Succeeded) {
                    return RedirectToAction("Index");
                } else {
                    AddErrorsFromResult(result);
                }
            }
            return View(name);
        }

        [HttpPost]
        public async Task<IActionResult> Delete(string id) {
            IdentityRole role = await roleManager.FindByIdAsync(id);
            if (role != null) {
                IdentityResult result = await roleManager.DeleteAsync(role);
                if (result.Succeeded) {
                    return RedirectToAction("Index");
                } else {
                    AddErrorsFromResult(result);
                }
            } else {
                ModelState.AddModelError("", "No role found");
            }
            return View("Index", roleManager.Roles);
        }

        private void AddErrorsFromResult(IdentityResult result) {
            foreach (IdentityError error in result.Errors) {
                ModelState.AddModelError("", error.Description);
            }
        }
    }
}
```

Roles are managed using the RoleManager<T> class, where T is the type being used to represent roles (the built-in IdentityRole class for this application). The RoleAdminController constructor declares a constructor dependency on RoleManager<IdentityRole>, which is resolved using dependency injection when the controller is created.

The RoleManager<T> class defines the methods and properties shown in Table 29-6, which allow roles to be created and managed.

Table 29-6. *The Members Defined by the RoleManager<T> Class*

Name	Description
CreateAsync(role)	Creates a new role
DeleteAsync(role)	Deletes the specified role
FindByIdAsync(id)	Finds a role by its ID
FindByNameAsync(name)	Finds a role by its name
RoleExistsAsync(name)	Returns true if a role with the specified name exists
UpdateAsync(role)	Stores changes to the specified role
Roles	Returns an enumeration of the roles that have been defined

The new controller's Index action method displays all the roles in the application. The Create action methods are used to display and receive a form, the data from which is used to create a new role using the CreateAsync method. The Delete action method receives a POST request and receives the unique ID of a role, which is used to remove it from the application using the DeleteAsync method, having located the object that represents it using the FindByIdAsync method.

Creating the Views

To display details of the roles in the application, I created the Views/RoleAdmin folder and added the Index.cshtml file with the markup shown in Listing 29-7.

Listing 29-7. The Contents of the Index.cshtml File in the Views/RoleAdmin Folder

```
@model IEnumerable<IdentityRole>

<div class="bg-primary m-1 p-1"><h4>Roles</h4></div>

<div class="text-danger" asp-validation-summary="ModelOnly"></div>

<table class="table table-sm table-bordered table-bordered">
    <tr><th>ID</th><th>Name</th><th>Users</th><th></th></tr>
    @if (Model.Count() == 0) {
        <tr><td colspan="4" class="text-center">No Roles</td></tr>
    } else {
        foreach (var role in Model) {
            <tr>
                <td>@role.Id</td>
                <td>@role.Name</td>
                <td identity-role="@role.Id"></td>
                <td>
                    <form asp-action="Delete" asp-route-id="@role.Id" method="post">
                        <a class="btn btn-sm btn-primary" asp-action="Edit"
                        asp-route-id="@role.Id">Edit</a>
```

```
                        <button type="submit"
                                class="btn btn-sm btn-danger">
                            Delete
                        </button>
                    </form>
                </td>
            </tr>
        }
    }
</table>
<a class="btn btn-primary" asp-action="Create">Create</a>
```

This view uses a table to display details of the roles in the application. The third column uses a custom element attribute, like this:

```
...
<td identity-role="@role.Id"></td>
...
```

I want to display a list of the users who are members of each role, which requires too much code to be included in a view. To keep the view simple, I added a class file called RoleUsersTagHelper.cs to the Infrastructure folder and used it to define the tag helper shown in Listing 29-8.

Listing 29-8. The Contents of the RoleUsersTagHelper.cs File in the Infrastructure Folder

```
using System.Collections.Generic;
using System.Threading.Tasks;
using Microsoft.AspNetCore.Identity;
using Microsoft.AspNetCore.Identity.EntityFrameworkCore;
using Microsoft.AspNetCore.Razor.TagHelpers;
using Users.Models;

namespace Users.Infrastructure {

    [HtmlTargetElement("td", Attributes = "identity-role")]
    public class RoleUsersTagHelper : TagHelper {
        private UserManager<AppUser> userManager;
        private RoleManager<IdentityRole> roleManager;

        public RoleUsersTagHelper(UserManager<AppUser> usermgr,
                                  RoleManager<IdentityRole> rolemgr) {
            userManager = usermgr;
            roleManager = rolemgr;
        }

        [HtmlAttributeName("identity-role")]
        public string Role { get; set; }

        public override async Task ProcessAsync(TagHelperContext context,
                TagHelperOutput output) {

            List<string> names = new List<string>();
```

```
            IdentityRole role = await roleManager.FindByIdAsync(Role);
            if (role != null) {
                foreach (var user in userManager.Users) {
                    if (user != null
                        && await userManager.IsInRoleAsync(user, role.Name)) {
                        names.Add(user.UserName);
                    }
                }
            }

            output.Content.SetContent(names.Count == 0 ?
                "No Users" : string.Join(", ", names));
        }
    }
}
```

This tag helper operates on td elements with an identity-role attribute, which is used to receive the name of the role that is being processed. The RoleManager<IdentityRole> and UserManager<AppUser> objects allow queries of the Identity database to build up a list of usernames in the role. In Listing 29-9, I have added the tag helper to the view imports file and added an @using expression so that I can refer to the EF Core types in the views without using a namespace.

Listing 29-9. Adding a Tag Helper in the _ViewImports.cshtml File in the Views Folder

```
@using Users.Models
@using Microsoft.AspNetCore.Identity
@addTagHelper *, Microsoft.AspNetCore.Mvc.TagHelpers
@addTagHelper Users.Infrastructure.*, Users
```

Next, I added a view called Create.cshtml to the Views/RoleAdmin folder and added the markup shown in Listing 29-10 to support adding new roles.

Listing 29-10. The Contents of the Create.cshtml File in the Views/RoleAdmin Folder

```
@model string

<div class="bg-primary m-1 p-1"><h4>Create Role</h4></div>

<div asp-validation-summary="All" class="text-danger"></div>

<form asp-action="Create" method="post">
    <div class="form-group">
        <label for="name"></label>
        <input name="name" class="form-control" />
    </div>
    <button type="submit" class="btn btn-primary">Create</button>
    <a asp-action="Index" class="btn btn-secondary">Cancel</a>
</form>
```

The only form data I need to create a role is the name, which is why I am able to use a `string` as the view model class in the `Create.cshtml` view. I want to take advantage of model validation to ensure that the user supplies a value when the form is submitted, but it isn't worth creating a dedicated model class for such a simple task. Instead, if you look at the `Create` method that accepts POST requests in Listing 29-6, you will see that I have applied the `Required` validation attribute directly to the parameter. This has the same effect as applying the attribute in a model class and allows me to take advantage of the built-in model validation process.

Testing, Creating, and Deleting Roles

To test the new controller, start the application and navigate to the /RoleAdmin URL. Click the Create button, enter a name in the input element, and click the second Create button. The new role will be saved to the database and displayed when the browser is redirected to the Index action, as shown in Figure 29-5. You can remove the role from the application by clicking the Delete button.

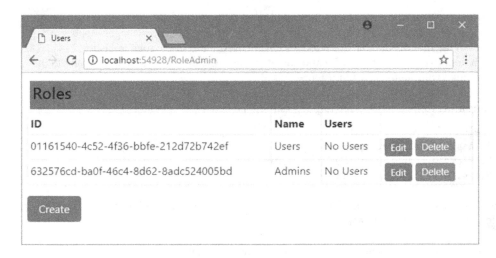

Figure 29-5. *Creating a new role*

Managing Role Memberships

The next step is to be able to add and remove users from roles. This isn't a complicated process, but it invokes taking the role data from the `RoleManager` class and associating it with the details of individual users.

I started by defining some view model classes that will represent the membership of a role and receive a new set of membership instructions from the user. Listing 29-11 shows the additions I made to the `UserViewModels.cs` file in the `Models` folder.

Listing 29-11. Adding View Models to the UserViewModels.cs File

```
using System.ComponentModel.DataAnnotations;
using System.Collections.Generic;
using Microsoft.AspNetCore.Identity;

namespace Users.Models {
```

```
public class CreateModel {
    [Required]
    public string Name { get; set; }
    [Required]
    public string Email { get; set; }
    [Required]
    public string Password { get; set; }
}

public class LoginModel {
    [Required]
    [UIHint("email")]
    public string Email { get; set; }
    [Required]
    [UIHint("password")]
    public string Password { get; set; }
}

public class RoleEditModel {
    public IdentityRole Role { get; set; }
    public IEnumerable<AppUser> Members { get; set; }
    public IEnumerable<AppUser> NonMembers { get; set; }
}

public class RoleModificationModel {
    [Required]
    public string RoleName { get; set; }
    public string RoleId { get; set; }
    public string[] IdsToAdd { get; set; }
    public string[] IdsToDelete { get; set; }
}
}
```

The RoleEditModel class represents a role and details of the users in the system, categorized by whether they are members of the role. The RoleModificationModel class represents a set of changes to a role.

Listing 29-12 shows the addition of new action methods in the RoleAdmin controller that use the view models from Listing 29-11 to manage role memberships.

Listing 29-12. Adding Action Methods in the RoleAdminController.cs File in the Controllers Folder

```
using System.ComponentModel.DataAnnotations;
using System.Threading.Tasks;
using Microsoft.AspNetCore.Identity;
using Microsoft.AspNetCore.Mvc;
using Users.Models;
using System.Collections.Generic;

namespace Users.Controllers {

    public class RoleAdminController : Controller {
        private RoleManager<IdentityRole> roleManager;
        private UserManager<AppUser> userManager;
```

```csharp
    public RoleAdminController(RoleManager<IdentityRole> roleMgr,
                              UserManager<AppUser> userMrg) {
        roleManager = roleMgr;
        userManager = userMrg;
    }

    // ...other action methods omitted for brevity...

    public async Task<IActionResult> Edit(string id) {

        IdentityRole role = await roleManager.FindByIdAsync(id);
        List<AppUser> members = new List<AppUser>();
        List<AppUser> nonMembers = new List<AppUser>();
        foreach (AppUser user in userManager.Users) {
            var list = await userManager.IsInRoleAsync(user, role.Name)
                ? members : nonMembers;
            list.Add(user);
        }
        return View(new RoleEditModel {
            Role = role,
            Members = members,
            NonMembers = nonMembers
        });
    }

    [HttpPost]
    public async Task<IActionResult> Edit(RoleModificationModel model) {
        IdentityResult result;
        if (ModelState.IsValid) {
            foreach (string userId in model.IdsToAdd ?? new string[] { }) {
                AppUser user = await userManager.FindByIdAsync(userId);
                if (user != null) {
                    result = await userManager.AddToRoleAsync(user,
                        model.RoleName);
                    if (!result.Succeeded) {
                        AddErrorsFromResult(result);
                    }
                }
            }
            foreach (string userId in model.IdsToDelete ?? new string[] { }) {
                AppUser user = await userManager.FindByIdAsync(userId);
                if (user != null) {
                    result = await userManager.RemoveFromRoleAsync(user,
                        model.RoleName);
                    if (!result.Succeeded) {
                        AddErrorsFromResult(result);
                    }
                }
            }
        }
```

```
        if (ModelState.IsValid) {
            return RedirectToAction(nameof(Index));
        } else {
            return await Edit(model.RoleId);
        }
    }

    private void AddErrorsFromResult(IdentityResult result) {
        foreach (IdentityError error in result.Errors) {
            ModelState.AddModelError("", error.Description);
        }
    }
  }
}
```

Most of the code in the GET version of the Edit action method is responsible for generating the sets of members and nonmembers of the selected role. Once all the users have been categorized, a new instance of the RoleEditModel class is passed to the View method so that the data can be displayed using the default view.

The POST version of the Edit method is responsible for adding and removing users to and from roles. The UserManager<T> class provides methods for working with roles, which I have described in Table 29-7.

Table 29-7. *The Role-Related Methods Defined by the UserManager<T> Class*

Name	Description
AddToRoleAsync(user, name)	Adds the user ID to the role with the specified name
GetRolesAsync(user)	Returns a list of the names of the roles of which the user is a member
IsInRoleAsync(user, name)	Returns true if the user is a member of the role with the specified name
RemoveFromRoleAsync(user, name)	Removes the user as a member from the role with the specified name

An oddity of these methods is that the role-related methods operate on role names, even though roles also have unique identifiers. It is for this reason that my RoleModificationModel view model class has a RoleName property.

Listing 29-13 shows the contents of the Edit.cshtml file, which I added to the Views/RoleAdmin folder and used to define the markup that allows the user to edit role memberships.

Listing 29-13. The Contents of the Edit.cshtml File in the Views/RoleAdmin Folder

```
@model RoleEditModel

<div class="bg-primary m-1 p-1 text-white"><h4>Edit Role</h4></div>

<div asp-validation-summary="All" class="text-danger"></div>

<form asp-action="Edit" method="post">
```

```
<input type="hidden" name="roleName" value="@Model.Role.Name" />
<input type="hidden" name="roleId" value="@Model.Role.Id" />

<h6 class="bg-info p-1 text-white">Add To @Model.Role.Name</h6>
<table class="table table-bordered table-sm">
    @if (Model.NonMembers.Count() == 0) {
        <tr><td colspan="2">All Users Are Members</td></tr>
    } else {
        @foreach (AppUser user in Model.NonMembers) {
            <tr>
                <td>@user.UserName</td>
                <td>
                    <input type="checkbox" name="IdsToAdd" value="@user.Id">
                </td>
            </tr>
        }
    }
</table>

<h6 class="bg-info p-1 text-white">Remove From @Model.Role.Name</h6>
<table class="table table-bordered table-sm">
    @if (Model.Members.Count() == 0) {
        <tr><td colspan="2">No Users Are Members</td></tr>
    } else {
        @foreach (AppUser user in Model.Members) {
            <tr>
                <td>@user.UserName</td>
                <td>
                    <input type="checkbox" name="IdsToDelete" value="@user.Id">
                </td>
            </tr>
        }
    }
</table>
<button type="submit" class="btn btn-primary">Save</button>
<a asp-action="Index" class="btn btn-secondary">Cancel</a>
</form>
```

The view contains two tables: one for users who are not members of the selected role and one for those who are. Each user's name is displayed along with a check box that allows the membership to be changed. The tables are contained in a form that is sent to the Edit action method and model bound to the RoleModificationModel class, providing easy access to the list of role membership changes to be made.

Testing and Editing Role Membership

To test the role membership feature, start the application, navigate to the /RoleAdmin URL, and create a new role called Users if you need to. Click the Edit button and you will see the users in the application are shown in the list of nonmembers, as shown in Figure 29-6.

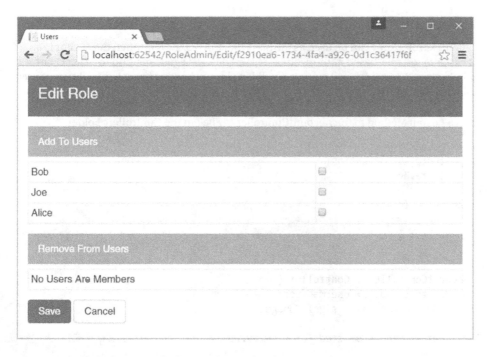

Figure 29-6. *Displaying and editing role membership*

Check the box to add Alice and Joe (two of the accounts added to the Identity system at the start of the chapter) and click the Save button. In the list of roles, you will now see Alice and Joe in the list of members, as shown in Figure 29-7.

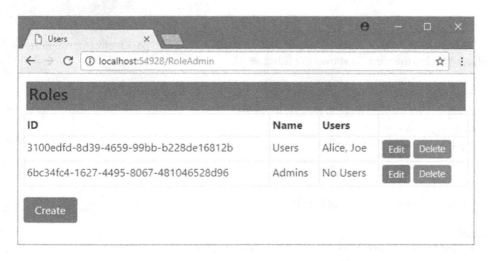

Figure 29-7. *Managing role membership*

Using Roles for Authorization

Now that the application has roles, they can be used as the basis for authorization through the Authorize attribute. To make it easier to test role-based authorization, I have added a Logout method to the Account controller, as shown in Listing 29-14, which will make it possible to log out and log in again as a different user to see the effect of role membership.

Listing 29-14. Adding a Logout Method to the AccountController.cs File om the Controllers Folder

```csharp
using System.Threading.Tasks;
using Microsoft.AspNetCore.Authorization;
using Microsoft.AspNetCore.Mvc;
using Users.Models;
using Microsoft.AspNetCore.Identity;

namespace Users.Controllers {

    [Authorize]
    public class AccountController : Controller {
        private UserManager<AppUser> userManager;
        private SignInManager<AppUser> signInManager;

        // ...other action methods omitted for brevity...

        [Authorize]
        public async Task<IActionResult> Logout() {
            await signInManager.SignOutAsync();
            return RedirectToAction("Index", "Home");
        }
    }
}
```

The next step is to update the Home controller to add a new action method and pass some information about the authenticated user to the view, as shown in Listing 29-15.

Listing 29-15. Enhancements to the HomeController.cs File in the Controllers Folder

```csharp
using System.Collections.Generic;
using Microsoft.AspNetCore.Mvc;
using Microsoft.AspNetCore.Authorization;

namespace Users.Controllers {

    public class HomeController : Controller {

        [Authorize]
        public IActionResult Index() => View(GetData(nameof(Index)));

        [Authorize(Roles = "Users")]
        public IActionResult OtherAction() => View("Index",
            GetData(nameof(OtherAction)));
```

```
    private Dictionary<string, object> GetData(string actionName) =>
        new Dictionary<string, object> {
            ["Action"] = actionName,
            ["User"] = HttpContext.User.Identity.Name,
            ["Authenticated"] = HttpContext.User.Identity.IsAuthenticated,
            ["Auth Type"] = HttpContext.User.Identity.AuthenticationType,
            ["In Users Role"] = HttpContext.User.IsInRole("Users")
        };
    }
}
```

The Authorize attribute unchanged for the Index action method, but I have set the Roles property when applying the attribute to the OtherAction method, specifying that only members of the Users role should be able to access it. I also defined a GetData method, which adds some basic information about the user identity, using the properties available through the HttpContext object.

■ **Tip** The Authorize attribute can also be used to authorize access based on a list of individual usernames. This is an appealing feature for small projects, but it means you have to change the code in your controllers each time the set of users you are authorizing changes, and that usually means having to go through the test-and-deploy cycle again. Using roles for authorization isolates the application from changes in individual user accounts and allows you to control access to the application through the memberships stored by ASP.NET Core Identity.

The final change is to the Index.cshtml file in the Views/Home folder, which is used by both actions in the Home controller, to add a link that targets the Logout method in the Account controller, as shown in Listing 29-16.

Listing 29-16. Adding a Sign-Out Link to the Index.cshtml File in the Views/Home Folder

```
@model Dictionary<string, object>

<div class="bg-primary m-1 p-1 text-white"><h4>User Details</h4></div>

<table class="table table-sm table-bordered m-1 p-1">
    @foreach (var kvp in Model) {
        <tr><th>@kvp.Key</th><td>@kvp.Value</td></tr>
    }
</table>

@if (User?.Identity?.IsAuthenticated ?? false) {
    <a asp-controller="Account" asp-action="Logout"
        class="btn btn-danger">Logout</a>
}
```

To test the authentication, start the application and navigate to the /Home/Index URL. Your browser will be redirected so that you can enter user credentials. It doesn't matter which of the user details from Table 29-2 you choose to authenticate with because the Authorize attribute applied to the Index action allows access to any authenticated user.

However, if you now request the /Home/OtherAction URL, the user details you chose from Table 29-2 will make a difference because only Alice and Joe are members of the Users role, which is required to access the OtherAction method. If you log in as Bob, then your browser will be redirected to the /Account/AccessDenied URL, which is used when a user is unable to access an action method. To handle this situation, I have added an AccessDenied method to the Account controller so that there is an action to handle the request, as shown in Listing 29-17.

■ **Tip** You can change the /Account/AccessDenied URL by setting the AccessDeniedPath configuration property. See the "Changing the Login URL" sidebar earlier in the chapter for a similar example.

Listing 29-17. Adding an Action Method in the AccountController.cs File

```
using System.Threading.Tasks;
using Microsoft.AspNetCore.Authorization;
using Microsoft.AspNetCore.Mvc;
using Users.Models;
using Microsoft.AspNetCore.Identity;

namespace Users.Controllers {

    [Authorize]
    public class AccountController : Controller {
        private UserManager<AppUser> userManager;
        private SignInManager<AppUser> signInManager;

        public AccountController(UserManager<AppUser> userMgr,
                SignInManager<AppUser> signinMgr) {
            userManager = userMgr;
            signInManager = signinMgr;
        }

        // ...other action methods omitted for brevity...

        [AllowAnonymous]
        public IActionResult AccessDenied() {
            return View();
        }
    }
}
```

To provide the AccessDenied action with a view to display, I created a file called AccessDenied.cshtml in the Views/Account folder and added the content shown in Listing 29-18.

Listing 29-18. The Contents of the AccessDenied.cshtml File in the Views/Account Folder

```
<div class="bg-danger mb-1 p-2 text-white"><h4>Access Denied</h4></div>
<a asp-action="Index" asp-controller="Home" class="btn btn-primary">OK</a>
```

Start the application, request the /Account/Login URL, and authenticate as bob@example.com. When the authentication process is complete, the browser will be redirected to the /Home/Index URL, which displays details of the account, as shown in the left screenshot in Figure 29-8, and which makes it clear that Bob is not a member of the Users role. Now request the /Home/OtherAction URL, which targets the action that has been protected with role-based access. Bob doesn't have the required role membership, and the browser is redirected to the /Account/AccessDenied URL, as shown in the right screenshot in Figure 29-8.

■ **Tip**   Roles are loaded when the user logs in, which means if you change the roles for the user you are currently authenticated as, the changes won't take effect until you log out and authenticate.

Figure 29-8. *Using role-based authorization*

Seeding the Database

One lingering problem in my example project is that access to my Admin and RoleAdmin controllers is not restricted. This is a classic chicken-and-egg problem because, in order to restrict access, I need to create users and roles, but the Admin and RoleAdmin controllers are the user management tools, and if I protect them with the Authorize attribute, there won't be any credentials that will grant me access to them, especially when I first deploy the application.

The solution to this problem is to seed the database with some initial data when the application starts. In Listing 29-19, I have added some new configuration data to the appsettings.json file to specify the details for the account that will be created.

Listing 29-19. Adding Configuration Data to the appsettings.json File

```
{
  "Data": {
    "AdminUser": {
      "Name": "Admin",
      "Email": "admin@example.com",
      "Password": "secret",
      "Role": "Admins"
    },
```

```
    "SportStoreIdentity": {
      "ConnectionString": "Server=(localdb)\\MSSQLLocalDB;Database=IdentityUsers;Trusted_Con
nection=True;MultipleActiveResultSets=true"
    }
  }
}
```

The Data:AdminUser category provides the four values that I need to create an account and assign it to a role that will be able to use the administration tools.

■ **Caution**   Putting passwords in plain-text configuration files means that you must make it part of your deployment process to change the default account's password when you deploy the application and initialize a new database for the first time.

Next, I added a static method to the AppIdentityDbContext class, as shown in Listing 29-20. The code to create the default account doesn't have to go in this class, but this is the location that feels natural to me and the one I use in my own projects. You can also use a separate class, which is what I did for the SportsStore application.

Listing 29-20. Adding a Method in the AppIdentityDbContext.cs File in the Models Folder

```
using Microsoft.AspNetCore.Identity;
using Microsoft.AspNetCore.Identity.EntityFrameworkCore;
using Microsoft.EntityFrameworkCore;
using Microsoft.Extensions.Configuration;
using Microsoft.Extensions.DependencyInjection;
using System;
using System.Threading.Tasks;

namespace Users.Models {

    public class AppIdentityDbContext : IdentityDbContext<AppUser> {

        public AppIdentityDbContext(DbContextOptions<AppIdentityDbContext> options)
            : base(options) { }

        public static async Task CreateAdminAccount(IServiceProvider serviceProvider,
            IConfiguration configuration) {

            UserManager<AppUser> userManager =
                serviceProvider.GetRequiredService<UserManager<AppUser>>();
            RoleManager<IdentityRole> roleManager =
                serviceProvider.GetRequiredService<RoleManager<IdentityRole>>();

            string username = configuration["Data:AdminUser:Name"];
            string email = configuration["Data:AdminUser:Email"];
            string password = configuration["Data:AdminUser:Password"];
            string role = configuration["Data:AdminUser:Role"];
```

```
            if (await userManager.FindByNameAsync(username) == null) {
                if (await roleManager.FindByNameAsync(role) == null) {
                    await roleManager.CreateAsync(new IdentityRole(role));
                }

                AppUser user = new AppUser {
                    UserName = username,
                    Email = email
                };

                IdentityResult result = await userManager
                    .CreateAsync(user, password);
                if (result.Succeeded) {
                    await userManager.AddToRoleAsync(user, role);
                }
            }
        }
    }
}
```

The CreateAdminAccount method receives an IServiceProvider object, which It uses to obtain the UserManager and RoleManager objects, and an IConfiguration object, which it uses to get the data from the appsetting.json file. The code in the CreateAdminAccount method checks to see whether the user already exists and, if not, creates it and assigns it to the specified role, which is also created if needed. In Listing 29-21, I have added a statement to the Startup class that calls the CreateAdminAccount method after the rest of the application has been set up and configured.

Listing 29-21. Calling the Database Method in the Startup.cs File in the Users Folder

```
...
public void Configure(IApplicationBuilder app) {
    app.UseStatusCodePages();
    app.UseDeveloperExceptionPage();
    app.UseStaticFiles();
    app.UseAuthentication();
    app.UseMvcWithDefaultRoute();
    AppIdentityDbContext.CreateAdminAccount(app.ApplicationServices,
        Configuration).Wait();
}
...
```

Because I am accessing a scoped service via the IApplicationBuilder.ApplicationServices provider, I must also disable the dependency injection scope validation feature in the Program class, as shown in Listing 29-22.

Listing 29-22. Disabling Scope Validation in the Program.cs File in the Users Folder

```
using System;
using System.Collections.Generic;
using System.IO;
using System.Linq;
using System.Threading.Tasks;
```

```
using Microsoft.AspNetCore;
using Microsoft.AspNetCore.Hosting;
using Microsoft.Extensions.Configuration;
using Microsoft.Extensions.Logging;

namespace Users {
    public class Program {
        public static void Main(string[] args) {
            BuildWebHost(args).Run();
        }

        public static IWebHost BuildWebHost(string[] args) =>
            WebHost.CreateDefaultBuilder(args)
                .UseStartup<Startup>()
                .UseDefaultServiceProvider(options =>
                    options.ValidateScopes = false)
                .Build();
    }
}
```

Now that there is a reliable default account in the Identity database, I can use the Authorize attribute to protect the Admin and RoleAdmin controllers. Listing 29-23 shows the changes to the Admin controller.

Listing 29-23. Restricting Access in the AdminController.cs File in the Controllers Folder

```
using Microsoft.AspNetCore.Identity;
using Microsoft.AspNetCore.Mvc;
using Users.Models;
using System.Threading.Tasks;
using Microsoft.AspNetCore.Authorization;

namespace Users.Controllers {

    [Authorize(Roles = "Admins")]
    public class AdminController : Controller {

        // ...statements omitted for brevity...
    }
}
```

Listing 29-24 shows the corresponding change I made to the RoleAdmin controller.

Listing 29-24. Restricting Access in the RoleAdminController.cs File in the Controllers Folder

```
using System.ComponentModel.DataAnnotations;
using System.Threading.Tasks;
using Microsoft.AspNetCore.Identity;
using Microsoft.AspNetCore.Mvc;
using Users.Models;
using System.Collections.Generic;
using Microsoft.AspNetCore.Authorization;

namespace Users.Controllers {
```

```
[Authorize(Roles = "Admins")]
public class RoleAdminController : Controller {
    // ...statements omitted for brevity...
}
}
```

Start the application and request the /Admin or /RoleAdmin URL. If you have already logged in as one of the other users, you will have to log out. Otherwise, you will be prompted for credentials, and you can authenticate as admin@example.com with the password secret to access the administration features.

Summary

In this chapter, I showed you how to use ASP.NET Core Identity to authenticate and authorize users. I explained how to collect and validate credentials users and how to restrict access to action methods based on the roles that a user is a member of. In the next chapter, I demonstrate some of the advanced features that ASP.NET Core Identity provides.

CHAPTER 30

■ ■ ■

Advanced ASP.NET Core Identity

In this chapter, I finish my description of ASP.NET Core Identity by showing you some of the advanced features it offers. I demonstrate how you can extend the database schema by defining custom properties on the user class and how to use database migrations to apply those properties without deleting the data in the ASP.NET Core Identity database. I also explain how ASP.NET Core Identity supports the concept of claims and demonstrate how they can be used to flexibly authorize access to action methods through policies. I finish the chapter by showing you how ASP.NET Core Identity makes it easy to authenticate users through third parties. I demonstrate authentication with Google accounts, but ASP.NET Core Identity has built-in support for Microsoft, Facebook, and Twitter accounts as well. Table 30-1 summarizes this chapter.

Table 30-1. *Chapter Summary*

Problem	Solution	Listing
Store custom data for users	Add properties to the user class and update the Identity database	1–3
Perform granular authorization	Use claims	4–7
Create custom claims	Use claims transformation	8, 9
Use claims data to assess user access	Create policies	10–14
Use policies to access resources	Assess policies within action methods	15–20
Allow third parties to perform authentication	Accept claims from authentication providers such as Microsoft, Google, and Facebook	21–24

Preparing the Example Project

In this chapter, I am going to continue working on the Users project I created in Chapter 28 and enhanced in Chapter 29. Start the application and make sure that there are users in the database. Figure 30-1 shows the state of my database, which contains the users Admin, Alice, Bob, and Joe from the previous chapter. To check the users, start the application, request the /Admin URL, and authenticate as the Admin user, using the e-mail address admin@example.com and the password secret.

© Adam Freeman 2017
A. Freeman, *Pro ASP.NET Core MVC 2*, https://doi.org/10.1007/978-1-4842-3150-0_30

Figure 30-1. *The initial users in the Identity database*

I also need some roles for this chapter. Navigate to the /RoleAdmin URL, create roles called Users and Employees, and assign users to those roles, as described in Table 30-2.

Table 30-2. *The Roles and Members Required for the Example Application*

Role	Members
Users	Alice, Joe
Employees	Alice, Bob

Figure 30-2 shows the required role configuration displayed by the RoleAdmin controller.

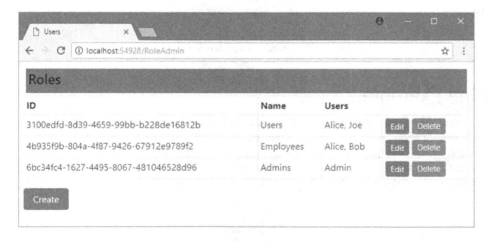

Figure 30-2. *Configuring the roles required for this chapter*

Adding Custom User Properties

When I created the AppUser class to represent users in Chapter 28, I explained that the base class defined a basic set of properties to describe the user, such as e-mail address and telephone number.

Most applications need to store more information about users, including persistent application preferences and details such as addresses—in short, any data that is useful for running the application and that should last between sessions. Because the ASP.NET Core Identity system uses Entity Framework Core to store its data by default, defining additional user information means adding properties to the user class and letting EF Core create the database schema required to store them.

Listing 30-1 shows how I added two simple properties to the AppUser class to represent the city in which the user lives and their qualification level.

Listing 30-1. Adding a Property in the AppUser.cs File in the Models Folder

```
using Microsoft.AspNetCore.Identity;

namespace Users.Models {

    public enum Cities {
        None, London, Paris, Chicago
    }

    public enum QualificationLevels {
        None, Basic, Advanced
    }

    public class AppUser : IdentityUser {
        public Cities City { get; set; }
        public QualificationLevels Qualifications { get; set; }
    }
}
```

The enumerations called Cities and QualificationLevels define values for some cities and different levels of qualification. These enumerations are used by the City and Qualification properties added to the AppUser class.

The actions added to the Home controller in Listing 30-2 allow the user to view and edit their City and Qualification properties.

Listing 30-2. Adding Support for Custom Properties in the HomeController.cs File in the Controllers Folder

```
using System.Collections.Generic;
using Microsoft.AspNetCore.Mvc;
using Microsoft.AspNetCore.Authorization;
using Users.Models;
using Microsoft.AspNetCore.Identity;
using System.Threading.Tasks;
using System.ComponentModel.DataAnnotations;

namespace Users.Controllers {
```

```
public class HomeController : Controller {
    private UserManager<AppUser> userManager;

    public HomeController(UserManager<AppUser> userMgr) {
        userManager = userMgr;
    }

    [Authorize]
    public IActionResult Index() => View(GetData(nameof(Index)));

    [Authorize(Roles = "Users")]
    public IActionResult OtherAction() => View("Index",
        GetData(nameof(OtherAction)));

    private Dictionary<string, object> GetData(string actionName) =>
        new Dictionary<string, object> {
            ["Action"] = actionName,
            ["User"] = HttpContext.User.Identity.Name,
            ["Authenticated"] = HttpContext.User.Identity.IsAuthenticated,
            ["Auth Type"] = HttpContext.User.Identity.AuthenticationType,
            ["In Users Role"] = HttpContext.User.IsInRole("Users"),
            ["City"] = CurrentUser.Result.City,
            ["Qualification"] = CurrentUser.Result.Qualifications
        };

    [Authorize]
    public async Task<IActionResult> UserProps() {
        return View(await CurrentUser);
    }

    [Authorize]
    [HttpPost]
    public async Task<IActionResult> UserProps(
            [Required]Cities city,
            [Required]QualificationLevels qualifications) {
        if (ModelState.IsValid) {
            AppUser user = await CurrentUser;
            user.City = city;
            user.Qualifications = qualifications;
            await userManager.UpdateAsync(user);
            return RedirectToAction("Index");
        }
        return View(await CurrentUser);
    }

    private Task<AppUser> CurrentUser =>
        userManager.FindByNameAsync(HttpContext.User.Identity.Name);
}
}
```

The new CurrentUser property uses the UserManager<AppUser> class to retrieve an AppUser instance to represent the current user. The AppUser object is used as the view model object in the GET version of the UserProps action method, and the POST method uses it to update the value of the new City and QualificationLevel properties.

The GetData method has been updated so that the dictionary it returns contains the values of the custom properties for the current user, which mean that the values of these properties will be seen in the views displayed by the Index and OtherAction action methods.

To provide the UserProps action methods with a view, I added a view called UserProps.cshtml to the Views/Home folder and added the markup shown in Listing 30-3.

Listing 30-3. The Contents of the UserProps.cshtml File in the Views/Home Folder

```
@model AppUser

<div class="bg-primary m-1 p-1 text-white"><h4>@Model.UserName</h4></div>

<div asp-validation-summary="All" class="text-danger"></div>

<form asp-action="UserProps" method="post">
    <div class="form-group">
        <label asp-for="City"></label>
        <select asp-for="City" class="form-control"
                asp-items="@new SelectList(Enum.GetNames(typeof(Cities)))">
            <option disabled selected value="">Select a City</option>
        </select>
    </div>
    <div class="form-group">
        <label asp-for="Qualifications"></label>
        <select asp-for="Qualifications" class="form-control"
            asp-items="@new SelectList(Enum.GetNames(typeof(QualificationLevels)))">
                <option disabled selected value="">Select a City</option>
        </select>
    </div>

    <button type="submit" class="btn btn-primary">Submit</button>
    <a asp-action="Index" class="btn btn-secondary">Cancel</a>
</form>
```

The view contains a form with select elements that are populated with the values from the enumerations defined in Listing 30-1. When the form is submitted, the AppUser object that represents the current user is retrieved from Identity, and the values of the custom properties are updated using the values selected by the user, like this:

```
...
AppUser user = await CurrentUser;
user.City = city;
user.Qualifications = qualifications;
await userManager.UpdateAsync(user);
return RedirectToAction("Index");
...
```

Notice that I have to explicitly tell the user manager to update the database record for the user to reflect the changes by calling the UpdateAsync method. I have not had to do this previously because the UpdateAsync method has been called for me within the methods that I have used to make Identity changes, but when you change properties directly, you are responsible for telling the user manager to perform an update.

Preparing for Database Migration

All of the application plumbing to support the new properties is in place, and all that remains is to update the database so that its tables will store the custom property values.

Entity Framework Core doesn't have integrated support for working with seed data, and care must be taken when creating migrations to disable seeding, as shown in Listing 30-4; otherwise, the new properties added to the model class in Listing 30-1 will cause an error. The seeding statement can be enabled again once the database migration has been created and applied.

Listing 30-4. Disabling Database Seeding in the Startup.cs File in the Users Folder

```
...
public void Configure(IApplicationBuilder app) {
    app.UseStatusCodePages();
    app.UseDeveloperExceptionPage();
    app.UseStaticFiles();
    app.UseAuthentication();
    app.UseMvcWithDefaultRoute();
    //   AppIdentityDbContext.CreateAdminAccount(app.ApplicationServices,
    //         Configuration).Wait();
}
...
```

With the seeding disabled, the next step is to create a new database migration, which will contain the SQL commands required to update the database schema. Use a command prompt or PowerShell window to run the following command in the Users project folder:

```
dotnet ef migrations add CustomProperties
```

When this command has finished, you will see a new file in the Migrations folder whose name contains CustomProperties. The exact name contains a numeric ID, but if you open this file, you can see a C# class that contains a method called Up, which performs the SQL commands required to add support for the custom properties to the database. There is also a method, called Down, that executes commands that downgrade the database to its previous schema.

The next step is to migrate the database to the new schema, which is done by running the following command:

```
dotnet ef database update
```

When the command has completed, the table in the database that stores user data will contain new columns that represent the custom properties.

■ **Caution**   Be careful when performing database migrations on production databases that contain real user data. It is easy to create a migration that drops columns or entire tables, which can have a devastating effect. Make sure that you test the effect of database migrations thoroughly and make sure you have a backup of critical data in case things go wrong.

Testing the Custom Properties

To test the effect of the migration, start the application and authenticate as one of the Identity users (by using, for example, the e-mail alice@example.com and the password secret123). Once authenticated, you will see the default values for the City and QualificationLevel properties. The properties can be changed by requesting the /Home/UserProps URL, selecting new values, and clicking the Submit button, which will update the database and redirect the browser back to the /Home URL, which will display the new values, as shown in Figure 30-3.

Figure 30-3. *Using custom user properties*

Working with Claims and Policies

In older user-management systems, such as ASP.NET Membership, which was the predecessor to ASP.NET Core Identity, the application was assumed to be the authoritative source of all information about the user, essentially treating the application as a closed world and trusting the data contained within it.

This is such an ingrained approach to software development that it can be hard to recognize that's what is happening, but you saw an example of the closed-world technique in Chapter 29 when I authenticated users against the credentials stored in the database and granted access based on the roles associated with those credentials. I did the same thing again in this chapter when I added properties to the user class. Every piece of information that I needed to manage user authentication and authorization came from within my application—and that is a perfectly satisfactory approach for many web applications, which is why I demonstrated these techniques in such depth.

ASP.NET Core Identity also supports an alternative approach for dealing with users, which works well when the MVC application isn't the sole source of information about users and which can be used to authorize users in more flexible and fluid ways than traditional roles allow. This alternative approach uses *claims*, and in this section, I'll describe how ASP.NET Core Identity supports *claims-based authorization*.

■ **Tip** You don't have to use claims in your applications, and as Chapter 29 showed, ASP.NET Core Identity is perfectly happy providing an application with authentication and authorization services without any need to understand claims at all.

Understanding Claims

A *claim* is a piece of information about the user, along with some information about where the information came from. The easiest way to unpack claims is through some practical demonstrations, without which any discussion becomes too abstract to be truly useful. To get started, I added a class file called ClaimsController.cs to the Controllers folder and used it to define the controller shown in Listing 30-5.

■ **Tip** You may feel a little lost as I define the code and describe the classes for this example. Don't worry about the details for the moment—just stick with it until you see the output from the action method and view that I define. More than anything else, that will help put claims into perspective.

Listing 30-5. The Contents of the ClaimsController.cs File in the Controllers Folder

```
using Microsoft.AspNetCore.Authorization;
using Microsoft.AspNetCore.Mvc;

namespace Users.Controllers {

    public class ClaimsController : Controller {

        [Authorize]
        public ViewResult Index() => View(User?.Claims);
    }
}
```

You can get the claims associated with a user in different ways. The User property (also available as the HttpContext.User property) returns a ClaimsPrincipal object, which is the approach that I have used in this example. The set of claims associated with a user is accessed through the ClaimsPrincipal methods and properties described in Table 30-3.

Table 30-3. *Selected Members of the ClaimsPrincipal Class*

Name	Description
Identity	Gets the IIdentity value that is associated with the current user, as described in the following sections.
FindAll(type) FindAll(<predicate>)	These methods return all the claims of a specific type or that are matched by the predicate.
FindFirst(type) FindFirst(<predicate>)	These methods return the first claim of a specific type or that is matched by the predicate.
HasClaim(type, value) HasClaim(<predicate>)	These methods return true if the user has a claim of the specified type with the specified value or if there is a claim that is matched by the predicate.
IsInRole(name)	Returns true if the user is a member of the role with the specified name.

As I explained in Chapter 28, the HttpContext.User.Identity property returns an implementation of the IIdentity interface, which is a ClaimsIdentity object when working using ASP.NET Core Identity, and Table 30-4 shows the members it defines that are relevant to this chapter.

Table 30-4. *Selected Members Defined by the ClaimsIdentity Class*

Name	Description
Claims	Returns an enumeration of Claim objects representing the claims for the user.
AddClaim(claim)	Adds a claim to the user identity.
AddClaims(claims)	Adds an enumeration of Claim objects to the user identity.
HasClaim(predicate)	Returns true if the user identity contains a claim that matches the specified predicate.
RemoveClaim(claim)	Removes a claim from the user identity.

Other methods and properties are available, but the ones in the table are those that are used most often in web applications, for reasons that will become obvious as I demonstrate how claims fit into the wider ASP.NET Core platform.

In Listing 30-5, I use the Controller.User property to get a ClaimsPrincipal object and pass the value of the Claims property as the view model for the default view. A Claim object represents a single piece of data about the user, and the Claim class defines the properties shown in Table 30-5.

Table 30-5. *Properties Defined by the Claim Class*

Name	Description
Issuer	Returns the name of the system that provided the claim
Subject	Returns the ClaimsIdentity object for the user who the claim refers to
Type	Returns the type of information that the claim represents
Value	Returns the piece of information that the claim represents

To display details of the claims associated with a user, I created the Views/Claims folder, created a file within it called Index.cshtml, and added the markup shown in Listing 30-6.

Listing 30-6. The Contents of the Index.cshtml File in the Views/Claims Folder

```
@model IEnumerable<System.Security.Claims.Claim>

<div class="bg-primary m-1 p-1 text-white"><h4>Claims</h4></div>

<table class="table table-sm table-bordered">
    <tr>
        <th>Subject</th><th>Issuer</th><th>Type</th><th>Value</th>
    </tr>
    @if (Model == null || Model.Count() == 0) {
        <tr><td colspan="4" class="text-center">No Claims</td></tr>
    } else {
        @foreach (var claim in Model.OrderBy(x => x.Type)) {
            <tr>
                <td>@claim.Subject.Name</td>
                <td>@claim.Issuer</td>
                <td identity-claim-type="@claim.Type"></td>
                <td>@claim.Value</td>
            </tr>
        }
    }
</table>
```

The view uses a table to display each of the claims provided in the view model. The value of the Claim. Type property is a URI for a Microsoft schema, which isn't especially useful. The popular schemas are used as the values for fields in the System.Security.Claims.ClaimTypes class, so to make the output from the Index.cshtml view easier to read, I added a custom attribute to the td element that displays the Type property like this:

```
...
<td identity-claim-type="@claim.Type"></td>
...
```

I added a class file called ClaimTypeTagHelper.cs to the Infrastructure folder and used it to create a tag helper that translates the attribute value into a more readable string, as shown in Listing 30-7.

Listing 30-7. The Contents of the ClaimTypeTagHelper.cs File in the Infrastructure Folder

```
using System.Linq;
using System.Reflection;
using System.Security.Claims;
using Microsoft.AspNetCore.Razor.TagHelpers;

namespace Users.Infrastructure {

    [HtmlTargetElement("td", Attributes = "identity-claim-type")]
    public class ClaimTypeTagHelper : TagHelper {
```

```
        [HtmlAttributeName("identity-claim-type")]
        public string ClaimType { get; set; }

        public override void Process(TagHelperContext context,
                                     TagHelperOutput output) {
            bool foundType = false;
            FieldInfo[] fields = typeof(ClaimTypes).GetFields();
            foreach (FieldInfo field in fields) {
                if (field.GetValue(null).ToString() == ClaimType) {
                    output.Content.SetContent(field.Name);
                    foundType = true;
                }
            }
            if (!foundType) {
                output.Content.SetContent(ClaimType.Split('/', '.').Last());
            }
        }
    }
}
```

To see why I have created a controller that uses claims without really explaining what they are, start the application and authenticate as the user Alice (using the e-mail address `alice@example.com` and the password `secret123`). Once you are authenticated, request the `/Claims` URL to see the claims associated with the user, as illustrated in Figure 30-4.

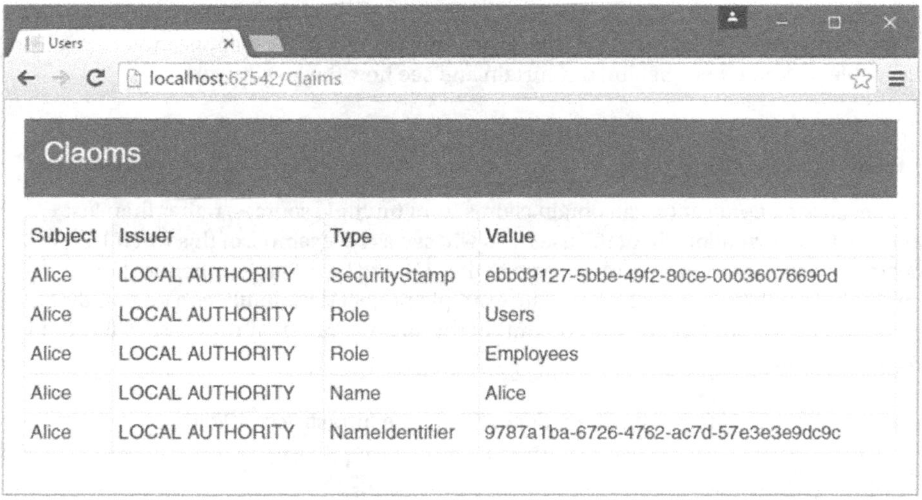
Users
localhost:62542/Claims
Claoms
Subject
Issuer
Type
Value
Alice LOCAL AUTHORITY SecurityStamp ebbd9127-5bbe-49f2-80ce-00036076690d
Alice LOCAL AUTHORITY Role Users
Alice LOCAL AUTHORITY Role Employees
Alice LOCAL AUTHORITY Name Alice
Alice LOCAL AUTHORITY NameIdentifier 9787a1ba-6726-4762-ac7d-57e3e3e9dc9c

Figure 30-4. *The output from the Index action of the Claims controller*

It can be hard to make out the detail in the figure, so I have reproduced the content in Table 30-6.

Table 30-6. *The Data Shown in Figure 30-4*

Subject	Issuer	Type	Value
Alice	LOCAL AUTHORITY	SecurityStamp	Unique ID
Alice	LOCAL AUTHORITY	Role	Users
Alice	LOCAL AUTHORITY	Role	Employees
Alice	LOCAL AUTHORITY	Name	Alice
Alice	LOCAL AUTHORITY	NameIdentifier	Alice's user ID

The table shows the most important aspect of claims, which is that I have already been using them when I implemented the traditional authentication and authorization features in Chapter 29. You can see that some of the claims relate to user identity (the Name claim is Alice, and the NameIdentifier claim is Alice's unique user ID in the ASP.NET Core Identity database). Other claims show membership of roles—there are two Role claims in the table, reflecting the fact that Alice is assigned to both the Users and Employees roles.

The difference when this information is expressed as a set of claims is that you can determine where the data came from. The Issuer property for all the claims shown in the table is set to LOCAL AUTHORITY, which indicates that the user's identity has been established by the application.

So, now that you have seen some example claims, I can more easily describe what a claim is: a claim is any piece of information about a user that is available to the application, including the user's identity and role memberships. And, as you have seen, the information I have been defining about my users in earlier chapters is automatically made available as claims by ASP.NET Core Identity. While claims can seem bewildering at first, there is no magic about them, and like every other aspect of MVC applications, they turn out to be far less formidable once you peek behind the curtain and see how they really work.

Creating Claims

Claims are interesting because an application can obtain claims from multiple sources, rather than just relying on a local database for information about the user. You will see a real example of this when I show you how to authenticate users through a third-party system in the "Using Third-Party Authentication" section, but for the moment I am going to add a class to the example project that simulates a system that provides claims information. Listing 30-8 shows the contents of the LocationClaimsProvider.cs file that I added to the Infrastructure folder.

Listing 30-8. The Contents of the LocationClaimsProvider.cs File in the Infrastructure Folder

```
using System.Security.Claims;
using System.Threading.Tasks;
using Microsoft.AspNetCore.Authentication;

namespace Users.Infrastructure {

    public class LocationClaimsProvider : IClaimsTransformation {

        public Task<ClaimsPrincipal> TransformAsync(ClaimsPrincipal principal) {
            if (principal != null && !principal.HasClaim(c =>
                    c.Type == ClaimTypes.PostalCode)) {
```

```
            ClaimsIdentity identity = principal.Identity as ClaimsIdentity;
            if (identity != null && identity.IsAuthenticated
                    && identity.Name != null) {
                if (identity.Name.ToLower() == "alice") {
                    identity.AddClaims(new Claim[] {
                        CreateClaim(ClaimTypes.PostalCode, "DC 20500"),
                        CreateClaim(ClaimTypes.StateOrProvince, "DC")
                    });
                } else {
                    identity.AddClaims(new Claim[] {
                        CreateClaim(ClaimTypes.PostalCode, "NY 10036"),
                        CreateClaim(ClaimTypes.StateOrProvince, "NY")
                    });
                }
            }
        }
        return Task.FromResult(principal);
    }

    private static Claim CreateClaim(string type, string value) =>
        new Claim(type, value, ClaimValueTypes.String, "RemoteClaims");
    }
}
```

The TransformAsync method, which is defined by the IClaimsTransformation interface, receives a ClaimsPrincipal and inspects it, casting the value of its Identity property to a ClaimsIdentity object. Then the value of the Name property is used to create claims about the user's ZIP code and state.

This class simulates a system such as a central HR database, which would be the authoritative source of location information about staff, for example. To register the source of the claims, I defined a service in the ConfigureServices method of the Startup class, as shown in Listing 30-9.

Listing 30-9. Enabling Claims Transformation in the Startup.cs File in the Users Folder

```
using Microsoft.AspNetCore.Builder;
using Microsoft.Extensions.DependencyInjection;
using Microsoft.Extensions.Configuration;
using Microsoft.AspNetCore.Identity;
using Microsoft.EntityFrameworkCore;
using Users.Models;
using Users.Infrastructure;
using Microsoft.AspNetCore.Authentication;

namespace Users {

    public class Startup {

        public Startup(IConfiguration configuration) =>
            Configuration = configuration;

        public IConfiguration Configuration { get; }

        public void ConfigureServices(IServiceCollection services) {

            services.AddTransient<IPasswordValidator<AppUser>,
```

```
                CustomPasswordValidator>();
            services.AddTransient<IUserValidator<AppUser>,
                CustomUserValidator>();
            services.AddSingleton<IClaimsTransformation,
                LocationClaimsProvider>();

            services.AddDbContext<AppIdentityDbContext>(options =>
                options.UseSqlServer(
                    Configuration["Data:SportStoreIdentity:ConnectionString"]));

            services.AddIdentity<AppUser, IdentityRole>(opts => {
                opts.User.RequireUniqueEmail = true;
                //opts.User.AllowedUserNameCharacters = "abcdefghijklmnopqrstuvwxyz";
                opts.Password.RequiredLength = 6;
                opts.Password.RequireNonAlphanumeric = false;
                opts.Password.RequireLowercase = false;
                opts.Password.RequireUppercase = false;
                opts.Password.RequireDigit = false;
            }).AddEntityFrameworkStores<AppIdentityDbContext>()
                .AddDefaultTokenProviders();

            services.AddMvc();
        }

        public void Configure(IApplicationBuilder app) {
            app.UseStatusCodePages();
            app.UseDeveloperExceptionPage();
            app.UseStaticFiles();
            app.UseAuthentication();
            app.UseMvcWithDefaultRoute();
        }
    }
}
```

Each time a request is received, the claims transformation middleware calls the
LocationClaimsProvider.TransformAsync method, which simulates my HR data source and creates
custom claims. You can see the effect of the custom claims by starting the application, authenticating as a
user, and requesting the /Claims URL. Figure 30-5 shows the claims for Alice. You may have to sign out and
sign back in again to see the change.

Figure 30-5. *Defining additional claims for users*

Obtaining claims from multiple locations means that the application doesn't have to duplicate data that is held elsewhere and allows integration of data from external parties. The Claim.Issuer property tells you where a claim originated from, which helps you judge how accurate the data is likely to be and how much weight you should give the data in your application. Location data obtained from a central HR database is likely to be more accurate and trustworthy than data obtained from an external mailing list provider, for example.

CREATING CUSTOM IDENTITY CLAIMS

If you want to add custom local claims to the application, then you can do so when you create new users. The UserManager<T> class provides AddClaimAsync and AddClaimsAsync methods that can be used to define local claims, which are then stored in the database and retrieved automatically when the user is authenticated (which means you don't need to rely on the claims transformation feature). However, before using these methods, consider how the data you store will be kept current and whether your application would be better served by retrieving the data dynamically from its source. As I explain in the next section, claims are used for authorization checks, and stale claim data can allow users to access parts of the application that they should have been barred from and prevent access to areas to which they have been granted.

Using Policies

Once you have some claims to work with, you can use them to manage user access to your application more flexibly than with standard roles. The problem with roles is that they are static, and once a user has been assigned to a role, the user remains a member until explicitly removed. This is, for example, how long-term employees of big corporations end up with incredible access to internal systems: they are assigned the roles they require for each new job they get, but the old roles are rarely removed.

Claims are used to build authorization *policies*, which are part of the application configuration and applied to action methods or controllers using the Authorize attribute. Listing 30-10 shows a simple policy that only allows access to users with a specific claim type and value.

Listing 30-10. Creating a Claim Policy in the Startup.cs File in the Users Folder

```
using Microsoft.AspNetCore.Builder;
using Microsoft.Extensions.DependencyInjection;
using Microsoft.Extensions.Configuration;
using Microsoft.AspNetCore.Identity;
using Microsoft.EntityFrameworkCore;
using Users.Models;
using Users.Infrastructure;
using Microsoft.AspNetCore.Authentication;
using System.Security.Claims;

namespace Users {

    public class Startup {

        public Startup(IConfiguration configuration) =>
            Configuration = configuration;

        public IConfiguration Configuration { get; }

        public void ConfigureServices(IServiceCollection services) {

            services.AddTransient<IPasswordValidator<AppUser>,
                CustomPasswordValidator>();
            services.AddTransient<IUserValidator<AppUser>,
                CustomUserValidator>();
            services.AddSingleton<IClaimsTransformation, LocationClaimsProvider>();

            services.AddAuthorization(opts => {
                opts.AddPolicy("DCUsers", policy => {
                    policy.RequireRole("Users");
                    policy.RequireClaim(ClaimTypes.StateOrProvince, "DC");
                });
            });

            services.AddDbContext<AppIdentityDbContext>(options =>
                options.UseSqlServer(
                    Configuration["Data:SportStoreIdentity:ConnectionString"]));
```

```
        services.AddIdentity<AppUser, IdentityRole>(opts => {
            opts.User.RequireUniqueEmail = true;
            //opts.User.AllowedUserNameCharacters = "abcdefghijklmnopqrstuvwxyz";
            opts.Password.RequiredLength = 6;
            opts.Password.RequireNonAlphanumeric = false;
            opts.Password.RequireLowercase = false;
            opts.Password.RequireUppercase = false;
            opts.Password.RequireDigit = false;
        }).AddEntityFrameworkStores<AppIdentityDbContext>()
            .AddDefaultTokenProviders();

        services.AddMvc();
    }

    public void Configure(IApplicationBuilder app) {
        app.UseStatusCodePages();
        app.UseDeveloperExceptionPage();
        app.UseStaticFiles();
        app.UseAuthentication();
        app.UseMvcWithDefaultRoute();
    }
  }
}
```

The AddAuthorization method sets up authorization policy and provides an AuthorizationOptions object that defines the members described in Table 30-7.

Table 30-7. *The Members Defined by the AuthorizationOptions Class*

Name	Description
DefaultPolicy	This property returns the default authorization policy, which is used when the Authorize attribute is applied without any arguments. By default, this policy checks that users are authenticated.
AddPolicy(name, expression)	This method is used to define a new policy, as described in the following text.

Policies are defined using the AddPolicy method, which works with a lambda expression that operates on an AuthorizationPolicyBuilder object to build up a policy in steps using the methods described in Table 30-8.

Table 30-8. *Selected Methods Defined by the AuthorizationPolicyBuilder Class*

Name	Description
RequireAuthenticatedUser()	This method requires that the request is associated with an authenticated user.
RequireUserName(name)	This method requires that the request is associated with the specified user.
RequireClaim(type)	This method requires that the user has a claim of the specified type. It is only the presence of the claim that is checked, and any value will be accepted.
RequireClaim(type, values)	This method requires that the user has a claim of the specified type and with one of a range of values. Values can be expressed as comma-separated arguments or as an IEnumerable<string>.
RequireRole(roles)	This method requires that the user has membership in a role. Multiple roles can be specified as comma-separated arguments or as an IEnumerable<string>, and membership of any one of the roles will meet the requirement.
AddRequirements(requirement)	This method adds a custom requirement to the policy, as described in the "Creating Custom Policy Requirements" section.

The policy in Listing 30-10 requires that a user has membership of the Users role and has a StateOrProvince claim with a value of DC. When there are multiple requirements, all of them have to be met for authorization to be granted.

The first argument to the AddPolicy method is the name by which the policy can be referred to when it is applied. The name of the policy in Listing 30-10 is DCUsers, and this is the name used in the Authorize attribute to apply the policy to the Home controller in Listing 30-11.

Listing 30-11. Applying an Authorization Policy in the HomeController.cs File in the Controllers Folder

```
using System.Collections.Generic;
using Microsoft.AspNetCore.Mvc;
using Microsoft.AspNetCore.Authorization;
using Users.Models;
using Microsoft.AspNetCore.Identity;
using System.Threading.Tasks;
using System.ComponentModel.DataAnnotations;

namespace Users.Controllers {

    public class HomeController : Controller {
        private UserManager<AppUser> userManager;

        public HomeController(UserManager<AppUser> userMgr) {
            userManager = userMgr;
        }

        [Authorize]
        public IActionResult Index() => View(GetData(nameof(Index)));
```

```
//[Authorize(Roles = "Users")]
[Authorize(Policy = "DCUsers")]
public IActionResult OtherAction() => View("Index",
    GetData(nameof(OtherAction)));

// ...other methods omitted for brevity...

private Task<AppUser> CurrentUser =>
    userManager.FindByNameAsync(HttpContext.User.Identity.Name);
    }
}
```

The Policy property is used to specify the name of the policy that will be used to protect the action method. The result is that a combined check on the roles and claims that a user has is performed when a request targets the OtherAction method. Only the Alice account has the right combination of role membership and claims, which you can check by running the application, authenticating as different users, and requesting the /Home/OtherAction URL.

Creating Custom Policy Requirements

The built-in requirements check specific values, which is a good starting point but doesn't allow for every authorization scenario to be handled. If access should be prohibited for a certain claim value, for example, then things start to get tricky with the built-in requirements, which just aren't set up for that kind of check.

Fortunately, the policy system can be extended with custom requirements, which are classes that implement the IAuthorizationRequirement interface, and custom authorization handlers, which are subclasses of the AuthorizationHandler class that evaluate the requirement for a given request. To demonstrate, I added a file called BlockUsersRequirement.cs to the Infrastructure folder and used it to define the custom requirement and handler shown in Listing 30-12.

Listing 30-12. The Contents of the BlockUsersRequirement.cs File in the Infrastructure Folder

```
using System;
using System.Linq;
using System.Threading.Tasks;
using Microsoft.AspNetCore.Authorization;

namespace Users.Infrastructure {

    public class BlockUsersRequirement : IAuthorizationRequirement {

        public BlockUsersRequirement(params string[] users) {
            BlockedUsers = users;
        }

        public string[] BlockedUsers { get; set; }
    }

    public class BlockUsersHandler : AuthorizationHandler<BlockUsersRequirement> {

        protected override Task HandleRequirementAsync(
                AuthorizationHandlerContext context,
                BlockUsersRequirement requirement) {
```

```
            if (context.User.Identity != null && context.User.Identity.Name != null
                && !requirement.BlockedUsers
                    .Any(user => user.Equals(context.User.Identity.Name,
                        StringComparison.OrdinalIgnoreCase))) {
                context.Succeed(requirement);
            } else {
                context.Fail();
            }
            return Task.CompletedTask;
        }
    }
}
```

The BlockUserRequirement class is the requirement and is used to specify the data that will be used to create a policy, which in this case is a list of users who will not be authorized. The BlockUsersHandler class is responsible for evaluating an authorization request using the requirement data and is derived from the AuthorizationHandler<T> class, where T is the type of the requirement class.

The Handle method is called on the handler class when the authorization system needs to check access to a resource. The arguments to the method are an AuthorizationHandlerContext object, which defines the members described in Table 30-9, and the requirement object that provides access to the data needed to perform the check.

Table 30-9. *Selected AuthorizationHandlerContext Members*

Name	Description
User	This property returns the ClaimsPrincipal associated with the request.
Succeed(requirement)	This method is called if the request meets the requirement. The argument is the IAuthorizationRequirement object received by the Handle method.
Fail()	This method is called if the request fails to meet the requirement.
Resource	This property returns an object that is used to authorize access to a single application resource, as described in the "Using Policies to Authorize Access to Resources" section.

The requirement handler in Listing 30-12 checks the name of the user to see whether it is in the forbidden list provided by the BlockUsersRequirement object and calls the Succeed or Fail method accordingly. Applying a custom requirement requires two configuration changes, as shown in Listing 30-13.

Listing 30-13. Applying a Custom Authorization Requirement in the Startup.cs File in the Users Folder

```
using Microsoft.AspNetCore.Builder;
using Microsoft.Extensions.DependencyInjection;
using Microsoft.Extensions.Configuration;
using Microsoft.AspNetCore.Identity;
using Microsoft.EntityFrameworkCore;
using Users.Models;
using Users.Infrastructure;
using Microsoft.AspNetCore.Authentication;
using System.Security.Claims;
using Microsoft.AspNetCore.Authorization;
```

```
namespace Users {

    public class Startup {

        public Startup(IConfiguration configuration) =>
            Configuration = configuration;

        public IConfiguration Configuration { get; }

        public void ConfigureServices(IServiceCollection services) {

            services.AddTransient<IPasswordValidator<AppUser>,
                CustomPasswordValidator>();
            services.AddTransient<IUserValidator<AppUser>,
                CustomUserValidator>();
            services.AddSingleton<IClaimsTransformation, LocationClaimsProvider>();
            services.AddTransient<IAuthorizationHandler, BlockUsersHandler>();

            services.AddAuthorization(opts => {
                opts.AddPolicy("DCUsers", policy => {
                    policy.RequireRole("Users");
                    policy.RequireClaim(ClaimTypes.StateOrProvince, "DC");
                });
                opts.AddPolicy("NotBob", policy => {
                    policy.RequireAuthenticatedUser();
                    policy.AddRequirements(new BlockUsersRequirement("Bob"));
                });
            });

            services.AddDbContext<AppIdentityDbContext>(options =>
                options.UseSqlServer(
                    Configuration["Data:SportStoreIdentity:ConnectionString"]));

            services.AddIdentity<AppUser, IdentityRole>(opts => {
                opts.User.RequireUniqueEmail = true;
                //opts.User.AllowedUserNameCharacters = "abcdefghijklmnopqrstuvwxyz";
                opts.Password.RequiredLength = 6;
                opts.Password.RequireNonAlphanumeric = false;
                opts.Password.RequireLowercase = false;
                opts.Password.RequireUppercase = false;
                opts.Password.RequireDigit = false;
            }).AddEntityFrameworkStores<AppIdentityDbContext>()
                .AddDefaultTokenProviders();

            services.AddMvc();
        }

        public void Configure(IApplicationBuilder app) {
            app.UseStatusCodePages();
            app.UseDeveloperExceptionPage();
            app.UseStaticFiles();
```

```
                app.UseAuthentication();
                app.UseMvcWithDefaultRoute();
            }
        }
    }
}
```

The first step is to register the handler class with the service provider as an implementation of the IAuthorizationHandler interface. The second step is to add the custom requirement to a policy, which is done using the AddRequirements method, like this:

```
...
opts.AddPolicy("NotBob", policy => {
    policy.RequireAuthenticatedUser();
    policy.AddRequirements(new BlockUsersRequirement("Bob"));
});
...
```

The result is a policy that requires authenticated users who are not Bob and that can be applied through the Authorize attribute by specifying the policy name, as shown in Listing 30-14.

Listing 30-14. Applying a Custom Policy in the HomeController.cs File

```
...
//[Authorize(Roles = "Users")]
[Authorize(Policy = "DCUsers")]
public IActionResult OtherAction() => View("Index", GetData(nameof(OtherAction)));

[Authorize(Policy = "NotBob")]
public IActionResult NotBob() => View("Index", GetData(nameof(NotBob)));
...
```

You will not be able to access the /Home/NotBob URL if you have authenticated as Bob, but all other user accounts will be granted access.

Using Policies to Authorize Access to Resources

Policies can also be used to control access to individual *resources*, which is a general term for any item of data that your application uses and which require more granular management than is possible at the action method level. As a demonstration, I added a file called ProtectedDocument.cs to the Models folder and used it to define a class that represents a document with some ownership attributes, as shown in Listing 30-15.

Listing 30-15. The Contents of the ProtectedDocument.cs File in the Models Folder

```
namespace Users.Models {

    public class ProtectedDocument {
        public string Title { get; set; }
        public string Author { get; set; }
        public string Editor { get; set; }
    }
}
```

This is just a placeholder for a real document, with the key point being that each document should be editable by just two people: the author and the editor. A real document would require content and change tracking and many other features, but this is enough for the example. I added a class file called DocumentController.cs to the Controllers folder and used it to create the controller shown in Listing 30-16.

Listing 30-16. The Contents of the DocumentController.cs File in the Controllers Folder

```
using Microsoft.AspNetCore.Authorization;
using Microsoft.AspNetCore.Mvc;
using System.Linq;
using Users.Models;

namespace Users.Controllers {

    [Authorize]
    public class DocumentController : Controller {
        private ProtectedDocument[] docs = new ProtectedDocument[] {
            new ProtectedDocument { Title = "Q3 Budget", Author = "Alice",
                Editor = "Joe"},
            new ProtectedDocument { Title = "Project Plan", Author = "Bob",
                Editor = "Alice"}
        };

        public ViewResult Index() => View(docs);

        public ViewResult Edit(string title) {
            return View("Index", docs.FirstOrDefault(d => d.Title == title));
        }
    }
}
```

The controller maintains a fixed set of ProtectedDocument objects. The ProtectedDocument objects are used in the Index action, which passes all the documents to the View method, and the Edit action, which selects one document based on a title argument. Both of the action methods use a view called Index. chstml, which I added to a new folder called Views/Document, as shown in Listing 30-17.

Listing 30-17. The Contents of the Index.cshtml File in the Views/Document Folder

```
@if (Model is IEnumerable<ProtectedDocument>) {
    <div class="bg-primary m-1 p-1 text-white">
        <h4>Documents (@User?.Identity?.Name)</h4>
    </div>
    <table class="table table-sm table-bordered">
        <tr><th>Title</th><th>Author</th><th>Editor</th><th></th></tr>
        @foreach (var doc in Model) {
            <tr>
                <td>@doc.Title</td>
                <td>@doc.Author</td>
                <td>@doc.Editor</td>
                <td>
                    <a class="btn btn-sm btn-primary" asp-action="Edit"
                        asp-route-title="@doc.Title">
```

```
                        Edit
                    </a>
                </td>
            </tr>
        }
    </table>
} else {
    <div class="bg-primary m-1 p-1">
        <h4>Editing @Model.Title (@User?.Identity?.Name)</h4>
    </div>
    <div class="m-1 p-1">
        Document editing feature would go here...
    </div>
    <a asp-action="Index" class="btn btn-primary">Done</a>
}
<a asp-action="Logout" asp-controller="Account" class="btn btn-danger">Logout</a>
```

If the view model is a sequence of ProtectedDocument objects, then the view displays a table with one row for each document, displaying the names of the author and editor and a link to the Edit action. If the view model is a single ProtectedDocument, then the view displays some placeholder content for where a real application would provide editing features.

At the moment, the only authorization restriction is the Authorize attribute applied to the DocumentController class, which means that any user can edit any document, not just the author and editor. You can see this by running the application, requesting the /Document URL, authenticating as any of the application users, and clicking the Edit button for the documents. Figure 30-6 shows the user Joe editing the Project Plan document, for example.

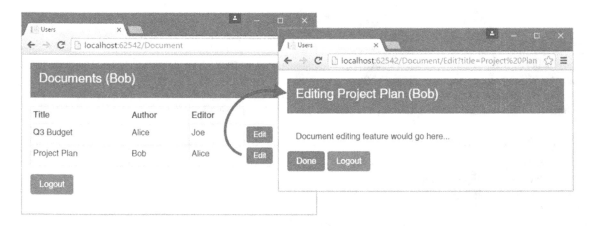

Figure 30-6. *Editing documents*

Creating the Resource Authorization Policy and Handler

Restricting access to individual documents at the action method level is difficult because the Authorize attribute is evaluated before the action method is invoked. This means the decision about authorization is made before the ProtectedDocument object is retrieved and can be inspected, and the details of which users should be allowed to access the document are revealed.

The solution to this problem is to create an authorization polic[y] with ProtectedDocument objects and to use them within the action m[ethod] revealed. To demonstrate, I added a file called DocumentAuthorization[.cs] and defined the classes shown in Listing 30-18.

Listing 30-18. The Contents of the DocumentAuthorization.cs File in the Infrast[ructure Folder]

```csharp
using System;
using System.Threading.Tasks;
using Microsoft.AspNetCore.Authorization;
using Users.Models;

namespace Users.Infrastructure {

    public class DocumentAuthorizationRequirement : IAuthorizationRequirement {
        public bool AllowAuthors { get; set; }
        public bool AllowEditors { get; set; }
    }

    public class DocumentAuthorizationHandler
        : AuthorizationHandler<DocumentAuthorizationRequirement> {

        protected override Task HandleRequirementAsync(
                AuthorizationHandlerContext context,
                DocumentAuthorizationRequirement requirement) {
            ProtectedDocument doc = context.Resource as ProtectedDocument;
            string user = context.User.Identity.Name;
            StringComparison compare = StringComparison.OrdinalIgnoreCase;
            if (doc != null && user != null &&
                (requirement.AllowAuthors && doc.Author.Equals(user, compare))
                || (requirement.AllowEditors && doc.Editor.Equals(user, compare))) {
                context.Succeed(requirement);
            } else {
                context.Fail();
            }
            return Task.CompletedTask;
        }
    }
}
```

The AuthorizationHandlerContext object provides a Resource property that provides access to an object that can be inspected for authorization. The DocumentAuthorizationHandler class checks to see whether the Resource property is a ProtectedDocument object and, if it is, checks to see whether the current user is the author and editor and whether the DocumentAuthorizationRequirement object allows editors or authors to access the document.

In Listing 30-19, I have registered the DocumentAuthorizationHandler class as a handler for DocumentAuthorizationRequirement requirements and defined a policy that has this requirement.

...and handler that know how to deal ...ethod, once the user details have been ...cs to the Infrastructure folder

...ucture Folder

he Startup.cs File in the Users Folder

```
ces) {



    onClaimsProvider>();
    JsersHandler>();
    ntAuthorizationHandler>();



    rovince, "DC");

        policy -> {
        policy.RequireAuthenticatedUser();
        policy.AddRequirements(new BlockUsersRequirement("Bob"));
    });
    opts.AddPolicy("AuthorsAndEditors", policy => {
        policy.AddRequirements(new DocumentAuthorizationRequirement {
            AllowAuthors = true,
            AllowEditors = true
        });
    });
});

services.AddDbContext<AppIdentityDbContext>(options =>
    options.UseSqlServer(
        Configuration["Data:SportStoreIdentity:ConnectionString"]));

services.AddIdentity<AppUser, IdentityRole>(opts => {
    opts.User.RequireUniqueEmail = true;
    //opts.User.AllowedUserNameCharacters = "abcdefghijklmnopqrstuvwxyz";
    opts.Password.RequiredLength = 6;
    opts.Password.RequireNonAlphanumeric = false;
    opts.Password.RequireLowercase = false;
    opts.Password.RequireUppercase = false;
    opts.Password.RequireDigit = false;
}).AddEntityFrameworkStores<AppIdentityDbContext>()
    .AddDefaultTokenProviders();

services.AddMvc();
}
...
```

The final step is to apply the authorization policy in the action method, as shown in Listing 30-20.

Listing 30-20. Applying the Policy in the DocumentController.cs File in the Controllers Folder

```
using Microsoft.AspNetCore.Authorization;
using Microsoft.AspNetCore.Mvc;
using System.Linq;
using Users.Models;
using System.Threading.Tasks;

namespace Users.Controllers {

    [Authorize]
    public class DocumentController : Controller {
        private ProtectedDocument[] docs = new ProtectedDocument[] {
            new ProtectedDocument { Title = "Q3 Budget", Author = "Alice",
                Editor = "Joe"},
            new ProtectedDocument { Title = "Project Plan", Author = "Bob",
                Editor = "Alice"}
        };
        private IAuthorizationService authService;

        public DocumentController(IAuthorizationService auth) {
            authService = auth;
        }

        public ViewResult Index() => View(docs);

        public async Task<IActionResult> Edit(string title) {
            ProtectedDocument doc = docs.FirstOrDefault(d => d.Title == title);
            AuthorizationResult authorized = await authService.AuthorizeAsync(User,
                doc, "AuthorsAndEditors");
            if (authorized.Succeeded) {
                return View("Index", doc);
            } else {
                return new ChallengeResult();
            }
        }
    }
}
```

The controller constructor defines an IAuthorizationService argument, which provides methods that can be used to evaluate authorization policies and which is resolved using dependency injection. In the Edit method, I call the AuthorizeAsync method, passing in the current user, the ProtectedDocument object, and the name of the policy that I want to apply. If the result from the AuthorizeAsync method is true, then authorization is approved, and the View method is called. If the result is false, then there is an authorization problem, and I return a ChallengeResult object, as described in Chapter 17, which tells MVC that there has been an authorization failure.

You can see the effect by running the application and requesting the /Document URL, authenticated as different users. If, for example, you authenticate as Joe, then you will be able to edit the budget document but not the project plan.

Using Third-Party Authentication

One of the benefits of a claims-based system such as ASP.NET Core Identity is that any of the claims can come from an external system, even those that identify the user to the application. This means that other systems can authenticate users on behalf of the application, and ASP.NET Core Identity builds on this idea to make it simple and easy to add support for authenticating users through third parties such as Microsoft, Google, Facebook, and Twitter.

There are some substantial benefits of using third-party authentication: many users will already have an account, users can elect to use two-factor authentication, and you don't have to manage user credentials in the application. In the sections that follow, I'll show you how to set up and use third-party authentication for Google users.

Registering the Application with Google

Third-party authentication services typically require applications to be registered before they can authenticate users. The result of the registration process is credentials that are included in the authentication request to the third-party service. The Google registration process is performed at http://console. developers.google.com, following the instructions at http://developers.google.com/identity/sign-in/web/devconsole-project. You must specify a callback URL, which for the default configuration is / signin-google. If you are in development, set the callback URL to be http://localhost:port/signin-google. For production applications, create a URL that includes the public hostname and port.

Following the registration process, you will receive a client ID, which identifies your application to Google, and a client secret, which is used as a security precaution to prevent other applications from pretending to be your application.

■ **Note** You must register your own application and use the client ID and client secret that the registration process produces. The code in this section will not work unless you change the credentials with the values that are unique to your application.

Enabling Google Authentication

ASP.NET Core Identity comes with built-in support for authenticating users through their Microsoft, Google, Facebook, and Twitter accounts as well more general support for any authentication service that supports OAuth. Each service has its own extension method that is used to register with the application in the Startup class, and Listing 30-21 shows how the Google service is set up. (I have removed the configuration statements from earlier examples for brevity.)

Listing 30-21. Enabling Google Authentication in the Startup.cs File in the Users Folder

```
...
public void ConfigureServices(IServiceCollection services) {

    services.AddTransient<IPasswordValidator<AppUser>,
        CustomPasswordValidator>();
    services.AddTransient<IUserValidator<AppUser>,
        CustomUserValidator>();
    services.AddSingleton<IClaimsTransformation, LocationClaimsProvider>();
    services.AddTransient<IAuthorizationHandler, BlockUsersHandler>();
    services.AddTransient<IAuthorizationHandler, DocumentAuthorizationHandler>();
```

```
    services.AddAuthorization(opts => {
        opts.AddPolicy("DCUsers", policy => {
            policy.RequireRole("Users");
            policy.RequireClaim(ClaimTypes.StateOrProvince, "DC");
        });
        opts.AddPolicy("NotBob", policy => {
            policy.RequireAuthenticatedUser();
            policy.AddRequirements(new BlockUsersRequirement("Bob"));
        });
        opts.AddPolicy("AuthorsAndEditors", policy => {
            policy.AddRequirements(new DocumentAuthorizationRequirement {
                AllowAuthors = true,
                AllowEditors = true
            });
        });
    });

    services.AddAuthentication().AddGoogle(opts => {
        opts.ClientId = "<enter client id here>";
        opts.ClientSecret = "<enter client secret here>";
    });

    services.AddDbContext<AppIdentityDbContext>(options =>
        options.UseSqlServer(
            Configuration["Data:SportStoreIdentity:ConnectionString"]));

    services.AddIdentity<AppUser, IdentityRole>(opts => {
        opts.User.RequireUniqueEmail = true;
        opts.Password.RequiredLength = 6;
        opts.Password.RequireNonAlphanumeric = false;
        opts.Password.RequireLowercase = false;
        opts.Password.RequireUppercase = false;
        opts.Password.RequireDigit = false;
    }).AddEntityFrameworkStores<AppIdentityDbContext>()
        .AddDefaultTokenProviders();

    services.AddMvc();
}
...
```

The AddAuthentication.AddGoogle method sets up the required services for authenticating users with Google and specifies the client ID and client secret that were created during the registration process.

When you authenticate a user with a third party, you can elect to create a user in the Identity database, which can then be used to manage roles and claims just as for regular users. In Chapter 28, I added a user validation class that prevents users from being created if their e-mail address isn't in the example.com domain. Since I will be dealing with users from any and all domains, I have to disable the e-mail check in the validator for this example, as shown in Listing 30-22.

Listing 30-22. Disabling Validation in the CustomUserValidator.cs File in the Infrastructure Folder

```
using System.Collections.Generic;
using System.Linq;
using System.Threading.Tasks;
using Microsoft.AspNetCore.Identity;
using Users.Models;

namespace Users.Infrastructure {

    public class CustomUserValidator : UserValidator<AppUser> {

        public override async Task<IdentityResult> ValidateAsync(
                UserManager<AppUser> manager,
                AppUser user) {

            IdentityResult result = await base.ValidateAsync(manager, user);

            List<IdentityError> errors = result.Succeeded ?
                new List<IdentityError>() : result.Errors.ToList();

            //if (!user.Email.ToLower().EndsWith("@example.com")) {
            //    errors.Add(new IdentityError {
            //        Code = "EmailDomainError",
            //        Description = "Only example.com email addresses are allowed"
            //    });
            //}

            return errors.Count == 0 ? IdentityResult.Success
                : IdentityResult.Failed(errors.ToArray());
        }
    }
}
```

Next, I added a button to the Views/Account/Login.cshtml file, which allows users to log in via Google, as shown in Listing 30-23. Google provides images for buttons to make them consistent with other applications that support Google accounts, but for simplicity, I have just created a standard button.

Listing 30-23. Adding a Button to the Login.cshtml File in the Views/Account Folder

```
@model LoginModel

<div class="bg-primary m-1 p-1 text-white"><h4>Log In</h4></div>

<div class="text-danger" asp-validation-summary="All"></div>

<form asp-action="Login" method="post">
    <input type="hidden" name="returnUrl" value="@ViewBag.returnUrl" />
    <div class="form-group">
        <label asp-for="Email"></label>
        <input asp-for="Email" class="form-control" />
    </div>
```

```
    <div class="form-group">
        <label asp-for="Password"></label>
        <input asp-for="Password" class="form-control" />
    </div>
    <button class="btn btn-primary" type="submit">Log In</button>
    <a class="btn btn-info" asp-action="GoogleLogin"
       asp-route-returnUrl="@ViewBag.returnUrl">
        Log In With Google
    </a>
</form>
```

The new button targets the GoogleLogin action on the Account controller. You can see this method—and the other changes I made to the controller—in Listing 30-24.

Listing 30-24. Adding Support for Google to the AccountController.cs File in the Controllers Folder

```
using System.Threading.Tasks;
using Microsoft.AspNetCore.Authorization;
using Microsoft.AspNetCore.Mvc;
using Users.Models;
using Microsoft.AspNetCore.Identity;
using System.Security.Claims;
using Microsoft.AspNetCore.Http.Authentication;

namespace Users.Controllers {

    [Authorize]
    public class AccountController : Controller {
        private UserManager<AppUser> userManager;
        private SignInManager<AppUser> signInManager;

        // ...methods omitted for brevity...

        [AllowAnonymous]
        public IActionResult GoogleLogin(string returnUrl) {
            string redirectUrl = Url.Action("GoogleResponse", "Account",
                new { ReturnUrl = returnUrl });
            var properties = signInManager
                .ConfigureExternalAuthenticationProperties("Google", redirectUrl);
            return new ChallengeResult("Google", properties);
        }

        [AllowAnonymous]
        public async Task<IActionResult> GoogleResponse(string returnUrl = "/") {
            ExternalLoginInfo info = await signInManager.GetExternalLoginInfoAsync();
            if (info == null) {
                return RedirectToAction(nameof(Login));
            }
            var result = await signInManager.ExternalLoginSignInAsync(
                info.LoginProvider, info.ProviderKey, false);
            if (result.Succeeded) {
                return Redirect(returnUrl);
```

```
        } else {
            AppUser user = new AppUser {
                Email = info.Principal.FindFirst(ClaimTypes.Email).Value,
                UserName =
                    info.Principal.FindFirst(ClaimTypes.Email).Value
            };
            IdentityResult identResult = await userManager.CreateAsync(user);
            if (identResult.Succeeded) {
                identResult = await userManager.AddLoginAsync(user, info);
                if (identResult.Succeeded) {
                    await signInManager.SignInAsync(user, false);
                    return Redirect(returnUrl);
                }
            }
            return AccessDenied();
        }
    }
    }
}
}
```

The GoogleLogin method creates an instance of the AuthenticationProperties class and sets the RedirectUri property to a URL that targets the GoogleResponse action in the same controller. The next part is a magic phrase that causes ASP.NET Core Identity to respond to an unauthorized error by redirecting the user to the Google authentication page, rather than the one defined by the application.

```
...
return new ChallengeResult("Google", properties);
...
```

This means that when the user clicks the Log In via Google button, their browser is redirected to the Google authentication service and then redirected back to the GoogleResponse action method once they are authenticated. Within the GoogleResponse method, I get details of the external login by calling the GetExternalLoginInfoAsync of the SigninManager, like this:

```
...
ExternalLoginInfo info = await signInManager.GetExternalLoginInfoAsync();
...
```

The ExternalLoginInfo class defines an ExternalPrincipal property that returns a ClaimsPrincipal object, which contains the claims provided for the user by Google. I sign in the user with the application using the ExternalLoginSignInAsync method, like this:

```
...
var result = await signInManager.ExternalLoginSignInAsync(
            info.LoginProvider, info.ProviderKey, false);
...
```

If the sign-in fails, then it is because there is no user in the database that represents the Google user, which I solve by creating the new user and associating the Google credentials with it, using these two statements:

```
...
IdentityResult identResult = await userManager.CreateAsync(user);
...
identResult = await userManager.AddLoginAsync(user, info);
...
```

■ **Note**   When I create the Identity user, I use the e-mail claim provided by Google for both the `Email` and `UserName` properties of the `AppUser` object so that I don't get any name conflicts with any of the existing users in the database.

To test authentication, start the application, click the Log In via Google button, and provide the credentials for a valid Google account. When you have completed the authentication process, your browser will be redirected back to the application.

Summary

In this chapter, I showed you some of the advanced features that ASP.NET Core Identity supports. I demonstrated the use of custom user properties and how to use database migrations to update the database schema to support them. I explained how claims work and how they can be used to create more flexible ways of authorizing users through policies. I also explained how policies can be used to control access to individual resources managed by an application. I finished the chapter by showing you how to authenticate users via Google, which builds on the ideas behind the use of claims. In the next chapter, I show you how some of the most important conventions used in MVC applications are actually implemented and how you can customize them in your own applications.

CHAPTER 31

■ ■ ■

Model Conventions and Action Constraints

Throughout this book, I have emphasized that there is no magic involved in MVC development and that a small peek behind the scenes reveals how everything fits together to deliver the features that I have described in previous chapters.

In this final chapter of the book, I describe two useful features that let you customize the way your MVC application works. *Model conventions* allow you to replace the conventions used to create controllers and actions, overriding those that are applied by default. *Action constraints* allow you to specify what kind of requests an action can be used for, which provides guidance to MVC when it comes to selecting an action to handle a request.

You can skip this chapter if you want (and you might want to, since it is heavy going in places), but keep it in mind the next time your application is misbehaving. You won't need to use the features that I describe in this chapter often—or at all, even—but the more you know about how MVC works, the better equipped you are to deal with problems when they arise. Table 31-1 summarizes the chapter.

Table 31-1. *Chapter Summary*

Problem	Solution	Listing
Customize the application model	Use one of the built-in attributes or create a custom model convention	1–14
Apply a customization throughout the application	Define a global model convention	15, 16
Differentiate between two action methods that could handle a request	Use action constraints	17–25

Preparing the Example Project

For this chapter, I used the ASP.NET Core Web Application (.NET Core) template to create a new Empty project called ConventionsAndConstraints. Listing 31-1 shows the Startup class, which sets up the MVC Framework and the middleware components useful for development.

© Adam Freeman 2017
A. Freeman, *Pro ASP.NET Core MVC 2*, https://doi.org/10.1007/978-1-4842-3150-0_31

Listing 31-1. The Contents of the Startup.cs File in the ConventionsAndConstraints Folder

```
using System;
using System.Collections.Generic;
using System.Linq;
using System.Threading.Tasks;
using Microsoft.AspNetCore.Builder;
using Microsoft.AspNetCore.Hosting;
using Microsoft.AspNetCore.Http;
using Microsoft.Extensions.DependencyInjection;

namespace ConventionsAndConstraints {

    public class Startup {

        public void ConfigureServices(IServiceCollection services) {
            services.AddMvc();
        }

        public void Configure(IApplicationBuilder app, IHostingEnvironment env) {
            app.UseStatusCodePages();
            app.UseDeveloperExceptionPage();
            app.UseStaticFiles();
            app.UseMvcWithDefaultRoute();
        }
    }
}
```

Creating the View Model, Controller, and View

For many of the examples in this chapter, it is helpful to know which method was used to respond to a request. To that end, I created a Models folder and added to it a class file called Result.cs, which I used to define the class shown in Listing 31-2. This class will allow the controllers in this chapter to pass information to the view about how the request was processed.

Listing 31-2. The Contents of the Result.cs File in the Models Folder

```
using System.Collections.Generic;

namespace ConventionsAndConstraints.Models {

    public class Result {
        public string Controller { get; set; }
        public string Action { get; set; }
    }
}
```

I require only a single controller and view for this chapter. I created the Controllers folder, added a class file called HomeController.cs, and used it to define the class shown in Listing 31-3.

Listing 31-3. The Contents of the HomeController.cs File in the Controllers Folder

```
using ConventionsAndConstraints.Models;
using Microsoft.AspNetCore.Mvc;

namespace ConventionsAndConstraints.Controllers {

    public class HomeController : Controller {

        public IActionResult Index() => View("Result", new Result {
            Controller = nameof(HomeController),
            Action = nameof(Index)
        });

        public IActionResult List() => View("Result", new Result {
            Controller = nameof(HomeController),
            Action = nameof(List)
        });
    }
}
```

Both of the action methods in this controller render a view called `Result`, which I defined by creating the Views/Home folder and adding a view file with the markup shown in Listing 31-4.

Listing 31-4. The Contents of the Result.cshtml File in the Views/Home Folder

```
@model Result
@{ Layout = null; }

<!DOCTYPE html>
<html>
<head>
    <meta name="viewport" content="width=device-width" />
    <link href="/lib/bootstrap/dist/css/bootstrap.min.css" rel="stylesheet" />
    <title>Result</title>
</head>
<body class="m-1 p-1">
    <table class="table table-sm table-bordered">
        <tr><th>Controller:</th><td>@Model.Controller</td></tr>
        <tr><th>Action:</th><td>@Model.Action</td></tr>
    </table>
</body>
</html>
```

The view depends on the Bootstrap CSS package for styling the HTML elements. To add Bootstrap to the project, I used the Bower Configuration File item template to create the `bower.json` file and added the Bootstrap package to the dependencies section, as shown in Listing 31-5.

Listing 31-5. Adding a Package in the bower.json File in the ConventionsAndConstraints Folder

```
{
  "name": "asp.net",
  "private": true,
  "dependencies": {
    "bootstrap": "4.0.0-alpha.6"
  }
}
```

The final preparation is to create the _ViewImports.cshtml file in the Views folder, which sets up the built-in tag helpers for use in Razor views and imports the model namespace, as shown in Listing 31-6.

Listing 31-6. The Contents of the _ViewImports.cshtml File in the Views Folder

```
@using ConventionsAndConstraints.Models
@addTagHelper *, Microsoft.AspNetCore.Mvc.TagHelpers
```

If you start the application, you will see the result shown in Figure 31-1.

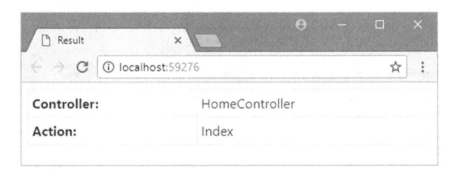

Figure 31-1. *Running the example application*

Using the Application Model and Model Conventions

MVC favors convention over configuration, which is why you can simply create a class whose name ends with Controller and start defining action methods. At runtime, MVC uses a discovery process to locate all of the controllers and actions in the application and inspects them to see whether they use features such as filters.

The end result of the discovery process is the *application model*, which is made up of objects that describe every controller class, action method, and parameter that has been found. The conventions that MVC relies on are applied to the application model as it is constructed. For example, when a controller class is discovered, the name of the class is used as the basis for the controller that represents it in the model; in other words, the HomeController class is used to create a Home controller. When the routing system identifies a request that has to be handled by the Home controller, it is the application model that provides the mapping to the HomeController class.

The application model can be customized using *model conventions*, which are classes that inspect the contents of the application model and make adjustments, such as synthesizing new actions or changing the way that classes are used to create controllers. In the following sections, I explain how the application model is structured, introduce the different types of model conventions, and demonstrate ways in which conventions can be used. Table 31-2 puts the application model and model conventions in context.

Table 31-2. *Putting the Application Model and Model Conventions in Context*

Question	Answer
What are they?	The application model is a complete description of the controllers and actions that have been discovered in the application. Model conventions allow custom changes to be applied to the application model.
Why are they useful?	Model conventions are useful because they allow changes to the way that classes and methods are mapped to controllers and actions. Other customizations can be performed, such as restricting the HTTP methods that an action accepts or applying action constraints (which are described later in this chapter).
How are they used?	Model conventions are defined using a range of interfaces, described in the following sections, and applied as attributes or configured in the Startup class.
Are there any pitfalls or limitations?	There are some oddities in the way that model conventions are applied, as described in the following sections.
Are there any alternatives?	No, although you can introduce your own components to create a custom application model if the default one doesn't suit your needs.

Understanding the Application Model

During the discovery process, MVC creates an instance of the ApplicationModel class and populates it with details of the controllers and actions that it finds. When the discovery process is complete, *model conventions* are applied to make any custom changes you specify. The starting point for understanding the application model is to examine the properties defined by the Microsoft.AspNetCore.Mvc. ApplicationModels.ApplicationModel class, which are described in Table 31-3.

Table 31-3. *Selected ApplicationModel Properties*

Name	Description
Controllers	This property returns an IList<ControllerModel> that contains all of the controllers in the application.
Filters	This property returns an IList<IFilterMetadata> that contains the global filters in the application.

■ **Note** This may seem like a dry place to start, especially if you want to begin digging into the detail, but it is worth taking a moment to appreciate how completely the classes described in this section describe the core parts of an MVC application. Understanding how the application model works will help you understand how more advanced features work behind the scenes, which will better equip you to diagnose problems when you get unexpected results in your own projects.

The important property for this chapter is `Controllers`, which returns a list containing a `ControllerModel` object for each controller that has been discovered in the application. Table 31-4 describes the most important `ControllerModel` properties.

Table 31-4. *Selected ControllerModel Properties*

Name	Description
ControllerName	This `string` property defines the name of the controller. This is the name that will be used to match the `controller` routing segment.
ControllerType	This `TypeInfo` defines the type of the controller class.
ControllerProperties	This property returns an `IList<PropertyModel>` that describes all of the properties defined by the controller, as described in Table 31-5.
Actions	This property returns an `IList<ActionModel>` that describes all of the actions defined by the controller, as described in Table 31-6.
Filters	This property returns an `IList<IFilterMetadata>` that contains the filters that apply to all of the actions in the controller.
RouteConstraints	This property returns an `IList<IRouteConstraintProvider>` that is used to restrict how routes target actions defined by the controller.
Selectors	This property returns an `IList<SelectorModel>` that contains details of the action constraints (described in the "Using Action Constraints" section) and the routing information applied to the controller through attributes, as described in Chapter 15.

You can see how some of the core functionality of MVC is captured by the application model classes. The `ControllerName` property, for example, is used to set the name that will be used by the routing system to match URLs, while the `ControllerType` property is used to set the controller class that the name relates to.

The `ControllerProperties` property returns a list of `PropertyModel` objects, each of which describes a property defined by the controller. Table 31-5 describes the most important `PropertyModel` properties.

Table 31-5. *Selected PropertyModel Properties*

Name	Description
PropertyName	This `string` property returns the name of the property.
Attributes	This property returns a list of the attributes that have been applied to the property.

The `Actions` property returns a list of `ActionModel` objects, each of which describes an action method defined by a single controller class. Table 31-6 describes the most important properties of the `ActionModel` class.

Table 31-6. Selected ActionModel Properties

Name	Description
ActionName	This `string` property defines the name of the action, which is the one that will be used to match the `action` routing segment.
ActionMethod	This `MethodInfo` property is used to specify the method that implements the action.
Controller	This property returns the `ControllerModel` that describes the controller to which this action belongs.
Filters	This property returns an `IList<IFilterMetadata>` that contains the filters that apply to the action.
Parameters	This property returns an `IList<PropertyModel>` that contains descriptions of the parameters required by the action method.
RouteConstraints	This property returns an `IList<IRouteConstraintProvider>` that is used to restrict how routes target the action.
Selectors	This property returns an `IList<SelectorModel>` that contains details of the action constraints (described in the "Using Action Constraints" section) and the routing information applied to the controller through attributes, as described in Chapter 15.

The final level of detail is accessed through the `Parameters` properties, which returns a list of `ParameterModel` objects that describe each of the parameters defined by the action method. Table 31-7 describes the most important properties of the `ParameterModel` class.

Table 31-7. Selected ParameterModel Properties

Name	Description
ParameterName	This `string` property is used for the name of the parameter.
ParameterInfo	This `PropertyInfo` property is used to specify the parameter.
BindingInfo	This `BindingInfo` property is used to configure the model binding process, as described in Chapter 27.

These types—`ApplicationModel`, `ControllerModel`, `PropertyModel`, `ActionModel`, and `ParameterModel`—are used to describe every aspect of the controller classes in the application, as well as their methods, properties, and the parameters each method defines.

Customizing the Application Model

MVC has some built-in conventions that it applies as it populates the `ApplicationModel` with `ControllerModel`, `PropertyModel`, `ActionModel`, and `ParameterModel` objects to describe the controllers it discovers.

Some of the conventions are explicit, such as removing `Controller` from the name of controller classes and using it to set the `ControllerName` property of `ControllerModel` objects. It is this convention that means you define a class such as `HomeController` but target it with URL segments that contain `Home`.

Other conventions are implicit, such as each class being used to create one controller and each method being used to create one action. Most MVC developers take these conventions for granted and don't give them any conscious thought, but every aspect of the application model can be changed.

In previous chapters, I described attributes that change the way that MVC works, and these are actually model conventions. Table 31-8 describes the attributes.

Table 31-8. *The Basic Attributes That Change the Default Application Conventions*

Name	Description
ActionName	This attribute allows the value for the ActionName property of an ActionModel to be specified explicitly rather than derived from a method name.
NonController	This attribute prevents a class from being used to create a ControllerModel object.
NonAction	This attribute prevents a method from being used to create an ActionModel object.

In Listing 31-7, I have used the ActionName attribute to change the name of the action that is created to represent the List method in the HomeController class.

Listing 31-7. Customizing the Application Model in the HomeController.cs File in the Controllers Folder

```
using ConventionsAndConstraints.Models;
using Microsoft.AspNetCore.Mvc;

namespace ConventionsAndConstraints.Controllers {

    public class HomeController : Controller {

        public IActionResult Index() => View("Result", new Result {
            Controller = nameof(HomeController),
            Action = nameof(Index)
        });

        [ActionName("Details")]
        public IActionResult List() => View("Result", new Result {
            Controller = nameof(HomeController),
            Action = nameof(List)
        });
    }
}
```

I have specified that the name Details should be used to create the action, replacing the default name of List. You can see the effect by starting the application and requesting the /Home/Details URL. As Figure 31-2 shows, the request is handled by the List method.

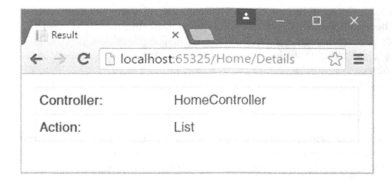

Figure 31-2. *Customizing the application model*

Understanding the Role of Model Conventions

The attributes described in Table 31-8 allow basic changes to be made to the application model but are limited in their scope. For more substantial customizations, *model conventions* (also known just as *conventions*) are required.

The attributes from Table 31-8 allow you to specify changes to the application model objects before they are created, such as by overriding the name used for an action. By contrast, creating a model convention allows you to change the application model by altering the model objects after they have been created, which allows for much broader changes to be applied. Four kinds of model conventions are available, each of which is defined by a different interface, as described in Table 31-9.

Table 31-9. *The Application Model Convention Interfaces*

Name	Description
IApplicationModelConvention	This interface is used to apply a convention to the ApplicationModel object.
IControllerModelConvention	This interface is used to apply a convention to the ControllerModel objects in the application model.
IActionModelConvention	This interface is used to apply a convention to the ActionModel objects in the application model.
IParameterModelConvention	This interface is used to apply a convention to the ParameterModel objects in the application model.

All four interfaces work in the same way, and only the level at which they operate within the application model changes. For example, here is the definition of the IControllerModelConvention interface:

```
namespace Microsoft.AspNetCore.Mvc.ApplicationModels {

    public interface IControllerModelConvention {

        void Apply(ControllerModel controller);
    }
}
```

991

The Apply method is called to provide the model convention with the opportunity to make changes to the ControllerModel to which it has been applied, which is received as the method argument. The other interfaces also defined Apply methods, and each receives a model object of the type it modifies, such that the IActionModelConvention interface receives an ActionModel object and the IParameterModelConvention interface receives a ParameterModel object.

Creating a Model Convention

Controller, action, and parameter model conventions can be applied as attributes, which makes it easy to set the scope of the changes they apply. As a demonstration, I created an Infrastructure folder and added a class file to it called ActionNamePrefixAttribute.cs, which I used to define the class shown in Listing 31-8.

Listing 31-8. The Contents of the ActionNamePrefixAttribute.cs File in the Infrastructure Folder

```
using System;
using Microsoft.AspNetCore.Mvc.ApplicationModels;

namespace ConventionsAndConstraints.Infrastructure {

    [AttributeUsage(AttributeTargets.Method, AllowMultiple = false)]
    public class ActionNamePrefixAttribute : Attribute, IActionModelConvention {
        private string namePrefix;

        public ActionNamePrefixAttribute(string prefix) {
            namePrefix = prefix;
        }

        public void Apply(ActionModel action) {
            action.ActionName = namePrefix + action.ActionName;
        }
    }
}
```

The ActionNamePrefixAttribute class is derived from Attribute and implements the IActionModelConvention interface. Its constructor accepts a string that is used as a prefix, which is applied by modifying the ActionName property of the ActionModel object received by the Apply method.

■ **Tip** Notice that I have restricted the use of the ActionNamePrefix attribute so that it can be applied only to methods. When applying model conventions as attributes, controller conventions take effect only when they are applied to classes, action conventions take effect only when they are applied to methods, and parameter conventions take effect only when they are applied to parameters. A convention applied at the wrong level will simply be ignored without any error. To avoid confusion, use AttributeUsage to limit the scope of the attributes you create.

In Listing 31-9, I have applied the model convention attribute to one of the action methods of the Home controller.

Listing 31-9. Applying a Model Convention in the HomeController.cs File in the Controllers Folder

```
using ConventionsAndConstraints.Models;
using Microsoft.AspNetCore.Mvc;
using ConventionsAndConstraints.Infrastructure;

namespace ConventionsAndConstraints.Controllers {

    public class HomeController : Controller {

        public IActionResult Index() => View("Result", new Result {
            Controller = nameof(HomeController),
            Action = nameof(Index)
        });

        [ActionNamePrefix("Do")]
        public IActionResult List() => View("Result", new Result {
            Controller = nameof(HomeController),
            Action = nameof(List)
        });
    }
}
```

When MVC goes through its discovery process, it will create an ActionModel object that describes the List method, detect the ActionNamePrefix, and call its Apply method. You can see the effect by running the application and requesting the /Home/DoList URL, which has replaced the URL that would target the List method under the default conventions, as shown in Figure 31-3.

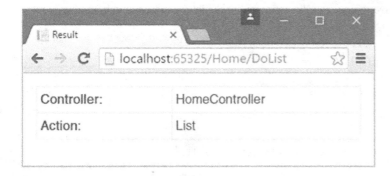

Figure 31-3. *Applying a model convention*

Using Conventions That Add or Remove Models

There is a quirk in the way that model conventions are applied that prevents them from adding or removing objects in the application model. For example, imagine if you wanted to create a convention that some methods could be reached through two different actions. To demonstrate the problem, I added a class file called AddActionAttribute.cs to the Infrastructure folder and used it to define the class shown in Listing 31-10.

Listing 31-10. The Contents of the AddActionAttribute.cs File in the Infrastructure Folder

```
using System;
using Microsoft.AspNetCore.Mvc.ApplicationModels;

namespace ConventionsAndConstraints.Infrastructure {

    [AttributeUsage(AttributeTargets.Method, AllowMultiple = true)]
    public class AddActionAttribute : Attribute, IActionModelConvention {
        private string additionalName;

        public AddActionAttribute(string name) {
            additionalName = name;
        }

        public void Apply(ActionModel action) {
            action.Controller.Actions.Add(new ActionModel(action) {
                ActionName = additionalName
            });
        }
    }
}
```

This action model convention uses an ActionModel constructor that duplicates the settings of an existing object and then changes the ActionName property of the new instance. The new ActionModel is added to the controller's collection of actions by navigating through the ActionModel.Controller property. In Listing 31-11, you can see how I have applied the model convention to the Home controller.

Listing 31-11. Applying a Model Convention in the HomeController.cs File in the Controllers Folder

```
using ConventionsAndConstraints.Models;
using Microsoft.AspNetCore.Mvc;
using ConventionsAndConstraints.Infrastructure;

namespace ConventionsAndConstraints.Controllers {

    public class HomeController : Controller {

        public IActionResult Index() => View("Result", new Result {
            Controller = nameof(HomeController),
            Action = nameof(Index)
        });

        [AddAction("Details")]
        public IActionResult List() => View("Result", new Result {
            Controller = nameof(HomeController),
            Action = nameof(List)
        });
    }
}
```

When you start the application, MVC will begin its discovery process and report the following error:

```
InvalidOperationException: Collection was modified; enumeration operation may not execute.
```

The model convention is trying to change the set of action model objects as they are being enumerated by the discovery process, which causes an exception. Avoiding an error requires a different approach, as shown in Listing 31-12.

Listing 31-12. Creating a Safe Convention in the AddActionAttribute.cs File in the Infrastructure Folder

```csharp
using System;
using Microsoft.AspNetCore.Mvc.ApplicationModels;
using System.Linq;

namespace ConventionsAndConstraints.Infrastructure {

    [AttributeUsage(AttributeTargets.Method, AllowMultiple = true)]
    public class AddActionAttribute : Attribute {

        public string AdditionalName { get; }

        public AddActionAttribute(string name) {
            AdditionalName = name;
        }
    }

    [AttributeUsage(AttributeTargets.Class, AllowMultiple = false)]
    public class AdditionalActionsAttribute : Attribute,
            IControllerModelConvention {

        public void Apply(ControllerModel controller) {
            var actions = controller.Actions
                .Select(a => new {
                    Action = a,
                    Names = a.Attributes.Select(attr =>
                        (attr as AddActionAttribute)?.AdditionalName)
                });

            foreach (var item in actions.ToList()) {
                foreach (string name in item.Names) {
                    controller.Actions.Add(new ActionModel(item.Action) {
                        ActionName = name
                    });
                }
            }
        }
    }
}
```

It isn't possible to modify the set of actions associated with a controller within an action model convention, but I still need some way to denote the changes that I require. For this reason, I have made the AddActionAttribute class just an attribute and not a model convention.

It is possible to change the set of actions within a controller model convention, which is why I created the AdditionalActionsAttribute class. The Apply method uses LINQ to locate the methods to which the AddActionAttribute class has been applied and creates new ActionModel objects with the names that are specified.

The most important part of this class is the call to the ToList method applied to the LINQ results.

```
...
foreach (var item in actions.ToList()) {
...
```

This method forces the evaluation of the LINQ query and puts the result into a new collection, which means that the foreach loop enumerates a different set of objects from the one that MVC is enumerating as it applies the model conventions. Without the ToList call, I would have received the same error message as the model convention from Listing 31-12 produced; with the ToList call, I am able to create new action model objects. Listing 31-13 shows how I have applied the revised attributes to the Home controller.

Listing 31-13. Applying the Revised Convention in the HomeController.cs File in the Controllers Folder

```csharp
using ConventionsAndConstraints.Models;
using Microsoft.AspNetCore.Mvc;
using ConventionsAndConstraints.Infrastructure;

namespace ConventionsAndConstraints.Controllers {

    [AdditionalActions]
    public class HomeController : Controller {

        public IActionResult Index() => View("Result", new Result {
            Controller = nameof(HomeController),
            Action = nameof(Index)
        });

        [AddAction("Details")]
        public IActionResult List() => View("Result", new Result {
            Controller = nameof(HomeController),
            Action = nameof(List)
        });
    }
}
```

You can see the effect of the revised model convention by starting the application and requesting the /Home/Details and /Home/List URLs. As Figure 31-4 shows, the model convention has added a new action that is handled by the List method, supplementing the action model that is created by default.

Figure 31-4. *The effect of creating an action model*

Understanding Model Convention Execution Order

Model conventions are applied in a specific order, starting with the broadest scope: controller model conventions are applied first, followed by action model conventions, and, finally, parameter model conventions. To demonstrate the order, I have applied both of the custom conventions I created in previous examples to the List method of the HomeController class, as shown in Listing 31-14.

Listing 31-14. Applying Multiple Conventions in the HomeController.cs File in the Controllers Folder

```
using ConventionsAndConstraints.Models;
using Microsoft.AspNetCore.Mvc;
using ConventionsAndConstraints.Infrastructure;

namespace ConventionsAndConstraints.Controllers {

    [AdditionalActions]
    public class HomeController : Controller {

        public IActionResult Index() => View("Result", new Result {
            Controller = nameof(HomeController),
            Action = nameof(Index)
        });

        [ActionNamePrefix("Do")]
        [AddAction("Details")]
        public IActionResult List() => View("Result", new Result {
            Controller = nameof(HomeController),
            Action = nameof(List)
        });
    }
}
```

The AdditionalActions attribute, which is a controller model convention, is applied first and creates a new action called Details. Next, the ActionNamePrefix attribute, which is an action model convention, is applied; it applies the Do prefix to all of the actions associated with the method. The result is that the List method implements two actions, DoList and DoDetails, which can be reached with the /Home/DoList and /Home/DoDetails URLs, as shown in Figure 31-5.

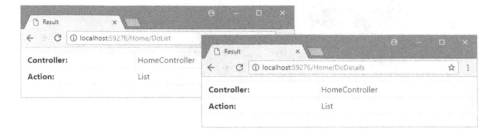

Figure 31-5. *The effect of model convention execution order*

Creating Global Model Conventions

If you need to change the default model conventions, then you may have to do so for every controller, action, or parameter in the application. If this is the case, then you can create a *global model convention*, rather than have to remember to apply attributes consistently to every controller class. Global model conventions are configured in the Startup class, as shown in Listing 31-15.

Listing 31-15. Creating a Global Filter in the Startup.cs File in the ConventionsAndConstraints Folder

```
using System;
using System.Collections.Generic;
using System.Linq;
using System.Threading.Tasks;
using Microsoft.AspNetCore.Builder;
using Microsoft.AspNetCore.Hosting;
using Microsoft.AspNetCore.Http;
using Microsoft.Extensions.DependencyInjection;
using ConventionsAndConstraints.Infrastructure;

namespace ConventionsAndConstraints {

    public class Startup {

        public void ConfigureServices(IServiceCollection services) {
            services.AddMvc().AddMvcOptions(options => {
                options.Conventions.Add(new ActionNamePrefixAttribute("Do"));
                options.Conventions.Add(new AdditionalActionsAttribute());
            });
        }

        public void Configure(IApplicationBuilder app, IHostingEnvironment env) {
            app.UseStatusCodePages();
            app.UseDeveloperExceptionPage();
            app.UseStaticFiles();
            app.UseMvcWithDefaultRoute();
        }
    }
}
```

The MvcOptions object received by the AddMvcOptions extension method defines a Conventions property. This property returns a list collection to which model convention objects can be added. The listing applies both of the custom model conventions globally, which means that all action names will be prefixed with Do and all methods will be inspected for the AddAction attribute. Since these model conventions are applied globally, I have removed the attributes from the HomeController class, as shown in Listing 31-16.

Listing 31-16. Removing Model Conventions in the HomeController.cs File in the Controllers Folder

```
using ConventionsAndConstraints.Models;
using Microsoft.AspNetCore.Mvc;
using ConventionsAndConstraints.Infrastructure;

namespace ConventionsAndConstraints.Controllers {

    //[AdditionalActions]
    public class HomeController : Controller {

        public IActionResult Index() => View("Result", new Result {
            Controller = nameof(HomeController),
            Action = nameof(Index)
        });

        //[ActionNamePrefix("Do")]
        [AddAction("Details")]
        public IActionResult List() => View("Result", new Result {
            Controller = nameof(HomeController),
            Action = nameof(List)
        });
    }
}
```

Global model conventions are applied before conventions applied directly to classes. If there are multiple global conventions, then they are applied in the order they are registered and with no regard to their type. I registered the action model convention before the controller model convention, which means that the Details action specified through the AddAction attribute is created after the ActionNamePrefixAttribute convention is applied to all of the action names. The result is that the List method implements two actions, DoList and Details, which can be reached with the /Home/DoList and / Home/Details URLs, as shown in Figure 31-6.

Figure 31-6. *The effect of global model convention ordering*

Using Action Constraints

Action constraints decide whether an action method is suitable for handling a specific request, which might lead you to think that action constraints are like the authorization filters that I described in Chapter 19.

In fact, the use of action constraints is much more limited. When MVC receives an HTTP request, it goes through a selection process to identify the action method that will be used to handle it. If there are multiple actions that could handle the request, then MVC needs some way to decide which one to use, and that's where action constraints are used. Table 31-10 puts action constraints into context.

Table 31-10. *Putting Action Constraints in Context*

Question	Answer
What are they?	Action constraints are classes that MVC uses to determine whether a request can be processed by a specific action.
Why are they useful?	If there are two or more actions that could handle a request, then MVC needs some means to decide which of them is the most suitable. Action constraints are used to provide that information.
How are they used?	Action constraints are applied as attributes, which allows them to be reused throughout an application and means that the logic that determines whether an action should process a request doesn't have to be defined within the action method itself.
Are there any pitfalls or limitations?	Action constraints can be applied too widely and prevent a request from being processed by any suitable action method, resulting in an unhelpful 404 - Not Found response being sent to the client.
Are there any alternatives?	Filters are more useful if you want to restrict access to actions under specific circumstances because you can redirect the client to display a helpful error page.

Preparing the Example Project

The purpose of action constraints is to help MVC choose between two or more similar action methods when any of them could be used to handle a request. This is the situation that I have created in Listing 31-17 by adding a new action method to the Home controller.

Listing 31-17. Creating Two Suitable Actions in the HomeController.cs File in the Controllers Folder

```
using ConventionsAndConstraints.Models;
using Microsoft.AspNetCore.Mvc;
using ConventionsAndConstraints.Infrastructure;

namespace ConventionsAndConstraints.Controllers {

    //[AdditionalActions]
    public class HomeController : Controller {

        public IActionResult Index() => View("Result", new Result {
            Controller = nameof(HomeController),
            Action = nameof(Index)
        });

        [ActionName("Index")]
        public IActionResult Other() => View("Result", new Result {
            Controller = nameof(HomeController),
            Action = nameof(Other)
        });

        //[ActionNamePrefix("Do")]
        [AddAction("Details")]
        public IActionResult List() => View("Result", new Result {
            Controller = nameof(HomeController),
            Action = nameof(List)
        });
    }
}
```

I added a new method called Other and applied the ActionName attribute so that it produces an action called Index. I also updated the Startup class to remove the global model conventions from the previous part of the chapter, as shown in Listing 31-18.

Listing 31-18. Removing Conventions in the Startup.cs File in the ConventionsAndConstraints Folder

```
using System;
using System.Collections.Generic;
using System.Linq;
using System.Threading.Tasks;
using Microsoft.AspNetCore.Builder;
using Microsoft.AspNetCore.Hosting;
using Microsoft.AspNetCore.Http;
using Microsoft.Extensions.DependencyInjection;
using ConventionsAndConstraints.Infrastructure;

namespace ConventionsAndConstraints {

    public class Startup {
```

```
        public void ConfigureServices(IServiceCollection services) {
            services.AddMvc().AddMvcOptions(options => {
                //options.Conventions.Add(new ActionNamePrefixAttribute("Do"));
                //options.Conventions.Add(new AdditionalActionsAttribute());
            });
        }

        public void Configure(IApplicationBuilder app, IHostingEnvironment env) {
            app.UseStatusCodePages();
            app.UseDeveloperExceptionPage();
            app.UseStaticFiles();
            app.UseMvcWithDefaultRoute();
        }
    }
}
```

This means that that there are two actions called Index on the Home controller, and if you start the application, you will see the error shown in Figure 31-7, which indicates that MVC doesn't know which action should be used.

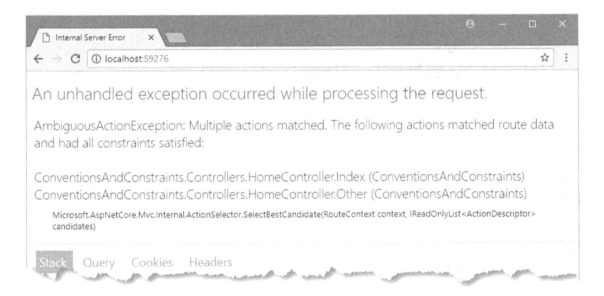

Figure 31-7. *The effect of creating two equally suitable action methods*

The error can be hard to read in a screenshot, so here is the relevant part of the message:

```
AmbiguousActionException: Multiple actions matched. The following actions matched route
data and had all constraints satisfied:
ConventionsAndConstraints.Controllers.HomeController.Index
ConventionsAndConstraints.Controllers.HomeController.Other
```

Understanding Action Constraints

Action constraints are used to tell MVC whether an action method can be used to handle a request and to implement the IActionConstraint interface, which is defined as follows:

```
namespace Microsoft.AspNetCore.Mvc.ActionConstraints {

    public interface IActionConstraint : IActionConstraintMetadata {

        int Order { get; }

        bool Accept(ActionConstraintContext context);
    }
}
```

When MVC goes through the process of selecting an action method to handle a request, it checks to see whether there are constraints associated with it. If there are, then they are arranged in sequence based on the value of the Order property, and the Accept method of each is called in turn. If any of the constraints return false from the Accept method, then MVC knows that the action method cannot be used to handle the current request.

■ **Tip** The IActionConstraint interface is derived from IActionConstraintMetadata, which is an interface that defines no members. It is not used directly, and you should always use the IActionConstaint interface when you define custom constraints or use the IActionConstraintFactory interface if you want to create a constraint that has dependencies to resolve, as described in the "Resolving Dependencies in Action Constraints" section.

To help action constraints to make their determination, MVC provides them with an instance of the ActionConstraintContext class for context data, which defines the properties described in Table 31-11.

Table 31-11. *The ActionConstraintContext Properties*

Name	Description
Candidates	This property returns a list of ActionSelectorCandidate objects that describe the set of action methods that MVC has shortlisted to handle the current request.
CurrentCandidate	This property returns the ActionSelectorCandidate object that describes the action method that the constraint is being asked to assess.
RouteContext	This property returns a RouteContext object, which provides information about the routing data (through the RouteData property) and the HTTP request (through the HttpContext property).

Creating an Action Constraint

The most common type of constraint examines the request to ensure that some policy has been met, such as a particular HTTP header value being present. To demonstrate how to create this kind of action constraint, I added a class file called UserAgentAttribute.cs to the Infrastructure folder of the example project and used it to define the class shown in Listing 31-19.

Listing 31-19. The Contents of the UserAgentAttribute.cs File in the Infrastructure Folder

```
using System;
using System.Linq;
using Microsoft.AspNetCore.Mvc.ActionConstraints;

namespace ConventionsAndConstraints.Infrastructure {

    public class UserAgentAttribute : Attribute, IActionConstraint {
        private string substring;

        public UserAgentAttribute(string sub) {
            substring = sub.ToLower();
        }

        public int Order { get; set; } = 0;

        public bool Accept(ActionConstraintContext context) {
            return context.RouteContext.HttpContext
                .Request.Headers["User-Agent"]
                .Any(h => h.ToLower().Contains(substring));
        }
    }
}
```

This is an action constraint attribute that prevents a request from matching actions when the User-Agent header doesn't contain a specified string. Within the Accept method, I get the HTTP headers from the HttpContext object and use LINQ to see whether any of them contain the substring that is received through the constructor.

Note   Don't rely on the User-Agent header to identify browsers in real applications because the header values are often misleading. For example, the version of the Microsoft Edge browser that is current as I write this sends a User-Agent header that contains Android, Apple, Chrome, and Safari, which makes it easy to mistake it for another browser. A more robust approach is to use a JavaScript library such as Modernizr (http://modernizr.com) to detect the features on which your application relies.

In Listing 31-20, I have applied the constraint to one of the methods in the HomeController class.

Listing 31-20. Applying an Action Constraint in the HomeController.cs File in the Controllers Folder

```
using ConventionsAndConstraints.Models;
using Microsoft.AspNetCore.Mvc;
using ConventionsAndConstraints.Infrastructure;

namespace ConventionsAndConstraints.Controllers {

    //[AdditionalActions]
    public class HomeController : Controller {

        public IActionResult Index() => View("Result", new Result {
            Controller = nameof(HomeController),
            Action = nameof(Index)
        });

        [ActionName("Index")]
        [UserAgent("Edge")]
        public IActionResult Other() => View("Result", new Result {
            Controller = nameof(HomeController),
            Action = nameof(Other)
        });

        //[ActionNamePrefix("Do")]
        [AddAction("Details")]
        public IActionResult List() => View("Result", new Result {
            Controller = nameof(HomeController),
            Action = nameof(List)
        });
    }
}
```

I applied the attribute to the Other method and specified that the action should not be allowed to receive requests whose User-Agent header does not contain the term Edge.

If you start the application and request the /Home/Index URL with Google Chrome and Microsoft Edge, you will see that the requests are handled by different methods, as illustrated in Figure 31-8.

Figure 31-8. *The effect of an action constraint*

UNDERSTANDING THE EFFECT OF A CONSTRAINT ON ACTION SELECTION

The previous example reveals an aspect of using constraints that may not be immediately obvious: an action with a constraint whose Accept method returns true for a request is given preference over an action to which no constraints have been applied.

There are two Index actions defined by the Home controller—created from the Index and Other methods—and both of them can be used to process requests whose User-Agent header contains the string Edge. The reason that the Other method is used to process the request from the Edge browser is because it has a constraint applied to it and that constraint's Accept method returns true. The idea is that an action that has a constraint that has accepted a request is a better candidate than an action with no constraints at all.

Creating a Comparative Action Constraint

Through the Candidates and CurrentCandidate properties of the ActionConstraintContext object, constraints are provided with details of the other actions that are candidates to handle a request. Each potential match is described using an instance of the ActionSelectorCandidate class, which defines the properties shown in Table 31-12.

Table 31-12. *The ActionSelectorCandidate Properties*

Name	Description
Action	This property returns an ActionDescriptor object that describes the candidate action.
Constraints	This property returns a list of IActionConstraint objects that comprise the set of constraints that have been applied to the candidate action.

The ActionDescriptor class is used to describe an action via the properties described in Table 31-13, many of which are similar to those provided by other context objects.

Table 31-13. *Selected ActionDescriptor Properties*

Name	Description
Name	This property returns the name of the action.
RouteConstraints	This property returns an IList<IRouteConstraintProvider> that is used to restrict how routes target the action.
Parameters	This property returns an IList<PropertyModel> that contains descriptions of the parameters required by the action method.
ActionConstraints	This property returns an IList<IActionConstraintMetadata> containing the constraints for this action.

Constraints can inspect the candidate actions and have insight into how and where they have been applied, which can be used to fine-tune how they work. As an example, consider the way that I have applied constraints to the Home controller in Listing 31-21.

Listing 31-21. Applying a Constraint in the HomeController.cs File in the Controllers Folder

```
using ConventionsAndConstraints.Models;
using Microsoft.AspNetCore.Mvc;
using ConventionsAndConstraints.Infrastructure;

namespace ConventionsAndConstraints.Controllers {

    public class HomeController : Controller {

        public IActionResult Index() => View("Result", new Result {
            Controller = nameof(HomeController),
            Action = nameof(Index)
        });

        [ActionName("Index")]
        [UserAgent("Edge")]
        public IActionResult Other() => View("Result", new Result {
            Controller = nameof(HomeController),
            Action = nameof(Other)
        });

        [UserAgent("Edge")]
        public IActionResult List() => View("Result", new Result {
            Controller = nameof(HomeController),
            Action = nameof(List)
        });
    }
}
```

There is only one List action in the application, and applying the constraint to it means that only requests whose User-Agent header contains Edge can use it. If you make a request with Chrome, for example, then you will receive a 404 - Not Found response.

This is not helpful because users won't understand why they have received the error, and there is no explanatory text that suggests using a different browser instead. Action constraints are helpful when you want to steer the selection of an action method to handle a request and not when you want to prevent a specific action from being used at all; if that is your goal, then using a filter will allow you to redirect the client to a descriptive error page, which is a substantially more helpful response.

To address this problem, I have updated the UserAgentAttribute class so that the constraint does not reject requests when there is only one candidate action available to handle the request, as shown in Listing 31-22.

Listing 31-22. Checking for Other Candidates in the UserAgentAttribute.cs File in the Infrastructure Folder

```
using System;
using System.Linq;
using Microsoft.AspNetCore.Mvc.ActionConstraints;
```

```
namespace ConventionsAndConstraints.Infrastructure {

    public class UserAgentAttribute : Attribute, IActionConstraint {
        private string substring;

        public UserAgentAttribute(string sub) {
            substring = sub.ToLower();
        }

        public int Order { get; set; } = 0;

        public bool Accept(ActionConstraintContext context) {
            return context.RouteContext.HttpContext
                    .Request.Headers["User-Agent"]
                    .Any(h => h.ToLower().Contains(substring))
                || context.Candidates.Count() == 1;
        }
    }
}
```

The additional LINQ query checks to see whether the candidate action returned by the CurrentCandidate property is the only one in the collection returned by the Candidates property. If it is, then the constraint knows that MVC doesn't have an alternative action available and allows the request. You can see the effect by starting the application and requesting the /Home/List URL using Google Chrome. Even though the User-Agent header sent by Chrome doesn't contain Edge, which is the term specified by the attribute on the List method, the constraint class determines that there are no other candidates and allows the request to proceed.

Resolving Dependencies in Action Constraints

The IActionConstraintFactory interface is used when you need to resolve dependencies for an action constraint through the service provider, which I described in Chapter 18. Here is the definition of the interface:

```
using System;

namespace Microsoft.AspNetCore.Mvc.ActionConstraints {

    public interface IActionConstraintFactory : IActionConstraintMetadata {

        IActionConstraint CreateInstance(IServiceProvider services);

        bool IsReusable { get; }
    }
}
```

The CreateInstance method is called to create new instances of the action constraint class, and the IsReusable property is used to indicate whether the objects returned by the CreateInstance method can be used for multiple requests.

To demonstrate the use of this interface, I need a dependency that will require resolution. To that end, I added a class file called `UserAgentComparer.cs` to the `Infrastructure` folder and used it to define the class shown in Listing 31-23.

Listing 31-23. The Contents of the UserAgentComparer.cs File in the Infrastructure Folder

```
using System.Linq;
using Microsoft.AspNetCore.Http;

namespace ConventionsAndConstraints.Infrastructure {

    public class UserAgentComparer {

        public bool ContainsString(HttpRequest request, string agent) {
            string searchTerm = agent.ToLower();
            return request.Headers["User-Agent"]
                .Any(h => h.ToLower().Contains(searchTerm));
        }
    }
}
```

The `UserAgentComparer` class defines a single method that looks for a string in the `User-Agent` header of an HTTP request. This is the same functionality I used earlier but packaged into a separate class so that I can use the service provider to manage its life cycle, which I have configured in Listing 31-24.

Listing 31-24. Registering a Type in the Startup.cs File in the ConventionsAndConstraints Folder

```
using System;
using System.Collections.Generic;
using System.Linq;
using System.Threading.Tasks;
using Microsoft.AspNetCore.Builder;
using Microsoft.AspNetCore.Hosting;
using Microsoft.AspNetCore.Http;
using Microsoft.Extensions.DependencyInjection;
using ConventionsAndConstraints.Infrastructure;

namespace ConventionsAndConstraints {

    public class Startup {

        public void ConfigureServices(IServiceCollection services) {
            services.AddSingleton<UserAgentComparer>();
            services.AddMvc().AddMvcOptions(options => {
                //options.Conventions.Add(new ActionNamePrefixAttribute("Do"));
                //options.Conventions.Add(new AdditionalActionsAttribute());
            });
        }

        public void Configure(IApplicationBuilder app, IHostingEnvironment env) {
            app.UseStatusCodePages();
            app.UseDeveloperExceptionPage();
```

```
            app.UseStaticFiles();
            app.UseMvcWithDefaultRoute();
        }
    }
}
```

I selected the singleton life cycle, which means that a single instance of the UserAgentComparer will be used. In Listing 31-25, I have updated the UserAgent constraint so that it delegates the inspection of the header to a UserAgentComparer object, which is obtained through the service provider.

Listing 31-25. Resolving Dependencies in the UserAgentAttribute.cs File in the Infrastructure Folder

```
using System;
using System.Linq;
using Microsoft.AspNetCore.Mvc.ActionConstraints;
using Microsoft.Extensions.DependencyInjection;

namespace ConventionsAndConstraints.Infrastructure {

    public class UserAgentAttribute : Attribute,  IActionConstraintFactory {
        private string substring;

        public UserAgentAttribute(string sub) {
            substring = sub;
        }

        public IActionConstraint CreateInstance(IServiceProvider services) {
            return new UserAgentConstraint(services.GetService<UserAgentComparer>(),
                substring);
        }

        public bool IsReusable => false;

        private class UserAgentConstraint : IActionConstraint {
            private UserAgentComparer comparer;
            private string substring;

            public UserAgentConstraint(UserAgentComparer comp, string sub) {
                comparer = comp;
                substring = sub.ToLower();
            }

            public int Order { get; set; } = 0;

            public bool Accept(ActionConstraintContext context) {
                return comparer.ContainsString(context.RouteContext
                        .HttpContext.Request, substring)
                    || context.Candidates.Count() == 1;
            }
        }
    }
}
```

In this model, the attribute that is applied to action methods is responsible for creating instances of the constraint class when its CreateInstance method is called. The argument to the CreateInstance method is an IServiceProvider object, which I use in the example to get a UserAgentComparer so I can create an instance of the private constraint class, which is then used in the selection process.

AVOIDING THE SCOPE TRAP

Like other attribute-based features, applying a constraint attribute to a controller class is equivalent to applying the attribute to each individual method. However, this usually produces undesirable results because the purpose of constraints is to help MVC select an action method, and that is not the effect that applying the same constraint to all of the actions in controller generally achieves.

For example, if I applied the UserAgent attribute to the HomeController class, the Index actions would no longer be reachable by any browser. Both Index actions would be equally suitable for those browsers that include Edge in the User-Agent string, which will result in an exception. For all other browsers, neither Index action would be suitable, which will result in a 404 - Not Found response.

It is possible to use the context object in a constraint to look for other constraints and see whether they are likely to reject the request, but this leads to the Accept method of each constraint being called many times for each request, which can be an expensive process and one that is best avoided.

Constraints work best when there are multiple action methods that can handle the same request and then the constraint is applied to those methods.

Summary

In this chapter, I described two features that are used to customize the way that MVC operates. I explained how model conventions can be used to change the way that classes and methods are mapped to controllers and actions. I also described how action constraints are used to restrict the range of requests that an action may process and how they are used to select an action from a list of candidates identified when a request arrives.

And that is all I have to teach you about ASP.NET Core MVC 2. I started by creating a simple application and then took you on a comprehensive tour of the different components in the framework, showing you how they can be configured, customized, or replaced entirely.

I wish you every success in your MVC projects, and I can only hope that you have enjoyed reading this book as much as I enjoyed writing it.

Index

Get the eBook for only $5!

Why limit yourself?

With most of our titles available in both PDF and ePUB format, you can access your content wherever and however you wish—on your PC, phone, tablet, or reader.

Since you've purchased this print book, we are happy to offer you the eBook for just $5.

To learn more, go to http://www.apress.com/companion or contact support@apress.com.

Apress®